THE WORLD

A History

Second Edition

Felipe Fernández-Armesto

UNIVERSITY OF NOTRE DAME

Volume One: To 1500

MAPS BY

DORLING KINDERSLEY

PRENTICE HALL
Upper Saddle River   London   Singapore
Toronto   Tokyo   Sydney   Hong Kong
Mexico City

Executive Editor: Charles Cavaliere
Editorial Assistant: Lauren Aylward
Production Project Manager: Lynn Savino Wendel
Senior Development Editor: Gerald Lombardi
Editor in Chief, History: Priscilla McGeehon
Editor in Chief, Development: Rochelle Diogenes
Editorial Director: Leah Jewell
Associate Supplements Editor: Emsal Hasan
Director of Marketing: Brandy Dawson
Executive Marketing Manager: Sue Westmoreland
Senior Marketing Manager: Laura Lee Manley
Marketing Assistant: Ashley Fallon
AV Project Manager: Mirella Signoretto
Manager, Rights and Permissions: Zina Arabia

Manager, Visual Research: Beth Brenzel
Image Permission Coordinator: Craig A. Jones
Cover Image Specialist: Karan Sanatar
Photo Researcher: Francelle Carapetyan
Composition/Full Service Project Management: Rebecca Dunn, Prepare, Inc.
Director, Media & Assessment: Brian Hyland
Media Editor: Sarah Kinney
Media Project Manager: Tina Rudowski
Senior Operations Specialist: Mary Ann Gloriande
Senior Art Director: Maria Lange
Interior and Cover Designer: QT Design
Printer/Binder: Courier Kendallville
Cover Printer: Lehigh-Phoenix Color/Hagerstown

DK Maps designed and produced by DK Education, a division of Dorling Kindersley Limited, 80 Strand, London WC2R ORL. DK and the DK logo are registered trademarks of Dorling Kindersley Limited.

This book was set in 11/13 Minion.
Credits and acknowledgments borrowed from other sources and reproduced, with permission, in this textbook appear on appropriate page within text or on page C-1.

Library of Congress Cataloging-in-Publication Data
Fernández-Armesto, Felipe.
  The world : a history / Felipe Fernandez-Armesto. -- Combined vol., 2nd ed.
    p. cm.
  Maps by Dorling Kindersley.
  Includes index.
  ISBN 978-0-13-606147-2 (combined)—ISBN 978-0-205-65501-4 (exam)—ISBN 978-0-13-606148-9 (v. 1)—
  ISBN 978-0-13-606149-6 (v. 2)—ISBN 978-0-205-68347-5 (v. a)—ISBN 978-0-13-608757-1 (v. b)—ISBN 978-0-13-606150-2 (v. c)
    1. Civilization--History. 2. Human ecology. I. Title.
  CB151.F48 2007
  909—dc22   2008050926

10 9 8 7 6 5 4 3 2 1

Prentice Hall
is an imprint of

www.pearsonhighered.com

ISBN 10:   0-13-606148-6
ISBN 13: 978-0-13-606148-9

Contents

PART 1   Foragers and Farmers, to 5000 b.c.e.   3

"So far, we know of nowhere else in the cosmos where so much has happened and is happening today. By galactic standards, global history is a small story—but it is a good one"   xviii

1 Out of the Ice: Peopling the Earth   4

"We all think we know what it means to be human, but if anyone asks us to define humankind, we cannot do it. Or at least we cannot do it satisfactorily."   5

2 Out of the Mud: Farming and Herding after the Ice Age   30

"Agriculture enabled humans to see the world in a new way—to imagine that magic and science had the power to change nature."   32

Contents

PART 2

Farmers and Builders, 5000 to 500 B.C.E. 61

"Interactions matter. Societies learn from each other, compete with each other, and exchange culture. Isolation retards." **90**

"Paradox racked the most ambitious states of the era. They were committed to population growth, which imposed unsustainable goals of expansion as conquered territory became farther and farther away from the center." **116**

"Political instability among competing states may not seem conducive to civilization, but it stimulated technological change: hotter furnaces, more iron. It also multiplied opportunities for artists and intellectuals. An age of sages would soon be apparent in Eurasia."   149

PART 3   The Axial Age, from 500 B.C.E. to 100 C.E.   155

"As a result of the spread of the work of the sages and their schools, the thought of the modern world has a familiar ring to a student of the axial age. It seems astonishing that today, after all the technological and material progress of the last 2,000 years, we remain so dependent on the thought of such a distant era and have added so little to it."   185

"Routes of commerce are the lifelines of empires: pumping them with resources, equipping them with new ideas and technologies, laying down tracks for their armies to follow."   190

"... the world that emerged in the last three centuries of the first millennium C.E. was deeply transformed. Rather than the world of empires that had dominated the densely populated belt of the axial age, it might be more proper to speak of a world of civilizations." 266

"Even as they changed the societies in which they triumphed, the new religions changed in their turn, compromising with vested interests, modifying their messages to suit mighty patrons, serving the needs of warriors and kings, even becoming organs of the state, instruments of government, means of training bureaucrats, and communicating with subjects." 296

"History is like climate, in which numerous cycles of varying duration all seem to be going on all the time, and where random or almost random changes frequently intervene." 332

"In the preindustrial world, the size of states and the scope of economies were functions of time as well as distance. Messages, armies, revenues, and cargoes took a long time to travel across broken country or, by sea, through variable winds."   369

"Yet the hostility of nomads and farmers arose, less perhaps, from conflicts of interest than from mutual misunderstanding: a clash of cultures, incompatible ways of seeing the world and coping with it."   403

PART 6

The Crucible: The Eurasian Crises of the Thirteenth and Fourteenth Centuries   409

"Without the Mongol peace, it is hard to imagine any of the rest of world history working out quite as it did, for these were the roads that carried Chinese ideas and transmitted technology westward and opened up European minds to the vastness of the world."   437

"Climate and microbes belong to two rebellious realms of nature that resist human power." 444

"The world did not wait passively for European outreach to transform it, as if touched by a magic wand. Other societies were already working magic of their own, turning states into empires and cultures into civilizations." 484

THE BIG PICTURE

A CLOSER LOOK

Special Features

Projection

A map projection is used to portray all or part of the round Earth on a flat surface, which cannot be done without some distortion. The projections in *The World* show the Earth at global, continental, country, and city scale and vary with each map. The map shown here uses a Robinson projection, which uses curvature to provide a good balance between the size and shape of the lands being depicted. As any number of projections could have been selected for each map in *The World*, great care was shown in choosing projections that best serve the goals of the author.

M aps use a unique visual language to convey a great deal of information in a relatively simple form. The maps in this book use a variety of different projections—techniques used to show the Earth's curved surface on a flat map—to trace the history of humans from about 150,000 years ago to the present. This brief guide explains the different features on the maps in *The World*, Second Edition and how to interpret the different layers of information embedded in them.

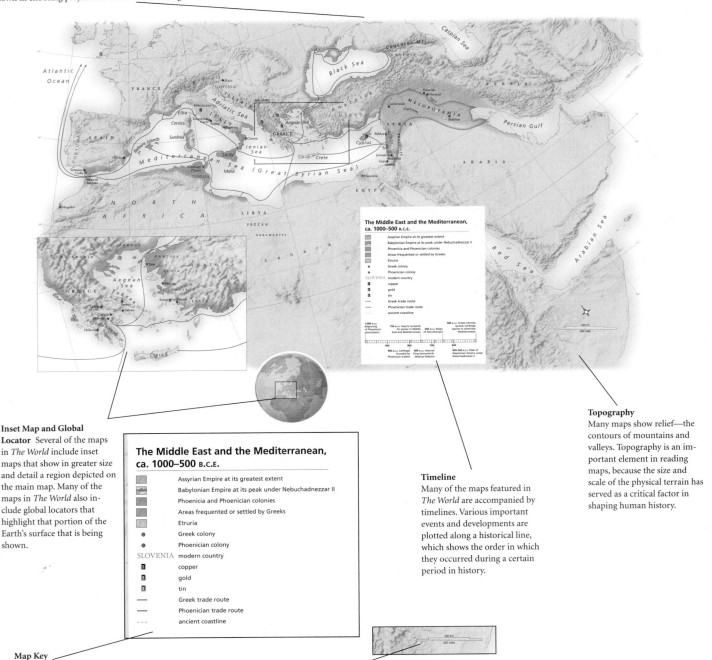

The Middle East and the Mediterranean, ca. 1000–500 B.C.E.

Inset Map and Global Locator

Several of the maps in *The World* include inset maps that show in greater size and detail a region depicted on the main map. Many of the maps in *The World* also include global locators that highlight that portion of the Earth's surface that is being shown.

The Middle East and the Mediterranean, ca. 1000–500 B.C.E.

	Assyrian Empire at its greatest extent
	Babylonian Empire at its peak under Nebuchadnezzar II
	Phoenicia and Phoenician colonies
	Areas frequented or settled by Greeks
	Etruria
●	Greek colony
●	Phoenician colony
SLOVENIA	modern country
▣	copper
▣	gold
▣	tin
—	Greek trade route
—	Phoenician trade route
---	ancient coastline

Timeline

Many of the maps featured in *The World* are accompanied by timelines. Various important events and developments are plotted along a historical line, which shows the order in which they occurred during a certain period in history.

Topography

Many maps show relief—the contours of mountains and valleys. Topography is an important element in reading maps, because the size and scale of the physical terrain has served as a critical factor in shaping human history.

Map Key

Maps use symbols to both show the location of a feature and to give information about that feature. The symbols are explained in the key that accompanies each map.

Scalebar

When using a map to work out what distances are in reality, it is necessary to refer to the scale of that particular map. Many of the maps in *The World* (such as the one shown here) use a linear scale. This only works on equal-area maps, where distances are true. On maps with projections that are heavily curved, a special "perspective-scale graphic" is used to show distance.

KEY TO MAP FEATURES IN *THE WORLD*, SECOND EDITION

PHYSICAL FEATURES

——— coastline

- - - - - ancient coastline

——— river

········· ancient river course

═══════ canal

☐ glacier

▦ ancient lake

▨ marshland

☐ ice cap / sheet

☐ ice shelf

△ elevation above sea level (mountain height)

⏃ volcano

⤫ pass

LATITUDE/LONGITUDE

——— equator

——— lines of latitude / longitude

- - - - - tropics / polar circles

45° degrees of longitude / latitude

BORDERS

——— international border

··········· undefined border

- - - - - maritime border

——— internal border

·········· disputed border

COMMUNICATIONS

——— major road

——— minor road

⊦⊦⊦⊦⊦ major railway

SETTLEMENT / POSSESSION

○ settlement symbol

◇ colonial possession

TYPOGRAPHIC KEY

REGIONS

state / political region..... LAOS

administrative region within a state..................... *HENAN*

cultural / undefined region / group.................... *FERGHANA*

MISCELLANEOUS

tropics / polar circles.......... Antarctic Circle

people / cultural group..... *Samoyeds*

annotation............................. **1914** British protectorate

PHYSICAL FEATURES

continent / ocean..... *AFRICA*

INDIAN OCEAN

landscape features.....*Mekong*

Lake Rudolf

Tien Shan

Sahara

SETTLEMENTS

settlement / symbol location / definition...... Farnham

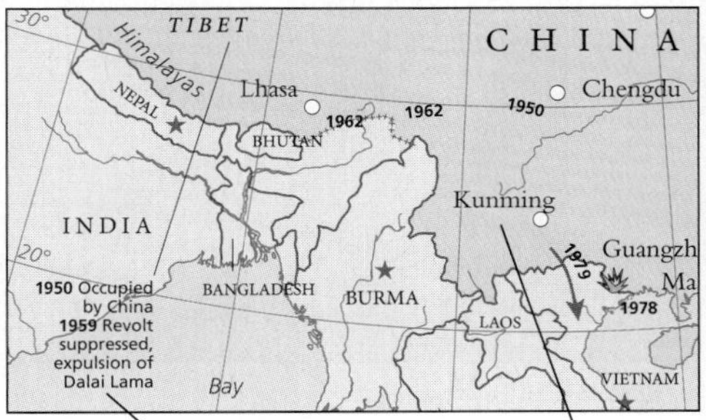

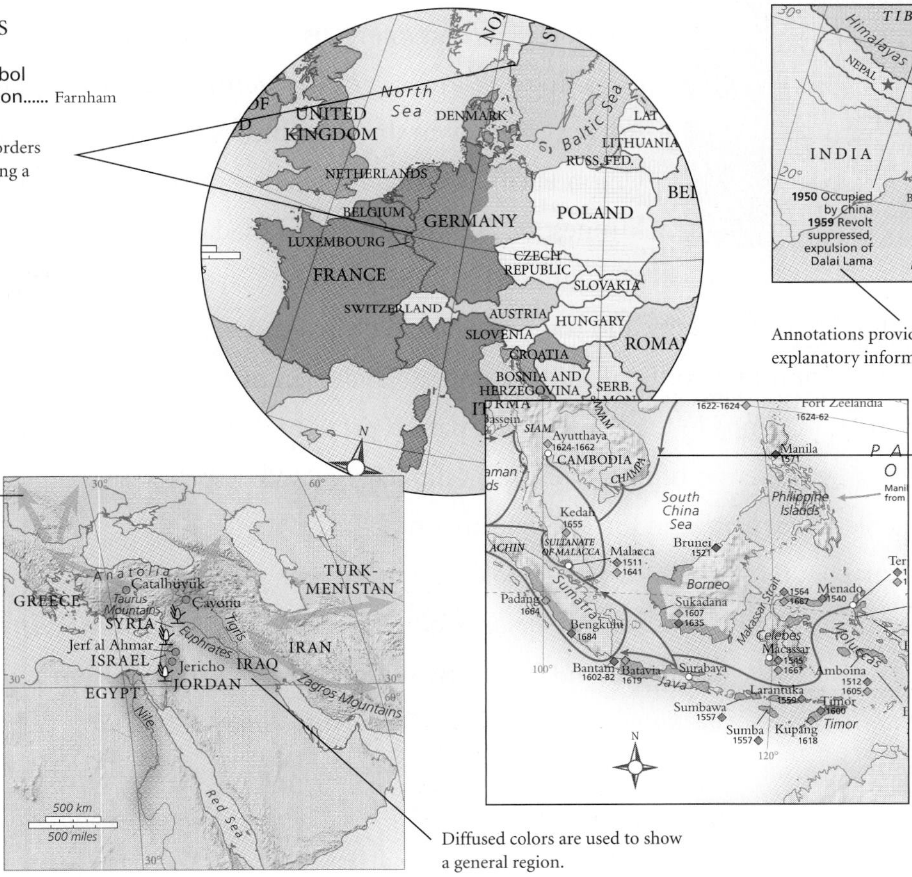

Major land borders are shown using a solid line.

Annotations provide additional explanatory information.

Political control is identified by color.

Broad arrows indicate general movement or spread of ideas, crops, or goods.

Thin arrows indicate journeys, trade routes, or campaigns.

Diffused colors are used to show a general region.

About Felipe Fernández-Armesto

Felipe Fernández-Armesto holds the William P. Reynolds Chair of History at the University of Notre Dame. He has master's and doctoral degrees from the University of Oxford, where he spent most of his teaching career, before taking up the Chair of Global Environmental History at Queen Mary College, University of London, in 2000, and the Prince of Asturias Chair at Tufts University (2005–2009). He is on the editorial boards of the History of Cartography for the University of Chicago Press, Studies in Overseas History (Leiden University), *Comparative Studies in Society and History, Journeys,* and *Journal of Global History.* Recent awards include the World History Association Book Prize (2007), Spain's Premio Nacional de Gastronomía (2005, for his work on the history of food), and the Premio Nacional de Investigación (Sociedad Geográfica Española, 2004). He has had many distinguished visiting appointments, including a Fellowship of the Netherlands Institute of Advanced Study in the Humanities and Social Sciences and a Union Pacific Visiting Professorship at the University of Minnesota. He won the Caird Medal of the National Maritime Museum in 1995 and the John Carter Brown Medal in 1999 and has honorary doctorates from La Trobe University and the Universidad de los Andes. He has served on the Council of the Hakluyt Society, on the Committee of English PEN, and as Chairman of the PEN Literary Foundation. His work in journalism includes regular columns in the British and Spanish press, and, among his many contributions to broadcasting, he is the longest-serving presenter of BBC radio's flagship current affairs program, *Analysis.* He has been short-listed for the most valuable literary prize in the United Kingdom.

Fernández-Armesto is the author, coauthor, or editor of 30 books and numerous papers and scholarly articles. His work has been translated into 25 languages. His books include *Before Columbus; The Times Illustrated History of Europe; Columbus; Millennium: A History of the Last Thousand Years* (the subject of a ten-part series on CNN); *Civilizations: Culture, Ambition, and the Transformation of Nature; Near a Thousand Tables; The Americas; Humankind: A Brief History; Ideas that Changed the World; The Times Atlas of World Exploration; The Times Guide to the Peoples of Europe; Amerigo: The Man Who Gave His Name to America;* and *Pathfinders: A Global History of Exploration.*

Dear Reader,

History is stories. There are hundreds of tales in this book about real, flesh-and-blood people—commoners and kings, sons and mothers, heroes and villains, the famous and the failed. I try to combine them in two narratives that crisscross throughout the book. One is the story of how people connect and separate, as cultures take shape and influence and change one another. Alongside this story, there is another one of how humans interact with the rest of nature—other species, the unstable natural environment, the dynamic planet.

History is global. The whole world stays in view in almost every chapter. Readers can compare and connect what was happening in every region and every continent in every period—like observers from another galaxy, gazing at the world from outer space and seeing it whole.

History is universal. This book tries to say something about every sphere of life—including science and art, suffering and pleasure, thought and imagination.

History is a problem-posing discipline. This book is full of provocations, contested claims, debated speculations, open horizons, and questions too complex and too interesting to answer easily. I employ facts not just for their own sake but also to make my readers—and myself—think.

History is evidence. Readers of this book confront the sources on every page—the words, images, and objects people really used in the past—to reveal vivid pictures of what history looked like and what it felt like to live in the past.

History enhances life. I believe that a textbook can be entertaining, even amusing, as well as instructive and accessible; challenging without being hostile; friendly without being cloying.

History isn't over. This book is about how the world got to be the way it is, confronting present problems and perspectives for the future—which is, after all, only the past that hasn't yet happened.

Felipe Fernández-Armesto

INTRODUCING THE WORLD

By the standards of astronauts, say, or science fiction writers, historians seem timid, unadventurous creatures who are only interested in one puny species—our species, the human species—on one tiny planet—our planet, Earth. But Earth is special. So far, we know of nowhere else in the cosmos where so much has happened and is happening today. By galactic standards, global history is a small story—but it's a good one.

Humans, moreover, compared with other animals, seem outward looking. Our concerns range over the universe, and beyond it, to unseen worlds, vividly imagined or mysteriously revealed. Not just everything we do but also everything that occurs to our minds is part of our history and, therefore, is part of this book, including science and art, fun and philosophy, speculations and dreams. We continually generate stories—new stories—at an amazing rate.

But the present passes instantly into the past. The present is always over, transformed into history. And the past is always with us, tugging at our memories, shaping our thoughts, launching and limiting our lives. Human history may seem narrowly self-interested, but it focuses on an undeniably riveting subject that is also our favorite subject—ourselves.

THE WAY OF HUMANKIND

Although the story of this book is a human story, it can never be merely human because, in isolation humankind does not make perfect sense. Humans are animals, and to understand ourselves thoroughly and to know what, if anything, makes us unique, we have to compare ourselves with other animals. As with other animals, we are best studied in our habitats. We cannot begin to comprehend our own history except in context. Our story is inseparable from the climates where it takes place and the other life forms that we depend on or compete with. We lord it over other species, but we remain linked to them by the food chain. We transform our environment, but we can never escape from it. We differentiate ourselves from nature—we speak loosely, for instance, of nature as if we were not natural creatures ourselves. We distance ourselves from our fellow-animals by adopting what we think are unnatural behaviors—wearing clothes, for instance, cooking food, replacing nature with culture. In short, we do what is natural to us, and all the elaborate culture we produce generates new, intimate relationships with the environment we refashion and the life forms we exploit.

We are exceptionally ambitious compared to other animals, consciously remodeling environments to suit our own purposes. We carve out fields, turn prairies into wheat lands, deserts into gardens, and gardens into deserts. We fell forests where we find them and plant them where none exist; we dam rivers, wall seas, cultivate plants, breed creatures, extinguish some species, and call others into being by selection and hybridization. Sometimes we smother terrain with environments we build for ourselves. Yet none of these practices liberates us from nature. As we shall see, one of the paradoxes of the human story is that the more we change the environment, the more vulnerable we become to ecological lurches and unpredictable disasters. Failure to establish the right balance between exploitation and conservation has often left civilizations in ruins. History becomes a path picked across the wreckage. This does not mean that the environment determines our behavior or our lives, but it does set the framework in which we act.

We are an exceptionally successful species in terms of our ability to survive in a wide range of diverse climates and landscapes—more so than just about any other creature, except for the microbes we carry around with us. But even we are still explorers of our planet, engaged in an ongoing effort to change it. Indeed, we have barely begun to change planet Earth, though, as we shall see, some human societies have devoted the last ten thousand years to trying to do it. We call ourselves lords, or, more modestly, caretakers of creation, but about 90 percent of the biosphere is too far underwater or too deep below the Earth for us to inhabit with the technology we have at present: These are environments that humans have only recently begun to invade and that we still do not dominate.

If we humans are peculiarly ambitious creatures, who are always intruding in the life of the planet, we are also odd compared to other animals in the way we generate change among ourselves. We are an unpredictable, unstable species. Lots of other animals live social lives and construct societies. But those societies are remarkably stable compared to ours. As far as we know, ants and elephants have the same lifeways and the same kinds of relationships that they have had since their species first appeared. That is not to say animals never change their cultures. One of the fascinating discoveries in primatology is that apes and monkeys develop cultural differences from one another, even between groups living in similar and sometimes adjacent environments. In one forest region of Gabon in West Africa, chimpanzees have developed a termite-catching technology. They "fish" with stripped branches that they plunge into termite nests but do not use tools to break open nuts. Chimps in a neighboring region ignore the termites but are experts in nut cracking, using rocks like hammers and anvils. In Sumatra in Indonesia, orangutans play a game—jumping from falling trees—that is unknown to their cousins in nearby Borneo. In Ethiopia in East Africa, males in some baboon groups control harems while others nearby have one mate after another. In some chimpanzee societies, hunting and meat eating seem to have increased dramatically in recent times.

These are amazing facts, but the societies of nonhuman animals still change little compared with ours. So, alongside the theme of human interaction with the rest of nature is another great theme of our history: the ways our societies have changed, grown apart from one another, reestablished contact, and influenced one another in their turn.

THE WAY OF THIS BOOK

This book, then, interweaves two stories—stories of our interactions with nature and stories of our interactions with each other. The environment-centered story is about humans distancing themselves from the rest of nature and searching for a relationship that strikes a balance between constructive and destructive exploitation. The culture-centered story is of how human cultures have become mutually influential and yet mutually differentiating. Both stories have been going on for thousands of years. We do not know whether they will end in triumph or disaster.

There is no prospect of covering all of world history in one book. Rather, the fabric of this book is woven from selected strands. Readers will see these at every turn, twisted together into yarn, stretched into stories. Human-focused historical ecology—the environmental theme—will drive readers back, again and again, to the same concepts: sustenance, shelter, disease, energy, technology, art. (The last is a vital category for historians, not only because it is part of our interface with the rest of the world, but also because it forms a record of how we see reality and of how the way we see it changes.) In the global story of human interactions—the cultural theme—we return constantly to the ways people make contact with each another: migration, trade, war, imperialism, pilgrimage, gift exchange, diplomacy, travel—and to their social frameworks: the economic and political arenas, the human groups and groupings, the states and civilizations, the sexes and generations, the classes and clusters of identity.

The stories that stretch before us are full of human experience. "The stork feeds on snakes," said the ancient Greek sage, Agathon, "the pig on acorns, and history on human lives." The only way to build up our picture of human societies and ecosystems of the past is to start with the evidence people have left. Then we reassemble it bit by bit, with the help of imagination disciplined by the sources. Anyone reading a history book needs to bear in mind that interpreting evidence is a challenge—half burden and half opportunity. The subject matter of history is not the past directly because the past is never available to our senses. We have only the evidence about it. This makes history an art, not a science, an art disciplined by respect for the sources, just as patterns impose discipline on poets or as the limitations of stagecraft discipline a play.

For a book like this, the sources set the limits of my imagination. Sometimes these are concrete clues to what people really did—footprints of their wanderings, debris of their meals, fragments of their technologies, wreckage of their homes, traces of diseases in their bones. Usually, however, the sources do not reflect the way things were but the way people wished to represent them in their arts and crafts and writings. In short, most sources are evidence of what happened only in the minds of those who made them. This means, in turn, that our picture of what went on in the world beyond human minds is always tentative and open to reinterpretation. The historian's job is not—cannot be—to say what the past was like, but rather, what it felt like to live in it because that is what the evidence tends to reveal.

One of the most admirable historians of the twentieth century, R. G. Collingwood, who was also a professor of philosophy at Oxford, said that "all history is intellectual history." He was right. History—even the environmental and cultural history that is the subject of this book—is largely about what people perceived rather than what they really saw, what they thought or felt rather than what happened outwardly, what they represented rather than what was real. The nineteenth-century philosopher Arthur Schopenhauer, one of the most pessimistic thinkers ever, who drew on Hindu and Buddhist writings for his inspiration, said that history's only subject was "humankind's oppressive, muddlesome dream." He thought that made history pointless. I think the dream makes it intriguing.

Because the evidence is always incomplete, history is not so much a matter of describing or narrating or question-answering as it is a matter of problem-posing. No one reading this book should expect to be instructed in straightforward facts or to acquire proven knowledge. The thrill of history is asking the right question, not getting the right answer. Most of the time, the most we can hope for is to identify interesting problems that stimulate debate. And we have to accept that the debate is worthwhile for its own sake, even if we have insufficient knowledge to reach conclusions.

There is no agreement among historians even about what are the right sorts of questions to ask. Some—including me—are interested in huge philosophical questions, such as how does history happen? What makes change? Is it random or is it subject to scientific laws? Do impersonal forces beyond human control—environmental factors or economics or some world force called fate or evolution or God or progress—determine it? Or is change the externalization of ideas, which arise in minds and are projected onto the world through human action? And if it's a mixture, what's the balance?

At a slightly lower level of analysis, some historians ask questions about how human societies function. How and why do societies grow and fragment and take different forms? How do some people get power over others? How and why do revolutions happen and states and civilizations rise and fall?

Other historians like to pose problems about the present. How did we get into the mess we're in? Can we trace the causes of present dilemmas back into the past and, if so, how far? Why do we have a globally connected world without global governance? Why is peace always precarious? Why does ecological overkill menace our global environment? Having accounted—or failed to account—for the present, some historians like to focus on the future. They demand lessons from history about how to change our behavior or cope with recurrences of past difficulties. Others, again, search to make sense of the past, to find an overall way of characterizing it or narrating it that makes us feel we understand it.

Yet others—the majority, in the current state of historical fashion, and again including me—like to study the past for its own sake and try to identify the questions that mattered to people at the time they first asked them. This does not mean that the sort of history found in this book is useless (although I do not necessarily think it would be a bad thing if it were). For to penetrate the minds of people of the past—especially the remote past of cultures other than your own—you have to make a supreme effort of understanding. The effort has dividends for the person who practices it. It enhances life by sharpening responses to the streetscapes and landscapes, art and artifacts, laws and letters we have inherited from the past. And understanding is what we need most today in our multicultural societies and multicivilizational world.

HOW THIS BOOK IS ARRANGED

After finding the time, accumulating the knowledge, posing the questions, stiffening the sinews, and summoning the blood, the big problem for the writer of a global history textbook is organizing the material. The big problem for the reader is navigating it. It is tempting to divide the world up into regions or cultures or even—as I did in a previous book—into biomes and devote successive chapters to each. You could call that "world history," if you genuinely managed to cover the world. But "global history" is different: an attempt to see the planet whole, as if from an immense, astral height, and discern themes that truly transcend geographical and cultural boundaries. In this book, therefore, I try to look at every continent in just about every chapter (there are a couple of chapters that, for reasons described in their place, focus only on part of the world). Each chapter concentrates on themes from the two great global stories: how human societies diverge and converge, and how they interact with the rest of nature.

Because history is a story in which the order of events matters, the chapters are grouped into 10 parts, arranged chronologically. There are 30 chapters—one for each week in a typical U.S. academic year (though of course, every reader or group of readers will go at their own pace)—and 10 parts. I hope there is plenty to surprise readers without making the parts perversely defiant of the "periods" historians conventionally speak of. Part I runs from roughly 150,000 to roughly 20,000 years ago, and, on the whole, the periods covered get shorter as sources accumulate, cultures diverge, data multiply, and readers' interests quicken. Of course, no one should be misled into thinking the parts are more than devices of convenience. Events that happened in, say, 1850, are in a different part of this book from those that happened in, say 1750. But the story is continuous, and the parts could equally well be recrafted to start and end at different moments.

At every stage, some parts of the world are more prominent than others because they are more influential, more populous, more world-shaping. For great stretches of the book, China occupies relatively more space; this is not for reasons of political correctness, but because China has, for much of the past, been immensely rich in globally influential initiatives. In the coverage of the last couple of hundred years, Europe and the United States get a lot of attention: this is not "Eurocentrism" or "Westocentrism" (if there is such a word), but an honest reflection of how history happened. But I have tried not to neglect the peoples and parts of the world that historians usually undervalue: poor and peripheral communities sometimes have a stunning impact on the world. The margins and frontiers of the world are often where world-changing events happen—the fault lines of civilizations, which radiate seismic effects.

Learning Features for the Second Edition of *The World*

The pedagogical program for the Second Edition of *The World* has been carefully devised to complement the narrative, reinforce important concepts, and prompt students to ask questions and formulate arguments.

Chapter-opening vignettes use dramatic and unusual stories to put the main themes of each chapter in relief. One-third of the chapter-opening vignettes in the Second Edition are new.

Focus Questions open each chapter and encourage students to think critically about the key questions raised in each chapter.

Making Connections tables throughout the text help students see the global linkages behind important historical developments. Praised by users of *The World*, every chapter in the Second Edition now includes at least one, and in some cases, as many as three, Making Connections tables. New Making Connections tables have been added to Chapters 9, 13, 15, 20, 21, 22, and 26. To further improve their visual efficacy, locator maps showing the regions examined in each Making Connections table have been added to the Second Edition.

A Closer Look sections, one per chapter, provide in-depth visual analysis of a specific cultural artifact. Praised by users for the way in which they connect the macro with the micro, detailed notes and tie lines draw the reader into close contact with the object, providing opportunities to pose larger questions. Users of *The World* have consistently cited the Closer Look sections as effective learning tools for their students. One-third of the Closer Look sections in the Second Edition are new. See page xxvii for a complete listing.

Maps Widely hailed by users of the First Edition, the maps in *The World* employ innovative perspectives to help the reader see world history in a fresh and dynamic way. A range of different maps—from two-page thematic maps to spot maps that pinpoint specific events—connect with the discussion on a variety of different levels. Each map in the Second Edition has been extensively checked for accuracy and/or re-drafted to improve its graphical presentation. The Second Edition includes 35 new full-size maps and 102 new locater maps. See page xxi for a listing of the maps in the Second Edition.

NEW The Big Picture Building on the success of the map program for the First Edition, each of the 10 parts in *The World* now ends with "The Big Picture," a two-page map of the world that graphically highlights an important, pivotal development in global history. Accompanied by text and questions, each Big Picture map provides the reader with a visual snapshot of what the world looked like at key intervals in human history. Interactive versions of the Big Picture maps can be found on MyHistoryLab. Short video clips of the author discussing developments in global history related to the Big Picture maps are also available on the MyHistoryLab that accompanies the text.

Visual Sources Users of *The World* consistently rank its photo program as the best found in any textbook available today. Intimately connected to the narrative, each photo provides a compelling visual record, from mammoth huts to satellite images of the Earth from space. Detailed captions, crafted by the author, explicate the meaning behind each visual source. There are over 100 new photos in the Second Edition of *The World*.

In Perspective sections conclude each chapter and do much more than summarize the preceding discussion. They put the developments covered in the chapter into historical perspective, and they make explicit for the student the process by which historians interpret the past.

Chronologies throughout each chapter arrange key historical developments in the order in which they occurred.

Key Terms are defined in the Glossary and set in boldface type in the text.

In-text Pronunciation Guides, embedded directly in the text, provide phonetic spellings for unfamiliar words.

CHANGES TO THE SECOND EDITION

The many helpful readers' reports and reviews of the First Edition by both users and non-users formed the basis for preparing the Second Edition. Every chapter was either updated with new and accepted scholarship or reorganized to clarify its presentation. In many chapters, more substantive changes were made in response to feedback and advice from teachers.

Chapters 1–15

Chapter 1 now begins with a discussion of Imo, the famous Japanese macaque. Chapter 2 examines the archaeological remains of an ancient feast to highlight the main problems of the chapter. Chapter 3 now begins with a discussion of Queen Hatshepsut's expedition to Punt. In Chapter 5, coverage of Babylon and classical Greece has been expanded. Chapter 6 now includes a new section on the Israelites and more discussion of Buddhism. Discussion of Rome has been increased in Chapter 7. Chapter 8 includes fuller treatment of Tang China. Chapter 9 now provides an overview of the main tenets of the major world religions. Chapter 10 opens with a story of Queen Gudit of Ethiopia. Both the Crusades and Ghana are examined in more depth in Chapter 12. The Renaissance receives more discussion in Chapter 15.

Chapters 16–30

The "In Perspective" section in Chapter 16 has been extensively revised and enhanced. The opening vignette for Chapter 17 now tells the story of Charles Ledger and quinine; the "In Perspective" section for this chapter has also been expanded. Chapter 18 now opens with a vignette about the experience of Siamese ambassadors in eighteenth-century France, and it examines the Protestant Reformation in more depth. The "In Perspective" sections in Chapters 19 and 20 have been expanded significantly. Chapter 21 provides more extensive treatment of the wars for independence in Latin America. Chapter 22 now includes more coverage of the French Revolution and the Napoleonic wars. Chapter 24 provides a new discussion of feminism in both Egypt and the United States. Chapter 25 has increased coverage of the Scramble for Africa. Chapter 26 includes new discussion of nationalism and state formation in Japan, Germany, Italy, and the United States. Chapter 29 now opens with the story of Dolores Jimenez and her role in the Mexican Revolution. Chapters 28 and 30 have been updated with important new information pertaining to the history of the twentieth century and the first decade of the twenty-first century: political and social developments, financial crises, and global warming.

SUPPORT MATERIALS

The World, Second Edition, comes with an extensive package of support materials for teachers and students.

For Instructors

◆ **The Instructor's Manual/Test-Item File** includes chapter outlines, overviews, key concepts, discussion questions, teaching notes, map quizzes, and suggestions for audiovisual resources, as well as approximately 1,500 test items. Particular emphasis is placed on essay questions that test students' understanding of concepts across chapters.

◆ **Test Manager** is a computerized test management program for Windows and Macintosh environments. The program allows instructors to select items from the test-item file to create tests. It also allows for online testing.

◆ **The Instructor's Resource Center** (*www.pearsonhighered.com*) Text-specific materials, such as the instructor's manual, the test-item file, map files, digital transparencies and PowerPoint™ presentations, are available for downloading by adopters.

For Instructors and Students

◆ *http://www.myhistorylab.com* MyHistoryLab for *The World* offers students and instructors a state-of-the-art, interactive learning tool for world history. Organized by the main subtopics of *The World*, and delivered within a course-management platform, MyHistoryLab supplements and enriches the classroom experience and can form the basis for an online course. New interactive Big Picture Maps and videos of the author outlining key developments in world history now enrich the MyHistoryLab for *The World*. Audio summaries of the main concepts in each chapter are also available for downloading to MP3 players. Please contact your Pearson representative for details.

◆  **NEW** *Around the World in Sixty Minutes Video Series.* In response to overwhelming requests from instructors and students around the country, Pearson Prentice Hall and Felipe Fernández-Armesto have teamed up to produce a ten-part video series that covers key, transformative developments in world history from the beginnings of agriculture to the world we inhabit today. Each segment in the Series is approximately 4-6 minutes in length and features Fernández-Armesto discussing pivotal changes in human history: the beginnings of agriculture, the axial age, the rise of world religions, the tensions between pastoralists and settled societies, the age of the plague, human transplantations, the Enlightenment, the Industrial Revolution, and the paradoxes of the twentieth century. Shot in various locations, and interspersed with photos and historical footage, each video in the Series can serve as an ideal lecture launcher in the classroom or as a self-directed review opportunity for students. Questions at the end of each segment allow students to respond with short essays and submit electronically via MyHistoryLab. A demo video clip can be viewed at www.pearsonhighered.com/theworld.

As a further enrichment to the Series, each video is part of an integrated "learning zone" that also includes an interactive version of the Big Picture map that ends each of the ten Parts in *The World*.

◆  **NEW Interactive Big Picture Maps** feature the same maps as those in the text, rendered as globes that can be spun. Interactive icons on the globe allow students to explore visual and textual sources, which are linked to the e-book that accompanies *The World*.

The result is a rich, dynamic, and integrated learning experience that combines video, audio, visual sources, and text documents to reinforce the inquiry-based approach that sets *The World* apart from other books. A demonstration map can be viewed at www.pearsonhighered.com/theworld.

POPULAR VALUEPACKS FOR *THE WORLD*

◆ Titles from the renowned **Penguin Classics** series can be bundled with *The World* for a nominal charge. Please contact your Pearson Arts and Sciences sales representative for details.

◆ **Connections: Key Themes in World History**. Series Editor Alfred J. Andrea. Concise and tightly focused, the titles in the popular Connections Series are designed to place the latest research on selected topics of global significance, such as disease, trade, slavery, exploration, and modernization, into an accessible format for students. Available at a 50% discount when bundled with *The World*. For more information go to www.pearsonhighered.com.

◆ Getz/Hoffman/Rodriguez, *Exchanges: A Global History Reader* introduces students to the discipline of world history. Unlike other source collections, *Exchanges* helps students look beyond strictly delineated regionalism and chronological structures to understand history as a series of ongoing debates. Available at a 50% discount when bundled with *The World*.

◆ Clark, *A Guide to Your History Course: What Every Student Needs to Know*. This concise, spiral-bound guidebook orients students to the issues and problems they will face in the history classroom. Available at a 50% discount when bundled with *The World*.

◆ **The Prentice Hall Atlas of World History, Second Edition** includes over 100 full-color maps in world history, drawn by Dorling Kindersley, one of the world's most respected cartographic publishers. Copies of the Atlas can be bundled with *The World* for a nominal charge. Contact your Pearson sales representative for details.

For Students

◆ Extensively revised and updated, the **Primary Source: Documents in Global History DVD** is both a rich collection of textual and visual documents in world history and an indispensable tool for working with sources. Extensively developed with the guidance of historians and teachers, the revised and updated DVD version includes over 800 sources in world history—from cave art to satellite images of the Earth from space. More sources from Africa, Latin America, and Southeast. Asia have been added to this revised and updated DVD version. All sources are accompanied by headnotes and focus questions, and are searchable by topic, region, or time period.

◆ **World History Study Site** (*www.pearsonhighered.com*) This course-based, open-access online companion provides a wealth of resources for both students and professors, including test questions, flash cards, links for further research, and Web-based assignments.

◆ **CourseSmart** **CourseSmart Textbooks Online** is an exciting new choice for students looking to save money. As an alternative to purchasing the print textbook, students can subscribe to the same content online and save up to 50% off the suggested list price of the print text. With a CourseSmart eTextbook, students can search the text, make notes online, print out reading assignments that incorporate lecture notes, and bookmark important passages for later review. For more information, or to subscribe to the CourseSmart eTextbook, visit *www.coursesmart.com*.

ACKNOWLEDGMENTS

Without being intrusive, I have tried not to suppress my presence—my voice, my views—in the text because no book is objective, other than by pretense, and the reader is entitled to get to know the writer's foibles and failures. In overcoming mine, I have had a lot of help (though there are sure still to be errors and shortcomings through my fault alone). Textbooks are teamwork, and I have learned an immense amount from my friends and helpers at Pearson Prentice Hall, especially my editors, Charles Cavaliere and Gerald Lombardi, whose indefatigability and forbearance made the book better at every turn. Laura Lee Manley, senior marketing manager, and Sue Westmoreland, Executive Marketing Manager, for their creativity. I also thank the picture researcher Francelle Carapetyan, and the members of the production and cartographic sections of the team who performed Herculean labors: Ann Marie McCarthy, senior managing editor; Lynn Savino Wendel, production project manager; Mirella Signoretto, map project manager; and David Roberts, cartographer.

I also owe a debt of gratitude to the senior management team at Pearson Prentice Hall who supported this endeavor every step of the way: Bill Barke, CEO, Pearson Arts & Sciences, Yolanda de Rooy, president of the Humanities and Social Sciences division; Leah Jewell, editorial director; Priscilla McGeehon, editor-in-chief for history; Rochelle Diogenes, editor-in-chief for development; and Brandy Dawson, director of marketing.

I could not have gotten through the work without the help and support of my wonderful colleagues at Queen Mary, University of London; the Institute of Historical Research, University of London; and the History Department of Tufts University. I owe special thanks to the many scholars who share and still share their knowledge of global history at the Pearson Prentice Hall Seminar Series in Global History, and through the World History Association, the *Journal of Global History*, the *Journal of World History*, and H-NET. David Ringrose of University of California, San Diego, was a constant guide, whose interest never flagged and whose wisdom never failed. Many colleagues and counterparts advised me on their fields of expertise or performed heroic self-sacrifice in putting all of the many pieces of the book together: Natia Chakvetadze, Shannon Corliss, Maria Guarascio, Anita Castro, Conchita Ordonez, Sandra Garcia, Maria Garcia, Hector Grillone, the late Jack Betterley, Jeremy Greene, Jai Kharbanda, Ernest Tucker (United States Naval Academy), Steve Ortega (Simmons College), David Way (British Library), Antony Eastmond (Courtland Institute), Morris Rossabi (Columbia University), David Atwill and Jade Atwill (Pennsylvania State University), Stephen Morillo (Wabash College), Peter Carey (Oxford University), Jim Mallory (Queens University, Belfast), Matthew Restall (Pennsylvania State University), Roderick Whitfield (School of Oriental and African Studies, University of London), Barry Powell (University of Wisconsin), Leonard Blussé (Harvard University), Guolong Lai (University of Florida), Frank Karpiel (The Citadel), George Kosar (Tufts University), David Kalivas and Eric Martin of H-NET and the many subscribers to their service who commented on the book or posted or e-mailed queries and suggestions, and the faculty, staff, and students of the many colleges where I got the chance to discuss the book (Boston College, Colorado State University, Essex Community College, Georgetown University, Jackson State University, Northern Kentucky University, Ohio State University, Penn State University, St John's University [New York], Salem State University, San José State University, Simmons College, U.S. Air Force Academy, U.S. Naval Academy, University at Buffalo, University of California [San Diego], San Diego State University, University of Arkansas [Little Rock], and University of Memphis) as well as the many good people whose assistance I may have failed to acknowledge.

Felipe Fernández-Armesto
Somerville, Massachusett

DEVELOPING *THE WORLD*

Developing a project like *The World* required the input and counsel of hundreds of individuals. David Ringrose, from the University of California at San Diego served as *The World*'s editorial consultant, closely reading and commenting on every draft of the book. His experience and understanding of classroom issues were invaluable to the development of *The World*. Nearly 100 reviewers critiqued portions of the manuscript from the first to the final draft. In addition, the manuscript was class-tested with over 1,000 students across the country who provided invaluable feedback and advice. Additionally, fifteen focus groups were held with teachers of world history to gather feedback and test ideas. An additional 75 reviewers of critiqued portions of *The World* to help prepare the Second Edition. We thank all those who shared their time and effort to make *The World* a better book.

Reviewers of the First Edition

Donald R. Abbott, San Diego Mesa College
Wayne Ackerson, Salisbury University
Roger Adelson, Arizona State University
Alfred J. Andrea, University of Vermont (Emeritus)
David G. Atwill, Pennsylvania State University
Leonard Blussé, Harvard University
Mauricio Borrero, St. John's University
John Brackett, University of Cincinnati
Gayle K. Brunelle, California State University—Fullerton
Fred Burkhard, Maryland University College
Antoinette Burton, University of Illinois
Jorge Cañizares-Esguerra, University of Texas—Austin
Elaine Carey, St. John's University
Tim Carmichael, College of Charleston
Douglas Chambers, University of Southern Mississippi
Nupur Chaudhuri, Texas Southern University
David Christian, San Diego State University
Duane Corpis, Georgia State University
Dale Crandall-Bear, Solano Community College
Touraj Daryaee, University of California, Irvine
Jeffrey M. Diamond, College of Charleston
Brian Fagan, University of California—Santa Barbara
Nancy Fitch, California State University—Fullerton
Alison Fletcher, Kent State University
Patricia Gajda, The University of Texas at Tyler
Richard Golden, University of North Texas
Stephen S. Gosch, University of Wisconsin—Eau Claire
Jonathan Grant, Florida State University
Mary Halavais, Sonoma State University

Shah M. Hanifi, James Madison University
Russell A. Hart, Hawaii Pacific University
Phyllis G. Jestice, University of Southern Mississippi
Amy J. Johnson, Berry College
Deborah Smith Johnston, Lexington High School
Eric A. Jones, Northern Illinois University
Ravi Kalia, City College of New York
David M. Kalivas, Middlesex Community College
Frank Karpiel, College of Charleston
David Kenley, Marshall University
Andrew J. Kirkendall, Texas A&M University
Dennis Laumann, The University of Memphis
Donald Leech, University of Minnesota
Jennifer M. Lloyd, SUNY—Brockport
Aran MacKinnon, University of West Georgia
Moria Maguire, University of Arkansas—Little Rock
Susan Maneck, Jackson State University
Anthony Martin, Wellesley College
Dorothea Martin, Appalachian State University
Adam McKeown, Columbia University
Ian McNeely, University of Oregon
Margaret E. Menninger, Texas State University—San Marcos
Stephen Morillo, Wabash College
William Morison, Grand Valley State University
Laura Neitzel, Brookdale Community College
Kenneth J. Orosz, University of Maine—Farmington
Michael Pavkovic, Hawaii Pacific University
Phyllis E. Pobst, Arkansas State University
Kenneth Pomeranz, University of California—Irvine

Sara B. Pritchard, Montana State University
Norman Raiford, Greenville Technical College
Stephen Rapp, Georgia State University
Vera Blinn Reber, Shippensburg University
Matthew Redinger, Montana State University—Billings
Matthew Restall, Pennsylvania State University
Jonathan Reynolds, Arkansas State University
Richard Rice, University of Tennessee—Chattanooga
Peter Rietbergen, Catholic University (Nijmegen)
David Ringrose, University of California—San Diego
Patricia Romero, Towson University
Morris Rossabi, Queens College
David G. Rowley, University of Wisconsin—Platteville
Sharlene Sayegh, California State University—Long Beach
William Schell, Murray State University
Linda Bregstein Scherr, Mercer County Community College
Patricia Seed, University of California, Irvine
Lawrence Sondhaus, University of Indianapolis
Richard Steigmann-Gall, Kent State University
John Thornton, Boston University
Ann Tschetter, University of Nebraska—Lincoln
Deborah Vess, Georgia College & State University
Stephen Vinson, SUNY—New Paltz
Joanna Waley-Cohen, New York University
Anne M. Will, Skagit Valley College
John Wills, University of Southern California
Theodore Jun Yoo, University of Hawaii—Manoa

Reviewers of the Second Edition

A NOTE ON DATES AND SPELLINGS

In keeping with common practice among historians of global history, we have used B.C.E. (before the common era) and C.E. (common era) to date events. For developments deep in the past, we have employed the phrase "years ago" to convey to the reader a clear sense of time. Specific dates are only given when necessary and when doing so improves the context of the narrative.

Recognizing that almost every non-English word can be transliterated in any number of ways, we have adopted the most widely used and simplest systems for spelling names and terms. The *pinyin* system of Chinese spelling is used for all Chinese words with the exception of such words as *Yangtze*, which are still widely referred to in its Wade-Giles form. Following common usage, we have avoided using apostrophes in the spelling of Arabic and Persian words, as well as words from other languages—thus, *Quran* and *Kaaba* instead of *Qu'ran* and *Ka'ba*, and *Tbilisi* instead of *T'bilisi*. Diacritical marks, accents, and other specialized symbols are used only if the most common variant of a name or term employs such devices (such as *Çatalhüyük*), if they are part of a personal noun (such as *Nicolás*), or if the inclusion of such markings in the spelling of a word makes pronouncing it easier (*Teotihuacán*).

Throughout the text the first appearance of important non-English words whose pronunciation may be unclear for the reader are followed by phonetic spellings in parentheses, with the syllable that is stressed spelled in capital letters. So, for example *Ugarit* is spelled phonetically as "OO-gah-riht." Chinese words are not stressed, so each syllable is spelled in lowercase letters. Thus, the city of Hangzhou in China is rendered phonetically as "hahngjoh." For monosyllabic words, the phonetic spelling is in lowercase letters. So *Rus* is spelled as "roos." The table below provides a guide for how the vowel sounds in *The World* are represented phonetically.

a	as in *cat, bat*
ah	as in *car, father*
aw	as in *law, paw*
ay	as in *fate, same*
eh	as in *bet, met*
ee	as in *beet, ease*
eye	as in *dine, mine*
ih	as in *if, sniff*
o	as in *more, door*
oh	as in *row, slow*
oo	as in *loop, moo*
ow	as in *cow, mouse*
uh	as in *but, rul*

THE WORLD

A History

Second Edition

PART 1

ENVIRONMENT

CULTURE

1.75 million to 1.25 million years ago
Homo erectus migrations out of East Africa

6 million years ago
Evolution of hominids/early humans

since 3 million years ago
Stone tools

Foragers and Farmers, to 5000 B.C.E.

◀ **The human imprint.** Hand stencils – painted, scratched or made by spraying with ocher, like this example from the Cosquer Cave on the south coast of France – are among the most common images in surviving Ice-Age decorated caves. Cosquer is a well-preserved gallery of them, because rising sea levels concealed the entrance to the cave until it was discovered by a diver, Henri Cosquer, in 1985. The practice of touching the rock surface with outstretched palm, and recording the visitor's presence in enduring form, lasted in the region for thousands of years: surviving examples cover a period of more than 12,000 years from about 30,000 B.C.E. This suggests remarkable continuities of belief and ritual among people who seem to have been trying to contact an immutable world of spirits inside the Earth.

160,000 to 20,000 years ago
Most recent Ice Age

since 20,000
Global warming

 since ca. 10,000
Agriculture

since ca. 150,000 years ago
Homo sapiens

150,000 years ago
Fire, fire-hardened wood spears

since at least 100,000 years ago
Art, ritual, religion; first migrations out of Africa

since 40,000 years ago
Bow and arrow

CHAPTER 1

Out of the Ice: Peopling the Earth

▲ **A macaque monkey** of Imo's tribe on Koshima Island in Japan washes a sweet potato while her baby looks on. Other macaque tribes have developed new cultural practices in recent times, including taking baths in hot springs—a practice otherwise confined to humans—and playing games with stones. Many non-human creatures are now known to be cultural, including all the great apes, and even capuchin monkeys in northern Brazil, who have had no common ancestors with other primates for 30 million years. Dolphins, whales, elephants, and rats are among other candidates for whom culture has been proposed but not proved.

Imo was less than two years old. But she displayed amazingly precocious talents as an innovator and teacher. Her tribe loved to eat freshly cleaned sweet potatoes, scraping the dirt off with their hands. But Imo figured out how to wash the vegetables clean and passed the knowledge on, first to her mother and then, gradually, to other relatives who in turn taught others, until most of the tribe had mastered the idea. Imo later found a new way to separate wheat grains from the sand that clung to them: she dropped them in water. The sand was heavier than the cereal, so that it sank while Imo scooped up the wheat. Again, she taught the practice to the tribe.

JAPAN

The most surprising thing about Imo's achievement, when scientists in Japan observed it in 1953, was that she was a monkey. Her tribe was a community of macaques or "snow monkeys", also most famous for their habits of bathing in a hot water spring. She excited the scientific world because she helped to prove that humans are not the only species with culture—that is, with behaviors transmitted by learning, not just sprung from instinct, which become routines or rites, practiced not necessarily because they are useful but because they are traditional or conventional. To this day, the monkeys of Imo's tribe wash their sweet potatoes before eating them and teach their youngsters to do the same, even if you give them ready-washed food from a supermarket shelf.

Meanwhile, examples of culture in nonhuman species have multiplied. Human culture is still special in curious ways: it changes much faster than that of other species, and it diverges much more widely, but we are now beginning to realize that to understand human peculiarities we have to take other cultural animals into account. Some of the most challenging recent discoveries have brought animal politics to light. Typically, "alpha males", who rule by force, with subordinate helpers or sometimes in gangs, dominate chimpanzee societies. But a few years ago, a clever, relatively weak male seized temporary control of a community of fellow-chimps in Tanzania by strewing boxes across the pathways used by the leaders: he bamboozled them into surrendering power. Even baboons can change their political systems. In Kenya in 1986, the aggressive elite that ruled a group of about 90 baboons all died suddenly after raiding a contaminated garbage dump for food. After that, the group adopted a much looser power structure, and taught male "immigrants" from other tribes to adopt collaborative approaches to power. Mutual grooming replaced force as the main way to gain authority and attract mates. New research is focusing on even more surprising examples of what looks like cultural behavior in dolphins, elephants, and rats.

So we are not alone. The assumption that humans are easily separable from the rest of creation now looks shaky. We all think we know what it means to be human, but if anyone asks us to define humankind, we cannot do it. Or at least we cannot do it satisfactorily.

FOCUS questions

Where in the evolutionary record do humans begin?

Why did the population of *Homo sapiens* grow so rapidly?

Why was the Ice Age a time of abundance?

What does its art tell us about Ice-Age society?

When did *Homo sapiens* migrate to the Americas?

How did human life change when the Ice Age ended?

SO YOU THINK YOU'RE HUMAN

We can call humankind a species, but species are just convenient categories for grouping together forms of life that are closely related. The boundaries between species are fuzzy and can change. There is no standard of how closely related you have to be to a fellow creature to be classed in the same species, or among species of the same sort, or, as biologists say, "genus." DNA evidence reveals that all the people we now recognize as human had a common ancestor who lived in Africa, probably more than 150,000 years ago. If we go back 5 to 7 million years, we share ancestors with chimpanzees. Double the length of time, and the fossils reveal ancestors whom we share with other great apes. Further back, the flow of evolution erodes the differences between our ancestors and other creatures. The differences are only matters of degree. If we accept the theory of **evolution**—and, in outline, it does present a true account of how life forms change—we cannot find any transforming moment in the past when humankind began. Species so like ourselves preceded us in the evolutionary record that, if we were to meet members of them today, we would probably embrace some of them as fellow humans and puzzle over how to treat others.

Even today, there are nonhuman species—especially among the apes—whose humanlike qualities so impress people who work and live with them that they seem morally indistinguishable from humans and should, according to some biologists and philosophers, be included in the same genus and even the same moral community as ourselves, with similar rights. In terms of the sort of cultures they have, emotions they reveal, societies they form, and behaviors they adopt, chimpanzees share many characteristics with the fellow apes we call humans. To a lesser extent, gorillas and orangutans are also like us. All of us apes use tools, learn from each other, practice altruism and deceit, like to play, detest boredom, and seem self-aware. Our bodies and our behaviors are so like those of chimpanzees that the physiologist and historian Jared Diamond has suggested we reclassify our species as a kind of chimp. Our relationship with other animals could come full circle. In the often-filmed story of *The Island of Dr. Moreau*, the British novelist H. G. Wells (1866–1946) fantasized about a scientist who strove to produce perfect creatures by surgically combining human characteristics with those of other animals. Today, in theory, genetic engineering can actually produce such hybrids, prompting us to wonder at what point a hybrid would become human. The first big question for this chapter, then, is where in the evolutionary record does it make sense to talk about humans? When does the story of humankind begin?

Human Evolution

Paleoanthropologists—the specialists responsible for answering or, at least, asking the question about which species are human—give conflicting responses. The usual place to look is among creatures sufficiently like us to be classified, according to the present consensus, in the same genus as ourselves: the genus called "Homo" from the Latin word that means

Hybrid human. The British actor Charles Laughton in the role of Dr. Moreau gives orders to one of his hybrid creatures in the 1933 movie *The Island of Lost Souls,* based on H.G. Wells's 1896 novel, *The Island of Dr. Moreau.* Moreau engineers his islanders by surgically combining human and animal body parts. "Are we not men?" the suffering creatures ask. Like Moreau, we are unable to answer that question, because we are uncertain about what it means to be human.

"human." A creature known as *Homo habilis* ("handy"), about 2.5 million years ago, chipped hand axes from stones. In calling this species the first humans, scholars defined humans as toolmakers—a now discredited concept. *Habilis* also had a larger brain than earlier predecessors and therefore demanded more nourishment, as brains use disproportionately more energy than other parts of the body. But ours is not the biggest-brained species in the evolutionary record. At one time, anthropologists backed a slightly later species, *Homo erectus* ("standing upright"), of about 1.5 million years ago, as the first human, largely because they admired the symmetrical flints for tools and weapons that *erectus* carved. From finds over 800,000 years ago, variant (or, perhaps, different) species called *Homo ergaster* ("workman") and *antecesor* ("predecessor") appeared, who later—at one site at least—stacked the bones of the dead. But reverence for the dead is not a uniquely human trait either. All these creatures, and others like them, have had champions who have claimed them as the first humans. Clearly, these instances of backing one set of ancestors over another reflect subjective criteria: supposed resemblances to ourselves. We are like the bereaved of some horrible disaster, scanning the remains of the dead for signs that we can recognize.

Species that occurred earlier than those we class under the heading "Homo," or who resembled us less, have tended to get labeled with less human-sounding names. Anthropologists used to call them "pithecanthropoi"—literally, ape-men. Current terminology favors "**australopithecines**" ("southern apelike creatures"), or "paranthropoi" ("next to humans"), as if they were identifiably nonhuman or prehuman. But in 1974, the archaeologist Dan Johansen made a discovery that blew away all notion of a clear dividing line. He spotted the bones of an australopithecine sticking out of the mud in Hadar in Ethiopia in East Africa. He dug her up and called her "Lucy" after the title of a song on a Beatles record he played that night in camp. Lucy had died over 3 million years ago. She was only about 3 feet tall, but she and her kind had characteristics that were thought to belong exclusively to later species of *Homo*. They walked on two legs and lived in family groups. Johansen discovered tools 2.5 million years old near the site the following year and, in 1977, he found footprints, dating back 3.7 million years, of creatures who stood and walked on two legs. Finds with similar characteristics may date as far back as 6 million years ago.

As evolution slowly grinds out species, the question that arises is who's human? Who's to say? It is tempting to try to settle the issue by reserving the term *human* for ourselves—members of the species we call **Homo sapiens**. Literally, the term *sapiens* means "wise," a grandiose name that betrays the foolishness of self-ascribed wisdom. For other species also have embarrassingly strong claims. One example is *Homo neanderthalensis*, who vanished only 30,000 years ago. The name means "of the Neander Valley"—the spot in northern Germany where remains of this species were found in 1856. We can be fairly certain that no one living today has a **Neanderthal** ancestor because there are no known cases of interbreeding between Neanderthals and our own ancestors. But *Homo neanderthalensis* and *Homo sapiens* coexisted for something like 100,000 years. Neanderthals had distinctive vocal tracts, so it is unlikely that they and our ancestors could speak each others' languages. They could have used nonverbal communication, however, just as we do today to talk with apes and even with humans whose spoken language we do not understand.

In most other respects, the two species of *Homo* were alike. Neanderthals were as big as *sapiens* and had a similar appearance; the brains were also similar, but, on average, the Neanderthal brain was slightly larger. They followed the same hunting,

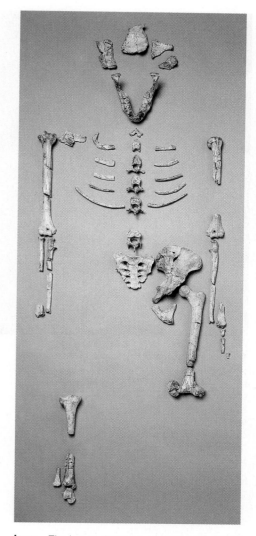

Lucy. The bones shown here aren't connected to each other, but modern imaginations have reconstructed the three-million-year-old skeleton known as "Lucy," as human or nearly so. Lucy walked on two legs and was closer to humans, in evolutionary terms, than any nonhuman creature that exists today.

(a)

(b)

The changing image of the Neanderthal. Gradually, over the last 30 years or so, the old image of a bestial, inhuman creature (b) has given way to a more sympathetic vision that acknowledges how like Neanderthals we are (a). An important conflict underpins the rival images: if we classify Neanderthals as human, where and how can we set the boundaries of humankind?

foraging ways of life in overlapping habitats. They made the same kinds of tools our ancestors made, lived in the same types of society, ate the same foods, and had many of the same customs and rites. They cared for their old and sick, and they buried their dead with signs of honor that suggest a sense of religion. They also seem to have expected an afterlife, burying bears' jaws with their dead, as if to protect them and perhaps—though the evidence is uncertain—strewing fragrant flowers on some graves as if to help, honor, or adorn the deceased. Yet some paleoanthropologists seem determined to deny Neanderthals the name of humans—using arguments startlingly, frighteningly reminiscent of those that nineteenth-century scientific racism employed to deny full humanity to black people: claiming, for instance, that they were inferior and doomed to extinction in competition for "the survival of the fittest." Typical anti-Neanderthal arguments are that their physiques were poorly adapted, that their efforts to articulate must have sounded like grunts, and that they had no art that we can recognize. Meanwhile, the evidence of their accomplishments is explained away. The ritual objects found at their graves, detractors say, must be "tricks of evidence," deposited accidentally by streams, winds, or animals.

Paleoanthropologists continue to dig up specimens that challenge believers in human uniqueness. In October 2004, excavators published news of a stunning find in Southeast Asia on the island of Flores in Indonesia, which included the remains of a female whose teeth, when they found her, were mashed to pulp, her bones rotted and soggy. She died 18,000 years ago. She was dwarfishly tiny. Her brain was barely as big as a chimpanzee's. But she had the power to subvert anthropological orthodoxy. *Homo floresiensis*, as her finders called her and her relatives whose bones lay alongside hers, proved that big brains do not make their possessors superior to other creatures. To judge from adjoining finds, these "hobbits," as the press dubbed them, had tools typical of early *Homo sapiens*, despite chimp-sized brains in imp-sized bodies. *Floresiensis* almost certainly made those tools. In known cases where nonhuman creatures lie alongside *sapiens*-made tools, *sapiens* ate them. But the remains of *floresiensis* showed no signs of having been butchered.

OUT OF AFRICA

Since no clear line separates human from nonhuman species, we might rationally start our story with our last common ancestor, roughly 150,000 years ago. All of us—as far as we can tell without actually testing everyone alive today—have a chemical component in our cells that a mother in East Africa passed on to her daughters at about that time. We nickname her Eve after the first woman in the biblical Book of Genesis, but of course she was not our first ancestor nor was she the only woman of her day. By the best available estimates, perhaps 20,000 individuals of the species *Homo sapiens* lived in the same region at that time. She may, however, have lived relatively early in the history of our species. No undisputed examples of *Homo sapiens* occur much earlier. We are therefore a young species, by the standards of evolution. In 2003, archaeological evidence of Eve's world turned up in Herto, in Ethiopia near the remains of a butchered hippopotamus. Three skulls—a child's and two adults'—dated to about 154,000 to 160,000 years ago, resemble those of humans today, except that they are larger than what is now average. They had been stripped of flesh and polished after death, which suggests that the culture they belonged to practiced some death-linked ritual. We can begin to picture not only the appearance of the African Eve—we can do that by looking in a mirror—but also something of her way of life or, at least, life at a time close to her own.

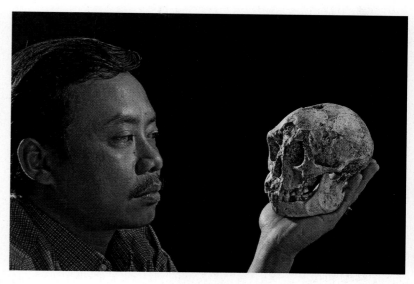

Homo floresiensis. The skull of *Homo floresiensis* is smaller than a chimpanzee's. Yet it held a brain with the same toolkit as our own species. So does size matter? Not, it seems, in brains. And the more discoveries we make about other species, the less special *Homo sapiens* seems.

Eve's homeland of mixed grassland and woodland was no Eden, but it was suitable for the creatures into which our ancestor and her offspring had evolved. In this environment they could make up for their deficiency as climbers by standing erect to look out around them. They could use fire to manage the grazing of the animals they hunted and could find materials to make into weapons and tools. They fire-hardened spears to kill game, and sharpened stones to butcher the carcasses. They could exploit their modest physical advantages over competitor species. Humans are poorly equipped physically, with inferior senses of sight, smell, and hearing, slow movements, unthreatening teeth and nails, poor digestions, and weak bodies that confine us to the ground. But we can sweat profusely over our hairless skins to keep cool during long chases, and we can ward off rival predators with our relatively accurate throwing-arms and well-coordinated eye–arm movements. In short, like most creatures, we are physically well equipped for a particular kind of habitat.

Peopling the Old World

From their beginnings in East Africa, Eve's descendants spread over the world (see Map 1.1). The first great problems these migrants pose for us are why they wanted to move, and what made them so adaptable to different environments. These are

Stone tools. Paleoanthropologists have long used stone tool-making technologies to classify hominid cultures, because these artifacts have survived in relatively large numbers. The chopper on the left, of a pattern that dates from over two million years ago, was made by striking cobblestones against each other. Chimpanzees can be taught to make similar tools. The more elegant axe-blade in the center is of a kind that predominated over much of the world between about 1.5 million and 150,000 years ago. Although the size, shape, and presumably function of these tools varied, as the examples on the right show, the technology was surprisingly uniform around the world. No bone tools, for example, from the period survive.

MAP 1.1

Early Human Migration 150,000–40,000 years ago

▢	*Homo erectus* migration, 1.75–1.25 million years ago
➤	*Homo sapiens* migration, 150,000–40,000 years ago
➤	Possible coastal migrations
◼	*Homo erectus* site described on page 14
◉	*Homo sapiens* sites described on pages 7-9
▼	Neanderthal sites described on page 7
▲	*Homo floresiensis* site
◼◉▼	other *Homo erectus, Homo sapiens,* and Neanderthal sites, 150,000–40,000 years ago
GABON	modern country
- - -	ancient coastline
⁓	ancient lake

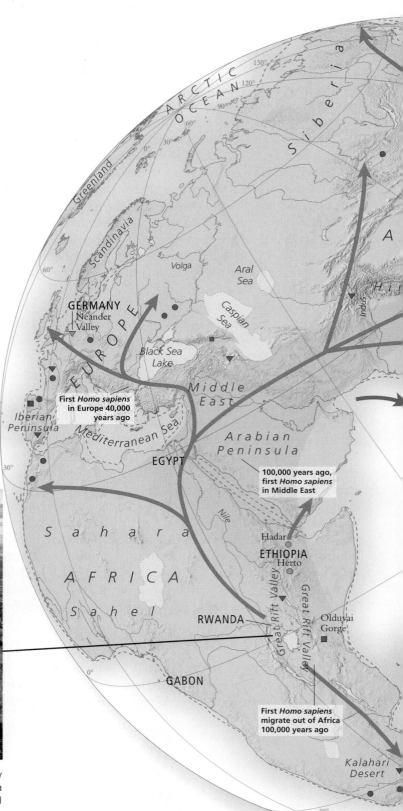

First *Homo sapiens* in Europe 40,000 years ago

100,000 years ago, first *Homo sapiens* in Middle East

First *Homo sapiens* migrate out of Africa 100,000 years ago

The Rift Valley is an almost continuous system of faults that stretches for nearly 3,000 miles across East Africa, from the northern coasts of what are now Eritrea and Somalia, across Ethiopia and south through Kenya and Tanzania to central Mozambique. Erosion of the surrounding highlands has helped to deposit and preserve extraordinary concentrations of prehistoric remains, including some of the most spectacular discoveries paleoanthropologists have made in the last 50 years.

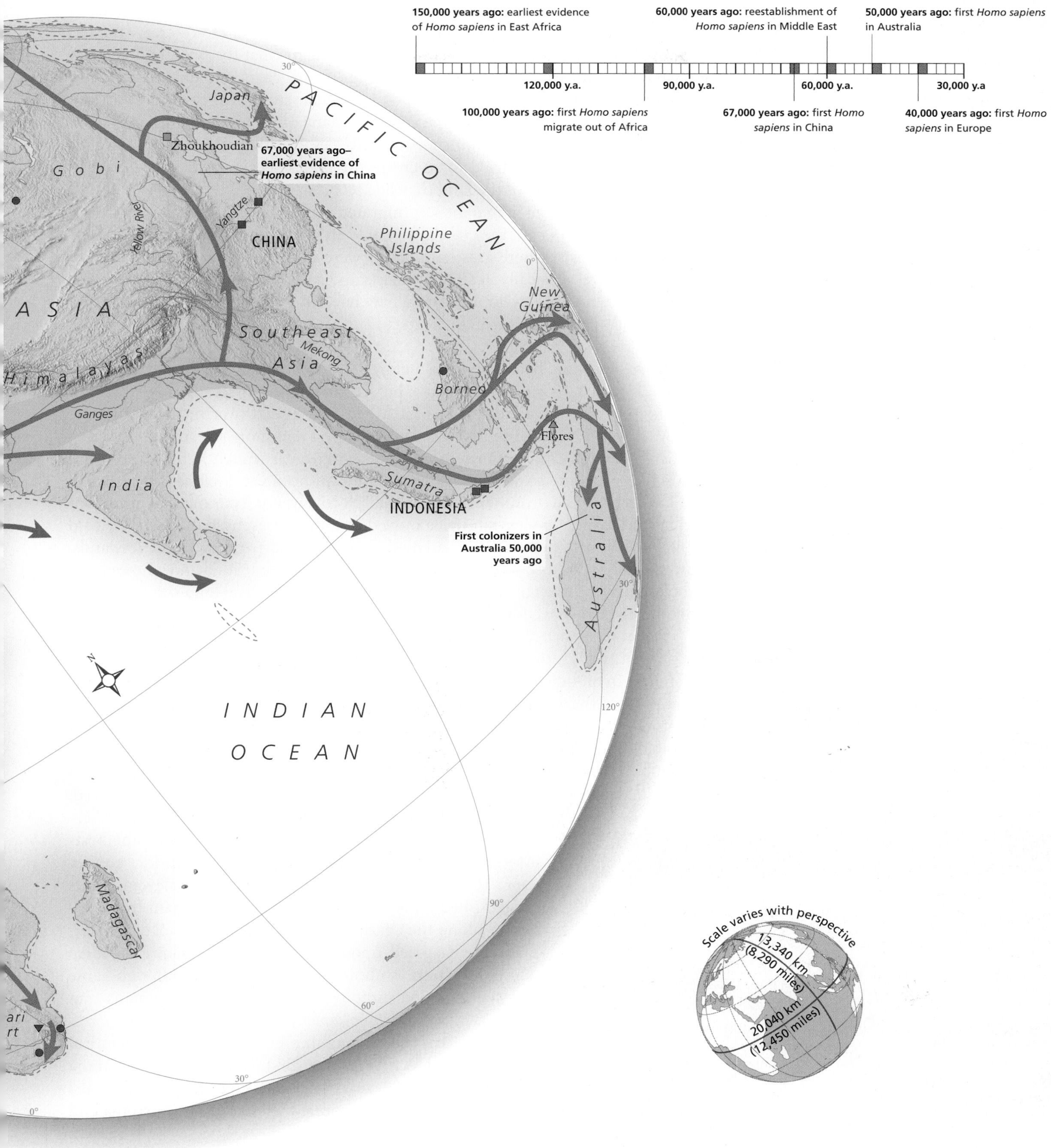

150,000 years ago: earliest evidence of *Homo sapiens* in East Africa

60,000 years ago: reestablishment of *Homo sapiens* in Middle East

50,000 years ago: first *Homo sapiens* in Australia

120,000 y.a.　　90,000 y.a.　　60,000 y.a.　　30,000 y.a

100,000 years ago: first *Homo sapiens* migrate out of Africa

67,000 years ago: first *Homo sapiens* in China

40,000 years ago: first *Homo sapiens* in Europe

PACIFIC OCEAN

Japan

Zhoukhoudian

G o b i

67,000 years ago—earliest evidence of *Homo sapiens* in China

Yellow River

Yangtze

CHINA

Philippine Islands

A S I A

S o u t h e a s t   A s i a

Mekong

New Guinea

Himalayas

Ganges

Borneo

India

Flores

Sumatra

INDONESIA

First colonizers in Australia 50,000 years ago

Australia

30°

INDIAN OCEAN

Madagascar

ari rt

Scale varies with perspective

13,340 km (8,290 miles)

20,040 km (12,450 miles)

big, perplexing problems because most species stay in the environments where they are best adapted. Even human populations rarely, if ever, seek new environments willingly, or adjust easily. When migrants move, they try to re-create the feel of home in their adopted country, carrying with them what the twentieth-century French historian Fernand Braudel called the "heavy baggage" of their **culture**. They transport familiar animals and transplant familiar crops, which usually means finding a new area similar to the one they left. Many of the early English settlers in America, for instance, were pioneers and refugees, but they called the place they chose New England and tried to re-create the landscapes and streetscapes, diet, houses, and ways of life of the land they had left.

Yet when groups of *Homo sapiens* migrated out of Africa to people the world, about 100,000 years ago, they often relocated in challengingly different environments: deep forests, where grassland habits were of limited use; cold climates, to which they were physically ill suited; deserts and seas, which demanded technologies they had not yet developed. These new habitats bred unfamiliar diseases. Yet people kept on moving through them and into them. We are still struggling to understand how it happened.

Such migration had happened before—or something like it had. Between about 1.75 and 1.25 million years ago, before *Homo sapiens* set out, *Homo erectus* migrated from a similar region in East Africa and spread over most of what are now Africa and Eurasia. But this was a much slower and more selective peopling of the Earth, and its circumstances are too obscure to cast much light on how and why *sapiens* became so widely dispersed. We can, however, look at other species that have crossed environments slowly and selectively. For example, the mountain gorillas of Rwanda in Central Africa moved into their present high, relatively cold habitat to escape the competitive environment of the tropical forest lowlands. Now, probably because food sources are relatively scarce in their new homeland, these exclusively vegetarian creatures are smaller and weaker than other gorillas. Nonetheless, they have forged a viable way of life.

We can reconstruct where and when *Homo sapiens* traveled while peopling the Earth, even though the archaeological evidence is patchy. One way is to measure differences in blood type, genetic makeup, and language among populations in different parts of the world (see Figure 1.1). The greater the differences, the longer the ancestors of the people concerned are likely to have been out of touch with the rest of humankind. This is inexact science, because people are rarely isolated for long. Over most of Eurasia and Africa, populations have moved about tremendously in recorded history. Groups of people have frequently been mixed and restirred.

There are, moreover, no agreed ways to measure the differences among languages. Still, for what it is worth, the best-informed research puts *Homo sapiens* in the Middle East by about 100,000 years ago. The colony failed, but new migrants reestablished it about 60,000 years ago. Settlement then proceeded along the coasts of Africa and Asia, probably by sea. The earliest agreed-upon archaeological evidence of *Homo sapiens* in China is about 67,000 years old (although some sites have yielded puzzlingly earlier dates for remains that seem like those of *Homo sapiens*).

It may seem surprising that humans developed nautical technology so early. Yet the first colonizers of Australia arrived over 50,000 years ago and must have used boats, because water already separated what are now Australia and

Chronology: Early Human Migration

150,000 years ago	Hypothetical African Eve (*H. sapiens*)
100,000 years ago	*H. sapiens* migrates out of Africa to Middle East
67,000 years ago	*H. sapiens* in China
60,000 years ago	*H. sapiens* reestablishes colony in Middle East
50,000 years ago	*H. sapiens* in Australia
40,000 years ago	*H. sapiens* in Europe
15,000 years ago	*H. sapiens* in the Americas

(All dates are approximate)

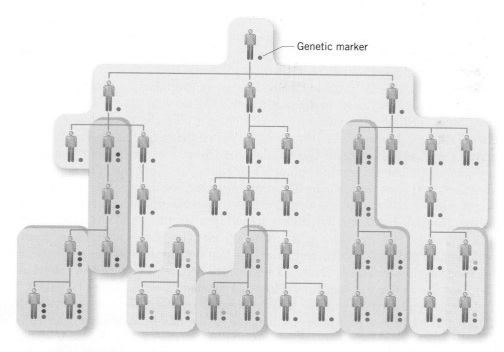

FIGURE 1.1 GENETIC DIVERSITY. Since genetic markers are inherited and are passed down from one generation to the next, they can be traced backward in time. Even through with each successive generation, new combinations of genetic markers are created, they all descend from one ancestor. The exact shape of this evolutionary tree is affected by other evolutionary forces, such as natural selection and migration. *National Geographic Genographic Project/Paula Willard. Reprinted by permission of National Geographic Image Collection.*

New Guinea from Asia. *Homo sapiens* reached Europe only a little later. Northern Asia and America—isolated by impenetrable screens of cold climate—were probably colonized much later. The most generally accepted archaeological evidence indicates the New World was settled no earlier than about 15,000 years ago.

If these dates are correct, the expansion of *Homo sapiens* implies an astonishing rate of population growth. Though, we have no idea—beyond guesswork—of the actual numbers that migrated, we can estimate a figure in millions by the end of the process. A handful of Eve's children had multiplied to the point where they could colonize most of the habitable Old World in less than 100,000 years. But was the increase in population cause or effect of the migrations? And how did it relate to the other changes migration brought? Migrating groups were doubly dynamic: not just mobile, but also subject to huge social changes—divisive and violent, but with constructive ways of organizing their lives.

Migration, Population, and Social Change

Migration changed people's relationships with each other, the size and organization of their groups, the way they saw the world, and the way they interacted with other species—including those they competed with, preyed on, and outlasted. As far as we know, everyone at the time lived by foraging and moved on foot. Because mothers cannot easily carry more than one or two infants, large numbers of children are unsuited to foraging life. Consequently, foragers usually limit their families, either by strictly regulating who can mate with whom (to reduce the numbers of breeding couples) or by practicing other forms of population control. Their main contraceptive method is a long period of lactation. Breast-feeding mothers are relatively infertile. The demographic growth that peopled the Earth is surprising, therefore, because it breaks the normal pattern of population stability in foraging communities. So how can we explain it?

Cooking with fire probably helped to make population growth possible, because it made food easier to digest. Creatures like us, who have short guts, weak jaws, blunt teeth, and only one stomach each, can only chew and digest limited energy sources. As a result, anything that increased the range of foods available to early humans and encouraged and enabled them to eat a lot was a major evolutionary advantage. The earliest indisputable evidence of cooking with fire dates back about 150,000 years, which coincides neatly with the beginning of the population boom, but we cannot be sure that fire-fueled cooking first happened then. The paleoanthropologist R. Wrangham has argued for a starting date more than 2 million years ago. His argument is based on the evolving shape of hominid teeth, which, apparently, got smaller and blunter at that time, presumably in response to the modification of food by flames. There is, however, no direct evidence that fire was used for cooking at that time. Fires that burned in caves between "500,000" and 1.5 million years ago appear to have been deliberately kindled, perhaps with cooking in mind. An almost irresistible case is that of Zhoukhoudian (joh-coh-dee-ehn) in China, where the great Jesuit scientist, Pierre Teilhard de Chardin (1881–1955), excavated the evidence and the Abbé Henri Breuil (1877–1961), the leading archaeologist of the day, identified it. "It's impossible," said the Jesuit, thinking the site was too early for the controlled use of fire, "it comes from Zhoukhoudian," "I don't care where it comes from," the Abbé replied. "It was made by a human, and that human knew the use of fire." We are similarly uncertain about when other technologies started that might have improved diet by improving hunting, such as making driving lanes and corrals to herd animals for killing, but, though much earlier dates have been proposed, the earliest known examples of fire-hardened spears are only 150,000 years or so old—again taking us back to a date near the start of the migrations.

Whether or not new technologies did empower humans to migrate, perhaps new stresses drove them on. Food shortages or ecological disasters might explain the necessity to move, but no evidence supports this or fits with the evidence of rising population. In every other case we know of, in all species, population declines when food sources shrink. Another possible source of stress is warfare. Among the four horsemen of the Apocalypse—war, plague, famine, and natural disaster in Revelation, the book of visions with which the Bible closes—war is the odd one out. The other three tend to inhibit human action, whereas war spurs us to new responses.

One of the most fascinating problems of history is how and when war started. According to one school of thought, war is natural to humankind. When people asked the commander of British forces in Europe in World War II, Bernard Montgomery (1887–1976), how he justified war, he would refer them to a book on *The Life of the Ant*. Some anthropologists agree, arguing that evolution implanted aggressive and violent instincts in humans as it did in other animals. Romantics defend the opposite point of view. Human nature, they say, is essentially peaceful until competition corrupts it. War, according to Margaret Mead, the great liberal anthropologist of the 1920s and 1930s, was an invention, not a biological necessity.

At first, the evidence seemed divided. The earliest archaeological proof we have of large-scale warfare is a battle fought at Jebel Sahaba, near the modern border of Egypt and Sudan, about 11,000 years ago. The victims included women

"Another possible source of stress is warfare. Among the four horsemen of the Apocalypse—war, plague, famine, and natural disaster in Revelation, the book of visions with which the Bible closes—war is the odd one out. The other three tend to inhibit human action, whereas war spurs us to new responses."

and children. Many were savaged by multiple wounds. One female was stabbed 22 times. At the time, agriculture was in its infancy. Today, both peoples who practice the simplest agriculture and those who supposedly represent modernity and civilization massacre others. These facts have encouraged speculation that warfare began—or, at least, entered a new, more systematic phase—when settled communities started to fight one another to control land and resources.

Yet organized warfare is probably much older than that. In the 1970s, the primatologist Jane Goodall observed something like what we would now call gang warfare among chimpanzee communities in West Africa. When chimpanzee splinter groups secede from their societies, their former fellows try to kill them. Similar conflicts may have made early human splinter groups migrate to safety. It is an intriguing speculation, but, even if it were to prove correct, it poses other problems. What stresses could have caused people to divide and fight each other 100,000 years ago? Rising population again? Or are we driven back to more speculation about increasing competition for supposedly diminishing food stocks, or even to assertions about innate animal aggression?

Chimp aggression. Humans obviously share aggressive individual tendencies with other apes. The American naturalist Jane Goodall discovered that chimpanzees organize conflicts with other groups of chimpanzees: they practice warfare, in other words. This seems to support what some philosophers and psychologists have long suspected: that war is a "natural" activity, or, if it is an effect of culture, that it arose early in the history of culture.

In societies of increasing violence, men have enhanced roles. This is because, among all primates, including humans, greater competitiveness in mating makes males, on average, bigger and stronger than females. Alpha males therefore rule, or at least boss, most ape societies. Human males usually seem to bond more closely with each other, or form more or stronger alliances, than females. This, too, is useful in competitive circumstances, such as those of war and politics. Yet women are, in at least one respect, more valuable in most societies than men. A society can dispense with most of its men and still reproduce itself. That is why societies more commonly risk men in war than women. Women, moreover, are more easily mistaken as sacred because of the obvious correspondences between the cycles of their bodies and the rhythms of the heavens. Menstruation and the cycle of female fertility match the phases of the moon.

So how did male domination come to be normal in human societies? One theory ascribes it to a deliberate, collective power-seeking strategy by males, inspired by dislike of women or resentment or envy or a desire to get control of the most elementary of resources—the means of reproducing the species. By analogy with chimpanzees, a rival theory suggests that male dominance is a consequence of hunting, which, in the few chimpanzee groups known to practice it, is an almost exclusively male activity. Hunting increases male dominance in chimpanzee society because the hunters distribute the meat, in almost ritual fashion. Females line up and, in effect, beg for morsels. Female chimps often exchange sex for food, especially meat. By contrast, among bonobos, who are like chimps but are strictly plant eating, both sexes share foraging, and females tend to be socially equal or even dominant. Hunting, however, seems to be a recent development in chimpanzee society and appears to have followed and strengthened male dominance—not caused it.

Without evidence to the contrary, it is unwise to assume that early in the migration period either sex monopolized political power. Still, migrating groups must have developed ways to liberate more women for childbirth or increase the fertile period of women's lives. Given the practical limitations on the number of children a woman can carry around with her, population can only have increased that way. Improved nutrition helped. Was there also some redistribution of economic activities, with men taking on more food-supplying roles?

Making Connections | THE FIRST POPULATION BOOM: REASONS FOR POPULATION GROWTH

Fire-managed grazing of animals; driving lanes; corrals	▷	control over food supply	▷	more food available for consumption
Throwing-arms; fire-hardened spears	▷	improved hunting	▷	improved diet
Cooking with fire	▷	improved taste and digestibility	▷	increase in range of available foods
Sexual economic specialization	▷	hunting and gathering	▷	women liberated for childbearing

As far as we know, in the earliest kind of economic specialization by sex, men did most of the hunting, while women did most of the gathering. Women's work seems to have been more productive in terms of calorific value per unit of energy expended. But we do not know when this specialization started or how rigid or widespread it was. In any case, the balance between hunted and gathered foods in the diets of the migrants varied according to the environment. In known cases, hunters supplied about a third of the nutrition. The migrations, and the accompanying demographic changes, would not have been possible without both hunting and gathering.

THE LAST GREAT ICE AGE

Whatever caused it, the peopling of the world spanned the most convulsive period of climatic change that *Homo sapiens* experienced before our own times. The cooling and warming phases of the planet are regular occurrences, and one or the other is always going on. Every 100,000 years or so, a distortion in the Earth's orbit tugs the Northern Hemisphere away from the sun. On more frequent cycles, the Earth tilts and wobbles on its axis. When these phenomena coincide, temperatures change dramatically and ice ages set in. A great cooling began about 150,000 years ago. The great migrations roughly coincided with the Ice Age, as if humans did not just welcome the cold, but actively sought it. We think of global warming as a current phenomenon, and indeed it is. The world only began to emerge from the last Ice Age about 15,000 to 20,000 years ago. The intensive global warming we experience today is the most dramatic phase of that trend.

This is how the world we inhabit today came about. As the Earth tilted and the sun blazed, the ice cap began to shrink. At its most extensive, about 20,000 years ago, it had reached the present lower courses of the Missouri and Ohio rivers in North America and deep into what are now the British Isles. It covered what is today Scandinavia. Most of the rest of what is now Europe was **tundra**, a treeless region with permanently frozen subsoil, or coniferous forest, with trees such as spruce, fir, and pine. In central Eurasia, tundra reached almost to the present latitudes of the Black Sea. **Steppe**—dry plain covered with scrub grass—licked the shores of the Mediterranean. In North America, tundra and coniferous forest extended to where Virginia is today (see Map 1.2).

Warming started about 18,000 years ago. Not long after, between about 16,000 and 8,000 years ago, the geological record shows enormous regional fluctuations in temperature. Melting ice meant cooling

Venus of Laussel. An image of a woman carved in relief on a cave wall in central France more than 20,000 years ago reveals much about Ice-Age life: esteem for big hips and body fat, the love of revelry suggested by the uplifted drinking-horn, the involvement of women in presumably sacred activity, and the existence of accomplished, specialized artists.

seas and temporary reversals of warming in affected latitudes. As the fluctuations subsided, temperatures leaped. Glaciers retreated worldwide. Seas flooded and spilled over land, until—broadly speaking—the world map as we know it today took shape.

Ice-Age Hunters

The severity of the Ice Age is unimaginable, but it was not an entirely hostile world. For the hunters who inhabited the vast tundra that covered much of Eurasia, the edge of the ice was the best place to be. Over thousands of years of cold, a lot of mammals had adapted by efficiently storing their own body fat—and that was the hunters' target. Dietary fat has a bad reputation today, but for most of history, most people have eagerly sought it. Relatively speaking, animal fat is the world's most energy-abundant source of food.

In some of the vast Ice-Age tundra, concentrations of small, easily trapped arctic hare could supply human populations. More commonly, however, hunters favored species they could kill in large numbers by driving them over cliffs or into bogs or lakes. The cave art of the time depicts the controlled use of fire and funnel-shaped drive lanes. The bones of 10,000 Ice-Age horses lie at the foot of a cliff near Solutré in France, and remains of 100 mammoths have turned up in pits at a site in the Czech Republic in Central Europe. About 20,000 years ago, the invention of the bow and arrow revolutionized killing technology. For the hunted species, such as the Old World's largest elephants and numerous kinds of deer, the new weapon hastened extinction, though climate change had perhaps already condemned them. But for the killers, while stocks lasted, the result was a fat bonanza, achieved with relatively modest effort.

It is rash to suppose that Ice-Age communities were small, limited to 30 or 50 people, like modern hunter–gatherers. Today, hunter–gatherers survive only in regions of great scarcity, where the modern world has driven them. Back then, community size varied according to the available resources; we can rarely put a figure to a group because only partial traces of Ice-Age dwellings have survived.

For Ice-Age artists, fat was beautiful. One of the oldest artworks in the world is the Venus of Willendorf—a plump little carving of a fat female, 30,000 years old and named for the place in Germany where she was found. Critics have interpreted her as a goddess, a ruler, or, since she could be pregnant, a means of conjuring fertility. However, her slightly more recent look-alike, the Venus of Laussel, carved on a cave wall in France, evidently got fat the way most of us do: by enjoyment and indulgence. She raises a horn, which must surely contain food or drink.

The remains of Ice-Age people reveal that, on average, they were better nourished than most later populations. Only modern industrialized societies surpass their intake of 3,000 calories a day. In some Ice-Age communities, people ate about 5 pounds of food a day. The nature of the plant foods they gathered—few starchy grains, relatively large amounts of fruit and plants that grow underground—and the high vitamin C content of animal organ meats provided five times the average intake of vitamin C of an American today. Abundant game guaranteed **Ice-Age affluence**. High levels of nutrition and long days of leisure, unequaled in most later societies, meant people had time to observe nature and think about what they saw. The art of the era shows the sublime results. Like all good jokes, *The Flintstones*—the popular

Chronology: The Ice Age	
150,000 years ago	Earth cools; last great Ice Age begins
18,000 years ago	Peak of Ice Age—farthest extent of ice cap
18,000 years ago	Warming of the Earth begins
16,000–8,000 years ago	Temperatures fluctuate; glaciers retreat; coastlines form
15,000–20,000 years ago	World emerges from Ice Age
(All dates are approximate)	

The Flintstones —the TV and movie "modern stone-age family" imagined by cartoonists William Hanna and Joseph Barbera—inspired childish fantasy and slapstick comedy. But the more we know of the humans of over 20,000 years ago, the more "modern" they seem, with arts, ambitions, religions, social forums, political practices, and mental and physical capacities recognizably like those of our own.

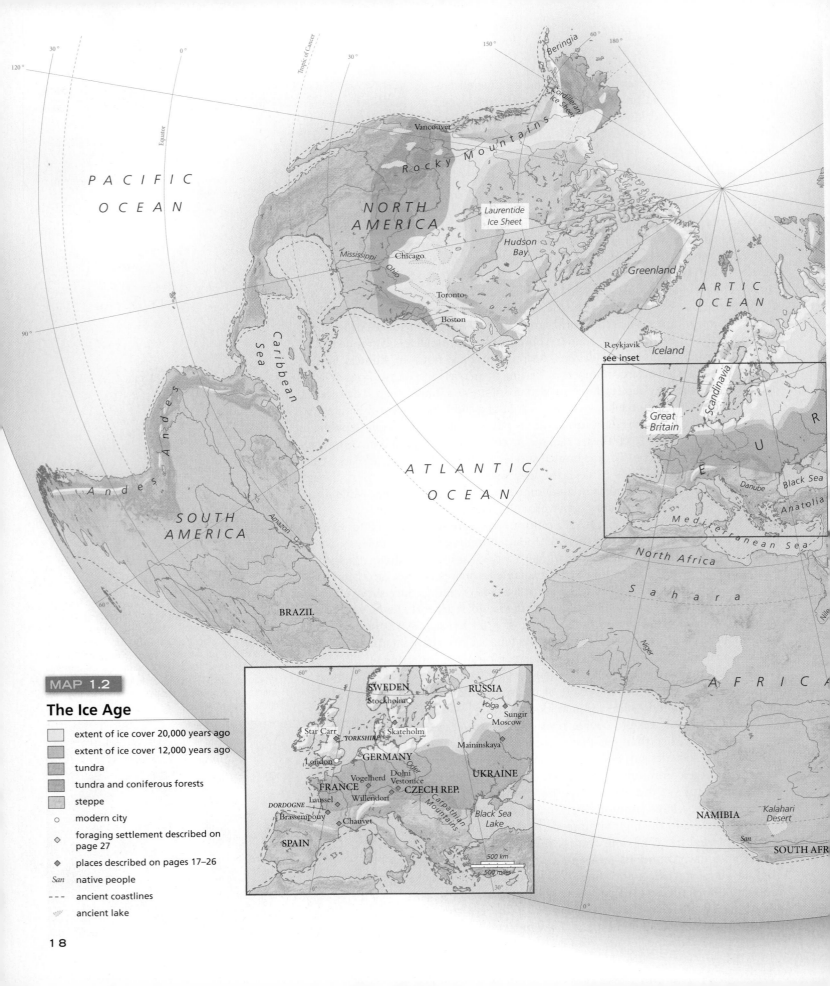

PACIFIC
OCEAN

NORTH
AMERICA

Rocky Mountains

Vancouver

Cordilleran
Ice Sheet

Beringia

Laurentide
Ice Sheet

Hudson
Bay

Greenland

ARTIC
OCEAN

Mississippi

Chicago

Ohio

Toronto

Boston

Reykjavik

Iceland

see inset

Caribbean
Sea

Andes

Andes

ATLANTIC
OCEAN

Great
Britain

Scandinavia

E U R

SOUTH
AMERICA

Amazon

Danube

Black Sea

Anatolia

Mediterranean Sea

North Africa

S a h a r a

Niger

Nile

BRAZIL

A F R I C A

NAMIBIA

Kalahari
Desert

San

SOUTH AFR

MAP 1.2

The Ice Age

extent of ice cover 20,000 years ago

extent of ice cover 12,000 years ago

tundra

tundra and coniferous forests

steppe

○   modern city

◇   foraging settlement described on
page 27

◆   places described on pages 17–26

San   native people

---   ancient coastlines

  ancient lake

SWEDEN

RUSSIA

Stockholm

Volga

Sungir
Moscow

Star Carr

YORKSHIRE

Skateholm

London

GERMANY

Maininskaya

Vogelherd

Dolni
Vestonice

UKRAINE

FRANCE

CZECH REP.

DORDOGNE

Laussel

Willendorf

Oder

Carpathian Mountains

Brassempouy

Chauvet

Black Sea
Lake

SPAIN

500 km

500 miles

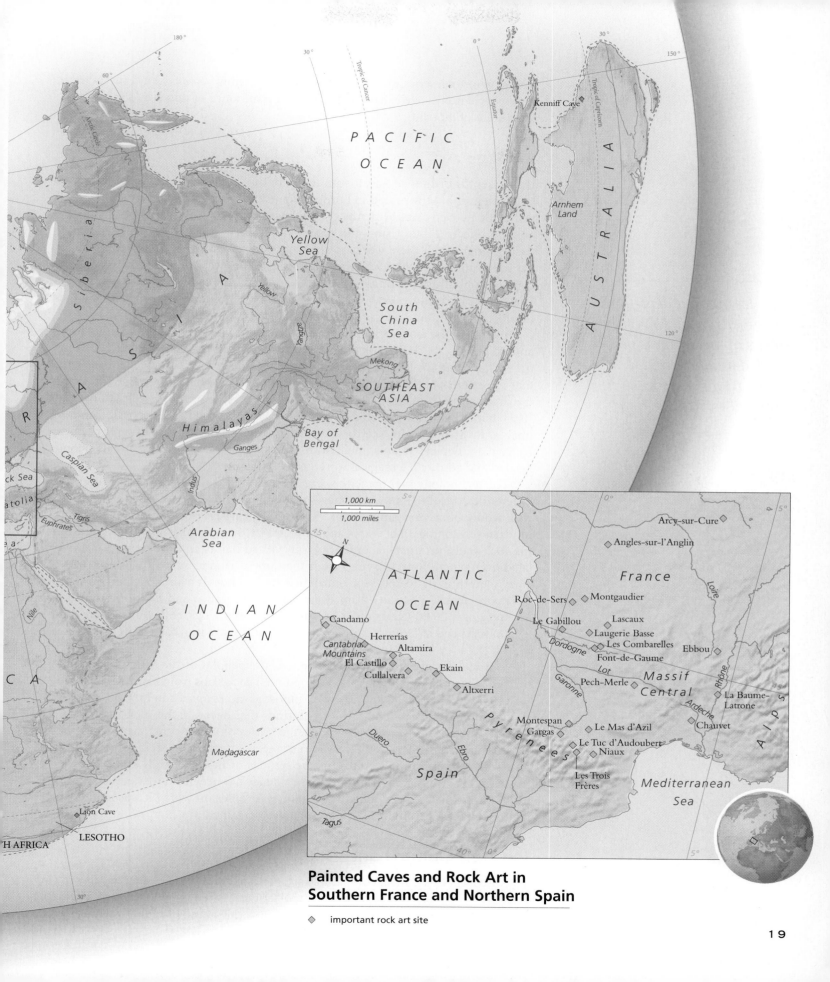

Map labels:

PACIFIC OCEAN

Siberia

A S I A

Arctic Circle

Yellow Sea

Yellow

Yangtze

South China Sea

Mekong

SOUTHEAST ASIA

Himalayas

Ganges

Bay of Bengal

Indus

Caspian Sea

ck Sea

atolia

Euphrates

Tigris

Arabian Sea

INDIAN OCEAN

Nile

Madagascar

Lion Cave

LESOTHO

H AFRICA

Kenniff Cave

Tropic of Cancer

Equator

Tropic of Capricorn

AUSTRALIA

Arnhem Land

180°
60°
30°
0°
30°
150°
120°

30°

Inset map:

1,000 km
1,000 miles

N

ATLANTIC OCEAN

France

Arcy-sur-Cure

Angles-sur-l'Anglin

Roc-de-Sers   Montgaudier

Le Gabillou   Lascaux

Candamo   Laugerie Basse

Herrerías   Les Combarelles   Ebbou

Cantabria Mountains   Altamira   Font-de-Gaume

El Castillo   Ekain   Massif

Cullalvera   Pech-Merle   Central

Altxerri   La Baume-Latrone

Dordogne

Garonne

Lot

Rhône

Ardèche

Alps

Montespan   Le Mas d'Azil   Chauvet

Gargas

Pyrenees   Le Tuc d'Audoubert

Niaux

Les Trois Frères

Spain   Mediterranean Sea

Duero

Ebro

Tagus

Loire

45°

5°

0°

5°

5°

40°

0°

5°

Painted Caves and Rock Art in Southern France and Northern Spain

◆   important rock art site

19

television cartoon series about a modern Stone-Age family—contains a kernel of truth. Cave people really were like us, with much the same kinds of minds and many of the same kinds of thoughts.

Ice-Age Art

In the depths of the Ice Age, a stunningly resourceful way of life took shape. We know most about the period in Europe, where extensive art has survived because it was made in deep caves evidently chosen because they were inaccessible. Only now are the effects of tourism—too many respiratory systems, too many camera flashes—damaging these works in their once-secret caverns. Most prehistoric art has been found in northern Spain and southwest France. About 50 cave complexes contain thousands of paintings, mostly of animals, and hundreds of smaller works. Examples of sculptures, carvings, and other art objects are also scattered across Europe, from Britain and the Atlantic to the Ural Mountains (see Map 1.2).

What was the art for? It surely told stories and had magical, ritual uses. Some animal images are slashed or punctured many times over, as if in symbolic sacrifice. When early artists traced around a pattern or an object, it seems believable that footprints and handprints inspired it. A good case has been made for seeing the cave paintings as aids to track prey. The shapes of hooves, the tracks, dung, seasonal habits, and favorite foods of the beasts are among the artists' standard images. By analogy with the rock-paintings of hunter–gatherers of later periods, Ice-Age art depicts an imagined world, full of the spirits of the animals people needed and admired: a magical world, accessed in mystical trances.

The technology that made the cave art was simple: a palette mixed from three different colors of the mineral ocher—red, brown, yellow—and animal fat, applied with wood, bone, and animal hair. Yet even the earliest works appeal instantly to modern sensibilities. The looks and litheness of the animal portraits spring from the rock walls, products of practiced, specialized hands and of learning accumulated over generations. Carvings from the same period exhibit similar elegance— ivory sculptures of 30,000-year-old arched-necked horses from Vogelherd in south Germany; female portraits from Brassempouy in France and Dolní Vestonice in Moravia, over 20,000 years old. Clay models of bears, dogs, and women were fired 27,000 years ago at Dolní Vestonice and at Maininskaya in what is now Russia (see Map 1.2).

Outside Europe, what little we know of the peoples of the time suggests that they created equally skillful work. Four painted rock slabs from Namibia in southwest Africa are about 26,000 years old, almost as old as any art in Europe, and bear similar animal images. The earliest paintings that decorate the rocks of Arnhem Land in northernmost Australia show faint traces of long-extinct giant kangaroos and scary snakes. A clue to the very idea of representing life in art fades today from a rock face in Kenniff, Australia, where stencils of human hands and tools were made 20,000 years ago. But most of the evidence has been lost, weathered away on exposed rock faces, perished with the bodies or hides on which it was painted, or scattered by wind from the earth where it was scratched.

Ice-Age Culture and Society

The discovery of so much comparable art, of comparable age, in such widely separated parts of the world suggests an important and often overlooked fact. The Ice Age was the last great era of what we would now call a kind of **globalization**. That

> *". . . Ice-Age art depicts an imagined world, full of the spirits of the animals people needed and admired: a magical world, accessed in mystical trances."*

is, key elements of culture were similar all over the inhabited world. Although languages and the structures of political and social life were probably already highly various, people practiced hunter–gatherer economies with similar kinds of technology, ate similar foods, enjoyed similar levels of material culture, and—as far as we can tell—had similar religious practices. Social change and intellectual shifts were challenging for people who experienced them, but they happened slowly by comparison with later periods. The earliest of the art-filled caves of southern France, at Chauvet, is 30,000 years old; that at Lascaux dates from 10,000 years later. Yet the subjects the artists painted, and the techniques and styles they used, hardly changed in all that time.

The **material culture**—concrete objects people create—that many archaeological digs yield provides clues to what goes on in the mind. A simple test establishes that fact. We can make informed inferences about people's religion, or politics, or their attitudes toward nature and society, or their values in general, by looking at what they eat, how they dress, and how they decorate their homes. For instance, the people who hunted mammoths to extinction 20,000 years ago on the Ice-Age steppes of what is now southern Russia built dome-shaped dwellings of mammoth bones on a circular plan 12 or 15 feet in diameter that seem sublime triumphs of the imagination. They are reconstructions of mammoth nature, humanly reimagined, perhaps to acquire the beast's strength or magically to assume power over the species. In fact, ordinary, everyday activities went on inside these extraordinary dwellings—sleeping, eating, and all the routines of family life—in communities, on average, of fewer than 100 people. But no dwelling is purely practical. Your house reflects your ideas about your place in the world.

Thanks to the clues material culture yields, we can make some confident assertions about other aspects of Ice-Age people's lives: their symbolic systems, their magic, and the kind of social and political units in which they lived. Although Ice-Age people had nothing we recognize as writing, they did have highly expressive symbols, which we can only struggle to translate. Realistic drawings made 20,000 to 30,000 years ago show recurring gestures and postures. Moreover, they often include what seem to be numbers, signified by dots and notches. Other marks that we can no long interpret are undeniably systematic. One widely occurring mark that looks like a P may be a symbol for female because it resembles the curves of a woman's body. What looks as if it might be a calendar was made 30,000 years ago in the Dordogne region in France. It is a flat bone inscribed with crescents and circles that may record phases of the moon.

Clues to the spiritual life of the time appear in traces of red ocher, the earliest substance that seems to have had a role in ritual. The oldest known ocher mine in the world, about 42,000 years old, is at Lion Cave in what is now Lesotho in southern Africa. The vivid, lurid color was applied in burials, perhaps as a precious offering, perhaps to imitate blood and reinvest the dead with life. People may also have used ocher to paint their living bodies.

Ice-Age people also used symbols and pigments in magic, and those who controlled them wielded power. In paintings and carvings, we can glimpse the Ice-Age elite, people considered special and set apart from the group. In figures wearing animal masks—antlered or lionlike—the wearer is transformed. From anthropological studies of the recent past, we know such disguises are normally efforts to

Lions from Chauvet Cave, France. In 1994, three cave explorers spent the Christmas holiday in the gorges of the Ardéche region in southeastern France. In the area, explorers had already discovered numerous caves that Ice-Age people had decorated between about 14,000 and 21,000 years ago. But nothing already known about the region prepared the team for the breathtaking find that awaited them. It soon became apparent that the Chauvet cave was one of the most extensive collections of Ice-Age art in the world. Furthermore, carbon dating from many of the images led to an inescapable conclusion. These were the world's oldest known paintings, yielding three dates of over 30,000 years, and none less than 23,000. The paintings also subverted everything previously thought about Ice-Age art. Scholarship had assumed that Ice-Age art had evolved in style from "primitive" sketches by the earliest artists to the sublime images painted toward the end of the era in the caves of Altamira in Spain and Lascaux in France. In technique and skill, the Chauvet paintings are equal to paintings done in similar environments 10,000 or 15,000 years later. The Chauvet painters' favorite subjects were rhinoceroses and lions often shown stalking like the group above.

A CLOSER LOOK

Mammoth Hut

Ninety-five jawbones with the chins facing down form a decorative outer wall that is lined with skulls and other bones.

Between 40,000 and 16,000 years ago, on what are now the Russian and Ukranian steppe, people built dwellings made out of the bones of woolly mammoths and other creatures. The biggest surviving dwelling at Mezhirich (Ukraine) has 385 bones from about 100 different beasts that, when alive, weighed over 46,000 pounds in all.

Wooden roof covered with hides

Generations of ancient steppe dwellers collected bones and stored them in pits. Some buildings used bones that were 8,000 years old when the buildings were constructed.

Tusks form the porch

Central hearth or shrine, ornamented by an erect mammoth skull painted with ocher carved with zigzag designs.

Right femur (male)

The floor area is between 13 and 23 feet wide. Extensive finds of ash, charcoal, and ocher suggest that rituals took place at these sites. Skulls, jaws, and shoulder blades form the foundations of the dwellings.

How does this Ice-Age dwelling demonstrate the close connection between environment and culture?

communicate with the dead or with the gods. Bringing messages from other worlds is the role of a **shaman**, someone who acts as an intermediary between humans and spirits or gods. The shaman may seek a state of ecstasy induced by drugs or dancing or drumming, to see and hear realms normally inaccessible to the senses. He becomes the medium through which spirits talk to this world. Among the Chukchi hunters of northern Siberia, whose way of life and environment are similar to those of Ice-Age peoples, the shaman's experience is represented as a journey to consult the spirits in a realm that only the dead can normally enter. The shaman may adopt an animal disguise to acquire the animal's speed or strength or identify with an animal ancestor. The shaman's role can be an awesome source of authority. Shamans can challenge alpha males. Like other religions, shamanism involves spiritual insight that people of both sexes, various levels of intellect, and all kinds of physical makeup can acquire. It can replace the strong with the seer and the sage. By choosing elites who had the gift of communicating with spirits, Ice-Age societies could escape the oppression of the physically powerful or those privileged by birth.

Although we cannot be sure about the nature of the Ice-Age power class, we know it existed because of glaring inequalities in the way Ice-Age people were buried. In a cemetery at Sunghir, near Moscow, dated about 24,000 years ago, the highest-status person seems, at first glance, to have been an elderly man. His burial goods include a cap sewn with fox's teeth and about 20 ivory bracelets. Nearby, however, two boys about 8 or 10 years of age have even more spectacular ornaments. In addition to ivory bracelets and necklaces and fox-tooth buttons, the boys have animal carvings and beautifully wrought weapons, including spears of mammoth ivory, each over 6 feet long. About 3,500 finely worked ivory beads had been drizzled over the head, torso, and limbs of each boy. Here was a society that marked leaders for greatness from boyhood and therefore, perhaps from birth.

In our attempt to understand where power lay in Ice-Age societies, the final bits of evidence are crumbs from rich people's tables, fragments of feasts. Archaeologists have found ashes from large-scale cooking and the calcified debris of food

Shaman. In many societies, communication with the spirit-world remains the responsibility of the specialists whom anthropologists call shamans. Typically, they garb and paint or disguise themselves to resemble spirits, or the animals deemed to have privileged access to realms beyond human sense. The shamans then "journey" to the spirits or ancestors in trances induced by dancing, drumming, or drugs. Shamans often acquire social influence and political authority as healers, prophets, and arbitrators.

Sunghir burial. A profusion of beads distinguishes the graves of people of high status at Sunghir in Russia, from about 24,000 years ago. The distribution of signs of wealth in burials suggests that even in the Ice Age inequalities were rife and that status could be inherited.

at sites in northern Spain, perhaps from as long as 23,000 years ago. The tally sticks that survive from the same region in the same period may also have been records of expenditure on feasts. What were such feasts for? By analogy with modern hunting peoples, the most likely reason was to forge alliances between communities. They were probably not male-bonding occasions, as some scholars think, because they were staged close to major dwelling sites where women and children would be present. Instead, from the moment of its emergence, the idea of the feast had practical consequences: to build and strengthen societies and enhance the power of those who organized the feasts and controlled the food.

Peopling the New World

The New World was one of the last parts of the planet *Homo sapiens* peopled. We can be sure of that much, but it is not easy to say exactly when or by whom. According to the formerly dominant theory, a gap opened between glaciers toward the end of the Ice Age. A race of hunters crossed the land link between North America and Asia, where the Bering Strait now flows, to enter a paradise where no human hunter had ever trod before. The abundance was so great and the animals were so unwary, that the invaders ate enormously and multiplied greatly. They spread rapidly over the hemisphere, hunting the great game to extinction as they went. The story appealed to an unsophisticated form of U.S. patriotism. The Clovis people, as these hunters were dubbed after an early archaeological site in New Mexico, seemed to resemble modern American pioneers. They exhibited quick-fire locomotion, hustle and bustle, technical prowess, big appetites, irrepressible strength, enormous cultural reach, and a talent for reforging the environment.

By comparison, the truth about the peopling of the hemisphere is disappointingly undramatic. These first great American superheroes—like most of their successors—did not really exist. Although archaeologists have excavated too few sites for a complete and reliable picture to emerge, a new theory now dominates. We have evidence of early human settlement scattered from the Yukon to Uruguay and from near the Bering Strait to the edge of the Beagle Channel—that is, from the waterway that divides North America and Asia to the southern limits of the South American mainland. This evidence is so widespread, spanning so long a period, embedded in so many different geological layers, and exhibiting such a vast range of cultural diversity that one conclusion is inescapable—colonists came at different times, bringing different cultures with them.

No generally accepted evidence dates any inhabited sites in the American hemisphere earlier than about 13,000 B.C.E. (see Map 1.3). The first arrivals came during a time when glaciers covered much of North America. They stuck close to the cold, where the game was fattest. They followed corridors between walls of ice or along narrow shores away from glaciers. Other arrivals came by sea and continued to come after the land bridge was submerged. Around 10,000 years ago, a catastrophic cluster of extinctions wiped out the mammoth, mastodon, horse, giant sloth, saber-toothed tiger, and at least 35 other large species in the Americas. New hunting techniques and perhaps new hunting peoples were probably partly responsible. But we can only explain the events in the context of vast climatic changes that affected habitats and the whole ecology on which these animals depended.

Many supposedly early sites of human habitation have proved to be delusions of overenthusiastic archaeologists—false, or, at best, unconvincing. A few sites, however, offer strong evidence of the antiquity and range of settlement. Most are in

"This evidence is so widespread, spanning so long a period, embedded in so many different geological layers, and exhibiting such a vast range of cultural diversity that one conclusion is inescapable—colonists came at different times, bringing different cultures with them."

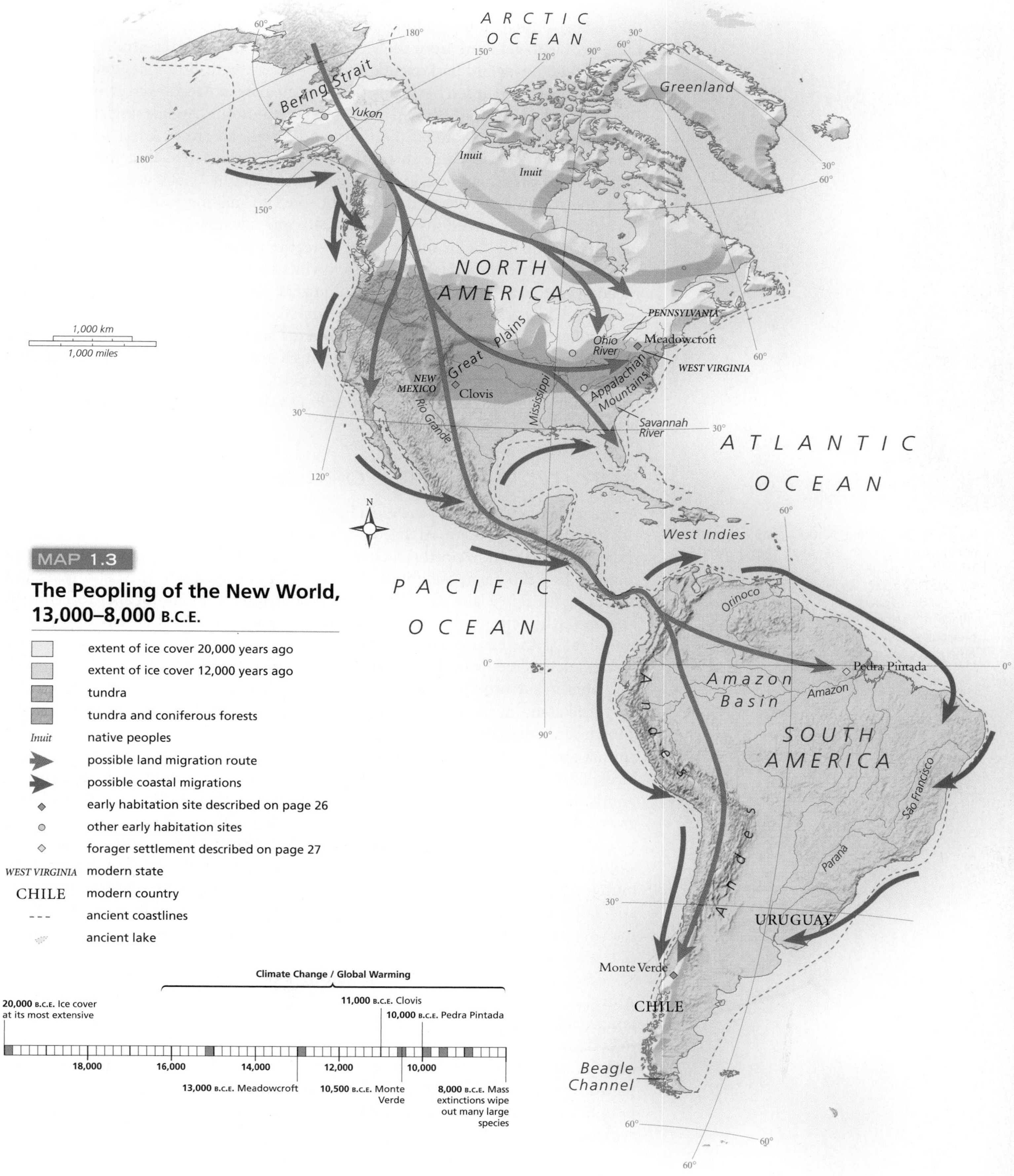

ARCTIC OCEAN

Bering Strait

Yukon

Greenland

Inuit

Inuit

NORTH AMERICA

PENNSYLVANIA

Great Plains

Ohio River

Meadowcroft

WEST VIRGINIA

NEW MEXICO

Clovis

Rio Grande

Mississippi

Appalachian Mountains

Savannah River

ATLANTIC OCEAN

1,000 km

1,000 miles

N

PACIFIC OCEAN

West Indies

Orinoco

Amazon Basin

Amazon

Pedra Pintada

Andes

SOUTH AMERICA

São Francisco

Paraná

URUGUAY

Monte Verde

CHILE

Beagle Channel

MAP 1.3

The Peopling of the New World, 13,000–8,000 B.C.E.

	extent of ice cover 20,000 years ago
	extent of ice cover 12,000 years ago
	tundra
	tundra and coniferous forests
Inuit	native peoples
➤	possible land migration route
➤	possible coastal migrations
◆	early habitation site described on page 26
⊙	other early habitation sites
◇	forager settlement described on page 27
WEST VIRGINIA	modern state
CHILE	modern country
- - -	ancient coastlines
⋯	ancient lake

Climate Change / Global Warming

20,000 B.C.E. Ice cover at its most extensive

11,000 B.C.E. Clovis

10,000 B.C.E. Pedra Pintada

18,000   16,000   14,000   12,000   10,000

13,000 B.C.E. Meadowcroft   10,500 B.C.E. Monte Verde   8,000 B.C.E. Mass extinctions wipe out many large species

Monte Verde. About 12,000 years ago, a young person trod in fresh clay that lined a hearth in Monte Verde, Chile. Peat sealed and preserved the footprint to be rediscovered by archaeologists in the 1970s. Excavations at Monte Verde revealed a village of mammoth hunters so old that it made previous theories about when people arrived in the Americas questionable or even untenable.

the eastern United States—a long way from Asia. It must have taken a long time for these people to get there from the vicinity of the modern Bering Strait. In the mid-1970s, 15,000-year-old basketwork and tools made with fine flints emerged from deep under the discarded beer cans that topped a dig at Meadowcroft, on the Ohio River, near the border of Pennsylvania and West Virginia. Archaeologists are investigating similar sites between the Ohio and Savannah rivers. Later in the 1970s, excavations at Monte Verde in southern Chile revealed a 20-foot long, wooden, hide-covered dwelling preserved in a peat bog for about 12,500 years. Nearby were a big mastodon-butchery and a space devoted to making tools. The inhabitants brought salt and seaweed from the coast, 40 miles away, and medicinal herbs from mountains equally far in the opposite direction. Half-chewed lumps of seaweed show the eaters' dental bites; a boy's footprints survive in the clay lining of a pit. If Meadowcroft is a long way from the colonizers' entry point near the Bering Strait, southern Chile is a world away again—almost as far as you can get in the Western Hemisphere. How long would it have taken the settlers of Monte Verde to cross the hemisphere, over vast distances and through many different kinds of environments, each demanding new forms of adaptation? Most specialists think it must have taken thousands of years. The question of the date of the first peopling of the New World therefore remains open.

SURVIVAL OF THE FORAGERS

As the ice cap retreated and the great herds shifted with it, many human communities opted to follow them. Archaeology has unearthed traces of their routes. Along the way, in what is now northern Germany, about 12,000 years ago, people sacrificed reindeer by deliberately weighting them with stones sewn into their stomachs and drowning them in a lake. About 1,000 years later, hunters as far north as Yorkshire in England, who left a well-preserved camp at Starr Carr, found an environment as abundant as the cave artists' had been. Not only was it filled with tundra-loving species such as red deer, elk, and aurochs—huge, shaggy wild cattle—but also with wild boar in surroundings that were becoming patchily wooded.

At Skatelholm in Sweden, about 8,000 years ago, hunters founded the largest known settlement of the era. It was a winter camp in an area where the 87 different animal species roamed that the inhabitants ate: trapping river-fish, netting sea-birds, harpooning seals and dolphin, sticking pigs, and driving deer into pits or ponds. In summer, the people must have moved farther north. They lie today in graves decorated with beads and ocher and filled with the spoils of their careers, including antlers and boar's tusks. Their dogs are buried nearby. These burly, wolflike companions are sometimes interred with more signs of honor than humans were given. Dogs were full members of societies where hunting prowess and skill in war determined status. Many of the human dead bear wounds from man-made weapons. Here, too, is evidence of sexual specialization. Women have only a third as many wounds as the men.

The most persistently faithful followers of the ice were the Inuit of North America. About 4,000 years ago, they invented the blubber-filled soapstone lamp enabling them that follow big game beyond the tundra and into the darkness of an arctic winter. They could track the musk ox to the shore of the ocean and the caribou on its winter migrations, when its fur is thickest and its fat most plentiful. This way of life persisted until the late twentieth century, although the people who first practiced it have disappeared. Migrants from the Arctic Ocean replaced them 1,000 years ago.

Climate change trapped other foraging peoples in environments where they had to develop new ways of life. Some of these environments offered new kinds of abundance. Here were broad-leaved forests, rich in acorns (which make nutritious food for any humans who have enough time to fine-grind them), and lakes and rivers full of aquatic life. New World prairies held apparently inexhaustible stocks of bison (though the largest bison species was rapidly hunted to extinction). Between the unstable periods of climate change around 12,000 years ago, foragers even colonized dense, tropical forests in Southeast Asia and in the New World at Pedra Pintada in Brazil where the Amazon River now flows. Today foragers in this region have to struggle to find foods they can digest, but it seems to have been more environmentally diverse toward the end of the Ice Age.

Some societies perpetuated their foraging life in hot, arid deserts, as different from the best hunting grounds of the Ice Age as it is possible to imagine. This required two forms of adaptation. First, the thinly dispersed populations had to create collaborative networks. Such interdependence explains why peoples who live in ecologically shaky homelands often require people to marry outside the group (a practice known as exogamy) and why they regard hospitality to strangers as a sacred obligation. Second, poor environments demanded that inhabitants develop what we might call orally transmitted science. For only with accurate and extensive knowledge of their habitat can people survive in harsh environments.

The San or Bushmen of southern Africa's Kalahari Desert illustrate the difficulties and solutions. Their domain has shrunk in the last few centuries, as Bantu farmers, Khoi herdsmen, and white invaders have overrun much of their former territory. But their heartland was already dry at the time of the San's first occupancy, about 14,000 years ago. The increased rainfall that usually followed the retreat of the ice hardly fell here. There are underground rivers but few permanent water holes. The people watch for rare signs of rain and hurry to gather the vegetation that accompanies it. The scrubland plant foods, including water-bearing tubers and a kind of cactus, supply 30 percent of their sustenance. The rest comes from game, which grazes on tough desert shrubs that humans cannot digest.

Laurens van der Post, a South African adventurer who has written about the Bushmen, once accompanied a band of San hunters in search of their favorite food, eland, a type of antelope. One morning just after sunrise, they found the tracks of a herd. By three in the afternoon, after nonstop pursuit at a trot, they came on the herd and took aim. To kill large game is almost impossible with a Bushman's bow. He wounds the beast with a poisoned barb and follows it until it drops from exhaustion and the effects of the drug. On this occasion, the hunters ran for 12 miles without stopping "and the final mile was an all-out sprint." The next time they made contact with the herd, one bull was seen to be tiring. It still took another full hour of pursuit until he fell. Then "without pause or break for rest they were fresh enough at the end to plunge straight away

Bushmen. Though now obliged to adopt a mixed economy, supported in part by farming and donations of food, the San or Bushmen of southern Africa have been among the most conservative of the world's peoples. They maintained their foraging way of life, essentially unchanged, for millennia—despite neighbors' attempts to exterminate them. This record of survival contrasts with the rapid turnover of more ambitious civilizations that radically modify their environments, usually with disastrous results.

Chronology

Over 3 million years ago	Lucy
2–1 million years ago	*Homo erectus* migrates from East Africa to Africa and Eurasia
100,000 years ago	*Homo sapiens* migrates out of Africa
67,000 years ago	*Homo sapiens* in Asia
50,000 years ago	*Homo sapiens* colonizes Australia and New Guinea, *Homo sapiens* reaches Europe
30,000 years ago	Last Neanderthals vanish
20,000–15,000 B.C.E.	World emerges from the Ice Age
20,000 B.C.E.	Invention of the bow and arrow
13,000 B.C.E.	*Homo sapiens* in the Americas
(All dates are approximate)	

into the formidable task of skinning and cutting up the heavy animal." Bushmen who persist with this demanding way of life to this day are obviously pursuing a commitment that has grown out of generations of invested emotion. As difficult as it may be for us to understand, the San would find it heart-wrenching to change a way of life for the mere sake of efficiency, convenience, or material gain.

In one sense, the world's food supply still depends on foraging. The amount of food from hunting actually increased in the twentieth century, which may go down in history not only as the last age of hunting but as the greatest. Throughout the world today, we practice a highly specialized, mechanized, and unusual form of hunting—deep-sea trawling. Fish farming is likely to replace it in the future, but in any case, deep-sea fishing is a historical throwback.

In Perspective
After the Ice

In the post–Ice-Age world, little by little, over thousands of years, most societies abandoned foraging and adopted farming or herding as the way to get their food. Among peoples who still live close to the ice cap, the Inuit remain faithful to their hunting tradition in North America. Most of their Old World counterparts, however, have long abandoned it. In Eurasia, though some hunting cultures still cling to the old ways at the eastern end of Siberia, the peoples on the western Arctic rim—the Sami (or Lapplanders) of Scandinavia and their neighbors, the Karelia, Samoyeds, and Nenets—adopted reindeer herding over 1,000 years ago. The Ice-Age way of life, if not over, is drawing to a close. Hunting is now thought of as a primitive way to get food, long abandoned except as an aristocratic indulgence in some countries or as a supposedly manly sport in others.

The disappearance of foraging lifeways seems a remarkable turnaround for a predator species such as *Homo sapiens*. There was a time, before hunting, when our ancestors were scavengers, but for hundreds of thousands, perhaps millions, of years, foraging was reliable and rewarding. It fed people through every change of climate. Its human practitioners spread over the world and adapted successfully to every kind of habitat. They dominated every ecosystem they became part of, and competed successfully with most other species. They achieved startling increases in their numbers, which we struggle to explain. They founded more varied societies than any other species (though the differences among these societies were slight compared to later periods.) They had art-rich cultures with traditions of learning and symbolic systems to record information. They had their own social elites, political customs, ambitious magic, and practical methods to exploit their environment.

Our next task is to ask why, after the achievements recounted in this chapter, people abandoned the foraging life? Renouncing the hunt and pursuing new ways of life after the Ice Age are among the most far-reaching and mysterious transformations of the human past. If the puzzle of why *Homo sapiens* spread over the Earth is the first great question in our history, the problem of why foragers became farmers is the second.

"If the puzzle of why Homo sapiens *spread over the Earth is the first great question in our history, the problem of why foragers became farmers is the second."*

PROBLEMS AND PARALLELS

1. When does the story of humankind begin? Is it possible to define what it means to be human? What characteristics do we share with chimpanzees and other apes?

2. How do Neanderthals and *Homo floresiensis* challenge definitions of *Homo sapiens?*

3. Why is it likely that all humans alive today are descended from a common ancestor whom anthropologists nickname "Eve"? Why did *Homo sapiens* migrate out of Africa? How did migration change people's relationships with each other and with their environment?

4. Why did the population of *Homo sapiens* grow so rapidly?

5. What stresses could have caused early peoples to divide and fight each other? What are the theories for why war started?

6. How did male domination come to be normal in human societies? What impact did sexual economic specialization have on early societies?

7. Why was the Ice Age a time of affluence? What role did shamans play in Ice-Age society? What do Ice-Age art and the remains of ancient feasts suggest about Ice-Age societies?

READ ON ▶ ▶ ▶

F. Fernández-Armesto, *Humankind: A Brief History* (2004) traces debates over the boundaries of the concept of humankind. Jared Diamond's book on the human overlap with apes is *The Third Chimpanzee* (1992). The works of F. de Waal, especially *The Ape and the Sushi Master* (2001), and those of J. Goodall, especially *The Chimpanzees of Gombe* (1986), are fundamental for understanding the issues. B. Sykes, *The Seven Daughters of Eve* (2001), is the best introduction to the use of DNA in paleoanthropology. C. Stringer and C. Gamble, *In Search of the Neanderthals* (1995), is an interesting review of human engagement with Neanderthal remains. The classic novel by W. Golding, *The Inheritors* (1963), is an imaginative attempt to envisage Neanderthal life.

Good general introductions to human evolution include R. G. Klein, *The Human Career* (1999), and I. Tattersall, *The Fossil Trail* (1997). They should now be read in conjunction with the critique of C. Gamble, *Origins and Revolutions* (2007). C. Gamble, *Timewalkers: The Prehistory of Global Colonization* (1994), is an excellent account of the migrations. On fire, J. Goudsblom, *Fire and Civilization* (1993), is a classic, which the author has kept up to date in recent editions. R. Wrangham's views appeared in "The Raw and the Stolen," *Current Anthropology*, vol: 40 (1999), 567–594. On war, K. Lorenz, *On Aggression* (1966), and R. Ardrey, *The Territo-*

rial Imperative (1997), are controversial classics. J. Haas, ed., *The Anthropology of War* (1990) and L. H. Keeley, *War before Civilization* (1997), survey the evidence.

On sex roles, G. Lerner, *The Creation of Patriarchy* (1987), and E. Martin, *The Woman in the Body: A Cultural Analysis of Reproduction* (1992), set the terms of debate. J. Peterson, *Sexual Revolutions* (2002), is an invaluable short survey.

On the conditions of Ice-Age life, M. D. Sahlins, *Stone Age Economics* (1972), is a stimulating classic. T. D. Price and J. A. Brown, eds., *Prehistoric Hunter-Gatherers* (1985), is an important collection of studies. On the art, the most illuminating works include S. J. Mithen, *Thoughtful Foragers* (1990), and J. D. Lewis-Williams, *Discovering Southern African Rock Art* (1990).

On the peopling of the New World, the challenging and readable work of J. Adovasio, *Before America* (2004), makes a stimulating starting point. S. Mithen, *After the Ice* (2004) is an engaging and imaginative introduction to the post–Ice-Age world.

The material on L. van der Post comes from his now much maligned classic, *The Lost World of the Kalahari* (1977). For up-to-date studies see L. Marshall, *The !Kung of Nyae Nyae* (1976), and E. Wilmsen, *Land Filled with Flies* (1989).

CHAPTER 2

Out of the Mud: Farming and Herding after the Ice Age

▲ **Preparing a feast.** Traditionally, the usual staple crop of the Amazonian Yanomami of northern Brazil and southern Venezuela is a variety of banana, but they also cultivate manioc, which now occupies up to 50 per cent of their fields. Bitter manioc is poisonous—which is an advantage against predators—and must be peeled, grated, and pulped to remove the toxic acid before being converted into soup or bread for human consumption.

It was a really big party. But no one now knows what the celebration was for. Early in the third millennium B.C.E., on a hilltop at Hambledon in southwest England, in the midst of a complex of ceremonial enclosures and defensive earthworks, people gathered for purposes we can no longer identify, but one thing is obvious from the archaeological record. They were there to eat and drink. They brought a mixture of food with them. They got some of it, such as venison, by hunting. Other items, especially the large quantities of hazlenuts, were the fruit of gathering. But there were also foods the people produced for themselves by herding and farming: cattle, pigs, sheep, and wheat and barley that had already been cleaned of chaff. They intended to eat the food, not store it, because the site is strewn with the fragments of broken plates and cups, but there are few remains of large containers. Some of the animals they reared were enormous, yielding 600 pounds of meat, organ meats, and fat, and on some of the days of feasting at the site, two or three such creatures were butchered at one time. So these were gatherings of hundreds or thousands of people, who knew how to breed livestock for size. The people who lived in the area at the time exhibited strikingly varied food habits, which implies that there were different ranks or orders of society, marked by differences of diet. Most people lived mainly on meat and milk, but some ate only vegetable foods. They probably washed their feast down with wine, because archaeologists have found the remains of grapes and grape vines at the site.

HAMBLEDON, ENGLAND

The feasting at Hambledon Hill perhaps sprang from a hunter–gatherer way of life, which people in the region had not yet altogether abandoned in favor of farming. Once hunters kill a large animal, such as a deer or even a wild ox, they have to eat the meat quickly in communal meals before it rots. Yet the eaters who gathered at Hambledon were engaged in a huge transformation of their way of life—from foraging for food to growing and breeding it—that had already been going on for centuries in their part of the world and, in some places, for thousands of years. The transition has been gathering pace ever since and now includes most of the Earth's inhabitants.

To most people, in most societies, for most of the time, food is and always has been the most important thing in the world. Nothing can happen without it. Changes in how we get food and whether we get it are among history's biggest changes. During the global warming that followed the Ice Age, **husbandry**—breeding animals and cultivating crops—began to replace hunting and gathering and introduced the biggest

FOCUS questions

Why are settled foragers often better off than farmers?

What kinds of environments are suited to herding?

What kinds of environments were suited to early agriculture?

Where did farming start, and what were the first crops farmers raised?

Given the disadvantages of agriculture, why did people in most areas of the world switch from foraging to farming?

The rice fields of Bali in Indonesia are among the most productive in the world, using varieties of rice and techniques for farming it that are about 1,000 years old. Irrigation channels, maintained and administered by farmers' cooperatives, distribute water evenly among the terraces. Though originally a lowland crop, favoring swampy conditions, rice adapts perfectly to upland environments and to terrace farming.

change of all. The menu at the Hambledon feast—the mix of wild and cultivated plants, and hunted and domesticated meat—raises one of the most perplexing sets of problems in history: when, where, how, and why did people abandon the life of foragers and take up farming? Why did food procurers become food producers?

THE PROBLEM OF AGRICULTURE

Husbandry happened in two distinct ways, involving different types of environments and different levels of environmental intervention. In some environments, people could exploit creatures that had a herd instinct by managing the herds, rather than by hunting them. Breeding enhanced qualities that evolution did not necessarily favor, such as docility; size; and yield of meat, milk, eggs, and fat. On the negative side, close contact between humans and animals often allowed disease-bearing organisms to thrive, threatening human lives and health and sometimes unleashing plagues. Otherwise, however, animal husbandry barely affected the environment. Herds, on the whole, kept to their traditional patterns of migration, and people continued to accompany them—driving the beasts rather than following them. Domesticated animals remained recognizably the heirs of their wild ancestors, and the landscapes through which they traveled did not change much, except that the herds' feeding and manure probably encouraged the grasses they ate to flourish at the expense of other plant species.

In other environments, however, plant husbandry involved massive human intervention. In the long run, tillage of the soil changed the world more than any previous innovation by *Homo sapiens*. From postglacial mud, people coaxed what we now call "civilization"—a way of life based on radically modifying the environment. Instead of merely trying to manage the landscape nature provided, farmers recarved it with fields and boundaries, ditches and irrigation canals. They stamped the land with a new look, a geometrical order. Agriculture enabled humans to see the world in a new way—to imagine that magic and science had the power to change nature. Such power, in turn, changed people's sense of where they fit into the panorama of life on Earth. Now they could become masters or, in more modest moments or cultures, stewards of creation.

Together, farming and herding revolutionized humans' place in their ecosystems. Instead of merely depending on other life forms to sustain us, we forged a new relationship of interdependence with those species we eat. We rely on them for food; they rely on us for their reproduction. Domesticated animals would not exist without humans. Husbandry was the first human challenge to evolution. Instead of evolving species through **natural selection**, farming and herding proceed by what might be called unnatural selection—sorting and selecting by human hands, for human needs, according to human agendas. In other words, we breed livestock and cultivate plants.

Herding and tilling also changed human societies. By feeding people on a vastly greater scale, agriculture allowed societies to get hugely bigger than ever before. We can only guess at the absolute figures, but in areas where farming has replaced foraging in modern times, population has increased fifty- or even a hundredfold. Larger populations demanded new forms of control of labor and food distribution, which, in turn, nurtured strong states and powerful elites. Society became more volatile and apparently less stable.

In almost every case, for reasons we still do not understand, when people begin to practice agriculture, the pace of change quickens immeasurably and cumulatively. States and civilizations do not seem to last long. Societies that we think of as being the most highly evolved turn out to be least fitted for survival. Compared with the relative stability of forager communities, societies that depend on agriculture are prone to lurch and collapse. History becomes a path picked among their ruins.

In other words, farming is a disastrous and even a self-destructive option for many of the societies that adopt it: as we shall see in this chapter, it commonly brings devastating new diseases, oppressive political systems, and recurrent famines to many of the societies that choose it as their means of life. It is worth pausing to think about the implications. It shows that cultures do not necessarily change like living organisms, according to the rules of evolution. Typically, living creatures evolve because successful adaptations, which help the species survive, become generalized. Cultures, however, often respond to changes in their environments by adopting dysfunctional new features.

Farming is a perfect example. But until recently, historians rarely stopped to think about the high costs people incurred when they took it up. After all, agriculture has obvious advantages. Farmers can select the best specimens of edible crops and creatures, collect them in the most convenient places, crossbreed the livestock, and hybridize the plants to improve size, yield, or flavor. By these methods, small farming societies grow into bigger communities and build up large populations. Usually they go on to create cities and develop ever more complex technologies. For people who like living amid this kind of complexity, or who believe that history has a single "course" and that the same kind of changes are bound to happen everywhere, peoples who clung to foraging seem baffling.

A Case in Point: Aboriginal Australians

In August 1770, the British navigator Captain James Cook reached the north coast of Australia, on the first of his spectacular voyages of exploration that charted the lands and limits of the Pacific Ocean. Near Cape York, he paused at an island he named Possession Island. For although his stated purpose was scientific, he was also an officer of the Royal Navy with orders to extend the British Empire. To Cook's mind, the island, though inhabited, was waiting to be grabbed. The natives could not be said to possess it because they had left no marks of possession on its soil. A wealth of plants that they could have domesticated—"fruits proper for the support of man"—was growing wild. Yet, Cook wrote, the people "know nothing of cultivation. . . . It seems strange."

Cook and others at the time saw only two explanations for why foragers, such as the **aborigines** in Australia, would reject agriculture: They were either stupid or subhuman. Early European painters in Australia depicted aborigines as apelike creatures, grimacing oddly and crawling in trees. The colonists ignored the natives, or, when they got in the way, hunted them down—as they would beasts. Not only did the native Australians reject agriculture, in some areas, they appeared to shun every technical convenience. On the island of Tasmania, in the extreme south of Australia, where the natives became extinct soon after European settlement began, they seemed to have forgotten every art of their ancestors: bows, boats, even how to kindle fire. In Arnhem Land, in the extreme north, they used boomerangs to make music but no longer as weapons for the hunt. Progress, which the European discoverers of Australia believed in fervently, seemed to have gone into reverse. Australia was not only on the exact opposite side of the world from England, it was a topsy-turvy place where everything was upside down.

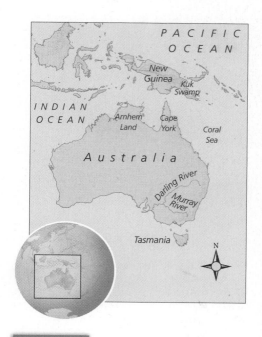

MAP 2.1

Australia

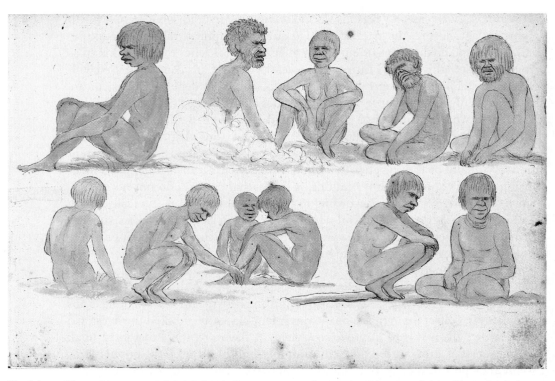

Aborigines. "One seldom sees such gaiety in a ballroom as among these untaught savages." John Glover devoted many years to making drawings and paintings of the aboriginal Palawa people of Tasmania from 1820, when he first arrived in the island. In finished paintings—for which these drawings are sketches—he usually showed them dancing, resting, swimming, or climbing trees, always innocent, peaceful, and alien. By the time he died in 1849, the settlers' campaign of extermination and deportation had left only about 40 Palawa alive in Tasmania.

We can be certain, however, that if aborigines rejected agriculture or other practices Europeans considered progressive, it must have been for good reasons. The aborigines did not lack the knowledge necessary to switch from foraging to farming if they had wanted to do so. When they gathered wild yams or the root known as nardoo, they ensured that enough of the plant remained in the ground so that it would grow back. In many regions, too, they used fire to control the grazing grounds of kangaroos and concentrate them for hunting. Fire was a common recourse among herders to manage pasture and among tillers to renew the soil. Along the Murray and Darling rivers, aborigines even watered and weeded wild crops and policed their boundaries against human and animal predators (see Map 2.1).

The aboriginal Australians could also have systematically planted and irrigated crops, farmed the grubs they liked to eat, penned kangaroos, and even tried to domesticate them. (Kangaroos are cantankerous creatures, but people do make pets of them. Breeding selected specimens would probably produce a domestic strain in a few generations.) In the far north of Australia, aboriginal communities traded with the farming cultures of New Guinea. So, even if they hadn't developed agriculture on their own, they could have learned it from outsiders. If the aborigines did not farm, it must have been because they did not want to. In short, they were doing well without it. Similar cases all over the world support this conclusion. Where wild foods are abundant, there is no incentive to domesticate them. Of course, people often adopt practices that do them no good. We can concede this general principle, but, case by case, we still want to know why.

Preagricultural Settlements

Under some conditions, people can settle in one place without the trouble of farming. Archaeological evidence in the region we now call the Middle East shows this. After the Ice Age ended about 15,000 B.C.E., a frontier zone between forest and grassland stretched across the eastern shore of the Mediterranean and what are now Iran, eastern Turkey, and Iraq (see Map 2.2). The forests were full of acorns, pistachios, and almonds, which gatherers ground into flour and paste. The grasslands bred vast quantities of wild grass with edible seeds. These foods could all be warehoused between harvests and had the additional advantage of ripening at different times. Dense herds of gazelle in the grasslands provided more nutrition for hunters to bring home. Food was so plentiful that foragers did not have to move around much to find it.

By about 14,000 to 15,000 years ago, permanent settlements arose throughout the region: clusters of dwellings with stone walls, or those made of wood on stone foundations, or cut from soft stone and roofed with reeds. The foragers who lived in these sedentary communities apparently kept to themselves.

MAP 2.2

Preagricultural Settlements in the Middle East

- forest
- grassland
- TURKEY   modern-day country
- preagricultural settlement described on page 36
- other preagricultural settlements
- ---- ancient coastlines

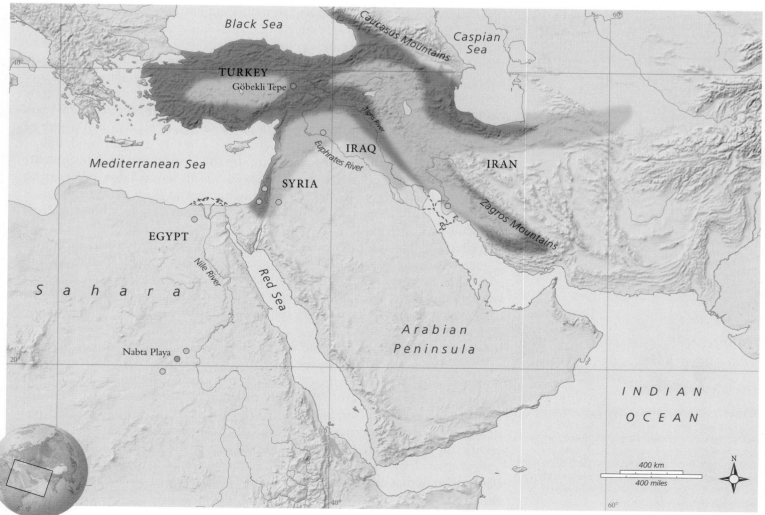

Jomon pottery. Ten thousand years ago, the Jomon potters of Japan produced the world's earliest known earthenware vessels. Other pottery-making peoples also practiced farming, but the Jomon people were sedentary foragers—living in permanent or long-term settlements, but managing the environment in minimal ways and relying on abundant wild foods, including nuts, seeds, acorns, some 70 marine animal species, and land mammals—eating not just boar, deer, and hare, but also wolves, wildcats, flying squirrels, and monkeys.

Women and work. Archaeology can reconstruct how ancient people behaved by measuring the deformities in their skeletons. The woman whose toe this was lived in a community of early sedentary foragers in what is now Syria. She evidently spent much of her time kneeling, presumably to grind the acorns and kernels of wild wheat on which her people relied for food.

Villages had distinctive identities and habits, which almost amounted to badges of identity. Some favored gazelle toe bones for jewelry; others preferred fox teeth and partridge legs. These people married within their own communities to judge from the evidence of inherited physical characteristics. For example, in some villages, people were relatively short, while in others, they had distinctive dental patterns. These settlers cut what look like plans of their fields on limestone slabs, which suggests that they were territorial—that they had a sense of possession that Captain Cook would have recognized.

In sum, the lives of preagricultural settlers were so much like the lives of the early farmers who succeeded them that when archaeologists first found the foragers' villages in the 1930s, they assumed the inhabitants were farmers. But the settled foragers were actually better off than farmers. Their remains, on the whole, show better health and nutrition than the farming peoples who followed later in the same region. A diet rich in seeds and nuts had ground down their teeth, but—unlike the farmers—they have none of the streaked tooth-enamel common among people who suffer from food shortages.

Similar evidence of preagricultural settlements exists in other places. Take a few conspicuous examples. The Jomon people of central Honshu Island in Japan lived in permanent villages 13,000 years ago, feeding themselves by fishing and gathering acorns and chestnuts. They made pots for display, in elaborate shapes, modeled on flames and serpents, and lacquered them with tree sap. Their potters were, in a sense, magicians, transforming clay into objects of prestige and ritual. Underwater archaeology has recently discovered what seem to be the remains of substantial stone buildings of the Jomon period submerged offshore as the result of an ancient landslide. In the Egyptian Sahara, at Nabta Playa, about 40 plant species, including sorghum, a type of cereal grass, grew alongside hearths and pit ovens, evidence of settled life from about 10,000 years ago. In other parts of the central Sahara in the same period that had plenty of water and a cooler climate than now, foragers found sorghum and millet, another cereal grass. At Göbekli Tepe, a hilltop site in southeast Turkey, contemporaries who lived mainly by gathering wild wheat hewed 7-ton pillars from limestone. They erected them in a sunken chamber in their village and decorated them with carvings of snakes, boar, gazelles, cranes, and symbols that look suspiciously like writing.

What was life like in these earliest settlements? Small, permanent houses suggest that nuclear families—parents and children—predominated, though some sites clearly have communal work areas for grinding seeds and nuts. As for who did the work, the most stunning finding of recent archaeology in the Middle East suggests that work was probably shared between the sexes. The way skeletons are muscled suggests that women did slightly more kneeling (and therefore slightly more grinding of nuts and seeds) than men, and men did more throwing (and therefore more hunting) than women. But both sexes did both activities. Male and female bodies began to reconverge after a long period during which they had evolved to look different. As food production replaced hunting and gathering, war and child rearing became the main sex-specific jobs in society. The convergence between the physical features of men and women seems still to be in progress today. Indeed, it seems to be accelerating as men and women share more and more tasks, and the need for heavily muscled or big-framed bodies diminishes along with physically demanding jobs in much of the world.

The Disadvantages of Farming

Preagricultural communities do not simply progress to farming. If foraging produces abundance and security, it does not necessarily follow that farming can deliver more of the same. The consequences of adopting agriculture are by no means all positive. In the early stages of moving from foraging to farming, the food supply actually becomes less reliable because people depend on a relatively small range of farmed foods or even on a single species. As a result, a community becomes vulnerable to ecological disasters. Famine becomes more likely as diet narrows. Moreover, when people have to plant and grow food as well as gather it, they have to use up more energy to get the same amount of nourishment (although domesticated foods, once harvested, tend to be easier to process for eating). The need to organize labor encourages inequalities and exploitation. Concentrations of domesticated animals spread disease, such as smallpox, measles, rubella, chicken pox, influenza, and tuberculosis.

So the problem is really the opposite of what Cook supposed. It is farmers' behavior, not foragers' behavior, that is strange. Husbandry is not a step along a march of improvement because in some ways, it makes life worse. No one has described the problem better than the historian of agronomy, Jack L. Harlan:

> [P]eople who do not farm do about everything that farmers do, but they do not work as hard. . . . They understand the life cycles of plants, know the seasons of the year, and when and where the natural plant food resources can be harvested in great abundance with the least effort. There is evidence that the diet of gathering peoples was better than that of cultivators, that starvation was rare, . . . that there was a lower incidence of chronic disease and not nearly so many cavities in their teeth.

The question must be raised: Why farm? Why work harder for less nutritious food and a more capricious supply? Why invite famine, plague, pestilence, and crowded living conditions?

Chronology: Early Forager Settlements	
15,000 years ago	World emerges from the Ice Age
14,000–15,000 years ago	Permanent settlements appear in Middle East
13,000 years ago	Honshu Island, Japan
10,000 years ago	Nabta Playa, Egypt; Göbekli Tepe, Turkey
(All dates are approximate)	

[Handwritten margin note: disadvantages: - famine : due to the reliances on food supply. - uses same amount of energy - organize labor - disease.]

HUSBANDRY IN DIFFERENT ENVIRONMENTS

Part of what is surprising about agriculture is that it is so common. Not only has almost the entire human world adopted it, but many peoples came to it independently of one another. Scholars used to suppose that agriculture was so extraordinary it must have begun in some particular spot and that **diffusion** spread it from there—carried by migrants or conquerors, or transmitted by trade, or imitated. The last 40 years of research have shown, on the contrary, that the transition to food production happened over and over again, in a range of regions and a variety of environments, with different foodstuffs and different techniques. The most obvious contrast in environments is between **herders** and **tillers**. Herding develops where plants are too sparse or indigestible to sustain

Chukchi herder. The choice between hunting and herding often depends on local and historical circumstances. Reindeer-herding is an ancient practice in much of northern Eurasia, whereas in North America, the caribou have remained wild. In extreme northeast Asia, close to America, the Chukchi long resisted the example of neighboring people and preferred hunting to herding. In the last two or three centuries, however, they have adopted the herdsman's vocation shown here.

Making Connections | FORAGERS AND FARMERS COMPARED

FORAGERS	FARMERS
Food procurers hunt and gather	**Food producers** husbandry (breed animals, cultivate crops)
Fit into nature little environmental impact	**Change nature** herders: some environmental impact tillers: massive environment impact
Manage the landscape	**Nature remade and reimagined**
Dependence on wild animals and plants	**Interdependence between humans, plants, and animals** animals and plants exploited and domesticated
Stable food supply nomadic foragers move in response to environmental change; sedentary foragers vulnerable to changes of climate	**Unstable food supply** small range of farmed foods increases vulnerability to ecological disasters
Stable population • relatively little labor needed • population control available, mainly by managed lactation	**Expanding population** • breeding livestock and cultivating plants leads to increased food supply and increased population • concentrations of domesticated animals spread disease
Stable society • kinship and age fix individual's place in society • sexes usually share labor by specializing in different economic tasks	**Radically changed, unstable society** • need to control labor and food distribution leads to social inequalities • work shared between the sexes, increased reliance on female labor • strong states develop with powerful elites, complex technologies

human life, but animals can convert these plants into meat—an energy source that people can access by eating the animals. Tilling develops where the soil is suitable or enough ecological diversity exists to sustain plant husbandry or mixed farming of plants and animals.

Herders' Environments

In three regions of the Earth—tundra, the evergreen forests of northern Eurasia, and great grasslands—it is not possible to grow enough humanly digestible plant foods to keep large numbers of people alive. In the tundra and evergreen forests, average temperatures are too low, the growing season is too short, the surface soil is too vulnerable to frost, and the subsoil, in some areas, is too frozen. These environments offer only two options. People can remain foragers—and primarily hunters, seeking the fat-rich species typical of such zones. The Inuit in the North American Arctic, for example, hunt seal and walrus. Or people can become herders, like the Sami and Samoyeds of northern Europe and northwest Asia, who live off reindeer.

Similarly, the soils of the world's vast grasslands—known as prairie in North America, pampa in South America, steppe in Eurasia, and the **Sahel** in Africa—have, for most of history, been unfavorable for tillage. The sod is mostly too difficult to turn without a steel plow. Except for patches of exceptionally favorable soil, herding has been the only possible form of husbandry in these areas. The peoples of the Eurasian and African grasslands were probably herding by about 5000 B.C.E. In contrast, native American grassland dwellers of the New World retained a foraging way of life because available species—bison, various types of antelope—were, for the most part, more abundant for the hunt and less suitable for herding (see Map 2.3).

For those who choose it, herding has three special consequences. First, it imposes a mobile way of life. The proportion of the population who follow the herds—and, in some cases, it is the entire population—cannot settle into permanent villages. Herder peoples are not unwilling or unable to build permanently or on a large scale. The Scythians, for instance, people of the western Asian steppe who first domesticated the horse and invented the wheel and axle about 6,000 to 7,000 years ago, built impressive stone structures. But these were underground tombs, dwellings for the dead, while the living inhabited temporary camps. Some herding societies in Asia and Africa have become rich enough to found cities for elites or for specialists working outside of food production, such as craftsmen or miners. Indeed, as we shall see (Chapter 13), in the thirteenth century C.E., a city of this type, Karakorum in Mongolia, was one of the most admired cities in the world. On the whole, however, herding does not favor the development of cities or the kind of culture that cities nourish, such as monumental buildings, large-scale institutions for education and the arts, and industrial technology.

Second, since herders breed from animals that naturally share their grassland habitats, their herds consist of such creatures as cattle, sheep, horses, goats—milk-yielding stock. To get the full benefit from their animals, herding peoples have to eat dairy products. To modern, milk-fed Americans, this may sound perfectly normal. But it required a modification of human evolution. Most people, in most parts of the world, do not naturally produce lactase, the substance that enables them to digest milk, after infancy. They respond to dairy products with distaste or even intolerance. Whereas the Masai of Kenya in East Africa get 80 percent of their energy intake from milk, their Kikuyu neighbors, who are tillers, detest the stuff. People from the steppes of Eurasia invented an amazing variety of products, including butter, yoghurt, and cheese to make milk digestible.

Third, the herders' diet, relying heavily on meat, milk, and blood, lacks variety compared to the diets of people in more ecologically diverse environments. This does not mean that the herders' diet is nutritionally deficient. If you eat organ meats (especially liver, kidneys, heart, lungs, and glands), drink animal blood, and prepare dairy products in a variety of ways to harness beneficial bacteria, you can get everything the human body needs, including adequate vitamin C. But this does not mean that herding peoples, although they often express contempt for farmers, despise the crops farmers grow. On the contrary, herders highly prize cultivated plants and import them at great cost or take them as tribute or booty. The same goes for the products of the sedentary industries that only farming folk have land or leisure for, or that are possible only in tree-rich environments, such as wood products, silk, linen, and cotton.

Violence between herders and farmers was common until about 300 years ago or so, when the war technology of sedentary societies left herding societies unable to compete. Conflict arose not from herders' hatred of farmers' culture but from a desire to share its benefits. On the other hand, farmers have not normally had to depend on herding cultures for meat or dairy products. Typically, they can farm

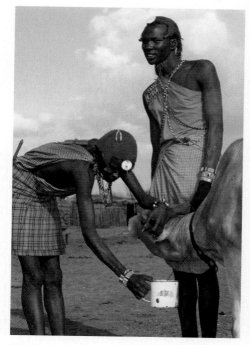

Masai. Humans need vitamin C, but the meat and dairy products from herds do not supply much of it. So people in herding cultures eat half-digested plants from animals' stomachs and organ meats, such as the liver, in which vitamin C tends to get concentrated. Fresh blood—drawn here from the veins of a calf by Masai women in Kenya—is also a useful source of the vitamin. Drinking blood confers an added advantage: nomads can draw it from their animals "on the hoof," without slaughtering them or halting the migrations of their flocks.

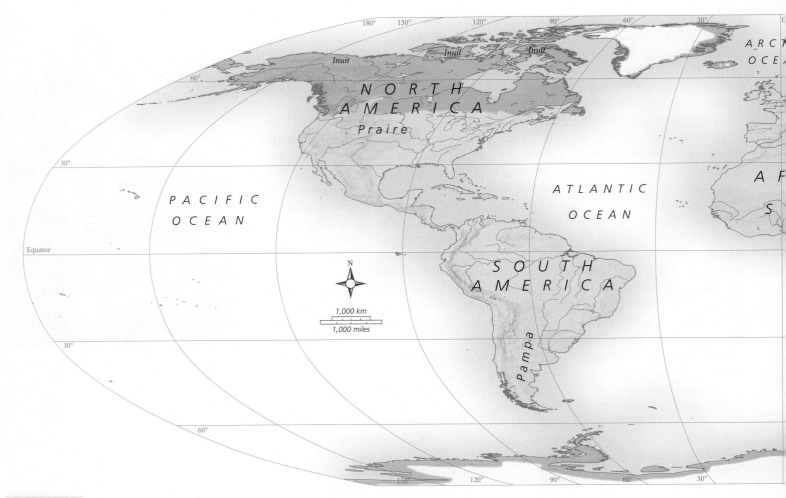

MAP 2.3

Herders' Environments

	tundra
	evergreen forests
	grasslands
Sami	hunters and herders described on pages 38–39
KENYA	modern country

their own animals, feeding them on the waste or surplus of their crops or by grazing them between their tillage. Or they can graze sheep or goats upland, at higher altitudes above their fields. Therefore, in herder–settler warfare, the herders have typically been aggressive and the settlers defensive.

Tillers' Environments

In the tundra, northern Eurasian evergreen forests, and great grasslands, tilling isn't an option. Husbandry is restricted to herding. But numerous other environments are suited to farming. The first essential prerequisite for farming was soil loose enough for a dibble—a pointed stick for poking holes in the ground—to work. At first, this was the only technology available. Where the sod had to be cut or turned—where, for instance, the soil was heavy clay or a dense or sticky mixture—agriculture had to wait for the slightly more advanced technology of the spade and the plow.

Equally necessary prerequisites for agriculture were sufficient water, by rain or flood or irrigation, to grow the crop; enough sun to ripen it; and some way to nourish the soil. This last was generally the hardest to ensure, because farming can exhaust even the richest soils fairly rapidly. Flooding and layering with silt or dredging and dressing new topsoil is needed to replace nutrients. Alternatively, farmers can add fertilizer: ash from burned wood, leaf mold from forest clearings, guano

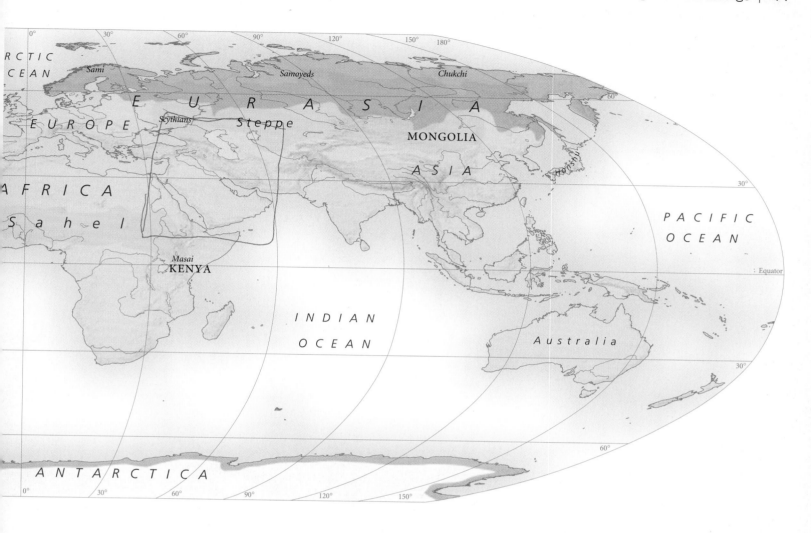

from bird colonies if there are any nearby, mined potassium, manure from domesticated animals, or night soil—if all else fails, for human excretion is poor fertilizer.

We can divide environments suited to early agriculture into three broad types: swampy wetlands, uplands, and alluvial plains, where flooding rivers or lakes renew the topsoil. (Cleared woodlands and irrigated drylands are also suitable for agriculture, but as far as we know, farming never originated in these environments. Rather, outsiders brought it to these areas from some place else.) Each of the three types developed with peculiar characteristics and specialized crops. It is worth looking at each in turn (see Map 2.4).

Swampland Swamp is no longer much in demand for farming. Nowadays, in the Western world, if we want to turn bog into farmland we drain it. But it had advantages early on. Swamp soil is rich, moist, and easy to work with simple technology. At least one staple grows well in waterlogged land—*rice*. We still do not know where or when rice was first cultivated, or even whether any of these wetland varieties preceded the dryland rice that has gradually become more popular around the world. Most evidence, however, suggests that people were producing rice at sites on the lower Ganges River in India and in parts of Southeast Asia some 8,000 years ago, and in paddies in the Yangtze River valley in China not long afterward.

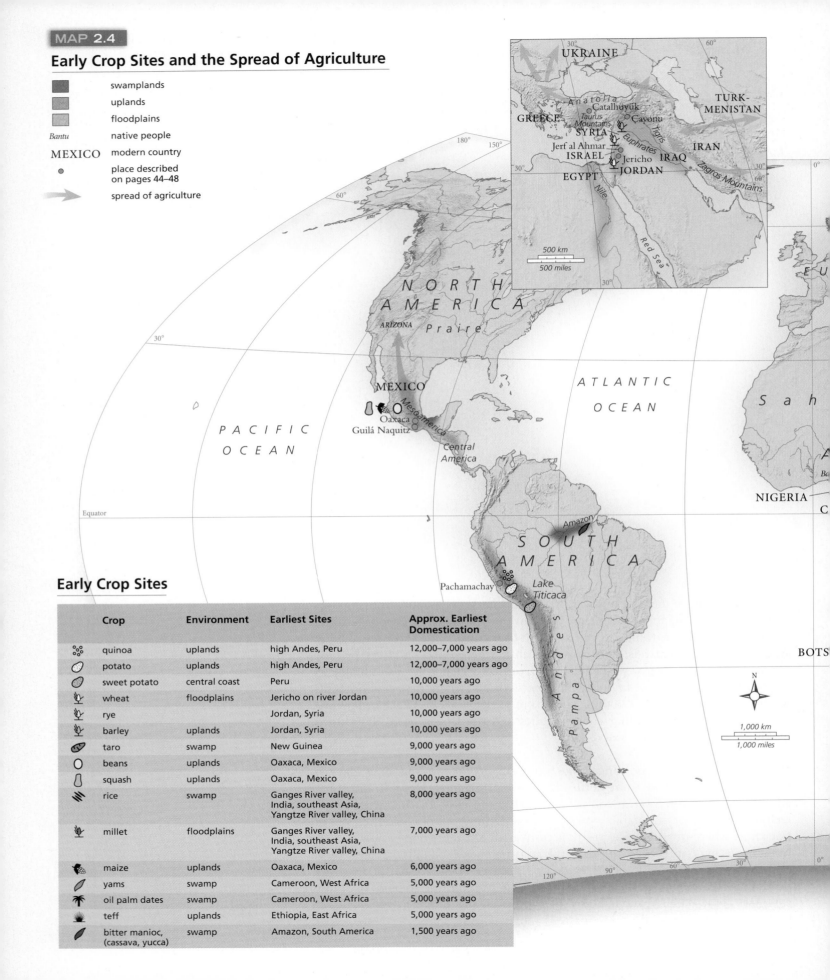

MAP 2.4

Early Crop Sites and the Spread of Agriculture

- swamplands
- uplands
- floodplains
- *Bantu* — native people
- MEXICO — modern country
- • — place described on pages 44–48
- → — spread of agriculture

Early Crop Sites

	Crop	Environment	Earliest Sites	Approx. Earliest Domestication
	quinoa	uplands	high Andes, Peru	12,000–7,000 years ago
	potato	uplands	high Andes, Peru	12,000–7,000 years ago
	sweet potato	central coast	Peru	10,000 years ago
	wheat	floodplains	Jericho on river Jordan	10,000 years ago
	rye		Jordan, Syria	10,000 years ago
	barley	uplands	Jordan, Syria	10,000 years ago
	taro	swamp	New Guinea	9,000 years ago
	beans	uplands	Oaxaca, Mexico	9,000 years ago
	squash	uplands	Oaxaca, Mexico	9,000 years ago
	rice	swamp	Ganges River valley, India, southeast Asia, Yangtze River valley, China	8,000 years ago
	millet	floodplains	Ganges River valley, India, southeast Asia, Yangtze River valley, China	7,000 years ago
	maize	uplands	Oaxaca, Mexico	6,000 years ago
	yams	swamp	Cameroon, West Africa	5,000 years ago
	oil palm dates	swamp	Cameroon, West Africa	5,000 years ago
	teff	uplands	Ethiopia, East Africa	5,000 years ago
	bitter manioc, (cassava, yucca)	swamp	Amazon, South America	1,500 years ago

Map labels: UKRAINE, GREECE, Anatolia, Çatalhüyük, Taurus Mountains, Çayönü, SYRIA, Euphrates, Tigris, TURK-MENISTAN, IRAN, Jerf al Ahmar, ISRAEL, Jericho, JORDAN, IRAQ, Zagros Mountains, EGYPT, Nile, Red Sea, 500 km, 500 miles

NORTH AMERICA, ARIZONA, Prairie, MEXICO, Oaxaca, Guilá Naquitz, Mesoamerica, Central America, PACIFIC OCEAN, ATLANTIC OCEAN, Equator, SOUTH AMERICA, Amazon, Pachamachay, Lake Titicaca, Andes, Pampa, Sah, NIGERIA, BOTS, 1,000 km, 1,000 miles

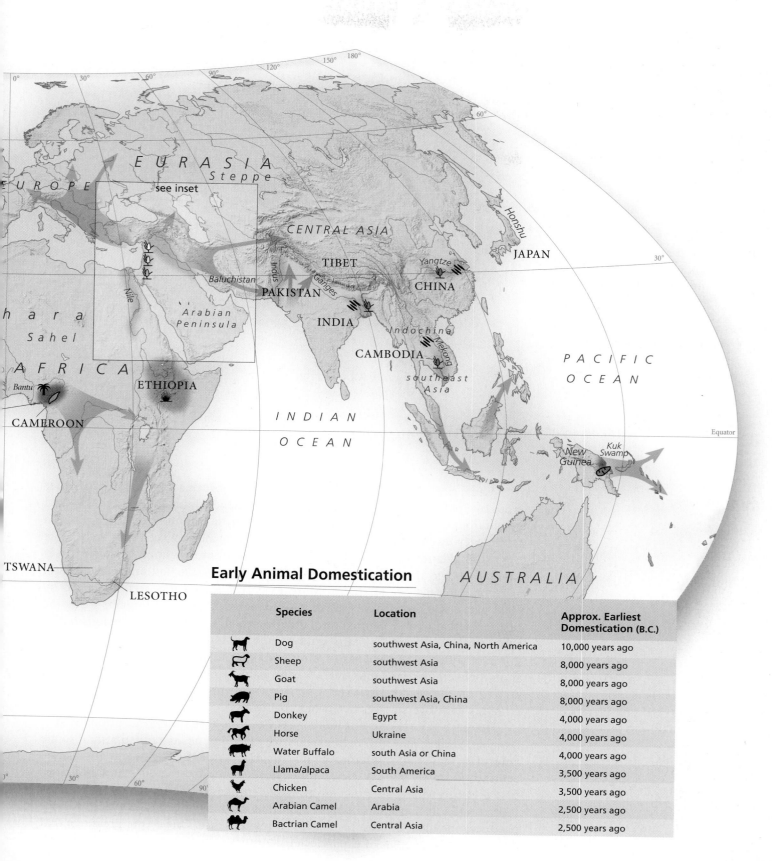

Early Animal Domestication

	Species	Location	Approx. Earliest Domestication (B.C.)
	Dog	southwest Asia, China, North America	10,000 years ago
	Sheep	southwest Asia	8,000 years ago
	Goat	southwest Asia	8,000 years ago
	Pig	southwest Asia, China	8,000 years ago
	Donkey	Egypt	4,000 years ago
	Horse	Ukraine	4,000 years ago
	Water Buffalo	south Asia or China	4,000 years ago
	Llama/alpaca	South America	3,500 years ago
	Chicken	Central Asia	3,500 years ago
	Arabian Camel	Arabia	2,500 years ago
	Bactrian Camel	Central Asia	2,500 years ago

Making Connections | HERDERS AND TILLERS COMPARED

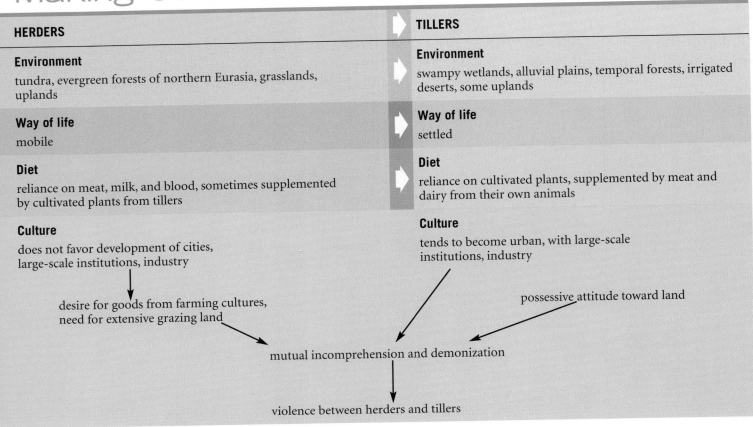

HERDERS		TILLERS
Environment		**Environment**
tundra, evergreen forests of northern Eurasia, grasslands, uplands		swampy wetlands, alluvial plains, temporal forests, irrigated deserts, some uplands
Way of life		**Way of life**
mobile		settled
Diet		**Diet**
reliance on meat, milk, and blood, sometimes supplemented by cultivated plants from tillers		reliance on cultivated plants, supplemented by meat and dairy from their own animals
Culture		**Culture**
does not favor development of cities, large-scale institutions, industry		tends to become urban, with large-scale institutions, industry

desire for goods from farming cultures, need for extensive grazing land

possessive attitude toward land

mutual incomprehension and demonization

violence between herders and tillers

Where rice is unavailable, swampland cultivators can adapt the land for other crops by dredging earth—which they can do by hand in suitable conditions—and by building up mounds. Not only can they plant the mounds, but they can also farm water-dwelling creatures and plants in the ditches between mounds. In the western highlands of New Guinea, the first agriculture we know of started fully 9,000 years ago in the boggy valley bottoms. Drains, ditches, and mounds still exist in the Kuk swamp there. More extensive earthworks were in place by 6000 B.C.E. The crops have vanished—biodegraded into nothingness—but the first farmers probably planted *taro*, the most easily cultivated, indigenous native root. Modern varieties of taro exhibit signs of long domestication. A diverse group of plants—native bananas, yams and other tubers, the sago palm, and nuts from the palmlike *pandanus* tree—was probably added early. At some point, pigs arrived on the island. However, a fierce and, on present evidence, unresolvable scholarly controversy rages over when that was.

Having a variety of crops made New Guinea's agriculture exceptionally sustainable. Variety may also help explain why farming has remained a small-scale enterprise there that numerous, politically independent villages, and not a large, centralized state, conduct. New Guinea never generated the big states and cities that grew up where the range of available crops was narrower and agriculture more fragile. It may sound paradoxical that the most advantageous crop range produces the most modest results, but it makes sense. One of the pressures that drives farming peoples to expand their territory is fear that a crop will fail. The more territory you control, the more surplus you can warehouse, the more manpower you command, and the more productive are your fields. Moreover, if you farm an environment with a narrow range of food sources, you can diversify only by conquering other people's habitats. The history of New Guinea has been as violent as that of other parts of the world, but its wars have always been local and the resulting territorial adjustments small. Empire-building was unknown on the island until European colonizers got there in the late nineteenth century.

We know of no other swamps that people adapted so early, but many later civilizations arose from similar sorts of ooze. We do not know much about the origins of **Bantu** agriculture in West Africa, but it is more likely to have begun in the swamp than in the forest. Swampland is suited to the native *yams* on which Bantu farming first relied. Waterlogged land is also the favorite habitat of the other mainstay of Bantu tradition, the *oil palm*. The earliest archaeological evidence of farming based on yams and oil palms dates from about 5,000 years ago in swampy valley bottoms of Cameroon, above the forest level.

Swampland also contributed to the agriculture that began along the Amazon River in South America 4,000 or 5,000 years ago. At first, the crops were probably richly diverse, supplemented by farming turtles and snails or similar mollusks. Later, however, from about 500 C.E., farmers increasingly focused on *bitter manioc*, also known as cassava or yucca, which has the great advantage of being poisonous to predators. Human consumers can process the poison out. Olmec civilization, which, as we shall see in Chapter 3, was enormously influential in the history of **Mesoamerica**, was founded in swamps thick with mangrove trees about 3,000 years ago.

Uplands Like swamplands, regions of high altitude are not places that people today consider good for farming. Farmers have usually left these regions to the herdsmen and native upland creatures, such as sheep, goats, yaks, and llamas. There are three reasons for doing so: First, as altitude increases, cold and the scorching effects of solar radiation in the thin atmosphere diminish the variety of viable plants. Second, slopes are subject to erosion (although this has a secondary benefit because relatively rich soils collect in valley bottoms). Finally, slopes in general are hard to work once you have come to rely on plows, but this does not stop people who do not use plows from farming them. Nonetheless, in highlands suitable for plant foods plant husbandry or mixed farming did develop.

The Andes Highlands usually contain many different microclimates at various altitudes and in valleys where sun and rain can vary tremendously within a short space. Some of the world's earliest farming, therefore, happened at surprisingly high altitudes. Evidence of mixed farming survives from between about 12,000 and 7,000 years ago near Lake Titicaca, elevation 13,000 feet, in the Andes of South America. Here, in the cave of Pachamachay, bones of domesticated llamas cover those of hunted camelios—the llamalike but smaller *vicuña* and *guanaco*. The domesticated animals fed on *quinoa*, an extremely hardy grainlike food that resembles some kinds of

The valley of Cuzco, Peru, the homeland of the Inca (Chapter 15). Potatoes—which were first cultivated in the Andes at least 7,000 years ago and spread from there to the rest of the world—remain a staple in this region. They are the only food that—if eaten in sufficient quantities—contains all the nutrients necessary to sustain life. Suitable varieties of potatoes flourish at over 13,000 feet above sea level. In mountain climates, they can be freeze-dried for year-round nutrition.

grass. It grows at high altitudes thanks to a bitter, soapy coating that cuts out solar radiation. The llamas ingested the leafy part and deposited the seeds in their manure. Their corrals therefore became nurseries for a food fit for humans to grow and eat.

The earliest known experiments in domesticating the *potato* probably occurred at about the same time in the same area. Potatoes were ideal for mountain agriculture. Not only were some naturally occurring varieties of potato hardy enough to grow at altitudes of up to 14,000 feet, but they also provided total nutrition. Eaten in sufficient quantities, potatoes provide everything the human body needs to survive. Moreover, the high-altitude varieties have a hidden advantage. Whereas wild kinds of lowland potatoes are poisonous and need careful processing to become edible, the concentration of poison in potatoes diminishes the higher you climb. There is an obvious evolutionary reason for this. The poison is there to deter predators, which are most numerous at low altitudes.

The potato gave Andean mountain dwellers the same capacity to support large populations as peoples of the valleys and plains, where a parallel story began in the central coastal region of what is now Peru. There, around 10,000 years ago, farmers grew *sweet potato* tubers similar to modern varieties. If agriculture did indeed produce sweet potatoes, they would have to be counted as the New World's earliest farmed crop. Once both regions had the capacity to feed dense populations, Andean history became a story of highland–lowland warfare, punctuated by the rise and fall of mountain-based empires.

FIGURE 2.1 TEOSINTE AND MAIZE. The form of teosinte from which early farmers in Mesoamerica developed maize no longer exists. But the diagram illustrates the stages through which Mesoamericans may have bred teosinte into maize, until they developed the characteristic thick, densely packed cobs familiar today. Unlike teosinte, maize cannot germinate without human help.
Permission of the University of Michigan Museum of Anthropology.

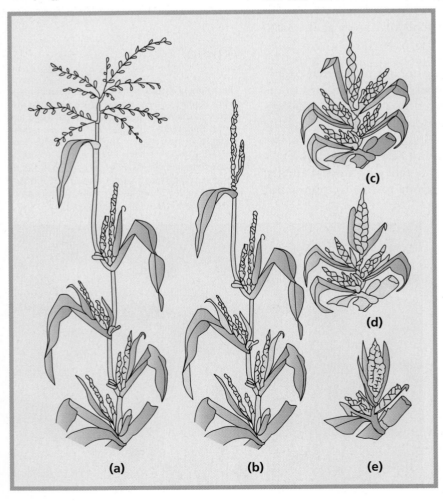

(a)   (b)   (c)   (d)   (e)

Mesoamerica The Mesoamerican highlands, which stretch from central Mexico to Central America and are less high and less steep than those of the Andes, produced their own kind of highland-adapted food: a trinity of *maize*, *beans*, and *squash*. This combination grows well together and when eaten together provides almost complete nutrition. The earliest surviving specimens of cultivated maize are 6,000 years old. People in Mesoamerica developed maize from a wild grass known as teosinte, of which a type still grows in the state of Oaxaca in central Mexico, along with the wild ancestors of modern domesticated beans (see Figure 2.1). By working out how long it would take wild species to mutate, botanists estimate that people domesticated beans about 9,000 years ago. The earliest domesticated squashes date from about the same period and are found at the same site as teosinte and wild beans, at Guilá Naquitz, in Oaxaca. The fact that their wild ancestors have disappeared suggests that farming here might have started with squashes when gatherers of wild beans and grains needed to provide food during droughts. Squash grows well during dry spells severe enough to wither teosinte and blight beans, so it would have provided a food reserve that people did not need to store.

The Old World   The Old World had no potatoes, quinoa, or even maize for highland farmers to work with. The hardiest staples available in most of Eurasia and Africa were *rye* and *barley*. Surprisingly, however, people in lowlands first domesticated both of them in what are now Jordan and Syria, probably about 10,000 years ago. Rye germinates at just a couple of degrees above freezing, but its drawbacks made it more popular as a winter crop in wheat-growing lowlands than as a mountain staple. Its yield is lower, and it is less nutritious than other grains. Rye is also extremely vulnerable to fungus infection. Barley did not fulfill its potential to be an Old World equivalent of quinoa or potatoes until the sixth century C.E., when it became the staple food of a farming society in Tibet (Chapter 10).

The only other Old World grain with similar potential was Ethiopia's indigenous grass called *teff*. Although its tiny grains make teff laborious to cultivate and process, it was suited to the region's fertile soil and temperate climate above 7,200 feet. Farmers in Ethiopia cultivated teff at least 5,000 years ago, but they never had to rely on it absolutely. Some varieties of *millet*—the name of a huge range of grasses whose seeds humans can digest—had superior yields. Over time, millet displaced teff, which never became a major staple outside Ethiopia.

Teff—the staple grain of early Ethiopian civilization—remains unique to the region, where it is still harvested regularly. But, as the picture shows, it more closely resembles wild grasses than modern high-yielding food grains. The starchy ears are tiny and require much labor to mill. So, like many traditional staples, teff faces the threat of extinction today from the competition of commercial hybrids or genetically modified varieties, promoted by powerful corporations.

Alluvial Plains   Although swamps and rain-fed highlands have produced spectacularly successful agriculture, farmers get the best help from nature in **alluvial plains**, flat lands where mud carried by overflowing rivers or lakes renews the soil. If people can channel the floods to keep crops from being swept away on these plains, alluvium, made up of sediment and other organic matter, restores nutrients and compensates for lack of rain. As we shall see in the next chapter, alluvial soils in arid climates sustained some of the world's most productive economies until late in the second millennium B.C.E. *Wheat* and barley grew in the black earth that lines Egypt's Nile, the floodplains of the lower Tigris and Euphrates rivers in what is now Iraq, and the Indus River in what is now Pakistan. People first farmed millet on alluvial soils in a somewhat cooler, moister climate in China, in the crook of the Yellow River and the Guanzhong Basin around 7,000 years ago. And in the warm, moist climate of Indochina in what is now Cambodia, three crops of rice a year could grow on soil that the annual counter flow of the Mekong River created. The Mekong becomes so torrential that the delta—where the river enters the sea—cannot funnel its flow, and water is forced back upriver.

Smaller patches of alluvium, deposited by floods, nourished the world's earliest known fully farming economies. Among the first of these farming economies was Jericho on the river Jordan. Today, the Jordan valley looks inhospitable: desert crusted with salt and sodium. Ten thousand years ago, however, Jericho overlooked an alluvial fan that trickling streams washed down from the Judaean hills, filling the river as it crept south from the Sea of Galilee. The Jordan was thick with silt. The banks it deposited formed the biblical "jungle

Jericho Skull.   No one knows why people in Jericho, in the eighth millennium B.C.E., kept skulls, painted them with plaster, and inserted cowrie shells into the eye sockets. But these decorated skulls have, in a sense, helped the dead to survive. Some of the skulls even show traces of painted hair and mustaches.
Ashmolean Museum, Oxford, England, UK

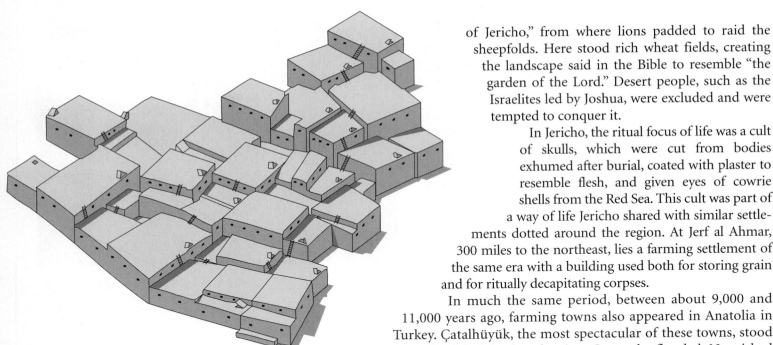

FIGURE 2.2 ÇATALHÜYÜK The houses of Çatalhüyük were linked not by streets as we know them, but by rooftop walkways, from which people presumably used ladders to reach different levels. The diagram reconstructs part of Çatalhüyük on the basis of archaeological findings. Wall paintings there show that other settlements in the region were constructed on similar principles. *Schematic reconstruction of houses and shrines from Level VI at Catalhoyuk by James Mellaart. Reprinted by permission of the Catalhoyuk Research Project.*

of Jericho," from where lions padded to raid the sheepfolds. Here stood rich wheat fields, creating the landscape said in the Bible to resemble "the garden of the Lord." Desert people, such as the Israelites led by Joshua, were excluded and were tempted to conquer it.

In Jericho, the ritual focus of life was a cult of skulls, which were cut from bodies exhumed after burial, coated with plaster to resemble flesh, and given eyes of cowrie shells from the Red Sea. This cult was part of a way of life Jericho shared with similar settlements dotted around the region. At Jerf al Ahmar, 300 miles to the northeast, lies a farming settlement of the same era with a building used both for storing grain and for ritually decapitating corpses.

In much the same period, between about 9,000 and 11,000 years ago, farming towns also appeared in Anatolia in Turkey. Çatalhüyük, the most spectacular of these towns, stood on an alluvial plain that the river Çarsamba flooded. Nourished by wheat and beans, the people filled an urban area of 32 acres. Walkways across flat roofs, not streets as we define them, linked a honeycomb of dwellings. The houses, built of mud bricks, were identical (see Figure 2.2). The wall panels, doorways, hearths, ovens, and even the bricks were a standard shape and size. You can still see where the occupants swept their rubbish—chips of bone and shiny, black flakes of volcanic glass called obsidian—into their hearths.

Çatalhüyük was not an isolated phenomenon. A wall painting there depicts what may be another, similar urban settlement. Even earlier sites, smaller than Çatalhüyük but on the same order, communicated with the Jordan valley—villages like Çayonu, inhabited by people who piled up skulls and performed sacrifices on polished stone slabs. By exchanging craft products—weapons, metalwork, and pots—for primary materials such as cowrie shells from the Red Sea, timber from the Taurus Mountains in Anatolia, and copper from beyond the Tigris, the inhabitants of Çatalhüyük became rich by the standards of the time. Archaeologists have unearthed such treasures as fine blades and mirrors made from local obsidian and products of the copper-smelting technology that these people gradually developed.

Yet the inhabitants of Çatalhüyük never got safely beyond the mercy of nature. They worshiped images of its strength: bulls with monstrous horns and protruding tongues, crouching leopards who guard goddesses leaning on grain bins, fuming volcanoes, giant boars with laughing jaws and bristling backs. This is surely farmer's art, animated by fear of the wild and loathing of the savage. Most people died in their late twenties or early thirties. Their corpses were ritually fed to vultures and jackals—as surviving paintings show—before their bones were buried in communal graves.

Çatalhüyük lasted for nearly 2,000 years, remarkable longevity by the standards of later cities. It became doomed as the waters that supplied it dried up. Even during its greatest prosperity, its space was limited and its resource base restricted. But, along with Jericho and other settlements of the era, it pointed to the future, showing how farming, despite all its short-term disadvantages and the sacrifices it demanded, could sustain life through hard times.

A CLOSER LOOK

The Fertility Goddess of Çatalhüyük

Her seated position and uptilted head suggest authority, as do the predatory felines that guard the throne, as if in obedience to someone able to command nature.

In recent times, the so-called fertility goddess or Earth Mother of Çatalhüyük has become a cult object for feminists, who make pilgrimages to the site. But what her image was for and what it represents are unknown.

The folds of fat around her joints suggest a degree of obesity amounting to clinical pathology or physical deformity. Most human societies, for most of history, have admired body fat on both men and women.

Her bulbous breasts and exaggerated sex organs suggest the importance of fertility to the society in which this image was crafted.

From this image, what can we infer about the status of women in early agricultural societies?

THE SPREAD OF AGRICULTURE

The development of food production in diverse environments with different foods and different techniques points to an important conclusion: It was not a unique occurrence—a one-of-a-kind accident or a stroke of genius. Rather, farming was an ordinary and fairly frequent process that could therefore be open to a variety of explanations.

Where we can be sure agriculture developed independently, we can see that early food producers focused on what they could grow or raise most easily in their particular environment. Examples include livestock herds in central Eurasia; wheat and barley in the Middle East; sweet potatoes, quinoa, and potatoes in the Andean region; the squash–maize–beans trinity in Mesoamerica; millet in China; and rice in Southeast Asia. In New Guinea agriculture was based on taro, in Ethiopia on teff, and in West Africa on yams and oil palms. Nevertheless, connections between neighboring regions were unquestionably important in spreading husbandry. Some crops were undoubtedly transferred from the places they originated to other regions (see Map 2.4).

Europe

It seems likely (though the evidence is slight and subject to reinterpretation) that migrants from Asia colonized Europe. They brought their farming materials and knowledge with them, as well as their **Indo-European languages**, from which most of Europe's present languages descend. Colonization was a gradual process, beginning about 6,000 years ago. Early farmers may have cleared land, but probably did not undertake large-scale deforestation. Later, well-documented cases from other forest environments suggest that early agriculturists in Europe found trees useful and even revered them. So large-scale deforestation more likely occurred naturally, perhaps through tree diseases. Between 4,500 and 5,000 years ago, for instance, in northern Europe, the broad-leaved forest receded, creating areas that were well suited to farming. When the woodland grew back after a few hundred years, farmers unquestionably cut it away.

Asia

Similar migrations probably spread farming to parts of Central Asia south of the steppeland. The farming that developed in alluvial environments in Anatolia and the Jordan valley colonized or converted every viable part of the region by 8,000 or 9,000 years ago. At altitudes above 1,800 feet, inhabitants of sites east of the Zagros Mountains (in what is now Iran) replaced their wild grains with cultivated varieties. Then, too, by about 6,000 years ago, comprehensive irrigation systems for farming crisscrossed the oases in southern Turkmenistan, which had a moister climate than it has now.

In the Indian subcontinent, the sudden emergence of well-built villages in the same period was probably the result of outside influence. No intermediate phase between foraging and farming occurred; there was no period when foragers led settled lives. We can trace the spread of farming from southwest Asia by way of Baluchistan (southern Pakistan). Here, remnants of domestic barley and wheat in mud bricks and the bones of domestic goats confirm the presence of agriculture about 9,000 years ago. This is also the site of the world's earliest surviving cotton thread, strung through a copper bead about 7,500 years ago.

Chronology: The Spread of Agriculture

9,000 years ago	Evidence of agriculture in Indian subcontinent; farming spreads by diffusion in the Egyptian Sahara and Nile valley
8,000–9,000 years ago	Farming spreads from Jordan valley and Anatolia to central Asia, south of the steppe
6,000 years ago	Migrants from Asia bring farming materials and knowledge with them to Europe
4,500–5,000 years ago	Bantu expansion spreads farming from West Africa southward
3,000 years ago	Maize moves northward from Mexico to southwestern United States
(All dates are approximate)	

The Americas

In much of North America, the spread of maize northward from its birthplace in central Mexico marked the transmission of agriculture. This process took thousands of years and demanded the development of new varieties as the crop crossed climate zones on its northward route. The best estimate puts maize farming in the southwestern United States about 3,000 years ago. Meanwhile, some North American peoples began to farm sunflowers and sumpweed for their edible seeds and roots. In South America, the idea of agriculture spread from, or across, the high Andes, through the upper Amazon Basin.

Africa

How agriculture spread in Africa is less clear than in other regions. People began to cultivate similar plant foods in the Egyptian Sahara and in the Nile valley about 9,000 years ago. It therefore appears that one region might have influenced the other. A little later, wheat cultivation along the Nile followed developments of a similar kind in the Jordan valley. Between 4,500 and 5,000 years ago, agriculture spread southward from West Africa along with Bantu languages. We can trace the path from what are now Cameroon and Nigeria in West Africa, southward and then eastward across the expanding Sahara to the Nile valley, before turning south again (see Map 2.5).

The Pacific Islands

Scholars debate when agriculture originated in the Pacific Islands. In particular, we do not know how or when the sweet potato—which, together with the pig, is the basis of food production in most of the region—got there. The most widely respected theory sees agriculture as the result of diffusion from New Guinea. It was a slow process requiring many adaptations as it spread across the ocean with seaborne migrants.

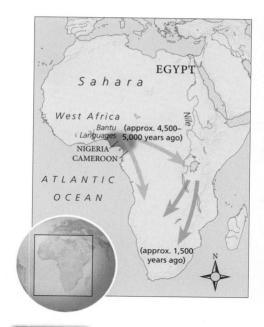

MAP 2.5

The Spread of Bantu Languages

SO WHY DID FARMING START?

Knowing or guessing about how food production started does not tell us why it started. Why, despite the short-term difficulties, did some peoples originate farming and others adopt it? Though scholars ferociously advocate rival explanations, we do not have to choose among them. Different explanations, or different combinations of the same explanations, may have applied in different places. Nor do we have to go through all the theories. We can group them under seven manageable headings.

Population Pressure

The first group of theories explains agriculture as a response to stress from population growth and overexploitation of wild foods. Examples include hunting game to extinction and overgathering plants, grubs, and mollusks. Logically, population should not grow if resources are getting scarce. But anthropological studies of contemporary cultures making the transition to agriculture in Botswana and Lesotho in southern Africa support the theory. Apparently, once farming starts, people cannot abandon it without catastrophe. A ratchet effect makes it impossible, while population rises, to go back to less intensive ways of getting food. As an explanation, however, for why agriculture arose in the first place, population pressure does not match the facts of chronology. Populations certainly grew in the most dedicated farming cultures, but, in most places, growth was probably more a consequence of agriculture than a cause.

> *"Knowing or guessing about how food production started does not tell us why it started. Why, despite the short-term difficulties, did some peoples originate farming and others adopt it?"*

The Outcome of Abundance

A group of theories has arisen in direct opposition to stress theory. These claim that husbandry was a result of abundance. Farming, it is said, was a by-product of the leisure of fishermen in Southeast Asia who devoted their spare time to experimenting with plants. Or it was invented by hill dwellers in northern Iraq, whose habitat was peculiarly rich in easily domesticated grasses and grazing herds. Or it was the natural result of concentrations of pockets of abundance in Central Asia in the post–Ice-Age era of global warming. As temperatures rose, oases opened up where different species congregated peacefully. Humans discovered they could domesticate animals that would otherwise be rivals, enemies, or prey. Abundance theory is a convincing description for why agriculture developed in some key areas, but it does not explain why, in good times, people would want to change how they got their food and take on extra work.

The Power of Politics

Stress theory and abundance theory may apply to why agriculture arose in different areas, but they cannot be true simultaneously. Therefore, beyond the food supply, it is worth considering possible political, social, or religious influences on food strategies. After all, food is for more than nourishment. It also confers power and prestige. It can symbolize identity and generate rituals. In hierarchically organized societies, elites nearly always demand more food than they can eat, not just to ensure their security but also to show off their wealth by squandering their waste.

In a society where leaders buy allegiance with food, competitive feasting can generate huge increases in demand, even if population is static and supplies are secure. Societies bound by feasting will always favor intensive agriculture and massive storage. Even in societies with looser forms of leadership or with collective decision making, feasting can be a powerful incentive to boost food production and storage, by force if necessary. Feasting can celebrate collective identity or cement relations with other communities. Then, too, people could process most of the early domesticated plants into intoxicating drinks. If farming began as a way to generate surpluses for feasts, alcohol must have had a special role.

Cult Agriculture

Cult agriculture. Chimú goldsmiths (Chapter 14) produced this ceremonial dish, which depicts the succession of the seasons, presided over by the central figure of the maize god, and offerings of the characteristic starches of the Peruvian lowlands—maize, cassava, sweet potatoes. By the time this object was made, however, around 1200 C.E., maize varieties had been adapted for varied environments, including uplands and temperate climates.

Religion may well have been the inspiration for farming. Planting may have originated as a fertility rite, or irrigation as libation (a liquid offering to the spirits or gods), or enclosure as an act of reverence for a sacred plant. To plow or dibble and sow and irrigate can carry profound meaning. They can be understood as rites of birth and nurture of the god on whom you are going to feed. In exchange for labor—a kind of sacrifice—the god provides nourishment. Most cultures have considered the power to make food grow to be a divine gift or curse or a secret that a hero stole from the gods. People have domesticated animals for use in sacrifice and prophecy as well as for food. Many societies cultivate plants that play a part at the altar rather than at the table. Examples include incense, ecstatic or hallucinatory drugs, the sacrificial corn of some high Andean communities, and wheat, which, in orthodox Christian traditions, is the only grain permitted for the Eucharist. And if religion inspired agriculture, alcohol as a drink that can induce ecstasy might have had a special appeal. In short, where crops are gods, farming is worship.

Climatic Instability

Global warming, as we saw in Chapter 1, presented some foragers with thousands of years of abundance. But warming is unpredictable. Sometimes it intensifies, causing droughts; sometimes it goes into reverse, causing little ice ages. Its effects are uneven. In the agrarian heartland of the Middle East, for example, warming squeezed the environment of nut-bearing trees but favored some grasses. The forest receded dramatically as the climate got drier and hotter. Between about 13,000 and 11,000 years ago a spell of cooling, when temperatures dropped a degree or so, seems to have affected much of the northern hemisphere. The new conditions encouraged people to rely more and more on grains for food and perhaps try to find ways to increase the amount of edible wheat. Gatherers who knew the habits of their plants tended them ever more carefully. It was, perhaps, a conservative, even a conservationist strategy: a way to keep old food stocks and lifestyles going under the impact of climate change.

Agriculture by Accident

In the nineteenth century, the most popular theory of how farming started attributed it to accident. One can hardly open a nineteenth-century book on the subject without encountering the myth of the primitive forager, usually a woman, discovering agriculture by observing how seeds, dropped by accident, germinated on fertilized soil. The father of the theory of evolution, Charles Darwin (1809–1882; see Chapter 25), thought something similar himself:

> The savage inhabitants of each land, having found out by many and hard trials what plants were useful . . . would after a time take the first step in cultivation by planting them near their usual abodes. . . . The next step in cultivation (and this would require but little forethought) would be to sow the seeds of useful plants; and as the soil near the hovels of the natives would often be in some degree manured, improved varieties would sooner or later arise. Or a wild and unusually good variety of a native plant might attract the attention of some wise old savage; and he would transplant it or sow its seed. . . . Transplanting any superior variety, or sowing its seeds, hardly implies more forethought than might be expected at an early and rude period of civilisation.

Darwin's reconstruction is plausible: He makes accident interact with human action. But this model leaves unsolved problems. Historians are never satisfied to fall back on what would or might have happened (though this may be necessary to help understand remote or poorly documented periods). We want to know— and it is the historian's job to try to tell us—what really did happen. Assuming that anything a "savage" does requires "little forethought" does not fit with what we now know of human nature. Cleverness occurs at every period of history and in every type of society—in New Guinea as well as in New York, in antiquity as well as in modernity.

Production as an Outgrowth of Procurement

Still, the accident theory may be right in one respect. Early practitioners may not have consciously thought of food production as a different strategy from foraging. It makes sense, for instance, to see herding as a natural development of hunting techniques, such as improving a species by culling weak or old animals, managing grazing by setting fires, driving herds down lanes to a place of

"Cleverness occurs at every period of history and in every type of society—in New Guinea as well as in New York, in antiquity as well as in modernity."

Einkorn is one of the few wild grasses that yield kernels that human stomachs can digest. It was a principal food source for the early sedentary foraging cultures of the Middle East, and one of the first species farmers adopted. But its grains are hard to separate from their tough husks, which helps explain why farmers strove to produce new varieties of grain by selection and hybridization.

slaughter, or corralling them for the kill. Similarly, farming and gathering might have been parts of a single continuous attempt to manage food sources. It is hard to tell where one leaves off and the other begins. "Even the simplest hunter–gatherer society," as archaeologist Brian Fagan has said, "knows full well that seeds germinate when planted." The Papago Native Americans of the Sonora Desert of Arizona drift in and out of an agrarian way of life as the weather permits, using patches of surface water to grow fast-maturing varieties of beans.

The archaeological evidence has begun to yield clues to how gatherer communities of southwest Asia transformed themselves into farming communities after the Ice Age. Grasses on the whole are naturally too indigestible to be human food. But the region produced wild barley and two kinds of wheat—einkorn and emmer. We know people ate them because archaeologists have found actual remains that grinders processed from 14,000 to 15,000 years ago. Kernels of these grains are hard to free from their tough, inedible covering, so people who ate large amounts of them may have had an incentive to try to breed varieties that were easier to process. At first, the gatherers beat sheaves of wheat with sticks where they grew and collected edible seeds in baskets as they fell. Increasingly, as time went on, they cut stalks with flint sickles, which meant that fewer seeds fell when the wheat was harvested. This new method suggests that people were selecting preferred seeds for replanting. Modern experiments show that this process could produce a self-propagating species within 20 years. Alternatively, the new method itself might have encouraged changes in the species because heavier, larger seeds would be more likely to fall to the ground at the point of harvesting. Eventually, new varieties would emerge, but the process would be much slower.

Even earlier, humans used a similar process with snails and other mollusks. Mollusks are an efficient food, self-packaged in a shell for carrying and cooking. Compared with the large four-legged beasts that are usually claimed as the first domesticated animal food sources, mollusks are readily managed. People can gather marine varieties, such as mussels and clams, in a natural rock pool. On land a snail-rich spot can be enclosed with a ditch. Moreover, snails are grazers and do not need to be fed with foods that humans would otherwise eat themselves. They can be herded without the use of fire, any special equipment, personal danger, or the need to train leashed animals or dogs to help. By culling small or undesirable types by hand, the early snail farmers could soon enjoy the benefits of selective breeding. Shell mounds from the late Ice Age or soon thereafter contain varieties of snails that are bigger on average than today's, so it looks as if the snail eaters were already selecting for size. Sometimes large-scale consumption of mollusks preceded that of foods that the more elaborate technologies of the hunt obtained. At Frankthi Cave in southern Greece, a huge dump of snail shells nearly 13,000 years old was topped first by red deer bones with some snail shells, and then, nearly 4,000 years later, by tuna bones.

Snails and other shell-dwelling mollusks are nature's "fast foods"—easily gathered and conveniently packaged. Discarded shells—heaps that are found all over the world, make a convenient record for archaeologists to study. In Frankthi cave in Greece, shown here, snail eaters piled huge residues nearly 13,000 years ago. Many ancient mollusks were bigger than modern species, which suggests that people were already selecting and encouraging large varieties.

A Conservative Revolution?

The archaeologist Martin Jones has suggested a speculative but attractive way of making sense of the competing theories about how agriculture started. In warming environments, where climate change threatened settled foragers' stands of crops, they would be bound to take increasing care of those crops to preserve their existing way of life. They would weed them, tend them, water them, winnow them to encourage the most high-yielding specimens, channel water to them, and even end up transplanting them to more favorable spots. They would adopt similar practices to conserve the creatures they hunted, gradually managing their grazing grounds ever more zealously, until eventually the humans and the species they ate became locked in mutual dependence—each unable to survive without the other. A conservative trait—a strategy of survival and resistance against change—ended by transforming the environment and committing people to a new way of life.

"So gathering, hunting, herding, and tillage, which our conventional chronologies usually place one after the other, were in fact complementary techniques to obtain food. They developed together, over thousands of years, in a period of relatively intense climatic change."

In Perspective
Seeking Stability

So gathering, hunting, herding, and tillage, which our conventional chronologies usually place one after the other, were in fact complementary techniques to obtain food. They developed together, over thousands of years, in a period of relatively intense climatic change. The warming, drying effects of the post–Ice-Age world multiplied the opportunities and incentives for people to experiment with food strategies in changing environments. Foragers turned to farming and herding by slow stages and one case at a time, as relationships between people and other species changed and accumulated little by little. The naturalist David Rindos described early farming as a case of human–plant symbiosis, in which species developed together in mutual dependence, and—in part at least—evolved together: an unconscious relationship. Eventually, foodstuffs developed that needed human involvement to survive and reproduce. For instance, emerging kinds of edible grasses, maize, for example, would not survive because their seeds would not fall to the ground unless a person took the seeds out of their husks.

The continuities in the worlds of the food procurers and early food producers are in many ways more impressive than the differences. The settled way of life, the art, the religious cults, even the kinds of foods

Chronology

15,000 B.C.E.	End of Ice Age
13,000–14,000 B.C.E.	First permanent settlements in Middle East
11,000 B.C.E.	Appearance of Jomon culture, Japan
10,000–5000 B.C.E.	Mixed farming and potato cultivation develop (South America)
9000–7000 B.C.E.	Farming towns appear in Anatolia and Egypt
8000 B.C.E.	Rye and barley cultivation in Jordan and Syria; farming spreads from Jordan and Anatolia to Central Asia
7000 B.C.E.	"Trinity" of maize, beans, and squash develops in Andes; farming spreads in Egyptian Sahara and Nile valley; evidence of agriculture in Indian subcontinent; earliest evidence of agriculture in New Guinea
6000 B.C.E.	Rice cultivation in India, Southeast Asia, and China
4000 B.C.E.	Scythians domesticate the horse and invent wheel and axle; Indo-European languages spread as migrants from Asia colonize Europe; millet farmed in Yellow River valley, China
5000–2000 B.C.E.	River valley civilizations flourish
3000 B.C.E.	Teff cultivated in Ethiopia; Bantu languages and agriculture begin to spread southward from West Africa; earliest specimens of cultivated maize (Mexico)
1000 B.C.E.	Maize cultivation moves northward from Mexico to southwestern United States

(All dates are approximate)

(though obtained by different means) are often of the same order. The similarities suggest a new way to look at the transition to agriculture. We can see it as an attempt to stabilize a world convulsed by climatic instability—a way to cope with environmental change that was happening too fast and to preserve ancient traditions. In other words, the peoples who switched to herding or farming and those who clung to hunting and gathering shared a common, conservative mentality. Both wanted to keep what they had.

Perhaps, then, we should stop thinking of the beginnings of food production as a revolution, the overthrow of an existing state of affairs and its replacement by an entirely different one. Rather, we should think of it as a **climacteric**—a long period of critical change in a world poised between different possible outcomes. Indeed, the concept of a climacteric can be a useful way to understand change. It is worth keeping it in mind throughout the rest of this book as we confront other so-called revolutions that were really uncertain, slow, and sometimes unconscious transitions. Yet if early farmers' motivations were indeed conservative, in most cases they failed to maintain the status quo. On the contrary, they inaugurated the spectacular changes and challenges that are the subject of the next chapter.

PROBLEMS AND PARALLELS

1. How was husbandry, with its emphasis on "unnatural selection," the first human challenge to evolution?

2. Why would some societies (such as the aborigines of Australia), with the ability to engage in agriculture, continue to live a hunter–gatherer lifestyle? What are the disadvantages of farming compared to foraging?

3. What was life like in preagricultural settlements? How did agriculture affect the pace of change in human society? Why were agricultural settlements less stable than foraging communities?

4. What are the relative benefits of farming and herding? Why was violence between farmers and herders common until recently?

5. What were the prerequisites for early agriculture? Why were alluvial plains the most hospitable environment for early agricultural communities?

6. Why did farming start at different places and at different times around the world? What are some of the rival theories advocated by scholars?

7. Why is the beginning of food production more of a climacteric than a revolution?

READ ON ▶ ▶ ▶

The lines of the argument are laid down in F. Fernández-Armesto, *Near a Thousand Tables* (2002). The method of classifying events in environmental categories comes from F. Fernández-Armesto, *Civilizations* (2001). Indispensable for the study of the origins of the agriculture are J. R. Harlan, *Crops and Man* (1992); B. D. Smith, *The Emergence of Agriculture* (1998); D. Rindos, *The Origins of Agriculture* (1987); and D. R. Harris, ed., *The Origins and Spread of Agriculture and Pastoralism in Eurasia* (1996). K. F. Kiple and K. C. Ornelas, eds., *The Cambridge World History of Food* (2000) is an enormous compendium.

I. G. Simmons, *Changing the Face of the Earth: Culture, Environment, History* (1989) is a superb introduction to global environmental history, as is B. De Vries and J. Goudsblom, eds., *Mappae Mundi: Humans and Their Habitats in a Long-term Socio-ecological Perspective* (2004).

The quotation from Darwin comes from his work of 1868, *The Variation of Animals and Plants under Domestication.*

On feasts, M. Dietler and B. Hayden, *Feasts: Archaeological and Ethnographic Perspective on Food, Politics, and Power* (2001) is an important collection of essays. *Feast: Why Humans Share Food* (2007) by Martin Jones is entertaining as well as instructive.

O. Bar-Yosef and A. Gopher, eds. (1991), *The Natufian Culture in the Levant* is outstanding. On Çatalhüyük, up-to-date information is in M. Özdogan and N. Basgelen, eds. (1999), *The Neolithic in Turkey: The Cradle of Civilization*, and I. Hodder, *Towards a Reflexive Method in Archaeology* (2000); but the classic J. Mellaart, *Çatal Hüyük* (1967) is more accessible. On Jericho, the classic work is by Kenyon, *Digging Up Jericho; the Results of Jericho Excavations* (1957).

The World in 5000 B.C.E.

The Ice Age was a dynamic time. But to us, who live amid convulsive change, it seems like an age of remarkable stability, continuity, and equilibrium. The retreat of the ice 20,000 years ago ended all that. Colonization quickened. Cultures diverged as communities tried different strategies for survival. From this point onward, societies could be classified in three types: hunters, who foraged for food, and herders and tillers, who produced it for themselves.

Hunters were the most successful survivors because they maintained their way of life relatively unchanged. Tillers (and to a lesser extent herders) had to embrace dynamic change: political change because they needed strong leaders to organize production and distribution of food; social and economic change because they needed large workforces and growing populations; changes in economic specialization and styles of living because ever larger populations had to be concentrated in relatively small spaces; changes in health and nutrition because of the need to survive on limited diets in a new disease environment; changes in warfare because they had to defend their flocks and fields or enlarge them at others' expense.

Yet more and more societies followed the tillers' example or adopted it independently, abandoning hunting or restricting it to elites. Peoples who remained loyal to hunting began to retreat into ever more marginal environments, to tundras, forests, and arid regions. The reasons for this withdrawal are hard to understand. To some extent, it was a simple matter of diminishing resources. As farming expanded, less game and land were available for hunting cultures. At another level, it was an effect of relative power. Though farming disrupted almost every society that adopted it, and often led to failure and collapse, it fed more people and generated more resources for war.

▶ QUESTIONS

1. How does this map show that gathering, hunting, herding, and farming were complementary techniques to obtain food? Does this perspective provide a new way to look at the transition to agriculture? If so, how?

2. If food production inaugurates change, which societies were the most poised for change in 5000 B.C.E.?

The World in 5000 B.C.E.

- intensive hunting and gathering
- centers of agricultural development
- secondary areas of settled agriculture
- → spread of farming
- ● early agricultural settlements and pre-urban sites 6000–5000 BCE
- ◇ hunter-gatherer sites

North America: hunting of small game and gathering of wild seeds and plant foods

Central America: intensive seasonal hunting and gathering

Amazon: forest hunting and gathering

Western South America: llama hunting

Japan and Korea: hunting and gathering supplemented by fishing

Northern China: millet cultivation; evidence of domesticated pigs and dogs

Yellow River and Yangtze Delta: early wet rice cultivation

Northern Europe: hunter-gathering supplemented by fishing

Mainland Southeast Asia: intensive hunter-gathering

Southern Europe: cereal cultivation; sheep and goat herding

Steppes: horse hunting

Mesopotamia: populations dependent on irrigation agriculture

Anatolia: farming villages, trade in flint, obsidian, timber, shells, and copper

New Guinea: upland drainage to encourage growth of wild taro

Near East: domestication of wild wheat and barley c.9000 BCE

Indus Valley: wheat and barley cultivation; cattle, sheep, and goat herding

Ganges Valley: intensive forest hunting and gathering

Sahara: cattle herding supplemented by intensive hunting and gathering

c.5000 BCE: start of desertification of Sahara

Nile Valley: wheat and barley cultivation

Maritime Southeast Asia: hunter-gatherers exploit rich marine resources

Australia: hunter-gatherers settle along major rivers

Greenland
Lena
Amur
JAPAN
Manchuria
KOREA
Gobi
Yenisey
Siberia
Volga
Steppes
ASIA
Yellow River
Yangtze
PACIFIC OCEAN
Philippine Islands
EUROPE
Anatolia
Himalayas
Ganges
Mekong
Euphrates
Tigris
Indus
Sahara
Nile
Arabian peninsula
Borneo
New Guinea
Sahel
Niger
AFRICA
Sumatra
Congo
INDIAN OCEAN
ATLANTIC OCEAN
Zambezi
Madagascar
Orange River
AUSTRALIA
Darling River
Antarctic Circle
ANTARCTICA
New Zealand

0°   30°   60°   90°   120°   150°

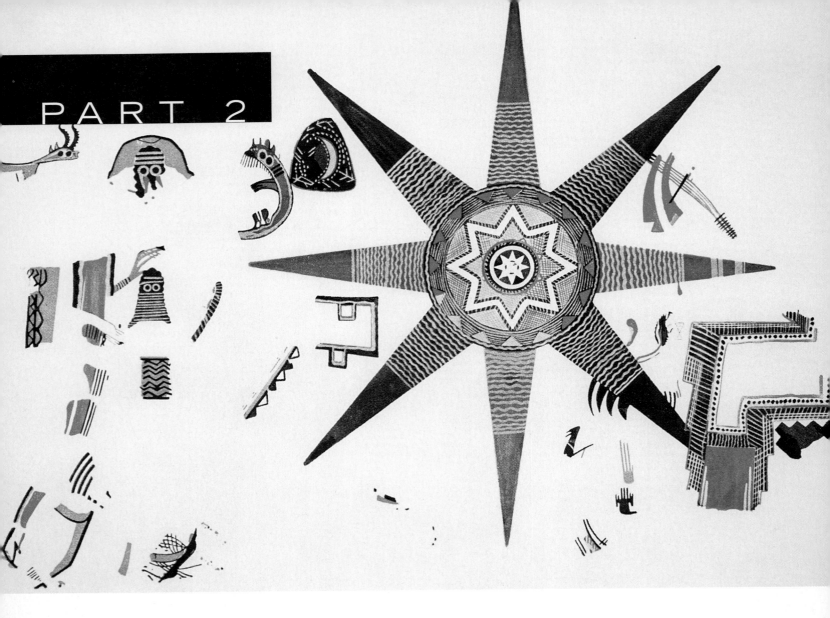

PART 2

ENVIRONMENT

ca. 4500 B.C.E.
Irrigation

ca. 3500 B.C.E.
Horses domesticated

since 5000 B.C.E.
Intensive agriculture, bronze metallurgy:
Tigris-Euphrates, Nile, Indus, Yellow Rivers

CULTURE

since ca. 3500 B.C.E.
Complex, hierarchical
societies and states

Farmers and Builders, 5000 to 500 B.C.E.

◀ **One of the World's Earliest Surviving Paintings** on plaster was found at Tel-Eilat Ghasuul in Jordan. It dates to about 4500 B.C.E., but the meaning of most of the images it depicts—veiled faces, a gazelle and other creatures, a hand apparently emerging from a sleeve—are too faded and fragmentary for us to decipher their meaning. The star-shaped diagram, however, seems to depict a vision of the Earth or the universe. The colors, markings, and forms are geometrically arranged to suggest an ordered array of mountains, plains, skies, and waters, within an enclosed world, from which alternating light and darkness radiate.

ca. 3000–1000 B.C.E.
Continued warming

ca. 1200–800 B.C.E.
Widespread environmental crises

ca. 1800 B.C.E.
Spread of iron technology

ca. 3200 B.C.E.
Writing

ca. 2000 B.C.E.
Epic of Gilgamesh

ca. 1000 B.C.E.
Mediterranean maritime
colonialism begins

CHAPTER 3

The Great River Valleys: Accelerating Change and Developing States

▲ **Diplomatic gifts.** Hatshepsut's envoy presents swords, ceremonial axes, and strung beads to the king and queen of Punt. More important, economically, than these diplomatic gifts were the vast amounts of grain and cattle the Egyptians shipped to Punt in exchange for the costly aromatic trees they acquired for the garden of the memorial temple Hatshepsut (r. c. 1503–1483 B.C.E.) was building for herself.

GREAT RIVER VALLEYS

Thinking about her death, around the mid-second millennium B.C.E., Queen Hatshepsut of Egypt chose her proudest achievements—the events she most wanted people to remember—to decorate her memorial temple. She devoted half a wall to scenes commemorating a shipborne expedition to the land of Punt, one of the remotest places in the world the Egyptians knew—a land of incense and ivory, panthers and monkeys, turtles and giraffes, gold and ebony. The location of Punt is uncertain, but many scholars think it was in East Africa in what is now Somalia. Hatshepsut needed crowning glories—exotic rarities that would make her admired and compensate for her lack of legitimacy as a ruler. For, uniquely among women, she had proclaimed herself pharaoh—sovereign of Egypt—and living god and ruled in place of the rightful heir, her young stepson Thutmoses III. These roles were not normally open to a living woman. In Egypt, and in many other societies of that time, imported riches conferred prestige in rough proportion to the distance they traveled. Hatshepsut wanted that prestige. And she wanted something more. She was planning a garden of incense trees, which only Punt could supply, as a gift to the god she claimed as her father. He had penetrated her mother's body, she said, "with the flood of divine fragrance, and all his odors were those of the land of Punt."

The idea of transplanting whole trees was daring enough. To get them, the Egyptian fleet had to sail the length of the Red Sea on a long voyage made hazardous by tortuous winds and rocks. Unless the surviving Egyptian text is just boasting—as it may well be—the people of Punt were astonished at the explorers' arrival. "How have you reached this land that Egyptians have never seen before?" they asked, with hands uplifted in surprise. "Have you descended hither by the paths of the sky or," they added, as if it were equally improbable, "did you come by way of the sea?"

The mission to Punt was more than an encounter between mutually unfamiliar peoples: it was also a meeting of contrasting ecologies and an occasion of exchange between them. Whereas Punt specialized in precious luxuries, Egypt was a mighty food producer, with an economy geared to massive output of grain and other foods. The incense trees were small objects of desire, but the Egyptians had to send five great ships to get them because the goods they offered in exchange were of small unit value and great bulk. Traders measured out the gold of Punt with bull-shaped weights, while the live incense-trees were potted and stowed aboard the Egyptian ships. The Egyptians paid for them with "bread, beer, wine, meat, and fruit." The exchange worked, because for all their wealth, the people of Punt could not produce food in such dazzling abundance.

Intensified agriculture widened the gaps among three already radically different types of economy: foraging, herding, and tillage (see Chapter 2). More spectacular, however, were the differences that separated farming cultures from each other. The societies of herders and tillers generated much more change of all kinds than those of foragers. Some of these herder and tiller societies came to occupy vast zones, to feed huge populations, and to sustain spectacular

63

FOCUS questions

Why did intensified agriculture lead to cultural differences?

Where did the first great river valley civilizations develop?

How can we account for the similarities and differences in political institutions, social structure, and ways of life in the four great river valleys?

How did the river valley states expand?

Is writing a defining characteristic of civilization?

Why is cultural divergence one of the main themes of human history since the beginning of agriculture?

material achievements—including cities, monumental arts, and world-changing technologies. Other societies remained relatively small and static. This does not mean they were backward or primitive. Their modest scale and relative isolation kept them stable. These were peoples who succeeded in adapting to climate change without subjecting their societies to social and political convulsions, which were often part of the price other peoples paid for material achievements that seem impressive to us. The big problem we need to look at in this chapter, then, is what made the difference.

It is also worth asking if we can detect any common patterns within these diverse societies. This is a long-standing quest for historians and, especially, for sociologists, who look for models that they can use to describe and predict how societies change. At a simple level, intensified agriculture clearly unlocks a potential pattern. More food makes it possible to sustain larger populations, to concentrate them in bigger settlements, and to divert more manpower into nonagricultural activities. But intensification also requires organization, and, broadly speaking, the more intensive the farming, the more organized it has to be. Someone with power, such as a landowner, ruler, or priest, or some group of such people has to divide the land, marshal labor, regulate the distribution of water and—if necessary—fertilizers, and, finally, store and guard surplus production, so that people can use it if crops fail or natural disasters strike. A more or less specialized legal elite is needed to resolve the frequent disputes that arise in thickly settled communities, where people have to compete for access to resources. So, intensively farmed areas tend to develop similar political institutions. Ruling groups in these areas must be able to command obedience and allegiance widely and deeply, which requires professional administrators and legal specialists.

We can see these changes in society and political organization that come with intensified farming in the history of many places, but especially from about 5000 B.C.E. in four regions with common environmental features. The "great river valleys," as they are traditionally called, in what are now Egypt, Iraq, Pakistan, and China, are the focus of this chapter, and their similarities and differences are among its principal themes. The next chapter follows their fortunes in the crises, catastrophes, and transformations they faced, in most cases toward the end of the second millennium B.C.E. Chapter 5 covers the recovery or renewal of ambitious states and cultural experiments after the crises had passed.

GROWING COMMUNITIES, DIVERGENT CULTURES

Most of the communities that early agriculture fed resembled the forager settlements that preceded them. They were small and did not change much over time. Owing to lack of evidence, we mostly have to infer what we think we know about them. So with no reason to think otherwise, we assume that early farming societies in New Guinea, North America, along the Amazon River in South America, and among the Bantu people in West Africa were like those in most of the rest of the world. They were extended family businesses where everyone in the community felt tied to everyone else by kinship. Elsewhere, owing to greater resources or to the enlivening effects of cross-cultural contacts through migration or trade, different patterns prevailed. Communities became territorially defined. Economic obligations, not kinship, shaped allegiance. Chiefs or economic elites monopolized or largely controlled the distribution of food.

Traditionally, scholars have tried to divide subsequent change in societies of this type into sequences or stages of growth—chiefdoms become states, towns become cities. But these are relative terms, and no hard-and-fast lines divide them. Nor do they have any mutually distinguishing characteristics. At most, differences are a matter of degree. For instance, we think of chiefdoms as having fewer institutions of government than states. In chiefdoms, the chief and a small group of counselors handle all the business of government. In a state, those functions get split among groups of specialists in, say, administering justice, handling revenue, or conducting war. In practice, however, we know of no community that does not delegate at least some power, or any state where the responsibilities of different government departments do not merge or overlap.

Similarly, no quality absolutely distinguishes some kinds of settlement from others. The difference between a small city and a big town or a small town and a big village is a matter of judgment. Some of the characteristics we traditionally associate with particular ways of life turn out, in the light of present knowledge, to provide little or no help for defining the societies in which they occur. We cannot, for instance, go on defining cities—or even towns or villages—as environments that promote the development of certain kinds of technology. Herding and nomadic peoples, for instance, practice metallurgy. Indeed, some of these peoples devised the earliest techniques of smelting and metalworking we know about and remained outstandingly skilled in them for most of history. Nor was weaving exclusive to settled communities. The Ice-Age creators of clay figurines understood the technique of making pottery artifacts, as we saw in Chapter 1. The earliest known pottery vessels come from the foragers' settlements of Jomon in Japan, as we saw in Chapter 2.

Where many people settle together, however, predictable changes usually follow. As markets grow, communities and settlements acquire more craftsmen, who engage in more specialized trades and who organize into more and larger units. As they get bigger, settlements and politically linked or united groups of settlements also expand the number of government functions. Where once there was just a chief and his counselors, now there are aides, advisers, officials, and administrators.

Densely settled communities also tend to divide their populations into more categories. This usually happens in two ways. On the one hand, as society gets bigger, people seek groups within it, of manageable size, with whom they can identify and to whom they can appeal for help in times of need. On the other hand, rulers organize subjects into categories according to the needs of the state, which include collective labor, taxation, and war. The categories get more numerous and varied as opportunities for economic specialization multiply and as more districts or quarters appear in growing settlements. In some cases, these categories resemble what, in our society, we call classes—that is, groups arrayed horizontally, one above or below another according to power, privilege, or prosperity. For most of history, however, it is misleading to speak of classes. Societies were more usually organized vertically into groups of people of widely varying rank and wealth, linked by some form of common allegiance. They might feel bound by a place of origin, or a locality or neighborhood, or a common ancestor, or a god, or a rite, or a family, or a sense of identity arising from shared belief in some myth (see Figure 3.1).

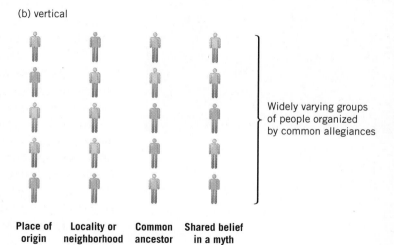

FIGURE 3.1 HORIZONTAL AND VERTICAL ORGANIZATIONS OF SOCIETY

(a) horizontal

Elites

Bureaucrats

Commoners

Classes of people differentiated by power, privilege, prosperity

(b) vertical

Widely varying groups of people organized by common allegiances

Place of origin · Locality or neighborhood · Common ancestor · Shared belief in a myth

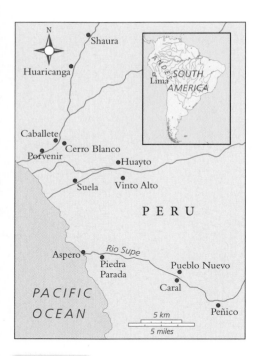

MAP 3.1

Coastal Peru, ca. 3500 BCE

• archaeological site

Trade enriches. Gold-laden graves in a 6,000-year-old cemetery at Varna, Bulgaria lie by an inlet beside a wood-built village that is quite different from mud-walled settlements in the interior, where the graves are under the houses. The Varna culture vanished—overwhelmed perhaps by horse-tamers from the nearby steppes.

So, if we want to try to trace the early history of cultural divergence, we should look for certain sorts of changes, namely, intensified settlement, population concentrated in relatively large settlements, multiplying social categories and functions of government, emergence of chiefs and fledgling states, and increasingly diversified and specialized economic activity. Between 5000 and 3000 B.C.E., we can detect these changes in widely separated places around the world. We can take a few examples in a selective tour through cultures launched into divergent futures.

Intensified Settlement and Its Effects

In the New World (see Chapter 1), Mesoamerica and Central America remained a region of small villages. We can document monumental cities and large states there only from about 2000 B.C.E. In North America, agriculture barely appeared. By contrast, at the base of the high Andes in South America, archaeology has unearthed early evidence of many different social rankings, economic specializations, and grossly unequal concentrations of wealth and power.

Five and a half thousand years ago— in about 3500 B.C.E.—large farming settlements began to appear on alluvial plains in coastal Peru, in the region north of present-day Lima, and especially in the Supe Valley, which has over 30 archaeological sites. The most impressive was Aspero, where by the mid–third millennium B.C.E. 17 mounds supported half a dozen platforms and various terraces, with large, complex dwellings and storehouses. The platforms were built up with loads of rubble in uniform containers, which suggests that a system existed to measure the labor of different groups of workers. An infant's grave gives us a glimpse into the society and perhaps the politics of the time. Under a grinding stone he lies painted with red ocher, wrapped in textiles, and scattered with hundreds of beads. This is evidence of inherited wealth and, perhaps, power in an economy dependent on grain where a flour-making tool literally marked the difference between life and death.

Covering over 32 acres, Aspero must have had a big population—uniquely big by the standards of the Americas at the time. There were, however, many settlements of between 2,000 and 3,000 people. They were trading centers where people exchanged the products of different ecosystems—marine shells, mountain foods, and featherwork made from the brightly colored birds that lived in the forests east of the Andes (see Map 3.1).

Comparable developments occurred across Eurasia (see Map 3.2). In parts of eastern Europe, for instance, innovations in technology and government emerged, without, as far as we know, any influence from outside the region. These settlements were of a scale we think of as villages rather than cities. In the shadow of the Carpathian Mountains, Europe's oldest copper mine at Rudna Glava, above the middle Danube River in modern Serbia, made the region a center of early metallurgy. In Tisza in what is now Hungary, over 7,000 years ago, smelters worked copper into beads and small tools—magic that made smiths powerful figures of myth. To the people who left offerings, the mines were the dwellings of gods.

In Bulgaria during the same period, trenches and palisades surrounded settlements, with gateways exactly aligned at the points of the compass, as in later Roman army camps. Here prospectors in metal-rich hills traded gold for the products of agriculture. No place in prehistoric Europe gleams more astonishingly than Varna on the Black Sea, where a chief was buried clutching a gold-handled axe, with his penis sheathed in gold, and nearly 1,000 gold ornaments, including hundreds of discs that must have spangled a dazzling coat. This single grave contained

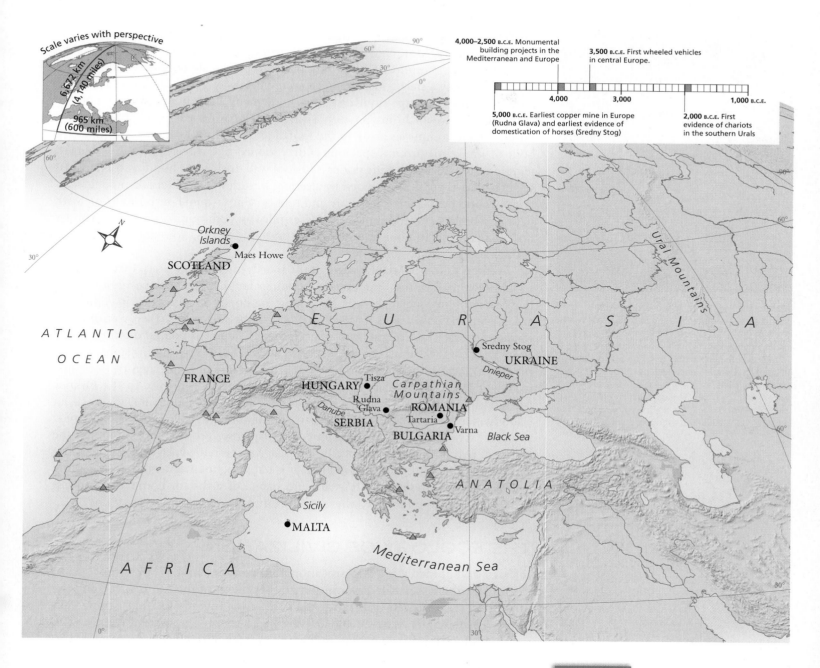

Scale varies with perspective

6,672 km (4,140 miles)

965 km (600 miles)

4,000–2,500 B.C.E. Monumental building projects in the Mediterranean and Europe

3,500 B.C.E. First wheeled vehicles in central Europe.

5,000 B.C.E. Earliest copper mine in Europe (Rudna Glava) and earliest evidence of domestication of horses (Sredny Stog)

2,000 B.C.E. First evidence of chariots in the southern Urals

4,000   3,000   1,000 B.C.E.

Orkney Islands

Maes Howe

SCOTLAND

ATLANTIC OCEAN

EURASIA

Ural Mountains

Sredny Stog

UKRAINE

Dnieper

FRANCE

Tisza

HUNGARY

Carpathian Mountains

Danube

Rudna Glava

ROMANIA

SERBIA

Tartaria

BULGARIA

Varna

Black Sea

ANATOLIA

Sicily

MALTA

Mediterranean Sea

AFRICA

more than three pounds of fine gold. Other graves were symbolic, containing earthenware masks without human remains. At Tartaria in Romania, markings on clay tablets look uncannily like writing.

A little to the east, also around 5000 B.C.E., at Sredny Stog, on the middle Dnieper River in what is now Ukraine, the earliest known domesticators of horses filled their garbage dumps with horse bones. In graves of about 3500 B.C.E., lie covered wagons, arched with hoops and designed to be pulled by oxen, rumbling on vast wheels of solid wood. These wagons were buried as if for use in an afterlife, evidence that rich and powerful chiefdoms could carry out ambitious building projects despite a herding way of life that required constant mobility. Few other societies in the world were rich enough to bury objects of such size and value. Central Eurasia became a birthplace for early transportation technology. For instance,

MAP 3.2

Intensified Settlements in Western Eurasia, 5,000–2,000 B.C.E.

●   Places described on pages 66–68

▲   other important archaeological sites

MALTA   modern country mentioned on pages 66–68

Malta. The world's oldest monumental stone buildings are temple complexes of the late fourth millennium B.C.E. on the Mediterranean islands of Malta and Gozo. All resemble this example at Mnajdra, with central corridors connecting kidney-shaped chambers, enclosed by fine-faced lime-stone, polished with stone tools. Inside, animals were sacrificed, and images of corpulent god-desses were stored. We do not know where the wealth that sustained the builders came from.

the earliest recognizable chariot dates from early in the third millennium B.C.E. in the southern Ural Mountains that divide Europe from Asia.

Meanwhile, monumental building projects, on a scale only agriculture could sustain and only a state could organize, were underway in the Mediterranean. The remains of the first large stone dwellings known anywhere in the world are on the island of Malta, which lies between Sicily and North Africa. Here, at least half a dozen temple complexes arose in the fourth and third millennia B.C.E. They were built of limestone around spacious courts shaped like clover leaves. The biggest temple is almost 70-feet wide under a 30-foot wall. Inside one building was a colossal, big-hipped goddess attended by sleeping beauties—small female models scattered around her. There were altars and wall carvings—some in spirals, some with deer and bulls—and thousands of bodies piled in communal graves. We wonder how Malta's soil, so poor and dry, could sustain a population large and leisured enough to build so lavishly.

Even on Europe's Atlantic edge, in the fourth millennium B.C.E., luxury objects could find a market and monumental buildings arose. Some of the earliest signs of the slow-grinding social changes lie among the bones of aristocrats in individual graves with the possessions that defined their status and suggest their way of life—weapons of war and drinking cups that once held liquor or poured offerings to the gods. Then come the graves of chiefs, buried under enormous standing stones (called megaliths), near stone circles probably designed to resemble the rings of trees, surrounding forest glades that preceded them as places of worship. In the Orkney Islands, for instance, off the north coast of Scotland, settled about 5,500 years ago, an elaborate tomb at Maes Howe lies close to a temple building, filled with light on midsummer's day. Nearby stone circles hint on a smaller scale at attempts to monitor the sun and, perhaps, control nature by magic. A stone-built village to the west has hearths and fitted furniture still in place. It is tempting to imagine this as a far-flung colonial station, preserving the styles and habits of a distant home in southwest Britain and northwest France, where the big tombs and stone circles are found.

THE ECOLOGY OF CIVILIZATION

In this world of increasing diversification, four regions stand out in terms of scale: the middle and lower Nile River in Egypt; the valleys of the Indus River, and the now dried-up Saraswati (sah-rah-SWAH-tee) river (mainly in what is now Pakistan); Mesopotamia, between and around the Tigris and Euphrates Rivers in what is now Iraq; and the Yellow River in China (see Map 3.3). Between 5000 and 2000 B.C.E., people in these regions exploited more land and changed at a faster pace than other regions. Change was measured in terms of intensified agriculture, technological innovation, development of state power, and construction of cities.

In recent times, these valleys have occupied disproportionate space in our history books and a privileged place in our store of images and memories. Their ruins and relics still inspire movie makers, advertisers, artists, toy makers, and writers of computer games. They shape our ideas of what civilizations ought to be. When we hear the word "civilization," we picture Egyptian pyramids, sphinxes, and mummies; Chinese bronzes, jades, and clays; Mesopotamian ziggurats—tall, tapering, steplike temples—and writing tablets smothered with ancient wedge-shaped letter forms. Or we conjure the windblown wrecks of almost-vanished cities in landscapes turning to desert. We even call these seminal—or nursery—civilizations, as if they were seed plots from which civilized achievements spread around the world. Or we call them great civilizations, and we begin our conventional histories of civilization by describing them.

Civilization is now a discredited word. People have abused it as a name for societies they approve of, which usually means societies that resemble their own. They have also denied the term to cultures they deem alien or lacking in material culture or institutions similar to their own. Or they have misapplied it as the name of a supposedly universal stage of social development, even though we have no evidence that societies follow any universal course of development. We can, however, understand a civilization simply as a society that, for good or ill, engages ambitiously with its environment, seeking to remodel the rest of nature to suit human purposes. That is, we can speak of the **ecology of civilization**, the interaction of people with their environment. In this sense of the word, the four river valleys housed societies more civilized than earlier cases we know of. They modified the landscape with fields and irrigation works or smothered it with monumental buildings on a scale that no people before attained or, perhaps, even conceived.

> *"We can, however, understand a civilization simply as a society that, for good or ill, engages ambitiously with its environment, seeking to remodel the rest of nature to suit human purposes."*

THE GREAT FLOODPLAINS

The four river valleys shared certain environmental features: a gradually warming and drying climate; relatively dry soils; and a reliance on seasonally flooding rivers and, therefore, on irrigation. If we consider them together, however, we can see how relentless divergence opened cultural chasms inside this common ecological framework.

MAP 3.3

The Great River Valleys

Great River Valley

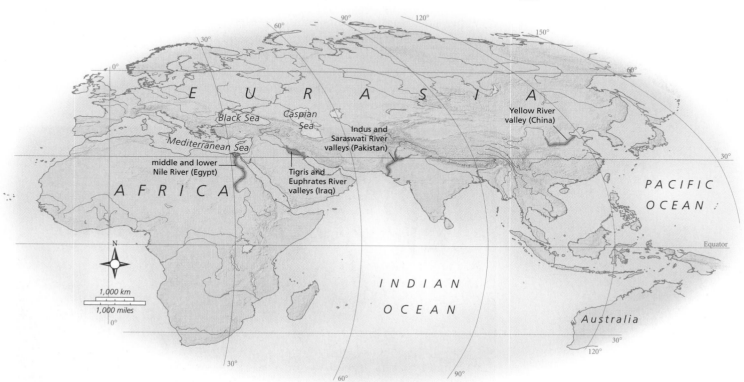

Nebamun's tomb from the fourteenth century B.C.E. shows the Egyptian vizier hunting in the lush Nile delta, abundant in fish below his reed-built boat, prolific in the bird and insect life flushed from the blue thickets at his approach. He grabs birds by the handful and wields a snake like a whip.

© *The British Museum/Art Resource, NY*

The Ecology of Egypt

In the north, where the lower Nile empties into the Mediterranean, Egypt had the advantage of a different kind of environment. Here, in the delta region, food sources and useful plants complemented what farmers could grow in the irrigated lands to the south. In the delta's teeming marshlands, birds, animals, fish, and plants clustered for the gatherer and hunter. A painter showed Nebamun—a scribe and counter of grain who lived probably about 3,500 years ago—hunting among reeds and bulrushes. Lotus and papyrus plants inspired carvers to decorate pillars. Contemporary praise of a city built in the delta paints the environment in lush colors, "full of everything good—its ponds with fish and its lakes with birds. Its meadows are verdant; its banks bear dates; its melons are abundant." The same source lists onions and leeks, lettuces, pomegranates, apples, olives, figs, sweet vines, and "red fish which feed on lotus-flowers." Thickets of rushes and papyrus provided rope and writing paper.

Most of Egypt, however, lay above the delta, as far upriver as the rocky rapids called cataracts. The Nile flows from south to north, from the highlands of Ethiopia in Central Africa to the Mediterranean, and where the ground breaks from higher altitudes or where the riverbed narrows, dangerous rapids hinder navigation. Soil samples reveal the history of climate change. By about 4,000 years ago, the valley was already a land of "black" earth between "red" earths. Floods fed the fertile, alluvial black strip along the Nile; slowly drying red desert lay on either side. Hunting scenes painted at Memphis, Egypt's first capital, in the Nile delta, showed game lands turning to scrub, sand, and bare rock. Rain became rare, a divine gift, according to a pious king's prayer to the sun, dropped from "a Nile in heaven." Thirst was called "the taste of death." Other lands had rain, as an Egyptian priest told a Greek traveler, "Whereas in our country water never falls on fields from above, it all wells up from below."

Making bread. Some of the activities portrayed in ancient Egyptian tomb-offerings seem humdrum. Beer-making or—as in this example, nearly 3,000 years old—bread-making, are among the most common scenes. But these were magical activities that turned barely edible grains into mind expanding drinks and a life-sustaining staple food.

In spring, when the Nile is low, rain in Central Africa swells the feed waters of the Nile, which turn green with algae in early summer, then red with tropical earth in August. In September and October, if all goes well, the river floods and spreads the dark, rich silt thinly over the earth. If the flood is too high, the land drowns. If the level of the river falls below about 18 feet, drought follows. In one of the oldest surviving documents of Egyptian history, probably of about 2500 B.C.E., a king reveals a dream. The river failed to flood because the people neglected the gods who ruled beyond the cataracts, where the waters came from. Still, compared to the other river valleys of the period, the Nile flood waters were—and still are—exceptionally regular and, therefore, easy to exploit.

Irrigation created little microclimates, like the paintings of orchards and gardens that adorn tombs in the city of Thebes, the second capital city of Egypt. From streams filled with water lilies, a gardener with a dog at his feet swings a bucket on a pole, called a *shaduf*, which a single operator can dip, hoist, reposition, and spill over the soil. It is an invention of maybe 6,000 years ago. Strips of cattle-raising grasslands lay between floodplain and desert. But the silt the water brought was vital because the nitrogen content of the soil decreases by two-thirds in the top 6 inches between floods. The annually renewed topsoil grew some of the densest concentrations of wheat in the ancient world.

The economy was dedicated to a cult of **everyday abundance**. That is, it guaranteed basic nutrition for a large population, not individual abundance. Most people lived on bread and beer (a much grainier, more nutritious brew than modern beer), in amounts only modestly above subsistence level. A surplus that had been gathered and guarded against hard times was at the disposal of the state and priests. Those whose food consisted exclusively of the wheat and barley of the irrigated dry lands were vulnerable to routine malnutrition and to famine in years of drought. Normally, however, there were greater quantities of the basic products of the economy than Egyptians could eat. The surplus-generated trade made up for the country's lack of timber and bought the plants Queen Hatshepsut craved for perfumes and incense. Most of the courtly luxuries that today's Western museum goers see in exhibits on ancient Egypt came from trade, raids, and conquest. Gold and ivory, for example, came from Nubia, an African kingdom beyond the cataracts, and copper and turquoise came from Sinai, a region of desert uplands that links Egypt to the Middle East (see Map 3.4).

Shifting Rivers of the Indus Valley

In the Indus valley, the sparse remains of the society called Harappan (after Harappa, one of its earliest excavated cities) lie frustratingly beyond historians' reach. The rising water table has drowned evidence of the earliest phases, and the literate period is obscure because scholars have not been able to decipher the

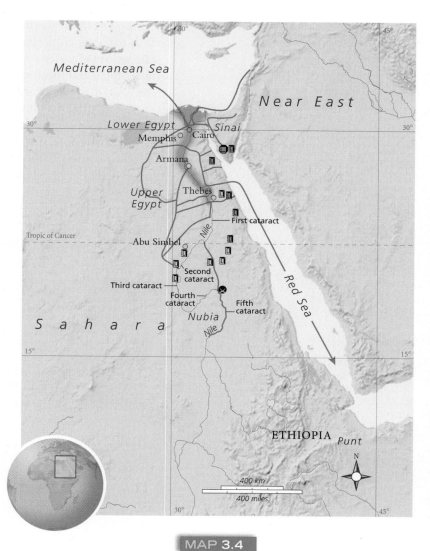

MAP 3.4

Ancient Egypt

▨	Nile River Valley
●	modern city
→	trade route

Trade Goods

▣	gold
▣	copper
◉	turquoise
⊗	ivory

writing system. Here the Indus and Saraswati rivers were more powerful and capricious than the Nile, changing course and cutting new channels that might deprive settlements of water supplies. Ultimately, perhaps, they were fatally unpredictable, for Egypt lasted thousands of years longer. When, the Indus altered course and the Saraswati dried up, Harappan cities dwindled to faint traces in the dust.

But 3,000 to 5,000 years ago, the Indus floodplain was broader than the Nile's. The Indus and Saraswati flooded twice a year—first with the spring snowmelt when the rivers rose and then in summer when warm air, rising in Central Asia, sucks moisture in from the sea. As a result, farmers here could grow two crops annually. The basic patterns were the same as in Egypt. Wheat and barley grew on rainless, irrigated soil, and cattle—mainly humped-back zebu, in Harappa— grazed on marginal grassland. No region was as rich as the Nile delta, but Harappa had a coastal outpost at the seaport of Lothal, on the Gulf of Cambay on the Indian Ocean, in a land of rice and millet (see Map 3.5).

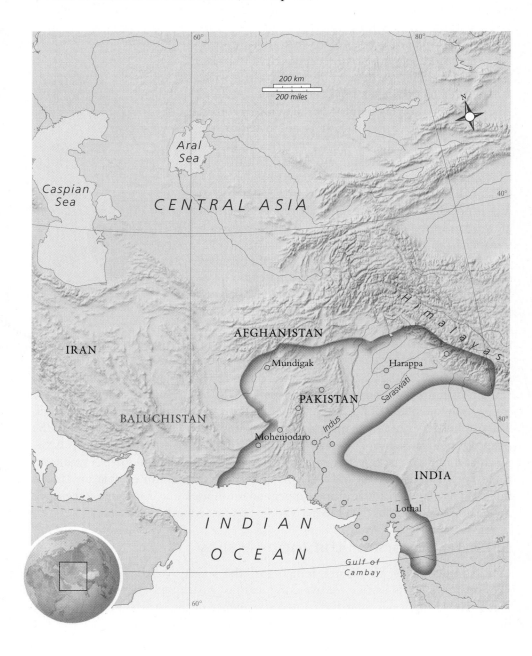

MAP 3.5

Harappan Civilization

▬	extent of Harappan culture
○	Harappan site
INDIA	modern country

The Harappan heartland had few valuables of its own. Again, as in Egypt, the basis of its wealth was the surplus of its agriculture. Around 2000 B.C.E., the Harappan-culture area was the biggest in the world, stretching over 500,000 square miles. This was, perhaps, evidence of weakness rather than strength. Territorial expansion was the Harrapan solution to feeding its increasingly dense population in the heartland, and no society can keep expanding forever.

Most surviving Harappan art is engraved on seals used to mark trading goods. These little masterpieces capture how people of the time saw their world. Some show naturalistic representations of animals, especially bearded zebus, feasting tigers, and elegant, humpless bulls, that are sniffing, it seems, at an object that looks like an incense burner. Violations of realism, however, are more characteristic and include comical elephants and rhinoceroses. Perplexing scenes, probably from Harappan mythology, include magical transformations of human into tiger, starfish into unicorn, horned serpent into flourishing tree. In one case, a human is transforming into a tree after sex with a rampant bull. A common motif shows an apelike figure defending a tree against a tiger; both creatures wear horns.

Fierce Nature in Early Mesopotamia

The waters of the Nile and the Indus spill and recede according to a reasonably predictable rhythm, but the Tigris and Euphrates flood at any time, washing away dikes, overflowing ditches. At other times, desert sandstorms choke the farmers and bury their crops. The writers of Mesopotamian literature—the earliest imaginative literature in the world to survive in written form—described an environment more violent and more hostile than those of Egypt and Harappa. Gods of storm and flood dominate, or at least shadow, the Mesopotamian world. In the wind, according to the poets, earth shattered "like a pot." "Will new seed grow?" asked a proverb. "We do not know. Will old seed grow? We do not know."

In lower Mesopotamia, where the first big cities sprang up around 3000 B.C.E., the rivers fell through a parched landscape from a distant land of rain, like trickles across a windowpane. Even with irrigation, the summers were too harsh and dry to produce food for the early cities, which had to rely on winter crops of wheat and barley, onions, chickpeas, and sesame. Rain fell more often then than it does today, but it was largely confined to winter when ferocious storms made the sky flare with sheet lightning. "Ordered by the storm-god in hate," according to a poet, "it wears away the country." The floods that created the life-giving alluvial soils were also life-threateningly capricious. Unleashed in early summer by mountain rains, rivers could swell and sweep away crops.

Meanwhile, earth and water, the benign forces that combined to create the alluvial soil, were also celebrated in verse. The goddess Nintu personified Earth—zealous, jealous mother, yielding nourishment, suckling infants, guarding embryos. Water, to awaken the land's fertility, was a male god, Enki, empowered "to clear the pure mouths of the Tigris and Euphrates, to make greenery plentiful, to make dense the clouds, to grant water in abundance to all ploughlands, to make corn lift its head in furrows and to make pasture abound in the desert." But Nintu and Enki were subordinate deities, at the beck and call of storm and flood.

The ferocity of the climate demanded hardy plants, so Mesopotamia produced much more barley than wheat. Exhausting digging raised dwellings above the flood and diverted and conserved water. By 5000 B.C.E., farmers throughout the region were using plows drawn by oxen. The people who lived along the lower stretches of the river depicted themselves in their art as dome-headed, potbellied lovers of music, feasts, and war. But they were necessarily resourceful people who made

Harappan seals. In the last couple of centuries, scholarly code-crackers have worked out how to read most of the world's ancient scripts. But the writing on Harappan seals remains elusive. The seals seem to depict visions and monsters—but the messages they conveyed were probably of routine merchants, data-stock-taking and prices. In most cases that we know of, writing was first devised to record information too uninteresting for people to confide to memory.

ships in a country with no timber, worked masterpieces in bronze in a part of the world where no metal could be found, built fabulous cities without stone by baking mud into bricks, and dammed rivers as the Marsh Arabs of southern Iraq do to this day—with brushwood, reeds, and earth.

The Good Earth of Early China

Mesopotamia and Harappa certainly traded with each other. Mesopotamia and Egypt were close to each other and in constant touch. The map shows, however, that China's Yellow River valley was relatively isolated by long distances and physical barriers—mountains, deserts, ocean (see Map 3.6). Nevertheless, perhaps in part because the environment was similar, developments here unfolded in familiar ways.

The Yellow River collects rain in the mountains of Shaanxi province, where rapid thaws bring torrents of water. Where it disgorges, the stream broadens suddenly and periodically overflows. Here the climate has been getting steadily drier for thousands of years. The region today is torrid in summer, icy in winter, stung by chill, gritty winds, and rasped by rivers full of ice. The winds blow dust from the Mongolian desert over the land, creating the crumbly, yellow earth that gives the river its name. This soil, called *loess*, is almost sterile if it is not watered, but the flood coaxes it into amazing fertility. Because of its ferocity and unpredictability,

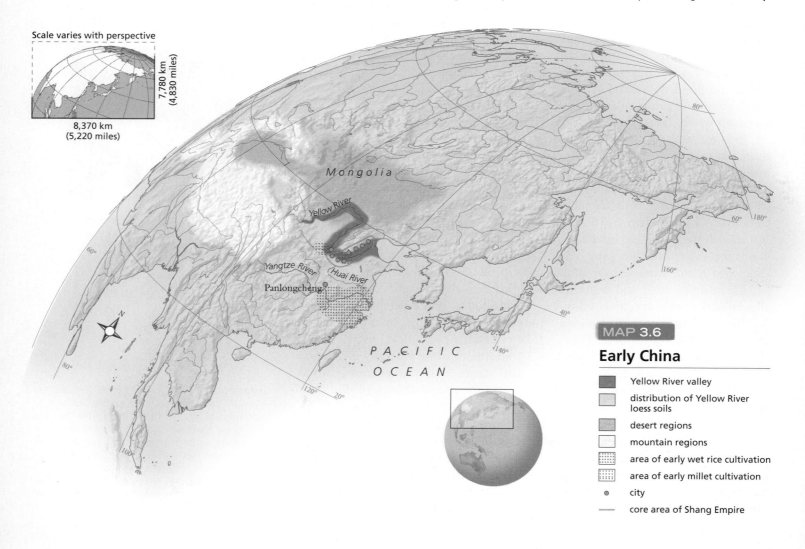

Scale varies with perspective

8,370 km
(5,220 miles)

7,780 km
(4,830 miles)

Mongolia

Yellow River

Yangtze River

Huai River

Panlongcheng

PACIFIC
OCEAN

MAP 3.6

Early China

- Yellow River valley
- distribution of Yellow River loess soils
- desert regions
- mountain regions
- area of early wet rice cultivation
- area of early millet cultivation
- • city
- — core area of Shang Empire

The Yellow River. The powdery, wind-blown soil from inner Asia that gives the Yellow River its name is highly fertile if irrigated. In a climate slightly warmer and slightly wetter than today's, it produced great quantities of millet in the third and second millennia B.C.E. What we now think of as Chinese civilization took shape when this region combined economically and politically with the moist, rice-producing Yangtze valley to the south.

the river needs careful management, with dikes to stem the flood, ditches to channel it, and artificial basins to conserve water against drought.

When farmers first began to till them, these lands were a sort of savanna, where grasslands mixed with woodland. Three or 4,000 years ago, water buffalo were still plentiful, together with other creatures of marsh and forest, such as deer, wild boar, silver pheasants, bamboo rats, and the occasional rhinoceros. In the *Shi Jing* (sher-jeeng)

> It was heavy, it was tall,
> it sprouted, it eared ...
> it nodded, it hung ...
> Indeed the lucky grains were sent down to us,
> The black millet, the double-kernelled,
> millet pink-sprouted and white.

During the Shang ruling dynasty, between about 3000 and 1000 B.C.E., millet sustained what were perhaps already the densest populations in the world and kept armies of tens of thousands of warriors in the field. The earliest known cultivators cleared the ground with fire before dibbling and sowing (see Chapter 2). They harvested each cluster of ears by hand and threshed seeds by rubbing between hands and feet. Crop rotation secured the best yields. Eventually soya beans provided the alternating crop, but it is not clear when soya cultivation began.

Even at its wettest, the Yellow River valley could not sustain a rice-eating civilization. Rice could only become a staple when people colonized new areas. Some later poets recalled expansion from the Yellow River southward as a process of conquest, grasping at the Yangtze River. But conquest makes more interesting myths than colonization does. Colonists and conquerors probably combined with other communities, where similar changes were already in progress, in a slow process of expansion on many levels, beginning more than 3,500 years ago.

CONFIGURATIONS OF SOCIETY

All four of the great river valleys faced the same problem—population was growing denser and society was becoming more complex, both of which demanded a strengthened state. Yet they adopted contrasting solutions.

Making Connections | THE ECOLOGY OF CIVILIZATIONS

	ENVIRONMENTAL DIVERSITY	PRIMARY MODIFICATIONS	ECONOMIC CONSEQUENCES
Egypt (Nile River)	Delta: marshlands, ponds, lakes; Upriver: "black earth," alluvial plain created from regular floods from central African headwaters; bordered by Sahara Desert, with scattered oasis	Exploitation of lush delta (*shaduf*); flooded alluvial plain with irrigation; microclimates with orchards, gardens	Everyday abundance of basic commodities (wheat, barley, cattle) leads to population increase, regional trade
Indus (Indus, Saraswati rivers)	Wide alluvial floodplain, frequent changing river courses, varied climate—coastal outposts, hot interior, upriver Himalayan headwaters; flooding twice a year from spring snowmelt and monsoon rains	Widespread irrigation of rainless upriver regions; grazing on grasslands, marsh areas	Agricultural surplus with two harvests a year; rapid population growth, urbanization
Mesopotamia (Tigris, Euphrates rivers)	Delta: marshlands, ponds, lakes, waterways; upriver alluvial plains flooded irregularly; harsh summer sandstorms, intense heat; winter floods, rainstorms; lack of forests, stone	Irrigation; dependence on winter crops: barley, wheat, onions, chickpeas; intensive plowing; digging of dikes and ditches to divert and store water	Widespread cultivation of grains leads to regional trade; use of mud brick for housing, temples
China (Yellow River)	Unpredictable river floods surrounding areas creating *loess* soil—basis of agriculture; probably more rainfall than the other three regions	Dikes, irrigation canals control flooding; creation of basins to conserve water; early exploitation of savanna grasslands, buffalo, and other animals; farming based on millet, later supplanted by soya	Gradual expansion/colonization southward toward rice-growing region of Yangtze River

The ziggurat of Ur. Typically, farming in any climate demands large-scale, highly disciplined labor, and generates seasonal manpower surpluses. Elites therefore have both the means and need to build on a monumental scale. This temple stairway at Ur in Mesopotamia is representative of the results: towering dimensions and precisely geometrical forms seem calculated to defy nature, symbolize order, and project triumphs of human imaginations.

Patterns of Settlement and Labor

We do not know how many people lived in the great river valley civilizations, but they surely numbered in the millions, and their numbers tended to grow, crowding their heartlands. In Egypt, instead of great cities, the people were spread fairly uniformly throughout the narrow floodplain of the Nile. Cities were strewn through the other three valleys.

By 3000 B.C.E., Sumer, as lower Mesopotamia (the part nearer the Persian Gulf) was called, was already a land of cities (see Map 3.7). Each city was sacred to the deity it housed, and a king who organized war against his neighbors ruled each city. The most famous city was one of the smallest. Ur had royal tombs of staggering wealth and towering ziggurats, built over 4,000 years ago. They were so impressive that centuries later, people venerated the biggest of them as a work of gods. In 2004, French archaeologists reported the discovery of the structures that seem to have inspired the ziggurats in what is now Iran, over an extensive area stretching from the Zagros Mountains eastward to Baluchistan. People at

Susa, for instance, built a terraced mound of mud bricks more than 240 feet square and 34 feet high, nearly 1,000 years before the earliest Mesopotamian ziggurats. From a slightly later date, the same excavations have yielded cylinders of colorful stone, carved with the facades of many-windowed buildings. So it looks as if the culture of Mesopotamian cities developed in part as a result of cultural exchanges with this previously unknown civilization.

By the beginning of the second millennium B.C.E., 1,000 years later, China, too, was a consciously urban culture. New frontier towns—modest places like Panlongcheng (pan-lung-chung), or Curled Dragon Town, in the northern province of Hubei—marked the growth of the kingdom. Its nearly one and a half acres provided for a governor's house surrounded by a colonnade of 43 pillars.

In any Harappan city of the same era, a citizen would have felt as at home as in any other. The streetscapes—the layouts of residential and administrative zones—were always much the same, as were the houses. Every brick was uniform—sometimes kiln baked, sometimes pan dried. Mohenjodaro (moh-hehn-joh-DAH-roh) was big enough to house perhaps 50,000 or 60,000 people and Harappa, over 30,000. No other settlements were anything like as big, but there were plenty of them—at least 1,500 are known to archaeologists.

In all these valleys, population density made specialization possible. People could devote themselves exclusively to particular crafts and trades. Although the evidence is deficient, each sex undoubtedly specialized in certain occupations, and women tended to be subordinated to men. There are several clues. First, there seemed to be a shift from matrilineal to patrilineal descent—systems, that is, inheriting status from the father rather than the mother. Then birth rates rose rapidly, which might have tied women to child rearing. About the same time—whether cause or result—art depicted women in servile roles. For instance, pouting, languid bronze dancing girls—or are they temple prostitutes?—figure among the few art works excavated from Harappan cities of the second millennium B.C.E. To judge from surviving Mesopotamian law codes and Chinese texts, women's talents became increasingly focused on the family home and child rearing. This is understandable because population increase created more strictly domestic work, while increasingly ambitious agriculture and construction were more efficiently entrusted to males.

So, along with other kinds of social differentiation, women seem to have been collectively disadvantaged, and men collectively privileged. Even at the most modest social levels, men had authority over women in their own households. Yet outside the home, urban life created new opportunities for specialized female labor. Women and children, for instance, were the textile workers in Ashur, a large city in northern Mesopotamia, and probably wove cotton in Harappan cities. Moreover, women were not necessarily excluded from power. These societies employed them as rulers, prophetesses, and priestesses and included them as subjects of art.

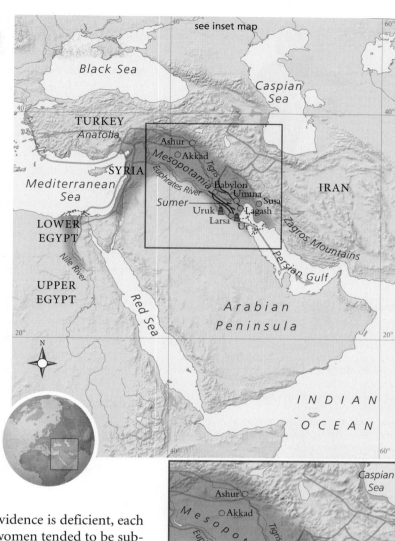

MAP 3.7

Early Mesopotamia

▨	fertile crescent
●	place described on pages 77–90
IRAN	modern country
- - -	ancient coastlines
——	ancient irrigation and water works
→	trade route
⛰	ziggurat

Dancing girl. One of a collection of bronze figures known as "dancing girls" unearthed at Mohenjo-daro. Their sinuous shapes, sensual appeal, and provocative poses suggest to some scholars that they may portray temple prostitutes. They are modeled with a freedom that contrasts with the formality and rigidity of the handful of representations of male figures that survive from the same civilization (see page 85).

Dancing girl. Bronze statuette from Mohenjo Daro. Indus Valley Civilization. National Museum, New Delhi, India. Borromeo/Art Resource, NY

Concentrating on domestic life also gave women opportunities to exercise informal power. Surviving texts show some of the consequences. Women had the right to initiate divorce, to recover their property, and, sometimes, to win additional compensation on divorce. A wife, says the Egyptian *Book of Instructions*, "is a profitable field. Do not contend with her at law and keep her from gaining control."

Politics

All four river valley societies shared, in one respect, a type of environment suited to tyranny, or, at least, to strong states exercising minute control over their subjects' lives. Indeed, for people living on the banks of silt-bearing, flood-prone rivers, intensified agriculture could have been a consequence—not a cause—of the political changes that accompanied it. That is, instead of an increased food supply requiring more political organization, a tyrannical leader may have forced people to farm more land to produce a surplus for trade, war, or feasts. Even without agriculture, people could have no security of life without collective action to manage the floods. Even foragers would need ditches and dikes to protect wild foodstuffs and defend dwellings. The mace head of an Egyptian king of the fourth millennium B.C.E. shows him digging a canal. Proverbially, a just judge was "a dam for the sufferer, guarding lest he drown," a corrupt one "a flowing lake." The importance of collectively managing the floods helps account for the obvious resemblances between the political systems of all these regions. All practiced divine or sacred kingship; all had rigid social hierarchies; all placed the lives and labor of the inhabitants at the disposal of the state.

We can see how one irrigation system worked, in Larsa in Mesopotamia, from the archive of a contractor named Lu-igisa, which has survived from around 2000 B.C.E. His job was to survey land for canal building, organize the laborers and their pay and provisions, and supervise the digging and the dredging of accumulated silt. Procuring labor was the key task—5,400 workers to dig a canal and 1,800 on one occasion for emergency repairs. In return, he had the potentially profitable job of controlling the opening and closing of the locks that released or shut off the water supplies. He was bound by oaths that were enforced by threat of loss. "What is my sin," he complained to a higher official when he lost control of a canal, "that the king took my canal from me and gave it to Etellum?"

The Egyptian State

It is tempting to attribute the loss of freedom in a forager society to the rise of a strong leader, but the one does not necessarily have to follow from the other. In ancient Egypt, the most common image of the state was of a flock the king tended like a herdsman. The comparison probably reflects the political ideas of earlier herder communities because farming as a way of life involves more competition for space than herding does. Disputes and wars over land strengthen rulership. Increased war and wealth would also shift patriarchs and elders out of supreme office in favor of stronger and wiser leaders.

In societies that rely on a single crop or a narrow range of crops, food shortages are a routine hazard. When normal weather patterns fail and reserves are inadequate, widespread famine can strike. As it is, shortages often occur annually in the unproductive season before the harvest. These problems are even worse for societies, like those of antiquity that cannot procure food through long-range trade. For these reasons, in Egypt—a scorching environment that floods periodically soak—defying nature meant more than refashioning the landscape. Above all, it meant stockpiling against disaster, to safeguard humans from the invisible forces that let loose the floods. The mortuary temple built to house the body of Rameses II, who probably ruled around 1300 B.C.E. (no dates in ancient Egyptian chronology are certain), had storehouses big enough to feed 20,000 people for a year. The taxation yields proudly painted on the walls of a high official's tomb are an illustrated menu for feeding an empire: sacks of barley, piles of cakes and nuts, hundreds of head of livestock. The state as stockpiler existed, it seems, not to redistribute goods but for famine relief.

Methods of collecting and storing grain were as vital as the systems of flood control, precisely because the extent of the flood could vary from one year to the next. The biblical story of Joseph, an Israelite who became a pharaoh's chief official and saved Egypt from starvation, recalls "seven lean years" at one stretch. Such bad times were part of folk memories, as were spells when "every man ate his children." A tomb scene from the city of Amarna (ah-MAHR-nah) shows a storehouse with only six rows of stacked victuals, including grain sacks and heaps of dried fish, laid on shelves supported on brick pillars. A strong state was an inseparable part of this kind of farsightedness. Grain had to be taxed under compulsion, transported under guard, and kept under watch.

If pharaohs were highly glorified storekeepers, what did the Egyptians mean when they said their king was a god? Furthermore, how could pharaohs bear the names and exercise the functions of many gods, each with a separate identity? A possible aid to understanding is the Egyptian habit of making images and erecting shrines as places where the gods could manifest themselves. The image "was" the god only when the god inhabited the image. The pharaoh's person could provide a similar opportunity for a god to take up residence. For example, the goddess Isis, in some characterizations, was her deified throne.

The idea of the god-king gave birth to royal power. In the collection of ancient Egyptian diplomatic correspondence known as the Amarna letters, the ruler of a city in Palestine around 1350 B.C.E. wrote, "To the king my lord and my Sun-god, I am Lab'ayu thy servant and the dirt whereon thou dost tread. At the feet of my king and my Sun-god seven times and seven times I fall." Some 400 years earlier, a father, Sehetep-ib-Re, wrote advice to his children—"a counsel of eternity and a manner of living aright." The king is the sun-god, but he is more. "He illumines Egypt more than the sun, he makes the land greener than does the Nile."

In Egypt the law remained in the mouth of the divine pharaoh, and the need to put it in writing was never strong. Instead, religion defined a moral code that the state could not easily modify or subvert. The evidence comes from Egyptian tombs. Early grave goods include the cherished possessions and everyday belongings of this world, suggesting that the next world would reproduce the inequalities and lifestyles of this one. At an uncertain date, however, a new idea of the afterlife emerged. This world was called into existence to correct the imbalances of the one we know. It is particularly well documented in ancient Egyptian sources that most of the elite seem to have changed their attitude toward the afterlife around 2000 B.C.E. Earlier tombs are antechambers to a life for which the world was practical training. Tombs built later are places of interrogation after a moral preparation for the next life.

Wall paintings from the later tombs show the gods weighing the souls of the dead. Typically, the deceased's heart lies in one scale, and a feather symbolizing truth lies in the other. The jackal-headed god of the underworld, Anubis, supervises the scales. The examined soul renounces a long list of sins that concentrate on

King Gudea (r. 2141–2122 B.C.E.) of Lagash in Sumeria, was one of ancient Mesopotamia's most determined propagandists, distributing dozens of statues of himself to other rulers. This example is typical, with his head bound by his characteristic lamb's fleece fillet, his overflowing oil flagon (signifying abundance under his rule), and the self-glorifying inscription that covers his robe. But the propaganda may have been born of despair. After his reign, Lagash vanishes from the historical record.

Weighing the soul. About 4,500 years ago, Egyptian sensibilities changed. Instead of showing the afterlife as a prolongation of life in this world, tomb-painters began to concentrate on morally symbolic scenes, in which gods interrogate the dead and weigh their good against their evil deeds.

three areas: sacrilege, sexual perversion, and the abuse of power against the weak. Then the good deeds appear: obedience to human laws and divine will, acts of mercy, offerings to the gods and the spirits of ancestors, bread to the hungry, clothing to the naked, "and a ferry for him who was marooned." The reward of the good is a new life in the company of Osiris, the sometime ruler of the universe. For those who fail the test, the punishment is extinction.

Statecraft in Mesopotamia

Unlike Egypt, which was a single state under a single ruler, Mesopotamia was divided into many small rival kingdoms called city-states because each was based on a single city. In Mesopotamia, kings were not gods, which is probably why the earliest known law codes come from there. The codes of Ur from the third millennium B.C.E. are fragmentary—essentially, lists of fines. But the code of King Lipit-Ishtar of Sumer and Akkad (ah-KAHD), around 2000 B.C.E., is clearly an attempt to regulate the entire society. It explains that the laws were divinely inspired and ordained "in accordance with the word of Enlil," the supreme god. Their purpose was to make "children support the father and the father children, . . . abolish enmity and rebellion, cast out weeping and lamentation . . . bring righteousness and truth and give well-being to Sumer and Akkad."

Hammurabi, ruler of Babylon in the first half of the 1700s B.C.E., gets undue credit because his code happens to survive intact, having been carried off as a war trophy to Persia. It is engraved in stone and shows the king receiving the text from the hands of a god. It was clearly intended to substitute for the physical presence and words of the ruler. "Let any oppressed man who has a cause come into the presence of the statue of me, the king of justice, and then read carefully my inscribed stone, and give heed to my precious words. May my stone make his case clear to him." These were not laws as we know them, handed down by tradition or enacted to restrain the ruler's power. Rather, they were means to perpetuate royal commands. Obedience was severely enforced in Mesopotamia—to the vizier in the fields, the father in the household, the king in everything. "The king's word is right," says a representative text, "his word, like a god's, cannot be changed."

Even if we had no written evidence to confirm it, royal power would gleam from the luxurious artifacts that filled rulers' tombs, evidence of the realm's wealth: a gilded harp carved in the form of a ram; dice and gaming boards of inlaid shell and polished stone; lively animals sculpted in gold and silver with eyes of shell and lapis lazuli (a blue stone); tapering vessels of gold, and golden cups modeled on ostrich eggs. The stunning collections of jewelry seem to have religious themes, as if each had a distinct ritual function.

In Mesopotamian carvings, the king is commonly the biggest figure in any scene that includes him. He drinks. He receives supplicants who petition his help and citizens and ambassadors who pay him tribute. He presides over armies and processions of chariots drawn by wild asses. He carries bricks to build cities and temples, purifying them with fire and consecrating them with oil. To form the first brick from the mud was the king's exclusive right, and bricks from the state kilns were stamped with royal names. Royal seals make plain why this was the case. They show gods building the world up out of mud. They mix it, carry it up ladders, and fling mud bricks up to the men who set them layer by layer. The transformation of mud into city was royal magic.

Oracles—means of supposed access to knowing the future—told kings what to do. Augurers were the hereditary interpreters of oracles. They read the will of the gods in the livers of sacrificed sheep, in the drift of incense, and, above all, in the movements of heavenly bodies. Their predictions of royal victory, danger, anger, and recovery from sickness fill surviving records. Religion, however, did not necessarily limit royal power. Normally, kings controlled the oracles. Kings themselves sometimes slept in temples to induce prophetic dreams, especially during a crisis, such as the failure of the floods. Of course, the predictions they reported may have merely legitimated the policies they had already decided to follow.

Yet these absolute rulers were there to serve the people: to mediate with the gods on behalf of the whole society, to organize the collective effort of tillage and irrigation, to warehouse food against hard times, and to redistribute it for the common good. A comic dialogue from Akkad illustrates the delicate politics and economics of control of the food supply in the second millennium B.C.E. "Servant, obey me," the master begins.

> I shall give food to our country.
> Give it, my lord, give it. The man who gives food to his country keeps his own barley
>   and gets rich on the interest other people pay him.
> No, my servant, I shall not give food to my country.
> Do not give, my lord, do not give. Giving is like loving . . . or like having a son. . . .
>   They will curse you. They will eat your barley and destroy you.

The most famous relic of ancient Mesopotamian literature, the epic of *Gilgamesh*, sheds further light on the nature of leadership, or at least of heroism, on which leadership is modeled. In the surviving versions, written down, perhaps about 1800 B.C.E., the same natural forces that molded the Mesopotamian environment shaped the story. When Gilgamesh, the hero of the poem, confronts a monster who breathes fire and plague, the gods blind the creature with a scorching wind. When Gilgamesh explores the Ocean of Death to find the secret of immortality, he encounters the only family to have survived a primeval flood. The disaster, wrought by divine whim, had destroyed the rest of the human race and even left the gods themselves "cowering like dogs crouched against a wall."

The character of Gilgamesh is a poetic invention, embroidered onto the stuff of legends. But there was a real Gilgamesh, too, or at least a king of that name in

"To form the first brick from the mud was the king's exclusive right, and bricks from the state kilns were stamped with royal names. Royal seals make plain why this was the case. They show gods building the world up out of mud. They mix it, carry it up ladders, and fling mud bricks up to the men who set them layer by layer. The transformation of mud into city was royal magic."

A CLOSER LOOK

A Board Game From Ancient Sumer

Elite pastime: The British archaeologist Sir Leonard Woolley (1880–1960) found the remains of two board games of the third millennium B.C.E. in a royal grave deep in the ruins of the Sumerian city of Ur. Rules in verse, apparently for a similar game, survive from early in the second century B.C.E. in Egypt.

Squares made of shells, set with the blue stone called lapis lazuli and red limestone. The squares were stuck to the wooden board with bitumen, a tar that the Sumerians used as glue. They derived it from the petroleum that bubbled to the surface in parts of Mesopotamia in what is today Iraq.

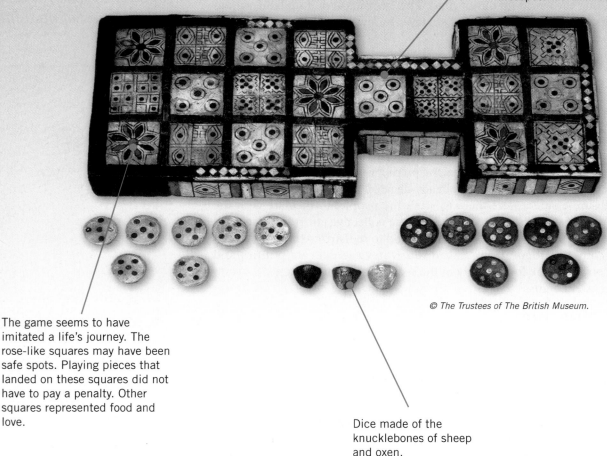

The game seems to have imitated a life's journey. The rose-like squares may have been safe spots. Playing pieces that landed on these squares did not have to pay a penalty. Other squares represented food and love.

Dice made of the knucklebones of sheep and oxen.

What does this board game tell us about the importance of leisure among members of the elite in the great river valleys?

historical sources. The poem quotes a proverbial saying about the historical Gilgamesh: "Who has ever ruled with power like his?" He was the fifth king recorded in the city of Uruk around 2700 B.C.E. (according to the most widely favored chronology). Some of the genuine wonders of the city appear during his reign—its walls, its gardens, the pillared hall where the deity was housed at the heart of the city.

The First Documented Chinese State

The earliest recorded kingship traditions of China resemble those of Egypt and Mesopotamia. They show the same connection between royal status and the management of water resources and the distribution of food. The legendary engineer—Emperor Yu the Great—was praised for having "mastered the waters and caused them to flow in great channels." Early folk poetry describes a period of city building after his time, so fast "that the drums could not keep pace." The legendary ruler Tan-fu "summoned the Master of Works,"

> He called the Master of Multitudes,
> He made them build houses.
> Their plumb-lines were straight.
> They lashed the boards and erected the frames
> They made the temple in careful order.

Gilgamesh, king of Uruk, hero of the world's earliest known work of imaginative literature, shown in a relief more than 3,000 years old, kills the Bull of Heaven. The bull was a personification of drought. It was part of a king's job to mastermind irrigation.
Royal Museums of Art and History, Brussels, Belgium. Copyright IRPA–KIK, Brussels, Belgium.

The earliest China we know of was a unitary state. The dynasty known as Shang dominated the Yellow River valley for most of the second millennium B.C.E. Vital evidence about the nature of the Shang state is inscribed on oracle bones, animal bones and turtle shells used to foretell the future. Diviners, whose job was to detect the oracles' messages, heated them to the breaking point and read the gods' answers to questions along the lines of the cracks. Scribes transcribed the answers onto the fragments, so the bones tell of the lives and duties of kings. The court treasury held millet, turtle shells, and oracle bones paid in tribute. The king was most often engaged in war and sometimes in diplomacy. Marriage was part of it; later emperors called it "extending my favor." To their soldiers, "our prince's own concerns" rolled them "from misery to misery" and gave them homes "like tigers and buffaloes . . . in desolate wilds."

Above all, the king was a mediator with the gods, performing sacrifices, preparing for and conducting oracle readings, breaking the soil, praying for rain, founding towns. He spent half his time hunting—presumably as a way to entertain counselors and ambassadors, train horsemen, and add meat to his diet. Scholars claim to detect an increasingly businesslike tone in the oracles. References to dreams and sickness diminish as time goes on, the style becomes terser, and the tone more optimistic. Sometimes the bones reveal revolutions in the conduct of rites from reign to reign, evidence that kings fought tradition and tried to give the world a stamp of their own. Tsu Jia, for instance, a king of the late second millennium B.C.E., discontinued sacrifices to mythical ancestors, mountains, and rivers and increased those to historical figures. Beyond reasonable doubt, he was modifying the practices of the longest-lived and most renowned of his dynasty, Wu Ding.

The chronology is uncertain, but Wu Ding must have ruled about 1400 B.C.E. He was remembered 1,000 years later as a conqueror who ruled his empire as easily "as rolling it on his palm." He was a glorious hunter, whose oracles predicted, on one occasion, a bag of "tigers, one; deer, forty; foxes, one hundred and sixty-four; hornless deer, one hundred and fifty-nine; and so forth." One of his 64 consorts

Oracle bones in China in the second millennium B.C.E. were heated until they cracked. Specialist diviners—shamans at first, later royal appointees—read the future along the lines of the cracks, scratching their interpretations into the bone. Most predictions were formal and even banal. This example says characteristically, "If the king hunts, there will be no disaster."

Bronze drinking vessel. The art of the bronze makers of the late second millennium B.C.E. in China has never been surpassed. Most of the bronzes, like this eleventh-century B.C.E. example in the form of a stylized tiger, were ritual drinking vessels, typically filled with grain alcohol to be offered to the spirits. Their symmetrical decoration suggests the influence of Daoism (see Chapter 6). Many have survived because they were buried as grave goods, for the use of ancestors in the afterlife.
Dagli Orti/PICTURE DESK KOBAL COLLECTION ART.

Chronology: The Great River Valleys	
5000 B.C.E.	Beginning of intense agriculture in great river valleys; use of plows widespread in Mesopotamia
4000 B.C.E.	*Shaduf* invented in Egypt
3000 B.C.E.	Menes unites Upper and Lower Egypt; large cities appear in lower Mesopotamia (Sumer)
2500 B.C.E.	Sargon of Akkad conquers Sumer; cities of Harappa and Mohenjodaro flourish
2250–2000 B.C.E.	Ziggurat of Ur
2000–1000 B.C.E.	Shang dynasty (China)
2000 B.C.E.	Law code of Lipit-Ishtar (Mesopotamia); concept of afterlife becomes more moralistic in Egypt
1800 B.C.E.	Epic of *Gilgamesh* written down
1700 B.C.E.	Law code of Hammurabi
1500 B.C.E.	Reading of oracle bones becomes secularized in China; beginning of gradual expansion of Yellow River valley southward toward Yangtze

(All dates are approximate)

was buried in the richest known tomb of the period, with her human servants, dogs, horses, hundreds of bronzes and jades, and thousands of cowrie shells, which were used as money. Although there is room for confusion because of the court habit of calling different people by the same name, court records probably identify her correctly. Wu Ding repeatedly consulted the oracles about her childbeds and sickbeds. She was one of his three principal wives and not only wife and mother, but active participant in politics. She had a domain of her own, including a walled town, and could mobilize 3,000 warriors on command.

As mediator with the gods, the king was a substitute for the shaman, as the person who normally fulfills that role in society is called (see Chapter 1). A shaman is the intermediary—the middleman—between humans and gods. He elicits the "sharp-eared, keen-eyed" wisdom of ghosts and spirits and restores contact with heaven after disordered times. By taking over the divination of bones and turtle shells, the king transferred the most important political functions of magic and religion—foretelling the future and interpreting the will of the spirits—to the state. No longer in the hands of diviners, recording and preserving the results of divination became a secular—or nonreligious— function. The king became the guardian of a secular bureaucracy—a slowly developing corps of court historians, who could acquire experience on which predictions could be based more reliably than on the shamans' supposed insights.

At this stage, the Chinese viewed kingship in practical terms—how well the ruler looked after his subjects. Shang rulers claimed to have come to power as executors of divine justice against an earlier—doubtless mythical—dynasty, the Xia (SHEE-ah), whose last representative had forfeited his right to rule by "neglecting husbandry": failing, that is, in his duty to look after the realm as a farmer cares for his fields. The earliest scholars' texts that describe the emergence of China probably reflect traditional propaganda fairly accurately. They depict kind, generous rulers who fostered the arts of peace. The Yellow Emperor, a mythical figure, was credited with inventing the carriage, the boat, the bronze mirror, the cooking pot, the crossbow, "and a kind of football." Poems and popular legends, however, reveal more of the bloody business of kingship, which inherited ancient clan leaders' rights of life and death. An axe engraved with the emblems of the executioner—hungry smiles and devouring teeth—signified the original term for rulership. "Bring your tongues under the rule of law," says a late Shang ruler in an approving poet's lines, "lest punishment come upon you when repentance will be of no avail."

Wealth and warfare were inseparable essentials of kingship. The tombs of Shang rulers around 1500 B.C.E. display the nature of their power: thousands of strings of cowrie shells, bronze axes and chariots, lacquer ware, and hundreds of intricately carved treasures of jade and bone. The greatest treasures were bronzes of unparalleled quality, cast in ceramic molds. Bronze making was the supreme art of Shang China, and its products were a privilege of rank. Thousands of human sacrifices, buried with kings to serve them in the next world or to sanctify their tombs, were—to those who buried them—among the cheapest sacrifices.

Ruling the Harappan World

In the Harappan world, the extraordinary consistency in urban layout and building design did not necessarily arise from political unity. Hierarchically ordered dwelling spaces hint at a class or even a more rigid caste structure. In a class system, individuals can rise or fall through the ranks of society. In a caste system they are stuck with the status with which they are born. In Harappan cities, the extensive communal quarters must have had something to do with the organization of manpower—soldiers, perhaps, or slaves, or scholars. Huge warehouses suggest a system to distribute food. The waste-disposal system looks like a masterpiece of urban planning, with clay pipes laid under the streets. The uniform bricks must have come from state kilns and pans. The imposing citadels or fortresses enclosed spaces that might have had an elite function, like the spacious bathing tank at Mohenjodaro (see Map 3.8). Harappan sites, however, have no rich graves, and the absence of kingly quarters or regal furnishings tempts us to imagine Harappan societies as republics or theocracies, god-centered governments run by priests.

For a society like Harappa's, whose writings we cannot read, normally archaeological evidence tells us what little we know. In particular, we would hope to learn something from works of art. But no pictorial art has survived, and Harappan artists seem to have produced little sculpture, except on a small scale in clay and sometimes bronze. One extraordinary figure from Mohenjodaro, of great seriousness, with almond eyes and rigidly fluted beard, wears a headband with what looks like the setting for a gem. He has a rich garment slung over one shoulder and extends what is left of his arm in what must surely have been a symbolic or ritual gesture. He has been called a priest-king or a philosopher-king, but these romantic terms are valueless. Since we know so little about Harappan politics, religion, and life, we have no context for interpreting him. We can only describe him.

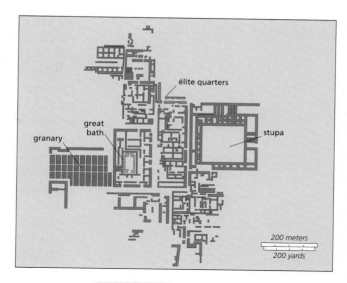

MAP 3.8

The Citadel at Mohenjodaro

The Politics of Expansion

Although just about everything in Harappan politics remains mysterious, the reach of the culture seems so vast it is hard to imagine how it can have spread so far, into a range of different environments, except by force of arms. A sense of what the Harappan frontier was like—expanding and violent—grips you when you see the garrisons that reached toward the interior of Asia, in unirrigatable deserts and siltless hills. In what is now northern Afghanistan, lapis lazuli and copper were traded at oasis settlements that reached westward toward the Caspian Sea. Mundigak, a fortified trading center, was equipped to house entire caravans. Today, behind formidable walls with square bastions, the wreck of a great citadel lunges over the landscape, baring rows of deep, round columns at its flank, like the ribs of a huge, squat beast crouched to guard the routes of commerce.

In Egypt, Mesopotamia, and China, the sources are ample enough to reveal how states grew by conquest. In Egypt, the Nile was the spine that supported a unitary state. More than the source of life-giving mud, the river was a highway through a long, thin land. Culture and trade could flow freely from the coast to the cataracts. When the owner of a fleet died, his ships were illustrated on the walls of his tomb, like that of the royal chancellor Merket-ra at Thebes, painted over 3,000 years ago, with yachts, barges, and fishing boats. Models and paintings of river craft

Harappan elite. Society and politics of ancient Harappa remain mysterious because little art survives as a clue to what went on, and we do not know how to decipher Harappan writings. A few sculptures, like this one from Mohenjodaro, depict members of an elite. The embroidered robe, jeweled crown, combed beard, and grave face all imply power—but is it priestly power, political power, or both?
Andy Crawford © Dorling Kindersley, Courtesy of the National Museum, New Delhi

are among the most common decorations of tombs. At Thebes, you can still see painted scenes of grain-laden barges, and others with oil jars and bundles of fodder, docking by the marketplace.

The river was politically unifying, too. Pharoahs took the river route for inspection tours of the kingdom, mooring at royal docks with brick shrines and exercise yards for chariots. Egypt was an empire shaped like the fans Egyptians used to rake and beat their wheat—the long staff of the Nile linked to the spread of the delta where the river meets the Mediterranean. Mythology preserved the memory of a prehistoric Egypt divided into two realms: an upriver South Kingdom, or Upper Egypt, and Lower Egypt, occupying the delta region. Pharaohs wore a double crown to recall this past. Egypt's traditional lists of dynasties began with Menes, the culture hero who supposedly conquered the delta from his own kingdom in the south around 3000 B.C.E. He united the kingdoms and founded Memphis, his capital, at the point on the Nile where Upper and Lower Egypt joined, a little to the south of modern Cairo.

Conveyance by river was one of the features this world had in common with heaven. To accompany the immortals as they were ferried across the sky, the pharaoh Cheops was provided with transport. In one pit adjoining his pyramid lies the barge that carried his body to the burial place. Egyptologists are currently excavating an adjoining pit, where his celestial boat is buried. In this sailing vessel, he would navigate the darkness, joining the fleet that bore the Sun back to life every night.

In retrospect, the unity of Egypt seems "natural"—river shaped. Mesopotamia was not so easy to unify. Competition was probably the driving force behind Mesopotamian city-states. Inscriptions addressed to their cities' patron gods are full of victories against rivals, each one's propaganda bewilderingly contradicting the others. Around 2000 B.C.E., the most boastful author of inscriptions, Lugal Zagesi, king of the city of Umma in Sumer, claimed more. The supreme god, Enlil, "put all the lands at his feet and from east to west made them subject to him" from the Persian Gulf to the Mediterranean.

This was almost certainly just a boast. Left to themselves, the warring Sumerian city-states could never have united for long. Around 2500 B.C.E., however, invaders from northern Mesopotamia forced political change. The conquering king, Sargon of Akkad, was one of the great empire builders of antiquity. His armies poured downriver and made him King of Sumer and Akkad. "Mighty mountains with axes of bronze I conquered," he declared in a surviving chronicle fragment and dared kings who came after him to do the same. His armies were said to have reached Syria and Iran.

Such a vast empire could not last. After a century or two, native Sumerian forces expelled Sargon's successors. Nevertheless, Sargon's achievement set a new pattern—an imperial direction—for the political history of the region. City-states sought to expand by conquering each other. For a time, Lagash, a northern neighbor of Ur, dominated Sumer. One of its kings was the subject of 27 surviving images. We have no better index of any ruler's power. But around 2100 B.C.E., Ur displaced Lagash. The new capital began to acquire the look for which it is renowned, with showy ziggurats and daunting walls. Within a few years more, tribute, recorded on clay tablets, was reaching Ur from as far away as the Iranian highlands and the Lebanese coast. A 4,000-year-old box—the soundbox of a harp, perhaps—gorgeously depicts the cycle of royal life in imperial Ur—victory, tribute-gathering, and celebration. Thereafter, leadership in the region shifted among rival centers, but it always remained in the south.

In China, itineraries for royal travel dating around 1500 B.C.E. reveal a different political geography. Kings constantly rattled up and down the great vertical artery of the realm, the eastern arm of the Yellow River, and frenziedly did the round of

Royal boat. The 143-foot-long boat that bore the body of Pharaoh Cheops or Khufu along the Nile to the Great Pyramid of Giza. The boat was modeled on images of the boat in which Egyptians depicted the sun sailing through the heavens. In what seems to have been part of the usual royal burial ritual, it was broken and buried in a ditch alongside the pyramid, from where archaeologists recovered it in 1954. It took 10 years to put the 154 fragments back together.

Making Connections | POLITICS AND STATE POWER IN GREAT RIVER VALLEY SOCIETIES

STATE	LEADER & SYMBOLIC ROLE	METHOD OF UNIFICATION	RULER'S MEANS OF CONTROL
Egypt	Pharaoh (herdsman) sometimes functions as god	Organizing labor to manage floods; distributing food; use of Nile River as highway to unify, control	Pharaoh's commands, policies function as law, regarded as divine
Mesopotamia city-states	Kings/royals meditate, lead worship, receive oracles	Organizing labor; distributing food; competition with other city-states	Earliest law codes; rituals performed by oracles guide decision making
China	Emperor/engineer, builder, hunter, takes on shamans' role in receiving prophecies	Organizing dike building, irrigation; use of Yellow River as highway to unify and control	Ritual divination using oracle bones—foretelling future, interpreting will of spirits
Harappa	Uncertain if singular ruler or priests dominated ruling class	Harnessing river, irrigation; distributing food; engineering and construction of complex urban systems	Unknown; widespread standardization of measurements and trade point to coordination/leadership

towns and estates to the south, as far as the river Huai. Occasionally, they touched the northernmost reach of the Yangtze River. This was a telltale sign. Shang civilization was expanding south from its heartlands on the middle Yellow River, growing into a regionally dominant superstate. Gradually, the worlds of Chinese culture and politics absorbed the Yangtze valley. The result was a unique state containing complementary environments: the millet-growing lands of the Yellow River, the rice fields of the Yangtze. The new ecology of China helped protect it against ecological disaster in either zone. It also formed the basis of the astonishingly resilient and productive state seen in subsequent Chinese history. The consequences will be apparent throughout the remainder of this book. For most of the rest of our story, China wields disproportionate power and influence.

Moreover, the broadening of China's frontiers stimulated rulers' ambitions. They became boundless. Religion and philosophy conspired. The sky was a compelling deity: vast and pregnant with gifts—of light and warmth and rain—and bristling with threats of storm and fire and flood. A state that touched its limits would fulfill a kind of "manifest destiny"—a reflection of divine order. Comparing the state to the cosmos prompted rulers to seek a dominion as boundless as the sky's. The Chinese came to see imperial rule over the world as divinely ordained. Emperors treated the whole world as rightfully or potentially subject to them. By the time of the Zhou, the dynasty that succeeded the Shang, the phrase **mandate of heaven** came into use to express these doctrines.

The concept of the mandate of heaven spread to neighboring peoples. On the Eurasian steppes, the immense flatlands and vast skies encouraged similar thinking. We have no documentation for the ambitions of the steppe dynasties until much later. But, as we shall see, steppelanders with conquest in mind repeatedly challenged empires around the edges of Eurasia in the first millennium B.C.E. It is probably fair to say that for hundreds, perhaps thousands, of years, the concept of a right to rule the world drove imperialism in Eurasia.

> "But, as we shall see, steppelanders with conquest in mind repeatedly challenged empires around the edges of Eurasia in the first millennium B.C.E. It is probably fair to say that for hundreds, perhaps thousands, of years, the concept of a right to rule the world drove imperialism in Eurasia."

Literate Culture

It used to be thought—some people still think—that one reason the early Egyptians, Mesopotamians, Chinese, and Harappans qualified as "civilized" was because they were the first to use symbolic methods to record information and pass it on to future generations.

Mesopotamians devised the wedge shapes of the writing known as **cuneiform** to be easily incised, or cut, in the clay tablets used to keep records. The hieroglyphs of the earliest Egyptian texts and the symbols carved on Chinese oracle bones were **logograms**, stylized pictures that provoked mental associations with ideas they were intended to represent or with the sounds of their spoken names (see figure 3.2). We can understand the writing from Mesopotamia, Egypt, and China, but scholarship has not yet cracked the code for Harappan writing. The surviving Harappan texts are on clay seals, which suggests they served commercial purposes. Though we cannot decipher them, they clearly mark the cord or sacks of merchants' goods. Archaeologists have retrieved many of them from heaps of discarded produce.

So, all these civilizations did indeed develop writing systems of great usefulness and perhaps great expressiveness. For three reasons, however, we can no longer claim that writing was a special and defining feature that made these the first civilizations. First, writing systems originated independently in widely separated parts of the world and were far more varied than traditional scholarship has supposed. Notched sticks and knotted strings can be forms of writing as much as letters on a page or in an inscription. Some writing systems were much older than the civilizations of the river valleys. We have already seen evidence of earlier symbolic-

FIGURE 3.2 ANCIENT WRITING SYSTEMS COMPARED

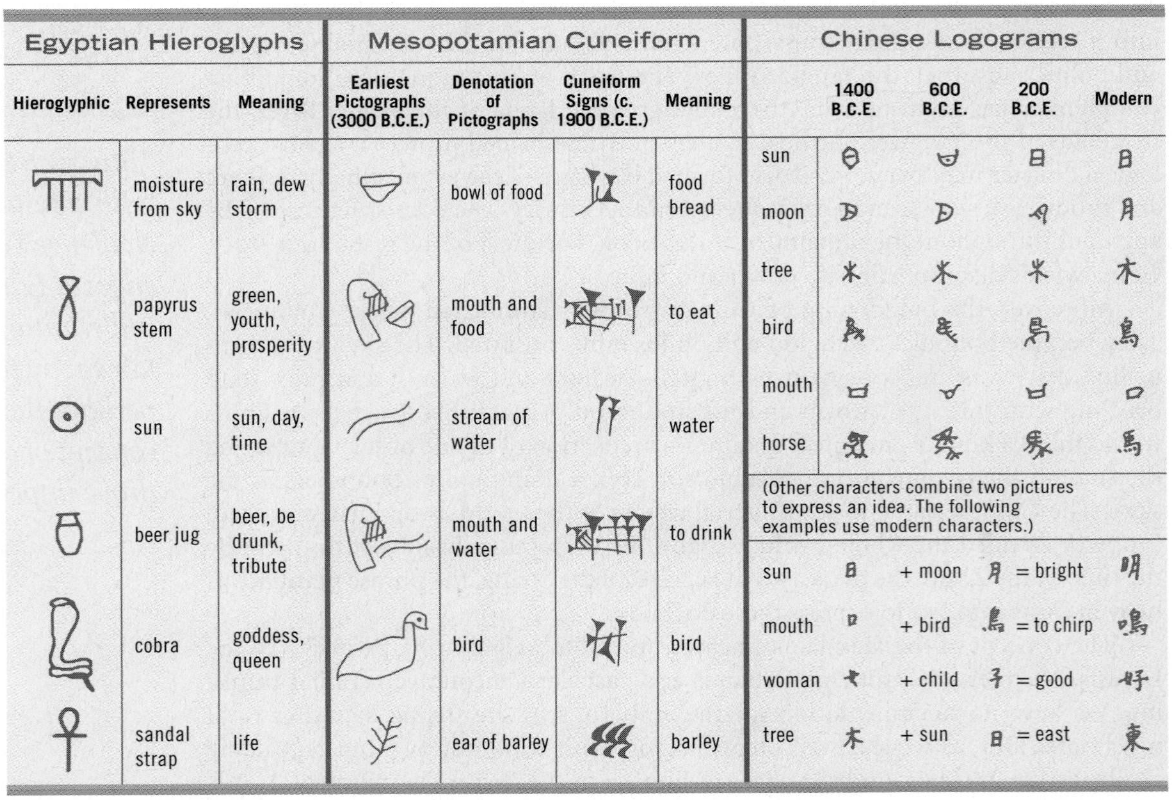

notation systems in Ice-Age cave paintings. Thanks to recent scholarship, our knowledge of early writing systems has grown so rapidly that the chronology and definition of writing are in turmoil.

Second, it is not clear why we should consider writing special compared to information-retrieval systems based on memory. The earliest writing systems were usually employed for trivia—merchants' price lists, tax collectors' memoranda, potters' marks, and similar jottings. Real art—the great creative poems and myths, like *Gilgamesh*—were too sacred for writing to taint and too memorable for such a crude method of transmission. Instead, for centuries, people memorized them and transmitted them orally from one generation to the next.

Finally, how much information does a system have to be able to convey before we can call it writing? Will knotted strings or notched sticks do? Surviving Shang oracle bones of the second millennium B.C.E. bear the ancestral language of modern Chinese. Yet a symbolic system of recording information seems undeniably represented on pottery more than 2,000 years older from Banpo in the Yellow River region. The symbols might be numerals and potters' marks. They do not seem to be connected sentences because the symbols are simple and used one at a time. So is this writing or something else unworthy of the name? Turtle shells recently discovered at Wuyang (woo-yahng) in China, which are even older, bear marks that we can only explain as part of a system of symbolic representation.

Instead of restricting our definition of writing, we ought to feel awe at the adventure of combining isolated symbols to tell stories and make arguments. But familiarity disperses awe. Some cultures may have taken thousands of years to make this leap, even while they used writing systems for other purposes, such as labels, oracles, bureaucracy, and magic charms.

Early writing. In almost all known cases, writing was devised to record neither wisdom nor art, but only tedious data, such as prices and tax returns. This clay tablet from a collection at the Library of Congress is written in Sumerian and concerns the wages paid to named supervisors of day laborers. It dates to 2039 B.C.E.

In Perspective
What Made the Great River Valleys Different?

Still, the fact remains that, thanks in part to their use of writing, the civilizations of the four great river valleys—or, at least, the three whose writings we can decipher—are, to us, the best known of their time. For that reason, not because of their supposed influence on other peoples, they fairly occupy so much space in books like this one. Studying their written works helps us identify at least two reasons for the cultural divergence of the era, of which they are extreme examples. First, in part, divergence was environmentally conditioned. That is, the greater or more diverse the resource base, the bigger and more durable the society it feeds. The great river valleys were large, continuous areas of fertile, easily worked soil, and for farming societies, exploitable land is the most basic resource of all. Environmental diversity gave the river valley peoples extra resources, compared with civilizations in less privileged regions. Egypt had the Nile delta at hand. In the Yellow River and Yangtze valleys, China had two complementary ecological systems. Mesopotamia had a hinterland of pastures, and Mesopotamia and Harappa had access to each other by sea.

Chronology

5000–2000 B.C.E.	Four great river valley civilizations develop: Middle and Lower Nile, Egypt; Indus and Saraswati rivers; Tigris and Euphrates rivers, Mesopotamia; Yellow River, China
4000 B.C.E.	*Shaduf* invented in Egypt
3000 B.C.E.	Menes unites Upper and Lower Egypt
2500 B.C.E.	Cities of Harappa and Mohenjodaro flourish; Sargon of Akkad conquers Sumer
2250–2000 B.C.E.	Ziggurat of Ur built
2000–1000 B.C.E.	Shang dynasty, China
1800 B.C.E.	*Epic of Gilgamesh* written down
1700 B.C.E.	Law code of Hammurabi

(All dates are approximate)

> *"The grandeur of the great river valley civilizations raises questions about their sustainability. Their wealth and productivity excited envy from outsiders and invited attack. Continued population growth demanded ever more intensive exploitation of the environment."*

Second, interactions matter. Societies learn from each other, compete with each other, and exchange culture with each other. The more societies are in touch with other societies, the more these activities occur. By contrast, isolation retards. Egypt was in touch with Mesopotamia and Mesopotamia with Harappa. China's relative isolation perhaps helps explain its late start in some of the common processes of change that these societies all experienced. All these societies enclosed, within their own bounds, relatively large zones of exchange. But all were remarkably self-contained. As we shall see in the next chapter, however, travel and trade were increasingly important. These were the means of communicating the cultures from the great river valleys to other regions, some of which were less environmentally fortunate. Invasions and migrations, too, were—and still are—effective forms of interaction because they shift many people around, and people carry their culture with them.

The grandeur of the great river valley civilizations raises questions about their sustainability. Their wealth and productivity excited envy from outsiders and invited attack. Continued population growth demanded ever more intensive exploitation of the environment. At the same time, climates and ecosystems continued to change. The vast collective efforts required for irrigation, storage, and monumental building left huge classes of people oppressed and resentful of elites. As a result of these and other stresses, beginning around 1500 B.C.E., transformation or collapse threatened all these societies. Meanwhile, peoples in less easily exploitable environments found the will and means to reproduce, challenge, or exceed the achievements of these four civilizations. The question of how well they succeeded is the focus of the next chapter.

Because they all made fairly extensive use of bronze, nineteenth-century archaeology—classifying societies according to their characteristic technology—called the era of the great river valley civilizations the Bronze Age. In the late second millennium B.C.E., the crises that afflicted them seemed to herald transition to an "Iron Age." Such labels no longer seem appropriate. Though there were bronze-using and iron-making societies, there was never an "age" of either. Some societies in Africa (see Chapter 5) never used bronze at all. Many societies never took up the use of iron. Where they did, they did not generally employ iron in ways that profoundly affected society—that is, to make tools and weapons—until well into the first millennium B.C.E. Although bronze making came to have an important place in the economies and art of many Eurasian peoples during the second millennium B.C.E., other societies achieved similar standards of material culture and developed comparable states without it. In any case, there are aspects of civilization—ways of thinking and feeling and behaving— more deeply influential than technology, "more lasting"—as a Roman poet said of his poems—"than bronze," and therefore more worthy of attention.

PROBLEMS AND PARALLELS

1. How did the distinctive ecological differences of the four river valleys affect their economic activity?
2. How did environmental transformations caused by humans (such as irrigation) affect the great river valley civilizations, both positively and negatively?
3. How did the role of leaders differ in the great river valleys? Why did Egypt have the most effective and long-lasting leadership structure? Why did Hatshepsut send an expedition to Punt?
4. What was the connection between religion and kingship in Egypt, Mesopotamia, and China? What is the evidence for these relationships?
5. How did rulers expand their states in China, Mesopotamia, the Indus valley, and Egypt? How did each area's environment affect this expansion?
6. What do the individual writing systems of China, Mesopotamia, the Indus valley, and Egypt tell us about each society's politics, religion, and economy?
7. Why are the ways a civilization thought, felt, and behaved not adequately conveyed by labels such as "Bronze Age"?

READ ON▶ ▶ ▶

R. L. Burger, *Chavín and the Origins of Andean Civilization* (1993) is an excellent introduction to the Peruvian material. H. Silverman, ed., *Andean Archaeology* (2004) contains some important recent research.

L. Nikolova, *The Balkans in Later Prehistory* (1999) is authoritative on the southeastern European sites. C. Renfrew, ed., *Problems in European Prehistory* (1979) includes some vital contributions. D. V. Clarke, *Skara Brae* (1983) is a useful pamphlet on those of the Orkneys. For the vexed question of the "rise" of "civilization" K. Wittfogel, *Oriental Despotism* (1967) is the now almost universally repudiated classic on the subject.

K. W. Butzer, *Early Hydraulic Civilization in Egypt* (1976) is a pioneering classic on the ecological dimensions. B. J. Kemp, *Ancient Egypt* (1989) is an excellent introduction.

G. Algaze, *The Uruk World System* (1993) is an important study of the origins of Mesopotamian civilization.

K. C. Chang, *Art, Myth and Ritual* (1983) and *Shang Civilization* (1980) are indispensable on China. E. L. Shaughnessy, *Sources of Western Zhou History* (1992) is immeasurably illuminating.

B. and R. Allchin, *The Rise of Civilization in India and Pakistan* (1982) is particularly useful for Harappa, on which the studies collected by G. Possehl, ed., *Harappan Civilization* (1993) are an important supplement.

CHAPTER 4

A Succession of Civilizations:
Ambition and Instability

▲ **Arrayed for war.** One measure of the influence of the Hittites is the durability of their art. This relief, from Carchemish in Phoenicia, dates from at least two centuries after the Hittite empire collapsed, but continues to reflect Hittite conventions and values. The winged sun was a symbol other regional empires adopted.

For a moment, the scribe thought the king was already dead. Called to the royal bedside to record the last words, he ruled a line under his notes.

They formed a grim, faltering record of an old man's incoherent regrets: his hatred of his treacherous sister—"a serpent" who "bellows like an ox"; the faithlessness of his adopted heir—"an abomination . . . without compassion"; the disloyalty of relatives "heedless of the word of the king. . . . No member of my family has obeyed me." The dying monarch railed against his daughter, too, whom rebels first kidnapped, then recruited. "She incited the whole land to rebellion." Rebels taunted him, "There is no son for your father's throne. A servant will sit on it. A servant will become king."

With his last bit of strength, Hattusili, the great king of the Hittites, ruler of the land of Hatti, south of the Black Sea, and of an empire that touched upper Mesopotamia and the Mediterranean, sought to keep a grasp on power from beyond the grave. With no suitable adult to succeed him, he decided that his infant grandson must be the next king. The administrators of the kingdom must protect the child and prepare him for manhood, reading to him every month his grandfather's testament, with its warnings against disloyalty in the realm and its exhortations to mercy, piety, and forgiveness.

Around the deathbed in the city of Kussara, in a room gleaming with lapis lazuli and gold, the assembled warriors and officials—"lords of the watch-towers," "supervisors of the messengers," "keepers of the storehouses"—contemplated an insecure future. But the king was not yet dead. He stirred, striving to speak. The scribe hastily picked up his stylus and, straining to catch the royal words, scratched hurried characters onto his clay tablet. A woman's name fell from the king's lips: Hastayar. Who was she? Wife or concubine, sorceress or daughter? No one now knows. But she was at the bedside, consulting with the old women who were the court's official prophetesses, even as the king's life ebbed. With Hattusili's last breath came these final words: "Is she even now interrogating the soothsayers? ... Do not forsake me. Interrogate me! I will give you words as a sign. Wash me well. Hold me to your breast. Keep me from the earth."

Hattusili dictated this deathbed testament—in about 1600 B.C.E. It is the most intimate and lively document to survive from its time, our only glimpse of a king with his guard down, disclosing his own personality. It also reveals the nature and problems of a state at this time: the all-importance of the person of a king, the sacred

FOCUS questions

Why were the Hittite, Cretan, and Mycenean states more fragile than the great river valley civilizations?

What fundamental problems to their survival did all large ancient civilizations face?

Why did Harappan civilization disappear?

What were the continuities between the Shang and the Zhou in China?

Where did the first states arise in the New World?

Why did Egypt survive when other ancient civilizations collapsed around 1000 B.C.E.?

nature of his word, the ill-defined rules of succession, the power and jealousies of military and administrative elites, an intelligence system that relied on soothsayers, and an atmosphere of danger and insecurity. In short, it was a political environment made to be volatile.

In the Hittite kingdom, we see the great themes of the second millennium B.C.E. First, features that characterized the great river valley civilizations of the previous chapter began to emerge in other environments. These features included intensive agriculture, densely distributed populations, stratified societies (with higher and lower classes), large cities, and states often seeking to build empires. Second, the number of complex states—those with large-scale systems to organize production, control distribution, and regulate life—rapidly increased. These new states also developed a great variety of political institutions and ways to structure society and organize economic activity. Finally, the accelerating pace of change claimed victims. By about 1000 B.C.E., war, natural disaster, environmental overexploitation, and social and political disintegration had strained or shattered most of the big states and civilizations that had emerged from the transition to agriculture.

Students of history often dislike this period, with its bewildering succession of empires and civilizations that rise and fall, sometimes with baffling speed. Textbook pages resemble a bad TV soap opera—crowded with action, empty of explanation, with too many characters and too few insights into their behavior. If we are to try to make sense of the millennium between 2000 and 1000 B.C.E., we need to understand the problems associated with accelerating change. This was a period of climacteric: an era of extended and critical change that extinguished some civilizations, changed others, and might have wiped all of them out. The question for this chapter, then, is, why were some ambitions in the world of around 3,000 years ago realized and others were not? What made the difference between success and failure for states and civilizations?

THE GROWTH OF TRADE

Hatti became a regional power through enrichment by trade. In the second millennium B.C.E., potential trading partners arose in nearby regions, as, for unknown reasons, the economic center of gravity in Mesopotamia gradually shifted upriver. Changes in the course of the Tigris and Euphrates rivers stranded formerly important cities. Accumulations of silt kept merchants offshore. Wars at the far end of the Persian Gulf and the disappearance of some of the great cities of the Indus valley probably disrupted commerce in the Arabian Sea and Persian Gulf. New opportunities, meanwhile, arose in the north as economic development created new markets, or expanded old ones, in Syria, the Iranian highlands, and Anatolia (see Map 4.1).

For instance, the archives of Ebla, an independent city-state in Syria, bear witness to its importance as a trading center, as well as to its cultural links with Mesopotamia. Its commerce was a state monopoly. Its merchants were ambassadors. A dozen foreign cities delivered gold, silver, copper, and textiles to its markets and treasury. Ebla was a center of textile production and metallurgy in gold, silver, and bronze. Not only was it a trading center, its fertile lands made it self-sufficient to overflowing. Its royal granary stored enough food for 18 million meals. The most complete surviving record of a tour of inspection of the state warehouses names 12 kinds of wheat, abundant wine and cooking oil, and more than 80,000 sheep. The city's manufactured products—ceramic seals, ivory figurines, metalwork—reached the courts of chiefs in central Anatolia.

With the shift of economic activity from Lower to Upper Mesopotamia and beyond, networks of traders spread to the east and north from growing upriver cities such as Ashur on the Tigris and Mari on the Euphrates. Thousands of documents—16,000 in Ebla, 17,000 in Mari—describe these traders, from wealthy private merchants underwritten by the state to stateless middlemen who served as deal makers. Trade is not just economic exchange. It also forges social obligations, establishes new relationships of power and legitimates old ones, and spreads culture. Some trade of the time was gift giving between palaces, carried by merchant-diplomats. The king of the city of Ugarit rewarded an official called Tamkaru for this kind of work with a grant of land in the mid-1200s B.C.E. On its new frontiers, trade generated unprecedented concentrations of wealth. Leaders who accumulated imported luxuries or who were tough enough to tax passing trade could reinvest in more goods or buy the allegiance of other chiefs. They might build palace centers like those of Mesopotamia and Egypt to redistribute goods.

Early in the second millennium B.C.E.—say, roughly 1800 B.C.E.—colonists from Ashur penetrated Anatolia and founded a new city at Kanes, 930 miles to the northwest. Thousands of clay tablets detail its imports of tin and textiles, its exports of gold and silver. Yet there was a human side of business then as now. The royal family of Ashur had a state farm at Sabi Abyad, which was also a frontier trading post on the routes to Anatolia and states along the eastern coast of the Mediterranean. Over 1,000 people lived there—migrants from Ashur, exiled foreigners, prisoners of war. The steward, permanently frustrated by impractical orders, frustrated the king in turn, who wrote: "What is this, that whatever I tell you, you fail to do as I say?" The supply of beer and tableware to entertain passing embassies provoked many quarrels. So did the problems of enforcing tolls on luxuries. The king berated the steward:

> Formerly I ordered you, "Caravans that come to me from Carchemish must not pass without your leave and you must stamp all goods with your seal." Now I have heard that caravans are on their way and I repeat: any caravan that comes my way, whether it belongs to [the governor] or princesses or nobles, every one must be sealed. I have also heard that they carry balsam. If any is missing, you will be executed.

Anitta, king of Kanes, early in the second millennium had "a throne of iron and a sceptre of iron." This is a revealing remark because iron was new, originating in this region but still rare. Soft iron, smelted at a temperature only slightly higher than that required for copper, was useless for weapons and plows. The technique of combining it with carbon to make it hard was difficult at the time and too unreliable to persuade investors to develop the technology. But the appearance of iron pointed to a future more durable than bronze, which remained the metal of choice for weapons and agricultural tools. One of the towns Anitta saw as a rival was Kussara, the hometown of the dynasty that later founded the kingdom of Hatti. According to one of his inscriptions, he demolished the place, sowed it with salt, and cursed it, so that it might never arise again. The curse failed. His example, however, inspired the Hittites and showed them how trade and conquest could build a state.

Ebla's palace walls in the mid-third millennium B.C.E. were 40 or 50 feet high. The ceremonial court in the foreground was 165 feet long. The holes show where pillars supported the roof. Akkadian invaders destroyed the palace around 2300 B.C.E., but left intact the precious archives that recorded the range of trade with Mesopotamia, Anatolia, and Egypt.

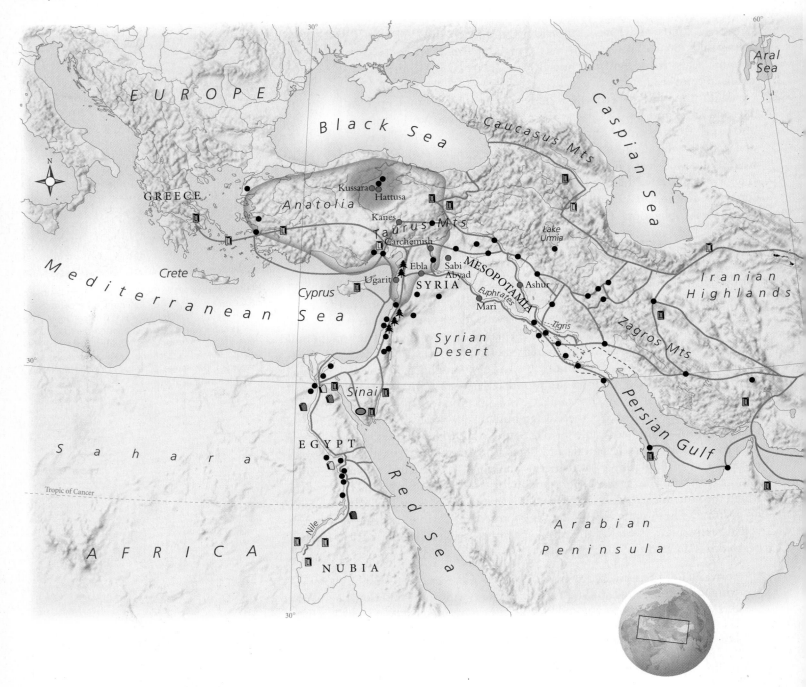

The Rise of the Hittites

Compared with the vast alluvial plains we discussed in the last chapter, the Anatolian plateau in what is today Turkey, where Hattusili's kingdom took shape, seems an unlikely place to found a large state. It had its patches of alluvium where small but spectacular towns like Çatalhüyük had flourished around 8000 to 7000 B.C.E., in a more favorable climate (see Chapter 2). But the environment had grown warmer and drier since then. Çatalhüyük's river had shifted and shrunk. By 2000 B.C.E., most of the plateau suffered alternating seasonal extremes that scorched and froze crops. Rainfall was, and still is, less than 20 inches a year. (The temperate

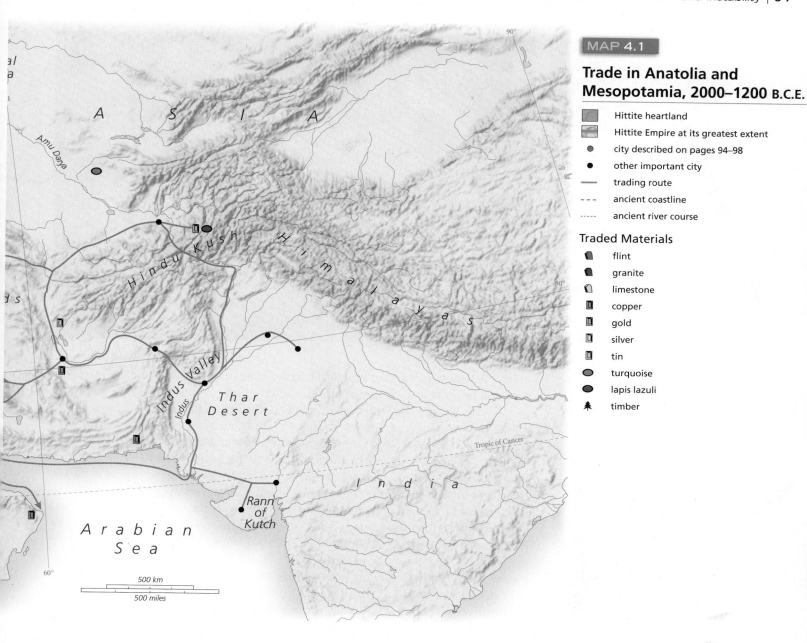

MAP 4.1

Trade in Anatolia and Mesopotamia, 2000–1200 B.C.E.

- Hittite heartland
- Hittite Empire at its greatest extent
- ● city described on pages 94–98
- ● other important city
- ── trading route
- - - - ancient coastline
- ----- ancient river course

Traded Materials

- flint
- granite
- limestone
- copper
- gold
- silver
- tin
- turquoise
- lapis lazuli
- timber

zones of Western Europe and North America receive two or three times more rain than that.) Desert tracts stretched between cultivatable patches.

Yet from the central part of this region, between about 1800 and 1500 B.C.E., the people who called themselves children of Hatti—Hittites—drew thousands of such patches and millions of people into a single network of production and distribution, under a common allegiance. They went on to build a state we can fairly call an empire. It had palace complexes, storehouses, towns, and—to take the example that the Hittites themselves would probably put at the top of the list—armies. All were comparable in scale with those of the river valley peoples of the last chapter. Egyptian pharaohs treated Hittite kings as equals. When one pharaoh died without

Hattusa. The site of the Hittite kings' palace-city of Hattusa near the modern city of Bogazkale in the heart of Turkish Anatolia. The citadel is visible toward the top of the picture, a temple, distinguished by its large courtyard, is to the left, and the remains of a monumental gate are on the right.

heirs, his widow sent to the king of Hatti for "one of your sons to be my husband, for I will never take a servant of mine and make him my husband."

We can picture the Hittites with the help of images they have left us of themselves: hook-nosed, short-headed, and—more often than not—arrayed for war. But how did their state and empire happen in such a hostile environment?

The strength of the Hittite kingdom was that it brought farmers and herders into a single state and economic system. This was how to make the most of the rugged Anatolian environment, with its small concentrations of cultivatable soil surrounded by marginal grazing land. The wool production of specialized herders combined with the food production of small farmers. Such mixed farming by independent peasants—not bonded or enslaved workers or wage earners—was of the highest importance. Livestock produce fertilizer, which can raise (or sustain) productivity and feed growing populations. Milk-rich diets, moreover, can provide the calories and nutrients that improve human fertility. Overall, the consequences are positive: more opportunity for economic specialization, urbanization, and the mobilization of manpower for war.

The surviving inventory of the estate of a typical Hittite peasant, Tiwapatara, lists one house for his family of five, three dozen head of livestock, one acre of pasture, and three and a half acres of vineyard, with 42 pomegranate and 40 apple trees. The pasture must have been for his eight precious oxen. His goats, hardier animals, presumably foraged where they could. Farmers like Tiwapatara were the manpower that, for a time, made Hatti invincible. Children such as his worked the farms during military campaigns, which usually coincided with sowing and harvest. He and his kind were willing, presumably, to support the state, which in turn protected them, for Hittite law laid down harsh penalties for theft or trespassing on private property. We do not know the total productivity of the economy, but a single-grain silo excavated in the major city, Hattusa, held enough grain for 32,000 people for a year.

Hatti developed its own political system, perhaps with some borrowings from Mesopotamia and Egypt. The king was the sun god's earthly deputy. Subjects called him "My sun," as modern monarchs are called "Your Majesty." His responsibilities were war, justice, and relations with the gods. Hardly any case at law was too trivial to be referred to the king, although, in practice, professional clerks dealt with most of them on his behalf. A vast household surrounded him: "the Palace servants, the Bodyguard, the Men of the Golden Spear, the Cupbearers, the Table-men, the Cooks, the Heralds, the Stable boys, the Captains of the Thousand." It was a bureaucratic court, where writing perpetuated the king's commands and conveyed them to subordinates, commanders, viceroys, and subject kings. The court was vast, too, because it had to house a huge harem. Royal concubines were rivets of the kingdom. The size and origins of the ruler's harem reflected his political reach. Moreover, he had to engender many daughters to contribute to the harems of allies and tributaries.

To judge from surviving law codes, Hittites observed many apparently arbitrary sexual taboos. Intercourse with pigs or sheep was punishable by death, but not cases involving horses or mules. Hittites evidently measured the civilization of other societies by the severity of their incest laws. Their own code forbade intercourse between siblings or cousins. Any sexual act, however, was polluting in some degree and had to be cleansed by bathing before prayer. If we knew more about Hittite religion, we might understand their morality better. Strong sexual taboos are usually found in "dualist" religions, alongside belief in the eternal struggle of forces of good and evil or spirit and matter. Hittite attitudes toward sex contrast with those in Mesopotamia, where—in what seems to have been a more typical pattern—sex was in some sense sacred, and temples employed prostitutes.

In some ways, Hatti was a man's world, with the masculine attitudes and values typical of a war state. The oath army officers took indicates this:

> Do you see here a woman's garments? We have them for the oath. Whoever breaks these oaths and does the king harm, let the oaths change him from a man to a woman! Let them change his soldiers into women, and let them dress in the fashion of women and cover their heads with a length of cloth! Let them break the bows, arrows and clubs in their hands and let them take up instead the distaff and the looking-glass!

Women, however, exercised power. Old women acted as diviners at court. Others, lower down the social scale, were curers, waving sacrificial piglets over the victims of curses, with the cry, "Just as this pig shall not see the sky nor the other piglets again, so let the curse not see the sacrificers!"

Fragility and Fall: The End of Hatti

The Hittite state was formidable in war. It had to be. Its domestic economy was fragile and its homeland poor in key resources. It needed to grow. Conquests were, in extreme circumstances, the only way to guarantee supplies of food for an increasing population and of tin to make bronze weapons. But even successful conflicts can weaken a state by overextending its power and disrupting its trade. In other words, growth is paradoxical. For many states, it is both a means of survival and an obstacle to survival. It butts against immovable limits. In Hatti's case, those limits were the frontiers of Egypt and Mesopotamia.

The Hittite kingdom suffered from other weaknesses. As with all communities that made the transition to agriculture, it was vulnerable to famine and disease. Around 1300 B.C.E., King Mursili II reproached the gods for a plague: "Now no one reaps or sows your fields, for all are dead! The mill-women who used to make the bread of the gods are dead!" A couple of generations later, there was reputedly "no grain in Hatti," when Puduhepa—a formidable royal spouse—wrote to Egypt demanding some as part

"But even successful conflicts can weaken a state by overextending its power and disrupting its trade. In other words, growth is paradoxical. For many states, it is both a means of survival and an obstacle to survival."

Chronology: The Hittites	
1800–1500 B.C.E.	Hatti develops into an empire
1800 B.C.E.	City of Kanes founded
1800 B.C.E.	Iron in use
1300 B.C.E.	Plague strikes Hatti
1210 B.C.E.	Last recorded mention of Hatti
(All dates are approximate)	

of the dowry of her daughter. For one of the last Hittite kings, Tudhaliya IV, an order not to detain a grain ship bound for his country was "a matter of life and death." Nomadic prowlers from the hinterlands were another common hazard. People the Hittites called *Kaska* invaded repeatedly to grab booty or extort protection. On at least one of their raids, they robbed the royal court.

In the late 1300s B.C.E., the Hittite state was in obvious decline. Hatti lost southern provinces and (by Tudhaliya's own admission in a letter scolding a negligent subordinate) at least one major battle to an expanding kingdom in Upper Mesopotamia. The oaths the king demanded from his subordinates have an air of desperation: "if nobody is left to yoke the horses and the king has not even one house in which to enter, you must show even more support. . . . If . . . the chariot-driver jumps down from the chariot, and the valet flees the chamber, and not even a dog is left, and if I do not even find an arrow to shoot against the enemy, your support for your king must be all the greater." Among the last documents the court issued are complaints that formerly subject kings were neglecting tribute or diplomatic courtesies. After 1210 B.C.E., the Hittite kingdom simply disappeared from the record.

INSTABILITY AND COLLAPSE IN THE AEGEAN

The Hittite story sums up the problems of global history in the second millennium B.C.E. It demonstrates how agrarian communities consolidated as states, expanded as empires, and—typically—failed to survive past 1000 B.C.E.

The civilization scholars call Minoan or Cretan, for instance, took shape in the second millennium on the large Mediterranean island of Crete, which lies between what are now Greece and Turkey (see Map 4.2). Nearby in the southern Peloponnese, the peninsula that forms the southern part of Greece, the civilization we call Mycenean emerged. Both have inspired Western imaginations. Europeans and Americans view Crete and Mycenae as part of their history, assuming that they can trace the civilization of classical Greece—and therefore of the Western world—to these glamorous, spendthrift cultures of 3,500 years ago. That now seems a doubtful assumption. By the time Plato and Aristotle formulated classical Greek philosophy in the fourth century B.C.E., the last cities of Mycenae had been ruins for 1,000 years. Crete and Mycenae were subjects of myth—civilizations almost as mysterious to the Greeks as they are to us, and almost as remote. Still, they are worth studying for their own sake and the light they cast on their times.

Knossos. Aquatic subjects abound in paintings on the palace walls of Knossos, Crete, from the mid-second millennium B.C.E. Dolphins were favored as food for elite feasts. The palace—at once an elite dwelling and a storehouse and distribution center for food—was rebuilt many times between destructions by earthquakes and, perhaps, invasions.

Cretan Civilization

Crete is 3,200 square miles, big enough to be self-sustaining, but mountains cover two-thirds of it, leaving little land to cultivate. To modern mainland Greeks, it is an impossible island, a land of devastating droughts and earthquakes. But to anyone looking today at the wall paintings from around 2000 B.C.E., when the first palace-storehouses arose there, ancient Crete seems a paradise of plenty. Fields of grain and vines; orchards of olives, almonds, and quince; forests of honey and venison, surround gardens of lilies and iris, gladioli and crocuses. The seas teem with dolphin and octopus, under skies where partridges and brightly colored birds fly.

This lavish world was painfully carved from a tough environment, harsh soil, and dangerous seas. And it depended on two

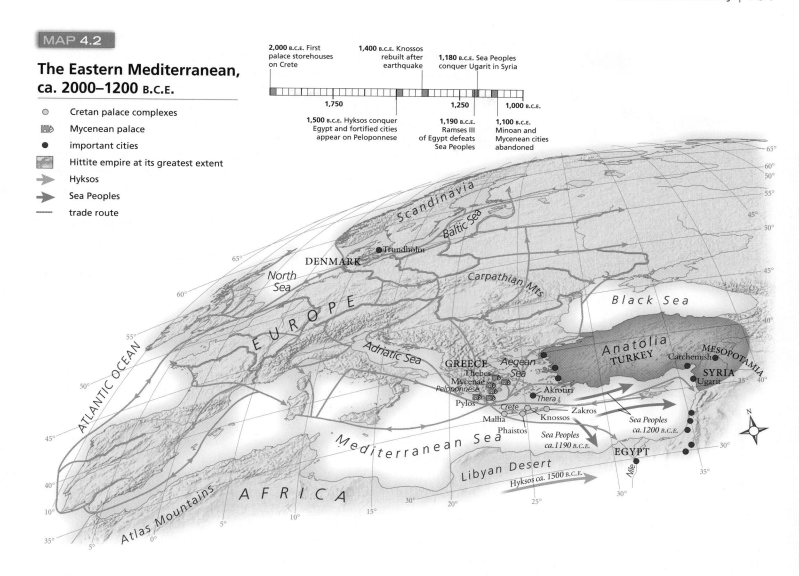

MAP 4.2

The Eastern Mediterranean, ca. 2000–1200 B.C.E.

○ Cretan palace complexes

🏛 Mycenean palace

● important cities

▨ Hittite empire at its greatest extent

➤ Hyksos

➤ Sea Peoples

— trade route

2,000 B.C.E. First palace storehouses on Crete

1,400 B.C.E. Knossos rebuilt after earthquake

1,180 B.C.E. Sea Peoples conquer Ugarit in Syria

1,750

1,250

1,000 B.C.E.

1,500 B.C.E. Hyksos conquer Egypt and fortified cities appear on Peloponnese

1,190 B.C.E. Ramses III of Egypt defeats Sea Peoples

1,100 B.C.E. Minoan and Mycenean cities abandoned

despotic methods to control an unpredictable food supply: organized agriculture, embracing, as in Hatti, both farming and herding, and state-regulated trade. The function of the palace as storehouse was a vital part of how the system worked. The greatest palace complex on the island, Knossos, covers more than 40,000 square feet. When it lay in ruins, visitors from Greece who saw its galleries and corridors imagined an enormous maze, built to house a monster who fed on human sacrifices. In fact, the labyrinth was an immense storage area for clay jars, 12 feet high, filled with wine, cooking oil, and grain, some still in place. The wool of 80,000 sheep was collected here.

Stone chests, lined with lead to protect the foodstuffs they contained, were like strongboxes in a central bank waiting to be distributed or traded. The Cretans were such skilled sailors that the Greeks said Cretan ships knew their own way through the water. Trade brought exotic luxuries to the elites. Ivory tusks and ostrich eggs can still be found at another palace complex at Zakros. Palace walls depict blue baboons from Egypt. Craft workshops inside the palaces added value to imports by spinning and weaving fine garments, delicately painting stone jars, and hammering gold and bronze into jewels and chariots. Palace records suggest a staff of 4,300 people.

Yet Knossos and buildings like it were also genuine palaces—dwellings of an elite who lived in luxury. Majestic stairwells rose to the noble floors, supported on squat columns with tops like fat pumpkins. These pillars, and those supporting the principal chambers, were lacquered red, and the wall paintings glowed with a wonderful sky blue—scenes of feasting, gossiping, playing, and bull leaping. At Zakros, a site that was never plundered, you can see marble-veined chalices, stone storage jars, and a box of cosmetic ointment with an elegant little handle in the form of a reclining greyhound. To judge from the frequency with which women occur in the wall paintings, they were active all over the palace complexes, as priestesses, scribes, artisans, and revellers in the dangerous, demanding game of bull-leaping, somersaulting between the horns of fighting bulls.

Lesser dwellings, grouped in towns, were tiny imitations of the palace. Many had columns, balconies, and upper-storey galleries. In the houses of more prosperous inhabitants, colorful pottery that was as thin as porcelain, elaborate stone vases ground into seductively sinuous shapes, and elaborately painted groundstone baths survive in large numbers. Yet at lower levels of society there was little surplus for luxury or time for leisure. Few people lived beyond their early 40s. If the purpose of the state was to recycle food, its efficiency was limited. Skeletons show that the common people lived near the edge of malnutrition.

The cities' environment was potentially destructive and, in combination with war, doomed the cities to eventual abandonment and the palaces to ruin. On the nearby island of Thera, which a volcanic eruption blew apart around 1500 B.C.E., the lavish city of Akrotiri was buried under layers of ash and rock. Knossos and similar palaces along the coasts of Crete at Phaistos, Mallia, and Zakros were all rebuilt once or twice on an increasingly generous scale, after unknown causes, possibly earthquakes, destroyed them.

The way the palaces were reconstructed suggests there was another hazard—internal warfare. Fortifications began to appear. Some of the elite from the eastern and southern ends of the island apparently moved to villas near Knossos about the time the palaces were rebuilt. There may have been a political takeover. At the time of the last rebuilding of Knossos, generally dated around 1400 B.C.E., a major change in culture occurred. The archives began to be written in an early form of Greek. As a result, we can now read them. The language previously in use is unknown, and its records are undecipherable. By this time, the fate of Crete seems to have become closely entangled with another Aegean civilization—the Mycenean.

Crystal vase. Under the elite apartments, Cretan palaces contained workshops where craftsmen made luxuries for elite consumption and for export, such as this crystal vase, about 3,500 years old, from the palace of Zakros, and the unguents and perfumes that vessels like these contained.

A Sun Chariot from Trundholm. The Trundholm bog in Denmark has preserved many objects and the remains of humans who were sacrificed in antiquity. The most elaborate find is a bronze and gold model of the sun, made in the mid-second millennium B.C.E. The use of precious bronze and gold to represent the sun suggests the veneration that the source of warmth and light attracted in cold, dark northern Europe. The bronze horse, modeled around a clay core, is mounted on bronze wheels, which suggests that the object was designed for use in religious rituals or astronomical demonstrations.

Mycenean Civilization

The fortified cities and gold-rich royal tombs of the Mycenean civilization began to appear in the 1500s B.C.E. States in the region already had kings who made war and hunted lions, shortly before these creatures became extinct in Europe. The kings' courts were centered in palace-storehouses like those of Crete. At Pylos, one of the largest Mycenean palaces, clay tablets list the vital and tiresome routines of numerous palace officials: levying taxes, checking that the landowner class observed its social obligations, mobilizing resources for public works, and gathering raw materials for manufacture and trade. In the palace of Pylos, workshops turned out bronzeware and perfumed oils for export to Egypt and the Hittite empire. The similarities with Cretan precedents are obvious. Women, however, seem to have been treated differently in Mycenae. Whereas Cretan art depicts women in public roles, Mycenean artists usually showed women in domestic roles, with their children close at hand.

The walls of Mycenae in southern Greece, built over 3,000 years ago, when warlike city-states arose in this region of modest agricultural productivity, apparently on the profits of the manufacture and export of luxuries for markets in Egypt and Anatolia. In the second half of the second millennium B.C.E., the language of Mycenae replaced that of Crete in official Cretan records, suggesting a change in political mastery.

Mycenean traders reached across northern Europe as far as Scandinavia (see Map 4.2). Unlike the minutely recorded trade transactions that helped spread civilization north from Mesopotamia, this commerce was not documented. Yet we know that eastern Mediterranean elites craved Baltic amber for glowing jewels. Scandinavia lacked tin for bronze making, which meant its craftsmen had to try to imitate Mediterranean dagger designs in flint. Trade changed Scandinavian society. The evidence was laid in graves, carved on rocks, and, above all, preserved in peat bogs. The most abundant of these natural archives are the bogs at Trundholm in Denmark, which mercilessly preserved corpses, some still with their hats on and their faces composed or contorted in death. The elite emerge from the peat, as they appear in engravings on the rocks in their tasseled garments and horned helmets. They had a taste for serpentine lines, displayed in the curving prows of engraved ships that curl like antlers, and sinuous bronze trumpets.

The volume of trade with Scandinavia was too small or perhaps too remote from state control to be included in Mycenean records. The essential duty of the palace bureaucrats was to equip their rulers for almost constant warfare. Unlike Cretan sites, the mainland palaces were heavily and cleverly fortified. As well as fighting each other, the kingdoms felt the threat of the barbarian hinterland, which may, in the end, have overwhelmed them. Paintings on the walls of Pylos show warriors, in the boar's-head helmets also worn on Crete and Thera, in battle with skin-clad savages.

Stunned by earthquakes, strained by wars, Mycenean cities followed those of Crete into abandonment by 1100 B.C.E. What is surprising is not, perhaps, that they should ultimately have perished, but that their fragile economies, sustained by elaborate and expensive methods of collecting, storing, and redistributing food, should have managed to feed the cities and support the elite culture for so long.

A GENERAL CRISIS IN THE EASTERN MEDITERRANEAN WORLD?

Although we could explain the extinction of Crete, Mycenae, and Hatti in terms of local political failures or ecological disasters, it is tempting to try to relate them to a general crisis in the eastern Mediterranean. For not only was the

Chronology: Crete and Mycenae	
2000 B.C.E.	First palace-storehouses on Crete
1500 B.C.E.	Fortified cities appear on the Peloponnese (Greece)
1400 B.C.E.	Knossos (Crete) rebuilt after earthquake; early Greek language used at Knossos
1100 B.C.E.	Cretan (Minoan) and Mycenaean cities abandoned
(All dates are approximate)	

Sea Peoples. "Now the northern peoples in their isles were quivering in their bodies," says the inscription that accompanies a ship-borne battle-scene of the reign of Ramses III. "They penetrated the channels of the mouths of the Nile. ... They are capsized and overwhelmed where they stand. ... Their weapons are scattered on the sea." Pharaohs' propaganda tended to lie or exaggerate, but the "Sea Peoples" really existed, and Egypt really escaped conquest or colonization by them.

grandeur of the Aegean civilizations blotted out and the Hittite empire of Anatolia overwhelmed, but nearby states also reported fatal or near-fatal convulsions. The Egyptians almost succumbed to unidentified **Sea Peoples**, who exterminated many states and cities in the region. Meanwhile, in Upper Mesopotamia, an anguished king of Ashur prayed to Assur, the city's god, "Darkness without sunshine awaits the evildoers who stretch out threatening hands to scatter the armies of Assur. Wickedly, they conspire against their benefactor."

The Egyptian Experience

Egypt had survived invasion before the Sea Peoples. Perhaps toward 1500 B.C.E., the Hyksos arrived, sweating from the Libyan Desert, to overwhelm the land and commission carvings of a sphinx seizing an Egyptian by the ears. Like so many nomadic conquerors of sedentary cultures around the world, the Hyksos adopted Egyptian culture and became Egyptianized before the natives expelled them. For their part, Egyptians considered all foreigners barbarians and viewed them with contempt.

But the narrowness of the Black Land, as the inhabitants called the fertile Nile valley, was a cause of unease, and Egyptians alternated between arrogance and insecurity. On the one hand, desert and sea gave protection against barbarian attack. Egypt was flanked by almost uninhabitable spaces, difficult to cross, whereas civilizations like those of Mesopotamia and Harappa with more attractive environments at their frontiers were under constant threat from marauders and invaders. On the other hand, sea and desert were the realm of Seth, the god of chaos who threatened to overwhelm the cosmic order of life along the Nile.

Exposure to invasion continued. The descent of the Sea Peoples—about 1190 B.C.E.—is well documented because the pharaoh who defeated them, Ramses III, devoted a long inscription to his achievement. It is glaring propaganda, a celebration of the pharaoh's power and preparation: "Barbarians," it says vaguely, "conspired in their islands. . . . No land could withstand their arms." A list of victims follows, including Hatti and a string of cities in southern Anatolia and along the eastern Mediterranean. "They were heading for Egypt, while we prepared flame before them. . . . They laid their hands on the land as far as the edges of the Earth, their hearts confident and trusting, 'We will succeed!'" The Nile delta, however, "made like a strong wall with warships. . . . I was the valiant war-god, standing fast at their head. Those who came forward together on the sea, the full flame was in front of them at the river mouths, while a stockade of lances surrounded them on the shore. They were dragged in, enclosed, and prostrated on the beach, killed and made into heaps."

The Roots of Instability

Yet even after unpicking the propaganda, we can be confident that the pharaoh's boasts reflect real events. Other documents confirm the existence of the Sea Peoples. For example, when the city of Ugarit in Syria fell, probably early in the twelfth century B.C.E., never to be reoccupied, messages begging for seaborne reinforcements were left unfinished. The reply from the governor of Carchemish (KAHR-keh-mihsh], an inland trading center on the way to Hatti and Mesopotamia, was typical—too little, too late: "as for what you have written me,

'Ships of the enemy have been seen at sea.' Well, you must remain firm. ... Surround your towns with ramparts. Have your troops and chariots enter there, and await the enemy with great resolution."

The image of a general crisis brought about by barbarian invasions has had an almost irresistible romantic appeal for Western historians influenced by a familiar episode of their own past: the decline and fall of the Roman Empire. A general crisis also fits with a popular conception of the past as a battlefield of barbarism versus civilization. However, such an idea is, at best, a gross oversimplification because both barbarism and civilization are relative, subjective terms. In any case, the difference between barbarism and civilization that became glaring in a later age was by no means always apparent to people at the time. Cultural divergence was in its infancy, and cultural gaps seemed bridgeable. As we have seen, the gap between herders and tillers was closed, and combined wool and grain production became the economic base for Hatti, Crete, and other societies that had limited farming land. Furthermore, there is no evidence, as some historians claim, that barbarian invaders enjoyed a technological advantage because they had iron weapons or a tactical advantage because they used massed infantry against chariots.

We can best understand the violent arrival of the Sea Peoples as a symptom of a broader phenomenon of the period: the widespread instability of populations driven by hunger and land shortages. Egyptian carvings show desperate migrations, would-be invaders with ox carts full of women and children. From Mesopotamia and Anatolia comes evidence of savage marauders in the late thirteenth century B.C.E. But migrants probably did not cause the decline of the states they ravaged. Rather, they were among the consequences of that decline. Environmental and economic historians have scoured the evidence for some sign of a deeper trauma, such as earthquakes or droughts or commercial failures that might explain grain shortages and disrupted trade. But they have found nothing of the sort at the time of the migrants' invasions.

The causes of the crisis lay in the common structural problems of the states that faltered or failed, namely, their ecological fragility and unstable, competitive politics. In this respect, the crisis was even more general, not just confined to the civilizations around the eastern Mediterranean where the Sea Peoples roamed. If we turn to trace the fate of communities elsewhere in Asia, and even to some examples in the New World, we can detect similar strains and comparable effects.

Chronology: Instability in the Eastern Mediterranean	
1500 B.C.E.	Hyksos conquer Egypt
1200 B.C.E.	Sea Peoples attack Mesopotamia and Anatolia
1190 B.C.E.	Ramses III defeats Sea Peoples
1180 B.C.E.	Sea Peoples conquer Ugarit in Syria
(All dates are approximate)	

"We can best understand the violent arrival of the Sea Peoples as a symptom of a broader phenomenon of the period: the widespread instability of populations driven by hunger and land shortages."

THE EXTINCTION OF HARAPPAN CIVILIZATION

In the Indus valley, city life and intensive agriculture were in danger of collapse even when they were at their most productive. Many sites were occupied only for a few centuries. Some sites were abandoned by about 1800 B.C.E., and by 1000 B.C.E., all had dwindled to ruins. Meanwhile, in Turkmenia, on the northern flank of the Iranian plateau, relatively young but flourishing fortified settlements on the Oxus River, such as Namazga and Altin, shrank to the size of villages. We know little about these places, and what brought about their end—or Harappan's—has provoked furious debate among scholars. Some believe in a sudden and violent invasion, while others think the end was the result of a gradual ecological disaster.

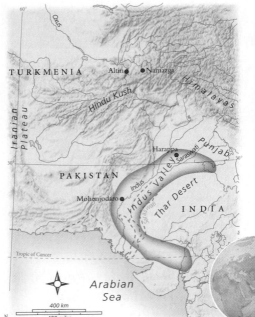

MAP 4.3

The Decline of Harappan Civilization

- ● place described on pages 105–107
- INDIA modern country
- - - - ancient coastline / river course
- *Saraswati* ancient river
- center of late Harappan civilization

The Evidence of the Rig Veda

Evidence for the theory that invaders destroyed Harappan civilization comes from a collection of hymns and poems called the ***Rig Veda***. The people who created this literature of destruction were a sedentary people living in what is now the Punjab, the area north of the Indus valley where India and Pakistan meet. They had probably been living there from about 1500 B.C.E. They were not newcomers or nomads. When poets wrote down the *Rig Veda*, some time around 800 B.C.E., after centuries of oral transmission, it still had the power to carry hearers and readers back to a lost age of heroes. The people of the Rig Veda spoke an Indo-European language—one of a group of languages prevalent over most of Europe and much of Southwest and South Asia today (see Figure 4.1). Scholars used therefore to suppose that their rampages in India were part of a vast pattern of violent migrations of the so-called Aryans—speakers of a single original language from which the entire Indo-European family of languages derives. But languages are spread by many means—including trade, missionary activity, and cultural exchange. There is no archaeological or DNA evidence that a single Indo-European people ever existed, nor any serious archaeological trace of the alleged migrations, though some archaeologists have argued that the spread of other forms of culture—such as farming and metallurgy—may be connected with the spread of the languages. In the present state of the evidence, it is pointless to speak of Aryans and hazardous to speak of Indo-European migrations. The people of the Rig Veda are best understood in their own terms.

Their hymns tell of a people who wanted a world of fat and opulence, basted with butter, flowing with milk, dripping with honey. Their strength in horses and chariots is not incompatible with a settled way of life. Elites of many essentially sedentary peoples have relied on horses in warfare. They valued boasting and drinking. Their rites of fire included burning down their enemies' dwellings. Their favorite god, Indra, was a "breaker of cities," but this was part of his generally destructive role, which included mountain smashing and serpent crushing.

Can these people have sacked the cities of the Indus and left corpses in Mohenjodaro buried in ash? Some of the cities seem already to have been in ruins when

Language Family	Modern Descendants
Indo-Iranian	Sanskrit, Hindi, Bengali, Persian, Urdu, Gujarati
Hellenic	Greek
Armenian	Western Armenian, Eastern Armenian
Balto-Slavic	Russian, Polish, Czech, Lithuanian, Serbo-Croatian
Illiryan	Albanian
Celtic	Irish-Gaelic, Welsh
Italic	Latin, Spanish, Italian, French, Romanian, Catalan, Portuguese
Germanic	German, English, Danish, Dutch, Swedish, Norwegian, Icelandic, Flemish, Afrikaans
Anatolian (extinct)	
Tocharian (extinct)	

FIGURE 4.1 INDO-EUROPEAN LANGUAGES

the *Rig Veda* poets beheld them. It would be surprising if invaders or rebels or neighbors or some combination of the three had not attacked these cities at some point in their history. But excavators who claimed that they could read such traumatic events at Mohenjodaro, in the bones of massacre victims and scorch marks on the walls, seem to have been wrong. Few of the supposed massacre victims have any wounds. Instead of a single violent event, the more likely explanation speaks of a gradual decline—a climacteric, a point at which Harappan civilization collapsed, and its cities were abandoned (see Map 4.3).

The Environment of Stress

The climate was getting drier in the Indus valley, and earthquakes may have shifted riverbeds. Unlike the crisis in the eastern Mediterranean, events in the Indus valley seem to fit with the chronology of environmental disaster. The Saraswati River, along which settlements were once densely clustered, disappeared into the advancing Thar Desert. Yet not even the loss of a river adequately explains the abandonment of the cities. The Indus River is still disgorging its wonderful silt, year by year, over vast, shining fields, which would have been sufficient to maintain the urban populations. Presumably, something happened to the food supply that was connected with the drying climate or human mismanagement of environmental resources—the cattle and other products that supplemented the wheat and barley of the fields.

In addition—or instead—the inhabitants apparently fled from some plague more deadly than the malaria that anthropologists have detected in buried bones. In an environment where irrigation demands standing water, mosquitos can breed. Malaria is inevitable. The people left, "expelled by the fire-god," as the *Rig Veda* says, and "migrated to a new land." This is probably an exaggeration. People stayed on or squatted in the decaying cities, inhabiting the ruins for generations. But the fall of Harappan civilization remains the most dramatic case of large-scale failure in the second millennium B.C.E. In broad terms, Harappa suffered essentially the same fate as the Hittite and eastern Mediterranean civilizations: The food distribution system outran the resource base. And when networks of power began to break down, invaders broke in.

The walled mounds of Mohenjodaro, a Harappan city abandoned in the late second millennium B.C.E. The walls were a defense against floods, not invaders. None of the "massacre victims" identified by archaeologists in the 1940s died by violence. Rather, a slow decline of population, a gradual impoverishment of material culture, and a relentless increase in disease set in as the river Saraswati dried up.

CONFLICT ON THE YELLOW RIVER

China experienced different problems toward the end of the second millennium B.C.E. from those of Egypt or Harappan. China suffered no large-scale population loss, no wholesale abandonment of regions, or wreck of cities. Nonetheless, what the Chinese of the period experienced was in some ways similar to other peoples in what looks increasingly like a global pattern.

The basis of the Shang state had always been shaky. War, rituals, and oracles are all gamblers' means of power, vulnerable to the lurches of luck. Manipulating the weather, the rains, the harvests, for instance, was a big part of the king's job, but in reality, of course, it was not one he could accomplish. Failure was built into his job description. It was a common problem for monarchs of the time, exposing pharaohs to blame for natural disasters, driving Hittite kings to depend on soothsayers.

Chronology: The Collapse of Harappan Civilization	
1800 B.C.E.	Some Harappan cities abandoned
1000 B.C.E.	All Harappan cities in ruins
800 B.C.E.	*Rig Veda* written down
(All dates are approximate)	

Bronze drum. This intricate geometric design on the face of a Vietnamese drum shows a sunburst at the center. Rulers often displayed these impressive bronze drums as emblems of their royal status.

The late Shang state was shrinking. Beginning about 1100 B.C.E., the names of subject, tribute-paying, and allied states gradually vanish from the oracle bones. The king's hunting grounds grew smaller. The king took on greater personal responsibility, becoming the sole diviner and army general, as the numbers of courtiers and commanders at his disposal fell. Former allies became enemies.

Meanwhile, just as Mesopotamian culture had been exported to Anatolia and Cretan ways of life to Mycenae, so Shang culture was exported beyond the Shang state, and its effects were becoming obvious. For one, new chiefdoms were developing in less favorable environments under the influence of trade. As far away as northern Vietnam and Thailand, bronze-making techniques similar to those of China, appeared at the courts of chiefs who delighted in personal ornaments, spittoons, and, in Vietnam, heavily decorated drums. More ominously and closer to home, right on the Shang border, a state arose in imitation and, increasingly, in rivalry: Zhou (jaow).

The Rise of Zhou

The earliest Zhou sites—of the 1100s B.C.E.—are burials in the Liang (lee-ahng) Mountains above the Wei (way) River in western China. This was probably not the Zhou heartland, but the area they had migrated to from grazing country farther to the north. Their own legends recalled time spent "living among the barbarians." Muye (moo-yeh)—the name of the battlefield where they reportedly overthrew the Shang—means "Shepherd's Wild." The Zhou were highland herders, an upland, upriver menace to the Shang just as Akkad was to Sumer in Mesopotamia (see Map 4.4).

Except for the material culture visible in their graves, we know nothing of the Zhou before they attacked and conquered the Shang—not their origin, or their economic or political systems, or even their language. We know them after they had fallen under the Shang's spell, imitating Shang culture and, presumably, envying its wealth. They had also learned the Shang's most accomplished art: bronze casting.

According to the chronicles, Shang-style turtleshell oracles had inspired the Zhou to conquest, and later Zhou rulers upheld that tradition. Chronicles composed in the third century B.C.E. tell the same story as texts hundreds of years older. If they can be believed, the Zhou "captured"—as they put it—the Shang state in a single battle in 1045 B.C.E. at Muye. They annexed it as a kind of colony and established garrisons all along the lower Yellow River to the coast. Archaeological evidence shows that they shifted the center of the empire north, to the hilly Shaanxi region, west of where the Yellow River turns toward the sea.

The Zhou Political System

Inscriptions on bronze loving cups are the only contemporary written sources to survive from the period of Zhou supremacy, which lasted from about 1000 through the 700s B.C.E. Those who could afford them—and, of course, few could—recorded their inheritances, their legacies to their families, and, above all, the key moments in their family's relationships with the imperial house. Documenting the family's achievements was related to a belief in inherited virtue. Indeed, as Shao Gong, uncle and adviser to an early Zhou king, put it: "there is nothing—neither wisdom nor power—that is not present at a son's birth."

Chronology: Zhou China	
1100 B.C.E.	Shang state in decline
1045 B.C.E.	Zhou overthrow Shang at Battle of Muye
1045–700 B.C.E.	Zhou supremacy

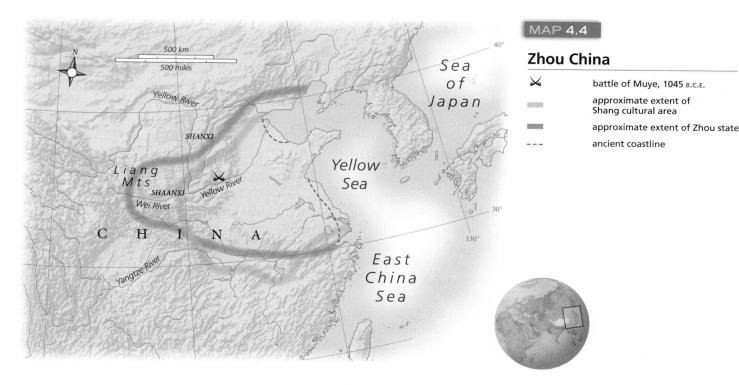

Zhou China

⚔	battle of Muye, 1045 B.C.E.
▬	approximate extent of Shang cultural area
▬	approximate extent of Zhou state
- - -	ancient coastline

The inscriptions tend to be long and give lots of detailed but unimportant information, perhaps in an effort to legitimize what they describe. Shortly before 1000 B.C.E., for instance, a king's nephew recorded how he had been made ruler of the colony of Xing (shing). He tells us first of the royal decision to make the appointment. Then we get the circumstances: The nominee performs a sacrificial libation—a drink offering to the gods—of gratitude. He accompanies the king on a lake hunt in a ship with a red banner. The king bags a goose and gives the nominee a black axe. "In the evening, the lord was awarded many axe-men as vassals, two hundred families, and was offered the use of a chariot-team in which the king rode; bronze harness-trappings, an overcoat, a robe, cloth and slippers." The gifts were apparently important because all such inscriptions mention them. The special clothes conferred status. The new lord then commissioned a commemorative cup, which bore the inscription. "With sons and grandsons, may he use it for ever to confer virtue, invoke blessings, and recall the order to colonize Xing."

Once the Zhou conquered the Shang, they did not continue all Shang traditions. Indeed, despite pious declarations, they gradually abandoned the most sacred Shang rite: divination by bone oracles. Although the Zhou extended China's cultural frontiers before their own state dissolved in its turn in the eighth century B.C.E., their leaders were not universal emperors in the mold of the Shang, ruling all the world that mattered to them. Rival states multiplied around them, and their own power tended to erode and fragment. But they originated the ideology of the **mandate of heaven**, which "raised up our little land of Zhou." All subsequent Chinese states inherited the same notion that the emperor was divinely chosen. Furthermore, all subsequent changes in rule appealed to the same claim that heaven transferred power from a decayed dynasty to one of greater virtue. The Zhou created an effective myth of the unity and continuity of China that dominated the way the Chinese came to think of themselves. This myth has been passed on and is now the standard Western view of China, too, as a monolithic state—massive, with a uniform culture of exceptional durability, and a tendency to claim dominion over all the world.

"The Zhou created an effective myth of the unity and continuity of China that dominated the way the Chinese came to think of themselves."

STATE-BUILDING IN THE AMERICAS

On a relatively smaller scale and over a longer time span, communities in parts of the New World experimented with some of the same processes of state-building and civilization that we have seen in the Old World. People in two areas—parts of the Andean region of South America and in Mesoamerica—were particularly ambitious in modifying their environments.

Andean Examples

About 3,500 years ago, experiments in civilization spread from alluvial areas on the Peruvian coast to a variety of less obviously favorable environments (see Map 4.5). In Cerro Sechín, only about 300 feet higher than the Supe valley in north-central Peru (see Chapter 2), an astounding settlement existed in about 1500 B.C.E. It occupied a site of about 12 acres dominated by a stone platform 170 feet square. Rites of victory seem to have been celebrated here. Hundreds of carved warrior images slash their victims in two, exposing their entrails, or slicing off their heads. By about 1200 B.C.E., nearby Sechín Alto was one of the world's great ceremonial complexes, with gigantic mounds erected to perform rituals, and monumental buildings arrayed along two boulevardlike spaces, each more than a mile long, at its heart. The biggest mound covers 30 square miles and is almost 140 feet tall.

These places, and others like them, suggest new experiments to manage the environment and coordinate food production in numerous small, hilly areas, each irrigated by a gravity canal and organized from a central seat of power. The violent carvings of Cerro Sechín show the price paid in blood to defend or enlarge them.

In the same period—in the last three centuries or so of the second millennium B.C.E.—farther up the coast, new settlements took shape around the Cupisnique (koo-pees-nee-keh) gorge. Though the environment was similar, the physical remains suggest a different culture and different politics. Huaca de los Reyes, for instance, had dozens of stucco-fronted buildings and colonnades of fat pillars, each up to 6.5 feet thick, guarded by huge, saber-toothed heads in clay. At Pampa de Caña Cruz, a gigantic mosaic, 170 feet long, made of thousands of fragments of colored rock, represented a similar head. It was embedded in the earth, so that a viewer could only appreciate its shape from a great height—a height the humans who made it could not reach, but their gods, perhaps, could. These regions traded with the nearby highlands, where building on a monumental scale followed soon afterward in the Cajamarca (ka-ha-MAR-kah) valley and the Upper Huallaga (wa-YAH-gah) valley. These sites constitute evidence of extraordinary cultural diversity among connected communities within a fairly small space.

Most Andean experiments in civilization were short lived. With modest technologies, they struggled to survive in unstable environments. **El Niño**—the periodic reversal of the normal flow of Pacific currents—was always a threat. At irregular intervals, usually once or twice a decade, El Niño drenches the region in torrential rain and kills or diverts the usually ample supply of ocean fish. Andean civilizations also faced crises their own success caused when population levels outgrew food supplies, or overexploitation impoverished the soil, or envious neighbors unleashed wars. Their traditions, however, lasted and spread to a great variety of environments, notably Chavín de Huantar.

Cerro Sechín. As urban life and monumental building spread upland from the river valleys of coastal central Peru in the second millennium B.C.E., warfare and rites of human sacrifice spread with them. Walls at Cerro Sechín are carved with scenes of warriors overseeing the severed heads and cleft bodies of their victims.

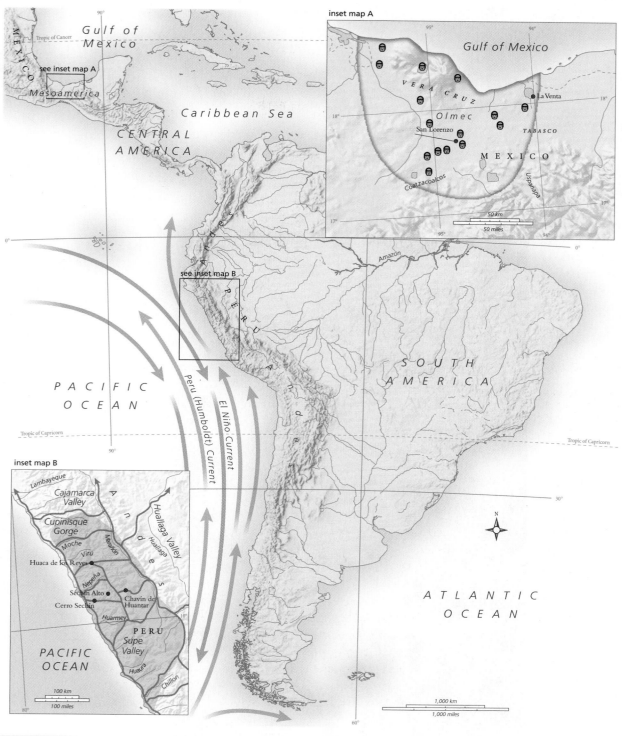

MAP 4.5

State-Building in the Americas, ca. 1500–1000 B.C.E

- Olmec cultural area
- Chavín cultural area
- → normal flow of Pacific Ocean current
- → El Niño current
- Olmec sculptural site
- **PERU** modern country
- *TABASCO* state province

A CLOSER LOOK

The Raimondi Stela at Chavín de Huantar

The Raimondi Stela, named after Antonio Raimondi, an Italian geographer who did excavations at Chavín de Huantar in the nineteenth century, is a 6-foot-high slab of carved granite that depicts an individual whom archaeologists call the Walking Sticks God. Later carvings with similar features occur in Andean sites for at least 1,000 years.

The god's elaborately layered feather headdress extends for over 3 feet and has carvings of snakes and gods' heads.

The god holds a thunder bolt in each fist.

With its horns and broad nostrils, the face of the Walking-Sticks God could be mistaken for that of a bull, except that no bulls or cattle of any kind existed in the pre-Hispanic Americas.

The god's belt and footwear culminate in serpents' heads.

What does the Raimondi Stela tell us about the dominance of a priestly or shaman elite in Chavín culture?

The city of Chavín de Huantar (cha-VEEN deh wantar) began to emerge about 1000 B.C.E., over 3,300 feet up in the Andes, on the Mosna River. Chavín demonstrates how people could achieve prosperity and magnificence at middling altitudes. The essential prerequisites were command of trade routes and the availability of diverse foodstuffs that grow in the microclimates of mountain environments like Chavín's (see Figure 4.2). Gold-working technology, which was already at least 1,000 years old in the highlands, provided objects for luxury trade, and forest products from east of the mountains were also in demand in the lowland cities. Chavín was in the middle of these trades, acting as a distribution center.

Even in the impressive world of early Andean civilizations, the sheer workmanship of Chavín stands out in architecture, water management, engineering, metalwork, and ceramics. People from all over the central Andes and lowlands admired and imitated Chavín and its arts. The many ceremonial spaces, storehouses, and barracklike dwellings have inspired much speculation about how this society was organized and ruled. The best clues, however, are probably in the sculptures. They are full of forest creatures: jaguars, anacondas, and the small crocodiles called caymans. But humans half-transformed into jaguars are dominant, often with traces of drug-induced ecstasy. Nausea and bulging eyes contort their faces; their nostrils stream with mucus. Here is the evidence of a society ruled by shamans—the go-betweens who rise above the level of their subjects by drug-induced ecstasies. Proof of their power lay in the messages they brought back from the gods and the spirit world.

Grassy plain: 13,000 ft. above sea level
Uplands: 10,500–12,500 ft. above sea level
Frost-free valleys: 7,500–10,000 ft. above sea level
Lower slopes of mountains: 2,400–7,000 ft. above sea level
Dry coastal region: 2,400 ft. above sea level

FIGURE 4.2 THE ANDEAN ENVIRONMENT packs tremendous ecological diversity into a small space, with various climatic zones at different altitudes, contrasting microclimates in the valleys, and tropical forest and the ocean close to hand. Maize grows on low slopes, coca and sweet potatoes above it, and potatoes at higher altitudes. The high grassland called puna provides grazing for llamas and their kin.

Developments in Mesoamerica

States developed in the Andes the same way they developed in the Old World—as responses to the stimulation of trade. Both followed the model described in Chapter 3: beginning with intensified agriculture, leading to population density, economic specialization, growing markets, and trade. In the Andes, the model emerged from the soil of Aspero in the Supe valley and climaxed in Chavín. In Mesoamerica, however, stunning experiments in civilization began, as far as we know, without the benefit of trade.

The culture we loosely call Olmec arose in what is now the province of Tabasco in southern Mexico in the second millennium B.C.E. (see Map 4.5). We can picture the Olmecs with the help of portraits they left: huge sculpted heads, carved from stones and columns of basalt, each of up to 40 tons, toted or dragged over distances of up to 100 miles. Some have jaguarlike masks or squat heads with almond eyes, parted lips, and sneers of cold command. Perhaps they, too, are shaman-rulers with the power of divine self-transformation, though they are never as thoroughly transformed as the coca-crazed shamans of Chavín.

The swamps of Tabasco had supported agriculture for at least 1,000 years before the first monumental art and ceremonial centers in the Olmec tradition appeared. The Olmec chose settlement sites near mangrove swamps and rain forest, close to beach and ocean, where they could exploit a variety of environments. Marshy lakes, full of aquatic prey, attracted settlers. They dredged mounds for farming from the swamp and, between the mounds, coaxed canals into a grid for raising fish, turtles, and perhaps caymans.

Olmec head. The Olmec carving known to archaeologists as Head No. 1, in San Lorenzo, Veracruz, in Mexico, where nine such sculptures, each over 6 feet high, are concentrated. San Lorenzo is far from the source of the basalt from which the heads were carved. Their close-fitting helmets have inspired the fantasy that they were representations of space men. Their thick-lipped faces have induced almost equally incredible speculations about prehistoric arrivals from Africa. More probably—like later monumental portraits in Mesoamerica—they represent stylized images of rulers.

The agricultural mounds became the model for ceremonial platforms. The earliest known ceremonial center was built on a rise above the river Coatzalcos around 1200 B.C.E. Two large centers soon followed; at La Venta, deep among the mangrove swamps on the Tonalá River, and at nearby San Lorenzo in what is now the state of Vera Cruz in Mexico. By about 1000 B.C.E., San Lorenzo had substantial reservoirs and drainage systems, integrated into a plan of causeways, plazas, platforms, and mounds. At La Venta, there are early examples of the ritual spaces that were fitted into these gridworks. The center was built with stones toted and rolled from more than 60 miles away. The focus of La Venta is a mound over 100 feet tall—evidently a setting for the most important rituals. One of the ceremonial courts has a mosaic pavement that resembles a jaguar mask that its creators appear to have deliberately buried. Similar buried offerings were placed under other buildings, perhaps the way some Christians bury relics from saints in the foundations and altars of churches. Although the stone buildings—those that survive—were designed for ritual life, these were cities: dense settlements clustered around the ceremonial centers.

Two unsolved problems exist about the Olmecs: How and why did intensive food production begin? And how and why did ambitious attempts to modify the environment begin? Monumental building requires ample food supplies to support manpower and generate spare energy. Many scholars still believe that the Olmecs could have produced sufficient food by slashing forest clearings, setting fire to the stumps, and planting seeds directly in the ash. But as far as we know, no society using such methods ever prospered the way the Olmecs did. It is more likely that the transition to city-building began when the Olmecs started farming high-yielding varieties of maize. With beans and squash, maize provided complete nourishment. The three plants together were so important to Olmec life that they depicted them on gods' and chieftains' headgear.

Although the evidence is scanty, it looks as if a determined, visionary leadership energized by shamanism drove Olmec civilization forward. An exquisite scene of what seems to be a ceremony in progress suggests the seemingly pivotal role of shamanism. Archaeologists found it buried in sand, perhaps as an offering. Carved figures with misshapen heads, suggesting that the skull was deliberately deformed, stand in a rough circle of upright stone slabs. They wear nothing but loincloths and ear ornaments. Their mouths are open, their postures relaxed. Similar figures include a *were-jaguar*—a small creature, half jaguar, half human. Others carry torches on phallic staffs. Or else they kneel or sit in a restless posture, as if ready to be transformed from shaman into jaguar, as other works depict. For the rites these figures suggest, the Olmecs built stepped platforms—forerunners, perhaps, or maybe just early examples of the angular mounds and pyramids typical of later New World civilizations.

Rulers were buried in the sort of disguises they wore for ritual performances. They became fantastic creatures with a cayman's body and nose, a jaguar's eyes and mouth, and feathered eyebrows that evoke raised hands. They lay in pillared chambers with bloodletting tools of jade or stingray spine beside them. We can still see their images carved on benchlike thrones of basalt, where they sat to shed blood—their own and their captives'. One of these carvings shows a throne with a submissive figure roped to a majestic character in an eagle headdress, who leans outward as if to address an audience.

Chronology: State-Building in the Americas

1500 B.C.E.	Cerro Sechín (Peru)
1200 B.C.E.	Sechín Alto (Peru)
1000 B.C.E.	Chavín civilization emerges
1000 B.C.E.	Olmec cities of San Lorenzo and La Venta flourishing
500 B.C.E.	End of Chavín civilization
300 B.C.E.	Olmec civilization in decline
(All dates are approximate)	

Believers in the diffusionist theory of civilization have often hailed the Olmecs as the mother civilization of the Americas. **Diffusionism** states, in brief, that civilization is such an extraordinary achievement that we can credit only a few gifted peoples with creating it. It then diffused—or spread by example and instruction—to other less inventive peoples. This theory is almost certainly false. Rather, several civilizations probably emerged independently, in widely separated places. The Olmec civilization was one among many, including the Egyptian, Mesopotamian, Harappan, and Chinese.

Nevertheless, Olmec influence seems to have spread widely in Mesoamerica and perhaps beyond. Many aspects of Olmec life became characteristic of later New World civilizations: mound building; a tendency to seek balance and symmetry in art and architecture; ambitious urban planning around angular temples and plazas; specialized elites, including chieftains commemorated in monumental art; rites of rulership involving bloodletting and human sacrifice; a religion rooted in shamanism with bloody rites of sacrifice and ecstatic performances by kings and priests; and agriculture based on maize, beans, and squash.

ASSESSING THE DAMAGE

By 1000 B.C.E., failed states littered the landscape. Some of the world's spectacular empires broke up, and mysterious catastrophes cut short the histories of many of its most complex cultures. Food distribution centers controlled from palace labyrinths shut down. Trade was disrupted. Settlements and monuments were abandoned. The Harappan civilization vanished, as did the Cretan and Mycenean. Hatti was obliterated.

In Mesopotamia, Akkadian armies spread their own language along the length of the Tigris and Euphrates. Sumerian speech slowly dwindled from everyday use to become—like Latin in the Western world today—a purely ceremonial language. The cities of Sumer crumbled. Their memory was preserved chiefly in the titles that invaders from uplands and deserts used to dignify the rule of their own kings. Ur declined to a cult center and tourist resort.

Something similar occurred in China, which succumbed to a new ruling elite of conquerors, the Zhou, from neighboring uplands. Aspects of the civilization survived, but its center of gravity was shunted upriver. As we shall see in Chapter 5, when numerous competing kingdoms in turn succeeded Zhou in the 700s B.C.E., continuity was not broken. Society and everyday life remained essentially intact. This was a pattern often repeated in Chinese history. In the New World, meanwhile, Mesoamerica and the Andean region undertook environmentally ambitious initiatives, but none of them showed much staying power.

The Survival of Egypt

Though there were more losers than winners after the climacteric of the second millennium B.C.E., the outstanding case of endurance was Egypt. Invasions in the late second millennium failed, and the basic productivity of the Egyptian agrarian system remained intact. But even Egypt was reined in.

Nubia—the region upriver of the cataracts, what is now Sudan—disappeared from Egyptian records by 1000 B.C.E. This was

"By 1000 B.C.E., failed states littered the landscape. Some of the world's most spectacular empires broke up, and mysterious catastrophes cut short the histories of many of its most complex cultures."

Tribute. Wall painting in the tomb of the vizir Rekhmire—one of hundreds of Egyptian nobles buried in sumptuous graves in Thebes around the mid–second millennium B.C.E. Part of Rekhmire's job was to receive "tribute" or, in effect, trade samples from foreign lands. Items depicted here include copper ingots with handles from the eastern or northern shores of the Mediterranean and exotic products from the Nubian frontier—ivory, apes, a giraffe.

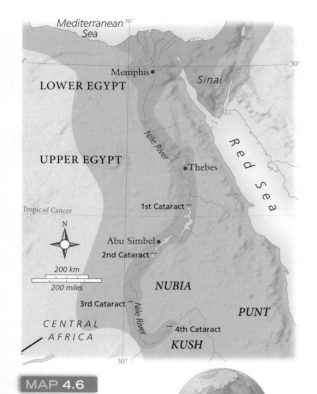

MAP 4.6

Egypt and Nubia, ca. 1500 B.C.E.

regions of control under Tut-mose I

a major reversal because extending its empire along the Nile had been one of Egypt's most constant objectives. The abundant ivory, the mercenaries that Nubia supplied, and the river trade that made gold in Egypt "as plentiful as the sand of the sea" had long drawn Egypt southward. Egypt originally became interested in Central Africa when the explorer Harkhuf made three expeditions around 2500 B.C.E. He brought back "incense, ebony, scented oil, tusks, arms, and all fine produce." Harkhuf's captive pygmy, "who dances divine dances from the land of the spirits," fascinated the boy pharaoh Pepi. Writing to the explorer, the pharaoh commanded the utmost care in guarding him: "inspect him ten times a night. For my Majesty wishes to see this pygmy more than all the products of Sinai and Punt."

Contact and commerce led to the formation of a Nubian state in imitation of Egypt, beyond the second cataract. From about 2000 B.C.E. on, Egypt tried to influence or control this state, sometimes by erecting fortifications, sometimes by invasion, sometimes by pushing its own frontier south to beyond the third cataract. Pharoahs' inscriptions piled curses on the Nubians as the latter became more powerful and more difficult to handle. Eventually, around 1500 B.C.E., Pharoah Tut-mose I launched a campaign beyond the fourth cataract, conquering the kingdom of Kush and making Nubia a colonial territory (see Map 4.6). Egypt studded Nubia with forts and temples. The last temple, to Ramses II, at Abu Simbel, was the most crushingly monumental that Egyptians had built for 2,000 years.

It has remained a symbol of power ever since. But during the reigns of his immediate successors, disastrously little flooding of the Nile, on which the success of Egyptian agriculture depended, was recorded. This was the era, toward the end of the thirteenth century B.C.E., when Egypt came closer to collapse than at any time since the invasion of the Hyksos. To abandon Nubia in the late second millennium B.C.E., after investing so much effort and emotion, shows how severe Egypt's need for retrenchment must have been.

In Perspective
The Fatal Flaws

The causes of instability in the four great river valleys and the smaller states that arose later were much more general than any general crisis theory suggests. If Harappan society was unsustainable in the silt-rich Indus valley, how realistic were the Hittite or Olmec or Cretan or Andean ambitions in much less favorable environments?

Paradox racked the most ambitious states of the era. They were committed to population growth, which imposed unsustainable goals of expansion as conquered territory became farther and farther away from the center. They were founded on intensified methods of production, which drove them to overexploit the environment. They concentrated large populations, making them more vulnerable to famine and disease. Enemies surrounded them, jealous of their wealth and resentful of their power. They created more enemies for themselves by inspiring rivals and imitators in their hinterlands. When their food distribution programs failed, disruptive migrations resulted. Their rulers condemned themselves to failure and

Making Connections

INSTABILITY: CONDITIONS LEADING TO DOWNFALL
OF KINGDOMS 2000–1000 B.C.E.

KINGDOM AND REGION	PRIMARY PROBLEMS	CONSEQUENCES
Egypt	Exposure to invasion; limited areas of soil fertility; occasional grain shortages	Famines, land shortages, and sizable migrations; invasion by Sea Peoples exploits instability
Northern Anatolia—Hatti	Growth overlaps with frontiers of Egypt, Mesopotamia; overextension of power; disruption of trade through warfare; vulnerability to famine and disease in early stages of agriculture	Nomadic prowlers attack during weak periods, conquered subjects revolt
Crete—Minoan Civilization	Uneven organization of labor; distribution of food; competition with other city-states; destruction of environment; little fertile soil; dangerous seas	Social inequality, internal warfare combine with nearby volcanic activity and earthquakes to force abandonment of cities, palaces
Greece—Mycenaean Civilization	Barbarian raiders from north attracted by wealth of palaces; earthquakes; social inequality; internal warfare	Social inequality, internal warfare combine with nearby volcanic activity and earthquakes to force abandonment of cities, palaces
Indus River—Harappa and Mohenjodaro	Gradually drying climate; evidence of earthquakes, shifting riverbeds, disease; overuse of environmental resources	Gradual collapse of food distribution system; political control; cities and towns abandoned
China—Shang and Zhou Dynasties	Overdependence of Shang leaders on rituals, oracles, war, conquest to manipulate harvest, weather	Collapse of Shang rule; rise of Zhou state; shifting center of empire; lessened dependence on divination by bone oracles
Andes—Supe Valley, Cajarmarca Valley, and Cupinisque Gorge	Vulnerability to climate change from El Niño; population levels dependent on sufficient food supplies	Overexploitation of soil leads to famines; envious neighbors unleash war; Chavín de Huantar emerges as dominant state.
Mesoamerica—Olmec	Intensive food production unable to support large populations	Building on large scale declines by 300 B.C.E.

Chronology

2500 B.C.E.	Egypt expands southward
2000–1000 B.C.E.	Climacteric: critical and accelerating change; state-building in Hatti, Crete, Egypt; Shang China, the Andes, and Mesoamerica
2000 B.C.E.	Nubian state formed, emulating Egypt, Cretan civilization emerges
1800–1500 B.C.E.	Hittite kingdom flourishes
1500 B.C.E.	Mycenae civilization appears; Cerro Sechín flourishes in Andes (Peru)
1210 B.C.E.	Last record of Hatti
1190 B.C.E.	Ramses III defeats Sea Peoples
1000 B.C.E.	Cretan and Mycenaean cities abandoned; Shang state in decline; Harappan cities in ruin; Chavín civilization emerges; Nubia disappears from Egyptian records
300 B.C.E.	Olmec civilization declines (Mesoamerica)

(All dates are approximate)

rebellion because they lived a lie, manipulating unreliable oracles, negotiating with heedless gods, bargaining with hostile nature.

In some cases, the traditions that failed or faltered during the great climacteric simply got displaced, to reemerge elsewhere. In others, dark ages of varying duration—periods of diminished achievement, about which we have little evidence—followed the climacteric. Chavín survived for about 500 years, until about 500 B.C.E., but during the following several centuries, people in the Andes attempted nothing on a comparable scale. After the Olmec stopped building on a large scale, probably in the 300s B.C.E., they had no successors for many centuries. Squatters occupied the cities of Harappa and Mycenae. The literacy of these civilizations was lost, their writing systems forgotten. When writing resumed in these regions hundreds of years later, the inhabitants had to invent new alphabets.

Our next problem is to penetrate that darkness and trace the displaced traditions from failed states. We want to examine the context that would produce a different world after the climacteric, post-1000 B.C.E. In the last millennium B.C.E.—thanks to an extraordinary blossoming of intellectual and spiritual life—the world was literally rethought.

PROBLEMS AND PARALLELS

1. How did the features that characterized the great river valley civilization begin to emerge in other environments in the second millennium B.C.E.?

2. Why did the number of complex states rapidly increase during this period?

3. Why was Egypt under Ramses III able to defeat the Sea Peoples while the Hittite kingdom fell? Why did Cretan and Mycenaean civilization collapse in this period?

4. What factors might account for the long-term survival of Chinese civilization and the collapse and disappearance of Harrapan/Indus valley civilization?

5. Why is the period between 2000 and 1000 B.C.E. a climacteric in global history?

READ ON ▶ ▶ ▶

T. Bryce, *Life and Society in the Hittite World* (2002) is incomparable in its field. To understand the nature and importance of trade, the books of M. W. Helms, *Ulysses' Sail* (1988) and *Craft and the Kingly Ideal* (1993) are of great help. M. Heltzer, *Goods, Prices and the Organisation of Trade in Ugarit* (1978), and E. H. Cline, *Sailing the Wine-Dark Sea* (1994) are valuable studies of particular trade routes.

The classic work on Malta is J. Evans, *Prehistoric Antiquities of the Maltese Islands* (1971). The best book on Crete is now O. Dickinson, *The Aegean Bronze Age* (1994). E. D. Oren, ed., *The Sea Peoples and Their World* (2000) is an important collection.

Leading works on the so-called Indo-Europeans are J. P. Mallory, *In Search of the Indo-Europeans* (1989), and C. Renfrew, *Archaeology and Language* (1987). The books listed for Chapter 3 by Shaghnessy, Posspehl, and Bulger remain important for this chapter.

Especially useful on the Olmecs are M. D. Coe, ed., *The Olmec World: Ritual and Rulership* (1996), and E. Benson and B. de la Fuente, eds., *Olmec Art of Ancient Mexico* (1996). D. O'Connor, *Ancient Nubia* (1994) is a good introductory work.

▲ **Byblos**—King Zeker Baal's city—on the shore of Lebanon. Baal, the god for whom the king was named, supposedly lived far away on the crest of the forested mountains. Byblos's ability to deliver timber to traders on the coast therefore demonstrated a divine relationship. Zeker Baal boasted that he could induce Baal to "fling trees down on the shore."

The time was high summer, a little over 3,000 years ago; the place, the eastern Mediterranean. "Guided," he says, "only by the light of the stars," Wenamun, an Egyptian ambassador, was on his way to the city-state of Byblos, in Phoenicia, on the shore of what is now Lebanon. His mission: to procure timber for the Egyptian fleet from the mountain forests the king of Byblos controlled. The mission was important because Egypt had no timber of its own.

On arrival he found a place to stay and set up an altar to Egypt's chief god, Amun. At first, King Zeker Baal refused to see him, preferring, he claimed, to reserve his forests for his own purposes. He kept Wenamun waiting for weeks. Then the king suddenly summoned the ambassador in the dead of night. Presumably, the summons was a negotiating ploy. Wenamun, however, reported it as a dramatic change of heart that Amun had brought about. "I found him," says Wenamun of the king, "squatting in his high chamber, and when he turned his back against the window, the waves of the Great Syrian Sea were breaking against the rear of his head." The ambassador recorded the dialogue that followed—doctored, no doubt, but still revealing.

"I have come," Wenamun began, "after the timber contract for the great and august ship of Amun, king of gods." He reminded Zeker Baal that his father and grandfather had sent timber to Egypt, but the king resented the implication that timber was due as tribute.

"They did so by way of trade," he replied. "When you pay me I shall do it." The two men bickered over the price, and each threatened to call off the negotiations. "I call loudly to the Lebanon which makes the heavens open," claimed Zeker Baal, "and the wood is delivered to the sea."

"Wrong!" retorted Wenamun. "There is no ship which does not belong to Amun. His also is the sea. And his is the Lebanon of which you say, 'It is mine.' Do his bidding and you will have life and health."

It was an impressive speech, but in the end, the Egyptians had to pay Zeker Baal's price: four jars of gold and five of silver, unspecified amounts of linen, 500 ox hides, 500 ropes, 20 sacks of lentils, 20 baskets of fish. Wenamun wrote: "And the ruler was pleased and he supplied 300 men and 300 oxen. And they felled the timber, and they spent the winter at it and hauled it to the sea."

The Egyptian ambassador's document is vivid and dramatic, a true story better than fiction. But its value goes deeper. It opens a window into a world recovering from the crises and climacteric of the late second millennium B.C.E. The confidence of a small city-state like Byblos in the face of demands from a giant like

PHOENICIA

Egypt seems astounding. But new opportunities that were opening up, thanks to increasing trade and cultural exchange in Eurasia, justified it.

The question for this chapter, then, is what happened between 1000 and 500 B.C.E. that led some places to recover from the failures of the second millennium? Investigating the nature and extent of those recoveries will equip us to approach a far bigger problem in the next part of this book: How do we explain the vitality and influence—the intellectual and spiritual achievements—of some groups and centers in Eurasia in the period that followed, beginning about 500 B.C.E.?

Equally important in its way is the problem of why new initiatives were so rare, late, and slow beyond Eurasia. In particular, why did the promising initiatives in parts of the Americas and sub-Saharan Africa wither instead of grow and thrive in this period? Why, for example, was Greece's dark age after the fall of Mycenae so much shorter than the dark ages of the Andes after Chavín or Mesoamerica after the Olmecs? Why did big states and monumental cities appear later in sub-Saharan Africa than in China, say, or India, or the Mediterranean? And why did so much historical initiative—the power of some human groups to influence others—become so concentrated in a few regions?

The best way to approach these questions is to look first at the regions that recovered from the disrupted traditions and overthrown states of the late second millennium. Recovery came about in the Middle East, where Hatti had vanished and Lower Mesopotamia—Sumer—declined; in the Mediterranean, where Crete and Mycenae were in ruins; in China, where Zhou had replaced Shang; and in India, where the Harappan cities disappeared. We will then look at the history of Africa and the Americas to see how isolation frustrated and slowed down certain changes.

TRADE AND RECOVERY IN THE MIDDLE EAST

Byblos was one of the largest city-states of Phoenicia, a maritime culture along the eastern coast of the Mediterranean (see Map 5.1). The name "Phoenicia" expresses the Phoenicians' chief interest—trade—for the word almost certainly means "suppliers of purple dye." Tyre, an even bigger port near Byblos, developed a deep, rich purple from the crushed shells of sea mollusks that became Western antiquity's favorite and most expensive color. (It took 12,000 shells to make the dye for just one cloak.) Beginning early in the first millennium B.C.E., Phoenician traders and colonists spread around the Mediterranean. Meanwhile, however, new, land-based empires arose that grew rich as much by conquest as by trade, threatening Phoenicia and, eventually, engulfing it (see Map 5.1).

The Phoenician Experience

In front of them, Phoenicians had waters accessible through excellent harbors. Behind them, they had mountains with forests of cedar and fir for shipbuilding and timber exports. What they did not have was much land to farm. They turned, therefore, to industry and trade. Their craftsmanship was the stuff of other peoples' stories. In legend, at least, Phoenician ships brought gold for King Solomon from distant Ophir, a mythical or lost kingdom. Timber from Tyre built the Temple of Solomon in Jerusalem, in exchange for food and oil. Phoenician cities stood, as the biblical prophet Ezekiel said of Tyre, "at the entry of the sea . . . a trader for the people of many isles. Their ports ring with precious metals, exude aromas of spice, and swirl with dye-steeped textiles. But the basis of everything is shipbuilding: the timbers from Lebanon, the oak for the oars, benches of ivory, sails of Egyptian linen, and mariners and builders from the Phoenician coast."

"This was a period when the only way to trade with a region that did not have its own merchant class or tradition of long-distance commerce was to colonize it."

This was a period when the only way to trade with a region that did not have its own merchant class or tradition of long-distance commerce was to colonize it. According to legend, the Phoenicians' earliest colonies were in what is now Tunisia in North Africa and at Cadiz in Spain. Phoenicians founded the city of Carthage near modern Tunis around 800 B.C.E. and colonized the Mediterranean islands of Malta and Sardinia by 700 B.C.E. From these bases, Phoenician navigators broke into the Atlantic and established a trading post as far away as Mogador on the northwest coast of Africa. Roman sources even credit them, probably mistakenly, with sailing around Arabia and Africa.

Where they built cities, the Phoenicians were agents of cultural exchange, borrowing from all over the eastern Mediterranean, while introducing clay-lined beehives, glass blowers' techniques, and their own vats for mixing Tyrian dye. They also exported some of their religious cults. In Carthage, newborn babies rolled from the arms of statues of their gods, Baal and Tanit, as sacrifices into sacred flames.

The colonies remained, even when the cities of Phoenicia fell to foreign raiders or rulers. In 868 B.C.E. the king of Assur (see Chapter 4) "washed his weapons in the Great Syrian Sea," and his successors continued to grab tribute from Phoenicia for over a century. Egyptian and Babylonian rulers—and by the early sixth century, conquerors from Persia—then preyed on the region in their turn. By 500 B.C.E., Carthage aspired to be an imperial capital of its own, fighting to control Mediterranean trade—first with Greek cities, then with Rome. It had a fine harbor just where a lot of shipping needed it—in the center of the Mediterranean—and a fertile hinterland of flocks, wheat fields, irrigated gardens of pomegranates and figs, and vineyards. Its aspirations seemed justified. The city's worst enemy, the Roman statesman, Cato the Elder (234–149 B.C.E.), preached, to the Roman Senate, "Carthage must be destroyed." To show why, he displayed plump, fresh figs, a delicate fruit that spoils quickly, newly imported from there. With this single gesture, he conveyed that the land was fertile, the city was rich and strong—and Rome was within its easy reach.

A Roman poet later recalled Phoenicians as "a clever people who prospered in war and peace. They excelled in writing and literature and the other arts, as well as in seamanship, naval warfare, and ruling over an empire." Their records might illuminate for us the dark age of lack of sources after the fall of Mycenae, but the Romans, who defeated Carthage in three wars and destroyed the city in 146 B.C.E., were too thorough in victory. The Phoenician language gradually yielded in North Africa and in Phoenicia itself to Latin and Greek—the languages the Romans introduced for administrative and literary purposes—and almost the whole of Phoenician literature disappeared. Only fragments of stone inscriptions survive, along with the Phoenicians' unique gift to the world, the alphabet.

Chronology: Phoenicia	
1000 B.C.E.	Phoenicia trades and colonizes in the Mediterranean
800 B.C.E.	Carthage founded as a colony
700 B.C.E.	Malta and Sardinia colonized
500 B.C.E.	Carthage seeks control of Mediterranean trade
146 B.C.E.	Carthage destroyed by the Romans
(All dates are approximate)	

Atlantic
Ocean

FRANCE

Race

SLOVENIA

ETRUSCANS

Elba

ILLYRIA

Adriatic Sea

Tarquinii

Caere

Rome

see inset

Corsica

Aegean Sea

Paestum

GREECE

SPAIN

PORTUGAL

Elche

Balearic Islands

Sardinia

*Ionian
Sea*

Croton

Mediterranean

Sicily

Crete

Tartessos
Cadiz

Carthage
(Tunis)

Malta

Sea (*Great Syrian S*

Pillars of
Hercules

TUNISIA

Mogador

N O R T H

A F R I C A

L I B Y A

F E Z Z A N

G A R A M A N T E S

S a h a r a

THRACE

MACEDONIA

PHRYGIA

Anatolia

Troy

L Y D I A

*Aegean
Sea*

Phocaea

GREECE

Euboea

I O N I A

Samos

Miletus

L Y C I A

Delphi

Eretria

Athens

Corinth

Mycenae

Peloponnese

Helicon

Crete

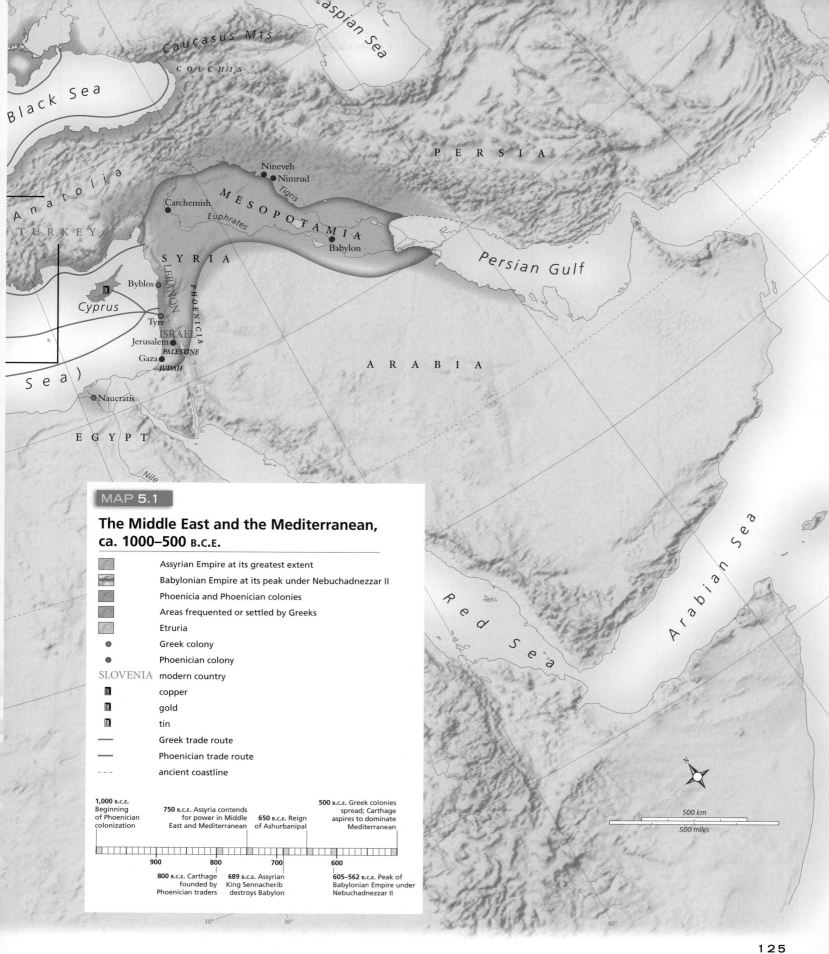

Black Sea

Caucasus Mts

COLCHIS

Caspian Sea

Anatolia

TURKEY

Nineveh
Nimrud

P E R S I A

Tigris

M E S O P O T A M I A

Carchemish

Euphrates

Babylon

Persian Gulf

Tropic of C

S Y R I A

Byblos

Cyprus

LEBANON

Tyre

PHOENICIA

ISRAEL

Jerusalem

PALESTINE

Gaza

JUDAH

A R A B I A

Sea)

Naucratis

E G Y P T

Nile

Arabian Sea

Red Sea

MAP 5.1

The Middle East and the Mediterranean, ca. 1000–500 B.C.E.

- Assyrian Empire at its greatest extent
- Babylonian Empire at its peak under Nebuchadnezzar II
- Phoenicia and Phoenician colonies
- Areas frequented or settled by Greeks
- Etruria
- ● Greek colony
- ● Phoenician colony
- SLOVENIA   modern country
- copper
- gold
- tin
- —— Greek trade route
- —— Phoenician trade route
- --- ancient coastline

1,000 B.C.E.
Beginning of Phoenician colonization

750 B.C.E. Assyria contends for power in Middle East and Mediterranean

650 B.C.E. Reign of Ashurbanipal

500 B.C.E. Greek colonies spread; Carthage aspires to dominate Mediterranean

900   800   700   600

800 B.C.E. Carthage founded by Phoenician traders

689 B.C.E. Assyrian King Sennacherib destroys Babylon

605–562 B.C.E. Peak of Babylonian Empire under Nebuchadnezzar II

500 km

500 miles

10°   30°   40°

All writing systems, as far as we know, except those indebted to the Phoenician, are based on syllables, logograms, or some combination of both. In the former, each sign represents a syllable, usually composed of one vowel sound and one consonant. In the second type, a sign stands for an entire word. Both methods require the user to know a large number of signs—typically, dozens in the syllabic system and hundreds or even thousands in a logographic one. But both methods have their advantages. Since only the leisured had time to learn them, they were secrets of a well-educated elite. They should also, in principle, consume less time and fewer valuable writing materials—stone or clay tablets, monuments, papyrus, or costly hides—than a system that demands at least one sign for every sound. Systems in the Phoenician tradition, on the other hand, suit societies with wide literacy and cheap writing materials. Easy to master and use, these kinds of writing systems encourage learning and make it easier to do the kinds of business—both political and commercial—in which written records are helpful. The simpler the writing system, the more people who can master it and use it. The Greeks seem to have gotten the idea of an alphabet and some of the symbols from the Phoenicians. From there, the idea spread to the Romans and other European peoples who, in turn, later transmitted it around the world.

The Assyrian Empire

By 1000 B.C.E., Hatti's extinction was Assur's opportunity (see Chapter 4). Kings of Assur, who were already wide-scale raiders, forged a state along the Upper Tigris, in the hills where enough rain fell to make agriculture possible without irrigation. By about 750 B.C.E., Assyrian rulers considered themselves successful enough to contend for more than regional power (see Map 5.1). King Tiglath-pilaser III adopted the title of King of the Four Quarters, or, as we would say, King of the World.

Close to home, within Upper (northern) Mesopotamia, Assyrian might reduced the traditional local rulers to purely ceremonial roles. To exercise real power in their place, the Assyrian kings appointed governors to run provinces, which were too small to mount successful rebellions. Beyond this core, Assyrian supremacy was looser, exercised by more varied means, adjusted according to local feeling and custom. In Babylon, for instance, the king of Assyria performed the annual rite of allegiance to the city god; in the city of Gaza, near the border between modern Israel and Egypt, he was enrolled among local divinities. Elsewhere, he destroyed temples and statues of gods to demonstrate his power and then restored them to show his generosity.

Fear was the cement of Assyria's empire. An ideology of domination is obvious in the remnants of Assyria that archaeologists have dug up: in the crushing weight of palace gates, the gigantic scale of the royal beasts that guard them, and the monumental sculptures, with their endless portrayals of battles and processions of tribute bearers. Colossal winged bulls carved for the palace at Nimrud were so heavy they sank the rafts when they were first transported. But, reported the governor, "Although it cost me a great deal of trouble, I have hauled them out again." The king was not divine, but heroic and intimate with gods. In portraits he kills bulls and lions and consults heaven, while winged spirits attend him. He literally entertained gods in his bedchamber: Attendants brought the statues of gods in and offered them food and libations.

Inscriptions from the reign of King Ashurbanipal (ah-shoor-BAH-nee-pahl) in the mid-seventh century B.C.E. best capture the character of the Assyrian state. He was probably the most self-celebrated monarch in the history of the Mesopotamian world. While never dethroning war as the Assyrians' priority, he made a cult of literacy, looting the learning of Babylon for his library at Nineveh (NIH-neh-veh). He was proud of the canals dug and the wine pressed in his reign, the 120 layers of bricks in the foundations of his palace, the offerings he made "of first fruits to [the god] Assur, my lord, and the temples of my land." We can picture him in his pleasure gardens, where pomegranates clustered as thick as grapes and "I, Ashurbanipal, pick fruit like a squirrel." A portrait survives of him picnicking with his wife under a vine; but dangling from it is the head of a captured enemy.

To celebrate a new palace and flaunt the wealth of his realm, Ashurbanipal held a banquet for 16,000 citizens, 5,000 visiting dignitaries, 1,500 palace officials, and 47,074 workmen "summoned from all over the kingdom." They consumed history's biggest meal: 10,000 jugs of beer; 10,000 skins of wine; 30,000 quarts each of figs, dates, and shelled pistachios; 1,000 each of lambs and fat oxen; 14,000 sheep; 20,000 pigeons; 10,000 eggs; 10,000 desert rats; and hundreds of deer. "For ten days I gave them food, I gave them drink, I had them bathed, I had them anointed. I honored them and sent them back to their lands in peace and joy." Palace-building, evidently, was politically functional, bringing subjects and tributaries together in a common enterprise. This, perhaps, was why Assyrian kings built so many of them.

But instability lay at the heart of the monarchy. Like Egyptian and Chinese rulers, the Assyrian kings sought to enhance their power by claiming to communicate with forces in Nature—a doomed enterprise. When their supposed magic failed, they lost power, and competing factions arose. Some Assyrian monarchs asserted their legitimacy so vigorously as to make us doubt it. Ashurbanipal's father tried to secure the succession against rebellion with 150 lines of oaths and curses:

> Just as the noise of doves is persistent, so may you, your women, your sons, your daughters have no rest or sleep. Just as the inside of a hole is empty, may your inside be empty. Just as gall is bitter, so may you, your women, your sons, your daughters, be bitter towards each other. Just as the water of a slit waterskin runs out, so may your waterskin break in a place of thirst and famine, so that you die of thirst.

In the background of internal conflicts, was a harem of ambitious women with time to conspire in favor of their own sons. In the early eighth century B.C.E.,

Winged bull. "May the guardian bull, the guardian genius, who protects the strength of my throne, always preserve my name in joy and honor until his feet move themselves from this place." An inscription left by King Esarhaddon, son of Sennacherib, explains the function of the winged bulls—usually carved with the portrait heads of kings—that guarded Assyrian gates and throne rooms.

Human-headed winged bull and winged lion (lamassu). Alabàster (gypsum); Gateway support from the Palace of Ashurnasirpal (ruled 883–859 B.C.E.). Limestone. H: 10' 3/1/2" W: 2' 1/2". The Metropolitan Museum of Art, Gift of John D. Rockefeller, Jr., 1932. (32.143.2) Photography © 1996 The Metropolitan Museum of Art.

King Ashurbanipal reclines to feast with his queen in the garden of his palace at Nineveh. Servants whisk flies and bring refreshments. In parts of the relief not shown here, birds sing, harpists play, and the head of the king of conquered Elam decorates a tree. The picnic is perhaps a victory celebration. Success in war bought Assyria's luxuries.

Sammuramat was one such woman who effectively ruled the empire and accompanied her son on military campaigns. Naqia was another. She was virtual co-ruler with her husband, Sennacherib (she-NAH-keh-rihb), the Assyrian monarch famed for descending on the Hebrew holy city of Jerusalem "like a wolf on the fold." She did everything kings did, from dedicating inscriptions to building a palace and receiving important war dispatches.

The Babylonian Revival

As the old cities of Lower (southern) Mesopotamia declined and trade shifted upriver, the city of Babylon became the heir of Sumer—the resting place of all the learning and much of the remaining wealth. To the Assyrians, Babylon was always the great prize, and it became part of their expanding empire. But Babylonians never forgot their independence and frequently tried to reclaim it. In 689 B.C.E., Sennacherib attempted a definitive solution. He massacred or dispersed the population, razed buildings to the ground, threw the debris into the river, and dug channels across the site of the city, with the deliberate aim of turning it into a swamp. His son relented and set to rebuilding the city, but in the next generation Ashurbanipal resumed the policy of vengeance.

In 649 B.C.E., Ashurbanipal was said to have deported 500,000 people to prevent anyone from stealing back to Babylon, "and those still living," he announced, "I sacrificed as an offering to the spirit of my grandfather, Sennacherib." Yet the name of Babylon still retained mythic power as a rallying point for native resistance to Assyria, and a reversal of fortunes was at hand. Overextended along the Euphrates River, Assyria succumbed to enemies on other fronts. In the late seventh century B.C.E., Nabopolassar—"the son of nobody," as his inscriptions admit—masterminded a Babylonian revival. His boast was that he "defeated Assyria, which, from olden days had made people of the land bear its heavy yoke."

Chronology: Assyria and Babylon	
750 B.C.E.	Assyria is an empire under Tiglath-pilaser III
689 B.C.E.	Sennacherib destroys city of Babylon
620s B.C.E.	Assyrian empire falls; Ashurbanipal is last king
605–562 B.C.E.	Peak of Babylonian empire under Nebuchadnezzar II
(All dates are approximate)	

Making Connections | CONDITIONS LEADING TO RECOVERY THE IN MIDDLE EAST, 1000–562 B.C.E.

STATE	TYPE OF LEADERSHIP AND INITIATIVES	EFFECTS
Phoenician city-states	Merchant elites; economy based on trade and proximity to forest, mineral, metal resources; colonization of Mediterranean	Spread of Phoenician technical knowledge, culture, and alphabet throughout Mediterranean
Assyrian Empire	Powerful king with provincial governors; cult of personality combined with ideology of domination; palace-building, other monumental architecture	Imperial state based on upper Tigris River spreads to lower Mesopotamia, Mediterranean coast
Babylonian Empire	Strong city-state asserts independence, becomes imperial center after decline of Assyrians; large-scale building projects; monumental architecture	Large metropolis becomes regional political/trade/cultural center; Babylon and Egypt battle for control of regional resources

Babylon now became once more an imperial metropolis, exploiting the vacuum Assyria's collapse left. Babylon's fame peaked during the long reign (605–562 B.C.E.) of Nebuchadnezzar (neh-boo-kahd-NEH-zahr) II, whose campaigns the Bible describes. He attacked the kingdom of Judah, destroyed King Solomon's temple at Jerusalem, and deported the Jews into exile. He fought off the Egyptians at Carchemish in Palestine. His building projects, however, made a more worthy monument. Ancient Greek guidebooks attributed two of the proverbial wonders of the world to him: the terraced "hanging" gardens of Babylon, supposedly built to please a concubine, and city walls broad enough to race four chariots abreast. Nebuchadnezzar was a master of theatrical gestures, a genius at attracting esteem. He cultivated an image of himself as the restorer of ancient glories by rebuilding ziggurats and city walls all over Mesopotamia. On what survives of his showy works, bulls, lions, and dragons strut elegantly in glazed brick.

Whether because Nebuchadnezzar overreached himself or because his dynasty could produce no more dynamic leaders, his was Babylon's last era of greatness. In effect, Babylon and Egypt fought each other to exhaustion in their efforts to replace Assyria. From 539 B.C.E., Babylon was merely a provincial center under the rule of foreigners (below, p. 198.) Five centuries later, the Greek geographer Strabo reported that Babylon had been "turned to waste" by the blows of invaders and the indifference of rulers. "The great city has become a great desert."

GREECE AND BEYOND

In the late second millennium B.C.E., when the Sea Peoples and other displaced communities disrupted the eastern Mediterranean and threatened Egypt (see Chapter 4), a similar upheaval took place on land. Migrants from the north swept into southern Greece, eradicating literate culture. Refugees streamed across the Aegean and Ionian Seas to Italy, Anatolia, and islands in the eastern and central Mediterranean.

Babylon. No king of Babylon built more grandly than Nebuchadnezzar II (r. 604–562 B.C.E.), who gave the city center a gate, shown here in reconstruction, dedicated to the goddess Ishtar. Precious lapis lazuli colored the tiles that smother the gate. Guardian bulls and dragons adorn it.

Olive harvest. The export of olive oil was vital to Greece's recovery from the so-called dark ages that followed the fall of Mycenaean cities. Greece's poor soils and hot climate could not produce much else that was salable abroad. Solon, the legendary lawgiver, supposedly compelled the Athenians to grow olives. Scenes of laborious techniques to harvest olives from their trees decorate this vase by the most prolific Athenian artist of the late sixth century B.C.E., known as the Antimenes Painter.

The Greek Environment

By early in the first millennium B.C.E., the massive Mycenaean palace centers were in ruins. The only stone or rubble buildings from this period that we know of in Greece were in the city of Eretria, on the island of Euboea. Few iron tools were available for farming. Barley was the staple crop, laboriously cultivated in Greek soil, where bones of rock poked through the emaciated earth. (The philosopher Plato coined the image.) Most Greeks lived by goat farming and in thatched huts.

Industry and trade were ways to escape rural poverty. In the tenth century B.C.E., Athens, Corinth, and a few other centers exported finely decorated pots, and pressed olives—the only surplus farm product—for their oil. Neighboring peoples considered the Greeks' barley unfit to eat. But olive oil was exportable and came from a crop with advantages. Its care was seasonal and left plenty of time for seafaring. It would grow in ground that grains disdained. It permitted farming at remarkably high altitudes, over 2,000 feet. It also had many uses. It added badly needed fat and flavor to the diet, could be burned as fuel in lamps, and, in a world without soap, could be used to clean the body by providing a lubricant for scraping off sweat and grime. Olive processors became rich and invested wealth in promoting more trade. Commercial enterprise soon lined the Aegean and Ionian seas with cities; then, from the mid–eighth century B.C.E. onward, spread all over the Mediterranean and the Black Sea. The Greeks lived, they said, "around a sea, like frogs around a pond."

The Greek poet Hesiod recorded a conversation that evokes the way Greece took to the sea. Perses, his younger brother, was lolling around their humble farm in the annoying manner younger brothers sometimes have, while Hesiod sweated at the plow. "Greece and poverty are sisters," Perses began, "How can I make money easily?" Hesiod recommended work on the land. But Perses insisted, "I want to avoid toil, Hesiod. You know me!"

"Get a house first," said the elder brother, "and a woman and a plowing ox—a slave woman, not a wife—a woman who can take her turn following the ox." But Perses was the type of person who asks for advice only because he wants to confirm his own opinion. He revealed what he really wanted: "to buy and sell in distant markets."

"Please don't be a fool," rejoined Hesiod. "Our father tried that. He came here in his black ship, fleeing from the evil poverty with which God punished us men. And where did he end up? In this miserable dump, bad in winter, hard in summer. . . . "

"But that's why my heart is set on escape. . . . "

"Not now. . . . Till the soil as I tell you, and wait for the sailing season and then haul your ship to the wine-dark sea and stuff it with cargo."

"What do you know about sailing? You've only been over the sea once, to Euboea, for the poetry contest. . . . "

" . . . Where I was victorious and carried off the prize. . . . But just as God taught me the secrets of composition, so shall he tell me the secrets of navigation for me to confide to you."

Hesiod went into the trancelike state poets of the time affected when composing. He revealed detailed sailing directions to his brother, along with typically Greek moral advice. "Money may be all you want in life, but it is not worth the risk of drowning. . . . Be moderate, my brother. Moderation is best in everything."

All over Greece, however, men like Perses won the arguments. Greek writers included merchants and explorers among their heroes; something unthinkable, for example, in China of the time, which valued only farmers, warriors, and scholars. In the 500s B.C.E., trade was growing so rapidly that some Greek states introduced their own coinage and designed and built new, larger types of ships.

Greek Colonialism

By Hesiod's time, iron tools had improved agriculture and increased food production, which in turn led to an increase in population. But more people meant more demands on food and land. Now, not only were the Greeks a trading people, they also became colonizers (see Map 5.1). Their settlements extended to wheat-growing areas in Sicily, southern Italy, the north shore of the Black Sea, and then to rich markets in what are now France and Spain. Greek experience echoed that of Phoenicia: city-states at home, outreach by sea, colonies abroad.

The Greeks founded colonies on the advice of gods who spoke through oracles, especially the one at Delphi, a cave in central Greece where smoke rose from deep crevices in the earth. Here, a priestess sat on a three-legged throne cast in the form of writhing serpents and uttered divine pronouncements. The oracle recommended colonization in a baffling array of cases. One supplicant went to the shrine to find a remedy for childlessness, with no thought of starting a colony, and received orders to found Croton in southern Italy. More understandably, others were told to colonize to escape famine. Founding colonies became so much a part of the Greek way of life that a comic playwright speculated on the chances of founding one in the sky. "Not that we hate our city," the would-be colonists protest, "for it is a prosperous mighty city, free for all to spend their wealth in, paying fines and fees." That is a Greek joke. Grasping humor across chasms of time and culture is one of the pleasures of studying the past.

Most colonists were outcasts, exiles, and criminals—frontiersmen forging a new society. But from nostalgia, need, and lack of imagination they clung to familiar ties and patterns. Wherever they went, they reproduced Greek ways of life. At Naucratis in the Nile delta, for example, colonists dedicated shrines to cults from their hometowns—Hera, queen of the gods, of Samos and the sun-god Apollo of Miletus. In the sixth- and fifth-centuries B.C.E., offerings to Aphrodite, goddess of love, show a steady stream of Greek sex-tourists to the lively local brothels. Such sober travelers as Solon, the great lawgiver of Athens, also visited Naucratis. They came to Egypt on business or in search of enlightenment from a great civilization.

Meanwhile, growing contacts inspired Greek artists and thinkers at home. The sea washed new cultural influences back toward Greece. The most striking example is the creation of a writing system, loosely based on Phoenician models. Unlike so many of the earlier systems that were developed to catalog merchandise or record trade transactions, the Greek alphabet was rapidly used to record creative literature and preserve epic poems that bards once recited at warriors' drinking parties. Poems attributed to the bard Homer, for instance, were written down in their surviving versions probably toward the end of the second century B.C.E. They have been revered—and imitated—ever since in the West for the brilliance with which they evoke war and seafaring. The *Iliad* tells a story of the interplay of gods and mortals during a military expedition from Mycenae to the city of Troy in what is now western Turkey. The *Odyssey* recounts the wanderings of one of the heroes of the same war on his way home. The *Iliad* bristles with ships' masts. The *Odyssey* is loud with waves. Greek literature rarely strayed far from the sea.

The influence of the *Iliad* and the *Odyssey* is part of a broader phenomenon: the way ancient Greece has helped to shape much of the modern world. Evidence is

Paestum. Around 600 B.C.E., Greek colonists founded the city now called Paestum in southern Italy. This view of the ruins of the Temple of Hera, queen of the gods, shows how faithfully the builders reproduced the style and feel of home. An upper gallery is visible on the left. No more perfect example of Greek architecture of the early sixth century survives in Greece itself.

The Parthenon. The temple of the goddess Athene, dominates the acropolis of Athens, a huge, natural, flat-topped rock that rises above the city. Here the civic life of the community centered in ancient times. Most of the surviving ruins are of buildings of the fifth century B.C.E., the product of a building program inaugurated by Pericles, who was a tireless advocate of democracy but who, in effect, used his popularity to seize power over the city and to be its ruler from about 461 to 429 B.C.E.

all around us. The most imitated building in the history of the world is the Parthenon—a temple built in the fifth century B.C.E. that still dominates the skyline of Athens, the capital of modern Greece. Of all the architectural styles available to builders, that of Greece of the fifth and fourth centuries B.C.E.—the only style we call "classical"—is still by far the most popular for buildings of public importance throughout Europe and the Americas. You find it in every possible context, from the White House and most of the palaces that house European and Latin American heads of state to municipal libraries, city halls, schools, museums, churches, and banks. The Disney Corporation chose the style—or a travesty of it—for its headquarters in Burbank, California. The former Beatle Paul McCartney chose it for the rock music school he founded in his native city of Liverpool in England. Most "great books" programs in American universities still start with ancient Greek poems that are roughly contemporary with those of Hesiod. Art courses pay homage to the surviving art of the ancient Greeks, most of which is sculpture depicting the human form. Until recently—in most contexts until the twentieth century—textbooks about ancient Greece figured prominently among the course materials for most subjects.

But who were the Greeks, and what did they do to make their achievements so enduring?

Early Greek Society

Greeks had a remarkably uniform set of ideas about themselves—"our community of blood and language and religion and ways of life." Some of their notions were mythical, and Western tradition has multiplied the myths. We have idealized the Greeks as originators of our civilization and embodiments of all our values. However, scholars have been revising almost everything that has traditionally been said about them. We now know that the pure white marble Greek buildings and statues we saw as chaste specimens of classical taste were painted in gaudy colors in their day. The Greek gods appear no longer as personifications of virtues and vices, but as unpredictable and often demonic manipulators. Their world—and the imagination of most Greeks who shared it—was run not by reason but by weird and bloody rites, goat dances, orgiastic worship, sacrifices, signs, and omens.

The Greeks formed two kinds of community, which they called *ethne* (EHTH-nay) and *poleis* (poh-lihs) *demokrateia* (to mean a state where supreme power belonged to an assembly of all citizens. But most Greeks disapproved of such an arrangement. The Greeks counted only privileged males as citizens, and normally only if both their paternal and maternal grandfathers had also been citizens. Women were excluded. So were slaves, who made up 40 percent of the population in fifth-century B.C.E. Athens. In some Greek states, citizens used bits of broken pottery as ballots on which to scrawl their votes to exile unpopular leaders. When we look at them now, we see fragments of an oppressive system that made slaves of captives, victims of women, battle fodder of men, and scapegoats of failures.

Families—groups based on monogamous couples and their descendants—were the basis of society in Greek communities. When Aristotle, the greatest Greek scholar, speculated in the fourth century B.C.E about the origins of the state, he assumed that it arose from the voluntary alliance of families. In Athens, some of the earliest group burials known to archaeologists are in family plots. Typically, girls were married at age fourteen or fifteen to men twice their age. So men dominated. "The Greeks," said a writer of the fourth century B.C.E., "expect their daughters to keep quiet and do wool-work." Myth cut women out of Athenian origins: the founders of the community supposedly sprang from the soil. Wives and daughters did not normally inherit property, unless their menfolk specifically said they could. They rarely appeared in public, except as extravagantly emotional mourners or as priestesses in religious cults. In art of the first half of the millennium, men are shown more and more in the company only of other men, women only with other women. Women's function was to serve the community by bearing and raising children and thereby increasing manpower for production and war. In the city-state of Sparta—which Greeks always regarded as "utterly different" from other Greek states—all women had to train for motherhood, and women who died in childbirth were commemorated in the same way as heroic warriors killed in battle. At times, Plato (see Chapter 6) called for women to be men's equal partners, but popular literature almost always presented women as despicable creatures. Even women who were intellectually superior to men were portrayed as dangerous or vulgar.

Scholars used to infer Greek values and morality from philosophical writings, but now we also look to popular plays and satires and find that the average Greek's social attitudes were different from the philosophers'. Athenian elites, for instance, tended to idealize homosexual relationships between older men and adolescents, but the playwrights' audiences despised them.

One of the discredited notions is of Greek "purity"—the idea that the Greeks were a self-made civilization, owing almost nothing to other cultures. To some extent, this was one of their myths of themselves: a way of differentiating themselves from foreigners, whom the Greeks equated with barbarians. Indeed, the Greeks went beyond mere imitation when they received influences, whether from abroad or from an antiquity that they saw as their own. But they were heavily indebted to what they called Asia, which to them included Egypt, and especially, to Lydia, Lycia, Phrygia in Anatolia, and to the Ionian islands in the Aegean. Here—as we shall see in the next chapter—the learning we call Greek first appeared. Helicon (the mountain sacred to the Muses, the nine goddesses who presided over the arts and learning) had, as scholars now say, an east face. Greece was not merely Greek. It was a land open to the eastern Mediterranean, and influences from around the sea's rim fashioned Greek culture. As we shall see in the next chapter, from the sixth century B.C.E. onward, the work Greeks did in philosophy, math, science, technology, and the creative arts and letters was abreast of—in some respects, perhaps, ahead of—that of other civilizations of the time.

Greek women. Women collecting water from a fountain was a common subject for Greek painters of water pots. This example from the Greek colony of Vulci in Italy, where the native population esteemed women more highly than the Greeks did, follows a standard Greek pattern. It shows the women in profile, forming a line at a fountain with a lion's-head spout under a roof supported by slender columns.

The Spread of State-Building and City-Building

Phoenician and Greek colonization and trade made the Mediterranean a highway of cultural exchange. Around and across its peninsulas lay a thick crust of peoples who could build up a large surplus of resources, strong states, monumental cities, literate culture, and vibrant art (see Map 5.1). Most of them tend to get left out of books on global history, because they are little known or underrated. But they help us see the Phoenicians and Greeks in context. Without the context of the many other flourishing civilizations of the Mediterranean world at the time, the Phoenicians and

Greeks seem to spring from nowhere and to possess an altogether improbable and unconvincing peculiarity. The other peoples who lived around the sea also help us understand the later role of the region in the world—what made the Mediterranean a potential forge of empires and fount of influence for the future. A tour is in order.

Thracian Horseback Hero. Pre-Christian fragments of Thracian art sometimes survive because Christians recycled them as building material for churches. This heroic figure on a horse was a favorite subject for Thracian artists. Goldsmiths had depicted a similar figure, known to historians as "The Master of the Animals," for centuries. Dominating a rearing horse and calmly feeding a lion, the hero has powers of control over sometimes unconquerable and savage forces of nature. The posture of the horse has signified command in Western art and imagery ever since.

The Thracians The lands of the Thracians lay along the Aegean Sea, north and east of Greece. Thracian history has to be felt and inferred, for their written works have perished. Perhaps this is because they chose odd materials, like the mushroom on which the last Thracian ruler wrote a message to a Roman emperor in the first century C.E. Scholars have not been able to decipher the only surviving Thracian inscription, even though it was written in Greek letters. But archaeology gives us inklings of their culture.

Because Thrace was close to the trading centers of the eastern Mediterranean, its chiefs made an early start accumulating wealth and state-building. They practiced rites of fire, commemorated in spiraling incisions that swirled on their hearths. A fine example imitates a shimmering sun. A horseback hero dominated their art, and defaced images at early Christian shrines leave no doubt that he was worshipped. In surviving examples he hunts with hounds, wrestles a three-headed monster, leads a bear in triumph, and does battle among severed heads.

Around 500 B.C.E., energetic rulers unified the Thracian city-states into a kingdom and sought to expand their domain. These were flesh-and-blood figures whom we know from Greek sources, not mythic heroes. In 429, the Thracian King Sitalkes invaded Macedonia in northern Greece with an army said to number 150,000. There he built a palace-city of 12.5 acres, mostly of mud bricks and painted stucco. His failure to build a permanent empire marks a new period, when Thracian states squirmed to survive alongside mightier neighbors.

The Illyrians and Garamantes On both shores of the central Mediterranean were thriving civilizations about which we now know little because few sources from them have survived. To the Thracians' west, along the coast of the Adriatic Sea around 500 B.C.E., lay Illyria, whose rulers and elites were buried with hoards of gold and silver and sacrifices of oxen and wild boar. The most famous object they are known to have left—an urn found at Vace in present-day Slovenia—depicts the luxurious life of an Illyrian court: Warriors parade. Hawkers and deer hunters stalk. Dignitaries display their authority with double-headed scepters or play on pipes. Voluptuous, long-haired women feed them.

Across the Mediterranean in North Africa, in the ferociously hot and dry region of Libya called the Fezzan (feh-ZAN), lived the Garamantes. They dug nearly 1,000 miles of irrigation tunnels under the Sahara Desert, carving out the limestone that lies between the water table and the sand. On all sides, desert surrounded their cities, of which, according to Roman reports, there were 14. The Garamantes grew wheat where they could and barley elsewhere. No records of their own survive, but early Greek descriptions call them a slave-trading elite, driving four-horse chariots. Romans depicted their tattooed and ritually scarred faces under ostrich-plume helmets.

The Etruscans On the north shore of the Mediterranean, stretching across central Italy, was Etruria, the land of the Etruscans. Their "loamy, fat and stoneless" soil had to be plowed nine times to make a furrow, so they needed the iron mines of Elba, a nearby island, and the most up-to-date smelting technology. Much of the region, however, lay under malarial marshes that the Etruscans drained. Their language, which their neighbors could not understand, became a soothsayers' tongue in Roman times and was then forgotten. So we cannot decipher their inscriptions.

We can, however, glimpse Etruscan culture through their arts. Theater was their specialty. They gave the Romans their word for actor: *hister*. After acting, soothsaying was the skill they esteemed most, reading omens from sheep's livers and the flight of birds. These were borrowed techniques. Sheep's livers, for example, were called "tablets of the gods" in ancient Mesopotamia. Like the Phoenicians (and perhaps thanks to trade with them), Etruscan culture drew from all over the Mediterranean.

Etruscan cities were the earliest in Italy. Caere covered 150 acres and Tarquinii 135. Each could have accommodated 20,000 inhabitants. The layout of their tombs imitated their houses, as if to prepare for an afterlife. In a tomb at Caere, a warrior lies alongside two chariots, with shields and arrows nailed to the walls. It is tempting to identify him as a king of Caere whom Roman sources reviled for having "mocked the gods" with cruelty to his captives. But the grave was not made for him. The tomb's best chamber houses a heavily bejeweled woman. Strewn around her, objects of gold, silver, and ivory are marked with her name: Larthia.

Among the Etruscans, women had freedom Greeks and Romans of the time mistook for immodesty. They could go out of their homes, attend games, and dine with men. In Greek art, the only women who did such things were prostitutes, but Etruscan wives routinely dined with their husbands. In one tomb, a married couple was buried under a portrait showing them reclining as companions, side by side on a couch, in the way Mediterranean elites of the time typically ate dinner. With easy affection, he draws her close, as she offers him a garland of flowers. Since mirrors and combs often display inscriptions, we can assume upper-class Etruscan women were literate.

In Greek and Roman eyes, Etruscans spent too much time on grooming and dress, like characters in ads on television, and wantonly displayed their bodies, like beach cultists in modern California. Accusations that Etruscans performed sexual acts in public may be only slight exaggerations. On the wall of one tomb, a half-naked couple shares a bed. Depictions of banquets show nude serving boys, as in Greece—but this may have been normal attire, or lack of it, for the young.

Spain In the mid-millennium, Greeks said, "The god of riches dwells in Spain." Treasures of Spain survive. From western Spain comes a belt decorated with a hero in combat with a lion and a huge funeral monument depicting a banquet of monsters—one with two heads, one with a forked tongue—feeding on wild boar. In another scene, a hero challenges a fire-breathing monster. The region evidently had an elite with the resources needed to build on a large scale and the power to inspire heroic and terrible images of authority.

From eastern Spain comes an imposing female sculpture—startling in its realism—called the Lady of Elche. Originally, she was probably enthroned in a tomb. A hollow space in her back may have held an offering to the gods or the ashes or bones of a human fellow occupant. Her luxurious dress, elaborate hairstyle, grand headdress, and enormous jewels, which bulge like Hollywood costume pieces, leave no doubt of her social status or the wealth of the society that produced her.

Soothsayer. A diviner between earth and heaven. The legendary Greek soothsayer, Chalcas, whose name is clearly legible in the inscription, sprouts wings in this late fifth-century B.C.E. bronze mirror, as he peers at the liver of a sacrificed animal, searching for auguries.

Chronology: Greece and the Mediterranean

1000–900 B.C.E.	End of Greek dark ages
750 B.C.E.	Trade expands and Greek cities line the Mediterranean
500s B.C.E.	Greek colonies spread
500 B.C.E.	Thracian city-states united
500 B.C.E.	Illyrian, Garamantine, Etruscan, and Spanish civilizations thrive
100 B.C.E.	*Iliad* and the *Odyssey* probably written down
(All dates are approximate)	

A CLOSER LOOK

An Etruscan Sarcophagus

A ceramic sarcophagus from a richly painted Etruscan burial chamber of the sixth century B.C.E. at Cerveteri in central Italy. A couple is shown together, hospitably sitting up as if to entertain visitors. They appear in death as they might have in life—reclining together at a dinner party, exchanging affection with vivid realism.

The man once raised a drinking cup.

The upper bodies of the husband and wife are vertical and square-shouldered, but their hips and legs seem to sink into the couch.

Uplifted eyes and benign smiles gesture as if to communicate something important to the viewer—perhaps an invitation to dine with them in eternity.

Sarcophagus of a married couple on a funeral bed. Etruscan, from Cerveteri, 6th BCE. Terracotta. Lewandowski/ Ojeda. Musee Louvre, Paris France. RMN Reunion Des Musees Nationeaux/ Art Resource, NY

How does this scene contrast with the status of women in Greece at this time?

From the Mediterranean to the Atlantic From deep inside the steamship age, it is hard to imagine how inhibiting was the strength of the eight-knot current—the "rapacious wave," a Greek poet called it—that stoppered the Atlantic entrance to the Mediterranean. Here, according to myth, the divine hero Hercules erected his pillars as a warning against the monster-haunted "sea of darkness" beyond. But Greek and Phoenician traders braved them. Tartessos, their first destination, was the Eldorado of its day. At its heart lay the iron pyrites belt—an area in southern Portugal and Spain, rich in iron, copper, silver, gold. The banks of the Rio Tinto are blotched with the flow of copper-bearing ores. Miners dug deep underground galleries, drained with siphons.

Greek tales help us reconstruct Tartessos's history. Early stories are of a shepherd king, Geryon, followed by Theron, a conqueror so powerful it took the strength of Hercules to halt him. Then, in the mid-first millennium B.C.E., King Arganthonios was said to have subsidized the city walls that protected the marketplace of Phocaea at the other end of the Mediterranean. For a transition of this kind, from pastoralism to plutocracy, trading partners were essential. But Tartessos belongs to a long tradition of civilization-building in Spain, dimly detectable in even earlier treasure hordes. Native cultures, given the resources, were capable of spontaneous economic growth.

EMPIRES AND RECOVERY IN CHINA AND SOUTH ASIA

Summaries nearly always distort. But it is probably fair to say that the story of this chapter so far is one of formerly marginal regions becoming—at least for a while—rich and powerful like Phoenicia and Greece, Assyria and Babylon, and parts of the western and central Mediterranean, as if to replace the old centers of power and wealth in Lower Mesopotamia, Hatti, and Crete. This suggests problems to bear in mind when confronting what happened in China and South Asia in the same period: Were the traditions of the Shang and Zhou, in China, and of Harappa in India passed on to successors in new places? Or was the continuity of history ruptured, and a new beginning made in new locations?

Lady of Elche. The limestone sculpture known as the Lady of Elche evokes the splendor of Iberian civilization in the first millennium B.C.E. Carved with startling realism, she was originally enthroned and housed in a tomb, with offerings concealed in a hollow in her back. Her luxurious dress, elaborate hair, and bulging jewels were glamorously painted.

The Zhou Decline

When the Zhou conquered the Shang, they explained their victory as a mandate from heaven—they were divinely chosen to rule the world because they were more virtuous than the Shang (see Chapter 4). This was all well and good, but as Zhou supremacy spread, the realm became increasingly decentralized. Moreover, the impossibility of using magic to manage the state undermined royal authority. Zhou rituals to appease the gods became ever more elaborate: The vessels got bigger, the ceremonies more elaborate, the hymns of praise to Zhou ancestors more extravagant. "Heaven's mandate is unending," intoned the court poets and congregations, with evident unease. A poet in the provinces disagreed: "Drought has become so severe, . . . glowing, burning. . . . The great mandate is about to end."

King Li (LEE) ascended the throne in 857 B.C.E. Chroniclers portrayed him as a failure—self-indulgent and heedless of advice. After all, if he had been virtuous, he would not have lost the mandate of heaven. A bronze inscription preserves Li's own version: "Although I am but a young boy, I have no leisure day or night," sacrificing to ancestors, elevating "eminent warriors" and well-recommended sages. But there was more urgent business than these ceremonial acts. In 842 B.C.E., rebels drove him from his capital, eventually installing the young heir, Xuan (shoo-ehn). For a reign of 46 years, Xuan held off the main external threat, the western barbarians, while trying to confront natural disasters with magic.

When Xuan died in 782 B.C.E.—reputedly murdered by the ghost of a subordinate he had unjustly executed—an earthquake hit. "The hundred rivers bubble and jump, the mountains and mounds crumble and fall." Following tradition, the poet blamed the disaster on the government's shortcomings. But the problems went much deeper. As wealth from Zhou trickled outward from trade, outlying states grew more powerful and insubordinate. In 771 B.C.E., people whom the Zhou called "Dog barbarians" drove them from their ancestral lands forever.

The Zhou moved east, to a region much changed since its glorious era under the Shang. Zhou garrisons had colonized it and divided it among 148 *fiefs* that Zhou relatives or nominees ruled. Consolidation and reconfiguration gradually reduced the number, and by the sixth century B.C.E., the former empire had been transformed into jostling states (see Map 5.2). Leadership among them was usually determined by war—and, within states, by assassination and massacre. In 541 B.C.E., at one of the periodic summits of rulers, Zhao Yang (jaow yahng), the leading minister of the largest state north of the Yellow River, summed up what Chinese historians came to call the "Warring States Period":

> Ever since the time when there has not been a true king, rulers of states have competed to preside at the inter-state conferences, which therefore rotate among the rulers. Is there a constant leader? . . . Which presiding state can pass judgment?

The kind of instability that Yang described seems bound to inhibit cultural and economic development and unleash violence. Yet the consequences were, in some respects, the opposite. As we shall see in the next chapter, the vibrant era of thinking and learning from the sixth century B.C.E. onward mainly coincided with the failures or absence of imperial initiatives. Politically, fragmentation encouraged intellectual creativity. Indeed, well before the turn of the mid-millennium, this fact was evident in the new initiatives and new thinking in South Asia.

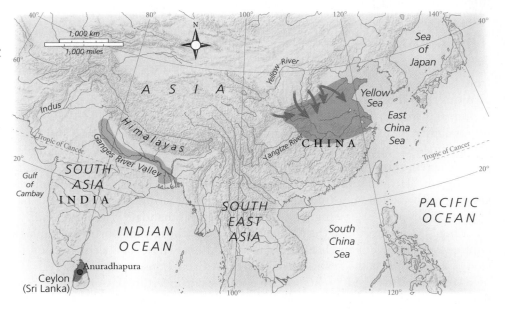

MAP 5.2

China and South Asia, ca. 750 B.C.E.

- China during Warring States Period
- barbarian incursions
- Ganges River Valley
- Sinhalese cultural area

South Asia: Relocated Centers of Culture

After the erosion and disappearance of the Harappan cities, Indian history differed in an important respect from other regions of large-scale state-building and city-building. In Europe, Mesopotamia, Phoenicia, and China, as we have seen, people tried to cope with the instabilities of the late second millennium in various ways. All depended on the survival or revival of previous traditions or on stimulation by outside influences. But India provides clear proof that such conditions were not necessary.

Historical orthodoxy has long insisted that something of the Harappan past—some migrants, some aspects of culture—must have survived. Indian civilization seems to deserve a pedigree as old as the Indus cities, and those cities, in turn, deserve to have left lasting traditions. But written and archaeological sources are few, and we have no evidence of real continuities or unmistakable transmissions of culture across the dark, undocumented centuries of Indian history. When civilization did reemerge in South Asia in the first millennium B.C.E., it was in two areas. One was the Ganges valley and the other was the island of Sri Lanka, which was once known as Ceylon.

The Ganges Valley

After a lapse of centuries, iron axes cleared the way for farming in the Ganges valley, a different environment from the hot, dry floodplains of the Indus valley. It was a region of abundant rain and rich forests. We have no knowledge that the Ganges received colonists from Harappa at the time. The only artifacts from the region during this period are fine copperware, which no one has found in the art of the Indus people, although some decorative designs may be similar.

Later Indian cultural history does not exhibit strong evidence that Harappan culture was transplanted to the Ganges either. Only pottery fragments exist, with glazes similar to Harappan wares. Moreover, the first urban sites and fortifications in the Ganges valley have none of the tell-tale signs of Harappan order: no seals, no weights and measures, no uniform bricks. This makes it hard to believe that the Ganges civilization could be the Harappan civilization transplanted. On the contrary, the lack of material evidence makes early Indian civilization seem even more distant from the Harappan than Greek civilization was from the Cretan and Mycenaean. In only one respect does the world of the Ganges clearly resemble that of Harappa—we know all but nothing about its political and social life.

The literature of its sages, however, survives in abundance. It is impossible to find evidence for traditional claims that the earliest texts originate from orally transmitted traditions from deep in the previous millennium. But surviving versions could have begun to be written down early in the first millennium B.C.E. The theoretical sections of these texts, the **Upanishads** (oo-PAH-nee-shahdz), show the recollection of a time when teaching passed from one generation to another by word of mouth. The very name "Upanishad" means something like "the seat close to the master."

One of the earliest Upanishads tells how the powers of nature rebelled against nature itself—how the lesser gods challenged the supreme god **Brahman** and failed. "But the fire could not burn straw without Brahman. The wind could not blow the straw away without Brahman." On its own, the story might suggest no more than divine omnipotence, similar to the doctrines Jews, Christians, and Muslims hold. But in the context of the other Upanishads, it seems part of a more

" . . . the lack of material evidence makes early Indian civilization seem even more distant from the Harappan than Greek civilization was from the Cretan and Mycenaean. In only one respect does the world of the Ganges clearly resemble that of Harappa—we know all but nothing about its political and social life."

general, mystical belief in the oneness of the universe, infinite and eternal. Such a "theory of everything" does not appear in the thought of earlier civilizations.

Sages of the time proclaimed two more stunningly new ideas. The first was that matter is an illusion. The world is Brahman's dream; the creation of the world was like falling asleep. Sense organs can tell us nothing that is true. Speech is illusory since it relies on lips and tongues. Thought is illusory, since it happens in—or at least passes through—the body. Most feelings are illusory because our nerves and guts register them. We can glimpse truth only in purely spiritual visions or certain kinds of feeling, like selfless love and unspecific sadness, which do not arise from particular physical stimuli. Second, the Upanishads describe a cycle of reincarnation or rebirth. Through a series of lives virtuously lived, the soul can advance toward perfection, at which time its identity is submerged in the divine "soul of the world" known as Brahman.

These profound ideas are so startling and innovative that we want to know how they occurred. And who were the patrons and pupils of the sages who uttered them? Why did society value such sublimely unworldly—such apparently use-less—speculations? We have no evidence on which to base answers to these questions. But these ideas are glimmerings of a new era of unprecedented and intense intellectual activity. Ideas from this period—from about the sixth century B.C.E. to about the first century C.E.—are antiquity's most influential legacy to us and are the subject of our next chapter. They still inform the questions that confront our religions and philosophies and still mold the way we think about them.

Building Anew in Sri Lanka

South Asia's other nursery of large-scale cities and states was in Sri Lanka, off the southern tip of India, in the Indian Ocean (see Map 5.2). Here, the *Mahavamsa*, chronicles of the long-lived "Lion Kingdom," are deceptive documents. In surviving versions, they were written down in what Westerners think of as the sixth century C.E., to serve a partisan political purpose: to justify the ruling *Sinhalese* people, sanctify their ground, legitimize their conquests. Their account of the early history of the kingdom features a prince born of a lion who battles with amorous female demons. The founders of the realm are characters in a familiar moral fable of the sea: storm-driven exiles, redeemed from sins that are bemoaned but never described. The chronicles begin the history of the kingdom with a credible event: colonization by seafarers from the Indian Ocean Gulf of Cambay, on the edge of the Harappan culture area. But the *Sinhalese* had no known connection with the Harappans. They became large-scale builders and irrigators but produced nothing to rival the logic, creative literature, mathematics, and speculative science written down along the Ganges about 2,500 years ago.

The heartland of the early kingdom was in the relatively dry northern plateau, where annual rainfall is heavy—about 60 inches a year—but painfully long dry spells are common. In summer, droughts crack the earth, shrivel the scrub, and scatter dust everywhere. Nowadays in the dry zone, rice cultivation relies on village reservoir tanks dug out of seasonal streams, dammed with earth. There is not always enough water for annual crops of rice. Even if we allow for changes in the climate, the *Sinhalese* colonists could not have built great cities without considerable feats of hydraulic ingenuity. At Maduru Oya, for instance, watertight valves dammed the flow of water from

Chronology: India and Sri Lanka

1000 B.C.E.	Civilization emerging in Ganges valley
800 B.C.E.	Upanishads probably written down
? B.C.E.	*Sinhalese* colonize Sri Lanka
500 C.E.	*Mahavamsa* probably written down
(All dates are approximate)	

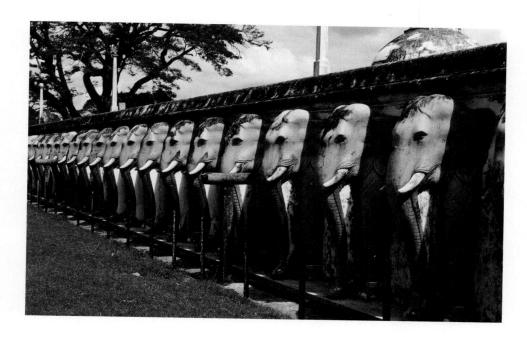

The elephant wall of Anuradhapura, the city in northern Sri Lanka that became a courtly center in the second half of the first millennium B.C.E., when kings endowed it with great irrigation cisterns, monumental trees, and sites of sacrifice, pilgrimage, and monastic life. The elephants guard a stupa—a dome-like spiritual dwelling place for the Buddha—built in the second century C.E. (See pp. 161–162.)

artificial lakes 6 miles long. Even before the adoption of Buddhism, which tradition dates to the third century B.C.E., Anuradhapura (an-uh-rad-PO-ra) was a large and splendid capital, with the largest artificial reservoir in the world (see chapter-opening illustration).

The new initiatives in the Ganges valley and in Sri Lanka exhibit so little connection to earlier civilizations or to others of this era that we have to acknowledge that civilizations can arise without the help either of recovered traditions or stimulation from outside influences. Yet the question remains, why didn't what happened in India occur in most of the rest of the world? If people in the Ganges valley and Sri Lanka could build states and cities without traditions from the past or influences from outside, why did something similar not occur in the Americas and most of Africa? Why were these vast regions relatively dormant for so long, despite the promising starts described in earlier chapters?

THE FRUSTRATIONS OF ISOLATION

In discussing developments in the Americas and Africa, we have to allow for a trick of the evidence. The cultures of Eurasia churned out huge amounts of documents and literature, much of which we can read today. This alone accounts for their dominant place in historical tradition, compared with cultures that employed other, less accessible ways to record events and ideas. In the West, prejudice also favors Eurasian cultures over others. That is, we pay more attention to history that seems to anticipate the way we live now. Sometimes we read into that history the origins of our own societies. Conversely, we overlook or fail to recognize history that appears too different from our own.

Compared to Eurasia, the geography of the Americas and sub-Saharan Africa discourages communication and cultural exchange (see Map 5.3). Much of Africa and Central and South America lies in the tropics, where dense rain forests make it difficult and unhealthy for outsiders attempting to cross them. Africa has relatively few rivers, and for the most part, they do not allow long-range navigation. In Eurasia, cultural exchange was rapid. It happened across zones of similar climate, with no need for either the people or the food plants and livestock they brought with

"In the West, prejudice also favors Eurasian cultures over others. That is, we pay more attention to history that seems to anticipate the way we live now. Sometimes we read into that history the origins of our own societies. Conversely, we overlook or fail to recognize history that appears too different from our own."

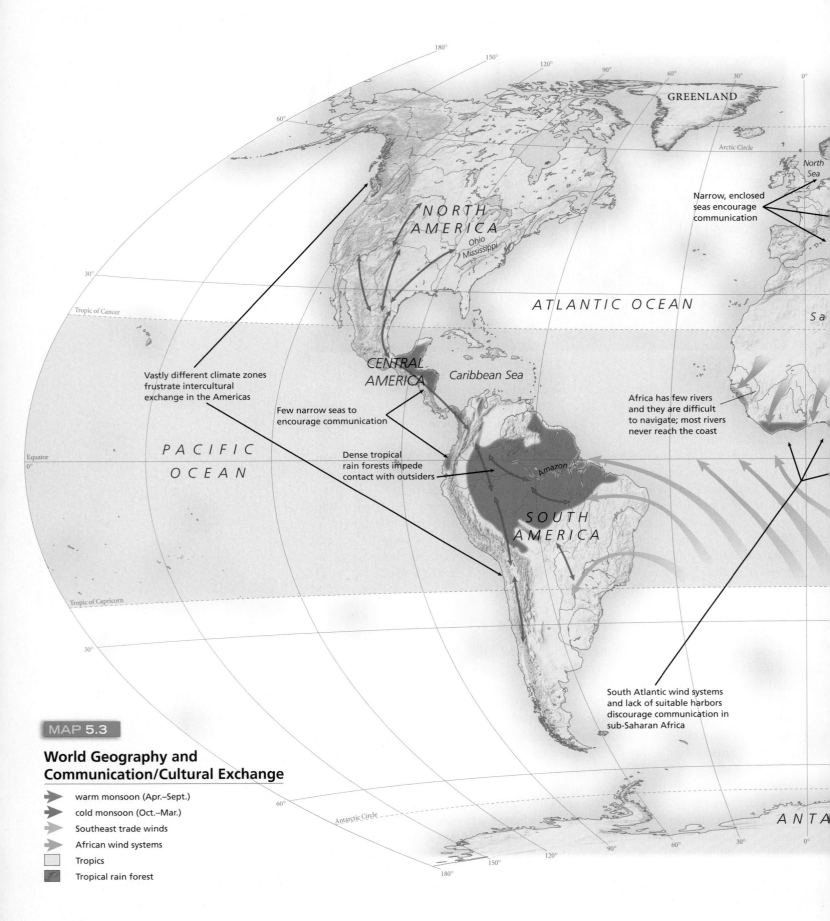

GREENLAND

North
Sea

Narrow, enclosed
seas encourage
communication

NORTH
AMERICA

Ohio
Mississippi

ATLANTIC OCEAN

S a

CENTRAL
AMERICA

Caribbean Sea

Vastly different climate zones
frustrate intercultural
exchange in the Americas

Africa has few rivers
and they are difficult
to navigate; most rivers
never reach the coast

Few narrow seas to
encourage communication

PACIFIC

OCEAN

Dense tropical
rain forests impede
contact with outsiders

Amazon

Equator
0°

SOUTH
AMERICA

Tropic of Capricorn

South Atlantic wind systems
and lack of suitable harbors
discourage communication in
sub-Saharan Africa

Antarctic Circle

ANTA

MAP 5.3

World Geography and
Communication/Cultural Exchange

warm monsoon (Apr.–Sept.)

cold monsoon (Oct.–Mar.)

Southeast trade winds

African wind systems

Tropics

Tropical rain forest

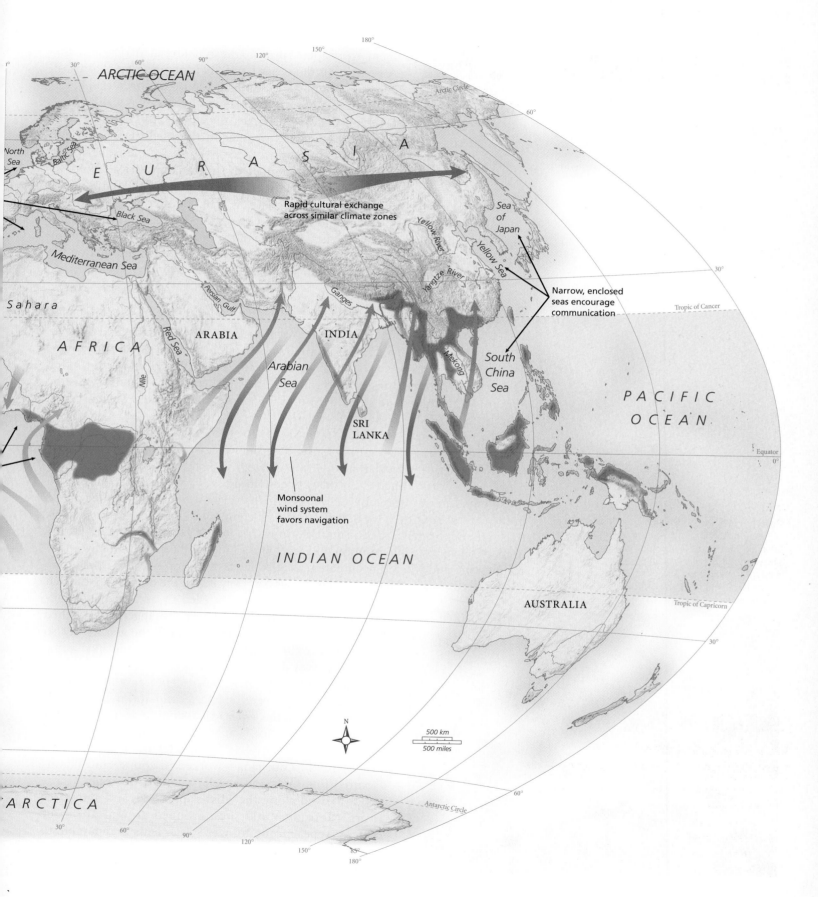

Rapid cultural exchange
across similar climate zones

Narrow, enclosed
seas encourage
communication

Monsoonal
wind system
favors navigation

ARCTIC OCEAN

EURASIA

North
Sea

Baltic Sea

Black Sea

Mediterranean Sea

Sahara

AFRICA

ARABIA

Red Sea

Nile

Persian Gulf

Ganges

INDIA

Arabian
Sea

SRI
LANKA

Yellow River

Yangtze River

Mekong

Sea
of
Japan

Yellow Sea

South
China
Sea

PACIFIC
OCEAN

INDIAN OCEAN

AUSTRALIA

ANTARCTICA

Arctic Circle

Tropic of Cancer

Equator

Tropic of Capricorn

Antarctic Circle

N

500 km
500 miles

Chronology: North America

Civilizations developing between 1000 and 500 B.C.E.	
Dorset culture—Northwest Canada to the Arctic	
Poverty Point—Gulf of Mississippi	
Foraging communities—Ohio River valley	
San Juan and Tucson basins—Southwest United States	

them to adapt. Cultural transmission in Africa and the Americas, on the other hand, had to cross vast chasms of climate from north to south and south to north, calling for different survival strategies along the way.

Monsoonal wind systems in much of maritime Asia and relatively stable weather in the Mediterranean favor navigation. By contrast, lee* shores and hostile winds enclose and hem in much of sub-Saharan Africa. Except in the Caribbean, the Americas have none of the narrow seas with which parts of Europe and Asia are relatively well endowed that encourage communication. Even the civilizations of the Ganges and Sri Lanka, though they originated independently, could take advantage of the communications systems of maritime Asia and trans-Eurasian trade routes early in their histories, linking up with China and southwest Asia by land and sea.

Developments in North America

In any case, there were plenty of developments in the world beyond Eurasia between 1000 and 500 B.C.E., but they tend to get left out of the global story, overshadowed by more spectacular changes in Eurasia. In the American far north, for instance, the Dorset culture, transformed life. People there began to build semisubterranean longhouses and stone alleys for driving caribou into lakes. Their art realistically depicted all the species that shared their environment.

The critical new technology was the blubber-fueled soapstone lamp, which enabled the Dorset people to colonize deserts of ice. Now hunters could go far from home in the Arctic darkness, tracking the musk ox to graveyards on the shore of the Arctic, devouring its entrails, boiled and dressed with seal oil. They could pursue the caribou to remote salt licks. For the caribou cannot be hunted at the hunter's pleasure. You have to wait until the beginning of winter, when its hair is thick enough to make the warmest clothing. No longer limited to the forest, the users of oil lamps could hunt on the ice, where abundant fat game waited without competitors and where the climate preserved carcasses. People of the Dorset culture speared seals and harpooned walruses from kayaks on the open sea. Now that their prey was too fat to be felled by arrows, they abandoned the bow for the barbed harpoon. Ingenious notched blades stayed in the victim's flesh, until the animal was so tired that it could be hauled in, butchered, and sped home on hand-drawn sleds with runners of walrus ivory.

Equally dramatic new ways of life developed in the same period—between the late-second and mid-first millennia B.C.E.—on the lower Mississippi River and the coast of the Gulf of Mexico (see Map 5.4). The culture—inappropriately called Poverty Point after the location of its biggest site in Louisiana—worked in copper and manufactured fine tools and jewelry of colorful stones. Trade goods arrived along the Mississippi, Red, and Tennessee rivers. More than 100 sites, grouped around 10 major centers, appear to be forager settlements comparable to settlements in the Middle East (see Chapter 2). The biggest covers a square mile and is divided by a series of

Poverty Point in Louisiana is the oldest and one of the most impressive of the mound-builders' sites of the lower Mississippi valley. The plaza shown in this drawing was in place by about 1000 B.C.E. The mound on the edge of the concentric ridges is 70 feet high.

Drawing by Jon L. Gibson

*Lee: the side away from the direction from which the wind blows.

ARCTIC OCEAN

GREENLAND

ARCTIC OCEAN

Arctic Circle

ARCTIC OCEAN

Dorset Culture

A R C T I C

NORTH

AMERICA

Mississippi

ATLANTIC OCEAN

PACIFIC OCEAN

San Juan Basin

SOUTHWEST

ARIZONA

Tucson Basin

Tucson

Red River

Poverty Point

LOUISIANA

Ohio River

Ohio River Valley

Tennessee River

Mississippi

Tropic of Cancer

Gulf of Mexico

MEXICO

of Cancer

MESOAMERICA

Olmecs

Caribbean Sea

N

MAP 5.4

North America, ca. 1000–500 B.C.E

- Dorset cultural area
- mound-building culture of Ohio River valley
- cultures of American Southwest
- *ARIZONA* modern country or state
- squash
- maize
- beans
- grains
- sunflower
- burial mounds
- musk
- aquatic mammals

500 km

500 miles

Equator

Heads sculpted from coarse-grained clay, in what is now central Nigeria, in the second half of the first millennium B.C.E., are not just fine works of art—as this example of the first century B.C.E. shows. They are also evidence of the technical accomplishments of the craftsmen who made clay tubing for the forges in which iron tools were made.
Nigeria, Nok head, 900 BC–200 AD, Rafin Kura, Nok. Prehistoric West African sculpture from the Nok culture. Terracotta, 36 cms high. © Werner Forman/Art Resource, NY

semicircular earthen ridges. Alongside is a mound almost 70 feet high, which appears oriented to the spring and autumn equinox. The mound is a ceremonial center utterly unlike anything seen earlier in Mesoamerica and therefore likely to have grown up independently.

Meanwhile, burial mounds in the Ohio River valley provide evidence of new social patterns and perhaps chiefdoms. Here, settled foragers planted grains and sunflowers to supplement the food they gathered and hunted, painted their dead in lively colors, and buried them with ornaments of copper and shell.

In the same period, contact with Mesoamerica brought about changes in parts of the North American Southwest. In the San Juan and Tucson basins in Arizona, people developed a new variety of maize that matured in 120 days. They could now cultivate maize in dryer areas where squash also grew. From around 500 B.C.E., the number of sites with traces of beans greatly increased. Farmers in the region were working their way toward the same complete system of nutrition—maize, squash, beans—that the Olmecs had developed in Mexico (see Chapter 4).

New Initiatives in Africa

As in North America, change in Africa between 1000 and 500 B.C.E. was slow and localized compared to the most dynamic parts of Eurasia. Nonetheless, events set a direction for the future. Four developments in particular are worth mentioning (see Map 5.5). First, around 750 B.C.E., Egypt weakened, and a Nubian state reemerged on the Upper Nile (see Chapter 4), with its chief cities at Napata and Meroe. Ever since Egypt had first colonized Nubia, Egyptian culture had heavily influenced it. Late in the millennium, however, the language of the Nubian royal court changed from Egyptian to an indigenous Nubian tongue. Scholars today have difficulty reading the distinctive script in which this language was written. This change shows that Nubia was becoming less Egyptian and more Sudanic, or, as some scholars like to say, more African.

Second, Africans developed hard-iron technology. This was almost certainly an independent discovery. African smiths had smelted soft iron and copper for centuries. The first iron foundries emerged along the Niger River in West Africa around 500 B.C.E., and again, perhaps independently, in Central Africa's Great Lakes region soon after. Natural drafts fanned the furnaces that melted the iron ore through long clay tubes. The people who made the tubes also left clay heads—wide-eyed, open-mouthed, partly shaved, with decoratively scarred foreheads. The use of fired clay suggests how Africans may have made the breakthrough in iron forging. These were people who knew the seemingly magical uses of fire—how fire turns hard what is soft and helps make art out of mud. Forging iron was a further stage in the process of exploring the potential of fire.

Third, Bantu languages continued their slow spread south (see Chapter 1), reaching the Great Lakes of Central Africa by about 1000 B.C.E. In this region, farmers could grow grains as well as yams, a major improvement in nutrition. Surplus production of food made trade with Nubia possible. Trade was part of a broader shift to new ways of life. At about this time, too, round dwellings with conical roofs replaced rectangular ones with ridged roofs. By the end of the first millennium B.C.E., thanks, perhaps, to improved tools made of iron, Bantu farmers reached what are now Kenya in East Africa and South Africa.

Finally, the growth of trade was pregnant with consequences for the future. The slaving activities of the Garamantes from what is today Libya suggest that one of the major routes to tropical Africa was already developing across the Sahara

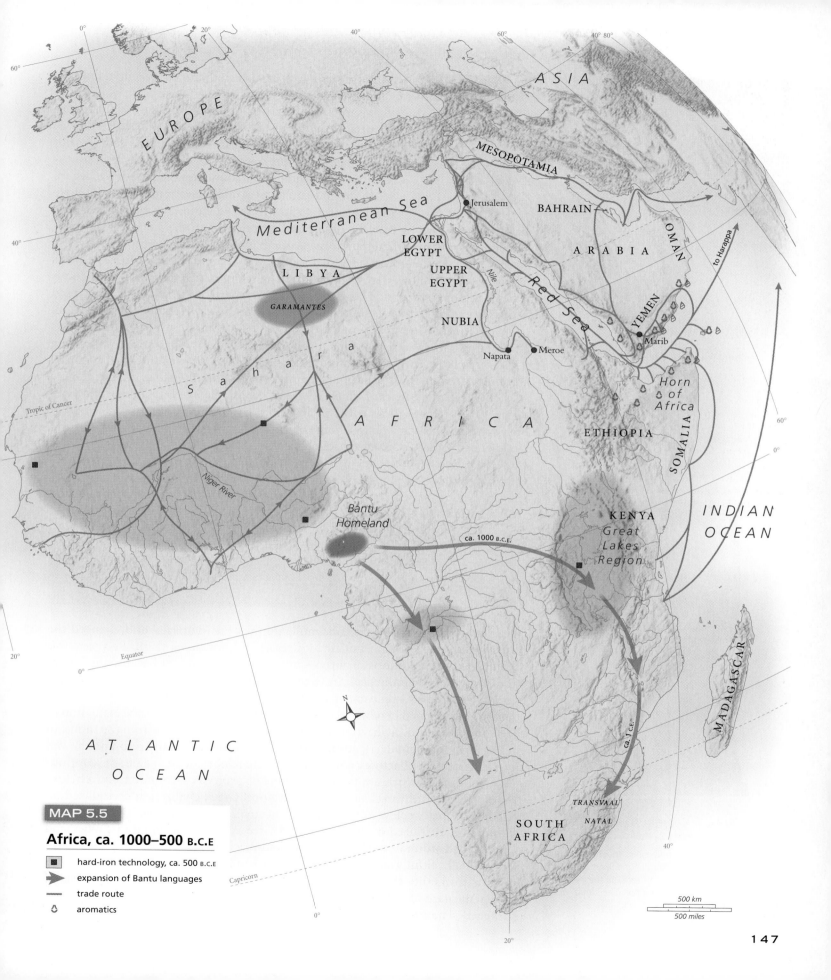

ASIA

EUROPE

MESOPOTAMIA

Mediterranean Sea

Jerusalem

BAHRAIN

OMAN

LOWER EGYPT

UPPER EGYPT

LIBYA

ARABIA

to Harappa

GARAMANTES

Nile

Red Sea

NUBIA

YEMEN

Marib

S a h a r a

Napata

Meroe

Tropic of Cancer

AFRICA

Horn of Africa

SOMALIA

ETHIOPIA

Niger River

INDIAN OCEAN

Bantu Homeland

ca. 1000 B.C.E.

KENYA
Great Lakes Region

Equator

MADAGASCAR

ATLANTIC OCEAN

ca. 1 C.E.

TRANSVAAL

NATAL

SOUTH AFRICA

Capricorn

MAP 5.5

Africa, ca. 1000–500 B.C.E

- ■ hard-iron technology, ca. 500 B.C.E
- ➤ expansion of Bantu languages
- — trade route
- ◊ aromatics

500 km

500 miles

Chronology: Africa/Southwest Arabia

1000s B.C.E.	Bantu languages expanding southward
900s B.C.E.	Sabaean empire grows
750 B.C.E.	Nubian kingdom reemerges
500 B.C.E.	First iron foundries along Niger River
100s B.C.E.	Bantu languages reach South Africa
(All dates are approximate)	

from the Mediterranean. The other great potential link was across the Indian Ocean from Asia to the Horn of Africa in what is today Somalia and Ethiopia. This link was at least as important for the history of civilization in East Africa as the link to the Mediterranean was to Europe. We do not know when this route opened, but developments in southern Arabia provide clues about how it may have begun. Southern and southeast Arabia have fertile valleys, where seasonal streams flow from the mountains before they soak into the desert and evaporate into the air. Here, the areas that are now Oman and Bahrain forged copper goods, and Yemen produced frankincense and myrrh, aromatic resins from trees that are used in perfumes and, as biblical accounts show, were in demand for religious rituals. Some of these goods reached Mesopotamia and Harappan cities. But when those civilizations collapsed in the second millennium B.C.E., so did most economic development in this region.

Only Saba, a state in the southwest corner of Arabia, closest to Africa, continued to grow. This was where the Queen of Sheba supposedly came from to King Solomon in Jerusalem in the tenth century B.C.E., if we can trust traditional biblical chronology. Numerous inscriptions survive from soon after that time. A temple outside Marib, the Sabaeans' chief city, bears bronze plaques commemorating victories—grisly scenes of warriors in triumph, brandishing the severed hands of their victims. This same temple houses bronze sculptures—tribute from kings and landowners, some, evidently, personal likenesses. Piecing together the inscriptions, we see how the Sabaean state expanded at its neighbors' expense. Understanding what happened in Saba is the best way to study one of the most intriguing problems in the next part of this book—the growth of great states, great buildings, and great ambitions in East Africa.

In Perspective
The Framework of Recovery

The climacteric of the late second millennium B.C.E. damaged and changed the frameworks of civilization but in most cases did not break them. Recovery was possible because traditions survived—or could be revived—or because there were stimulating outside influences. In Greece and India, people forgot the art of writing, and they had to reinvent it from scratch after hundreds of years. Recovery sometimes happened in new places and among new peoples. After the extinction of the Harappan world, civilization gradually emerged in India, far from the Indus. In Sri Lanka, monumental irrigation works and buildings arose. In Mesopotamia and China, the centers of activity and initiative were relocated, but, again, the continuities of tradition, which are the foundations of progress, were never entirely lost. Traditions spread through neighboring regions. Greek civilization crystallized on the edges of the Greek world, in islands and small colonies around the Ionian and Aegean seas. Fertilized by Phoenicia and Greece, a ring of ambitious cities and states formed around the Mediterranean and Black seas.

Gradually, fitfully, and despite reversals, people continued to make ambitious attempts to modify the environment, transforming new areas. In some parts of Eurasia, the pace of state-building and economic expansion not only resumed, but quickened. The imperial experiments between 1000 and 500 B.C.E. failed to take

Incense burner. An alabaster incense burner from Saba in southern Arabia, made in the third century B.C.E. The inscription records the name of the donor who gave it to a temple. The camel rider is carrying a pod of incense.
© *The Trustees of the British Museum.*

Making Connections | AMERICAN, AFRICAN, AND EURASIAN CIVILIZATIONS: 1000–500 B.C.E.

REGION	MEANS OF CULTURAL, ECONOMIC, POLITICAL DEVELOPMENT	DISTINCTIVE ACHIEVEMENTS
Greece	Seaborne trade; colonization of Mediterranean basin; extensive cultural exchange	New forms of government (*demokrateia*) and communities (*poleis, ethne*); colonial autonomy; highly developed written literature
Zhou Dynasty/ Warring States Period (China)	Centralized rule; elaborate court rituals; ancestor worship; trade and taxation; constant threat from barbarians	Political instability fosters intellectual endeavors
Ganges Valley	Highly developed spiritual literature (Vedas, Upanishads); agriculture with iron tools; little understanding of political, economic policies	First philosophies focused on doctrine of reincarnation, *maya* (matter as illusion), large-scale urban settlements, fortifications
Sri Lanka	Sophisticated water-management systems combined with urbanization	Large-scale cities, early adoption of Buddhism from neighboring India
North America	In the far north: decentralized communities, simple technologies, group hunting techniques; South/ Midwest: widespread trade networks connecting to Mesoamerica, settlements	Northern regions: long-term adaptation to hostile environments, gradual depletion of wildlife; South/Midwest: forager settlements, mound building, mixed agriculture/hunting–gathering culture
Sub-Saharan Africa/ Southwest Arabia	Widespread trade, cultural exchange with hard-iron technology accelerating tool and weapon making, spread of Bantu language	Growth of Nubian state south of Egypt; sophisticated art, industry in Niger region; building and farming techniques spread with Bantu speakers; trade and state-building in southwest Arabia (Saba)

hold, but efforts to expand borders and dominate other states became a typical feature of regions where change was accelerating. Political instability among competing states may seem unfavorable, but it stimulated technological change: hotter furnaces, more iron. It also, perhaps, multiplies the opportunities of patronage for artists and intellectuals. An "age of sages" was detectable in India and would soon be apparent in other parts of Eurasia.

In the Mediterranean and what we think of as the Middle East, between 1000 and 500 B.C.E., state-building and growing trade led to imperial ambitions that eventually failed. Elsewhere, imperial projects ran out of steam or into trouble—as in China—or simply did not happen. Was this because the contenders were too well matched? Or was it because the economic environment was too undeveloped or the ecological environment too fragile? Or was it because no conqueror had found an enduring formula, or a means to solidify states that were prone to failure? Whatever the problems that frustrated imperial ambitions in the first half of the

Chronology

1000–500 B.C.E.	Traditions and states of the late second millennium recover; dorset culture in American far north thrives; peoples of lower Mississippi and Gulf of Mexico develop new ways of life
1000 B.C.E.	Civilization reemerges in Ganges valley; Bantu languages continue slow spread southward
800 B.C.E.	Phoenicians colonize the Mediterranean
771 B.C.E.	Zhou driven eastward from their ancestral lands
750–500 B.C.E.	Rapid expansion of Greek trading and colonization
750 B.C.E.	Egypt declines and Nubian state reemerges
605–562 B.C.E.	Peak of Babylonian empire
500 B.C.E.	Carthage seeks control of Mediterranean trade until defeated by Romans in 146 B.C.E.; West Africans develop and spread hard-iron technology southward
100s B.C.E.	Bantu languages reach present-day South Africa

(All dates are approximate)

millennium, states soon found ways to overcome them. The second half of the millennium was remarkable not only as an age of sages in Eurasia, but also as an age of robust empires. A zone of connected, communicating cultures began to take shape across Eurasia and the Mediterranean, from the Pacific to the Atlantic. They nourished each other. Faint links were beginning to put parts of this central zone in touch with northern Europe and parts of Africa. In the rest of the world, isolated cultures, still organized in kinship groups or chiefdoms or small states, were able, at best, to develop regional networks on a relatively small scale.

As a result, the focus of the next part of this book is on Eurasia and, in particular, the regions where sages founded well-rooted intellectual traditions that have continued, ever since, to shape the way we think: in China, India, southwest Asia, and Greece. These were homelands of huge ambitions to understand the world, change it, or—in some cases—conquer it. Their stories occupy the next chapters.

PROBLEMS AND PARALLELS

1. Why was the ruler of the city-state of Byblos able to stand up to a giant nation-state like Egypt?

2. Why did the Phoenician writing system play such an important role in the "recovery" of the Mediterranean world?

3. How did rulers such as Ashurbanipal and Nebuchadnezzar II enhance and extend their imperial states?

4. Why was Greek cultural influence so important for the Mediterranean world? How has Greek influence persisted in Western culture today?

5. What evidence for the continuity of Harrapan/Indus valley culture exists in the civilizations of South Asia in the first millennium B.C.E.?

6. How did the interplay of cultures in the Mediterranean and Indian Ocean basins in the first millennium B.C.E. affect the development of civilizations in those areas? How did the isolation characteristic of cultures in the Americas and Africa affect the development of civilizations there?

READ ON ▶ ▶ ▶

H. Goedicke, ed., *The Report of Wenamun* (1975) is a first-rate edition of the text. S. Moscati, ed., *The Phoenicians* (1968), and M. A. Aubet, *Phoenicians and the West* (1993) introduce the Phoenicians and their colonies. The standard works by H. W. F. Saggs, *The Might that Was Assyria* (1984), and *The Greatness that Was Babylon* (1962) are still valuable introductions, as is J. Oates, *Babylon* (1979). J. and D. Oates, *Nimrud* (2001) describes the palace.

S. Hornblower, *Greek World* (1983), and O. Taplin, *Greek Fire* (1989), make exciting introductions to the Greeks. J. Boardman, *The Greeks Overseas* (1964), covers Greek colonization admirably. C. Morgan, *Athletes and Oracles* (1990) is a splendid study. S. B. Pomeroy, *Goddesses, Whores, Wives, and Slaves: Women in Classical Antiquity* (1995); C. B. Patterson, *The Family in Greek History* (1998); and L. Foxhall and J. Salman, eds., *When Men Were Men* (1998), deal with women. The long quotation from Hesiod on page 128 is from I. Morris and B. Powell, *The Greeks* (2006). M.L. West, *The East Face of Helican* (1997) shows where the Greeks got much of their mythic and literary culture from.

R. F. Hoddinott, *The Thracians* (1981); J. Wilks, *The Illyrians* (1992); C. M. Daniels, *The Garamantes of Southern Libya* (1970), and R. Harrison, *Spain at the Dawn of History* (1988) are outstanding on their respective subjects.

For the Zhou see page 000 above. On the Upanishads, J. Mascaro, *The Upanishads* (1965) is the best edition in translation; N. S. Subrahmanian, *Encyclopedia of the Upanishads* (1985) is a valuable companion.

On North America, B. Trigger and W. E. Washburn, *The Cambridge History of the Peoples of North America* (1996–2000) is an invaluable guide. B. Fagan, *Ancient North America: The Archaeology of a Continent* (1991), is a helpful introduction.

For Bantu languages in particular and the African background in general, J. Ki-Zerbo, ed., *The UNESCO General History of Africa*, (1993) is of great value.

The World in 500 B.C.E.

Because farming societies at first developed in isolation from each other—as agriculture emerged independently in many places around the world and grew different crops in contrasting environments—they were incomparably more diverse than hunter societies. As we saw in Chapter 3, both herders and tillers found that the demands of food production and war drove them to new political expedients. Different kinds of states emerged and grew and sometimes turned into empires.

Just as cities were relatively unstable environments, so states and empires were relatively unstable (and mutually hostile) forms of political organization. Although some states lasted for centuries or even millennia, their internal histories were full of the changes we have tried to follow, which as time went on tended to make them more unlike each other. Conflicting ideologies arose. States and empires adapted religions to justify the differences between them and competing states, and, in their turn, religions stoked hostility and helped to cause wars.

Meanwhile, the ambition to modify nature grew in the minds of the world's farmers. Across the globe—in East, Southwest, and Southeast Asia, in the Indian subcontinent, in parts of the Americas, Africa, and Europe, and around the Pacific—farmers recarved the landscape into fields and scored it with irrigation ditches.

In extreme cases, elites in farming societies smothered the landscape with towns and cities, environments of their own building. Urban environments are ecologically fragile, and the societies that lived in them began to experience the turbulent history—full of declines and falls, crises and collapses, confrontations and conflicts—that makes the broad outline of history so hard to discern and crowds the relatively stable hunting peoples out of the story.

▶ QUESTIONS

1. What causes led to so much instability in the period from 2000 B.C.E. to 1000 B.C.E.? Are there any connections or parallels among the different civilizations that faltered or declined in this period?

2. By 500 B.C.E., which regions were experiencing recovery or the emergence of new traditions? Which regions had yet to witness renewed state building and economic expansion?

3. Looking ahead to Chapters 6 and 7, what is the link, if any, between political instability and cultural and technological change?

To view an interactive version of this map, as well as a video of the author describing key themes related to this Part, go to www.myhistorylab.com

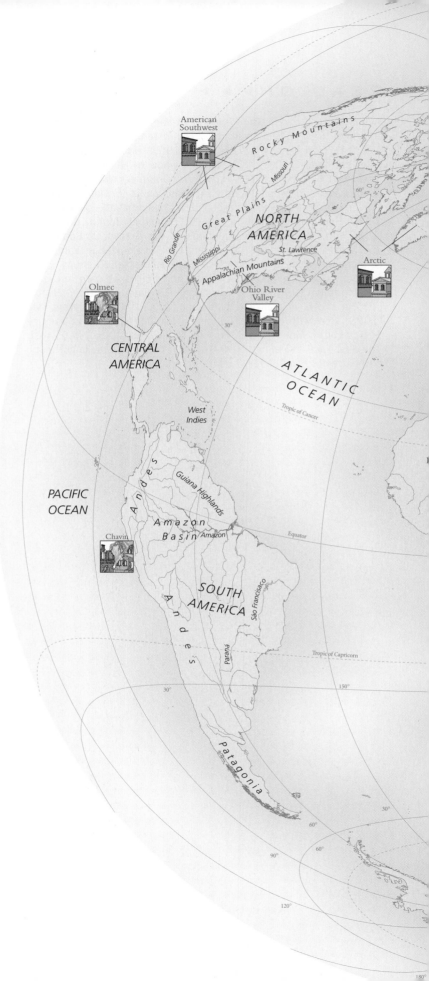

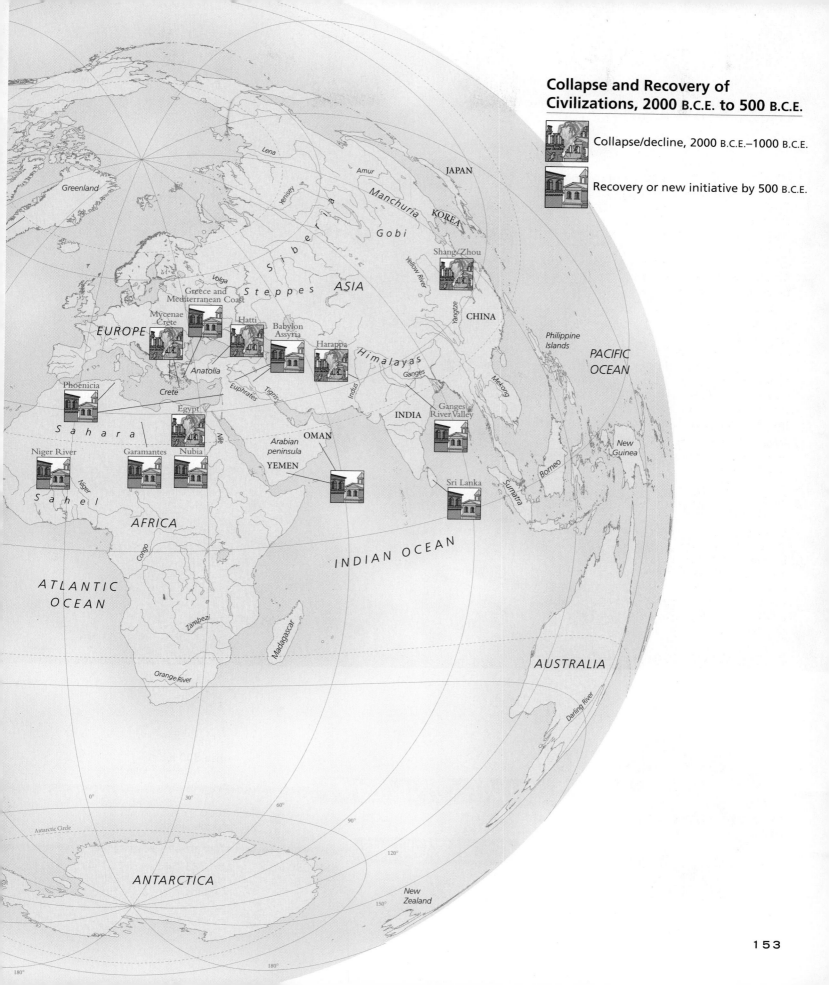

Collapse and Recovery of Civilizations, 2000 B.C.E. to 500 B.C.E.

Collapse/decline, 2000 B.C.E.–1000 B.C.E.

Recovery or new initiative by 500 B.C.E.

Greenland

Lena

Amur

JAPAN

KOREA

Manchuria

Gobi

Siberia

ASIA

Steppes

Yenisey

Volga

Shang-Zhou

Yellow River

Yangtze

CHINA

Greece and
Mediterranean Coast

Mycenae
Crete

Hatti

Babylon
Assyria

Harappa

Himalayas

Philippine
Islands

PACIFIC
OCEAN

EUROPE

Anatolia

Crete

Euphrates

Tigris

Ganges

Mekong

Indus

Phoenicia

Sahara

Egypt

Nile

Arabian
peninsula

OMAN

INDIA

Ganges
River Valley

New
Guinea

Niger River

Garamantes

Nubia

YEMEN

Sri Lanka

Sumatra

Borneo

Niger

Sahel

AFRICA

INDIAN OCEAN

ATLANTIC
OCEAN

Congo

Zambezi

Madagascar

AUSTRALIA

Orange River

Darling River

ANTARCTICA

New
Zealand

Antarctic Circle

0°

30°

60°

90°

120°

150°

180°

180°

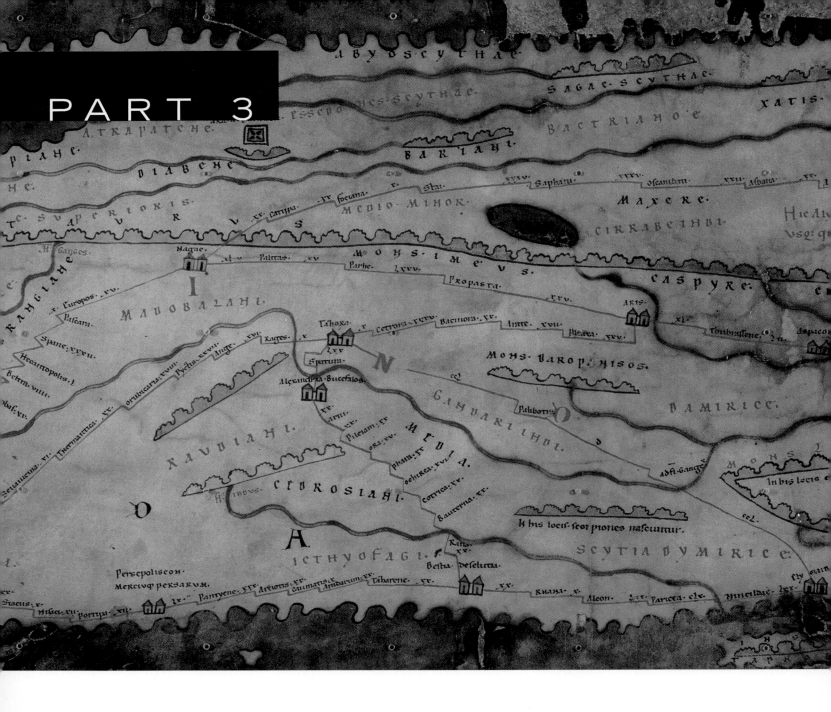

PART 3

since 800 B.C.E.
Trans-Mediterranean trade

since 3000 B.C.E.
Steppe pastoralism

650–550 B.C.E.
Zoroaster

ca. 623–543
B.C.E.
Buddha

551–479
B.C.E.
Confucius

The Axial Age, from 500 B.C.E. to 100 C.E.

◀ **A Roman road map**. A fragment of the 6.82 metres-long Peutinger Table, a thirteenth-century attempt to map Roman itineraries, showing routes from Georgia on the left, here called Hiberia, to India on the right. The legends that say "Here Alexander received a reply" and "Thus far Alexander went" can be read on the right, a little over half way up.

since 300 B.C.E.
Silk Roads; Monsoon–driven
Indian Ocean trade

since 100 B.C.E.
Mediterranean–Atlantic trade

ca. 550–334 B.C.E.
Persian Empire

427–347 B.C.E.
Plato

334–323 B.C.E.
Alexander's
Empire

**ca. 300–223
B.C.E.**
Mauryan
Empire

**240 B.C.E.
–400s C.E.**
Roman Empire

**221 B.C.E.
–220s C.E.**
Han Empire

ca. 3–33 C.E.
Jesus Christ

▲ **The Temple of Confucius** in Qufu, Shandong Province, court city of the kings of Lu and presumed birthplace of the sage. Emperors offered sacrifices in Confucius's honor at this shrine regulary from 205 B.C.E., when the first Han Emperor restored Confucianism as the giuding ideology of the state. The present building dates to a major reconstruction after a fire in 1499.

In This Chapter

J

Just over halfway through the first millennium B.C.E., a frustrated administrator in the police service set out from the small Chinese state of Lu (loo), south of the Yellow River, in search of a worthy master. Conflicting traditions claim him as the descendant of kings and the child of a humble home. By what is said to be his own account, he was a studious child, who worked his way through his education, learning menial jobs, including grain counting and bookkeeping. He could never get ahead in the bureaucracy of Lu, perhaps because he was openly disgusted with the immorality of its politics. A book later published under his name recounts the history of his times in deadpan fashion, listing the violence and injustice of the kings and aristocrats, without any apparent moralizing. The effect heightens the reader's revulsion.

CHINA

China had fragmented into the warring kingdoms described in the last chapter. It was a time of heightened warfare, in which ruthlessness replaced ritual combat. Thanks to the growth of populations, increasingly wealthy kingdoms mustered ever-larger armies of mass infantry, instead of relying on the more restrained battlefield traditions of professional soldiers and warrior aristocrats. There were plenty of rulers' courts where a sharp-witted official could find employment. But the exile from Lu never found the ideal ruler he sought. Instead, he lived by attracting pupils and left a body of thought that still influences ideas on the conduct of politics and the duties and opportunities of daily life. For him—and for most other thinkers in an era disfigured by the disintegration of China—loyalty was the key virtue: loyalty to God, to the state, to one's family, and to the true meanings of the words one uses. Most of the world knows him today by a name that is a corruption of his honorific title: "Master Kong"—Kong Fuzi (koong foo-tzeh) in Chinese, "Confucius" in the West.

The importance of Confucius is a reminder of how much the world of our own day owes to the world of his—how thinkers of the time anticipated and influenced the way we think now. Heroic teachers gathered disciples and handed down traditions. Typically, followers treated the founders with awestruck reverence, recast them as supermen or even gods, and clouded our knowledge of them with legends and lore. We can unpick enough evidence, however, to get tentative pictures of outstanding examples of some of them—some we even know by name—and an impression of what they taught.

Ideas are more than just part of history. They are what make history happen. Environment and evolution set the framework, supply our equipment, and impose the limits within which humans act. But, as far as we can tell, everything we go on to do arises first in the mind. We see the world as we think it is, imagine it differently, and act to realize our imaginings.

Between them, sages in parts of Eurasia in the period this chapter covers came up with ideas so influential that they justify a term that has become popular with scholars: the *axial age*. Different writers assign different meanings to this term. In this chapter and the next, it designates the 500 years or so, roughly up to the beginning of the Christian era. The image of an axis suits the period, for three reasons. First, as a glance at the map shows, the areas in which the thought of the sages and their schools unfolded stretched, axislike, across Eurasia, in regions that more or less bordered on and influenced each other (see Map 6.1). Second, the thought of the period has remained central to, and supporting of, so much later thought—not just in the lands where it originated, but all over the world, as its influence spread with developments described throughout the rest of this book. The religious leaders of the time founded traditions of such power that they have huge followings. The secular thinkers ran out, as if with their fingernails, grooves of logic and science in which people still think. They raised the problems of human nature—and of how we can devise appropriate social and political solutions to these problems—that still preoccupy us. And because disciples wrote down much of their teaching, a body of texts has survived to become reference points for later study.

No one should try to study this material expecting it to be easy. Part of the fun, part of the excitement, is engaging with minds active long ago, but still—with a bit of effort—intelligible to us today, and with ideas we can still recognize. We could dodge the difficulties by talking about the personalities instead of the problems of the axial age. But this chapter is designed to concentrate on what the axial-age sages thought and why they thought it—not on their own lives and characters. So, after first outlining who the sages were and where they operated, we shall turn to the common content of their minds: the religious, political, and scientific ideas that characterized the age and made it "axial"—the shared features, which for students of global history are the most interesting.

Finally, we examine the big problem that arises: Why was there an axial age at all? Why did so much thinking—so much enduring thinking, so much thinking that has shaped the world ever since—happen in such a relatively concentrated period? We will try to answer this question, toward the end of the chapter, by investigating the networks to which the sages and their disciples belonged. The way those networks operated is inseparable, of course, from the political and economic history of the age: The last chapter sketched the context from which axial-age thinking arose; the next chapter describes the political world that axial-age thinking formed, and the empires that surrounded, nourished, and transmitted it across the centuries to us.

China, India, Greece, and Southwest Asia, as we shall see, were the linked locations in which axial thinking happened. So we also have to keep in mind the problem of why other parts of the world seem to have experienced nothing similar. If Africa, or the Americas, or the Pacific world, or Western Europe, or northern or Central Asia had comparable sages and schools, they have left no record, and we know nothing of them. But of course, people who lived in those areas did initiate traditions of thought that had local or regional influence, inviting us to try to understand why evidence of those other traditions has not survived and to make comparisons between the Eurasian arena of the axial age and other parts of the world.

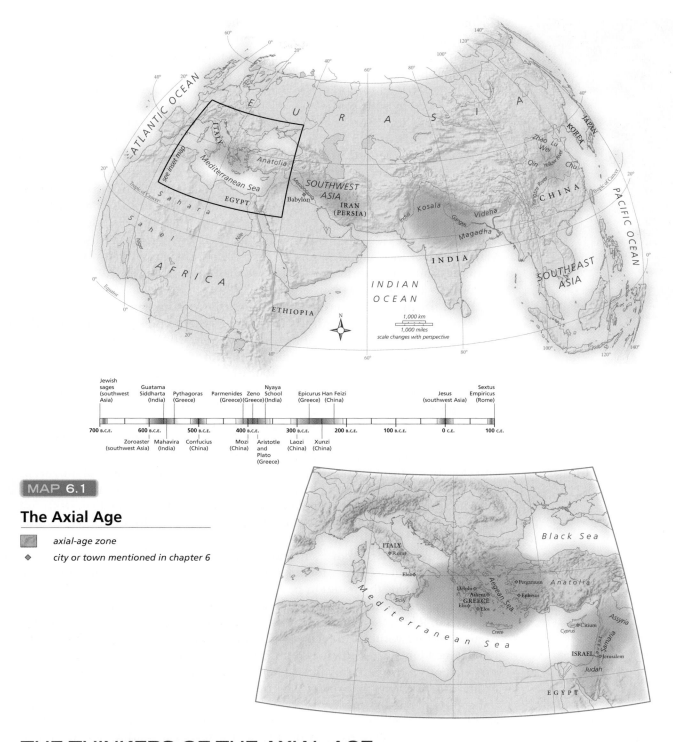

MAP 6.1

The Axial Age

axial-age zone

city or town mentioned in chapter 6

THE THINKERS OF THE AXIAL AGE

As we saw in the last chapter, the work of thinkers of great depth and complexity was recorded earlier in India. But that does not necessarily mean that it had happened nowhere else. The idea of writing down thoughts as profound, as precious, or as sacred as those of the sages took hold little by little. To the sages' early disciples, it seemed sacrilege to confide their secrets to writing. Gradually, however, evidence emerged that issues similar to those the Indian Upanishads raised (see

Zoroastrians. Though persecuted almost to extinction in Iran, the land of its birth, Zoroastrianism survives among exiled communities, especially in India, the United States, and Western Europe. Here Zoroastrian priests in London mark the New Year by kindling sacred light.

Chapter 5) were also attracting attention—whether independently, or as a result of contacts with India, we cannot say—in other parts of Asia.

In Iran, for instance, the influential sage usually known as Zoroaster (zoh-roh-AHS-tehr) is insecurely dated to the late seventh and early sixth centuries B.C.E. Texts ascribed to him are so partial, corrupt, and obscure that we cannot reconstruct them with confidence. As practiced by his followers, however, and twisted by tradition, Zoroastrianism assumed that conflicting forces of good and evil shaped the world. The single good deity, Ahura Mazda (ah-HOO-rah MAHZ-dah), was present in fire and light; the rites of his worshippers were connected with dawn and fire-kindling, while night and darkness were the province of Ahriman, the god of evil. This **dualist** way of making sense of the world, as an arena of conflict between opposing principles of good and evil, dominated mainstream thinking in Iran for 1,000 years. By influence or coincidence, it has appeared in the ideas of other Eurasian religions (see the discussion of Manichaenism in Chapter 9, pp. 271, 273). Zoroastrian communities are still scattered around the world. For reasons we shall come to, however, Zoroaster had no comparable successor in his homeland.

In India, meanwhile, around the middle of the millennium, texts of the Veda multiplied. In particular, teachings about Brahman, handed down in the early Upanishads and described in Chapter 5 were studied and written down. Alongside this defining—as we might call it—of Brahmanism in written texts, new thinking explored the moral implications of religious life, in a world of competing states comparable to that of China during its Warring States period. Vardhamana Jnatrputra, for instance, whose life is traditionally assigned to the sixth or early fifth century B.C.E., is universally known as "Mahavira" (ma-ha-VEE-rah)—"the great hero." He founded **Jainism**, a way of life designed to free the soul from evil by ascetic practices: chastity, detachment, truth, selflessness—and charity so complete that a religious Jain (JAH-een) should accept only what is freely given, preferring starvation to ungenerous life. Jainism, though it attracted lay followers, is so demanding that it could only be practiced with full rigor in monasteries and religious communities. It never drew a following outside India.

Gautama Siddharta, however, who probably lived between the mid-sixth and early fourth centuries B.C.E., founded in India a religion of potentially universal appeal. Or perhaps the tradition he launched is better described as a code of life than as a religion, since Gautama himself seems never to have made any assertions about God. Rather, he prescribed practices that would liberate devotees from the troubles of this world. Gautama, whose followers called him "the Buddha" or "the Enlightened One," taught that a combination of meditation, prayer, and unselfish behavior, of varying intensity for different individuals according to their vocations in life, could achieve happiness. The object was to escape desire—the cause of unhappiness. For the most privileged practitioners of what came to be called *Buddhism*, the aim was the ultimate extinction of all sense of self in a mystical state, called **nirvana** or "extinction of the flame." Devotees gathered in monasteries to help guide each other toward this end—but individuals in worldly settings could also achieve it. Many early Buddhist stories of the attainment of enlightenment concern people in everyday occupations, including merchants and rulers. This helped create powerful constituencies for the religion.

Buddhists now avoid the word "soul" because the Buddha decried the notion that there is anything essential or immutable about an individual person. But most early Buddhist texts clung to the notion that the self survives the death of the body—perhaps many such deaths in the course of a long cycle of death and rebirth. To liberate the self from the world, either by individual self-refinement or by losing oneself in selflessness, was likely to be a long job. Most religions of Indian origin agreed about that and expected reincarnation to recycle the soul. The distinctive element in the Buddhist view of this process was that it was ethical. A principle of justice—or at least of retribution—would govern the fate of the soul, which would be assigned a "higher" or "lower" body in each successive life according to how virtuous its deeds had been in its previous incarnation. In a famous text, recorded in eighth-century China, the Buddha promises that a righteous person can be born as an emperor for hundreds or thousands of eons. And he can also remember what happened in his previous life.

Critics sometimes claim that these new religions were really forms of old magic: that the desire to "escape the world" or "extinguish the self" or achieve "union with Brahman" was, in effect, a bid for immortality, and that mystical practice was a kind of alternative medicine designed to prolong or enhance life. Or else such practices as prayer and self-denial could be seen as a bid for the charismatic power of self-transformation of the shaman (see Chapter 1), obtained without using mind-bending drugs. These analyses may have some validity. The Buddha called himself healer as well as teacher. Many legends of the era associate miracles of therapy with founders of religions. The identification of detachment from the world with the pursuit of immortality is explicit, for instance, in writings attributed to Laozi (low-tzeh), who probably lived in the fourth-century B.C.E. and founded **Daoism** in China. His doctrine was obviously a response to the insecurities of life among the warring states described in the last chapter. Disengagement would give the Daoist power over suffering—power like that of water, which erodes even when it seems to yield: "There is nothing more soft and weak; for attacking the hard and strong there is nothing better."

Yet, however much the new religions owed to traditional magic, they were genuinely new. They upheld the effectiveness of moral practice, alongside formal

"Yet, however much the new religions owed to traditional magic, they were genuinely new. They upheld the effectiveness of moral practice, alongside formal rituals, as ways to adjust humans' relationship with nature or with whatever was divine: not just sacrificing prescribed offerings fittingly to God or gods, but modifying the way people behaved toward each other."

Nature worship. This rare Daoist scroll from about 1150 C.E.—only a portion of which is reproduced here—depicts some of the feats of the "Eight Immortals," the most famous characters in Daoist folklore. The serene landscape is typical of Daoist painting.

A CLOSER LOOK

The Buddha's Footprints

One of the 32 marks of a "superman" in Buddhist tradition is that his toes are long and straight.

This carved slab formed part of a Buddhist shrine in India. It depicts the Buddhapada, or footprints of the Buddha. Tradition holds that the Buddha's feet were imprinted with 108 auspicious symbols. Elaborate cults developed around the Buddhapada, particularly in South and Southeast Asia.

This three-pointed symbol represents the triple jewel, or *triratna.* The three jewels are the Buddha, his teachings (dharma), and the community of monks (sangha), who preserve and transmit those teachings.

The *makara*, a mythological sea monster with an elephant's trunk and a fish's tail, acts as a protector for the Buddha's footprints here.

The central wheel is symbolic of the Buddha's teachings, which set the wheel of dharma in motion.

A lotus blossom joins the *triratna* symbol. Because the lotus has its roots in mud, but flowers into pure open space, it symbolizes both the doctrine of the Buddha and the state of enlightenment that a person can reach through that doctrine.

The swastika is a traditional Indian symbol of good fortune, usually found on depictions of the palms of the Buddha's hands and the soles of his feet.

How does this carving symbolize the teachings of the Buddha?

rituals, as ways to adjust humans' relationship with nature or with whatever was divine: not just sacrificing prescribed offerings fittingly to God or gods, but modifying the way people behaved toward each other. They attracted followers with programs of individual moral progress, rather than with rites to appease nature. In other words, they were emerging as religions of salvation, not just of survival. They promised the perfection of the human capacity for goodness, or "deliverance from evil"—attainable in this world or, if not, by transfer to another world after death, or by a total transformation of this world at the end of time. Traditions developed during the axial age among the people later known as Jews also showed a drift in this direction.

The Jews

The Jews were relatively few in number and of little political significance, surrounded by more numerous peoples and by states more powerful than theirs. But they demand attention because of the long-term contribution they and their descendants made to almost every aspect of the life of Western societies—especially to the arts and sciences, to economic development, and, above all, to religion. Jewish religious thinking shaped Christianity (which ultimately became the most widely diffused religion in the West and, indeed, the world.) Later, Jewish religion also deeply affected Islam. In the long run, Christians and Muslims spread Jewish influence throughout the world.

Moreover, during the second half of the first millennium B.C.E., Jewish settlements began to spread around the Mediterranean and, ultimately, in Europe beyond the reach even of Phoenician and Greek traders. The Jews did not generally found towns of their own, but settled in small numbers, perhaps on the scale of family businesses, in already established cities, often as traders or artisans (though, at an uncertain but later date, Jewish farming communities took shape in Eastern Europe.)

When first recorded in documents, or traceable in archaeological evidence, late in the second millennium B.C.E., the ancestors of the Jews inhabited part of the war zone between Mesopotamia and Egypt, west of the Dead Sea and the Jordan River. Their own chronicles—written centuries later—claimed that they got there during a period of war and wandering after enslavement in Egypt, from where a divinely inspired leader, Moses, liberated and led them. No other evidence confirms this claim. The Jews were, however, self-consciously a people of pastoral origins. Their recollections of a nomadic past show this, and the biblical story of Cain and Abel confirms it. The blood sacrifice of Abel, the herdsman, was more "acceptable" to God than were the crops that his brother Cain, the "tiller of soil," offered. Other stories Jews told of their ancestors confirmed their self-perception as descendants of wandering herders and associated them with tales of exile from other centers of civilization. Abraham, their supposed common ancestor, allegedly came from distant Ur, in Mesopotamia or perhaps Turkey. His nephew Lot was a refugee from Phoenician cities.

From the eighth or ninth century B.C.E., neighboring peoples' inscriptions confirm essential features of the story told in Jewish writings. By then, the Jews were settled in and around the Jordan valley, raising sheep, goats, and donkeys, and farming wheat and barley in a climate of extremes. The harvest was expected to fail, on average, three times a decade, and the warehousing of grain stocks was a major public preoccupation, attested in many biblical stories about precautions against famine. The law forbade "moving your neighbor's boundary stone," but much land seems to have been held in common by the inhabitants of an entire settlement; and the poor could ask to glean fields after the harvest. Women were valuable both for their own labor and as producers of children. Suitors had to pay for them with years of labor service or hefty bride-prices. But women's economic and social value—"more precious than jewels." according to a proverb—was not echoed in legal rights. It was relatively easy for a man to obtain a divorce, and in cases of adultery, the onus of proof was on a woman accused by her husband.

The Jews inhabited two kingdoms, which they called Israel and Judah, fighting each other between brief periods of unity, which subsequent writers recalled as ideal times of power and prosperity under kings they called Saul, David, and Solomon (see Map 6.2). Warehousing food (and defending it from marauders and invaders) was, to judge from biblical texts, the main function of the state. This in turn required huge levies of forced labor, which war captives could provide when available but which normally had to come from the king's subjects—as many as 180,000 at a time, or so the royal chroniclers claimed, under 3,300 supervisors. The administration of justice—"winnowing evil with his eyes," as a proverb says—was the king's other principal function. The Bible is full of evidence of political tension between kings and priests or sometimes self-appointed "prophets," to whom kings frequently deferred.

Israel and Judah were always small, poor kingdoms by the standards of many of their neighbors and their feuds weakened them. They fell victim to neighboring empires: most of our data from the ninth century comes from inscriptions left by conquering kings from the upper reaches of the Tigris and Euphrates, who "washed their spears" in the Mediterranean or "slew all the people of the city of the king of Israel" to dazzle other peoples of the region. Large-scale deportations—including a massive forced migration to Babylon after the fall of the Jews' holy city of Jerusalem in the 580s (see Chapter 5)—incited a "diaspora mentality," exiles' sense of loss, resignation, nostalgia, defeat, and hope. "By the waters of Babylon," as the writer of the psalm put it, "we lay down and wept. . . . If I ever forget Jerusalem, let my tongue cleave to the roof of my mouth."

During traumas of conquest, dispersal, return to Jerusalem, and submission to foreign rule, from the seventh to the fifth centuries B.C.E., the Jews defined their sense of identity—expressed in writings now generally called the Old or Hebrew Testament. Instead of turning the Jews against their deity, their disasters inspired them to re-evaluate their relationship with him, and to see him not just as superior to the gods of other peoples, but as the only true God, beside whom all other gods were false. Sufferings were trials of faith and punishments for sin—especially, for failures to acknowledge God's uniqueness. By means of a "Covenant," God promised deliverance, if not in this life, then in the after-life, or at the end of history, or, at best, in a remote future, as a reward for present fidelity. Jews signified that fidelity by adhering to prescribed rituals and rules of life, known as "the Law." Jews differed among themselves about what deliverance would mean. For some, it would be individual immortality; for some, relief from a sense of sinfulness; for some, the elimination of evil from the world; for some, national independence; for some, an empire over their enemies.

The last great teacher of the age—the greatest, in terms of the scale of his influence—was the Jew we usually call Jesus, who died in or about 33 C.E. He was

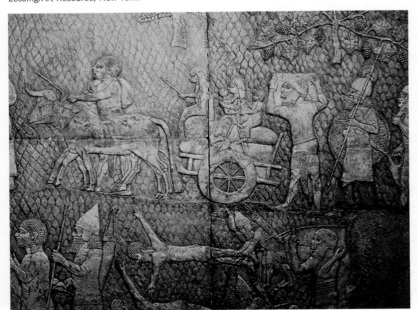

Exile of the Jews. "The king of Assyria carried the Israelites away to Assyria." This relief from the palace of the invading king seems to illustrate the scene described in the biblical Book of Kings (II.18:11), as soldiers take prisoners from the fortress of Lachish, which the Assyrians captured in 701 B.C.E. The Bible says that the Hebrew king then "stripped the gold from the doors of the Temple of the Lord" in an attempt to buy off the invaders.
Relief, Israel, 10th–6th Century: Judean exiles carrying provisions. Detail of the Assyrian conquest of the Jewish fortified town of Lachish (battle 701 BC). Part of a relief from the palace of Sennacherib at Niniveh, Mesopotamia (Iraq). British Museum, London, Great Britain. Erich Lessing/Art Resource, New York.

the last great teacher of the axial age—the greatest in terms of the scale of his influence. Scholars have questioned traditions concerning his life, on the grounds that his own followers were virtually the only ones who collected and wrote down the sources, and that we have almost no independent confirmation that he even existed. Actually, however, we are much better informed about him than we are about most other figures of his time or type. Collections of stories and sayings were written down within 30 or 40 years of his death. The brevity of this interval makes them unusually reliable by the standards of most such sources for ancient history.

To the secular historian, Jesus is best understood as an independent-minded Jewish rabbi, with a radical message. Indeed, some of his followers saw him as the culmination of Jewish tradition, embodying, renewing, and even replacing it. The name *Christ*, which his followers gave him, is a corruption of a Greek attempt to translate the Hebrew term *ha-mashiad*, or **Messiah**, meaning "the anointed," which Jews used to designate the king they hoped for at the end of history to bring heaven to earth. Jesus' message was uncompromising. The Jewish priesthood should be purged of corruption, the temple at Jerusalem "cleansed" of money-making practices. Even more controversially, some of his followers understood him to claim that humans could not gain divine favor by appealing to a kind of bargain with God—the "Covenant" of Jewish tradition. God freely gave or withheld his favor, or grace. According to Jewish doctrine, God responded to obedience to laws and rules. But Jesus' followers preferred to think that, however righteously we behave, we remain dependent on God's grace. No subsequent figure was so influential until Muhammad (moo-HA-mahd), the founder of Islam, who died six centuries later, and none thereafter for at least 1,000 years.

The religious teachings of the sages of the axial age were highlights in a world teeming with other new religions, most of which have not survived. In a period when no one recognized a hard-and-fast distinction between religion and secular life, spiritual ferment stimulated all kinds of intellectual innovation. It is still hard to say, for instance, whether Confucius founded a religion. After all, he ordered rites of veneration of gods and ancestors, but disclaimed interest in worlds other than our own. The other schools of the axial age in China—so numerous that they were called the Hundred Schools—shared similar priorities, but mixed what we would now think of as secular and religious thinking. Confucius's opponent, Mozi (moh-tzeh), is a case in point. He taught a philosophy of **universal love**, on secular grounds, 400 years before Jesus' religious version.

Some other innovators of the age, however, formulated ideas that belong without doubt in the realm of what we would now classify as secular thought. Greek sages, for instance, whose work overlapped with that of the founders of new religions in Asia, taught techniques for telling good from evil and truth from falsehood that we still use. The towering figures were two teachers of the fourth century B.C.E.: Aristotle, a physician's son from northern Greece, who was, perhaps, the most purely secular thinker of the age, and his teacher, the Athenian aristocrat, Plato. Aristotle left a body of work on science, logic, politics, and literature that had

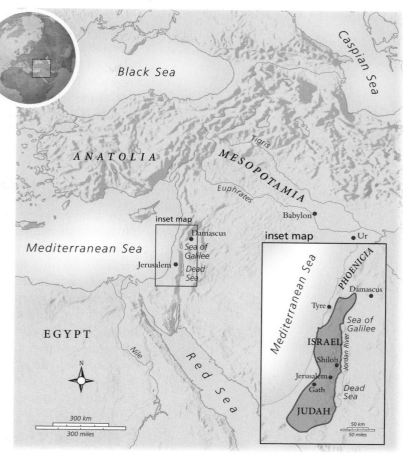

MAP 6.2

Ancient Israel

☐ territory ruled by David and Solomon, ca. 1000–900 B.C.E.

▨ Kingdom of Israel, 9th–8th c. B.C.E.

▨ Kingdom of Judah, 9th–8th c. B.C.E.

no equal in the West for centuries. It is commonly said that the whole of Western philosophy since the classical age of Athens in the fourth century B.C.E. has been "footnotes to Plato." Logicians and scientific observers and experimenters who belonged to the Hundred Schools in China and thinkers in India of the school known as Nyaya paralleled these achievements. We can only reconstruct the teachings of the Nyaya school, uncertainly, from later or, in some cases, hostile texts, because few original sources have survived. But together with logicians of the era in Greece and China, the Nyaya school shared confidence in reason and the urge to analyze it, resolving arguments step by step.

THE THOUGHTS OF THE AXIAL AGE

There is no easy way to analyze the thinking of the axial age. Textbook writers usually divide the subject by regions, because scholars tend to specialize in regions. This method, however, conceals the fact that an almost continuous zone across Eurasia stretching from China, through India, Southwest Asia, and the Mediterranean Levant, to Greece linked these regions together (see Map 6.1).

A thematic approach, of the kind we will attempt over the next few pages, helps to reveal the connections and contrasts, under the headings, first, of religion and morals, then of politics, and finally of reason and science. Of course, no such classification is watertight. No sage saw these headings as separate from each other. But between them, these categories cover the most explosive new ideas of the axial age. We start with religious ideas, bearing in mind the now-familiar warning that religion and secular life were overlapping categories for most thinkers at the time.

Religious Thinking

Of new thoughts of God formulated or developed in the axial age, three proved especially influential in global history: the idea of a divine creator, responsible for everything else in the universe; the idea of a single God, uniquely divine, or divine in a unique way; and the idea of an involved God, actively engaged in the life of the world.

Creation Gods and spirits are hard to imagine. It is even harder to imagine nothing: an idea, beyond experience, at the uttermost limits of thought. The idea of nothing enabled thinkers to understand the order of nature in a new way. For, once you have got your head around the concept of nothing, you can imagine creation from nothing. This is the key to a tradition of thought that is crucial to most modern people's religions. How did it come about?

Before the axial age, creation narratives, as far as we know, were not really about creation, but were explanations of how the universe came to be the way it is. Ancient Egyptian creation myths, for instance, tell of a creator transforming chaos into a world endowed with time: but the chaos was there for him to mold. The big bang theory—today's favorite scientific explanation of how the universe began to expand from an almost infinitesimally small core—resembles many early creation myths: Matter was already there when the bang redistributed it in space.

Some of the masters of the early Upanishads in India certainly had a notion of nothing, which they called "the void." We know this because they poured scorn on it. "How could it be so," sneered one text, "that being was produced from non-being?" The eternal being whom early Indian writings call Brahman created the world out of himself, "as a spider spins its web." In Greece in the fifth century

"For, once you have got your head around the concept of nothing, you can imagine creation from nothing. This is the key to a tradition of thought that is crucial to most modern people's religions."

B.C.E., Leucippus (who is credited with devising **atomic theory**—the theory that matter is not a continuous whole, but is composed of tiny particles) raised an apparently invincible logical objection: "the void is a non-being; and no part of what is can be a non-being, for whatever is, is absolutely." Plato's creator-god did not start from nothing, but rearranged what was already there.

Some ancient Greek poetry, however, described a world-beginning without prior matter. Emotion or thought was the prime mover of the universe. Indeed, feeling and thought can be defined in terms of each other. Feeling is thought unformulated, thought is feeling expressed in communicable ways. This Greek idea informed the mysterious notion of a world spawned by an intellectual act. As the Gospel according to John put it in the late first century C.E., "In the beginning was the logos"—literally, the thought, which English translations usually render as "the word." Of all the early Christian accounts of Jesus' life, John's was the gospel Greek thought influenced most heavily. Most other Christian accounts relied heavily on traditions peculiar to Jesus' own people, the Jews.

For the most challenging account of creation from nothing arose among the Jews, who brought an unusual philosophical twist to divine thinking: the idea of a creator who always existed but who made everything else out of nothing. Conclusions followed. The creator was unique, for nothing else could precede creation; he was purely spiritual, since there was no matter until he made it; he was eternal—he existed, that is, outside time—since he was not himself a product of creation; he was therefore unchanging; nothing greater than he could be conceived—his power had no limits.

Since its conception, the idea of creation from nothing has gradually convinced most people who have thought about it and has become the unthinking assumption of most of those who have not. It seems problematical, but so does the idea of eternal matter: If matter is eternal, how come it changes?

Monotheism The idea of a unique God, who monopolizes power over nature, is now so familiar, at least in the West, that we can no longer sense how strange it is. Yet, until the first millennium B.C.E., as far as we know, most people who imagined an invisible world—beyond nature and controlling it—supposed that it was diverse: crowded with gods, the way creatures crammed nature. To systematize the world of the gods in the axial age, Greeks arrayed gods in order. Persians reduced them to two—one good, one evil. In Indian *henotheism*, a multiplicity of gods collectively represented divine unity.

Once again, the most powerful formula developed in the sacred writings of the Jews. Yahweh (YAH-weh), their tribal deity, was, or became, their only God. The chronology is insecure, and we do not know whether the Jewish creation theory was cause or consequence of this development. Their writings called him "jealous"—unwilling to allow divine status to any rival. Fierce enforcement of his sole right to worship was part of the Covenant in which Yahweh's favor was exchanged for obedience and veneration. "I am Yahweh your God. . . . You shall have no other gods to rival me."

Jews were not obliged to impose the Yahweh cult on others. On the contrary, for most of history, they treated it as a treasure too precious to share with non-Jews. Elsewhere, monotheism seemed unappealing. Buddhism dispensed with the need for a creator by upholding that the universe was itself infinite and everlasting. When

The Creator. The British poet and artist William Blake (1757–1827) was explicit; he painted visions. His version of the Creation—probably now the most famous in the world—is certainly visionary, but has obvious sources. It calls the Bible to mind, as God measures "a world without form, and void." The use of rushing wind to suggest the Holy Spirit, and of sun rays to signify Jesus, are among the oldest conventions of Christian art. God's stooped posture and his dividers, flashing like lightning, recall medieval paintings of God as the architect of the cosmos (see Chapter 13).

asked about the existence of God, Buddha, in the recollection of his disciples, always answered evasively. In India, China, and Greece, the idea of a unique creator left options for polytheism: If one being inhabited eternity, why—in strict logic—might not others? Other forms of uniqueness can be divided: You can shatter a rock, parse a statement, refract light. So maybe the uniqueness of God is of this kind. Alternatively, it could be a kind of comprehensiveness, like that of "Nature," "the Earth," or the sum of everything. God is one—any good Brahmanist would acknowledge—in the sense that everything is one. In any case, if God's power is without limits, surely he can create other gods.

Despite these arguments, three developments have conspired, in the long run, to make the God of the Jews the favorite God of much of the world. First, the Jews' own "sacred" history of sacrifices and sufferings gave a compelling example of faith. Second, a Jewish splinter group, which recognized Jesus as—so to speak—the human face of God, opened its ranks to non-Jews. Christianity built up a vigorous and sometimes aggressive tradition of trying to convert non-Christians every-where. Thanks in part to a message that has been adaptable to all sorts of cultural environments, it became, over nearly 2,000 years, the world's most widely diffused religion. Finally, early in the seventh century C.E., the Prophet Muhammad studied Judaism and Christianity, and incorporated the Jewish understanding of God in Islam. In its turn—in many of the places where it was preached and spread—Islam became at least as appealing as Christianity and today has almost as many follow-ers. Well over a third of the world's population belongs to the tradition that includes Jewish, Christian, and Muslim monotheism (see Figure 6.1).

Divine Love Having created, did God remain interested in creation? Most Greek thinkers of the era ignored or repudiated the idea. Aristotle's description of God is of a perfect being: therefore one who needs nothing else, who has no uncompleted purposes, and who feels neither sensibility nor suffering. "The benevolence of heav-en" was a phrase much used in China around the mid-millennium, but this seems far short of love. Mozi, as even his philosophical adversaries admitted, "would wear out his whole being for the benefit of humankind." But his vision of humankind bound by love was not theologically inspired. Rather, he had a romantic vision of a golden age of "Great Togetherness" in the primitive past.

Contrasting systems inspired similar ethics of unselfishness, even in different contexts. We have seen unselfishness recommended in Brahmanism, for instance, where the world is illusory, or in some Greek thought, where the world is divine, or

FIGURE 6.1   THE ABRAHAMIC TRADITION

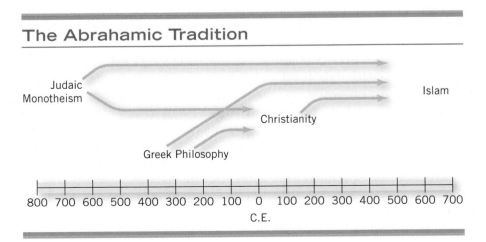

The Abrahamic Tradition

in Confucianism, where it is morally neutral, or in Zoroastrianism, where the world is actually evil, or Christianity, where it is good, or in Buddhism, where it is transient. Indeed, Buddhism's teachings of universal sympathy are so like those ascribed to Jesus that scholars have suspected Buddhist influence on the making of Christianity.

For humans, the claim that God's interest is specially focused on them seems suspiciously self-centered. Gradually, however, axial-age thinking made it believable by insisting that humankind was special—higher than other animals. There were dissenting traditions. Philosophers in southern Italy in the late sixth century B.C.E. taught that "All things that are born with life in them should be treated as kindred." Religious Jains' reverence for animals' souls is so intense that they sweep the ground to avoid walking on insects. But the biblical God makes "man in His own image" as the last word in creation and gives humans dominion over all other animals.

In the second half of the millennium, thinkers in other traditions formulated similar ideas. In the mid-fourth century B.C.E., Aristotle developed a hierarchy of living souls, in which the human soul was superior to those of plants and animals, because it had rational as well as "vegetative" and "sensitive" faculties. The Chinese formula was similar, as, for example, Xunzi (shoon-tzeh) put it early in the next century: "Man has spirits, life, and perception, and in addition the sense of justice; therefore he is the noblest of earthly beings." Humans could exploit stronger creatures because they were able to form societies and act collaboratively. Buddhism ranked humans as higher creatures than others for purposes of reincarnation.

These new thoughts on humans' place in creation left open the question of whether they were its lords or its stewards. But humankind now occupied a special relationship to God. Late in the axial age, some Jews began to use the image of **divine love** to express this relationship—perhaps to cope with the frustrations of their history, in which they had never been able to maintain political independence. Jesus and his followers seized on the identification of God with love. It was emotionally satisfying, for love is a universal emotion. By making God's love embrace all humans—rather than favoring a chosen race or a righteous minority—Christianity acquired universal appeal. Creation became an act of love consistent with God's nature. This solved a lot of problems, though it raised another—why does a loving God permit evil and suffering?

New Political Thinking

The evidence was glaringly ambiguous: Were misdeeds the result of corrupted goodness or inherent evil? Were human beings by their very nature good or bad? "The nature of man is evil—his goodness is only acquired by training," said Xunzi, for instance, in the mid–third century B.C.E. He believed that the original state of humankind was a grim swamp of violence, from which progress painfully raised people. "Hence," he continued, "the civilizing influence of teachers and laws, the guidance of rites and justice. Then courtesy appears, cultured behavior is observed and good government is the consequence." Confucius, on the other hand, thought that "Man is born for uprightness. If he lose it and yet live, it is merely luck." Since the axial age, political solutions to the problem of human nature have always been of two contrasting kinds: those that emphasize freedom, to release human goodness, and those that emphasize discipline, to restrain human wickedness. Either way, in liberating goodness or impeding evil, for axial-age thinkers, the state was an agent for virtue.

Divine love. "I am the good shepherd," said Jesus, according to the Gospel of John (10:14), "and I lay down my life for my sheep." During the persecutions that punctuated the first 300 years of the history of the Church, Christian artists interpreted the New Testament's many texts about "straying" and "lost" sheep as metaphors for the souls of martyrs, whom Jesus gathered into his fold. This third-century example shows how Christians continued the heroic and aesthetic conventions of classical sculpture.

"The Good Shepherd," marble, height: as restored 99 cm, as preserved 55 cm, head 15.5 cm. Late 3rd century A. D. Vatican Musuems, Pio-Christian Museum, Inv. 28590. Courtesy of the Vatican Museums.

Original sin. "For better, for worse." The embrace of Adam and Eve suggests sanctified love. Their unashamed nakedness (concealed later by an over-painter) signifies innocence. But the serpent is stroking Eve's hand, and sin and death are about to enter the world. This is one of at least 30 depictions of the scene by Lucas Cranach (1427–1553), one of the first Protestant painters, who longed to reverse humankind's self-alienation from God.

The biblical account of the creation of humans, in the book of Genesis, contained the most widely favored compromise. God made humans good and free. The abuse of freedom made people bad. Logically, however, this was unpersuasive. If Adam was good, how could he use freedom for evil? To escape this trap, Genesis added a diabolical device. The serpent (or other devilish agents in other traditions) corrupted goodness from outside. This has left politics with a difficult balancing act to perform, which no system has ever adequately accomplished, between freedom and force. In consequence, we can categorize most of the rest of the history of political thought as a debate between those who are pessimistic about human evil, and those who are hopeful of human goodness.

Political Pessimism For pessimists, the way to overcome human deficiencies was to strengthen the state. Plato was a member of an Athenian gang of rich, well-educated intellectuals and aristocrats, who felt qualified for power and therefore resented democracy. His rules for the ideal state were harsh, reactionary, and illiberal. Their many objectionable features—censorship, repression, militarism, regimentation, extreme communism, and collectivism, selective breeding of superior human beings, austerity, rigid class structure, active deception of the people by the state—all had a distressful influence. The key idea was that political power should be concentrated in a self-electing class of philosopher-rulers called **Guardians**.

Their qualification for office would be intellectual superiority, guaranteed by a mixture of heredity and education, that would make them selfless in their private lives and godlike in their ability to see what was good for the citizens. They would achieve Plato's declared objective in the construction of the state: the greatest happiness of the whole, and not that of any one class. He wrote so brilliantly and so persuasively that this reasoning has continued to appeal to state builders ever since. "There will be no end to the troubles of states, or indeed, of humanity," he claimed, "until philosophers become kings in this world, or till those we now call kings and rulers really and truly become philosophers." His Guardians, however, became the inspiration and the intellectual ancestors of elites, aristocracies, party hacks, and self-appointed supermen whose justification for tyrannizing others has always been that they know best.

Chinese counterparts exceeded the severity even of Plato's thinking. For most of the time, they were in the minority: The consensus among the sages was that the ruler should be bound by law (a point in which Aristotle, at the other end of Eurasia, agreed.) Confucius even said that ethics should override obedience to the law. The age-old tension between rules and rights showed, however, that law could function without any respect for ethics. In the fourth century B.C.E., a school of thought in China known as the **Legalists** made a virtue—or pretended virtue—of this deficiency. Their basic principle was that "goodness" was meaningless. Society

Political pessimism. Legend assigns the Great Wall of China to the Warring States period in the third century B.C.E., it took centuries to build and was often rebuilt thereafter. Little of the surviving workmanship, which stretches for some 4,000 miles, is more than 500 years old. Chinese culture now extends way beyond it, but it has an important place in the formation of Chinese identity—defining the supposed boundary of the non-Chinese world, displaying the ambition and achievement of Chinese civilization.

required only obedience. What the law actually said was irrelevant. All that really mattered was that it should be obeyed. Morality was nonsense. The only good was the good of the state. Law and order were worth tyranny and injustice. Ethics was a "gnawing worm" that would destroy the state.

This was a remarkable new twist in the history of thinking about law. All previous schools had tried to make human law more moral by aligning it with divine or natural law. The explanation lies in the terror of the times. Legalist doctrine was born in a time of civil disaster and has tended to resurface in bad times ever since. The Chinese Legalists were reacting against generations of disastrous feuding among the "Warring States." The ethics-based thinking of the Confucians and Daoists had done nothing to prevent this feuding. The legalists laughed off earlier sages' belief in the innate goodness of people. The best penalties were the most severe: cutting off people's heads, slicing people in half, pulling their bodies apart with chariots, boring a hole in their skulls, roasting them alive, or cutting out a wrongdoer's ribs. As well as in the worship of order, ancient Chinese Legalism anticipated modern fascism, for instance, in advocating and glorifying war, recommending economic self-sufficiency for the state, denouncing capitalism, praising agriculture, and insisting on the need to suppress individualism in the interests of state unity.

Political Optimism But most sages of the axial age were optimists. They thought human nature was essentially good. The political doctrines of Confucianism, for example, demanded that the state should liberate subjects to fulfill their potential. And some Greek sages advocated democracy, which entrusted citizens (though not, of course, excluded groups, such as women or slaves) with a voice in affairs of state, even if the citizens were poor or badly educated. The citizens and their participation in the governing of the state were ends in themselves, according to the underlying ideology of these beliefs, and, though to serve rulers or support society was an inescapable duty, it was not the purpose of life.

Chinese thinkers applied similarly individualistic doctrines, which gathered strength during the axial age, to the state. But they did not question the role of

Render unto Caesar. If the coin the Pharisees showed Jesus was up to date, it showed the head of Tiberius Caesar (r. 14–37 C.E.). "Render unto Caesar that which is Caesar's," said Jesus. Later ages misinterpreted him to mean, "Pay taxes." But he was probably making an ironic, rabbinical joke, and really meant the opposite—that nothing was Caesar's because everything belonged to God.

monarchy. The state, after all, was meant to reflect the universe. Its unity could not be compromised. All that could be expected was that the ruler should consult the people's interests and views and should face, in case of tyranny, the subject's right to rebel. In Daoist political thought, the ruler's job is to enforce virtue. Confucius advocated a return to a golden age supposedly located at the foundation of the Zhou dynasty (see Chapter 4). He called aristocracy and subordinate kings to an allegiance ordained by heaven. "Heaven sees according as the People see," said Mencius, Confucianism's outstanding spokesman. "Heaven hears according as the people hear." This was a reminder to the ruler, not a recipe for republicanism. Nor does Indian literature of the time mention popular institutions. But some Indian states did have elites numbered in the hundreds—perhaps in the thousands in some cases—which ruled as a group, electing leaders for fixed terms among themselves.

Meanwhile, in Greece, sages considered states to be purely practical mechanisms to be tinkered with at need. An enormous variety of political experiments unfolded, including republican or aristocratic systems, and even democratic ones. Aristotle made a masterly survey of them in the fourth century B.C.E. He thought monarchy was the best system in theory, but not in practice, because it was impossible to ensure that the best man would always be the ruler. More practical was aristocratic government, in which a manageable number of superior men administered the state. But it tended to degenerate into the self-interested rule of the wealthy or permanent power for an hereditary clique. Democracy, in which all the citizens shared, had—as we saw in Chapter 5—a long, if fluctuating, record of success in Athens. From early in the sixth century B.C.E., Athenian lawmakers appealed to the body of citizens to legitimate the laws. "Being master of the vote the people became master of the constitution." Aristotle denounced this system because it could lead to demagogues and mob rule. The best system was a carefully crafted mixture in which aristocracy predominated, under the rule of law. Broadly speaking, this was embodied in the Roman state of the second half of the millennium (see Chapter 8), which became, in turn, the model for most republican survivals and revivals in Western history. Even when, toward the end of the axial age, Rome abandoned republican government and restored what was in effect a monarchy, Romans still spoke of their state as a republic and the emperor as merely the chief magistrate.

In politics, Jesus preached a subtle subversion. A new commandment to "love one another," he claimed, could replace virtually all laws. The Kingdom of Heaven was more important than the empire of Rome. In one of history's great ironic jokes, Jesus advised fellow Jews, in effect, to despise or even ignore the state: "Render unto Caesar that which is Caesar's and unto God that which is God's." All Jews at the time would have understood what this meant, for everything, to them, was God's.

For society at large, Jesus was equally dangerous, welcoming social outcasts—prostitutes, tax collectors, "sinners," and people from Samaria, whom Jews despised as both sinners and heretics. He favored the weak against the strong: children, women, the lame, the blind, and beggars—the "meek," who, he promised, "shall inherit the earth." Given the radical nature of this bias, it is unsurprising that Jewish and Roman authorities combined to put him to death. His followers then turned from political activism to spiritual preparation for personal salvation.

Challenging Illusion

New thinking about reason and reality, and the relationship between them, flourished alongside or within the work of the religious leaders. Perhaps the most startling feature that united the thought of the axial age across Eurasia was the sages' struggle against illusion—their effort to see beyond appearances to underlying realities. "Behold," for instance, "people dwelling in a cavern," said Plato. "Like us, they see only their own shadows, or each other's shadows, which the fire throws onto the wall of their cave." Our senses deceive. We are mental cave dwellers. How can we see out of our cave? For convenience, we can group the novelties this quest inspired under the headings of mathematics, reason, and science (from which we can separate medicine as a distinct category). After reviewing the axial ages' achievements in those fields, we can turn to skepticism—mistrust of all of them and, in general, of human capacity to achieve more than practical happiness, a trend of thought that was, in some ways, an outcome of the others.

"Perhaps the most startling feature that united the thought of the axial age across Eurasia was the sages' struggle against illusion—their effort to see beyond appearances to underlying realities."

Mathematics

Evidence of the previously unperceived complexity of reality accumulated during the axial age. Indian sages, building on their early speculations about the possibility of nothing and of infinity, discovered in numbers a genuinely limitless universe. Jain speculators about the age of the cosmos involved the concept of mind-boggling big numbers, partly to demonstrate how impossible it was to attain the infinite. Workers in arithmetic discovered unreachable numbers: ratios that could never be exactly determined, yet that seemed to underpin the universe—for instance, those that determined the size of a circle, or the complex ratio that Greek mathematicians called "the Golden Number" (roughly 1.618), and that seemed to represent perfection of proportion. The invention of geometry showed how the mind can reach realities that the senses obscure or warp: a perfect circle, a line without magnitude. Reality can be invisible, untouchable, and yet accessible to reason.

A figure of enormous importance in unfolding these mysteries (for that is what they were to people at the time) was Pythagoras. His life spanned the Greek world. He was born on an island in the Aegean, around the mid-sixth century B.C.E., but spent most of his teaching life in a Greek colony in southern Italy. He attracted stories—he communed with the gods; he had a golden thighbone; he was not a mere man but a unique being, between human and divine.

Pythagoras is most famous today for two relatively trivial insights: that musical harmonies can be expressed as arithmetical ratios; and that consistent ratios characterize the lengths of the sides of right-angled triangles. His importance goes much deeper. He was the first thinker, as far as we know, to formulate the idea that numbers are real. They are obviously ways we have of classifying objects—two flowers, five flies. But Pythagoras thought there was more to it than that—that two and five really exist, quite apart from the objects they enumerate. They would still exist, even if there were nothing to count. He went further. Numbers are the basis on which the cosmos is constructed. "All things are numbers" was his way of putting it. Numbers determine shapes and structures—we still speak of "squares" and "cubes"—and numerical proportions underlie all relationships. Geometry, Pythagoras thought, is the architecture of the universe.

Not everyone was equally enthusiastic about the cult of numbers. "I sought the truth in measures and numbers," said Confucius in a text, which, though he probably did not really write it, reflects the prejudices of the third-century B.C.E. Daoist who compiled it, "but after five years I still hadn't found it." Still, the exploration of numbers was a widespread interest among axial-age sages. **Rationalism**—the doctrine that unaided reason can reach the truth and solve the world's problems—was among the results.

Reason

The first pure rationalist we know by name was Parmenides, who was from a Greek colony of southern Italy in the early fifth century B.C.E. He started with the geometry Pythagoras had taught. If you believe geometrical figures are real, you believe in the truth of a super-sensible world—for a perfect triangle, for instance, is like God: No one has ever seen one, though crude manmade approximations are commonplace. "It is natural," as Bertrand Russell—reputedly one of the twentieth century's clearest thinkers—said, "to go further and to argue that . . . the objects of thought are more real than sense-perception." The only triangles we know about are those in our thoughts. Parmenides therefore suggested that the same might be true of trees—and of everything else.

In some ways, the consequences are impressive. If, say, a pink rose is real by virtue of being a thought rather than a sensible object, then a black rose is equally real. The nonexistence of anything is an incoherent concept. Few of Parmenides's followers were willing to go that far, but reason did seem able to open secret caverns in the mind, where truths lay. "Fire is not hot. Eyes do not see": These were the numbing, blinding paradoxes of the fourth-century B.C.E. Chinese philosopher Hui Shih (hway-sheh), who wrote five cartloads of books. They show that data act directly on the mind, which processes them before they become sensations. Thought needs no objects outside itself. It can make up its own. It is pure. It does not have to arise from experience. For a true rationalist, the best laboratory is the mind, and the best experiments are thoughts.

In partial consequence, rationalism became an escapist's alternative to reality. Parmenides, for instance, thought he could prove that change was illusory and differences deceptive, and that only the unchanging and eternal were real. One of his successors, Zeno of Elea, invented famous paradoxes to demonstrate this: An arrow in flight always occupies a space equal to its size, therefore it is always at rest. You can never complete a journey because you always have to cross half the remaining distance first. Matter is indivisible because "if a rod is shortened every day by half its length, it will still have something left after ten thousand generations" (see Figure 6.2).

Despite rationalists' excesses, reason has helped to temper or restrain rival approaches to regulating the world—systems founded on dogma or charisma or emotion or naked power or lies. Philosophers have often dangled the tempting hope that reason could do more. It could reshape the world, formulate laws, and construct society. In practice, chapters on an "Age of Reason" in history books usually turn out to be about something else. Reason has never had much appeal outside elites and has only rarely ruled entire societies. It did, however, give axial-age thinkers a systematic way of organizing thoughts.

Early in the second half of the millennium, teachers in India, Greece, and China showed intense interest in proposing rules for the correct use of reason. Practical issues probably underpinned these movements. For pleading in courts, arguing between embassies, persuading enemies and praising rulers, it was important to make arguments watertight. Logic was a fascinating by-product of these practical needs.

The most rigorous and systematic exposition was Aristotle's, strapping common sense into intelligible rules. If we think we understand him, it is because he taught us how to think. To

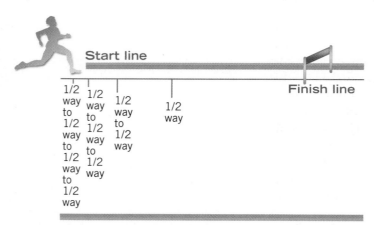

FIGURE 6.2 A PARADOX OF ZENO. Zeno used paradox to suggest that the world was illusory, observation absurd, and change logically impossible. Take motion: the runner can never reach his destination or make any real progress because before traversing a given distance he must first get to the halfway point, but because every halfway has its own halfway point, he'll never get anywhere. *Baird, Forrest E., Philosophic Classics Volume I: Ancient Philosophy 4th edition, ©* *2003. Electronically reproduced by permission of Pearson Education, Inc., Upper Saddle River, New Jersey.*

this day, even people who have barely heard of him use the techniques he taught, which have seeped into mental habits through the channels of tradition. He was the best-ever analyst of how reason works, in as much as it works at all. According to Aristotle, we can break valid arguments down into phases, called **syllogisms**, in which we can infer a necessary conclusion from two premises that prior demonstration or agreement have established to be true. If the premises are, "All men are mortal" and "Socrates is a man," it follows that "Socrates is mortal."

At roughly the same time in India, the Nyaya school of commentators on ancient texts analyzed logical processes in five-stage breakdowns that resembled syllogisms. Their conception, however, was in one fundamental way different from Aristotle's. They claimed reason was a kind of extraordinary perception that God conferred. Nor were they strictly rationalists, for they believed meaning did not arise in the mind. God, tradition, or consensus conferred it on the object of thought.

Science

Meanwhile, another route through the thought of the axial age led to science. As with the exploration of reason, the starting point was distrust of the senses. As the Daoist text, the *Lü Shi Chong Qiu* (lew-sheh-chuhng-chee-oh) of the third century B.C.E., points out, some metals may seem soft but can be combined to form harder ones; lacquer feels liquid but can be made dry by the application of another liquid; herbs taste poisonous but can be mixed to make medicine. First appearances are deceptive. "You cannot know the properties of a thing merely by knowing those of its components." The science of the axial age sought to penetrate the veil and expose underlying truths. Greeks agreed. "Truth," said Democritus around the turn of the fifth and fourth centuries B.C.E., "lies in the depths." Although no strictly scientific texts from India survive from this period, the Upanishads contain similar warnings about the unreliability of appearances (see Chapter 5).

The idea of a distinction between what is natural and what is supernatural was, as far as we can tell, new. Previously, the two realms seemed so thoroughly combined that science seemed essentially sacred, medicine magical. The earliest clear evidence of a shift in thinking is Chinese. In 679 B.C.E., the sage Shen Xu (shehn-shoo) is said to have taught that ghosts were just the products of the fears and guilt of those who see them. Confucius deterred his followers from thinking "about the dead until you know the living" and defined wisdom as aloof respect for gods and demons. Confucians professed interest in human affairs—politics and practical morality—and indifference to the rest of nature. But as far as his followers did study nature, it was in an effort to dig out what they regarded as superstition: the claim that inanimate substances had feelings and wills, the notion that spirits inhabit all matter, the claim—advanced sometimes even by sophisticated thinkers on the grounds that everything in the universe is connected to everything else— that the natural world is responsive to human sin or goodness. "If one does not know causes, it is as if one knew nothing," says a Confucian text of about 239 B.C.E. "The fact that water leaves the mountains is not due to any dislike on the part of the water but is the effect of height. The wheat has no desire to grow or be gathered into granaries. Therefore the sage does not enquire about goodness or badness but about reasons." Thus "natural" causes displaced magic.

In Greece, the origins of science are inseparable from a background of magic, nature worship, and shamanistic attempts to penetrate the mysteries of unseen worlds by rites and ecstasies. Most ancient Greeks, indeed, probably never escaped

"In Greece, the origins of science are inseparable from a background of magic, nature worship, and shamanistic attempts to penetrate the mysteries of unseen worlds by rites and ecstasies."

Delphi. Around Mount Parnassus, north of Athens, Greeks found or founded many shrines consecrated to Earth and Nature, as well as the most famous oracular site, at Delphi, where priestesses uttered obscure prophecies, supposedly under the influence of hallucinogenic fumes that rose from a fissure in the ground. Nearby, the circular sanctum known as the Tholos was built in the fourth century B.C.E., at or near the place where the Greeks' predecessors had located the navel of the Mother-Goddess or, as we might now say, the center of the Earth.

belief in the supernatural. From the late sixth century B.C.E., however, nature worship was beginning to encourage naturalistic explanations of curious phenomena. Texts, for instance, denounce attempts to understand omens or to foretell the future through magic as useless or delusive, and use observed data as the basis of speculations about the material nature of the universe. But for science to thrive in a world that, in most people's minds, gods and sprites and demons still ruled, a method was needed to observe nature systematically, order the information, and test the resulting hypotheses. Aristotle was the best representative of Greek science in its maturity. "We must have facts," he said, and he proceeded to gather them in enormous quantities. Like the perfect example of a "nutty professor," he prowled around his lecture room, dissected flies, and noted every stage in the incubation of birds' eggs. Other highlights of Greek science of the period included Archimedes's discovery of the mechanics of leverage in the mid-third century B.C.E., and, slightly later, the work of Eratosthenes, who produced an almost exactly accurate calculation of the size of the Earth (see Map 6.3).

Chinese practical science—systematic investigation of nature through observation and experiment—probably arose, around the same time that it did in Greece, from Daoist doctrines of nature. Habits of observation and experiment developed from the magical and omen-seeking practices of early Daoism. The Daoist word for a "temple" means *watchtower*—a platform from which to observe the natural world and launch naturalistic explanations of its phenomena. Daoism has, in Confucian eyes, a reputation for magical mumbo-jumbo because its priests practice strange ceremonies, many of which seem indebted in their origins to the magical fallacy that nature responds to human ritual. But Daoism also teaches that Nature—to the one who would control it—is like any other beast to be tamed or foe to be dominated—it must be known first.

Part of the result is that Daoism encouraged the beginnings of scientific practice: observation, description, classification, and experiment. In second-century B.C.E. China, for instance, the Daoist legend told of Yi (YEE) the archer, who on the advice of sages sought the medicine of immortality away in the West, when the herb that would confer it was growing outside his door. Daoist texts often have amusing dialogues between craftsmen who know their work and rationalists who persuade them to do it in a different way, with ruinous results. Grand theory is discouraged as an intrusion of reason into the workings of wisdom, which can be attained only by gaining knowledge. Chinese science has always been weak on theory, strong on technology.

Medicine

Controversy followed between magic and medicine—or was it just between rival forms of magic? Illness, like any abnormal state, including madness, could be the result of possession or infestation by a spirit, a "demon"—to recycle a commonly used

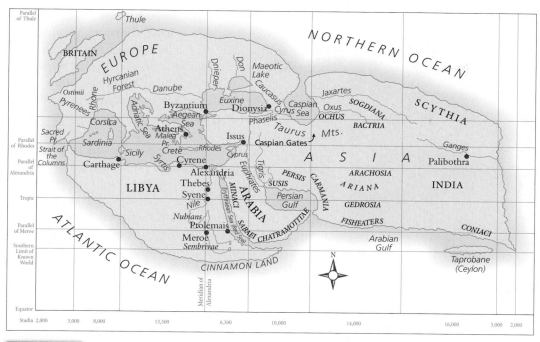

MAP 6.3

The World According to Eratosthenes

Eratosthenes (ca. 275–195 B.C.E.) directed the Library of Alexandria and made a remarkably accurate estimate of the size of the globe. His world map has not survived but a version can be reconstructed from ancient descriptions.

word for it. Or some diseases could have material causes, others spiritual. Or all could be a mixture of the two. Or sickness could be a divine affliction, the result of sin.

In an incident in China that took place in 540 B.C.E. according to the chronicle that recorded it, an official told his prince to rely on diet, work, and personal morale for bodily health, not on the spirits of rivers, mountains, and stars. Officials, however, usually command little prestige as physicians. The controversy that mattered occurred within the ranks of professional healers. In Greece in the late fifth century B.C.E., a secular school known as the Hippocratics tried to monopolize the medical profession, at the expense of rival healers who were attached to temples. The Hippocratics thought that health was essentially a state of balance among four substances in human bodies: blood, phlegm, and black and yellow bile. Adjust the balance, and you alter the patient's state of health. This condemned patients in the West for centuries to treatment mainly by diet, vomiting, laxatives, and blood-letting. The theory was wrong—but it was genuinely scientific, based on observation of the substances the body expels in pain or sickness.

A treatise sometimes attributed to Hippocrates himself—supposed founder of the school—advocates a naturalistic explanation for epilepsy, which many people at the time assumed to be a form of divine possession. The test is: Find a goat exhibiting the same symptoms that a human epileptic does. "If you cut open the head, you will find that the brain is . . . full of fluid and smells foul, convincing proof that the disease and not the deity is harming the body." The method sounds bizarre, but the conclusion is impressive. "Personally," the Hippocratic writer went on, "I believe that human bodies cannot be polluted by a god." A similar shift of business into the hands of secular medical specialists occurred in China. Xunzi, who died in 235 B.C.E., scorned a man who "having got rheumatism from damp-

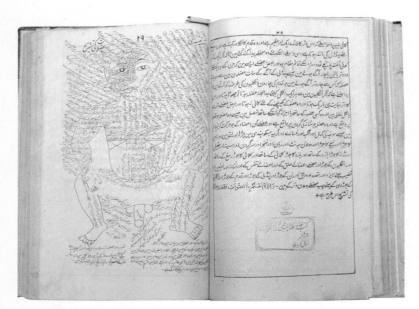

Ayurvedic medicine. This medical textbook, first published in 1593, and based on *The Canon of Medicine* written by the great Muslim scholar Avicenna early in the eleventh century, is still used by students at the Unani Medical College in Hyderabad, India. Ayurvedic treatments are usually herbal, although diet and exercise are also important remedies. The illustration and text shown here concern the muscles of the human body.

ness beats a drum and boils a suckling pig as an offering to the spirits." Result: "a worn-out drum and a lost pig, but he will not have the happiness of recovering from sickness." Religious explanations of disease remained. But the Hippocratics and their Chinese counterparts started a presumption that has gained ground ever since: that nothing needs to be explained in divine terms. The physical world is all there is.

These changes had close parallels in India. In the earliest known Indian work of medicine, the *Arthaveda* (ahr-thah-VEH-dah), which dates from the early first millennium B.C.E., diseases and demons are more or less identical and are treated with charms or drugs. From the sixth century B.C.E. onward, however, we see evidence of professional medical training and literature. Work largely complete by the second century C.E. summarizes these medical teachings. Writings attributed to Susutra, who probably lived in the sixth century B.C.E., concern surgery; writings attributed to Charaka (which may be the name of a school rather than a person) concentrate exclusively on diet and drugs. A saying attributed to Charaka is strikingly similar to the morals of the Greek Hippocrates: "If you want your treatment to succeed, to earn wealth, to gain fame, and to win heaven hereafter . . . seek the good of all living creatures, strive with your whole heart to cure the sick." The similarities among Indian, Greek, and Chinese axial-age medicine are so remarkable that historians often assume that they influenced each other. There is, however, no direct evidence for this influence.

Skepticism

A consequence of the rise of a scientific point of view was the suspicion that the world is purposeless. In particular, this line of thinking raised an idea that challenged another axial-age orthodoxy: If the world had no purpose, it was not made for human beings, who were reduced to insignificance. The idea Aristotle called the "Final Cause"—the purpose of a thing, which explains its nature—becomes incoherent. The world is a random event.

In around 200 B.C.E., this was such a dangerous idea that a skeptical Chinese treatise, the *Liezi* (lee-ay-tzeh), avoided direct advocacy of it by putting it into the mouth of a small boy, who challenged a pious host for praising the divine bounty that provided good things for his table. "Mosquitoes suck human blood, wolves devour human flesh but we do not therefore assert that Heaven created man for their benefit." The greatest-ever exponent of a cosmos without purpose was the Chinese philosopher of the first century C.E., Wangchong (wahng chohng). Humans, he said, live "like lice in the folds of a garment. When fleas buzz in your ear, you do not hear them: How could God even hear men, let alone concede their wishes?" Some materialist thinkers still take pride in asserting that the whole notion of purpose is superstitious and that asking why the world exists or why it is as it is is pointless.

Chronology: Axial-Age Science and Medicine	
Sixth century B.C.E.	Susutra (India)
Late fifth century B.C.E.	Hippocrates (Greece)
ca. 250 B.C.E.	Archimedes (Greece)
d. 235 B.C.E.	Xunzi (China)
ca. 200 B.C.E.	Eratosthenes (Greece)

In a world without purpose, there is no need for God. The name of the Greek philosopher Epicurus, who died in 270 B.C.E., has become unfairly associated with the pursuit of physical pleasure—which he certainly recommended, albeit with restraint. A far more important element of his thought was his interpretation of the atomic theory. In a world of atoms and voids, there is no room for "spirits." Since atoms are subject to "random swerves," there can be no fate. Since they are perishable, and everything is composed of them, there can be no immortal soul. Gods, if they exist at all, inhabit an imaginary world from which "we have nothing to hope and nothing to fear." Epicurus's arguments were formidable, and materialists and atheists kept returning to them. At about the end of the first century C.E., the Roman writer Sextus Empiricus suggested, like a modern Marxist, that "some shrewd man invented fear of the gods" as a means of social control. The doctrines of an all-powerful and all-knowing god were devised to suppress freedom of conscience. "If they say that God controls everything, they make him the author of evil," he concluded. "We express no belief and avoid the evil of the dogmatizers."

In revulsion from the big, unanswerable questions about the nature of reality, skeptical thinkers and their schools refocused philosophy on practical issues. One of the great anecdote-inspiring characters of ancient Greece was Pyrrho of Elis, who accompanied Alexander the Great's invasion of India in 327–324 B.C.E. (see Chapter 7) and imitated the indifference of the naked sages he met there. On board ship on the way home, he admired and shared the calm response of a pig to a storm. He was absent minded and accident prone, which made him seem unworldly, but his deepest indifference was to reason. The achievements of the Greek rationalists of the previous hundred years left him cold. Since, he argued, you can find equally good reasons on both sides of any argument, the only wise course is to stop thinking and judge by appearances. More effective was the argument that all reasoning starts from assumptions; so none of it is secure. Mozi had developed a similar insight in China around the beginning of the fourth century B.C.E. Most problems were matters of doubt. "As for what we now know, is it not mostly derived from past experience?"

Later Greek philosophy focused on systems that concerned the best practical choices for personal happiness or for the good of society. **Stoicism** is the outstanding example of this kind of philosophy, both for the coherence of stoic ideas and because these ideas were so influential. Stoicism appealed to the Roman elite and through them had an enormous effect on Christianity. First taught in the school that Zeno of Citium founded in Athens in the late fourth century B.C.E., stoicism started from the insight that nature is morally neutral—only human acts are good or evil. The wise man therefore achieves happiness by accepting misfortune. Further stoic prescriptions—fatalism and indifference as remedies for pain—were similar to teachings preached at about the same period at the far end of Eurasia, especially by the Buddha and his followers, or Laozi and his. People have sought the "happiness priority" in so many contrasting ways that it is hard to generalize about its overall effect on the history of the world. Stoicism, however, was certainly its most effective manifestation in the West. It has supplied, in effect, the source of the guiding principles of the ethics of most Western elites since it emerged.

Chronology: Skeptics and Stoics	
Fourth century B.C.E.	Pyrrho of Elis (Greece)
Late fourth century B.C.E.	Zeno of Citium (Greece)
d. 270 B.C.E.	Epicurus (Greece)
First century C.E.	Wangchong (China)
First century C.E.	Sextus Empiricus (Rome)

THE STRUCTURES OF THE AXIAL AGE

Monotheism, republicanism, Legalism, rationalism, logic, science (including scientific medicine), skepticism, the most enduring religions and ethical systems—the tally of new thinking in the axial age looks impressive by any standards, but especially because of its legacy to us. We have to confront the problems of why this period was so productive and why—though widely dispersed in Eurasia—it was confined, by global standards, to so few societies around the globe.

Clearly, the structures that underpinned the work of the axial-age thinkers were important for making it happen. The schools and sages formed four obvious and sometimes overlapping categories. First, there were professional intellectuals, who sold their services as teachers, usually to candidates for professional or public office, but perhaps also to those who sought happiness or immortality or, at least, health. A second class sought the patronage of rulers or positions as political advisers. Many sages belonged to both these groups: Aristotle, for instance, taught in Athens but also served as a tutor to the prince who later became Alexander the Great (see Chapter 7). Confucius eked out life as a teacher, but not because he did not want to serve states. A third category was made up of prophets or holy men, who emerged from ascetic lives with inspired messages for society; a fourth was composed of charismatic leaders with visions to share with and, if possible, impose on their peoples.

Most sages fitted into networks. Though lonely, hermitlike existence was an ideal that many of them recommended, affected, and even sought, few, if any, of these sages were genuinely isolated thinkers. Those, at least, who founded schools or established enduring influence depended on contacts to make and spread their reputations. Networks also stimulated innovation. They nourished competition, fertilized ideas through discussion and debate, and gave innovators emotional support. Plato wrote all his works in the form of dialogues and conversations—which make the function of the network visible. The Confucian Mencius, the Daoist Zhuangzi (Jwahng-tzeh), and Hui Shi, the analyst of language, were contemporaries of each other. Competition and debate probably sharpened their views and helped make them famous. Similarly, Plato's teacher Socrates was probably the most famous sage of Greece in the early fourth century B.C.E. and was in conflict with all the Greek schools of his day, attacking those known as Sophists for allegedly valuing the elegance of an argument as more important than its truth. Epicurus and Zeno of Citium established schools in Athens within a few years of each other toward the end of the fourth century B.C.E. (see Map 6.4).

Formal institutions of education played their part in defining networks and stimulating competition. We know little of how they functioned, but the Academy of Athens, founded in 380 B.C.E., had a garden and student lodgings that Plato purchased. Members ate together and contributed to costs according to their means. Master–pupil relationships created traditions or what we might call cross-generational networks. Socrates taught Plato, who taught Aristotle. Traditions of this sort can get rigid, but clever pupils often innovate by reacting against their masters' teaching (something all textbook writers

The Academy of Athens. Romans continued to admire the philosophy of classical Greece. The Acropolis of Athens is recognizable in the background of this mosaic, preserved in the ruins of Pompeii. The columns and gardens recall what the setting of Plato's Academy at Athens was really like.

MAP 6.4

Philosophical Schools in the Mediterranean Region, 600 B.C.E.–100 C.E.

● Schools mentioned or described in Chapter 6

should bear in mind) and set up chains of revisionism from one generation to the next. Confucius was a critic of the establishment of his day. Mohists, similarly, opposed Confucians. A succession of masters as well as a series of conflicts linked Mozi to Confucius. Han Feizi (hawn-fay-tzeh), a Confucian pupil, founded the Legalist school in reaction to his teacher, Xunzi (see Figure 6.3).

Disciples and pupils confided masters' works to writing. Literacy is not necessary for great thinking, but it helps. Many sages were hostile or indifferent to writing. The Upanishads were probably transmitted orally before they were finally written down. Socrates wrote nothing. Jesus wrote nothing that has survived—only, as far as we know, a few words scratched in the dust. The Buddha's teachings were too sacred—his first disciples thought—to confide to writing and had eventually to be retrieved from memories when it was finally decided to write them down. Does this mean that the axial age is a trick of the evidence? That the ideas of its sages became so influential only because they were eventually written down? Not entirely, but it does mean that its thoughts have come down to us in a way that other regions and other periods did not have or did not use.

Some thinkers of the axial age were rich men. Plato was an aristocrat who could endow his own school with his own money. The Buddha and Mahavira, the founder of Jainism, were princes. Usually, however, intellectuals need patrons or employers to survive. The politically fragmented worlds of axial-age Greece, China, and India, had plenty of potential patrons. A wandering scholar like Confucius might not retain a patron for long—but he could turn to others. This made for independence of thought and liberated political philosophy to criticize rulers. Every subsequent age has successfully adapted Confucius's message, but he addressed it to his own time—hence his emphasis on the renewal of tradition, the resumption of sacred rites, the restoration of land and property to their rightful owners. Of course, royal patrons are rarely disinterested. In mid-fourth century B.C.E. China, Mencius found his patron, the King of Wei, interested only in schemes to improve military efficiency. Also at the court of Wei, Hui Shi turned his talent for argument to negotiations with other states.

To patronize sages became, in itself, a source of princely prestige. In China the prince of Zhao allegedly had 1000 scholars at his court toward the mid-third

FIGURE 6.3 NETWORK OF CHINESE
PHILOSOPHERS, 400–200 B.C.E.

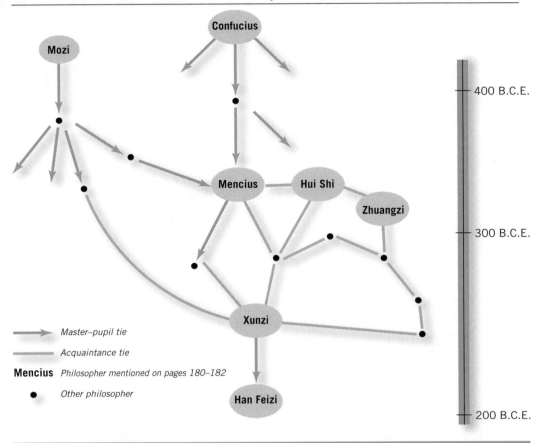

Network of Chinese Philosophers, 400–200 B.C.E.

century B.C.E. Intellectual wars paralleled bloodshed between states. The Chinese state of Chu supported the followers of Mozi against the Confucians. Qin, supposedly a "barbarian" kingdom on the edge of the Chinese culture area, was home to thousands of scholars. When its ruler burned books in the 220s B.C.E., it was less perhaps an act against learning than a gesture of partisanship on behalf of thinkers he favored.

In India, too, among the 12 or 16 states that shared the Ganges valley in the period, similar rivalries and opportunities existed. The Veda contains fragments of sages' dialogues with kings, in which the kings sometimes out argued the sages. Buddhism relied on rulers' patronage in the kingdoms of Kosala and Magadha. Mahavira was related to the rulers of Videha, where his doctrines enjoyed official favor. His followers debated with Buddhists for supremacy in Magadha. As we shall see in the next chapter, political unification and large-scale imperialism did not promote intellectual productivity. One of the reasons Zoroaster had no comparably influential successors in Persia is probably that Persia rapidly became an imperial power. In China, India, and Greece the axial age waned as empires grew at the expense of small states, even though the empires themselves spread axial-age ideas.

In some places, alongside state patronage, public values and popular support may have nourished the intellectuals. The sage and the holy man are most useful to the public in times of political dissolution. Their wisdom and objectivity make them sought after to arbitrate between neighbors or to take the place of absent

justice. Public interest is apparent in the multiplicity of schools and the willingness of pupils to seek the benefit of masters' expertise. Learned writings attracted readers. Democritus, an exponent of atomic theory in the early fourth century B.C.E., was credited with 60 books. Heraclitus, one of the first generation of Greek sages around the beginning of the sixth-century B.C.E., was a notorious loner who refused to take on pupils. But he nonetheless deposited his writings in the famous temple of the goddess Artemis at Ephesus on the western coast of Anatolia—in effect, his local public library.

In Perspective
The Reach of the Sages

Although the new thinking of the axial age was confined to parts of Asia and Europe, it was a worldwide story because of the way axial-age thinking later spread and shaped thoughts and feelings in every clime and continent. Empires that are the subject of the next chapter helped to spread it. Trade and colonization, which can be traced at intervals throughout the rest of this book, took axial thought further, until it had spread across the planet. The Roman empire carried Greek science and philosophy into Western Europe. Buddhism became a state ideology in the first empire to cover most of India. The Chinese Empire became a growing arena in

Making Connections | THINKERS AND THOUGHTS OF THE AXIAL AGE

REGION ➡	SAGE/THINKER ➡	PHILOSOPHY/ RELIGION ➡	DISTINCTIVE IDEAS ➡
Southwest Asia	Jewish sages, ca. 700–500 B.C.E.	Judaism	Monotheism; trials of faith; punishments for sin; covenant with God
	Zoroaster, ca. 600 B.C.E.	Zoroastrianism	Eternal conflict between good and evil (dualism)
	Jesus, ca. 30 C.E.	Christianity	Importance of faith, divine love
India	Gautama Siddharta, ca. 560 B.C.E.	Buddhism	Meditation; karma; Four Noble Truths; escaping desire
	Mahavira, ca. 559 B.C.E.	Jainism	Sanctity of life; nonviolence (*ahimsa*)
	Nyaya school, 350 B.C.E.	Rationalism	Logic; reason as an extraordinary perception conferred by God
Greece/Asia Minor	Pythagoras, ca. 550 B.C.E.	Mathematics	Geometrical and mathematical ideas; ratios; ideas that numbers are real
	Parmenides, ca. 425 B.C.E.	Rationalism	Objects of thought are more real than sense perception
	Zeno of Citium, ca. 390 B.C.E.	Stoicism	Nature is morally neutral; happiness achieved by accepting misfortune
	Aristotle and Plato, ca. 380 B.C.E.	Secular philosophy	Logic; science; political thought
	Epicurus, ca. 280 B.C.E.	Skepticism	Centrality of matter; soul is not immortal; if God exists he is indifferent to human affairs
China	Confucius, ca. 500 B.C.E.	Secular philosophy	Loyalty to God, state, and family; importance of ethics and right conduct
	Mozi, ca. 400 B.C.E.	Secular philosophy	Universal love
	Laozi, ca. 300 B.C.E.	Daoism	Detachment from world; quest for immortality
	Xunzi, ca. 250 B.C.E.	Secular philosophy	Human goodness can be attained through progress and freedom
	Han Feizi, ca. 225 B.C.E.	Legalism	Only good is the good of the state; law and order more important than tyranny and injustice

which Buddhism, as well as native Chinese thought, spread within and across China's widening borders. Japan and Korea fell under Chinese cultural influence, and their intellectual traditions developed from Chinese-inspired starting points. Migration and trade bore Indian thinking into parts of Southeast Asia. Christianity fused Jewish and Greek intellectual traditions and spread them—ultimately—all over the world. Islam shared much of the same heritage and spread it almost as far. Buddhism is the third, in terms of numbers of followers, of the three world religions of today. Alongside Christianity and Islam, both of which developed after the axial age, it has spread over many different countries and cultures, whereas most religions tend to remain specific to their cultures of origin. We do not fully understand why Buddhism succeeded in this way, but we shall trace its history in this book. The scale of demands Buddhism makes on its followers is well suited to a variety of walks of life.

As a result of the spread of the work of the sages and their schools, the thought of the modern world has a familiar ring to a student of the axial age. It seems astonishing that today, after all the technical and material progress of the last 2,000 years, we should remain so dependent on the thought of such a distant era and have added so little to it. We debate the same issues about the nature of reality, using the same tools of logic and science. We struggle with the same problems about the relationship of this world to others, and most of us still follow religious traditions that axial-age sages founded. We search for a balance between the same kinds of optimistic and pessimistic assessments of human nature that people of the axial age identified, and we seek to resolve similar conflicts of political ideas that arise as a result. To a remarkable extent, we express ourselves in terms the ancient sages taught.

Although the sages and schools of the axial age were confined to Eurasia, comparisons with other parts of the world help us understand how cultural contacts shape and spread what people think and believe. Over and over again, readers of this book will see and will have seen, for example, how ways of thought and life and worship radiated outward from kernel regions: from Mesoamerica, for example,

"As a result of the spread of the work of the sages and their schools, the thought of the modern world has a familiar ring to a student of the axial age. It seems astonishing that today, after all the technical and material progress of the last 2,000 years, we should remain so dependent on the thought of such a distant era and have added so little to it."

The Library of Celsus. In Heraclitus's day, the Temple of Artemis at Ephesus, in what is today Turkey, served as a repository of books that citizens could consult. Early in the second century C.E., however, Ephesus acquired the Library of Celsus, erected in memory of a Roman governor, specifically to house the city's collection of books. The facade—the only surviving part of the library—is modeled not on a temple but on a Greek theater, where knowledge, wisdom, intellect, and virtue played like characters in a drama.

Chronology

600 B.C.E.–100 C.E.	Teachers and their disciples influence thinking all across Eurasia
	Spread of Zoroastrianism for next 1,000 years primarily in present-day Iran
	Teachings about Brahman begin to be written down; Buddhism develops in India
	Confucianism, Daoism, and Legalism spread in China Legacy of Plato and Aristotle to Western philosophy
	Proponents of Secular Medicine (Susutra in India, Hippocrates in Greece, and Xunzi in China)
580 B.C.E.	Forced migration of Jews from Jerusalem to Babylon creates a "diaspora mentality," influential up to present times
33 C.E.	Jesus and spread of Christianity over the next two millennia

(All dates are approximate)

into North and Central America; or from parts of the Andes along the coasts and mountain chains of South America and across the Amazon valley; or from the Ethiopian highlands into East Africa and South Arabia; or from centers on the Niger River into the Sahel and the forests of West Africa; or as we shall see in later chapters from East Asia across Polynesia deep into the Pacific But the relatively isolating geography of the Americas, sub-Saharan Africa, and the Pacific worked against the kinds of comparatively intense exchange that were possible across Eurasia.

It is impossible to trace to their outer limits the networks that bound the axial-age sages. But the similarities between their thoughts across Eurasia suggest that long-range cultural exchanges must have been going on among them. This was perhaps the critical difference that made Eurasian societies relatively prolific in a period when we know of no comparable achievements in intellectual life anywhere else in the world. Our next task is therefore to look not only at the changing political frameworks of the axial age, but also at the evidence of the spread and strength of long-range cultural contacts in the world of the time.

PROBLEMS AND PARALLELS

1. What were the similarities among the ideas of the great sages of the axial age? How do they influence the way we think now?

2. How did the concept of nothing enable thinkers to understand nature in a new way?

3. How did the idea of divine love alter humankind's relationship with God and the world? What were the similarities between the ideas of Jesus and Mozi?

4. How did religious ideas affect political thought in the axial age? Why were most axial sages optimists rather than pessimists?

5. How did axial-age science investigate nature? How did axial-age medicine distinguish itself from magic?

6. What roles did networks, schools, and patrons play in spreading axial-age thinking? Why did Zoroaster have no influential intellectual disciples in Persia?

7. What comparisons can be made between the spread of ideas during the axial age and the way culture radiated outward from kernel regions in other parts of the world?

READ ON ▶ ▶ ▶

The Analects of Confucius is the best work with which to begin study of the sage. Many editions are available: R. Dawson, *Confucius* (1982) is perhaps the best general introductory account of the subject. E. L. Shaughnessy, *Before Confucius* (1997) gives the background to the thought of the period of the Hundred Schools. T. De Bary, ed., *Sources of Chinese Tradition* (2000) is an excellent introductory anthology of extracts from key texts. J. Needham, *Science and Civilisation in China* (1961), I and II, with vol. VII by C. Habsmeier, set Chinese thought—not only on science—in global context, stressing the priority of Chinese achievement in antiquity and the Middle Ages. N. Sivin, *Medicine, Philosophy and Religion in Ancient China* (1996) collects essays on the links between Tao and science. For Chinese political thought, see S. DeGrazia, *Masters of Chinese Political Thought* (1973), for a selection of texts and B. I. Schwartz, *The World of Thought in Ancient China* (1985), for a critical guide.

R. Zaehner, *The Dawn and Twilight of Zoroastrianism* (2003) is an unsurpassed classic. R. Gotshalk, *The Beginnings of Philosophy in India* (1998) can be recommended on the Upanishads; for texts, E. Deutsch, *A Source Book of Vedanta* (1971) has a good selection. A. T. Embree, ed., *Sources of Indian Tradition* (1988) collects some useful texts. R. Gombrich, ed., *The World of Buddhism* (1991) is a superb introduction to its subject, especially good on Buddhist monasticism. K. H. Potter, ed., *Encyclopedia of Indian Philosophies* (1994) 6 vols, is a comprehensive guide to Indian thought.

On the Jewish and Jesusian concept of God, K. Armstrong, *A History of God* (1993), and J. Miles, *God: A Biography* (1995) are suggestive and instructive; the revisionist M. S. Smith, *Origins of Biblical Monotheism* (2001) can also be recommended. C. S. Lewis, *The Four Loves* is a classic work contrasting the Jesusian notion of divine love with other traditions. The version in *The New Jerusalem Bible* is the most reliable modern translation of the gospels and has manageable and instructive notes. On Jesus, G. Vermes, *Jesus the Jew* (1973) is provocative, enlightening, and gripping. C. P. Thiede and M. D'ancona, *The Jesus Papyrus* (1997), too, offers an invigorating challenge to conventional thinking. M. Staniforth, trans., *Early Jesusian Writings* (1968) collects some of the texts that did not make it into the Bible. On the Jews, F. E. Deist, *The Material Culture of the Bible* is particularly useful.

W. K. C. Guthrie, *A History of Greek Philosophy* (1962) is a model of scholarship; the sixth and last volume, *Aristotle: An Encounter* is also an intensely personal and fascinating study of the single most important thinker in the history of Western thought. A. A. Long, *Hellenistic Philosophy* (1974) takes up the story where Guthrie leaves off. The classic work by E. R. Dodds, *The Greeks and the Irrational* (1957) remains a valuable corrective to conventional thinking. O. Taplin, *Greek Fire* (1990) is an accessible and up-to-date study of ancient Greek thought. M. L. West, *The East Face of Helicon* (1997) settles the controversy about where Greek ideas "originally" came from. R. Collins, *The Sociology of Philosophies* (1998) makes an important contribution to tracing the connections that made schools of thinkers and forged the contacts between them.

CHAPTER 7

The Great Empires

▲ **China and Rome on the Silk Roads.** A face with Caucasian features on a woolen weaving from the first or second century C.E. is evidence that the Chinese and the Romans were linked by trade. The cloth was discovered in a grave on the Silk Roads in Xinjiang. The face was stitched into a pair of pants and woven in a style not used by the Chinese.

In this Chapter

In about 33 B.C.E, Maecenas, one of the Roman Empire's leading ministers, gave a small farm to a penniless poet. It was a gift in appreciation of the brilliant satirical verses the poet—whose name was Horace—wrote as evening entertainment for Roman intellectuals and elites. The farm was just what Horace wanted. For the rest of his days, he devoted much of his best poetry—some of the cleverest, loveliest work any wordsmith has ever forged—to celebrating the simple, rural life and praising his patrons. In one poem, he imagined Maecenas worrying over what the Chinese might be plotting. In others, Horace pictured Augustus, the Roman emperor, intimidating them with his power and fathering a future conqueror of China. This was outrageous flattery, since there was no likelihood of the Roman and Chinese empires having much contact of any kind, let alone going to war. In 97 C.E., China did send an envoy, Gan Ying, to Rome, but he turned back at the Black Sea, deterred by warnings from local enemies of Rome, who did not want the mission to succeed. They said to Gan, "If the ambassador is willing to forget his family and home, he can embark." So Gan sent home a favorable report on the Romans: "The people have an air comparable to those of China. . . . They trade with India and Persia by sea."

ROME

That was as close as the Roman and Chinese empires ever came to dealing directly with each other. But that Horace was aware of China, and realized that events at the far end of Eurasia could affect Roman interests, shows how the world was changing. It was, as we say now, getting smaller. The rise of unprecedentedly big empires, which are the focus of this chapter, was part cause, part effect of this shrinking world.

The world began shrinking during the period known as the axial age, from about 500 B.C.E. to 100 C.E., for three main reasons. First, land trade routes opened communications across Eurasia. Second, traffic grew along the existing maritime routes of the Indian Ocean. And, finally, sea travel began to connect the Mediterranean with northern Europe's Atlantic shores. The trade routes of the Phoenician and Greek trailblazers described in Chapter 5 led north from the Strait of Gibraltar to the tin-producing British Isles. Their colonies were staging posts in the making of a new economy—helping goods, people, and ideas cross or get around the sharply divisive watershed that separates Mediterranean from Atlantic Europe.

Not only did travelers and trade expand communications, but the need for big armies and the growth of commerce created a demand for stronger, bigger states. The axial age became an age of empires, with states of unprecedented size, including within their borders many political communities in common allegiance to a single source of authority. The new empires of the period took shape first in Southwest Asia, then around the Mediterranean, and finally in China and India. They established common frontiers or frontier zones of conflict and culture exchange. Around the axes of travel, chiefs, enriched by trade, turned into kings.

The empires spilled some of their people, technology, and means of life into frontier areas that had been little populated. Cultivated crops and domesticated livestock transformed previously undisturbed ecosystems. At an increasing rate, neighbors who had lived by hunting and foraging for wild plants adopted agriculture, following the empires' example. They developed or adapted varieties and species of plants and animals for their own environments. Those who continued to resist change were cast as enemies and savages. In the great grasslands, the steppes of central Eurasia, where tilling the soil was impossible, empires formed with a different sort of economy, based on herding livestock. A pattern began, lasting some 2,000 years, of violence between these nomad empires that lived by herding and the sedentary farmers who lived near them.

Meanwhile, beyond the routes that connected Eurasian empires, people still had the option of remaining foragers and small-scale farmers. They could minimize risk by minimizing change. Most of them took this option. In parts of the New World, however, experiments in embracing change and attempting to control it continued. Large-scale interventions in the environment and imaginative adaptations of human society took forms that were familiar from Eurasia. Agriculture led to urbanization, long-range commerce, and eventually imperialism. Seen from today's perspective, the Americas seemed to be reliving the history of the Old World.

ROUTES THAT DREW THE OLD WORLD TOGETHER

As a general rule in history, bigger states mean more exchange over longer distances. In part, this is simply because they facilitate trade and travel within their own expanding borders; in part, because they generate increasing contacts with each other by way of commerce, diplomacy, and war. To understand the cultural exchanges of the period—how and why they happened and to what extent—we therefore have to understand the political framework: where and how new states formed; how their horizons broadened; what were the new institutions—the mechanisms for conveying commands and exacting obedience—that enabled them to function over unprecedented distances.

State-building and the development of communications are mutually dependent processes. Routes of commerce are the lifelines of empires: pumping them with resources, equipping them with new ideas and technologies, laying down tracks for their armies to follow. Eurasia would have had no great empires—or, at least, the

Making Connections | THE DYNAMICS OF EMPIRE

ENVIRONMENT	SOCIETY	ECONOMY	COMMERCE	POLITICS
Cultivated crops and livestock transform ecosystems across Eurasia	Foragers adopt agriculture	Urbanization leads to increased trade over longer distances	Increased contact between regions leads to conflict, war, diplomacy, and cultural exchanges	Increased commerce, conflicts, numerous routes of communication provide opportunities for stronger, bigger states that can manage many political communities more efficiently

empires there would have been smaller—if new or developing avenues of communication had not become available. Indeed, this is a large part of why Eurasian empires in this period were bigger, and exercised more power over their subject-peoples, than empires elsewhere in the world, where no comparable long-range routes emerged. We must begin, therefore, by drawing in the long-range causeways of the period: the sea lanes and land routes that crossed Eurasia, making possible the cultural exchanges of the axial age and the new political developments in the empires the routes linked (see Map 7.1).

The Sea Routes of the Indian Ocean

The world maps Indian geographers of the axial age drew look like the product of stay-at-home minds. Four—then, from the second century B.C.E. onward, seven—continents radiate from a mountainous core. Around concentric rings of rock flow seven seas, made up respectively, of salt, sugarcane juice, wine, ghee (butter), curds, milk, and water. One should not suppose on the basis of this formal, sacred image of the world that Indians of the time were ignorant of geography. That would be like inferring from the stylized subway map that New Yorkers could not build railways.

We can detect real observations under the metaphors of the maps. The world is grouped around the great Himalaya Mountains and the triangular, petal-like form of India, with the island of Sri Lanka falling from it like a dewdrop. The ocean is divided into separate seas, some imaginary or little known, but others representing real routes to frequented destinations and commercial centers. The Sea of Milk, for instance, corresponds roughly to what we now call the Arabian Sea, and led to Arabia and Persia. The Sea of Butter led to Ethiopia.

Stories of Indian seafaring from late in the first millennium B.C.E. appear in the *Jatakas*, collected tales of Buddhahood—guides to how to become enlightened. Here, piloting a ship "by knowledge of the stars" is a godlike gift. The Buddha saves sailors from cannibalistic goblin-seductresses in Sri Lanka. He puts together an unsinkable vessel for a pious explorer. A merchant from the city of Benares (beh-NAH-res), following the advice of an enlightened sage, buys a ship on credit and sells the cargo at a profit of 200,000 gold pieces. Mani-mekhala, a guardian-deity, saves shipwreck victims who have combined commerce with pilgrimage "or are endowed with virtue or worship their parents." These are legends, but the surviving tales contain so many practical details that they only make sense against a background of real navigation. Similar legends appear in Persian sources, like the story

"State-building and the development of communications are mutually dependent processes. Routes of commerce are the lifelines of empires: pumping them with resources, equipping them with new ideas and technologies, laying down tracks for their armies to follow."

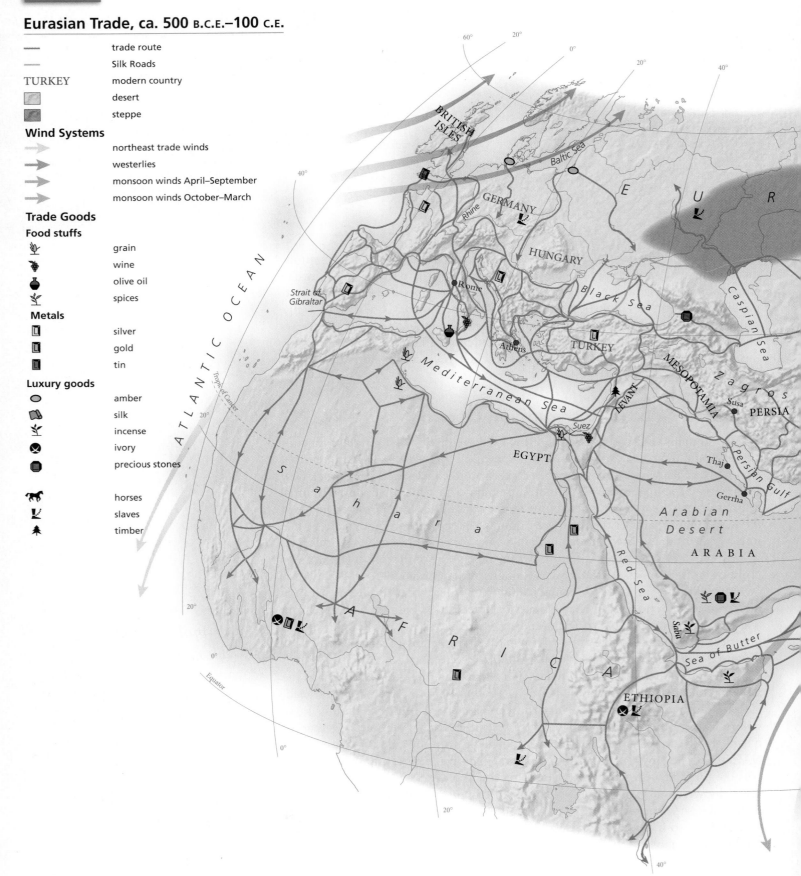

MAP 7.1

Eurasian Trade, ca. 500 B.C.E.–100 C.E.

Legend:

- ———— trade route
- ———— Silk Roads
- TURKEY modern country
- ▢ desert
- ▢ steppe

Wind Systems

- → northeast trade winds
- → westerlies
- → monsoon winds April–September
- → monsoon winds October–March

Trade Goods

Food stuffs
- grain
- wine
- olive oil
- spices

Metals
- silver
- gold
- tin

Luxury goods
- amber
- silk
- incense
- ivory
- precious stones
- horses
- slaves
- timber

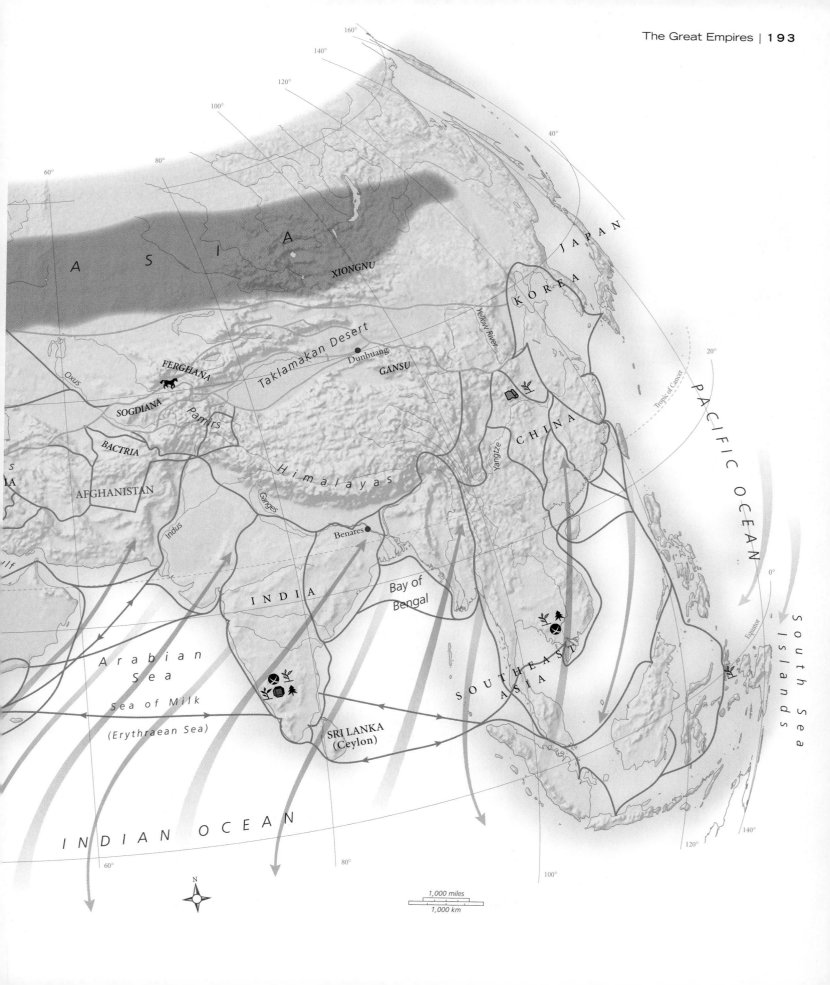

A   S   I   A

XIONGNU

160°
140°
120°
100°
80°
60°
40°

JAPAN

KOREA

Yellow River

20°

Tropic of Cancer

FERGHANA

Taklamakan Desert

Dunhuang

GANSU

PACIFIC OCEAN

Oxus

SOGDIANA

Pamirs

CHINA

Yangtze

BACTRIA

H i m a l a y a s

AFGHANISTAN

Ganges

IA

Indus

Benares

0°

INDIA

Bay of
Bengal

Arabian
Sea

SOUTHEAST
ASIA

South Sea Islands

Sea of Milk

Equator

(Erythraean Sea)

SRI LANKA
(Ceylon)

lf

INDIAN   OCEAN

120°

140°

60°

80°

100°

N

1,000 miles
1,000 km

An Indian globe of the early eighteenth century depicts a traditional view of the world. The island of Sri Lanka is the central dot located on the equator. A squat representation of the subcontinent, reminiscent of the shape of the subcontinent in most earlier Arab and European maps, occupies most of the space to the north. The small blue arc represents the Himalaya Mountains.

of Jamshid (jahm-SHEED), a hero who is both king and shipbuilder and who crosses oceans "from region to region with great speed."

Accounts of real voyages back these stories. Toward the end of the sixth century B.C.E., Darius I—an emperor enthusiastic for exploration—ruled Persia. He ordered a reconnaissance of the Indian Ocean from the northern tip of the Red Sea, around Arabia, to the mouth of the Indus River in northern India. This venture no doubt extended the range of navigation in the region, since the Red Sea, with its concealed rocks and dangerous currents, was notoriously hard to navigate. Among the consequences were penal colonies on islands of the Persian Gulf. A canal built from Suez on the Red Sea to the Nile indicates there must have been traffic for it to serve, traffic that the canal increased.

What Indian mapmakers called the Seas of Milk and Butter were, to Greek merchants, "the Erythraean Sea," from which traders brought back aromatics—especially frankincense and myrrh—and an Arabian cinnamon substitute called cassia. Many important ports for long-range trade lined Arabia's shores. At Gerrha, for instance, merchants unloaded Indian manufactures. Nearby, Thaj also served as a good place to warehouse imports, protected by stone walls more than a mile and a half in circumference and 15 feet thick. From Ma'in, one of the south Arabian states that Saba conquered (see Chapter 5), a merchant supplied Egyptian temples with incense in the third century B.C.E. We know this because he died in Egypt, and the story of his life is engraved on his stone coffin.

The reason for the long seafaring, sea-daring tradition of the Indian Ocean lies in the regularity of the monsoonal wind system. Above the equator, northeasterlies prevail in winter; but when winter ends, the direction of the winds reverses. For most of the rest of the year, the winds blow steadily from the south and west, sucked toward the Asian landmass as air warms and rises over the continent. By timing voyages to take advantage of the predictable changes in the direction of the wind, navigators could be confident of a fair wind out and a fair wind home.

It is a fact not often appreciated that, overwhelmingly, the history of maritime exploration has been made into the wind, presumably because it was at least as important to get home as to get to anywhere new. This was how the Phoenicians and Greeks opened the Mediterranean to long-range commerce and colonization (see Chapter 5). The same strategy enabled South Sea Island navigators of this period to explore and colonize islands of the Pacific (see Chapter 10). The monsoonal wind system in the Indian Ocean freed navigators from such constraints. One must try to imagine what it would be like, feeling the wind, year after year, alternately in one's face and at one's back. Gradually, would-be seafarers realized how the changes of wind made outward ventures viable. They knew the wind would change and so could risk an outward voyage without fearing that they might be cut off from returning home.

Still, the Indian Ocean is dangerous. Storms wrack it, especially in the Arabian Sea, the Bay of Bengal, and the deadly belt of bad weather that stretches across the ocean below about 10 degrees south of the equator. But the predictability of a homeward wind made this the world's most benign environment for long-range voyaging. The fixed-wind systems of the Atlantic and Pacific were almost impossible to cross with ancient technology. We know of no round trips across them. Even compared with other navigable seas, the reliability of the monsoon season offered other advantages. No reliable sources record the length of voyages in this period, but, to judge from later statistics, a trans-Mediterranean journey from east to west, against the wind, would take 50 to 70 days. With the monsoon, a ship could cross the entire Erythraean Sea, between India and a port on the Persian Gulf or near the Red Sea, in three or four weeks in either direction.

Land Routes: The Silk Roads

In the long run, sea routes were more important for global history than land routes. They carried a greater variety of goods faster, more economically, and in greater amounts. Nevertheless, in the early stages, most Eurasian long-range trade was small scale—in goods of high value and limited bulk. It relied on **emporium trading**—goods moved through a series of markets and middlemen, rather than an expedition across entire oceans and continents. In the axial age, the land routes that linked Eurasia were as important as the sea routes in establishing cultural contacts: bringing people from different cultures together, facilitating the flow of the ideas of the axial-age sages, transmitting the works of art that changed taste and the goods that influenced lifestyles.

Bit by bit, the evidence helps us see where and how these routes emerged, as a result of a mixture of economic and political initiatives, and what extremities they connected. From around the mid-first millennium B.C.E., Chinese silks appeared here and there across Europe—in Athens, and at the site of present-day Budapest in Hungary, and in a series of south German and Rhineland burials. By the end of the millennium, we can trace the flow of Chinese manufactured goods from the southern Caspian to the northern Black Sea, and into what were then gold-rich kingdoms in the southwest stretches of the Eurasian steppe. Meanwhile, roads that kings built and maintained crossed what are now Turkey and Iran, penetrated Egypt and Mesopotamia, reached the Persian Gulf, and, at their easternmost ends, touched the Pamir Mountains in Afghanistan and crossed the Indus River.

Merchants could also use these routes. The first written evidence of presumed commerce across Eurasia appears in a report from Zhang Qian (jyhang-chee-an), a Chinese ambassador who set out for Bactria, one of the Greek-ruled kingdoms established in Central Asia in the wake of Alexander the Great—in ca. 139 B.C.E. His main objectives were, first, to recruit allies against the aggressive steppeland dwellers on China's northern borders and, second, to obtain horses for the Chinese army from the best breeders, deep in Central Asia (see Map 7.1).

Zhang Qian's mission was one of the great adventures of history. Captured en route, he remained a hostage with the steppelanders for 10 years. He escaped and continued across the Pamir Mountains and the River Oxus. He was captured again, escaped again, and finally reached home, with a steppeland wife in tow, after an absence of 12 years. He never encountered potential allies, but from a commercial point of view, his reports were highly favorable. The kingdoms beyond the Pamir Mountains had "cities, houses and mansions as in China." In Ferghana (fehr-GAH-nah) in what is today Central Asia, the horses "sweat blood and come from the stock of the heavenly horses." Zhang Qian saw Chinese cloth in Bactria. "When he asked how they obtained these things, the people told him their merchants bought them in India. From the time of his mission, "specimens of strange things began to arrive" in China "from every direction."

In 111 B.C.E., a Chinese garrison founded the outpost of Dunhuang (doon-hwang)—the name means "blazing beacon"—beyond China's western borders.

"It is a fact not often appreciated that, overwhelmingly, the history of maritime exploration has been made into the wind, presumably because it was at least as important to get home as to get to anywhere new."

Heavenly horse. Chinese artists have favored horses as subjects in almost every period, but never more than during the Han dynasty (206 B.C.E.–220 C.E.), when an intense effort to import fine horses from Central Asia enriched China's equine bloodstock. More than for their utility, horses inspired artists—as in this example from Wuwei (Gansu province) of the second century C.E.—as symbols of the fleeting, ever-changing nature of human life.

General Wudi worships the Buddha. In the early second century B.C.E., shortly after the founding of Dunhuang, the Chinese General Wudi invaded Central Asia along the Silk Roads in search of horses. "Two golden men" were among the other booty he captured. Buddhist painters at Dunhuang assumed that these statues were Buddhas and depicted Wudi worshipping them.

It was a desolate region of desert and mountains. Here, according to a poem inscribed in one of the caves where travelers sheltered, was "the throat of Asia," where "the roads to the western ocean" converged like veins in the neck. We now call them the **Silk Roads**. They led to the markets of Central Asia—in the trading states of Bactria, and Ferghana and neighboring Sogdiana—and linked up with other routes: those that branched off into Tibet, or doubled back from beyond the Pamir Mountains toward India, or continued westward across the Iranian plateau toward Anatolia, Arabia, the Levant, and, ultimately, the Mediterranean.

From the neighborhood of Dunhuang, the Silk Roads skirted the Taklamakan (tahk-lah-mah-KAHN) Desert, under the mountains, to the north and south. It was a terrible journey, haunted, in Chinese accounts, by screaming demon drummers—personifications of the ferocious winds. But the desert was so demanding that it deterred even bandits, and the mountains offered some protection from the predatory nomads who lived beyond them. The Taklamakan took 30 days to cross—clinging to the edges, where water drains from the surrounding mountains.

A few years after the founding of Dunhuang, a Chinese army, reputedly of 60,000 men, traveled to secure the mountain passes at the western end and to force the horse breeders of Ferghana to trade. A painted cave shows the general, Wudi (woo-dee), kneeling before the "golden men"—idols taken, or perhaps mistaken, for Buddhas—that Chinese forces seized. In ca. 102 B.C.E., the Chinese invaded Ferghana, diverted a river, and obtained 30,000 horses in tribute. Meanwhile, caravans from China reached Persia, and Chinese trade goods became common along the eastern Mediterranean.

Trade across Eurasia exposed great disparities in wealth between East and West. These differences helped to shape the history of that region over the next 2,000 years. Already in the first century C.E., the Roman geographer Pliny worried about it. The Roman world produced little that its trading partners wanted, whereas the silks of China and the spices and incense of Arabia and the Indian Ocean were much in demand in Rome. The only way people in Europe could pay for them was in cash—gold or, more commonly, silver. Nowadays, we would call this an adverse **balance of trade**—the value of Europe's imports from Asia far surpassed the value of its exports. The problems of financing it, by finding enough silver, and ultimately of overcoming and reversing it, by finding and supplying goods Asians wanted to buy, became a major theme of the history of the West and, in the long run, as we shall see, of the world.

THE FIRST EURASIAN EMPIRE: PERSIA

A glance at the map shows how the region we know today as Iran commanded a central position in the developing trade across Eurasia, linking Central Asian markets to those of Southwest Asia and the Mediterranean. So—in view of the way trade and empire are mutually nourishing—it is not surprising that the first of the great empires of the axial age originated here.

In earlier periods, Akkadians and Assyrians had carried the traditions of lowland Mesopotamia north into their hills, like booty. Now conquerors from the adjoining and even higher tableland used the same traditions to create a new state. This state became the biggest the world had yet known: the Persian Empire.

Chronology: China and the Silk Road	
ca. 500 B.C.E.	Chinese silks appear in Europe
ca. 139 B.C.E.	Zhang Qian sets out for Bactria
111 B.C.E.	Chinese found Dunhuang
102 B.C.E.	Chinese invade Ferghana

Making Connections | TRADE ROUTES AND THEIR CONNECTIONS

LONG-RANGE ROUTES	ADVANTAGES	GEOGRAPHICAL SCOPE	COMMERCE AND EXCHANGE	POLITICAL SYSTEMS
Sea Route: Indian Ocean	Changeable, predictable monsoon winds lead to reliable schedules; great variety and amount of goods can be carried via ship (emporium trading); seaborne trade usually faster than land routes	East Africa, Arabia, India, Southeast Asia; canal between Red Sea and Nile River eventually connects to Mediterranean	Aromatics (incense), spices, gold, and "thousands of other things" (including wild animals)	African kingdoms, Indian empires and kingdoms, Arabian tribal chiefdoms, Mediterranean empires
Land Route: Silk Roads across Eurasia	Less investment needed to embark on small-scale trading expeditions; more cultural contacts between vastly different peoples; widespread trade of high-value items	China, Bactria, Sogdiana, Persia, Mesopotamia, Anatolia, Caspian/Black Sea, Mediterranean	Spices, silk, gold, silver, cloth, horses, aromatics	Imperial China, Central Asian kingdoms, Egypt, nomadic tribes of Middle East, Persian Empire, Roman Empire, Mediterranean city-states
Sea Route: Mediterranean	Relatively high population densities along the coastal Mediterranean provides more opportunities for trade, numerous ports; shorter distances, calmer waters than vast Indian Ocean routes	Europe, North Africa, Southwest Asia, Black Sea, with Red Sea–Nile canal connections to Arabia, Indian Ocean route	Grain, wine, olive oil, timber, metals	Greek city-states/colonies, Egypt, North African city-states, Roman Empire

The Persian Heartland

The heartland of the Persian Empire in what is today Iran consisted of scatterings of good soil and precious water in a vast, arid plateau. Ragae, with its brackish streams and sweet wells, overlooked the Zagros Mountains. Hamadan lay in a valley watered with springs, known for good fruit and inferior wheat. The Kur valley of Fars was the richest area in ancient times. Water from the Zayinda Rud—a modest stream much glorified in poetry—enriched the plain of Isfahan (IHS-fah-hahn, where the inhabitants used pigeon droppings for fertilizer. Rivers—including the Tigris and Euphrates—laced the southwest. Here, at the old trading city of Susa, on the border of the Mesopotamian world, the Persians established the capital of their state. Generally, between mountains and deserts, lay narrow strips of good pasture and land, watered by seasonal streams that could be irrigated for farming. Like the old Hittite Empire (see Chapter 4), Persia was another alliance of farmers and

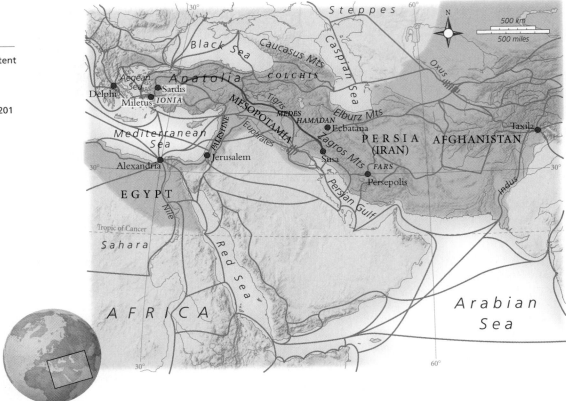

MAP 7.2

The Persian Empire

▨ Persian Empire at its greatest extent

— Persian royal road

▨ irrigation works

● place mentioned on pages 197–201

---- present-day coastline/river

— trade route

flocks. Hymns, which are among the earliest sources for Iranian history, praise herders and husbandmen as followers of truth and pronounce their nomadic enemies "adherents of lies, who uproot crops and waste livestock," which would be better employed fertilizing farmland. Farming communities' depictions of bull sacrifice show spurting blood transformed into sprouting wheat.

The founding of the Persian Empire is traditionally credited to Cyrus the Great, a general from the province of Fars. Toward the mid-sixth century B.C.E., he launched a coup to take over one of the biggest successor-states of Assyria, the kingdom of the Medes. His subsequent campaigns stretched from Palestine to Afghanistan. His power reached almost the farthest limits the Persian Empire would ever attain. Legends credited him with dreams foretelling the conquest of Europe and Asia. This seems doubtful. His inscriptions call him simply, "I, Cyrus, the Achaemenid" (ah-KEE-meh-nihd)—the name of a proud but previously provincial family to which he belonged. He headed a conquest state, poor in resources, with a need to keep growing. The Persian Empire gradually adopted the old world–conquering ambitions of Sargon of Akkad (see Chapter 3) and the Assyrians but with a difference: The Persians put these ambitions into practice.

The empire joined two regions—Mesopotamia and Persia—that mountains had formerly divided. At its greatest extent, it encompassed Greek cities on the Aegean coast, Egypt, and the Indian city of Taxila beyond the Indus River (see Map 7.2). It was an empire of unprecedented scale that relied on long-range trade and, therefore, needed to invest in communications. By early in the fifth century B.C.E., nearly 1,700 miles of road crossed the empire from Susa to Sardis in western Anatolia. Royal armies tramped them at a rate of 19 miles a day, and "Nothing mortal," it was said, "travels as fast as the royal mes-

Persepolis. Reliefs that line the approach to the audience chamber of the ruler of Persia at Persepolis show exactly what went on there: reception of tribute, submission of ambassadors. The figures look uniform at first, but their various styles of beards, headgear, and robes indicate the diversity of the lands from which they came and, therefore, the range of the Great King's power.

sengers." The road was also a channel for tribute. Carvings at the imperial city of Persepolis (puhr-SEH-poh-lees), founded deep inside Iran around the end of the sixth century B.C.E., show ivory, gold, and exotic animals arriving at the court of the ruler of Persia, the "Great King."

Persian Government

Persia was more than a robber empire. Persian rule gave good value to subjects in remote regions. The empire provided a canal linking the Nile to the Red Sea and irrigation works on the Oxus and the Karun rivers. Forts beyond the Caucasus Mountains kept steppe nomads at bay. At Jerusalem, Cyrus the Great undertook to rebuild the temple that symbolized the city's sanctity for the Jews, whom the Babylonians had deported to Mesopotamia (see Chapter 6). Cyrus's gesture was typical of the way Persian rulers conciliated the subjects they acquired. In gratitude, the biblical prophet Isaiah hailed Cyrus as God's anointed.

Greeks accused Persians of treating their kings like gods, in the Egyptian manner, because Persians had to prostrate themselves before the king, but this charge was unjust. Persian kings were not gods, but their right to rule was god given. Many inscriptions describe Ahura Mazda, god of light, as investing the king with power. The court religion—which was, effectively, for much of the time, the state religion—was the cult of fire and light that Zoroaster supposedly founded (see Chapter 6).

The other Persian practices that Greeks found peculiar were the Persian love of luxury—a criticism excused, perhaps, by envy—and their respect for women. Surviving Achaemenid ration lists—the records of wages and payments in kind that court personnel received—assign professions by sex. These show that royal attendants could be of either sex and that women could supervise mixed groups of men and women and earn higher wages than men. It was not, however, a society of sexual equality. Scribes had to be male, while servers of rations—the lowest category by

Winged lions were among the most common motifs in Persian jewelry and gold work of the mid-first millennium B.C.E., especially in drinking vessels. This example typically retains the shape of a horn but with a flat bottom that the drinker could rest easily on a table. The Persians probably took this motif from the symbolism of Assyrian royal monuments of the ninth century B.C.E., in which huge guardian figures, placed at gates and doorways, represented gods or rulers with the strength of the lion and the swiftness of a bird in flight.

MAP 7.3

The World According to Hecataeus

In 500 B.C.E., the ruler of Miletus, a Greek city on the coast of Anatolia, commissioned a world map in bronze to encourage a Greek alliance against Persia. The map showed a big Europe dominating Asia and Africa and probably resembled this reconstruction.

pay—had to be female. Mothers got extra rations for the birth of boys. Nevertheless, women could hold property in their own right. This gave them a political role as what, in modern American politics, would be called "campaign funders"—backers and patrons of men who sought power. Greek sources, exaggerating the amount of power women enjoyed as a result, blamed every lurch of palace politics on female willfulness. For Greeks, who barred women from political life in their own communities, saw them as dangerous agents of chaos in other cultures' states.

The Persian–Greek Wars

Greeks who lived on and beyond the western edge of the Persian Empire were in a giant's shadow. They needed to cope with insecurity and defeat fear. In about 500 B.C.E., the ruler of Miletus, a Greek colony on the Ionian shore of western Anatolia, showed a map of the world to the rulers of Sparta, a city in mainland Greece with a great reputation in war. Engraved on a bronze tablet, the map showed two roughly equal areas—an exaggeratedly large Europe at the top, like a protruding lip over Asia and Africa crammed into the lower half (see Map 7.3). The image was unrealistic, but the agenda was clear. Asia was reduced to a manageable conquest. The Miletian proposed an alliance against Persia.

Was the map a sign of confidence or bravado? It looked brash, but it concealed unease. Some combined raids by Greeks states followed Miletus's initiative, but they ended in failure. The Persian Empire had already conquered the mainland north of Ionia and launched into the sea, controlling Samos and all islands to the north. Rumors claimed that the Persians wanted to conquer Europe because "its trees were too fine for anyone but the Great King to possess." More likely, the empire was committed to expanding because it needed tribute from subject-lands to support it. In any event, the Greeks saw the Persians as a threat, but did not feel threatened enough to stop feuding with each other even when the Persians prepared to invade Greece.

The Greek world was in panic—but the panic was not strong enough to make Greeks unite. The oracle of Delphi (Chapter 5) even advised submitting to Persian rule, with its reputation for efficiency, generosity, and respect for trade. In the wars that followed, intermittently, throughout the fifth century and into the fourth, Greek unity was sporadic, occurring only in dire moments of Persian invasion. Persia, after testing the difficulties of conquering Greece in unsuccessful invasions in 490 and 480 B.C.E., was generally content to keep these enemies divided, while prioritizing Persian rule over rich, soft Egypt.

The sea became the effective frontier between the Greek and Persian worlds. A Persian decree of 387 B.C.E. sums it up: the king "deems it right that the cities in Asia be his. . . . The other Greek cities, both small and great, shall be independent," while most of the Greek colonies on the islands of the Aegean were divided between Persia and Athens. This was an indication that Athens—best resourced of the Greek cities because it controlled silver mines—had imperial ambitions of its own, which many Greek states found more menacing than those of Persia.

The Empire of Alexander the Great

Not even Athens could assert long-term hegemony in Greece. Macedon, however, could. Macedon is an example of a now familiar fact: On the edges of civilizations, chiefdoms developed into states. This northern kingdom had what to southern

Greeks was a barbarian background, but Greece profoundly influenced its culture. Increasingly, in the fourth century B.C.E., Macedonians saw themselves as Greeks: Aristotle (see Chapter 6) served as a tutor to the royal court.

In 338 B.C.E., King Philip of Macedon imposed unity by force on the Greeks and revived the idea of conquering Persia. When he was assassinated two years later—allegedly by a Persian-backed conspiracy—Philip's 19-year-old son, Alexander, inherited his father's ambitions. For Philip, attacking Persia was probably intended to focus his uneasily united realm on an external enemy. Alexander's motivation, however, has baffled historians. Was he seeking to vindicate his dead father? Or to reenact legendary romances of Greek campaigns in Asia, which filled his head from his boyhood reading? Or was he full of insatiable ambition to leave "no world unconquered" as some early biographers claimed? Did he have humdrum economic aims? He certainly showed interest in opening up Indian Ocean trade or seizing control of its routes. He ordered reconnaissance by sea of the routes between India, Persia, and Arabia, and began, just before his death, to plan the conquest of Arabia.

Alexander's ambitions probably grew with his success. He destroyed the Persian Empire at lightning speed in three years' campaigns from 334 B.C.E. (see Map 7.4). When the last Persian emperor died at his own officers' hands, perhaps because he had decided to abandon resistance, Alexander proclaimed himself "Great King." His success seems inexplicable except in terms of the interconnected skill and luck of the battlefield. The Persian Empire was essentially strong, well run, and easily governed. Alexander took it over intact, maintained its methods of control, and divided it among his generals.

Chronology: Rise and Fall of the Persian Empire

Sixth century B.C.E.	Cyrus the Great founds Achaemenid dynasty
Early fifth century B.C.E.	Completion of royal road from Susa to Sardis
490 and 480 B.C.E.	Unsuccessful efforts to conquer Greece
334 B.C.E.	Alexander conquers Persian Empire

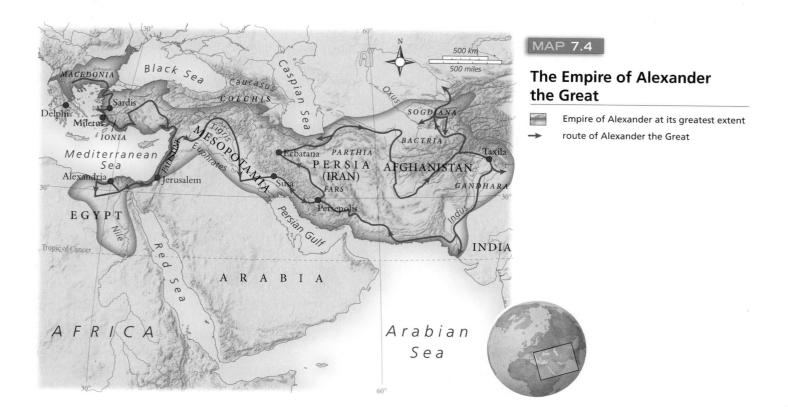

MAP 7.4

The Empire of Alexander the Great

Empire of Alexander at its greatest extent

route of Alexander the Great

Gandharan sculpture. Soldiers of Alexander the Great (r. 336–323 B.C.E.) founded the kingdom of Gandhara. Greek influence is unmistakable in its art: in the realistic modeling, the sculptural plasticity, the deep reliefs. Buddhist piety dominates the subject matter. Here the artist illustrates the legend of how King Sibi became a Buddha by sacrificing his eyes and flesh to save the life of a pigeon while gods look on.

Copyright The British Museum.

Success and flattering omens convinced Alexander that he enjoyed divine favor—perhaps, even, that he was divine. His methods became increasingly arbitrary, his character increasingly unpredictable. He dealt with disloyalty first by judicial murder, then assassination, then slaughter by his own hand, then arbitrary executions. In the last years of his life, his control slipped. He failed to impose Persian rituals of homage on his Greek and Macedonian followers who felt that it was demeaning to prostrate themselves before a mere mortal, even if he was a king. He sought conquests beyond Persia's frontiers, but his troops became insubordinate, and he had to halt his invasion of India, shortly after crossing the Indus. Characteristically, Alexander saved face by pretending he had submitted not to the demands of his men, but to warnings from the gods. He had just set the conquest of Arabia as his next objective when he fell dead at age 32, from unknown causes, during a drinking bout—the favorite Macedonian form of excess.

It was what modern publicists might call "a great career move." Alexander became the world's most written-about hero. Epic romancers embroidered his life with wonder stories of his uncontainable prowess. They credited him with exploring the depths of the ocean and ascending to heaven in a chariot drawn by ravens. An epic poem celebrated him in Malay. Kings in India, Ethiopia, and Scotland named themselves after him.

Alexander's material legacy was surprisingly meager. His empire did not outlast him. But long-term, long-range cultural exchanges flourished in the states among which it fragmented. On the frontiers of India, the kingdom of Gandhara (gahn-DAH-rah) combined Buddhist religion and Greek-style art. In Alexandria, the city Alexander founded at the Nile delta, Greek and Egyptian traditions fused. Through the kingdoms of Bactria and Sogdiana, the trade of the Silk Roads funneled. The successor-states helped spread Greek as a common language throughout the Middle East and western Asia. A Persian rump state, Parthia (PAHR-thee-ah), arose in the Iranian heartland and soon conquered Mesopotamia, but the defeat of Persia's empire and the collapse of Alexander's left a power vacuum in the eastern Mediterranean that none of Alexander's many imitators and heirs could fill. The eventual beneficiary was Rome.

THE RISE OF ROME

One of the great unsolved puzzles of history is how a small city-state of obscure origins and limited manpower conquered the Mediterranean, extended its frontiers to the Atlantic and North Sea, and transformed almost every culture it touched. The Romans started as a community of peasants, huddling for defense in an unstrategic spot. Though later Roman writers insisted on Rome's inevitable 'destiny' and praised the founders' choice of site, Rome had poor soil, no metals, and no outlet to the sea. Its inhabitants became warlike by necessity. They had no way to gain wealth except at their neighbors' expense.

The Romans organized their society for war and made victory their supreme value. Roman citizens owed the state at least 16 years of military service. They learned—to quote Horace again—that "to die for the fatherland is sweet and fitting." Their generals celebrated victories in triumphal public parades, showing off booty and prisoners.

Roman education emphasized the virtues of patience and endurance. As a result, Rome was exceptionally well equipped to tough out defeats. Like those other great imperialists, the nineteenth-century British, they could "lose battles but win wars."

This was particularly evident in the Punic Wars the Romans fought against Carthage (see Chapter 5) for domination of the western Mediterranean. The background against which they began is clear enough. In the late third century B.C.E., Roman armies reached the limits of landward expansion in Italy. They were therefore tempted further afield. First, they turned their aggression westward, toward the wealth of Sardinia, Sicily, and Spain. They were not, however, the only imperialists drawn toward those lands. Carthage, the most formidable naval empire of the western Mediterranean, already had colonies, allies, and subject-communities there. Reluctantly, the Romans built a fleet to fight the Carthaginians. This was remarkable, as the Romans hated the sea. "Whoever first dared to float a ship," wrote Horace in about 30 B.C.E., "must have had a heart of oak covered with a triple layer of bronze." Carthage recovered from every defeat, until in 146 B.C.E. Rome finally destroyed it and turned the western Mediterranean into a zone free of rivals. Historians generally regard these wars as the crucial episode in the rise of Rome.

Meanwhile, on its eastern flank, Rome invaded the islands of the Adriatic Sea and then engaged the major powers of the eastern Mediterranean. Macedon was first to fall, annexed to Rome in 148 B.C.E., after 50 years of intermittent wars. The rich kingdom of Pergamum, in Anatolia, once part of the Persian Empire, was next. When its last king died, he willed his kingdom to the Roman people in 133 B.C.E. Then came Syria and Palestine. When Rome annexed Egypt in 30 B.C.E., it controlled virtually all the shores of the Mediterranean (see Map 7.5).

"One of the great unsolved puzzles of history is how a small city-state of obscure origins and limited manpower conquered the Mediterranean, extended its frontiers to the Atlantic and North Sea, and transformed almost every culture it touched."

The Roman Frontiers

The Roman Empire was an empire of coasts, with the sea as it central axis. It therefore exposed long, vulnerable frontiers to landward. On the African and Levantine shores, Roman territory seemed protected—delusionally, as it turned out—by deserts. The European flank, however, despite 100 years of further conquests, never seemed satisfactorily established. There was no reliable barrier against attack. An endless quest for security led beyond the Mediterranean to the Rhine and the Danube rivers. In the late first and early second centuries C.E., Rome lavished resources on the conquest of Dacia (in part of what is now Romania), where deadly womenfolk were said to torture prisoners, flaying them with staves, clawing them with fingernails, burning them with torches. The Romans subdued Dacia, but the result was an even longer and more irrational frontier.

Roman expeditions also tested German defenses as far east as the Elbe River, but the Germans seemed worse than the Dacians—too barbaric to absorb. They were "wild creatures" incapable of laws or civilized arts, according to Velleius, a Roman cavalry officer who fought them around 4 B.C.E. Julius Caesar (d. 44 B.C.E.), whose methodical generalship extended the empire to the Rhine, regarded that river as the limit of civilization. So Rome abandoned the Germans to their own devices. This was probably a mistake. Almost all speakers of Germanic languages outside those in Switzerland, Austria, and the Rhineland were left outside the empire, seething with resentment and vengefulness at their exclusion from the wealth they associated with Rome. If Rome had absorbed them and the other sedentary peoples beyond its frontiers, as China did at the other end of Eurasia, the Roman Empire might have proved as durable as China's. The sedentary peoples China absorbed on its frontiers formed a formidable coalition, guarding the Chinese Empire against nomadic outsiders.

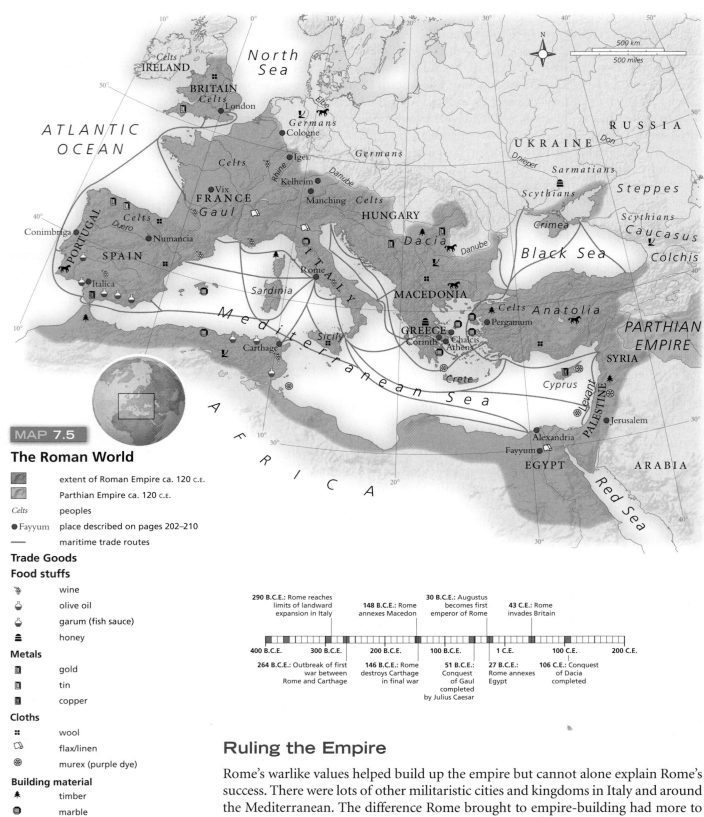

MAP 7.5

The Roman World

	extent of Roman Empire ca. 120 C.E.
	Parthian Empire ca. 120 C.E.
Celts	peoples
● *Fayyum*	place described on pages 202–210
——	maritime trade routes

Trade Goods

Food stuffs

	wine
	olive oil
	garum (fish sauce)
	honey

Metals

	gold
	tin
	copper

Cloths

	wool
	flax/linen
	murex (purple dye)

Building material

	timber
	marble
	slaves
	horses

290 B.C.E.: Rome reaches limits of landward expansion in Italy

148 B.C.E.: Rome annexes Macedon

30 B.C.E.: Augustus becomes first emperor of Rome

43 C.E.: Rome invades Britain

264 B.C.E.: Outbreak of first war between Rome and Carthage

146 B.C.E.: Rome destroys Carthage in final war

51 B.C.E.: Conquest of Gaul completed by Julius Caesar

27 B.C.E.: Rome annexes Egypt

106 C.E.: Conquest of Dacia completed

400 B.C.E. 300 B.C.E. 200 B.C.E. 100 B.C.E. 1 C.E. 100 C.E. 200 C.E.

Ruling the Empire

Rome's warlike values helped build up the empire but cannot alone explain Rome's success. There were lots of other militaristic cities and kingdoms in Italy and around the Mediterranean. The difference Rome brought to empire-building had more to do with political strategies for following up victory and consolidating power.

Though Romans used terror and violence as instruments of policy, Rome's was essentially a collaborative empire, which encompassed many existing elites among

its subject-peoples, turning them into what Romans called "allies" and "federates" and ultimately treating them as Romans, instead of taking the trouble (and running the risk) of trying to displace them. Representatives of people the Romans conquered or intimidated into submission would come to Rome and make offerings and take oaths in the temples of the universal deities of the empire, who were also the special patrons of Rome—especially Jupiter, the ruler of the gods, whose temple on the Capitoline hill stored records of the oaths of loyalty to Rome that subject and allied communities made.

Oath-taking rituals created real bonds between Romans and regional elites. When, for instance, the Greek city of Chalcis stepped up from the status of occupied conquest to ally in 191 B.C.E., the young girls of the city turned out to dance in celebration, singing, "We revere the good faith of the Romans, which we have solemnly sworn to cherish." Of course, the song and dance were mainly for show, but Chalcis stayed loyal thereafter. Oaths also served an obviously cruder purpose: the oath-takers returned home aware of what they would be up against, if they broke their obligations to their rich and powerful conquerors, and they became aware of how useful the Romans were as partners and protectors.

Where the Romans failed to tie existing elites to the empire with rewards and rites, rebellions followed. One of the most famous cases occurred in Britain in 60 C.E., when Roman soldiers abused Boudicca, the chief of a local tribe, and raped her daughters. She raised neighboring tribes in revolt and wiped out three Roman settlements, including London, before Rome rallied enough troops to defeat her. The repeated rebellions of the Jewish provinces were more serious—leading to some of the heaviest defeats Rome ever endured. The causes were manifold, but at their root was an intractable problem: Jews, who identified wholeheartedly with the worship of a unique God, could never join in the institutions of a polytheistic empire.

Roman methods were part predatory, part placatory. You can still sense the predatory character today, in the scenes Roman sculptors carved of soldiers carrying off precious booty, such as the eight-branched candlesticks from the Temple in Jerusalem, in 79 C.E., when the Romans destroyed the city after crushing a major Jewish revolt. Or you can see the spoils of empire today in Turkish Istanbul, where, at the highest point of the city, amid billowing exhaust fumes and flurries of dust, the Romans who built the city in the early fourth century C.E. scooped together

The sack of Jerusalem. The Jews were among the most intractable subjects of the Roman Empire. A scene carved on the Arch of Titus, built in 81 C.E., shows the sack of Jerusalem two years earlier, when Titus and his father mounted a major expedition to thwart Jewish resistance, destroyed the Temple, and carried off spoils to Rome including the seven-branched candlestick of pure gold, known as the menorah, the tablets of the laws of Moses (one of which is shown in the carving, hoisted on a pole), and the golden table and sacred trumpets, which appear on the right of the picture.

treasures from three continents to give the civic center instant dignity. The serpent throne of the Delphic oracle (see Chapter 5)—sacred to the Greeks—still lies here, charred, broken, and half-buried. The collected loot included obelisks from Egypt, a fragment of the True Cross and the nails of Christ's Passion from Palestine, and, from Asia Minor, an icon of the goddess Athene said to have belonged to the remotest ancestor of Rome's earliest kings.

Terror and intimidation also played a part in securing supremacy, as the fate of Carthage and Corinth make clear—cities the Romans looted and razed to the ground. Looting and destruction went hand in hand. When the Romans conquered what is now France, they denuded the country of gold and silver, as we know from the quality of surviving coins. Long lists of booty survive. During wars for the conquest of northern Greece, in 167 B.C.E., the Romans sacked 70 enemy towns so thoroughly that the region was still a desert 100 years later. They piled up the enemies' captured weapons and burned them as an offering to the gods, "to whom it is right," they explained, "to dedicate the spoils of the enemy." The conquerors shipped the riches of the plundered cities to Rome, where the loot went on display before being sold to pay the army's wages: "statues, paintings, textiles, vessels of gold, silver, bronze and ivory, made with great pains in the palace workshops. . . . The gaze of the crowd that came was no more drawn to a stage show, or athletic contests or chariot races than to all the booty of Macedonia."

At the same time, 150,000 captives from the war glutted Rome's market with slaves. War made the Roman economy dependent on slaves, both as domestic servants and as workers on aristocrats' huge farms and ranches. Though most of the sources speak of the relatively comfortable lives and prestigious jobs of domestic slaves, slavery in the Roman Empire was as brutal and corrupting a business as ever it was in other cultures and environments. In scale, nothing like it would be seen again in the history of Western civilization until the mass enslavement of black Africans from the sixteenth to the nineteenth centuries. As in that later episode, most of the slaves of Roman times worked on large-scale agricultural

Galley slaves. Hollywood's version of galley slaves at the oar from the film *Ben Hur* (1959). In reality, Roman navies employed professional oarsmen for what was a skilled, well-paid job, though the layout of the deck in this photo, with three banks of oars and a coxswain beating time, is authentic.

enterprises, with no hope of freedom or alleviation of their sufferings, or they worked in mines until—generally quickly—the work killed them. The statesman and stern moralist Cato (234–149 B.C.E.) was criticized for "getting full use out of his slaves, as if they were pack animals, and then, when they got old, driving them off and selling them."

Roman rule could be harsh and exploitative. Loot meant a lot to Rome, but for the victim-peoples of the Roman Empire the regular taxes were more oppressive. Yet people paid them, for most of the time, without rebelling, because in some respects the empire gave good value. For this was an empire that gave as well as took—run, on the whole, by an elite that knew the empire could only succeed by bringing benefits to its subjects. The empire provided security, the "Roman peace," as the peoples of the empire called it. Peace lengthened trade routes and nourished prosperity. The Romans' supreme skill, according to the incomparable poet of Roman propaganda, Virgil (70–19 B.C.E.), was "to rule the nations, to keep the world in peace, to spare the humbled, and to crush the proud." So good intentions tempered Roman injustices and atrocities. Although Rome never succeeded entirely in eliminating pirates from the sea or bandits from the highways, the Roman peace did work, on the whole, to the advantage of the entire empire. To the benefits of security, moreover, Rome added those of culture and commerce.

Imperial Culture and Commerce

Retired soldiers—Latin-speaking and schooled in allegiance to Rome—helped spread a common culture across the empire, settling in lands where they had been stationed and often marrying local women. On his tombstone in Cologne, in the Rhineland, the image of a retired veteran from southern Spain reclines; his wife and slave serve food and wine from an elegant, claw-footed table. A tomb-

Tombstone of a Roman Soldier. The Roman Empire shifted people across vast distances. This tombstone in Cologne, Germany, records a veteran soldier, Marcus Valerius Celerinus, who married and settled locally after his legion was transferred to Germany from his home in southern Spain, late in the first century C.E.

stone in northern Britain commemorates a 16-year-old boy from Roman Syria. He died, says the inscription, "in the land of the Cimmerians"—the rainy, foggy land that the Greek poet Homer (see Chapter 5) had imagined on the way to the underworld.

Roman culture was so well known in Britain, despite the remoteness of the province, that mints in the third century C.E. could stamp coins with references to the poetry of Virgil—who, in the reign of Augustus (r. 27 B.C.E.–14 C.E.), celebrated Rome's foundation myth. Everywhere, the empire promoted the same classical style for buildings and urban planning: symmetrical, harmonious, regular, and based on Greek architecture. The artistic traditions of subject-peoples became provincial styles. For instance, the last monuments of the funerary art of the pharaohs are the Fayyum portraits, which stare from the surfaces of burial caskets in Roman Egypt. They are recognizably in an ancient Egyptian tradition, yet faces as realistic and sensitive as these might be found in portraits anywhere in the Roman Empire.

Engineering was the Romans' ultimate art. They discovered how to make cement, which made unprecedented feats of building possible. Everywhere the empire reached, Romans invested in infrastructure, building roads, sewers, and aqueducts. Amphitheaters, temples, city walls, public baths, and monumental gates were erected at public expense, alongside the temples that civic-minded patrons usually endowed. The buildings serviced new cities, built in Rome's image, where there were none before, or enlarged and embellished cities that already existed. The biggest courthouse in the empire was in London, the widest street was in Italica, a Roman city in Spain. Colonists in Conimbriga, on the coast of Portugal, where salt spray corroded the mosaic floors, demolished their town center in the first century C.E. and rebuilt it to resemble Rome's. Trade as well as war shipped elements of a common culture around the empire. Rome exported Mediterranean amenities—the building patterns of villas and cities, wine, olive oil, mosaics—to the provinces, or forced Mediterranean crops like wine grapes, figs, and olive trees to grow in unlikely climates.

As industries became geographically specialized, trade and new commercial relationships crisscrossed the entire empire. In the first century C.E., merchants from the Duero valley in Spain were buried in Hungary. Greek potters made huge jars to transport wine from Spain to southern France. In southwest Spain, huge evaporators survive from the factories where garum—the empire's favorite fish sauce—was made from the blood and entrails of tuna and mackerel. The lives of cloth merchants from northeast France are engraved on a tomb at Igel, on the frontier of Germany. They conveyed bales of cloth by road and river and sold it in elegant shops, lavishing their profits on banquets to lord it over their farming neighbors.

Of course, as the empire grew, its political institutions changed. When Rome was a small city-republic, two annually elected chief executives, called consuls, shared power between themselves, subject to checks by the assembly of nobles and notables known as the Senate, and by the tribunes, representatives of the common citizens. Increasingly, however, as the state expanded, in the emergencies of war, power was confided to individuals, called dictators, who were expected to relinquish control when the emergency was over. In the second half of the first century B.C.E., this system finally broke down in a series of struggles between rival contenders for power. In 27 B.C.E., all parties accepted Augustus, who had emerged as

Fayyum portrait. When Egypt became a Roman province in 30 B.C.E., burial practices remained the same: Mummies were encased in painted caskets. But the style of painting that depicted the deceased gradually took on Roman conventions of portraiture, as in this lovely example of a young woman from the mid-second century C.E.

Aqueduct. Nearly 3,000 feet long and rising to 115 feet high, the second-century C.E. aqueduct of Segovia, Spain, is one of the surviving marvels of Roman engineering. In laying the infrastructure of communications and supply, the Romans were not only building up their own power and their ability to shift and sustain armies, they were also spectacularly demonstrating the benefits, self-confidence, and durability of their rule for their subject and "allied" peoples.

victor from the civil wars, as head of state and of government for life, with the right to name his successor.

Effectively, henceforth, Rome was a monarchy, though Romans, schooled in republicanism, hated to use the word. Part of the consequence of Roman distaste for kings was that the rules of succession to supreme power were never perfectly defined. Although the hereditary principle tended to prevail, it was never fully respected. Augustus called himself *princeps*—a word roughly equivalent to "chief" in English. Gradually, however, "emperor" took over as the name people normally used to designate the ruler. The Latin term—*imperator*—originally meant an army commander, and the army, or parts of the army, often in rivalry with each other, increasingly took to itself the role of dethroning and electing emperors.

One constant feature of politics was that women were always excluded—at least formally. Because Rome developed under the influence—and probably for many generations under the rule—of Etruscan kings, women enjoyed essentially the same privileges in society as their Etruscan forbears. The probably legendary story of Coriolanus (which became the subject of a play by Shakespeare) shows that the power-mother was a familiar figure in Rome. Coriolanus was a renegade general, marching on Rome at the head of a foreign army in the early fifth century B.C.E., when the republic was young and vulnerable. His mother countermarched out of the city, rebuked him, and sent him meekly away. "We rule all men," said a moralist of the third century B.C.E., "and who rules us? Our wives." It was an exaggeration, for in law at that date, at least nominally, the state recognized two forms of marriage: in the first, women were bound to obey every lawful command of their fathers and husbands. But by the time we have clear evidence about marriage customs—in the last century or two of the republic—the second form of marriage was general: wives kept their own property in marriage and could, and often did, divorce their husbands.

In consequence, widows and divorcees often headed businesses or, if they were landowners, ran their own estates. Henpecked husbands and manipulative women were stock figures in Roman literature. More surprising than their oblique role in politics is the silence of women in Roman literature: because most Roman writers were moralists and some of the rest were pornographers, it sometimes seems that Rome was overrun with sex-crazed, exhibitionistic women who acted like prostitutes. More normal, however, were the women commemorated in epitaphs on grave markers of the second and first centuries B.C.E.: "Claudia loved her husband with all her heart, buried one son, raised another, maintained charming conversation, kept house, and made wool. "Graxia Alexandria, in what was probably an everyday Roman story of suffering womanhood, was "a woman of exemplary chastity, who fed her sons at her breast. She lived 24 years, three months, and 16 days."

Roman marriage was a private arrangement, easily entered into between consenting individuals, with no religious connotations. Typically, however, especially among the prosperous, the families of the bride and groom met for a formal ceremony, often accompanied, as in the example depicted here, by a written contract—which gets pride of place in this expensive sculpture, evidently made to reinforce and commemorate the contract.

The Celts

This was by no means a uniform empire. It was so big that it could only work by permitting the provinces to retain their local customs and religious practices. At one level it was a

Chronology: Roman Expansion

ca. 290 B.C.E.	Rome reaches limit of expansion in Italy
146 B.C.E.	Rome destroys Carthage
148 B.C.E.	Rome annexes Macedon
133 B.C.E.	Pergamum added to Roman Empire
51 B.C.E.	Conquest of Gaul completed
30 B.C.E.	Rome annexes Egypt
43 C.E.	Rome invades Britain
106 C.E.	Conquest of Dacia completed

federation of cities, and at another a federation of peoples. Everywhere, Rome ruled with the collaboration—sometimes enforced—of established elites. Spanish notables with barbarous names followed Roman law in legal decisions that they ordered to be carved in bronze. Hebrew princes and Germanic chiefs ruled as imperial delegates. Greeks were Rome's partners in the east, where Greek rather than Latin was the most widespread common tongue and served at most levels as the official language of government. In the western half of the empire, the crucial collaborators were Celts.

The Celts dominated Western Europe by the mid-first millennium B.C.E. They occupied present-day France, Britain, Ireland, and most of Spain. Their settlements were widespread in Central Europe and even reached Anatolia. Everywhere they lived in numerous chiefdoms and small states. What united them was language. They all spoke mutually intelligible versions of a single tongue.

Stories about the Celts made Roman gooseflesh ripple. They hunted human heads and hung them on their saddles. They stitched sacrifice victims inside wicker images of gods and burned them alive. They had a reputation for drunkenness. A 35-year-old Celtic hostess at Vix in central France was buried with a Greek wine vessel so large that it had to be imported in sections and assembled on arrival. The Celts' courage was also renowned. Roman sculpture shows them dead or dying but never giving up.

Despite their fierce and undisciplined reputation, the Celts had a way of life that Romans recognized as civilized. For one thing, the Celts had a professional learned class, the Druids. They were supposedly suspicious of writing wisdom down, but many inscriptions survive, including laws, administrative records, and a calendar to foretell the future. When Julius Caesar conquered the Celts in Gaul (modern France and Belgium) in the 50s B.C.E., he used captured census returns to calculate the number of men he faced.

Town life thrived among the Celts, at least by the third century B.C.E. Roman propaganda has misled historians—especially the story of a captured British chief, who, on removal to Rome, marveled that the builders of such a city could covet his people's hovels. But Celtic cities had civilized amenities. There were modest Celtic towns in France and Spain. The town of Numancia, which was rich in iron, was a minor metropolis by Celtic standards. Covering almost 1,800 square feet, it was arranged in neat streets up to 21 feet wide. Here, on one terrible campaign, the Romans took 3,000 oxhides and 800 horses in booty. The dwellings of Numancia were of mud and thatch on a rubble base, but the inhabitants enjoyed fresh water supplies and sanitary drainage. Some Celtic towns were big. Manching in southern Germany, founded in the third century B.C.E., stretched over 1,000 acres. Nearby Kelheim was half as big again. Most towns minted coins and included workshops for bronze and iron manufacture, glass jewelry, and leather goods.

By the time Rome seriously began to wage war on them—early in the last quarter of the second century B.C.E.—the Celts of what is now France had a society Romans acknowledged as like their own: no longer organized along tribal lines but according to wealth, prowess, and ancestry. Nobility was measured in livestock, not land. Peasant-tenants paid their rents in calves, pigs, and grain. After ferocious initial resistance to Roman conquest, Celts usually accepted Romanization and became enthusiastic subjects of and collaborators in the Roman Empire. Generally, they welcomed the enriching economic consequences of the peace the Romans enforced.

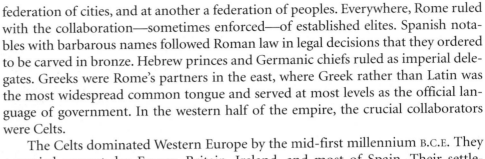

Celtic conspicuous consumption: This wine vessel, buried with the queen or princess to whom it belonged in the mid-first millennium B.C.E., was as tall as she was. Too big and heavy to handle, it was just for show. Like the wine it contained, it was imported from the Mediterranean. Greek soldiers and chariots decorate the rim. Serpent-haired Gorgons form handles, inside which lions climb—all symbolizing the owner's power.

THE BEGINNINGS OF IMPERIALISM IN INDIA

Meanwhile, beyond the eastern frontiers of Persia, in India, Alexander's threat seems to have had an immediately galvanizing effect. When one of his generals re-crossed the Indus in 305 B.C.E., he found the states of the Ganges valley confederated under a leader from the delta region, Candragupta (chahn-drah-GOOP-tah). The sources are hazy, however, until the next reign, that of Asoka (ah-SHOH-kah), which began in the 260s B.C.E. The *Arthasastra* (ahr-tha-SHAS-trah), purportedly the work of a servant of Candragupta, describes the political world of Asoka. More importantly, his thoughts and deeds come to life in the many decrees and self-reflexive thoughts he had inscribed on pillars and rock faces. Although it is an awful pun, one can say that the rock inscriptions are hard evidence.

The sources show, first, the extraordinarily long reach of Asoka's power. The inscriptions are scattered around the Indian subcontinent, but concentrated in three areas: the Ganges valley, a frontier zone in and around the Krishna (KREESH-nah) valley, and a northwest mountain zone on the upper Indus (see Map 7.6). Second, the evidence reveals an expanding realm, constantly reforging environments. "The king shall populate the countryside," says the *Arthasastra*, "by creating villages on virgin land or by reviving abandoned village sites. Settlement

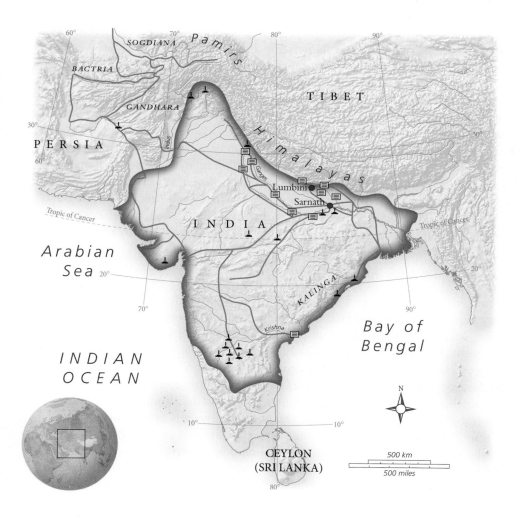

The Reign of Asoka, ca. 268–223 B.C.E.

- ▨ maximum extent of Asoka's empire
- ⊥ pillar edict of Asoka
- ▤ rock inscription of Asoka
- — trade route

can be effected either by shifting some of the population of his own country or by immigration of foreigners. . . . The villages shall be so sited as to provide mutual protection. . . . Like a barren cow, a kingdom without people yields nothing."

The same source describes two main types of environment—one rainy and the other requiring irrigation—and specifies suitable crops for both: two varieties of rice, two of millet, wheat, and barley, six sorts of beans, four types of oil seeds, various vegetables, herbs, and spices. The king is responsible for irrigation and should encourage others to irrigate by exempting them from the water tax. Pasture, mines, and forests (for obtaining war elephants) are all worthy objects of conquest. Roads are emphasized, with signposts and wells at 9-mile intervals. Regulating trade—including coinage, weights, and measures—and processing the raw materials of royal lands are also part of the ruler's job.

Government

Methods and means of government reflected central control. Peasants paid a quarter of their produce in tax, apparently directly to the king, with no mention of any intermediate rulers. (In Lumbini, where the Buddha was born, they paid only an eighth, as a mark of the king's piety.) Army leaders received pay in cash, rather than being given a share of royal power, as was customary in later Indian states. Asoka's inscriptions portray him as what we would now call a hands-on ruler. He "received reports at all times"—in his harem or gardens, his carriage, or his barns, where he inspected his livestock. "And whatever I order by word of mouth, whether it concerns a donation or proclamation or whatever urgent matter is entrusted by my officers, if there is any dispute or deliberation about it at the Council, it is to be reported to me immediately."

The *Arthasastra* expresses an ideology of universal rule and emphasizes the supremacy of "the king's law" and the importance of uniform justice. It is hard to know, however, what this meant in practice. India was already becoming a **caste** society, where social rank was inherited, unchangeable, and made sacred by religious sanctions. Brahmanical literature (see Chapter 5) treated women as if they were imperfectly human, though Buddhism admitted them to one form of high status as nuns. Few other occupations were open to them. There were state-run weaving shops for unmarriageable women, including retired prostitutes, the elderly, and the deformed. The king had female bodyguards, but this was because women's social exclusion made them trustworthy: They had nothing to gain by rebelling.

Asoka and His Mental World

The rock inscriptions are, in a sense, Asoka's autobiography, disclosing an extraordinary personal story of spiritual development. The first secure date in his reign is the conquest of Kalinga, a kingdom in eastern India around 260 B.C.E. In his commemorative inscription, he expresses regret for the suffering he caused: 150,000 deportees, 100,000 killed, "and many times that number who perished." He goes on "The Beloved of the gods [meaning Asoka himself] felt remorse, for, when an independent country is conquered the slaughter, death and deportation of the people is extremely grievous to the Beloved of the gods, and weighs heavily on his mind." The inscription then gets to what one suspects is the real point: "The Beloved of the gods believes that one who does wrong should be forgiven. . . . And the Beloved of the gods conciliates the forest tribes of his empire, but he warns them that he has power even in his remorse, and he asks them to repent, lest they be killed."

"India was already becoming a caste society, where social rank was inherited, unchangeable, and made sacred by religious sanctions."

A CLOSER LOOK

The Great Stupa of Sanchi

The Emperor Asoka (r. ca. 272–223 B.C.E.) built the first shrine at Sanchi near Bhopal in India, to honor a place made holy by the footprints of the Buddha. Enriched by the donations of pilgrims, it was adorned by dozens of elaborate structures over thousands of years.

Wheels are universal Buddhist symbols, for the Buddha "set the wheel of the law (dharma) in motion."

The northern gateway, shown here, is elaborately carved with scenes of legends of the Buddha's life and with tales of exemplary charity.

Elephants and tree spirits, in the form of dancers entwined with mango trees, hold up the upper crossbeams.

How does the Great Stupa at Sanchi show Asoka's use of Buddhism to consolidate political power?

So, in part at least, Asoka's remorse was intended as a warning, and he could hardly have won such a large empire except by war. Still, within a few years, the repudiation of conquest became a major theme of his inscriptions. "Any sons or grandsons I may have should not think of gaining new conquests. . . . The Beloved of the gods considers victory by the teaching of the Buddha to be the foremost victory. . . . The sound of the drum has become the sound of the Buddha's doctrine, showing the people displays of heavenly chariots, elephants, balls of fire, and other divine forms." Asoka put the policy of conquest-by-conversion into practice, sending missionaries to the kingdoms that replaced the old Persian Empire and to Sri Lanka (see Chapter 5). His descendants, he hoped, would adhere to this policy "until the end of the world."

How are we to explain Asoka's extraordinary behavior? His realm was expanding into areas where city life was only starting or, in northwest India, only reviving after the disappearance of the Harappan civilization. In the absence of existing bureaucracies, Asoka had to resort to the one disciplined, literate group available: the Buddhist clergy. This was the period when Buddhist scriptures were being recorded. Asoka recruited the scribes to his service. In an early inscription, he assured them of his fidelity to the Buddha. He listed the scriptures the scribes were writing down and declared his desire that monks, nuns, and his lay subjects should hear the scriptures frequently and meditate upon them.

These words are the tell-tale trace of Asoka's bargain with the clergy, probably made in the tenth year of his reign, 258 B.C.E. About this time, too, he made a much-publicized pilgrimage to the scene of the Buddha's enlightenment. In a further inscription, of perhaps two and a half years later, he admitted that his personal faith had made little progress for a year, but then he "drew close to the monks and became more ardent." He had made society holy, or, as he put it, he made "gods mingle with men" for the first time in India.

As the Buddhist clergy became more powerful, however, the monks' rivalry for the gifts of the pious and their disputes over matters of theology threatened the peace of the realm. So Asoka forbade them to speak ill of one another. "Concord is to be recommended, that men may hear one another's principles and obey them." Asoka's alliance with religion was the shape of things to come. As we shall see, it became a practice of kings all over the world, bringing problems and advantages.

Buddhist ideology underlies Asoka's many decrees against the unnecessary killing of animals. "Formerly in the kitchens of the Beloved of the gods many hundreds of thousands of living animals were killed daily for meat," but Asoka cut the kill rate to two peacocks and one deer per day and promised, "Even these three animals will not be killed in future." He banned outright the slaughter of particular species, including geese, queen ants, and iguanas, perhaps because these creatures were used in sorcery. He proclaimed that his duties embraced "care of man and care of animals. Medicinal herbs, useful to man or beast, have been bought and planted wherever they did not grow; similarly roots and fruit have been bought and planted wherever they did not grow. Along the roads wells have been dug and trees planted for the use of men and beasts."

The language of Buddhism also infused Asoka's declarations of policy: "All men are my children. . . . There is no better work than promoting the welfare of the whole world. And whatever may be my great deeds, I have done them to discharge my debt to all beings. I work for their happiness in this life, that in the next they may gain heaven." The disadvantaged were specifically included—slaves and servants, women and prisoners. In the twenty-sixth year of his reign, he likened the role his administrators played for his people to the way nurses cared for children.

Officials toured the empire to instruct people in Asoka's version of Buddhist ethics: family loyalty, piety for holy men, mercy toward living creatures, and personal austerity. He made such tours himself, taking more pleasure in distributing alms and consulting holy men, he said, than in all other pleasures. These activities replaced hunting, formerly a royal obligation, now banned.

Toward the end of Asoka's reign, it appeared that his enlightenment was beginning to damage the empire. He tightened laws on the treatment of animals, forbidding the slaughter of young livestock and animals that were nursing their young. He forbade the castration of roosters. Fishless days were imposed. "Chaff, which contains living things must not be set on fire. Forests must not be burned to kill living things or without good reason. An animal must not be fed with another animal." Gelding and branding were restricted. These decrees must have caused outrage and threatened livelihoods. The emperor's pride in the 25 amnesties he granted to imprisoned criminals can hardly have endeared him to their victims. His condemnation of all rituals as trivial and useless compared with a life in accordance with Buddhist doctrine alienated ordinary people. Perhaps worst of all, his policy against conquests meant the empire could not expand and turned the violence of the military classes inward.

Only 25 years after Asoka's death in 232 B.C.E., his empire (which historians call the Mauryan Empire) broke up into separate states. But state-forming, environment-modifying habits had spread throughout India. The economic infrastructure—the routes of commerce, the enhanced range of resources—was not invulnerable. But the Mauryan infrastructure was unforgettable, and it could usually be repaired or reconstructed, if necessary, after future wars and environmental disasters.

Chronology: The Reign of Asoka	
ca. 268–232 B.C.E.	Reign of Asoka
260 B.C.E.	Conquest of Kalinga
258 B.C.E.	Conversion to Buddhism
ca. 200 B.C.E.	Breakup of Asoka's empire

"Only 25 years after Asoka's death in 232 B.C.E., his empire broke up into separate states. But state-forming, environment-modifying habits had spread throughout India."

CHINESE UNITY AND IMPERIALISM

Even after 500 years of division among warring states, the ideal of imperial unity had not been forgotten in China. The Hundred Schools (see Chapter 6) kept it alive. The return of real unity, however, owed less to nostalgia than to a ruthless and innovative program of renewal, imposed by force. Of all the warring states, Qin was the most marginal, occupying relatively infertile uplands, far from the rice-growing regions. The intelligentsia of most other states considered its people imperfectly civilized.

Toward the mid-third century B.C.E., Qin began what, in retrospect, looks like a systematic strategy of rejecting the very idea of empire. In 256 B.C.E., its ruler discontinued all imperial rites, in effect dissolving the empire. Ten years later, a new king of Qin, Shi Huangdi (shee hwang-dee), declared that having been dismantled, the empire could be replaced. Over the next 25 years, he systematically isolated and conquered all rival kingdoms and declared himself "First Emperor" of a new monarchy. "If," he declared, "the whole empire has suffered and has been the prey of wars and rivalry, which have destroyed peace, it is because there were nobles and kings." In other words, with himself as sole ruler, a unified China would enjoy peace and prosperity.

Our picture of his reign comes from histories compiled one or two generations later. They are distorted partly by the awe Shi Huangdi inspired and partly by revulsion from his oppressive rule. They were based not on what he actually did, but on the sometimes unrealistic ambitions his decrees reveal. To judge by these sources, he

Terracotta Warriors. Though his life and reign were short, everything else about Shi Huangdi (r. 221–210 B.C.E.), the Qin ruler who conquered China, was on a monumental scale. The size and magnificence of his tomb, guarded by an army of terracotta warriors, echoes the grandeur of his engineering works and the scope of his ambitions and uncompromising reforms.

aimed to break the aristocracy, abolish slavery, outlaw inheritance practices that concentrated wealth in noble hands, and replace the power of kings and lords with a uniform system of civil and military districts under his own appointees. He ordered the burning of hundreds of people he considered disloyal and, reputedly, of thousands of books. Only useful technical manuals and the writings of the Legalist school (see Chapter 6) were allowed. Uniformity was the keynote of the new state. Laws, coinage, measures, script, even axle lengths of carts had, by decree, to be the same all over the kingdom. Unauthorized weapons were melted down.

Even if some of his plans went unfulfilled, Shi Huangdi's demonic energy is obvious in everything he attempted. He mobilized 700,000 laborers to build a network of roads and canals. He knocked the Great Wall of China together out of a series of older fortifications, as protection against nomad attacks. When he died, he was buried with thousands of life-size clay models of soldiers and servants—each with different facial and body features—to accompany him into the next life. He was a showman of power on a huge scale—which is usually a sign of insecurity. His empire was too fragile to last, but sweeping away the warring states made it easier for his successors to rebuild an enduring Chinese Empire.

Unity Endangered and Saved

The first instinct of the rebels who overthrew Shi Huangdi's feeble son in 207 B.C.E. was to break up the empire again and restore the system of the Warring States period. The result was chaotic warfare, with one of the rebel leaders, Liu Bang (lee-oh-bahng), emerging victorious over all the others. He put in place a carefully tempered version of Shi Huangdi's system. Restored kings had small territories within military districts. Peasants owed the state two years' military service plus one month's labor a year on state projects, which must have seemed lenient compared to Shi Huangdi's enforced labor and heavy taxation.

Legalism remained the dominant political philosophy. Liu Bang put most of his former allies to death and showed contempt for Confucianism. In the long run, however, Liu Bang's policies were not sustainable. Only Confucian scholars and officials could supply the literate administrators that a growing state needed. Gradually, especially in the 50-year reign of Han Wudi (hawn woo-dee), beginning in 141 B.C.E., Legalism was repudiated, and Confucianism again became the state ideology. A new elite—a Confucian-educated aristocracy dedicated to serving the state—replaced the old ruling class of kings and warrior aristocrats. The new regime invoked the Confucian myth of a golden age (see Chapter 6) and claimed to be restoring ancient virtue.

Liu Bang called his dynasty "Han" after the portion of the country he received in the carving up of Shi Huangdi's realm. In the period of expansion that began in the late second century B.C.E., Han China became the essential China that we see on maps of later eras. It occupied not only the Yellow River and Yangtze basins but also the West River valley, which joins the sea at Guangzhou (gwang-joh), stretching from the Great Wall in the north to Vietnam in the south. It also occupied northern Korea, and in the west reached toward Tibet and the Silk Roads between the Kunlun (kwuhn-lwuhn) and Tian Shan (tee-en shahn) Mountains. Chinese began to call themselves Han (see Map 7.7).

The return of peaceful conditions under the Han dynasty stimulated a population explosion. The figures recorded in the bureaucracy's censuses fluctuate unconvincingly. But the population of 20 million in Shi Huangdi's day probably tripled by the end of the millennium. In part, the huge increase was also a consequence of the increased size and environmental diversity of the state. Rice-growing and millet-growing regions could again exchange supplies in each other's bad times. The government coped with disasters, such as drought, famine, or earthquakes, by massive frontier colonization programs and redistributing population on a large scale. Forced migrations peopled newly conquered provinces in the southeast at the same time that settlers were encouraged to migrate south toward the Huai valley. These movements shifted the distribution of population, making the Yangtze River the main axis of China. Meanwhile, in the north in 120 B.C.E., 700,000 families were moved into a new conquest beyond the province of Shaanxi, which famine had devastated.

The Han dynasty lasted for 400 years (from 206 B.C.E. to 220 C.E.), despite a succession system that bred palace conspiracies. Succession was determined by designating a principal wife to be the mother of each emperor's heir. This gave empresses' families a unique opportunity to profit from the emperor's favor. But the advantage rarely lasted more than two generations—less, if the empress failed to produce a future emperor. Consequently, every empress's family was tempted to seize power for itself—and most tried. In these circumstances, a dynasty that survived a long time was a triumph against the odds.

The Menace from the Steppes

The other main problem China faced in this period emerged from the steppelands, north of the Great Wall and the Silk Roads. The region had a bad reputation with the Chinese. Its climate was inhospitable, its soil was unworkable, and its native herdsmen were reputedly savage. In some ways, however, it was a good place in which to start

Chronology: The Qin and the Han

ca. 400 B.C.E.	Beginning of Warring States period
ca. 256 B.C.E.	Ruler of Qin discontinues imperial rites
ca. 247 B.C.E.	Shi Huangdi becomes ruler of Qin state; beginning of Qin expansion
214 B.C.E.	Construction of Great Wall begins
210 B.C.E.	Death of Shi Huangdi
206 B.C.E.	Beginning of Han dynasty
141 B.C.E.	Han Wudi becomes Han emperor
ca. 139 B.C.E.	Embassy of Zhang Qian to Central Asia
220 C.E.	Collapse of Han dynasty

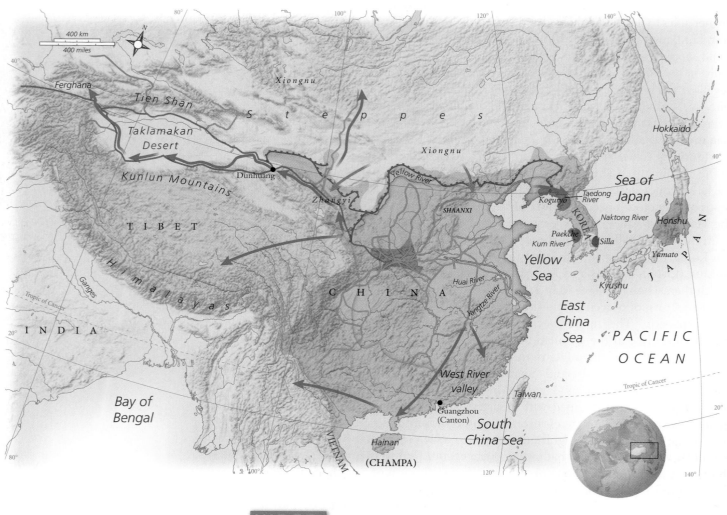

MAP 7.7

China and Its Neighbors, 250 B.C.E.–200 C.E.

▨ Qin Homeland	▨ Yayoi culture
▨ Maximum extent of Qin Empire	▨ Silla
▨ Han Empire, 2 C.E.	▨ Paekche
➤ Han expeditions	▨ Koguryo
➤ Xiongnu incursions	VIETNAM modern country
▬ Silk Road	*SHAANXI* region
▬ Chinese imperial canals	*Xiongnu* people
▬ Great Wall	
▬ Chinese imperial roads	

building an empire. It bred plenty of horses and men accustomed to the saddle. Its people were voracious because they were poor. It was a vast, flat tract of land, with few geographical obstacles to the creation of a large state. Because the steppeland fringed the region of the Silk Roads, leaders of steppeland war bands could conduct raids, amass treasure, and use their wealth to build up large followings. For the steppelander chiefs who lived closest to China, among the people the Chinese called Xiongnu (shee-ohng-noo), Chinese wealth was another means to transform themselves into kings and emperors.

In the absence of adequate evidence, guesswork can tentatively reconstruct how the Xiongnu Empire came into being. Chinese booty, ransom, and protection money enriched war chiefs who became wealthy enough to extend their followings beyond their own kin and mobilize ever-larger forces. According to Chinese evidence, compiled much later—which is all we have—the first Xiongnu state emerged late in the third century B.C.E., under a leader who styled himself "Son of Heaven," which was a Chinese imperial title and therefore perhaps suggests Chinese influence. His warriors hunted heads—exhibiting scalps from their bridles, making the skulls of their enemies into cups. The basis of their success in war was their skill in mounted archery. Sheep, horses, cattle, and camels were the basis of their economy—guaranteeing the advantages of mixed pastoralism, with milk yields of different species of animals peaking at different times. In about 176 B.C.E., they conquered Gansu (gohn-soo), at the western end of the Great Wall, and became a serious, constant nuisance to China.

Modern Steppelanders. Modern-day steppelanders: Two Kazak horsemen gallop across a plain with golden eagles used for hunting perched in their arms.

Confucian doctrine advocated what we would now call appeasement: "Your Majesty has but to manifest your virtue towards them and extend your favors to cover them, and the northern Barbarians will undoubtedly come of their own accord to pay you tribute at the wall." This policy was not as feeble as it sounds. Many neighboring peoples genuinely felt the "peaceful attraction" of Chinese rule, and Chinese culture proved remarkably adept at absorbing huge numbers of subject-peoples. The Xiongnu, however, were unresponsive to such methods.

In the late second century B.C.E., Han efforts to recruit allies against them failed. Zhang Qian's mission, described earlier in this chapter, was part of the effort and part of the failure. But between 127 and 120 B.C.E., the Chinese General Wei Qing (way-cheeng) mounted a series of successful operations against the Xiongnu and induced some of their bands or tribes into Chinese service. The fortification of the Silk Roads followed. Xiongnu victories became infrequent. Chinese defenses prevailed. For a while around the turn of the millennium, the Xiongnu even abandoned hostilities.

Thereafter, weakened by civil wars, the Xiongnu succumbed to a series of celebrated campaigns by General Ban Zhao (ban-jaow) in the late first century C.E. He recruited nomads to fight nomads and secured victories at small cost in Chinese lives. His most daring march took him to the shores of the Caspian Sea. In the exaggerated reports of Chinese chroniclers, he slaughtered thousands of foes and captured hundreds of thousands of head of livestock. He also "cut off the right arm of the Xiongnu" when he captured their permanent court. By the time Ban Zhao retired in 102 C.E., the Xiongnu themselves had come under increasing pressure from neighbors to the north and east, who, in their turn, were beginning to move toward statehood.

BEYOND THE EMPIRES

Evidently, in the second half of the first millennium B.C.E., the edges of empires bred states. The Xiongnu were not the only example of economic and political development in China's

Chronology: The Han and the Xiongnu	
Third century B.C.E.	First Xiongnu state emerges
ca. 176 B.C.E.	Xiongnu conquers Gansu
127–120 B.C.E.	Chinese mount successful operations against the Xiongnu
78–94 C.E.	Ban Zhao leads celebrated campaigns against the Xiongnu

Chronology: At the Edge of Empires

Seventh century B.C.E.	First written evidence of the Scythians
ca. 500 B.C.E.	Silla, Paekche, and Koguryo states dominate Korea
Fourth century B.C.E.	Yayoi culture emerges in Japan
ca. 200 B.C.E.	Sarmatians displace Scythians

shadow. Large-scale state formation also occurred in the same period in Japan and Korea, under Chinese influence, and at the other end of Eurasia, among the Scythians and Sarmatians, pastoral peoples whose lands bordered the Roman and Persian empires. The proximity of empires, however, was a sufficient, though not necessary, condition for new states to thrive. When, after discussing these Eurasian cases, we turn to the other side of the globe, we shall face the problem of how states formed in different contexts in Mesoamerica.

Japan and Korea

In the fourth century B.C.E., a rice-growing, bronze-using culture known to archaeologists as Yayoi emerged in Japan. It gradually developed into a state system, under the stimulus of contacts with China. In 219 B.C.E., for instance, a Chinese expedition visited Japan in search of the Isles of the Immortals, fabled in Daoist tales (for Daoism, see Chapter 6). According to Chinese records, in about 200 C.E., one of the Japanese states, Yamatai, conquered the others, under the rule of a female shaman. When she died, 1,000 attendants were burned at her burial. This is the first inkling we have of a unified Japanese state.

Korean states developed faster. The Chinese were in touch with three Korean states—Silla on the Naktong River, Paekche (pek-jay) on the Kum River, and Koguryo on the Taedong River. The Chinese sources are so vague, and the archaeological evidence so scanty, that historians can say nothing reliable about the political history of these realms. But their rulers were buried in impressive tombs—usually with a wooden chamber at their core, piled with stone and earth. Grave goods reveal something of the nature of power and trade: iron weapons, fabulous gold diadems and chains, bronze ornaments that imitate Chinese work.

The Western Eurasian Steppe

Meanwhile, at the other end of the Eurasian steppe, in what is modern-day Ukraine and southern Russia, states were forming among the pastoral peoples known as Scythians and Sarmatians. Scythian states formed in and around Crimea (creye-MEE-ah), a peninsula that juts into the Black Sea, where the Scythians came into contact with Greek colonies. Here was the Scythian center of Neapolis, a ruler's court covering 40 acres and surrounded by a stone wall. Evidence of Sarmatian royal courts is concentrated in an area to the east, beyond the rivers Dneiper and Don.

On one level, Greek writers sensed this pastoral, nomadic world was alien, wild, and menacing. The fifth-century B.C.E. Greek historian, Herodotus, told of a legendary traveler who undertook a mysterious, dreamlike journey to their land, beyond the river Don in modern Ukraine. He returned to tell the tale—but as a ghost. On another level, the nomads were familiar trading partners. Greek craftsmen depicted them in everyday scenes, milking sheep or stitching their cloaks of unshorn sheepskin. Greek and Celtic trade goods filled princely graves in the last half of the first millennium B.C.E.

Much of this art was produced under the patronage of Scythian and Sarmatian princes and is echoed in their own goldsmiths' work. A gold cup, for instance, from a royal tomb at Kul-Oba, near the Black Sea, shows bearded warriors in tunics and leggings at peace or, at least, between wars. They tend one another's wounds, fix

A gold cup of the mid-first millennium B.C.E. shows why Scythian art was admired in the classical world. Despite the Scythians' fierce reputation, their goldwork usually shows peaceful images of camp life, vividly depicted, such as this scene in which one warrior binds another's leg.

their teeth, mend their bowstrings, and tell campfire tales. A Sarmatian queen of the first century C.E. stares, in Greek clothes and hairstyle, from the center of a gold crown. She looks as if she fancied herself a Greek goddess. Above her head, what look like deer feed on golden fig leaves, or, perhaps, in the steppeland tradition, the artist meant them to be magical horses, crowned with antlers. When we look at their art, we can never be sure whether these people were happy in their own traditions or envious of the sedentary empires—probably a bit of both.

Mesoamerica

Far more remarkable than these cases of state-building by peoples on the edges of existing empires, are independent but comparable developments that began in this period in Mesoamerica (see Map 7.8). As we have seen, chiefdom-formation and state-building had a long history in this region and in other parts of the Americas, but every innovation had been blocked or frustrated. The geography and vast climate zones of the Americas discouraged communication and cultural change (see Chapter 5).

Now, at least two centers sprang into what might fairly be called a potentially imperial role. Monte Albán (MON-tay al-BAHN) in what is now the Mexican state of Oaxaca was the first. In a period of social differentiation early in the millennium, the region had deer-fed elite, buried in stone-lined graves with their jade-bead lip studs and earrings. Population growth accompanied their supremacy, with increasing exploitation of irrigation and the spread of settlement into areas of sparse rainfall. Around the middle of the millennium, ever-larger settlements appeared, with ritual mounds and the first engraved picture-writing, or glyphs. We do not know how to read this writing, and the inscriptions are all short—perhaps no more than names and dates. From about the same time and place, we have the first evidence of what the ritual platforms were for: a carving of a human sacrifice, with blood streaming from a chest sliced open to pluck out the heart.

Not long after this, Monte Albán began to draw in population from surrounding settlements. It was a natural fortress, enhanced by defensive walls. From a modest village, Monte Albán became a city of perhaps 20,000 people by about 200 B.C.E., when the population stabilized. Faded carvings proclaim its warlike values in parades of sacrifice victims. A palace and a reservoir that could have held 20,000 gallons of water suggest a familiar story: collective effort under strong rule. The

"From about the same time and place, we have the first evidence of what the ritual platforms were for: a carving of a human sacrifice, with blood streaming from a chest sliced open to pluck out the heart."

Monte Albán. The builders of Monte Albán (Oaxaca, Mexico) reshaped the 1,500-foot-high mound on which it stands to fit their idea of how a city should be: 50 acres of terraces supporting temples, palaces, and garrisons. This was truly an imperial metropolis, decorated with gaudy, gory slabs depicting dismembered captives.

Monte Albán and Teotihuacán

⇨	Monte Albán
⇨	Teotihuacán
○	settlement
●	place mentioned on page 221–223
OAXACA	modern province

main plaza contains 40 huge carved stones—probably of the second century B.C.E. These are "conquest slabs," listing the names of subject-cities from as far as 53 miles away, perhaps as many as 90, if the most daring readings are correct. The slabs record the tribute these cities had to pay.

Monte Albán casts light on the later and, in the long run, more spectacular case of Mesoamerican empire-building. Teotihuacán (tay-oh-tee-wah-KAHN), in the valley of Mexico, about 450 miles north of Albán, was destined to be a far greater metropolis. At 6,000 feet above sea level, a little higher than Monte Albán, its agriculture was based on what were by then the region's standard products: maize, beans, and squash. Around the end of the millennium, perhaps as the result of a war, a migration as sudden as Albán's shifted almost the entire population of the valley of Mexico to Teotihuacán. The building of the towering Sun Pyramid began. By about 150 C.E., 20 monumental pyramids were in place. The other buildings

included some structures apparently for housing people from distant lowland sites: ambassadors, tribute bearers, hostages.

The art of Teotihuacán suggests an ecologically fragile way of life, dependent on rainfall and unreliable gods to deliver fertile soil and crops. The artists imagined the sky as a serpent whose sweat fell as rain and fed the plant life of Earth, where sacrificers in serpent masks scattered blood from hands lacerated with cactus spikes or impaled human hearts on bones. Yet the city and the reach of its trade and power continued to grow for over 350 years. At its peak, Teotihuacán was big enough to house well over 100,000 people. Carvings over 625 miles away depicted its warriors, and its trade goods and tribute came from a similarly wide area. Teotihuacano artifacts of the period have turned up in archaeological digs as far away as Alta Vista in Zacatecas to the north and what is today Honduras in the south.

In Perspective
The Aftermath of the Axial Age

The axial age left three legacies: a remarkably durable heritage of ideas, less secure though lengthening routes for trade and cultural exchange in Eurasia, and a fragile group of empires. In some ways, these legacies seemed interdependent. The empires did little to add to the intellectual achievements that preceded them, but they did safeguard, enshrine, and nurture them. The Roman Empire, for example, adopted and fostered Greek learning and, as we shall soon see, did the same service for Christianity.

Persian emperors adopted Zoroastrian rites. Asoka became the patron of Buddhism in India. The Han dynasty rehabilitated Confucianism as the dominant ideology of China. And although the empires had probably been as much the effect as the cause of improved sea and land communications in Eurasia, they unquestionably helped them develop further. The road-building programs of all the empires, the Chinese effort to scout out the Silk Roads and build forts to guard them, and the interest Alexander and his Persian predecessors took in Indian Ocean navigation all demonstrate that.

The collapse of the Persian Empire and the rapid unraveling of Asoka's empire showed that the world was not yet safe for large-scale imperialism. But the pattern of state-building seems to have been irresistible. The new states that emerged on the edges of the existing Eurasian empires—and, as we shall see in the next chapter, in parts of Africa where contacts with Eurasia were multiplying—suggest this. The New World resembled a "parallel universe," where, despite the environmental differences, histories similar to those of parts of Eurasia and Africa were beginning to unfold.

In some ways, the next part of the story is of the continuation and extension of these themes: of growing convergence, in these respects, between the New World and the Old, and of more, roughly parallel developments in parts of Africa and the Pacific island world, where previously they had been absent or undetectable in the evidence. More puzzling—and therefore worth more attention in the next few chapters—are the problems of how, and how far, the intellectual legacy and communications framework of the axial age survived the crises, collapse, or transformation of the empires that had nurtured and transmitted them.

Chronology

Seventh century B.C.E.	First written evidence of the Scythians
Sixth century B.C.E.	Cyrus the Great founds Persian Empire
Fifth century B.C.E.	1,700 miles of road cross Persian Empire Chinese silks appear in Europe Silla, Paekche, and Koguryo states dominate Korea
Fourth century B.C.E.	Yayoi culture emerges in Japan
334 B.C.E.	Alexander conquers Persian Empire
Third century B.C.E.	Roman Empire expands beyond Italy First Xiongnu state emerges north of China
ca. 268–232 B.C.E.	Reign of Asoka (India)
206 B.C.E.	Beginning of Han dynasty in China
200 B.C.E.	Population of Monte Albán reaches 200,000 (Mesoamerica)
127–120 B.C.E.	Chinese mount successful operations against the Xiongnu
27 B.C.E.	Augustus becomes first emperor of Rome
ca. 150 C.E.	Teotihuacán at peak of its influence (Mesoamerica)
220 C.E.	Collapse of the Han dynasty

PROBLEMS AND PARALLELS

1. How do increased travel and trade create a demand for stronger, bigger states? How do the ensuing cross-cultural contacts, larger road networks, and increased communication benefit or disadvantage states?

2. Both Rome and Persia offered their conquered peoples many benefits and considerable autonomy. What were the benefits and drawbacks of these policies for both the imperial power and the subject-peoples?

3. What were the relative advantages and disadvantages of sea routes versus land routes for commerce and communication in the ancient world?

4. What common factors contributed to the fall of the empires discussed in this chapter? Why did Alexander's empire disintegrate after his death?

5. How did each empire in this chapter try to meld together diverse peoples into a single state? Did they succeed or fail? Was Asoka's adoption of Buddhism a wise imperial policy?

6. Beyond the great Eurasian empires, other states and societies thrived. Can they justifiably be termed *empires*? Why or why not?

READ ON ▶ ▶ ▶

For Indian maps, J. B. Harley and D. Woodward, eds., *History of Cartography* (1987), vol. 2, is fundamental. L. Feer, *A Study of the Jatakas* (1963) is a good introduction to those texts. The texts I cite on the Erythraean Sea are easy to consult in L. Casson, ed., *The Periplus of the Erythraean Sea* (1989), and S. Burstein, ed., *Agatharchides of Cnidos: On the Erythraean Sea* (1989). P. Horden and N. Purcell, *The Corrupting Sea* (2000), and D. Abulafia, ed., *The Mediterranean in History* (2003) are the best histories of the Mediterranean; for the link to the Atlantic, see B. Cunliffe, *Facing the Ocean* (2001). On the Indian Ocean, M. Pearson, *The Indian Ocean* (2003) is a masterly survey; the demanding work of K. Chaudhuri, *Asia before Europe* (1991) repays the effort it requires.

On the Silk Roads, the outstanding book is now the British Library exhibition catalog edited by S. Whitfield, *The Silk Roads* (2004). On Dunhuang, see R. Whitfield et al., eds., *Cave Temples of Dunhuang* (2000). J. Mirsky, *The Great Chinese Travelers* (1976), collects extracts from key texts, including the journey of Zhang Qian.

On the Persian Empire, *The Cambridge History of Iran* (1993) is unbeatable. On women, I follow M. Brosius, *Women in Ancient Persia* (1998). On the Persian Wars, P. Green, *The Greco-Persian Wars* (1996) is authoritative. S. Hornblower, *The Athenian Empire* (2000) is a superb study. The same author's *The Greek World* (1983) provides the backdrop down to the time of Alexander, on whom R. Lane Fox, *Alexander the Great* (1973) is both scholarly and irresistibly readable. My remarks on Alexander's legacy are indebted to G. Cary, *The Medieval Alexander* (1967), which is a wonderful book.

On the Romans, T. Cornell, *The Beginnings of Rome* (1995) takes the story down to the Punic Wars. A. Goldsworthy, *The Fall of Carthage* (2004) is a history of those wars. R. Syme, *The Roman Revolution* (1939) is a classic of abiding interest and importance, centered on the rise of Augustus and a monarchical system of government. The best study of Virgil is probably R. Jenkyns, *Virgil's Experience* (1999).

For Celtic history, N. K. Chadwick, *The Celts* (1971) remains standard. H. D. Rankin, *Celts and the Classical World* (1987) is particularly interesting on Greek and Roman images. M. J. Green, *Celtic Art* (1997) is a good introduction.

On India in this period, F. R. Allchin, ed., *The Archaeology of Early Historic South Asia* (1995) is fundamental. R. Thapar, *Asoka and the Decline of the Mauryas* (1961) is insightful and close to the sources. R. McKeon and N. A. Nikam, *The Edicts of Asoka* (1959) analyzes these important sources.

For the Qin-Han revolution, D. Twitchett and M. Loewe, eds., *The Cambridge History of China* (1986) is invaluable. Li Xueqin, *Eastern Zhou and Qin Civilizations* (1985) is excellent on the background. For the Xiongnu, as for all steppeland history, the classic work of R. Grousset, *The Empire of the Steppes* (1970) remains fundamental.

For Japan and Korea, *The Cambridge History of Japan* (1993) is inescapably useful. W. Hong, *Paekche of Korea and the Origins of Yamato Japan* (1994) is helpful on the links between the two regions. K. Mizoguchi, *An Archaeological History of Japan* (2002) surveys the archaeological evidence.

The Scythians and Sarmatians have inspired much good work. Useful introductions are supplied in T. Talbot Rice, *The Scythians* (1957); E. Phillips, *The Royal Hordes* (1965); and T. Sulimirski, *The Sarmatians* (1970). On Mesoamerica, J. A. Hendon and R. A. Joyce, *Mesoamerican Archaeology* (2004) has the most up-to-date account.

For Monte Albán, R. E. Blanton, *Monte Albán* (1978) is the standard work. For Teotihuacán, important works include J. C. Berlo, ed., *Art, Ideology and the City of Teotihuacán* (1993), and R. Storey, *Life and Death in the Ancient City of Teotihuacán* (1992).

The World in 100 C.E.

When most peoples around the world adopted agriculture, cultural divergence became dominant in the remainder of the period this volume covers. Uncrossable oceans still divided many of the world's peoples from each other. Some—especially in Australia and New Guinea and in dense forest environments elsewhere—were isolated from contact with outsiders except for their immediate or near neighbors. Poor communications tended to keep peoples apart in most of sub-Saharan Africa and the Americas and to inhibit long-range exchanges of culture and ideas. In consequence, some of those parts of the world independently experienced changes similar to those we can see elsewhere—including the rise of agriculture, cities, states, and empires. The pace of change in these isolated societies was slower, however, and the scale less widespread than in Eurasia and North Africa.

Even within Eurasia, across the great axis of communications that eased exchanges of influence, ideas, and technologies between regions as widely separated as Europe and China, the effects were markedly different from place to place. Although, as we saw in Chapter 6, the sages of the axial age in China, India, Iran, Palestine, and Greece shared many of the same thoughts, the results of their ideas were so different that they stimulated conflict: mutually hostile religions, mutually antagonistic world visions.

▶ QUESTIONS

1. By 100 CE, about half the population of the world lived within three major empires—Rome, Parthia, and Han China. How did environmental factors stimulate empire building in Eurasia? How did environmental factors inhibit the growth of states in other parts of the world?

2. How did the group of empires shown on this map safeguard, enshrine, and nurture the heritage of ideas produced during the axial age?

3. Despite the environmental differences, where in the New World were histories similar to those in parts of Eurasia and Africa beginning to unfold?

To view an interactive version of this map, as well as a video of the author describing key themes related to this Part, go to www.myhistorylab.com

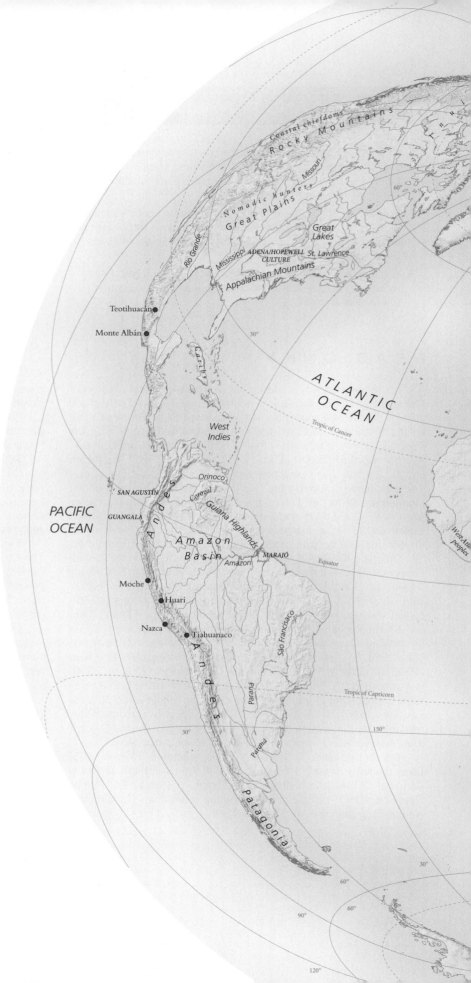

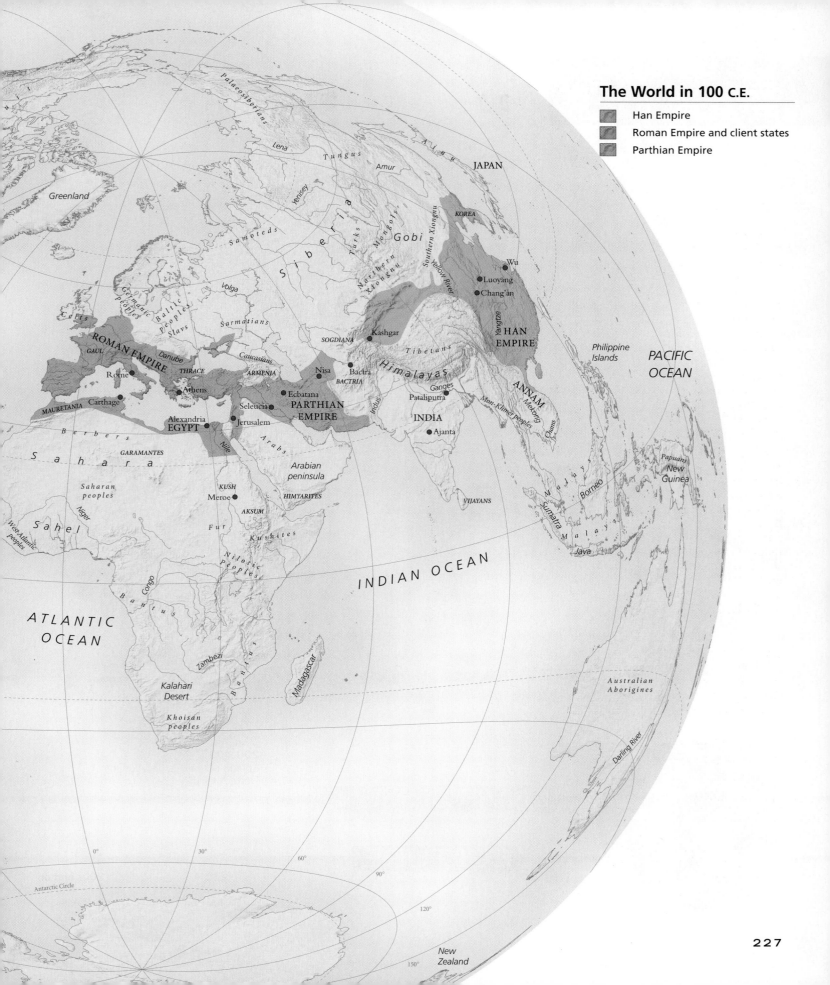

The World in 100 C.E.

- Han Empire
- Roman Empire and client states
- Parthian Empire

Greenland

Palaeosiberians

JAPAN

Lena

Tungus

Amur

Ainu

yenisey

Samoteds

Siberia

Turks

Mongols

Gobi

KOREA

Northern Xiongnu

Southern Xiongnu

Wu

Volga

Luoyang

Yellow River

Chang'an

Germanic peoples

Baltic Peoples

Sarmatians

Celts

Slavs

Kashgar

SOGDIANA

Tibetans

Yangtze

HAN EMPIRE

ROMAN EMPIRE

Danube

Caucasians

ARMENIA

Nisa

Bactra

Himalayas

Philippine Islands

PACIFIC OCEAN

GAUL

THRACE

Rome

Athens

Ecbatana

BACTRIA

Indus

Ganges

ANNAM

Seleucia

PARTHIAN EMPIRE

Pataliputra

Mekong

Mon-Khmer peoples

Chams

MAURETANIA

Carthage

Alexandria

EGYPT

Jerusalem

Arabs

INDIA

Ajanta

Berbers

GARAMANTES

Nile

Papuans

New Guinea

Sahara

Saharan peoples

Arabian peninsula

KUSH

Malays

Borneo

Niger

Meroe

AKSUM

HIMYARITES

VIJAYANS

Sahel

West Atlantic peoples

Fur

Kushites

Sumatra

Malays

Java

Nilotic peoples

Congo

Bantus

INDIAN OCEAN

ATLANTIC OCEAN

Zambezi

Madagascar

Australian Aborigines

Kalahari Desert

Bantus

Khoisan peoples

Darling River

0°   30°   60°   90°

Antarctic Circle

120°

New Zealand

150°

PART 4

ENVIRONMENT

200–400
Spread of maize cultivation into
North America

CULTURE

220
Breakup of
Han Empire

200s and on
Spread of Buddhism
East Asia

Fitful Transitions, from the Third Century to the Tenth Century

◀ **Polynesian reed map.**   Traditional Polynesian maps of the Pacific show routes across the ocean in the form of linked reeds between islands symbolized by small shells. The patterns of the reeds enable navigators to identify changes in the ocean swell.

mid–500s
Plague in Arabia and eastern Mediterranean

600–800
Growing trans-Saharan trade; Polynesian diaspora

800–1000
"Internal colonization" in China, Japan, western Europe

300s on
Spread of Christianity in Roman world

400s
Break up of Roman Empire

630 on
Rise and spread of Islam

Postimperial Worlds: Problems of Empires in Eurasia and Africa, ca. 200 to ca. 700 C.E.

▲ **Detail from a Mayan vase, early sixth century C.E.**   The color scheme of red on a gold background is characteristic of ceramics from Tikal, while the bird-like symbols with forked, blood-sucking tongues on the bottom row have similarities with glyphs from Teohituacán.

They arrived in January 378, soon after the beginning of the annual rainy season, in the moist, tropical lowlands of what is now eastern Guatemala. They came from Teotihuacán, 7,500 feet high in the mountain-ringed valley of central Mexico. The weather was unfamiliar. Teotihuacán had its rainy season in summer. They were not numerous or heavily armed, to judge from a picture an artist made of them, or travelers like them, as they completed their journey. Some of them looked and behaved like ambassadors, wearing the tasseled headdresses that signified ambassadorial rank and carrying ceremonial vessels, carved or painted with mythic scenes and political messages, as diplomatic gifts. They crossed hundreds of miles of mountains and forests, or perhaps descended by sea along the coast, to the land of the Maya, whose environment, culture, and language were different from their own. The Maya called the leader of the group Siyaj K'ak (SEE-ah kah-AK), meaning "fire born." Previously, historians called him "Smoking Frog"—a literal interpretation of his name-glyph. Contemporaries in the Maya world added a nickname, "The Great Man From the West." But why had he come?

His destination was the city of Tikal (tee-KAHL), over 625 miles from his home, in the region now called the Petén, where the limestone temples and gaudily painted roof combs of the city rose above the dense forest. Tikal was one of the oldest and clearly the largest of the many city-states among which the Maya world was divided. Its population at the time was perhaps over 30,000. But if Tikal was a great city by Maya standards, Teotihuacán dwarfed it, at probably more than three times its size. Teotihuacán, moreover, was no mere city-state but the nerve center of an empire that covered the valley of Mexico and spilled into neighboring regions, now called Tlaxcala and Morelos. Teotihuacano influence and tribute gathering probed further still. Traders from central Mexico had penetrated deep into the Maya lands for many decades. Contacts with the jade-rich highland Maya, who lived in the mountainous regions to the south and west of Tikal, were multiplying.

Relations between Tikal and Teotihuacán were important for both cities, because of the complementary ecologies of their regions (see Map 8.1). The Maya supplied Mexico with products unavailable in the highlands, including the plumage of forest birds for ornament,

MESOAMERICA

FOCUS questions

rubber for the ball games the elites of the region favored, cacao (which provided the elite with a mildly narcotic drink), jade for jewelry, and incense for rituals. But visitors like Siyaj K'ak and his Teotihuacanos were rare, or even, perhaps, unprecedented. As they approached, day by day, along the river now called San Pedro Mártir, the communities they passed through recorded their passage without comment but presumably with apprehension, and handed on the news to neighbors down the line. What were the newcomers' intentions? Were they invaders or invitees? Conquerors or collaborators? Envoys or adventurers? Were they mercenaries, perhaps, or a marriage party? Had they come to arbitrate disputes or to exploit them for their own purposes?

The inscriptions that record the events are too fragmentary to answer these questions. But they tell a suggestive story. When Siyaj K'ak reached Tikal on January 31, his arrival precipitated a revolution. On that very day, if the inscriptions can be taken literally, the life of the city's ruler, Chak Tok Ich'aak (chak tok eech-AH-AK)(or "Great Jaguar Paw," as historians used to call him), came to an end. He "entered the water," as the Maya said, after a reign of 18 years, ending the supremacy of a royal line that had supplied the city with 13 kings. The monuments of his dynasty were shattered into fragments or defaced and buried: slabs of stone on which images of kings were carved, with commemorations of the wars they fought, captives they took, astronomical observations they recorded, and sacrifices they offered to the gods—sometimes of their own blood, sometimes of the lives of their captives.

Tikal. The roof-combs of the Maya city of Tikal—hoisted facades set over the temples like mantillas in ladies' hair—rise over the forest of the Petén in Yucatán. Gaudily painted in their day, they warned off enemies, invited trade, celebrated kings. The small stones lining the plaza bear images and records of the deeds of rulers. The great temple in the middle ground was built as a tomb for King Jasaw Chan K'awiil (682–734), who restored the city's fortunes, after a period of impoverishment and defeat, and embarked on the most ambitious building program in Tikal's history.
Dagli Orti/Picture Desk, Inc./Kobal Collection

MAP 8.1

The Maya and Teotihuacán

	Maya
	Teotihuacán and directions of influence
⛩	Mayan temple
△	important Mayan site
△	important Teotihuacano site
●	obsidian mine
MEXICO	modern country
PETÉN	modern province or region
○	city described or mentioned on pages 231–234

Products Supplied from Maya to Teotihuacán

	cacao
	incense
	jade
	plumage
	rubber

Products Supplied to Teotihuacán from Neighboring Colonies

	avocado
	cacao
	cotton
	lime

To judge from the portraits his court sculptors left, the new king, whom Siyaj K'ak' placed on the throne, dressed in the style of his Teotihuacano patrons, wore adornments with images of central Mexican gods, and carried weapons of central Mexican design. His chocolate pots came from Teotihuacán or were copied from models made there. When he died early in the next century, he was buried with a carving of an underworld god, seated on a throne of human bones, holding a severed head.

Siyaj K'ak' installed new rulers not only in Tikal but also in other, smaller cities in the region over the next few years. Imperfect inscriptions suggest that some, perhaps all, of the affected cities professed allegiance to a ruler whose name-glyph shows an owl with a spear-thrower. This is also an image associated with war and power at Teotihuacán, suggesting that the supremacy of Teotihuacán, or at least of Teotihuacanos, was part of the new order. Moreover, a rash of new cities in the lowlands was founded from Tikal over the next few years, though they seem quickly, in most cases, to have asserted or exercised independence. It would exceed the evidence to speak of the birth of a new regional state, or the foundation of a new province of the empire of Teotihuacán. But we can confidently assert that contacts across Mesoamerica were growing, that state formation was quickening and spreading, and that a complex political pattern was emerging: jealous Maya cities, competing and combining, with elites often drawn or sponsored from central Mexico.

The influence and power of Teotihuacán were close to their maximum. Whether or not Maya cities were becoming formally dependent on Teotihuacán, they were certainly submitting to Teotihuacano influence. In the lowlands, that influence seems rapidly to have waned. In the highlands, however, it grew for a century and a half. Meanwhile, Teotihuacanos founded colonies wherever their city needed supplies. Chingú, near the later site of Tula, was one, where lime was exported for Teotihuacán's gigantic building projects. San Ignacio in Morelos was another, supplying avocados, cacao, and cotton, which would not grow in the highlands but was vital for everyday clothing and—increasingly—for the quilted armor warriors favored.

In part, pressure of population drove this expansion. Teotihuacán probably produced or attracted more people than it could contain. In any case, to sustain a growing city, Teotihuacán needed a growing empire. The basic foodstuffs the city consumed—maize and beans—were part of the ecosystem of its own region. But the concentration of population that had to be fed was enormous by the standards of preindustrial cities anywhere in the world and probably required extra supplies from farther away. The cotton and the luxuries and ritual objects on which elite life depended had to come from other climes. Teotihuacán had its own mines of obsidian—the glasslike substance of which the cutting blades of tools and weapons were made. But it had no other resources to export. It had to be a military state.

We do not know how the state was organized. Unlike the Maya, the Teotihuacanos produced no art depicting kings and, as far as we know, no chronicles of royal activities. Some curious features, however, show up in the archaeological record. During the fourth century, many families were shifted from small dwellings into large, lavishly built compounds, as if the city were being divided among rival, or potentially rival, focuses of allegiance. From the mid-fifth century, there are signs of internal instability. One of the most lavish temples was demolished. Thick, high internal walls divided different quarters of the city from each other. New building of other kinds gradually ceased. Meanwhile, Teotihuacano influence over areas far from the city withered. At an uncertain date, probably around the mid-eighth century, a traumatic event ended Teotihuacán's greatness. Fire wrecked the great temples and pyramids in the center of the city, and much of the population fled. We do not know what the state ideology was—but, whatever it was, it looks as if it was abandoned or replaced. Teotihuacán remained a city of perhaps 30,000 people, but it never again displayed imperial trappings or ambition. It is hard to resist the impression that the empire had overreached itself, committed to expansion that was increasingly hard to keep going, nurturing resentment abroad at its unparalleled power, and restlessness at home over the division of the spoils. No single city or empire of comparable dimensions replaced Teotihuacán. But people in Mesoamerica remembered it, conserved its influence, and tried to imitate it, as they entered a period of kaleidoscopic change, in which small, well-matched states fought among themselves without ever settling into an enduring pattern.

Teotihuacán was one of the world's most out-of-the-way empires—isolated from most of the others that arose in or after the axial age. Yet it was typical of its time. Other new imperial initiatives of the era—in the formative Islamic world and in Ethiopia—succumbed to remarkably similar challenges. Even the old empires struggled with similar problems. In Rome, India, China, and Persia, imperial traditions inherited from the axial age were extinguished or suffered periods of fragmentation or submersion by invaders whom the natives regarded as barbaric. And on the edges of empires in transformation, as well as within them, new states felt the effects.

"Teotihuacán was one of the world's most out-of-the-way empires—isolated from most of the others that arose in or after the axial age. Yet it was typical of its time. Other new imperial initiatives of the era—in the formative Islamic world and in Ethiopia—succumbed to remarkably similar challenges."

In this chapter and the next two, we have to face the questions of how, if at all, these stories are connected, and why their outcomes differed. How, for instance, imperial unity revived in China but not in the other affected areas, or why Christianity and Islam, but not Buddhism, became almost monopolistic ideologies in the areas they dominated. Less pressing, perhaps, but no less interesting, is the problem of how the history of the rest of the world echoes or connects with the fates of Eurasia's empires.

The political history of the period, chiefly in Eurasia and Africa, is the subject of this chapter, as we look in turn at each major area of imperial and state development, first filling in the stories of the third, fourth, and fifth centuries C.E. before focusing on a protracted spell of critical challenges in the sixth and seventh centuries. The ascent of the Christian, Muslim, and Buddhist religions is the theme of the next chapter. The last chapter in this part of the book provides an opportunity to explore global and environmental contexts and trace the world that emerged from the transformations, in the last two or three centuries of the millennium.

THE WESTERN ROMAN EMPIRE AND ITS INVADERS

On the summit of the Capitoline, one of Rome's seven hills, sits a bronze statue of the Emperor Marcus Aurelius, victoriously horsed, formerly carrying a globe. Since the emperor's death in 180, no image has been so often copied for rulers' portraits. For most beholders, the statue evokes Rome's peace through strength. Yet the reign of Marcus Aurelius (r. 161–180) has traditionally been regarded as the far edge of the high plateau of Roman achievement, after which decline set in, punctuated only by the lower peaks of ever more desperate recoveries.

The empire suffered from abiding problems: its sprawling size, its long, vulnerable land frontier; the unruly behavior of its politicized soldiery, with Roman armies fighting each other to make and unmake emperors; the uneasy, usually hostile relationship with rivals in Persia. Two new, growing dangers were increasingly apparent. First, for most of the elite, Christianity seemed subversive. To the pious, Rome's greatness was at the disposal of the gods. To the practical, Roman unity depended on the maintenance throughout the empire of politically charged cults: the worship of the emperor as divine, the cults of the patron gods of Rome. Second, Germanic peoples beyond the empire's borders in Europe coveted Roman wealth. The prosperity gap was like that between "North and South," on a global level, today—inspiring fear in the prosperous and envy in the poor. Increasingly, Germans from beyond the Rhine and Danube rivers raised problems of war and diplomacy as hard to manage as those the Persians posed on the empire's eastern frontiers.

Marcus Aurelius anticipated ways in which the empire would try to cope with these problems for the next three centuries. He sensed the need to divide responsibility for governing the vast empire, admitting his adoptive brother to the rank of co-emperor and delegating to him responsibility for guarding the eastern frontier. This sort of division of responsibility at the summit of government was to be a recurrent formula for saving the state from crisis. And Marcus Aurelius practiced stoicism—the philosophy, as we have seen, in which pagans and Christians could be reconciled (see Chapter 6). He repudiated fancy theories in favor of practical ethics—appropriate for the ruler of an empire racked by economic slumps and wars. His was a dark world, glinting with campfire light, as he fought to keep the Danube frontier secure. He snatched moments on campaign to write his

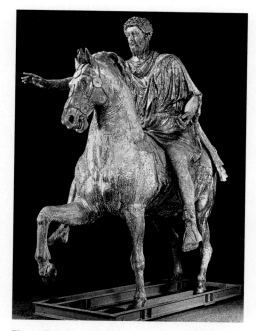

The philosopher at war. *The Meditations* of the Emperor Marcus Aurelius (r. 161–180) were written in military camps while he was campaigning against the barbarians on the empire's northern frontiers. His statue atop the Capitol at Rome has always symbolized dynamism and power, not only because of the commanding gesture of the emperor, but also because of the power his horse displays with its flared nostrils and stamping hoof.

Meditations in Greek, which was still the common language of the eastern half of the empire and still the prestige language favored for philosophy. "Renew yourself," he wrote in a memo to himself, "but keep it brief and basic."

In combination with the strain of threats from Persia and the convulsions of Roman politics, Germanic invasions in the third century almost dissolved the empire. In the late fourth century, the struggle to keep the immigrants out became hopeless. Some bands of Germans were drawn into the empire, while others were driven in. They usually came in relatively small, highly mobile war parties, numbering hundreds or at most a few thousand. They were composed of men detached from their traditional kinship structures by loyalty to a "ring giver"—a warlord who could buy their allegiance with the rewards of booty, protection money, ransom, extortion, or mercenary service. Trinkets of war-band service survive in burial sites: armbands set with jewels or onyx or inscribed with reminders of loyalty, rings bulging with garnets.

The biggest bands of migrants, numbering tens of thousands at a time, and traveling with women and children, were driven by stresses that arose beyond their borders, in the Eurasian steppelands. Here, the mid- and late fourth century was a traumatic time, when war or hunger or plague or exceptional cold or some combination of such events induced unprecedented mobility, conflict, and confusion. The Roman historian and retired soldier, Ammianus Marcellinus, reported a conversation with some Huns, reputedly the most ferocious of the steppeland peoples of the time. "Ask," he said, "who they are and whence they came—and they cannot tell you." Fear of the Huns glistens between the lines of every account: fear of their monstrous appearance, which Roman writers suspected must be produced by self-deformation; fear of their relationship with their horses, which made their mounted archery deadly; fear of their merciless treatment of enemies, which cowed resistance. (Fear of their smell too, since reputedly they never bathed.) Late in the fourth century, the Huns broke out of their heartlands in the depths of Asia—perhaps on the northeast borders of China, where many scholars identify them with the people the Chinese called Xiongnu (see Chapter 7). A kind of ricochet effect set in, as peoples collided and cannoned off each other, like balls on a pool table. Or perhaps all the turbulence of peoples, Germans and steppelanders alike, was the result of common problems: cold weather, shrinking pastures; or new sources of wealth, such as trade and booty, enriching new classes and disrupting the traditional stability of the societies concerned. Whatever the reasons, in the late fourth and early fifth centuries, displaced communities lined up for admission into the enticing empires of Rome, Persia, China, and India.

The hardest part of the story to appreciate is what it felt like for those who took part. In volatile conditions, illiterate masses leave few sources. Inklings emerge from the earliest surviving poem in what is recognizably German: the *Hildebrandslied*, the story of a family split between the war bands of rival chiefs in the chaos of the fifth century. Hildebrand's wife was left "in misery"; his baby grew into his battlefield adversary. The boy, raised in ignorance of his father's identity, unwittingly rejected his present of gold and jewels, "which the King of the Huns had given him." Only the first few lines survive of the terrible climax, in which father and son fight to the death. The story obviously has origins in a standard, traditional tragic

Hunnic cauldrons. The Huns' passage across Eurasia is marked by remains of the great bronze cauldrons they carried with them. The design, more or less uniform for centuries, seems to be inspired by the shape of Chinese temple bells, upended and perched on a stand. The handles at the top are typical. The mushroom-capped notches seem designed to hold ladles or spoons in place.

theme of conflict between the generations of a single family. But it also shows something peculiar about the predicament of Germanic peoples at the time: the chaotic, divisive effects of the migrations, the interdependence of the worlds of the Germans and the Huns.

Germans were not nomadic by custom but, according to their own earliest historian, Jordanes, who wrote in the sixth century, were "driven to wander in a prolonged search for lands to cultivate." The Ostrogoths, or Eastern Goths, for example, farmed on the banks of the Don River in what is now Ukraine from the late second century until the 370s, when Hun invaders forced them over the Dniester River into the territory of the Visigoths or Western Goths. In 376, a reputed 200,000 Visigothic refugees were admitted into the Roman Empire. But the Romans then left them to starve, provoking a terrible revenge at the battle of Adrianople in 378 when the Goths killed a Roman emperor along with most of his army. From 395 to 418, the Visigoths undertook a destructive migration across the empire, terrorizing areas they crossed. In 410, they sacked Rome, inspiring speculations about the end of the world among shocked subjects of the empire, before settling as paid "guests" and, in effect, the masters of the local population in southern France and northern Spain. Other Germanic peoples found the Visigoths' example irresistible. Rome's frontier with the Germans was becoming indefensible (see Map 8.2).

Changes within the Roman Empire

Meanwhile, the center of power in the dwindling empire shifted eastward into the mostly Greek-speaking zone, where barbarian incursions were more limited. Constantinople replaced Rome as the principal seat of the emperors. In 323, the Emperor Constantine elevated this dauntingly defensible small garrison town, surrounded on three sides by water and close to the threatened Danube and Persian frontiers, into an imperial capital.

From here, the emperors were able to keep invaders out of most of the eastern provinces of the empire in the fourth and fifth centuries, or limit immigration to manageable proportions or, in some places, to numbers needed for imperial defense. In the west, however, the empire could not control the incursions. In part, the greater durability of the eastern empire was the result of the direction invaders took. The Rhine River was an easily crossed frontier—especially in the cold winters of the early fifth century, when the river often froze. From there, invaders usually swung through northern France toward Spain, or turned south to reach Italy. Moreover, the eastern provinces of the empire—from Italy's Adriatic coast eastward—were relatively easy to reach, supply, and garrison from Constantinople, whereas the western Mediterranean lay beyond the terrible navigational bottlenecks between Italy, Sicily, and North Africa. The extra time it took to reach the west had not mattered much when the empire was politically stable; but it mattered now. Finally, the eastern provinces—especially those east of the Adriatic—were better equipped for survival by the presence of the emperor and by the wealth of great estates in regions where mountain barriers, deserts, and seas deterred at least some invaders.

By founding Constantinople, Constantine ensured that the city of Rome would continue to stagnate. Though the Roman Senate—the assembly of noblemen and notables responsible for the government of the city—continued to meet, civic projects gradually ceased. The western empire was beset with problems. Impeded by war, long-range exchanges of personnel and commerce became increasingly impractical. Communications decayed. Aristocrats withdrew from

"By founding Constantinople, Constantine ensured that the city of Rome would continue to stagnate. Though the Roman Senate—the assembly of noblemen and notables responsible for the government of the city—continued to meet, civic projects gradually ceased."

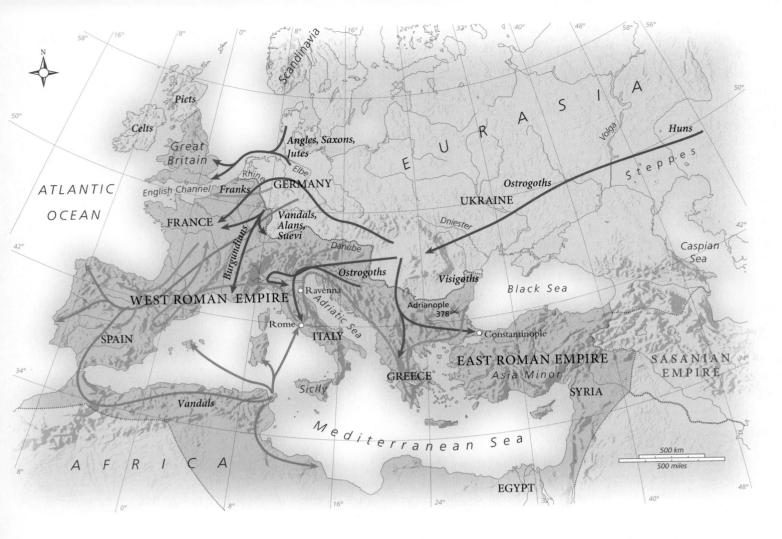

MAP 8.2

The Western Roman Empire and Its Invaders

■ extent of Roman Empire, 390 C.E.

Barbarian Migrations:

➤ Huns
➤ Ostrogoths
➤ Visigoths
➤ Angles, Saxons, Jutes
➤ Burgundians
➤ Franks
➤ Vandals, Alans, Suevi

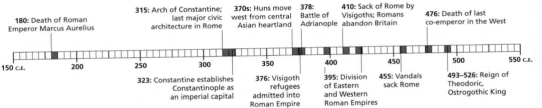

180: Death of Roman Emperor Marcus Aurelius

315: Arch of Constantine; last major civic architecture in Rome

370s: Huns move west from central Asian heartland

378: Battle of Adrianople

410: Sack of Rome by Visigoths; Romans abandon Britain

476: Death of last co-emperor in the West

323: Constantine establishes Constantinople as an imperial capital

376: Visigoth refugees admitted into Roman Empire

395: Division of Eastern and Western Roman Empires

455: Vandals sack Rome

493–526: Reign of Theodoric, Ostrogothic King

150 C.E.   200   250   300   350   400   450   500   550 C.E.

traditional civic responsibilities—struggling to keep their estates going amid invasions. Bishops replaced bureaucrats. In localities from which imperial authority vanished, holy men took on the jobs of judges. Almost everywhere, barbarian experts in warfare took military commands. Garrisons withdrew from outposts of empire beyond the Rhine, the Danube, and the English Channel. After 476, there was no longer a co-emperor in the west. Regional and local priorities replaced empirewide perspectives. The most extreme form of the dissolution of authority inside the empire was the establishment of kingdoms led by foreigners, as Germans—settled as uneasy allies, entrusted with tasks of imperial defense, and quartered at the expense of their host communities—gradually usurped or accepted authority over non-Germanic populations. Where such kingdoms delivered peace and administered laws, they replaced the empire as the primary focus of people's allegiance (see Map 8.3).

Stilicho. The late Roman Empire increasingly relied on immigrant mercenaries for its defense. The Vandal Stilicho (right) was one of the best, defending—as a Roman poet of the time said—"all within the sun's fiery orbit" in trust for the emperors of Rome. "All virtues meet in thee." He married an emperor's niece and maneuvered to make his son, Eucherius, also shown here, emperor. His daughter married an emperor. But, falsely accused of treachery, he loyally gave himself up for execution in 408 C.E. These ivory panels are examples of an art form traditionally used to commemorate Roman consuls.

The "Barbarian" West

At the time, writers of history and prophecy, peering through the twilight of the empire, could not believe Roman history was over. Rome was the last of the world monarchies that the Bible had foretold. Its end would mean the end of time. Everyone, including barbarian kings, connived in pretending that the empire had survived. Germanic settlers were all, in varying degrees, susceptible to Romanization, and their kings usually showed deference to imperial institutions. A Visigothic leader, Athawulf, vowed "to extirpate the Roman name," but ended by marrying into the Roman imperial family and collaborating with Rome. Burgundian kings in what is now eastern France continued a flattering correspondence with the emperors in Constantinople for as long as their state survived. The Franks, who occupied most of France in the late fifth and early sixth centuries, adorned their monarchs with emblems of Roman governors and consuls. No barbarians were proof against the appeal of Roman culture. Vandals, whose name has become a byword for destruction, had themselves portrayed in Roman-style mosaics. Even the Germanic settlers of Britain, most of whom had had virtually no contact with the Roman Empire, recalled the rule of Roman "giants" in their poetry.

Yet to Romans, the new rulers remained barbarians—foreigners of inferior culture. In turn, the limits of barbarian identification with Rome were of enormous importance. The notion of Roman citizenship gradually dissolved. Although the barbarians envied Roman civilization, most of them hankered after their own identities and—not surprisingly amid the dislocation of the times—clung to their roots. Many groups tried to differentiate themselves by upholding, at least for

MAP 8.3

The Barbarian West ca.526

- kingdom of the Vandals
- kingdom of the Ostrogoths
- kingdom of the Franks
- kingdom of the Suevi
- Burgundian kingdom
- Eastern Roman Empire
- Sasanian Empire

Chronology: The Transformation of Empire in the West	
162–180	Reign of Emperor Marcus Aurelius, high point of Roman Empire
Third and fourth centuries	Germanic migrants enter empire in increasing numbers
323	Founding of Constantinople
378	Battle of Adrianople, Roman emperor killed
Late fourth century	Huns break out of Central Asia
410	Visigoths sack Rome
476	Last Roman emperor in the west deposed

a time, unorthodox versions of Christianity. Some of their scholars and kings took almost as much interest in preserving their own traditional literature as in retaining or rescuing the works of classical and Christian writers. Law codes of barbarian kingdoms prescribed different rules for Germans and Romans.

The realm of the Ostrogothic king, Theodoric, was typically hybrid. He ruled Italy from 493 to 526. A church wall in his courtly center at Ravenna displays his palace, with throne room of gold, curtained like a sanctuary. His tomb is the burial mound of a Germanic king but is also in the style the Roman aristocracy of his era favored. Boethius, his chief minister, who was a Roman senator, not a Goth, worked hard to Romanize him. In a world of bewildering change, where traditional values vaporized and traditional institutions collapsed, Boethius clung to the old order, insisting on the continuity of the Roman Empire, reveling in his sons' election to ancient Roman offices of diminishing significance, and banking on the domestication of barbarian invaders. Imprisoned by Theodoric, he wrote *The Consolation of Philosophy*, fusing the stoical value system of happiness with the Christian tradition of deference to God. Happiness and God, Boethius argued, were identical.

Barbarian invaders had not extinguished the Roman Empire, but they had transformed it, in the areas they occupied, into what were, in effect, independent kingdoms with hybrid cultures. Historians have quarreled over whether to call this transformation a "decline," but in some ways archaeological evidence makes the term seem appropriate: towns shrank; inscriptions were fewer and less literate; the range of circulation of manufactures narrowed; and the

The Church of San Apollinare Nuovo. Though Arians—who rejected the doctrine of the equality of the Persons of the Trinity—and other Christians denounced one another for heresy, they designed and decorated their churches in Ravenna in the early sixth century in remarkably similar ways, with processions of mosaic saints and martyrs lining the nave. Here the palace of the Arian king Theodoric, who endowed this church, is also depicted—with the skyline of Ravenna behind it, as if the city were itself a sacred space.

quality of the goods people produced—especially pottery—diminished. Imperial institutions survived outside the barbarian kingdoms, and even within them people clung to a sense of continuity with the Roman past. But it is hard to resist the impression that that past was over and that in the Western empire, at least, a poorer, harder way of life had succeeded it.

STEPPELANDERS AND THEIR VICTIMS

Because Germanic peoples lined the zone between Rome's frontier and the Eurasian plains, steppeland peoples like the Huns made relatively few and brief forays into the Roman Empire. Empires centered in China, Persia, and India, by contrast, had to cope with the steppelanders directly. In some ways, invading herdsmen were easier to deal with than the Germans who were used to settled agriculture. The herdsmen's techniques of warfare were less flexible. Reliant, in this period, on mounted archery, they were ill equipped for mountain warfare on the frontiers of Persia or India, or in the rice paddy–scored terrain of central and southern China. When successful as conquerors, the steppelanders were usually easier to wean from their cultural traditions than the Germans, assimilating to Chinese or, in some cases, to Indian ways within a few generations.

China

China's empire, moreover, was better adapted for long-term survival than Rome's. Thanks to China's roughly round shape, Chinese armies could get quickly to any point on its frontiers. No invaders threatened the long sea coast. China also had excellent internal communications systems, based on rivers and

Making Connections | CHINA AND ROME COMPARED

	CHINA	**ROME**
Geography	Round shape ensures that centrally located armies can get quickly to any point on frontier. Numerous rivers and canals facilitate communication	Long land frontier and narrow sea lanes impede movement of troops and information
Culture	Subject peoples embrace Chinese identity; barbarian immigrants adopt Chinese customs and language	Germanic peoples beyond empire's borders covet Roman wealth. "North–South" prosperity gap leads to envy and hostility. Limited identification by barbarians with Rome
Economy	Size, productivity, and technical inventiveness lead to self-sufficiency	Adverse balance of trade drains wealth out of the empire

enhanced by canals. Chinese culture was more absorbent than Rome's. Subject-peoples tended to embrace Chinese identity with a surprising degree of commitment and even enthusiasm. *Barbarian* immigrants—the Chinese, like the Romans, used a contemptuous term for foreigners—commonly discarded their traditions and adopted Chinese customs, language, and identity. Above all, size, productivity, and technical inventiveness made China self-sufficient, if necessary. There was no adverse balance of trade, such as Rome endured, to drain wealth out of the empire—as Gaius Pliny the Elder, the nearest thing Rome had to an economist, complained in 77 C.E. China's internal market was huge—more internal trade meant more wealth.

But, like Rome in the same period, China under the Han dynasty never solved the most basic problem of imperial government: how to secure the succession of emperors. As we saw in the last chapter, factionalism and rebelliousness tended to breed in the families of imperial Chinese consorts. To offset the danger, emperors relied ever more heavily on the services of **eunuchs,** whom Roman emperors, too, regarded as perfect servants, and whose inability to father families of their own made them proof against dynastic ambitions. The long-term result was to create another faction and a new focus of resentment, as eunuchs usurped control over the succession. As in Rome, armies in China contended for the power to make and unmake emperors. Rivalry between armies and eunuchs precipitated civil war in 184, when Chang Chueh, a wandering medic, whose plague remedy made him a popular hero, proclaimed rebellion against eunuch rule. The army emerged ascendant from nearly 40 years of war that followed.

In 220, the last Han emperor was forced to abdicate in favor of a new, army-backed dynasty, known as Jin. But the former patterns of politics resumed. Civil war became chronic, made worse by emperors' efforts to divide their responsibilities along lines similar to those Rome adopted, giving members of the imperial family regions to run. Steppeland migrants and marauders played increasingly important roles in the wars. In 304, contenders for the disputed succession called in rival barbarian armies. The leader of one of these armies proclaimed himself emperor, and his son, Liu Cong (lee-oh tsohng), drove the Jin south, into the Yangtze valley. The old capital, Chang'an (chanhng-ahn), filled with "weeds and thorns."

Northern China became a kaleidoscope of kingdoms and self-styled empires, continually reshaken by warlords, adventurers, and new migrants, variously Turkic and Mongol (see Map 8.4). These migrants fitfully—but in the long term, irrepressibly—adopted Chinese ways. Buddhist missionaries promoted it; the development of the silk routes favored it. Toward the end of the fifth century, the ruler of the ascendant barbarians, the Xianbei (see-on bay), was deeply committed to Buddhism. Xiaowen (r. 471–499), or Toba Hung II, to give him his name in his native language, abolished traditional Xianbei rites and language in favor of Chinese practices. Aspiring to make a reality of his ancestors' claims to the mandate of heaven, he revived the state cult of Confucius that the Han had established, and moved to a new capital at Luoyang (lwoh-yahng). But the state he founded fragmented in its turn. The old aristocracy resisted Chinese values, while the court practiced Chinese-style cycles of factionalism, family rifts, and civil wars.

"A Parthian shot" now means a cutting parting remark—so-called from the tactics Parthian mounted archers used in defending their homeland in what is now Iran and Iraq against the Romans. Retreating, or pretending to retreat, they turned in their saddles to shoot at their pursuers. Steppelander armies copied or developed this technique on their own. This 2,000-year-old Chinese design shows a Turkic warrior wielding a double-curve bow, constructed to be compact but with high tensile strength for use on horseback.

India

For the sedentary civilizations that lined Eurasia to the south, stability was impossible as long as the steppeland churned out uncontainable migrant hordes, as India's case also shows. The Huns who began to infiltrate India around 415—working their way west and south around the mountain barrier, were, presumably, part of the fallout of the same catastrophes that spilled steppelanders into the Roman and Chinese empires. On the way, they wiped out Bactria and Gandhara, states that, founded in the era of Alexander the Great, had developed distinctive cultures by blending Greek and Buddhist ideas (see Chapter 7).

Although the invasion routes into India from the steppes look formidable on the map, they were poorly guarded at the critical time (see Map 8.4). In the fourth century, a ruler of Maghada who called himself Candragupta (CHAHN-drah GOOP-tah), after a hero of the time of Alexander the Great, attempted to restore the unity of the Indian subcontinent. His dynasty, the Guptas, never established as wide a dominion as that of Asoka (see Chapter 7), but they did weaken the states of India's northwest frontier, where the Huns got in. The loose-knit Gupta political system, which covered most of India as far south as the Deccan, linked many diverse layers of intermediate authority. So it was easily overthrown.

The morale of the population also favored the invaders. Writers generally agreed that they were living in the *Kaliyuga*, the age of decline. A play written by Kalidasa—who probably lived in the fourth century—depicted alienated classes in a morally corrupt state, where crooked officials tortured a fisherman charged with stealing the king's signet ring. The fisherman, however, had saved the ring by catching the fish that swallowed it. He paid his torturers off with the reward the king sent him and, at their suggestion, treated them

Chronology: The End of Dynasties in China and India	
220	Last Han emperor forced to abdicate
304	Contenders for Chinese throne call in barbarian armies
415	Huns begin to infiltrate India
ca. 467	Demise of Gupta Empire

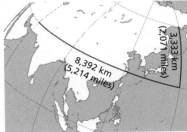

MAP 8.4

Steppelanders and Asian Kingdoms, ca. 300–700 C.E.

- farthest extent of Toba Hung II, ca. 500 C.E.
- kingdom of Candra Gupta I
- farthest extent of Gupta dynasty, ca. 500 C.E.
- —— Harsha's empire, ca. 650 C.E.
- ➡ Hun invasions
- ➡ Steppeland migrants into China
- → Journey of Faxian, 405-411 C.E.
- ⌇⌇⌇ Great Wall
- —— Grand Canal
- —— Silk Roads
- ○ city mentioned or described on pages 243-245

Xianbei people

Scale varies with perspective

to drinks in a wine shop. It was hard for the empire's poorest subjects to identify with a system that perpetuated their poverty by making social rank inherited. According to Faxian (faw-shee-ehn), a Chinese Buddhist pilgrim in India in 405–411, the "untouchables" of the lowest caste had to sound a clapper in the street to warn against their polluting presence (see Map 8.4 for the path of Faxian's journey).

In the 450s, when the Huns broke in—"kings of churlish spirit," who killed "women, children and cows"—their customs included reliance on flesh foods and, within the royal family, rituals in which kings sacrificed their mothers. Not surprisingly, against such a background, they persecuted Buddhists, as well as followers of native Indian traditions, who revered cows as sacred. The Gupta Empire showed little resilience. Its decline is conventionally dated from 467—less than a decade before the last emperor in Rome was forced to abdicate and was pensioned off. Subsequent Gupta emperors are shadowy—barely known, except by name, from contemporary sources. Yet within another 50 years or so, the Hunnic realm seems to have become one Indian state among many. Indian unity—such as it was—dissolved among a multitude of principalities in the north and a few relatively large, unstable kingdoms in the south.

NEW FRONTIERS IN ASIA

For the Chinese and Gupta empires the barbarian invasions inaugurated times of troubles, but it was a time of opportunity for developing states on their frontiers, where imperial power might otherwise have inhibited or repressed development. An early Gupta inscription mentions developing states around the frontiers: the Shaka dynasty in western India and the Vakatakas, whose daughters the Guptas took in marriage in the Deccan. The conditions favored similar effects in other parts of Asia.

Korea

Refugees from China, for instance, fled from the nomad invaders in search of tamer barbarians, to whom they could offer their services as technicians or sages. Dong Shou—to take a case in point—was a scholar who escaped from the Xianbei in 337 and took refuge in neighboring Koguryo (koh-goo-ryuh), an emerging state that occupied parts of what are now southeastern Manchuria and northern Korea. After a prosperous career, he was buried at Anak, amid wall paintings that document the history of Koguryo at the time. Buddhist and Daoist emblems mingle with scenes of the life of the kingdom: proudly displayed images of prosperity and strength, including irrigation works, rice production, people and horses eating, and a procession of well-armored soldiers. While China dissolved, Koguryo expanded. A memorial of King Kwanggaet'o, erected at the time of his death in 413, credits him with the conquest of 64 walled towns and 1,400 villages. Continuing prosperity—the result of the introduction of ox-drawn plows and irrigation for rice fields—can be measured in the results of the census the Chinese took when they eventually conquered Koguryo in 667–668. The country had 176 walled cities and 697,000 families. Unlike other communities whom the Chinese considered barbarians, however, Korean states had, by then, too much self-pride and too long a history of achievement to adopt Chinese identity.

Meanwhile, similar histories unfolded in the southern Korean kingdoms of Silla (shil-lah)and Paekche (pek-jay). There, royal tombs were full of gold—spangled crowns in the shape of stylized antlers, golden belts with pendants of gold, jade, and glass. Although the iron trade contributed to the enrichment of the state, Korean states were agrarian kingdoms whose wealth was in manpower. They fought one another to gain population. Paekche paid a ransom of 1,000 households, for instance, when raiders from Koguryo occupied its capital. Silla was particularly resolute in following Chinese models of state-building. In 520, King

Korean crown. Before Buddhism became rooted there in the sixth century C.E., Korean rulers were buried with fabulous treasures. This crown, with antler-like ornaments, is from one of the many royal burial mounds of the kingdom of Silla. It shows the influence of Chinese and Central Asian goldsmiths' work.

Pophung began to give positions of power and prestige to Confucian scholars. The kingdom, however, also had a caste system of its own. Many positions were open only to those ranked as possessing "sacred bone"—the rank of the royal family—and "true bone," the birthright of the courtly elite. (This distinction, however, disappeared after 653, when a true bone became king.) Silla unified the Korean peninsula in over 100 years of warfare from the mid-sixth century.

Funan

Meanwhile, the turbulence of central Eurasia, which periodically disrupted the Silk Roads, favored states along the maritime route across Eurasia, beside monsoonal seas. Chinese travelers' accounts give us glimpses into their world. The land of Funan occupied a stretch of territory, wrapped around the coast of the Gulf of Thailand. Chinese officials singled it out as a possible tributary or trading partner during a surge of interest in the potential of the region in the third century. Its culture was almost certainly borrowed from India. By Chinese reports, it was a repository of learning, rich enough to levy taxes in "gold, silver, pearls and perfumes." Its success depended on its role as a middleman in Chinese trade with Indonesia and the Bay of Bengal.

THE RISE OF ETHIOPIA

"The most remarkable product of growing commerce across monsoonal seas was not Funan but, unquestionably, Ethiopia, a country at the limit—almost beyond the reach—of the Indian Ocean network, a land that surrounding deserts and high mountains made hard to reach."

The most remarkable product of growing commerce across monsoonal seas was not Funan but, unquestionably, Ethiopia, a country at the limit—almost beyond the reach—of the Indian Ocean network, a land that surrounding deserts and high mountains made hard to reach (see Map 8.5). The right balance between accessibility and isolation was the key to Ethiopia's success. High altitude made the emergent state defensible and guaranteed it a temperate climate in tropical latitudes. Axum, the capital, was around 7,200 feet up, on a spur of the loftiest highlands.

Outsiders saw Axum (AHK-soom) as a trading state, where all the exotic goods of black Africa awaited: rhino horn, hippo hides, ivory and obsidian, tortoise shell, monkeys, and slaves. Objects manufactured in China and Greece found their way to Axumite tombs. The frequent use of Greek in inscriptions, alongside the native Ge'ez (geh-EHZ) language, indicates a cosmopolitan community. Ethiopian products could reach the outside world through links with the Mediterranean via Roman and later Byzantine Egypt and with the Indian Ocean via the Red Sea. The highlands could dominate the long Rift valley land route to the south, to lands rich in gold, civet (the glands of civet cats were used to make perfumes), slaves, and ivory.

But the corridor from the Ethiopian highlands to the port of Adulis on the Red Sea is long, and the Red Sea is hard to navigate. For the people of Axum, intent on their own agrarian way of life, trade was probably a sideline. They stamped ears of wheat on their coins. Terraces of grains sprang from valley soils, plowed with oxen and irrigated by stone dams across mountain streams. The highlands were fertile enough to produce two or three crops a year. Food mentioned in inscriptions includes wheat, beer, wine, honey, meat, butter, vegetable oils, and the world's first recorded coffee.

The material remains of the culture include finely worked ivory, metalwork, and huge, cubical tombs lined with brick arches. Axum contained an elaborate mausoleum of 10 galleries opening off a central corridor. Three enormous stone pillars, each of a single slab of locally quarried granite, towered over the city. The largest was 160 feet tall and weighed nearly 500 tons—bigger than any other monolith ever made. Depictions of many-storied buildings or figures of hawks and crocodiles adorned the pillars. According to a Greek visitor's description, the central plaza of the city had a four-towered palace and thrones of pure marble, smothered with inscriptions, and statues of gold, silver, and bronze.

Chronology: The Rise of Ethiopia	
340s	Spread of Christianity in Ethiopia
Early sixth century	King Kaleb begins conquest of southern Arabia
530s	Environmental crisis undermines control of south Arabia

Inscriptions from early in the fourth century recorded what people at the time regarded as the key events of politics: numbers of captives; plunder in live-stock; oaths of submission; doles of bread, meat, and wine granted to captives; their punitive relocation in distant parts of the empire; thankful offerings for gods who bestowed victory—native gods at first, then, from the 340s, the Christian God. The ambitions of the kings seemed to tug across the strait to Arabia (see Chapter 5). Early in the sixth century, King Kaleb launched an expedition to conquer southern Arabia, much of which the Ethiopians occupied for most of the rest of the century (see Map 8.5).

THE CRISES OF THE SIXTH AND SEVENTH CENTURIES

Ethiopian control of south Arabia probably faltered because of an environmental crisis in the 530s. Plague played a part in the collapse of the irrigation states of southern Arabia and drove migrants northward, some seeking refuge in Roman-controlled Syria, others swelling the cities of Mecca and Medina. Twice during the Ethiopian occupation, the great dam at Marib broke. The losses of irrigation water were so traumatic that they became a major theme for poets' laments.

These disasters roughly coincided with other, more widespread catastrophes. In 535, the skies of the Northern Hemisphere darkened. A massive volcanic eruption in Indonesia split Java from Sumatra (soo-MAH-trah) and spewed ash into the atmosphere. Thanks to the diminished sunlight, temperatures fell. The new conditions suited some disease-bearing microorganisms. A plague-bearing bacillus ravaged Constantinople. A disease that resembled smallpox devastated Japan. Even Mesoamerican graves contain evidence of a severe decline in health in what is now central Mexico toward the mid-sixth century. In the same period, the Eurasian steppes overspilled anew, impelling horseborne war bands into Europe: refugees, perhaps, from plague. Historians still debate how far these events are connected and whether a single volcanic explosion can account for them. Still, the sixth century marked a trough—a low point from which reformers, with varying fortunes, could launch revivals of endangered traditions and rally weakened states.

In India, for instance, early in the seventh century, Harsha, king of Thanesar, tried to fill in the political fissures and reconstruct an empire (see Map 8.4). He devoted his exceptionally long reign of 41 years to reunifying most of the Ganges Basin. Rulers in Punjab, Kashmir, and Nepal paid him tribute. He made tireless tours of his realm, collecting tribute, giving alms, and dispensing judgments. But even in the biography Harsha commissioned, practical compromises with kingly ideals are evident. The book describes the poor, gathering

Stela of Axum. Until the rulers of Ethiopia adopted Christianity in the mid-fourth century, they invested huge amounts of capital and labor to create gigantic stelae—still the biggest structures made of single blocks of stone anywhere in the world. The largest examples—which reach well over 100 feet high—stood on ground long used for burials and probably marked important tombs. They have the skyscraper-like form of towering buildings. This art form climaxed in the early fourth century, just before Ethiopian priorities switched to church building, and the last stelae were left to topple or perhaps were never even hoisted into position.

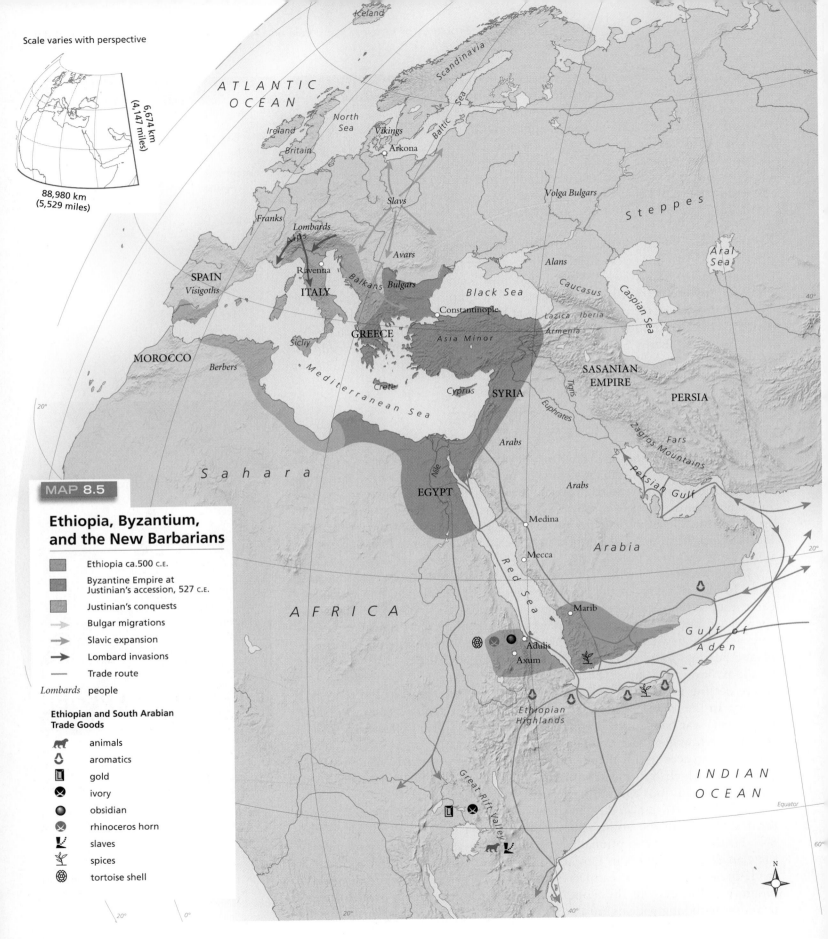

Scale varies with perspective

6,674 km
(4,147 miles)

88,980 km
(5,529 miles)

ATLANTIC
OCEAN

Iceland

Ireland

North
Sea

Britain

Vikings

Arkona

Scandinavia

Baltic Sea

Slavs

Volga Bulgars

Steppes

Aral
Sea

Franks

Lombards

Alps

Avars

Alans

Caucasus

Caspian Sea

SPAIN

Visigoths

Ravenna

ITALY

Balkans

Bulgars

Black Sea

Lazica

Iberia

Constantinople

Armenia

GREECE

Asia Minor

MOROCCO

Berbers

Sicily

Mediterranean Sea

Crete

Cyprus

SYRIA

SASANIAN
EMPIRE

Tigris

Euphrates

Zagros Mountains

PERSIA

Fars

Sahara

Arabs

Nile

Persian Gulf

EGYPT

Arabs

AFRICA

Medina

Mecca

Arabia

Red Sea

Marib

Gulf of
Aden

Adulis

Axum

Ethiopian
Highlands

INDIAN
OCEAN

Equator

Great Rift Valley

MAP 8.5

Ethiopia, Byzantium, and the New Barbarians

	Ethiopia ca. 500 C.E.
	Byzantine Empire at Justinian's accession, 527 C.E.
	Justinian's conquests
→	Bulgar migrations
→	Slavic expansion
→	Lombard invasions
—	Trade route
Lombards	people

Ethiopian and South Arabian Trade Goods

	animals
	aromatics
	gold
	ivory
	obsidian
	rhinoceros horn
	slaves
	spices
	tortoise shell

fragments of grain left after the king's camp has moved on. The king's elephants trample the hovels of peasants who can defend themselves only by hurling clods of earth. Harsha's dominion was an improvised conquest, and his achievement did not survive him. He had, however, more successful counterparts in China and Rome.

JUSTINIAN AND THE EASTERN ROMAN EMPIRE

Though the eastern Roman Empire remained a single state, it, too, was transformed. In the perceptions of its leaders, it remained "Roman," even after 476, when the emperors no longer had any power in Rome itself. Nowadays, however, historians of the period tend to stop calling the empire "Roman," at least from the sixth century onward, preferring the term *Byzantine Empire*, from "Byzantium," the former name of Constantinople. From the sixth or seventh century onward, the use of Latin—always restricted in the eastern provinces to fairly high levels of administration—dwindled. Although most invaders were defeated, turned away, bought off, or deflected by diplomacy, and no Germanic kingdoms took shape inside the eastern provinces, migrants seeped through the frontiers, especially in the eighth century. Meanwhile, the empire effectively abandoned ambitions to reconquer the western provinces. In the late sixth and early seventh centuries, emperors concentrated on the struggle with Persia and largely left the western provinces to the barbarians.

Justinian, emperor from 527 to 565, was the last emperor to adopt a grand strategy of imperial reunification, giving equal importance to recovery in the west and defense and expansion in the east (see Map 8.5). At its height, the Roman world spanned two contrasting environments: the Mediterranean and the Atlantic, uniting for the first time in history the two great economic zones of Western Europe, straddling the strait and the mountainous watersheds that naturally separate them. Now, shorn of any possibility of controlling Rome's Atlantic provinces, the empire reverted to being a purely Mediterranean enter-

Hagia Sophia. The minarets of the mosque of Hagia Sophia in Istanbul conceal the building's origins as the greatest Christian church of its day, built at the command of the Emperor Justinian to defy time and display the largest dome in the world at the time. The dome collapsed some 20 years after its completion. So the emperor had it rebuilt on an even more ambitious scale. Daring perforations around the base of the dome—over 100 feet wide and nearly 200 feet high—bathed the sanctuary in light.

Theodora. According to court gossip, Theodora (ca. 500–548), wife of the Roman Emperor Justinian (r. 527–565), was a former prostitute of insatiable sexual appetite. But the propagandist who portrayed her in mosaic, in the church of San Vitale at Ravenna, depicted her as a sacred figure, towering over priests and nobles and equal in stature to her husband. She approaches the altar arrayed in jewels—a convention used in the art of the time to personify the Church—bearing a gift of communion wine to be converted miraculously into the blood of Christ.

prise. More particularly, its weight was distributed toward the eastern end of the sea. Beyond the narrows around Sicily that divide the Mediterranean into two zones of navigation, traversible with difficulty, the empire clung only to narrow coastal strips, patches, and enclaves.

Justinian aimed to be a restorer but was more suited to be a revolutionary—"a born meddler and disturber," as a chronicler who knew him called him. As the heir of a peasant-turned-soldier whom the army had elected to rule, he enjoyed thumbing his nose at established elites. At a time when the Church legitimized authority, he infuriated bishops with his attempts to reconcile conflicting theological opinions. The monarchy needed its traditional supporters, but Justinian's tax policies made the rich howl with anguish. He was a great lawgiver who had himself depicted as the biblical Moses and yet exploited his prerogative as lawmaker to break all the rules himself. Typically, he outraged straitlaced courtiers by choosing a notoriously dissolute actress named Theodora to be his empress. He relied on her strength and intellect. She was the counselor of every policy and the troubleshooter of every crisis. In the famous mosaic portrait of her in the church of San Vitale at Ravenna in Italy, she wears jewels of triumph and a cloak embroidered with images of kingship and wisdom.

Justinian had the ill-disciplined energy of all insomniacs as he paced the palace corridors at night, "like a ghost," as hostile courtiers said. He thought big. He had himself depicted in a statue, toting a globe in one hand and spreading the other toward the rising sun. His projects included importing silk from China and allying with Arabs and Ethiopians against Persia. He built Hagia Sophia in Constantinople to be the biggest church in the world and, when its great dome fell down, built it again. He urged his armies against barbarian kingdoms with fanatical perseverance, at crippling cost. The outcome reunited most of the Mediterranean world. Buildings Justinian erected stretched from Morocco to the Persian frontier. He left his partially restored empire impoverished but enlarged.

The robust performance of the eastern empire in the crises that followed was impressive. In the West, however, where Justinian's wars devastated Italy, he probably did more in the long run to dissolve the empire than renew it, for it emerged more vulnerable to subsequent invaders. It was a hag-ridden, doom-fraught world, in which bishops and holy men took over the functions of vanishing public authorities, and relics of saints kept demonic powers at bay.

The Lombard ruler Agilulf (r. 590-616), optimistically characterized as "King of all Italy," depicted on a plaque of gilded copper from a ceremonial helmet. Elected and acclaimed king in traditional Germanic fashion by being hoisted on a shield, Agilulf chose—for the first time among Germanic kings—to be shown enthroned, like a Roman emperor, attended by winged victories brandishing standards and tributaries approaching the throne with bags of gold. In contrast to the warriors who shout acclamations with open mouths, Agilulf is a still, priest-like figure, holding his sword by the scabbard and raising his hand in a gesture of peace and blessing.

THE NEW BARBARIANS

For the barbarian invasions were not yet over. The next invaders of Italy, the Lombards, entered the peninsula in 568 from the north, just in time to gather the spoils of Justinian's wars, in which Romans and Goths had exhausted each other. On a plaque made to adorn the helmet of their King Agilulf, winged figures brandish drinking horns of a traditional Germanic court along with placards marked "Victory" of a kind carried in Roman triumphs. Agilulf's sumptuous cross—all Christian barbarian kings had something similar—is a wand of victory: a sign to conquer by. In the late seventh century, the Bulgars, another invader-people from the steppes, crossed the Danube and set up as the elite of a state that stretched from the northern Balkans almost to the walls of Constantinople. In his shrine at Arkona, on the Baltic, the four-headed deity of the Slavs was perhaps already developing the thirst for wine for which he later became notorious. During the seventh and eighth centuries, in an expansion almost undocumented and never explained, Slavs spread over most of Eastern Europe from the Baltic to southern Greece (see Map 8.5). Meanwhile, in North Africa, the Berbers, upland pastoralists, mobilized camel-borne war bands to terrorize the southern Mediterranean shore. In Scandinavia, in the eighth century, warriors who fought on sleds with prows carved with the heads of monsters took to the sea.

THE ARABS

These all proved formidable enemies of what was left of the Roman world. But most formidable of all the loiterers on the threshold were the Arabs, or, more precisely, nomadic, Arabic-speaking peoples of central Arabia. They lived astride the trade routes of the peninsula, between Romanized communities and city-states in the north and the maritime-oriented kingdoms of the seaboard. In the seventh century, they were transformed from a regional nuisance into a dynamic force. The preceding period in Arabia has received bad press—represented as chaotic and morally clueless, until the Prophet Muhammad brought peace and justice in the 620s and early 630s. But the contrast between the periods before and after the Prophet's arrival may be too sharply drawn.

The few glimpses the sources give us suggest that Arab society was already demographically robust, militarily effective, and—at least in its poetry—artisti-

"More than a religion, Islam—literally "submission" to God—was also a way of life and a blueprint for society, complete with a demanding but unusually practical moral code, a set of rules of personal discipline, and the outline of a code of civil law."

cally creative. "Poetry, horses, and numbers of people" were the standards by which different communities measured their rival merits. It is true, however, that Arabia was politically divided and riven by internal wars among tribes. The best-documented war was said to have started when the tribe of Dhubyan cheated in a horse race against the Abs. It lasted for generations and inspired the work of Antarah ibn-Shaddad al-Absi, the most renowned poet and warrior of the age.

It is also true that the economy of the tribes had come to depend on war: raiding the Byzantine, Persian, and Arab cities that were scattered around the edges of the region and milking their trade. In one respect, the transformation of these Arabs resembled that of other nomadic peoples mobilized for war by social change. As trade and banditry concentrated wealth, new styles of leadership dislocated the traditional, kinship-based structures of society and created an opportunity for a single, charismatic leader to unite an overwhelming force. In the Arabs' case, however, Muhammad's distinctive character marked him out from all other such leaders. His impact changed every aspect of life it touched. The Prophet taught a religion that was as rigorously monotheistic as Judaism, as humane and potentially as universal as Christianity, as traditional as paganism, and—for its time—more practical than any of them. More than a religion, Islam—literally "submission" to God—was also a way of life and a blueprint for society, complete with a demanding but unusually practical moral code, a set of rules of personal discipline, and the outline of a code of civil law.

Islam

A belief central to Islamic scholars represents Muhammad as God's mouthpiece and therefore, in human terms, utterly original. His teachings crackle and snap with the noise of a break with the past, but from Arab merchant communities he picked up Jewish concepts: monotheism, providence, history ruled by God. His earliest followers regarded themselves as descendants of the biblical patriarch Abraham through Abraham's maidservant Hagar and their son Ishmael. The inspiration of Islam combined elements borrowed from Judaism and Christianity with a measure of respect for some of the traditional rites and teachings of pagan traditions in Arabia.

Muhammad claimed to have received his teaching from God, through the Archangel Gabriel, who revealed divine words into his ear. The resulting writings, the **Quran** were so persuasive and so powerful that hundreds of millions of people believe him to this day. By the time of his death, Muhammad had equipped his followers with a dynamic form of social organization, a sense of their own unique access to the truth of God, and a conviction that war against nonbelievers was not only justified but also sanctified. Warriors were promised an afterlife in a paradise where sensual pleasures were like those of this world—pleasure gardens, young women. Muhammad's legacy gave Muslims (those who "submit" to God's message) administrative and ideological advantages against potential enemies. Yet the opportunity for the Arabs to become an imperial people arose as much, perhaps, from the weakness of the Byzantine and, especially, the Persian empires, as from the dynamics of their own society.

The Arabs against Persia and Rome

Of the old Eurasian empires, Persia's was the most successful in fending off steppeland turbulence. The Parthians, the Iranian dynasty that had come to power after the death of Alexander the Great (see Chapter 7), had favored the western regions of their empire and Mesopotamia. The Sasanians, however, who succeeded the Parthians as Persia's ruling dynasty from 226, concentrated their power in the most defensible part of the empire, building heavily in their own heartlands in the highlands of Fars and in and beyond the Zagros Mountains (see Map 8.5). A commanding position in the world, along the trade routes that linked the Mediterranean to the Indian Ocean and the Silk Roads, gave them the resources to maintain their traditional hostility to Rome—symbolized in a rock carving of 260, where the Roman emperor, Valerian, grovels at the feet of his Persian captors. Yet mutual respect tempered Persia's wars against Rome. Each empire recognized the other as civilized, while condemning all other neighbors as barbarians. In the 380s, Rome and Persia responded to the barbarian menace by making peace.

The peace lasted throughout the steppeland turbulence of the fifth century, but at the beginning of the sixth century, as other dangers seemed to recede, war between Romans and Persians resumed with deadly intent—like a fistfight between sparring partners that becomes deadly. By the time of the Arab conquests, the two giant empires had worn each other out. After more than a century of almost continuous conflict, the Roman Empire was close to exhaustion and the Persian, which got the worse of the fight, was near collapse. In consequence, neither empire could deal with the sudden rise of the Arabs. Mountains had protected Persia from northern steppeland invaders—but the Arab frontier to the southwest was flat. The Muslim Arabs absorbed the Persian Empire in its entirety in a series of campaigns from the late 630s to the early 650s. The Roman provinces of Syria, Palestine, Egypt, and North Africa—Rome's wealthiest and most populous subject-areas—fell to Arab or Arab-led armies by the early eighth century.

Sasanian victory. Huge rock carvings were traditional media of propaganda for Persian kings. None celebrates a more spectacular victory than that of Shapur I (r. 241–272) at the battle of Edessa in 260 C.E., when he took the Roman Emperor Valerian captive. The sculptor captured Valerian in another sense by showing him bending the knee in submission, while his cloak billows in the wind. The realism of the art enhances its symbolic significance, suggested by Shapur's huge crown, bulging physique, imperious gestures, and the stamp of his horse's hoof.

The Quran

The earliest known Arabic texts, from the fourth century C.E. onward, are inscribed in stone. Yet the earliest versions of the Quran, which date from the eighth century, are in a rounded script designed to be written with a brush. This form of written Arabic is known as Kufic—from the town of Kufa in Iraq, where it supposedly originated. Below are three lines from a Quran written in Kufic.

"This [divine writ], behold, is no less a reminder to all the worlds—and you most certainly grasp its purport after a lapse of time!" (Quran 38:87–88)

"In the name of God, the merciful the compassionate." (This is the *bismallah*, which begins all but one chapter of the Quran.)

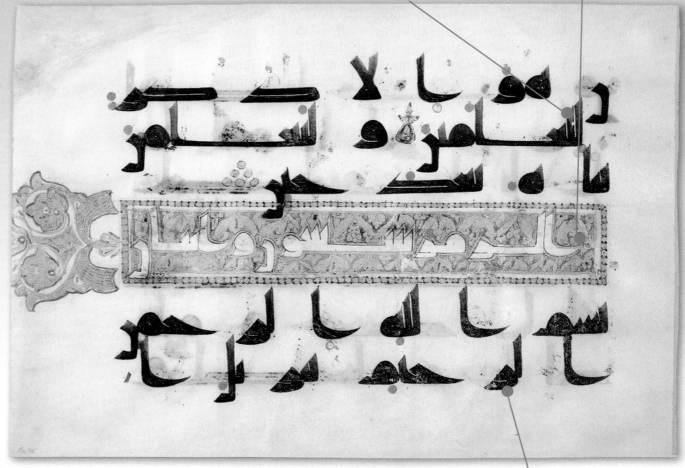

Arabic Manuscript: 30.60 Page from a Koran, 8th-9th century. Kufic script. H: 23.8 x W: 35.5 cm. Courtesy of the Freer Gallery of Art, Smithsonian Institution, Washington, D.C.: Purchase, F1930.60r

"The bestowal from on high of this divine writ..." (Quran 39:1)

What advantages did the Quran confer on early believers in Islam?

THE MUSLIM WORLD

Most of the area comprised within these limits became, in effect, a Muslim world (see Map 8.6). In some respects, it functioned remarkably cohesively, like a single empire, gradually spreading Islam, the Arabic language, and a common Muslim identity wherever it went, and introducing more or less uniform principles of law and government. Flexibility brought success. Although Arabs and descendants of the Prophet's own tribe enjoyed social privileges, every male Muslim could share a sense of belonging to an imperial elite. Although women were repressed, they at least had important rights: to initiate divorce (albeit under much stricter conditions than those that applied to men); to own property and retain it after divorce; and to conduct business in their own right. Christians and Jews, though vulnerable to periodic persecution and compelled to pay extra taxes, were normally allowed to worship in their own way. So, at first, were the Zoroastrians of Persia, who, though despised as pagans, were too numerous to alienate. Although other forms of paganism were forbidden, many traditional shrines and pilgrimages were resanctified as suitable for Muslim devotion.

But the Islamic world was too big to remain a single empire for long. And the precepts Muhammad left his followers at his death were not intended for a large state. For his followers, he was both prophet and ruler. Whereas Jesus invited individuals to respond to God's grace, Muhammad, more straightforwardly, called them to obey God's laws. Whereas Moses legislated for a chosen people, the Jews, and Jesus preached a "kingdom not of this world," Muhammad aimed at a code of behavior covering every department of life. He failed, however, to leave a code that was anything like comprehensive. So schools of jurisprudence set out to fill in the gaps by inferring Muhammad's principles from such laws as he did make in his lifetime, applying them more generally and, in some cases, adding insights from reason, com-

MAP 8.6

The Muslim World, ca. 756

- ◼ Muslim-ruled lands by 634
- ◼ Muslim-ruled lands by 656
- ◻ Muslim-ruled lands by 756
- → Muslim invasions, with dates
- — Byzantine Empire ca. 610
- — Sasanian Empire ca. 610

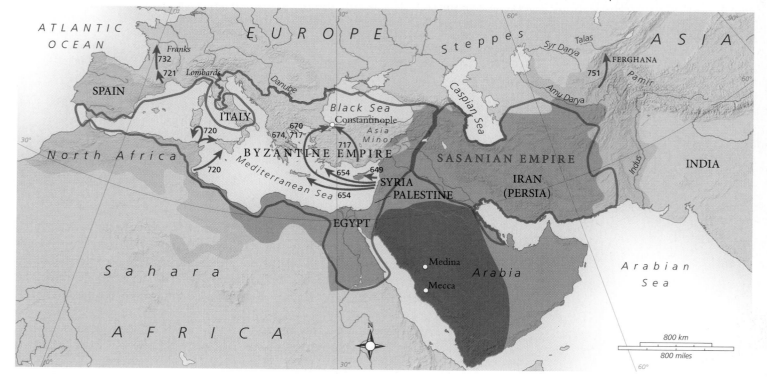

Making Connections | EMPIRES IN TRANSFORMATION

EMPIRE/ REGION	EXTERNAL ENEMIES	INTERNAL WEAKNESSES	STRENGTHS	SURVIVAL STRATEGIES	SUCCESSOR STATE
Teotihuacán/ Mesoamerica	Resentful tributary city-states	Overpopulation; reliance on imports; limited resources to export	Widely emulated culture; extensive trade network	Continual expansion to sustain population growth; installing friendly rulers in neighboring regions	
Roman/ Mediter-ranean	Germanic border peoples; Huns from Eurasian steppes; Persians	Sprawling, vulnerable land frontiers; politicized military; Christian threat to paganism; internal disorder; mass migrations; uncertain succession of leadership; adverse balance of trade	Occasional strong leaders; strong military tradition; eastern provinces easily defended and supplied	Division of leadership responsibility under Marcus Aurelius (162); division of empire after Constantine (d. 337); transfer of capital to Constantinople	Byzantine Empire in east; Germanic and barbarian kingdoms in west
Han/China	Steppeland raiders and migrants	Uncertain succession of leadership; feuding imperial factions; warlords	Circular shape facilitates move-ment of troops and information; Chinese culture imitated by barbarians; strong internal economy	Use of eunuchs for administration; promotion of Chinese customs and language among barbarians	Jin dynasty, followed by civil war and political fragmentation
Gupta/India	Huns	Cultural pessimism (age of Kaliyuga); poor defenses; inequality fostered by caste system; corrupt bureaucracy	Several strong leaders (Candra Gupta)	Differing layers of local authority linked together	Hunnic states and other principalities; kingdom of Harsha
Sasanian/Persia	Romans; nomadic Arabs	Exhaustion after continuous wars with Rome	Commanding geographic position; strong defenses; effective diplomacy	Concentrating power in most defensible areas; diplomacy with Rome	Islamic caliphate

mon sense, or custom. The **Sharia**—literally, "the camel's way to water"—was both a religious discipline and a law code for the state. The principles of law were unchange-able: revealed to the masters of the eighth and ninth centuries, whose interpretations of Muhammad's tradition were regarded as divinely guided. The reconciliation of the various schools' opinions, however, has always allowed some opportunities for devel-opment.

One consequence of the way Islam developed was that where Jesus had pro-claimed a sharp distinction between the secular and the spiritual, Muslims acknowledged no difference. The supreme Islamic author-ity, the **caliph**—literally, the "successor" of the Prophet—was, Christians said, both pope and emperor. The problem of identifying who was caliph split Islam between rival claimants and incompatible methods of choosing a caliph within a generation of Muhammad's death. The major division that eventually developed was between **Shia (SHEE-ah)** (meaning the "party" of Ali), which regarded the caliphate as the prerogative of Muhammad's nephew, Ali, and his heirs, and **Sunni** (SOO-nee) (meaning "tradi-tion"), which maintained that the Muslim community could designate any mem-ber of Muhammad's tribe to hold the office. The rift has never healed, and although Sunnism became the dominant tradition in the Islamic world, the schisms multiplied and, with them, internal conflicts, rival caliphates, and seces-sionist states.

Chronology: Islamic Expansion	
570–632	Life of Muhammad
630–early 650s	Muslim conquest of Iraq, Syria, Palestine, Egypt, Persian Empire
ca. 700	Muslim conquest of North Africa
ca. 715	Muslim conquest of Spain
751	Battle of Talas; Arabs victorious against Chinese

For as long as unity prevailed, the limits of Arab expansion show both its explo-sive nature and its reliance on mobilizing the resources and manpower of conquered or converted communities to make further conquests. When Arab expansion began to run out of impetus, in the second decade of the eighth century, armies owing alle-giance to the successors of Muhammad, under Arab generalship, were operating in northern Spain. More or less at the same time, they were destroying Zoroastrian tem-ples beyond the Jaxartes River in Central Asia and a Buddhist shrine in northern India. At its northeast extremity, the Arab effort even touched the outermost frontier of Chinese imperialism, west of the Pamir Mountains, where, in the first half of the eighth century, local rulers played off the Chinese against the Arabs in their efforts to maximize their own power. In 751, Chinese and Arab armies met in direct conflict for the first and last time, on the banks of the Talas River. The result was total victory for the Arabs and their Turkic allies. After this, China withdrew permanently behind the Pamirs, and most of Central Asia became securely part of the world of Islam—but that is part of the stories of chapters still to come.

RECOVERY AND ITS LIMITS IN CHINA

At home, China faced relatively familiar problems, with only internal conflicts to weaken it and only the well-known threat from the steppelands to hold at bay. China's recovery from the crisis of the sixth century started later than Rome's under Justinian but lasted longer. In the 570s, a professional soldier, Yang Jian (yahng jhee-en), became arbiter of power in the Yellow River valley—elevated to civil command because of his outstanding record in wars that had reunited the region. In 581, he proclaimed himself emperor, put to death 59 princes of the dynasty he had formerly served, and launched a strategy to re-create the empire by conquering the Yantgze valley. It proved remarkably easy—accomplished in about seven years, perhaps because dynastic instability had undermined the loyalty of southern Chinese to their existing rulers. As a Chinese who had proved that he could master barbarians on the battlefield, Yang Jian was an attractive candidate for the throne.

Conscious of his lack of all traditional credentials except success, the new emperor looked to Buddhism to legitimize his rule and to Legalism (see Chapter 6) for practical guidance in government. Law, Yang Jian said, should "suit the times." In other words, there were no sacred, everlasting, or universal principles. He vowed "to replace mercy with justice"—and demonstrated his commitment by endorsing the condemnation of his own son to death for embezzlement. He affected contempt for Confucian bookworms and controlled the court by violent displays of temper, personally beating underlings who displeased him, sometimes to death. His workaholic and frugal ways—he rationed the palace women's cosmetics—were the characteristics that most impressed observers.

Yang Zian's brutal, strong-arm methods were appropriate to a time of reunification by force. His successor, Yangdi (yahng-dee), who came to the throne in 605, reverted to tradition, announcing the revival of clemency, Confucian learning, and "ancient standards." The great triumph of his reign was the reintegration of the

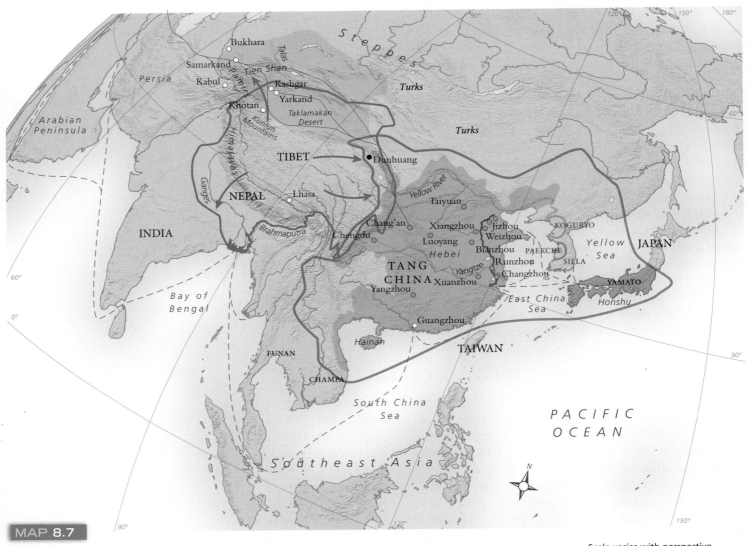

MAP 8.7

Tang China, Tibet, and Japan, ca. 750 C.E.

- Tang Empire at its greatest extent
- areas of temporary Tang control
- Yamato state
- approximate extent of Chinese cultural influence
- → Tibetan invasions
- Tibetan Empire ca. 750 C.E.
- Silk Roads
- ᵕᵕᵕ Great Wall
- — Grand Canal
- - - maritime trade routes
- ● city with over 300,000 inhabitants
- ○ other major city

Scale varies with perspective

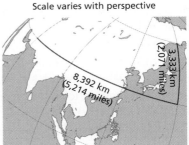

Yellow River and Yantgze valleys by an improved and extensive canal system, the Grand Canal. This was the kind of project that ought to have identified the dynasty with the "ancient virtue" Confucians prized. It was in the tradition of the great engineering emperors of legend, back to Yu the Great (see Chapter 3). Yangdi, however, forfeited this potential goodwill by the forced labor and taxes the canal-building effort demanded. From about the fourth or fifth year of his reign, moreover, he became prey to dreams of expansion. His policy of attempting to conquer Korea at the same time as his building projects strained the finances of the empire and the loyalty of the elite. He attempted unsuccessfully to buy the alliance of the nomad states on the northern border, but China was compelled to undertake the Korean adventure unaided. The effort was ruinous and unsuccessful—the usual prelude to a political revolution.

Rise of the Tang

In 617, Yangdi was deposed, but his sons could not agree on which of them should rule. Provincial armies rebelled. The most respected family in the kingdom, the Li, led a rebellion. Loyalty was not an option for the Li. Obsessed by fears of the Li's power and prophecies of their elevation to imperial status, Yangdi had attempted to exterminate their entire family. Li Yuan (lee yoo-ehn), head of the family after the massacre, was well connected in the army after having held many commands. By promises of future favor, he secured neutrality or support from the nomad princes. The reconquest of the country from rival rebels was not complete until about 624, but the exhaustion and disenchantment of the country favored a period of peace (see Map 8.7). The new dynasty, which called itself Tang (Tahng) relied at first on this comfortable mood. The second emperor of the dynasty, Taizong (teye-tzong), took an interventionist, reformist line. He favored the skeptical, scientific tradition, derided omens and magic potions, and held ceremonies when he pleased, not when seers told him to. He rationalized methods of administration, cutting down the number of posts and administrative divisions and subdivisions, creating a new, hand-picked bureaucracy for the provinces that he selected by examination, and simplified the law codes.

Empress Wu

Taizong's reforms did much to stabilize the empire. Dynastic crises no longer threatened to dissolve the state. A grueling test occurred in 690, when a woman seized the throne. On the face of it, this was unlikely to happen. Two collections of anecdotes—the *Nüjie* (noo-jay) and *Nüchunyu* (noo-chuhn-yoo)—dominated perceptions of women. They urged women to avoid idleness and promiscuity: A virtuous woman got up early and applied herself to household chores. Women were largely excluded from education—a limitation against which the *Nüjie* protested—and barred from the examinations for the state service. The only route to power was through the dangerous, overpopulated imperial harem. According to later sources, who may have deliberately tried to blacken her reputation because they were appalled at the very idea of a woman ruler, Wu Zhao (woo-jow) started as a lowly concubine, but her combination of beauty and brains impressed Taizong. Her recommendation of torture, brutality, and slaughter as methods of government supposedly amused him. It arose during a conversation about horse training, but, Wu Zhao said, "the emperor understood my meaning." She sought power by a characteristically bold stroke: seducing the emperor's heir. As the former emperor's concubine, she was ineligible to be the next empress, but she maneuvered her way around that obstacle with ease. In 655, she married the heir to the throne, replacing his official wife, whom she tortured to death. Similar methods ensured her ascendancy during her husband's lifetime and as effective regent during the next two reigns. To secure her own elevation to the rank of emperor, she mustered every disaffected faction. The Buddhist clergy were her agents, proclaiming her as an incarnation of God, circulating propaganda on her behalf around the empire. Urged by 60,000 petitioners, she became emperor—literally, because she did not rule as an empress but used the masculine title emperor.

Tang Decline

These extraordinary and—to most people at the time—unnatural events hardly disturbed the continuity of the Tang and provoked no serious attempts at provincial succession of the kind that had been routine under previous dynasties. Resentment accumulated, however, under the less resolute rule of Wu's successors. In the mid-eighth century, the defenses of the empire were beginning to look shaky as defeats by nomads became increasingly frequent. A frontier general, An Lushan (ahn loo-shawn), was selected as scapegoat. He had therefore little recourse except to rebel. The ensuing civil war confirmed the militarization of society, which, owing to the demands of frontier wars, was already happening anyway. In the 750s, 750,000 men were under arms. Governors became virtually autonomous rulers of their provinces. About a quarter to a third of the empire was effectively outside imperial control. In the late 770s, Dugu Ji (doo-goo gee) reported that 90 percent of peasants of Shuzhou (shoo-joh) and Anhui (ahn-hway) lived "without a penny to their name."

The emperors Dezong (r. 779–805) and Xianzong (shee-ehn-tzohng) (r. 805–820) tried to restore central power. To "bring the provinces under the rule of law" was now the watchword. "Only then can proper order be restored to the realm." Tax reforms in 782 decreed a single, uniform system throughout the empire. In practice, local authorities were left to fulfill quotas. Both emperors took the initiative against the autonomous provinces and even began to restore control of provincial armed forces to the central government. But they failed to control the most wayward province, Hebei (huh-bay), which was effectively independent by 822. Meanwhile, the provinces that remained supposedly subject to direct imperial control gained power at the expense of a central government that the efforts at recovery had impoverished. Governors enjoyed long tenures, levied unauthorized taxes, appointed local nominees to powerful administrative positions, and acquired ever-larger revenues and retinues. Central government recovered some taxpayers. There were 2.5 million registered households in 807 and 5 million in 839. This was still little more than half the figure attained before An Lushan's revolt. Imperial power became confined to the Yangtze valley.

Still, the Tang achievement was impressive. None of the other old empires—in Europe, Southwest Asia, India, or Ethiopia—managed a comparable record of continuity in the seventh and eighth centuries. Chinese achievements in the period were especially conspicuous in the allied fields of art and technology. The tools sculptors, potters, and bronze casters developed enabled artists to attain new heights of excellence. Surviving art works show where the wealth came from to sustain the output: dazzlingly fired, vividly realistic clay horses and camels are among the most common Tang objects museum visitors see in the West, attesting to the

Lady-in-waiting. Though the politics of Tang China could be turbulent, they never disturbed the serenity of the arts of the imperial court. Women were frequently depicted. Many images of women as servants or, as in this example, as imperial ladies-in-waiting, have survived because they were often placed as offerings in tombs. But portraits of female artisans—especially silk-makers—poets, students, equestrians, and matriarchs are also common, showing that, in an era that produced a female emperor, many occupations and roles were open to women.
Dagli Orti/Picture Desk, Inc./Kobal Collection

importance of trade with Central Asia. The biggest surviving concentration of Tang era paintings is in the caves of Dunhuang, where merchants on the Silk Road stayed and endowed grottoes for worship. The prominence of Buddhist themes in much of the art of the era confirms China's opening to exchanges of culture with South and Central Asia.

From a global perspective, the most important technological innovation was gunpowder, which was first described in an eighth- or ninth-century Chinese work on chemistry. As usual in the history of preindustrial technology, Chinese inventors were ahead of the rest of the world, and it was from China that the invention spread, slowly but with world-transforming impact. At first, it was used only as an incendiary device—no surviving text before the eleventh century describes its explosive properties. But awareness of its potential for warfare was acute in China, and scholars have long puzzled over why Chinese armies made so little use of it and left its development to engineers in the Islamic world and the West. It is normal, however, for leaders in any field to discourage innovations that might undermine their supremacy, and Chinese efforts were largely directed, at first, toward preventing the secret of gunpowder from leaving the country.

IN THE SHADOW OF TANG: TIBET AND JAPAN

In the shadow of Tang China, promising states emerged. Tibet and Japan provide contrasting examples (see Map 8.7).

Tibet

At the time of the presumed beginnings of the first Tibetan state in the sixth century, the Chinese spoke of Tibetans in the conventional language used for barbarians, as pastoralists who "sleep in unclean places and never wash or comb their hair. They do not know the seasons. They have no writing and keep records only by means of knotted cords or notched tally sticks." In the river valleys of Tibet, however, sedentary agriculture was possible. A little-understood agricultural transformation in the fifth century brought barley to these areas as a staple crop. Once a cereal food was available in large amounts, the advantages of a cold climate for storage helped to create large food surpluses. A land from which small numbers of nomads eked a precarious living now became a breeding ground of armies that could march on far campaigns with "ten thousand" sheep and horses in their supply trains.

Before the seventh century, divine monarchs ruled Tibet, "descended," according to early poems, "from mid-sky, seven stories high," and aspiring to rule "all under heaven." Like other divine kings, they were liable to be sacrificed when their usefulness expired. They were given no tombs, for it was believed

Tang pottery. The popularity of camels as subjects of fine pottery in Tang China shows the importance of communications with Central Asia along the desert Silk Roads. Here the potter manages to combine realism and idealism. No camel was ever so lovely, but the tilt of the head, the shape of the braying mouth, the details of the musculature, and the intricacies of the saddle are all lively and typical.

Chronology: Recovery and Its Limits in China	
581	Yang Jian proclaims himself emperor (Sui dynasty)
605	Yangdi becomes emperor
609	Grand Canal completed
617	Yangdi deposed; rebellion ensues
618	Li Yuan begins reconquest of China from rival rebels; beginning of Tang dynasty
626	Beginning of reign of Taizong, second Tang emperor
690	Wu Zhao (Empress Wu) seizes throne
755–763	Rebellion of An Lushan
822	Province of Hebei effectively independent

The Potala Palace, towering above the valley of Lhasa, stands on the supposed site of the palace of the kings of Tibet in the seventh and eighth centuries. The present construction, however, began to rise in the mid-seventeenth century. The building is designed to suggest mystical power—cloud-shrouded, hard of ascent, overwhelming.

that they ascended back into heaven. At an unknown date in the sixth century, kings who ruled until they died a natural death replaced this system. Long reigns, with stability and continuity, were now possible. The first king known from more than fragmentary mentions was Songtsen Gampo. His reign, from about 627 to 650, marked an unprecedented leap in Tibetan power. China bought him off with a Chinese bride in 640. Preserved among a cache of documents in a cave on the Silk Road is the oath of allegiance he exacted: "Never will we disobey any command the king may give." In practice, however, in most of the communities he conquered, he simply levied tribute, rather than practicing direct rule or close supervision.

Tibetan aggression continued for most of the next 250 years. Tibetan armies conquered Nepal and invaded Turkestan in Central Asia. A pillar at Lhasa, the Tibetan capital, erected before 750, records campaigns deep inside China. On the western front, Tibetans collaborated with Arab forces in the conquest of Ferghana, in 715. In 821 a Chinese ambassador described the Tibetan war camp, where shamans in tiger skins banged drums before a tent "hung with gold ornaments in the form of dragons, tigers and leopards." Inside, in a turban "the color of morning clouds," the king watched as chiefs signed the treaty with China in blood.

The kings' tastes were increasingly cosmopolitan. Ten of them, including Songtsen Gampo, lie under small mounds at Phyongrgyas, where "dead companions" attended them—now no longer sacrificed but appointed to guard and tend the graves without direct contact with the outside world. Pillars in Indian, Central Asian, and Chinese styles, and a guardian lion modeled on a Persian original attest to the role of Tibet as a cultural crossroads. Their metal smiths' ingenuity was famous. Mechanical toys of gold dispatched as gifts to the Chinese court included a horse with moving limbs and a tiger with roaring jaws. Tibetan chain mail had an almost magical reputation for deflecting missiles. Yet even this could not protect the Tibetans from the effects of the instability of the

Chronology: The Rise and Decline of Tibet

Fifth century	Barley introduced as a staple crop
627–650	Reign of Songtsen Gampo
715	Tibetan and Arab conquest of Ferghana
Early ninth century	Beginning of Tibetan decline

era of Tang decline, which must have disrupted trade, while the power of the step-pelanders limited Tibetan opportunities to raid or expand. In the early ninth century, Tibet suffered a dreary sequence of defeats on all fronts. Rebellions ensued. Tibet signed its last treaty as an equal with China in 823. Its last known king was assassinated in 842.

Japan

Better prospects of enduring experiments in statecraft existed on the remoter edges of Chinese cultural influence, in Japan, where the steppeland menace could not reach. Chinese culture began to arrive in Japan from Korea when the Buddhist monk Wani became tutor at a Japanese court in about 400. The Korean kingdom of Paekche sent scholars and Buddhist scriptures. The leading state in Japan, Yamato, was a maritime kingdom, attracted by Korean and Chinese civilization, and at least as interested in expanding onto the mainland of Asia as in growing within the Japanese islands. Around 475, Yuryaku, king of Yamato, applied to China for the rank of general and minister when he was preparing an expedition against the Korean kingdom of Koguryo. He claimed his ancestors had conquered "55 kingdoms of hairy men to the east and 65 barbarian kingdoms to the west." Crossing the sea to the north, he added, they had subjugated 95 kingdoms. "The way to govern is to maintain harmony and peace, thereby establishing order." Communications with China were still via Paekche. The advice of counselors from Korea reflects the restraining influence of Buddhist and Confucian precepts on the warlike culture of Yamato. The ruler, one of the Korean advisers suggested, should "try to make farmers prosperous. ... After he has followed this policy for three years, food and soldiers will become plentiful." From the mid-sixth century, Japan was following this sort of program, organizing royal estates, taking censuses.

Japanese tomb. In the second and third quarters of the first millennum C.E., Japanese elite burials took place in underground stone chambers that were often elaborately painted with scenes that recalled the deceased's life, anticipated the afterlife, and "quoted" from the deceased's astrological charts. The whole tomb would then be covered with mounds of earth. This example from a tomb in Asuka shows female attendants, with fan and torch, symbolically accompanying the deceased in the afterlife.

Early in the seventh century, direct contact with China opened. The first Japanese embassy to China presented greetings "from the Son of Heaven in the land where the sun rises to the Son of Heaven in the land where the sun sets." The Chinese dismissed this as impertinence. Their accounts make the queen who ruled Japan at the time say, "As barbarians living in an isolated place beyond the sea, we do not know propriety and justice." It is not clear that the Japanese really saw themselves like that. They staked a claim to equality with China—and imperial rank—that subsequent Japanese regimes never entirely abandoned.

In the 640s, the dynasty narrowly beat off a bid for the throne from a Chinese immigrant family. Reform of the administration then began in earnest. The drive to centralize by breaking up and replacing traditional power structures is reflected in a decree of 645 that blamed clan chieftains for dividing up the land, engaging in conflict, unjustly exploiting labor, and impoverishing peasants "who lack enough land to insert a needle." Landlords were forbidden "to increase, by one iota, the miseries of the weak." Indirectly, China's invasion of Korea in the 660s boosted imperial rule in Japan. One hundred Korean refugees were appointed to court rank. After victory in a civil war of 672, the ruling dynasty of Japan was unchallenged. Japan solved the problem that bedeviled the politics of other empires—devising a secure means to ensure the succession—by two means. First, women's aptitude to rule was accepted. This increased the

Making Connections | DEVELOPING FRONTIER STATES

STATE/REGION/PERIOD	IMPERIAL NEIGHBOR	RESOURCES/ ORGANIZATION:	ACHIEVEMENTS
Koguryo, Silla, Paekche/ Korea ca. 300–500	China	Chinese religious influence— Buddhism and Daoism; Chinese migrants and technical knowledge	Complex irrigation system for rice cultivation; hundreds of walled towns; strong military
Funan/Southeast Asia ca. 100–400	India, China	Indian cultural influences; commercial traders strategically located between India and China	Sophisticated culture; wealthy mercantile class; expansion around Gulf of Thailand
Ethiopia/Africa ca. 300–500	Rome, Byzantine Egypt	Accessible to Indian Ocean trade routes, isolated enough to be defensible; temperate climate; trade center connecting Africa to India, Arabia, and Mediterranean ports	Productive agriculture system—up to three crops a year; developed industry (metalwork, ivory) and large-scale urbanization
Tibet/Central Asia ca. 500–800	China, India	Development of barley as primary cereal crop for vast high-altitude plateau; food surpluses and strong military	Long-term alliance/tributary, relationship with China; stable leadership; conquest of neighboring kingdoms
Japan/East Asia ca. 400–600	China, Korea	Chinese/Korean cultural influences; strategic position for maritime trade; isolated and defensible; organization of royal estates; censuses	Long-term tributary relationship with China; gradually centralized power structure to maximize productivity; stable power structure with some women emperors

dynasty's stock of suitable candidates for the throne. Indeed, until the 770s, when a disastrous empress inspired lasting revulsion against women rulers, most rulers were women. Second, from 749, it became normal for rulers to abdicate and watch over the transmission of power to their heirs. The system worked well until the mid-ninth century, when a single courtly family, the Fujiwara, established an effective monopoly over supply of the chief wives for successive emperors. Thereafter, in the Japanese system of government, the emperor presided over the realm, but a dynasty of court favorites or chief ministers usually did the ruler's job. The last big political development—the search for a means to harness Buddhism for state service while preserving Japan's native religion—belongs in the next chapter.

In Perspective
The Triumph of Barbarism?

Had Siyaj K'ak been able to continue his journey from Teotihuacán and cross the ocean to Eurasia, he might have been gratified by the contrast between the stability and growth of the empire he represented and the perils that beset the empires of the Old World. In the year of his arrival, the Visigoths challenged Roman might at Adrianople. The crises that accompanied the traumas of the Eurasian steppelands and the migrations of Germanic and steppelander peoples into neighboring empires were already beginning. One measure of the instability that ensued is particularly striking. In much of Europe and India, the fifth and sixth centuries were so chaotic that recordkeeping collapsed, and we can no longer reconstruct a complete outline even of the most basic facts of political history—the names and chronology of kings and dynasties. By contrast, in the same period, for the Maya world Siyaj K'ak visited, we know far more about the rulers of many city-states, whose records are inscribed in stone in meticulous detail.

Yet, despite the waves of migrants and invaders that washed over Old World empires in the half millennium or so from about 200 onward and the crises they provoked, the most remarkable feature of the period is perhaps the durability of old orders. Cultural conflicts usually follow battlefield victories. And even where the so-called barbarians defeated the empires, they tended to get conquered in their turn by the cultures of their victims. The German invaders of the Roman world were partly Romanized, while the eastern Roman Empire survived, centered on Constantinople. Steppeland conquerors played havoc with the political unity of India—but the cultural transformations of India happened from within. "Barbarians" disrupted China politically but did not disturb the continuity of Chinese civilization. On the contrary, when barbarians settled within China, they adjusted to Chinese ways. Indeed, Chinese civilization overspilled China into new areas, such as Korea, Japan, Southeast Asia, and Tibet. The instability of the steppes damaged the land-bound trade of Eurasia, but the commerce of the Indian Ocean continued to grow, and the development of Ethiopia was among the consequences.

Chronology

220	End of Han dynasty in China
323	Founding of Constantinople
340	Spread of Christianity in Ethiopia
Third and fourth centuries	Germanic invasions of Roman Empire; Huns break out of Central Asia
ca. 375	Teotihuacán (Mesoamerica) at peak of its influence and power
Fifth century	Introduction of barley as a staple crop in Tibet
400	Beginning of Chinese influence in Japan
410	Visigoths sack Rome
415	Huns begin to infiltrate India
467	Death of last-known Gupta emperor (India)
476	End of west Roman Empire
493–526	Reign of Theodoric, Ostrogothic king in Italy
527–565	Reign of Justinian, Byzantine emperor
ca. 535	Massive volcanic eruption in present-day Indonesia
570–632	Life of Muhammed
Seventh century	Beginning of Slav expansion in Eastern Europe
609	Grand Canal completed in China
627–650	Reign of Songtsen Gampo in Tibet
630–720	Rapid Arab expansion
667–668	Chinese conquest of Koguryo (Korea)
690	Beginning of reign of Empress Wu (China)
751	Arabs defeat Chinese at battle of Talas

(All dates are C.E.)

> "Still, despite continuities that survived the barbarians, the world that emerged in the last three centuries of the first millennium C.E. was genuinely, deeply transformed. Rather than the world of empires that had dominated the densely populated belt of the axial age, it might be proper to speak of a world of civilizations."

Still, despite continuities that survived the barbarians, the world that emerged in the last three centuries of the first millennium C.E. was genuinely, deeply transformed. Rather than the world of empires that had dominated the densely populated belt of the axial age, it might be proper to speak of a world of civilizations. Western civilization was a hybrid—partly Germanic, partly Christian, partly Roman in heritage. The Islamic world was far more innovative, but it had, in some respects, a similar profile: with a biblical heritage, reinterpreted by Muhammad, and the learned legacies of Rome, Greece, and Persia, under an Arab elite from outside the empires, established by conquest but susceptible to the cultural influence of its victims. In both the Islamic world and Christendom, notions of universal empire survived: the caliphate, Byzantium. But neither could maintain unity in practice, and the respective regions became arenas of states contending for the imperial legacy or ignoring it. In India, political fragmentation under the impact of barbarian invasion was more thoroughgoing, in China less so. In both, however, the invaders and immigrants were like chameleons, taking on the cultural hues of their new environments. In both, moreover, the traditional culture spread into new areas and new states, such as those of south India, and China's neighbors. So nowhere, by the eighth century, except in Ethiopia, was there any longer a civilization that was confined to a single state.

Even at the end of a chapter crowded with politics, we still have not reached the deepest transformative influences on the period. One of the traditional limitations of history textbooks is that politics, which generates most of the sources, tends to dominate the foreground. But politics is full of short-term changes, while ideas and environmental influences generate the sea changes. The next two chapters explore the religious transformations that made this world of civilizations distinct, in particular, from the empires that preceded them, and the discovery and development of resources that not only renewed the Old World, but also opened up new frontiers in other parts of the globe.

PROBLEMS AND PARALLELS

1. How were imperial traditions inherited from the axial age extinguished or fragmented by the year 500?

2. How does the history of Teotihuacán echo Eurasian developments in this period?

3. What were the differences between the ways that China and Rome dealt with steppeland migrants and invaders? Why was China more successful?

4. How did the Byzantine Empire and the barbarian kingdoms in Western Europe continue the traditions of Rome? How did Justinian try to revive Roman power in the West?

5. To what extent was Ethiopia able to achieve a balance between accessibility and isolation?

6. How did states develop on the edges of empires during this period?

7. Why were the Arabs able to conquer a vast empire in so short a time? What role did the teachings of the Prophet Muhammad play making the Arabs an imperial people?

8. How was the world that recovered from the crises of the third through seventh centuries a world of civilizations?

READ ON▶ ▶ ▶

Helpful information on relations between Teotihuacán and the Maya is in D. Drew, *The Lost Chronicles of the Maya Kings* (1999); R. Hassig, *War and Society in Ancient Mesoamerica* (1992); and S. Martin and N. Grube, *Chronicle of the Maya Kings and Queens* (2000), which is also a lavish compendium of facts and images. G. Braswell, *The Maya and Teotihuacán* (2003) is an important revisionist study that challenges the account of Siyaj K'ak above.

On the transformation of the Roman world, Peter Brown, *The World of Late Antiquity* (1989) is the ideal introduction—sprightly and subtle. A. H. M. Jones, *The Later Roman Empire* (1964) is a classic study of undiminished interest. J. Herrin, *The Formation of Christendom* (1987) is assured, fluent, and in touch with the sources. A. Cameron et al., eds., *The Cambridge Ancient History*, xiv (2000) is forbiddingly comprehensive and magisterial. R. Collins, *Early Medieval Europe* (1991) is a vigorous, thoughtful textbook. The classic works by F. Lot, *The End of the Ancient World and the Beginning of the Middle Ages* (2000), and by H. Pirenne, cited below, can still be recommended in combination with more recent scholarship. B. R. Ward-Perkins, *The Fall of Rome and the End of Civilization* (2005) and P. Heather, *The Fall of the Roman Empire* (2005) are archaeologically informed appraisals of the catastrophic effects of the invasions.

There are many editions of the *Meditations of Marcus Aurelius*. On Constantine, R. Macmullen, *Constantine* (1987) is standard. Sources on his conversion are collected in M. Edwards, trans., *Constantine and Christendom* (2003). D. Bowder, *The Age of Constantine and Julian* (1978) is valuable in setting the context. M. Grant, *The Emperor Constantine* (1993) is lively and readable. R. Macmullen, *Christianity and Paganism in the Fourth to Eighth Centuries* (1997) is a valuable introduction. A. Momigliano, *The Conflict of Paganism and Christianity in the Fourth Century* (1964) is a collection of classic studies. R. Lane Fox, *Pagans and Christians* (1987), and K. Hopkins, *A World Full of Gods* (1999) are also helpful. On the transformation of the city of Rome, B. R. Ward-Perkins, *From Classical Antiquity to the Middle Ages* (1985) sets the context of urban change in Italy, while P. Llewellyn, *Rome in the Dark Ages* (1993) is a graphic account of the reemergence of Rome as the pope's capital.

W. Goffart, *Barbarians and Romans* (1980) is an introductory overview. E. A. Thompson, *A History of Attila and the Huns* (1972) is a classic study, still vital. There are many editions of the *Hildebrandslied*, but I know of no substantial critical studies in English except F. Norman, *Three Essays on the Hildebrandslied* (1973). The most useful study of the Christianity of Germanic invaders of the Roman Empire is E. A. Thompson, *The Visigoths in the Time of Ulfila* (1966). J. M. Wallace-Hadrill, *The Barbarian West* (1952) is the best possible introduction to the Germanic kingdoms; his *The Long-Haired Kings* (1962) is an absorbing collection of essays on the same subject, which should be read in conjunction with I. N. Wood, *The Merovingian Kingdoms* (1994). *The Consolation of Philosophy* is widely available in many editions. For Boethius's life and thought, J. Marenbon, *Boethius* (2003) is excellent, and H. Chadwick, *Boethius* (1981) is both authoritative and concise. S. Williams and G. Friell, *The Rome That Did Not Fall* (1999) is a helpful essay on the survival of the empire in the east. See now the revisionist, archaeologically informed survey of B. R. Ward-Perkins, *The Fall of Rome and the End of Civilization* (2005).

The steppes are covered in R. Grousset, *The Empire of the Steppes* (1970). Volume 3 of *The Cambridge History of China* (1978) covers this period admirably. S. A. M. Adshead, *Tang China* (2004) provides an introduction to that dynasty. C. P. Fitzgerald, *The Empress Wu* (1955) is a captivating classic biography. R. K. Dwivdki and D. L. Vaish, *A History of the Guptas* (1985), and S. Goyal, *History and Historiography of the Age of Harsha* (1992) provide a political and cultural outline of India. W. E. Henthorn, *A History of Korea* (1971) is particularly good on this period.

On Axum, see the works of Munro-Hay and Phillipson mentioned in Chapter 9.

On Justinian, *The Secret History of Procopius* (1927) is an irresistibly engaging, albeit cruelly prejudiced, source. Balanced modern studies include J. A. S. Evans, *The Age of Justinian* (1996), and R. Browning, *Justinian and Theodora* (1971). G. Greatrex, *Rome and Persia at War* (1998) admirably covers the Persian wars of this period.

For an understanding of Byzantium in this period, A. Cameron, *Changing Cultures in Early Byzantium* (1996) is an authoritative, clear, and insightful collection. M. Grant, *From Rome to Byzantium* (1998) is a readable narrative. M. Whittow, *The Making of Orthodox Byzantium* (1996) is invaluable on the development of a distinctive religious culture. A. Cameron and J. Herrin, *Constantinople in the Early Eighth Century* (1984) is helpful. M. Angold, *Byzantium* (2001) is a good overview. W. E. Kaegi, *Byzantine Military Unrest* (1981) takes an interesting approach. On eunuchs see K. Ringrose, *The Perfect Servant: Eunuchs and the Social Construction of Gender in Byzantium* (2003). On the Bulgars, O. Minaeva, *From Paganism to Christianity* (1996) wields fascinating artistic evidence. On Lombard Italy and its context, C. Wickham, *The Long Eighth Century* (2000) and *Early Medieval Italy* (1990) are excellent.

A. Hourani, *History of the Arab Peoples* (2003) is probably the best overall survey of Arab history. M. A. Cook, *Muhammad* (1983) is a brief and brilliant introduction. Some of the same author's important essays are collected in *Studies in the Origins of Early Islamic Culture and Tradition* (2004). M. Cook and P. Crone, *Hagarism: The Making of the Islamic World* (1977) is a ground-breaking study. M. Hodgson, *The Venture of Islam*, 3 vols., (1974) is a marvelous classic. G. R. Hawting, *The First Dynasty of Islam* (2000) is an efficient narrative of the early caliphate. On the impact of the Arab conquests, all students should read—critically, of course—the classic by H. Pirenne, *Mohammed and Charlemagne* (1939).

CHAPTER 9
The Rise of World Religions: Christianity, Islam, and Buddhism

▲ **Pilgrim's return.** Priests, officials, and bystanders (shown prostrating themselves, on the right) greet the pilgrim Xuanzang on his return to China from India, where he had traveled to find Buddhist scriptures. Pack horses bear the 75 sacred texts he had acquired to a temple on the left. Monks at the rear carry holy relics.

In this Chapter

In 872, Ibn Wahab, a Muslim traveler from Basra in Iraq, arrived in China at the Tang court. The emperor called for a box of scrolls, which he ordered to be put before the visitor, saying, "Let him see his master."

Ibn Wahab recognized the portraits of biblical prophets and patriarchs.

"I said," his account continues, "Here is Noah with his ark, which saved him when the world was drowned. . . ."

At these words, the emperor laughed and said, "You have identified Noah, but, as for the ark, we do not believe it. It did not reach China or India."

"That is Moses with his staff," I said.

"Yes," said the emperor, "but he was unimportant and his people were few."

"There," I said, "is Jesus, surrounded by his apostles."

"Yes," said the emperor. "He lived only a short time. His mission lasted only thirty months."

Then I saw the Prophet on a camel . . . and I was moved to tears. "Why do you weep?" asked the emperor. . . . "He and his people founded a glorious empire. He did not live to see it completed, but his successors have." Above each picture was an inscription which I supposed to contain an account of their history. I saw also other pictures, which I did not recognize. The interpreter told me that they were the prophets of China and India.

It would be rash to believe every word of this story. The remarks Ibn Wahab puts into the emperor's mouth seem calculated to favor Islam at the expense of Judaism and Christianity. Nevertheless, the anecdote does illustrate three important themes of the time. First, the effectiveness of communications across Eurasia is clear from Ibn Wahab's presence in China and from the extent of Chinese knowledge of Islam and the West. Second, the superiority of Chinese knowledge appears from the fact that the emperor knew a lot about the three Abrahamic faiths (Judaism, Christianity, and Islam claimed, each in its own way, to be based on the covenant between God and the biblical patriarch Abraham), while his visitor knew nothing about the Buddhist sages displayed in the same box of scrolls. Finally, the story raises the subject of this chapter: the beginnings of the ascent of Christianity, Islam, and Buddhism as *world religions*, with followings in all sorts of physical and cultural environments. Most religions tend to be culturally specific—they only appeal to peoples with certain cultural profiles and do not spread beyond their cultures of origin. Christianity, Islam, and Buddhism were unusual in aspiring to be universal, and in becoming global.

CHINA

IRAQ

Historians often claim to be interested in the past for its own sake. If we also want to understand our own world, and trace the emergence of its key features, we have to confront the problem of why Christianity, Islam, and Buddhism began to acquire the global acceptance they have today. So in this chapter, we have to stay in Eurasia and Africa—in the parts where these three religions had penetrated by Ibn Wahab's time—and catch up in the next chapter with changes that were occurring in other parts of the world.

There has never really been an "age of faith." Of course, there are plenty of sincere individual conversions, spiritually inspired or intellectually induced. Sometimes they can have enormous impact, not only on the lives of the people who experience them but also on society, inspiring mass movements and initiating social, political, and economic reforms. Most people, however, in most periods, experience religion only superficially. If they do undergo real conversion or spiritual rebirth, it happens sporadically and rarely lasts long. Nor should we judge the spread of religion by the extent of people's intellectual grasp of it. If you ask most Christians or Muslims or Buddhists about the doctrines of their faiths, they will usually give you, at best, a shallow account (for the facts about the doctrines of each of these faiths, see the Making Connections table on p. 298). Instead of understanding religion as belief, or spiritual experience, or doctrine, we can treat it, for our present purposes, as cultural practice, and say that a religion has "spread" where and when people in large numbers take part in its rites and identify with their fellow worshippers as members of a community. Four processes made possible the spread of religions in this sense during the period of takeoff for Islam, Buddhism, and Christianity: war, trade, missionary activity, and elite—especially royal—sponsorship (see Map 9.1).

COMMERCE AND CONFLICT: CARRIERS OF CREEDS

Forcible conversion is—strictly speaking—no conversion at all. "There is no compulsion in religion," says the Quran. Though Christians have sometimes done it, the law of the Catholic Church forbids using force to spread faith. Buddhism, too, has no place for coercion. But force sometimes works.

In the Islamic World

The Arabic word **jihad** (jee-HAHD) literally means *striving*. Muhammad used the word in two contexts: first, to mean the inner struggle against evil that Muslims must wage for themselves; second, to denote real war, fought against the enemies of Islam. These have to be genuine enemies, who "fight against you to the death." But in Muhammad's day the community he led was almost constantly at war, and Chapter Nine of the Quran seems to legitimate war against all "polytheists" and "idolaters." After the Prophet's death, his successors turned the doctrine of jihad against the "apostates" who abandoned Islam because they considered that their obligations to Muhammad had ended when he died. Jihad was then used to pro-

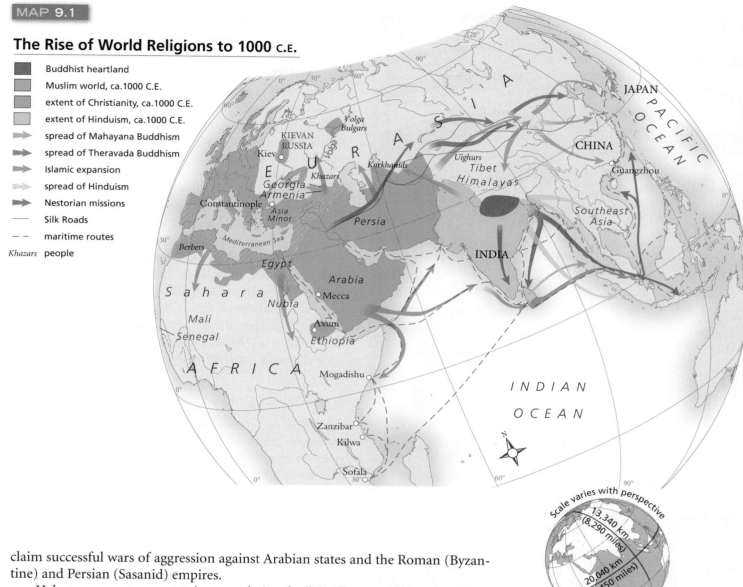

MAP 9.1

The Rise of World Religions to 1000 C.E.

- Buddhist heartland
- Muslim world, ca.1000 C.E.
- extent of Christianity, ca.1000 C.E.
- extent of Hinduism, ca.1000 C.E.
- → spread of Mahayana Buddhism
- → spread of Theravada Buddhism
- → Islamic expansion
- → spread of Hinduism
- → Nestorian missions
- — Silk Roads
- -- maritime routes
- *Khazars* people

claim successful wars of aggression against Arabian states and the Roman (Byzantine) and Persian (Sasanid) empires.

Holy war seems an appropriate translation for "jihad": an enterprise sanctified by obedience to what are thought to be the Prophet's commands and rewarded by the promise of martyrdom. According to a saying traditionally ascribed to Muhammad, the martyr goes straight to the highest rank of Paradise, nearest to the throne of God, and has the right to intercede for the souls of his loved ones. This is not far from the words of the Quran: "Allah has purchased of the believers their persons and their belongings in return for the promise that they shall have Paradise, for they fight in the cause of Allah and they slay the enemy or are slain." This is no more bloodthirsty than many passages in the Bible and needs no more to be taken literally than Paul's injunction to Christians to "fight the good fight." But it makes a handy justification for war and implies a link between war and the spread of Islam. The tenth-century Muslim jurist, al-Kayrawani (ahl keye-rah-WAH-nee), summed up the tradition as it had evolved by that time. Enemies could either submit to Islam or pay a poll tax for the privilege of persisting in their own religion. "Failing that, we will make war against them."

That was theory. Practice was not always so clear-cut. But in the first couple of centuries of Islamic expansion, victorious Muslim armies did normally aim to wipe out religions they classed as idolatrous, such as Hinduism, and to tax Christians, Jews, and, at times, other privileged groups, such as Zoroastrians in Persia. The result would not necessarily be to convert people to Islam, in the sense of changing their hearts and minds. But the elimination of traditional priesthoods and the destruction of former places of worship opened up spaces in which Islam, the religion of the conquerors, could take root. Moreover, God seemed to endorse Islam. The astonishing conquests of Muslim armies in the seventh and eighth centuries set up a framework within which people were both exposed to Islam and impressed by its victories. If traditional religion became a badge of resistance to conquest, it withered when that resistance failed. Among the pagan Berbers of northwest Africa, for instance, Muslim writers complained of the rejection of Islam during the seventh century. But when the last great Berber revolt against the Arabs failed in 703, the woman who had led it sent her sons to receive instruction in Islam.

In Christendom

So, slowly, faith followed the flag of conquest. Within the narrower limits of their lesser success, Christian conquerors also abused religion to justify war and imposed new forms of worship along with the terms of peace. In the eighth century, the Frankish king Charlemagne gave the pagan Saxons in eastern Germany a choice of baptism or death. In the ninth, Alfred the Great of England imposed baptism on defeated pagans as a condition of peace. Olaf, king of Norway in the early eleventh century, massacred, mutilated, or blinded pagans who refused Christianity. It seemed consistent with the nature of the Lord of Hosts, as the Bible frequently referred to God, to spread Christianity by war. Yet in all these cases, and others like them, however violent and arbitrary the beginnings of Christianity, the affected communities joined Christian civilization and built springboards for further missions elsewhere.

The Islamic Paradise. Especially in Iran, where this miniature was painted, perhaps as early as the eleventh century, portraiture was not considered offensive to Islam, and the Prophet himself was a frequent subject of art. Here, Muhammad, outlined in flame, seems to be appearing before God, depicted as pure flame in a tradition that goes back to Zoroastrianism. The archangel Gabriel and Buraq, the mythical winged creature who, Muslims believed, carried Muhammad to and from Paradise, look on.

In the Buddhist World

Less well known is that much of the early spread of Buddhism relied on similar strategies by royal strongmen. As in Christendom, Buddhist rulers practiced remarkable intellectual contortions to justify the imposition by violence of a doctrine of peace and love. Asoka (see Chapter 7) was not alone in priding himself on conquests allegedly achieved "by **dharma**"—the teachings of Buddha. Asoka's near contemporary, Kaniska, King of Peshawar in what is today Pakistan, enforced Buddhism on his own subjects, as did King Vattagamani, whose efforts we know from inscriptions in Sri Lanka, early in the first century B.C.E. In the mid-eleventh century C.E., when King Anuruddha (ah-noo-ROOD-dah) introduced Buddhism to Burma (present-day Myanmar), he showed his piety by waging war on the neighboring Mon kingdom to gain possession of holy scriptures.

Trade

But even if we accept that war can spread religions, we still need wider, deeper explanations for the rise of the potential world religions of our period. After the time of Asoka, Buddhism never became the ideology of a widely successful conqueror until the sixteenth century; nor did Christianity, until European empires began to spread it around the world. Meanwhile, though enlarged by conquest on and around the edges of Christendom, Christianity had, by comparison with Islam, relatively unsuccessful champions. To achieve wide-ranging conversions, it had, like Buddhism, to spread with individual journeys beyond political frontiers. Even Islam, as a religion, spread beyond the boundaries of Muslim political expansion.

Trade was probably at least as important as war for spreading religion. The temples of Dunhuang are full of images of the role of the Silk Roads in spreading Buddhism. Merchants who rested at the monastery there on their way along the road endowed thousands of paintings that still line chambers carved from the rock. According to tradition, a Chinese monk began to hollow the caves out of the cliff face in 366, when, "traveling the wilds with his pilgrim's staff, he arrived at this mountain and had a vision of a golden radiance in the form of a thousand Buddhas." Many of the paintings portray individual merchants in acts of worship, often with their families, and sometimes in the company of their ancestors. In one image, brigands, converted by a Buddhist merchant they have captured, join him in prayer. In others, merchants ransom themselves from bandits by acts of piety. In others, famous Buddhas and sages travel roads familiar to the merchants. These works of art are metaphors of spiritual redemption that people like merchants whose business requires constant travel, with its deadly dangers and distant rewards, could easily interpret. Networks of monasteries accommodated these merchants as well as pilgrims who traveled the roads from China to visit Buddhist shrines in India and acquire sacred texts and teachings.

Manichaeanism and the Uighurs

Buddhism met rival religions along the Silk Roads. The Uighurs were a pastoral, Turkic-speaking people who dominated the steppeland north of the roads for 100 years from the 740s. On service as mercenaries during the Chinese civil wars of the mid-eighth century, they picked up **Manichaeanism**, a religion of obscure origin, probably rooted in a heretical form of Zoroastrianism (see Chapter 6). Mani, its supposed founder in Persia in the third century, divided the universe into realms of spirit—which was good—and matter—which was evil. This kind of dualism, with its stark moral teaching and suspicion of sex, was an ancient and influential idea. But although Mani relentlessly sought to spread his religion, it had never previously captured the allegiance of a state. On the contrary, Zoroastrians, Christians,

Dunhuang. The Silk Roads spread Buddhism as well as trade. Here—in a tenth-century example of the thousands of devotional paintings merchants endowed at the monastery of Dunhuang in Central Asia—a convert and his family pray at the feet of a Bodhisattva. Many Chinese converts to Buddhism retained the family values characteristic of Confucianism.

A CLOSER LOOK

A Buddhist Pilgrim of the Seventh Century C.E.

Xuanzang was the foremost Chinese Buddhist of the seventh century. He went along the Silk Roads on a pilgrimage to India to visit the sites where the Buddha had lived and taught and to retrieve Buddhist manuscripts. Here he is depicted, some 250 years after his death, with much of the typical items a Buddhist monk took on pilgrimage.

A censer to burn incense in worship.

A rattle to attract alms from pious passersby.

The tiger alludes to his visit to the spot where, according to legend, the Buddha, moved by compassion, gave his life to feed a starving tiger.

How does this painting show the importance of missionaries in spreading world religions?

Muslims, and even—on at least one occasion, in China, in 732—Buddhists perse-cuted it. Now, however, the Uighur ruler proclaimed himself the "emanation of Mani," and Manichaean zealots became his counselors, rather as Buddhist and Christian rulers chose clergy as advisers and bureaucrats. Indeed, a Uighur bureau-cracy developed, using its own language and script. According to a ninth-century inscription, Manichaeanism transformed "a barbarous country, full of the fumes of blood into a land where the people live on vegetables, from a land of killing to a land where good deeds are fostered." Uighur monarchs endowed temples in China and sponsored the collecting of Manichaean scriptures. However, Buddhism and, to a lesser extent, Christianity ultimately replaced Manichaeanism among the Uighurs, and the creed of Mani never caught on to the same extent anywhere else.

Christianity on the Silk Roads

By comparison with Buddhism and even Manichaeanism, Christianity was only moderately successful along the Silk Roads. Relatively few Christians, especially from Western Europe, engaged in long-range trade. Among Christian peoples who did have strong vocations for commerce, the Armenians kept to themselves and avoided trying to convert others so as not to invite persecution by non-Christian rulers. **Nestorians**—Christians in a tradition of fifth-century origin named after Nestorius, Bishop of Constantinople, who regarded the human Jesus as merely human, quite distinct from the divine Jesus—had a network of monasteries and communities that reached China and spread the faith among adherents who came to number millions. But the Nestorians remained a thin and patchy presence across a vast area.

Islam on Trade Routes

If Buddhism dominated much of the Silk Roads, Islam spread almost equally effec-tively by trade along the sea routes of maritime Asia and across the Sahara. As Mus-lim merchant communities dispersed, they founded their own mosques, elected or imported their own preachers, and sometimes attracted local people to join them. Muhammad's commands for peaceful conversion were at least as strong as those for jihad. "Call unto the way of thy Lord with wisdom and fair exhortation," the Quran commands. "Say to those who have received the Book and to those who are ignorant, 'Do you accept Islam?' Then . . . if they turn away, it is thy duty to convey the message." In the ninth century, the major Chinese ports acquired mosques. According to a contemporary estimate, thousands of Muslims constituted the biggest of the foreign merchant communities who perished in what is now Guangzhou in a rebel massacre in 879. Seaborne pilgrims began to arrive at Mecca in the ninth century. In the same period, as East African ports became integrated into the trade routes of the Indian Ocean, so they developed Muslim communities, composed at first of Arab and Persian merchants and gradually attracting local people to the new religion. Although it did not penetrate far inland, Islam by the twelfth century was probably the most influential religion of the East African coast in the region lapped by the monsoons.

In West Africa, way beyond the African frontiers of the caliphates, Arab visitors to Soninke chiefdoms and kingdoms from the ninth century noted that some peo-ple followed "the king's religion," while others were Muslims. Although Islam made little documented progress in West Africa before the eleventh century, immigration and the spread of the Arabic language and Islamic culture along the Saharan trade

"Although it did not penetrate far inland, Islam by the twelfth century was probably the most influential religion of the East African coast in the region lapped by the monsoons."

Camel caravan is still the most practical way to cross the Sahara, and camels still carry part of the traditional salt trade there. Like other long-range trade routes, those across the Sahara in the Middle Ages were avenues for the transfer of culture, spreading Islam, for example, from North Africa to the kingdoms of the West African Sahel and the Niger valley.

routes prepared the way for Islamization. On this frontier, Islam lacked professional missionaries. Occasionally, however, a Muslim merchant might interest a trading partner or even a pagan ruler in Islam. A late eleventh-century Arab compiler of information about West Africa tells such a story, from Malal south of the Senegal. At a time of terrible drought, a Muslim guest advised the king that if he accepted Islam, "You would bring Allah's mercy on the people of your country, and your enemies would envy you." Rain duly fell after prayers and Quranic recitations. "Then the king ordered that the idols be broken and the sorcerers expelled. The king, together with his descendants and the nobility, became sincerely attached to Islam, but the common people remained pagans."

MONARCHS AND MISSIONARIES

Although not much practiced by Muslims in this period, conversion of kings was one of the main strategies Buddhist and Christian missionaries employed to spread their faiths. They learned to start at the top of society because religion, like other forms of culture, tends to trickle down, encouraged by the example the power of leaders imposes.

For Christians, in particular, the strategy of targeting elites marked a profound innovation in the history of the Church. Christianity in antiquity was branded—not altogether justly—as a "religion of slaves and women." It was deliberately addressed to outcasts. It appealed to a low level of society and, at first, to those with a low-level education. In its earliest days, it was actually unwelcoming to persons of high status, like the rich young man in the Gospels whom Jesus sent away grieving, or the well-to-do for whom admission to the Kingdom of God was as if through the eye of a needle. In apostolic times, converts of respectable status were few and modest: a Roman army officer; a tax collector; the "most excellent Theophilus," who was probably a Roman official addressed at the beginning of the Gospel of Luke and the Acts of the Apostles; an Ethiopian eunuch who was a royal official. Over the next two to three centuries, the Church grew and embraced people of all classes in the towns of the empire—thanks especially to Christian women, who became the evangelizers of their own husbands and children. But Christianity remained a minority religion, unable to capture the allegiance of rulers or the institutions of states. In the first half of the fourth century,

Chronology: War, Trade, and Religion	
366	Founding of Dunhuang
Fifth century	Nestorius, bishop of Constantinople
Seventh and eighth centuries	Rapid Islamic expansion
Mid-eighth century	Uighurs adopt Manichaeanism
Ninth century	Seaborne pilgrims begin to arrive in Mecca; Muslim merchant communities thrive in major Chinese ports
Mid-eleventh century	King Anuruddha introduces Buddhism to Burma; Islam begins to penetrate East and West Africa

however, three spectacular conversions inaugurated an era in which efforts at conversion targeted the top. The rulers of three great states adopted Christianity: the Roman Emperor Constantine, King Ezana of Ethiopia, and King Trdat (tuhr-DAHT) of Armenia.

Constantine

Like so many future invaders and tourists from the north, Constantine, commander of the Roman army in Britain from 306, was seduced by the feel and flavor of Mediterranean culture. The standard tale of the beginning of his conversion to Christianity is not credible. In 312, he was heading south, intent on capturing the Roman throne in the West for himself. Approaching the decisive battle of his bid for power, at Milvian Bridge, not far from Rome, he saw a vision that he later described as "a cross of light, superimposed on the sun"—perhaps like the crosslike clouds mountaineers have reported in the Alps, or perhaps an unusual grouping of planets, or perhaps just a dream. As Constantine already worshipped the sun, the image seemed calculated to appeal to him. The priorities reflected in the accompanying message, "In this sign, conquer!" seem to have reflected Constantine's own. He was looking for a Lord of Hosts rather than a God of Love. An alternative account of the conversion may be Constantine's own. It is a stock story of revelation by grace. "I did not think that a power above could see any thoughts which I harbored in the secret places of my heart . . . but Almighty God, sitting on high, has granted what I did not deserve."

Galla Placidia. As matriarchs of households, and sometimes as powerful agents in the Roman state, women played vital roles in spreading and shaping Christianity. In the early fifth century, Galla Placidia, an emperor's daughter, depicted here on a gold coin as "Principessa Augusta," with titles normally reserved for emperors, converted her first husband, the Visigoth King Athaulf, from heresy and from opposition to Rome. She not only built churches; she also intervened in the elections of popes and bishops and tried to influence church doctrine.

Everywhere politics was so deeply implicated in royal religion that it is hard to resist skepticism about the spirituality of royal converts and the sincerity of their conversions, just as today we prudently question politicians who claim to be "born again." Bet hedging was the usual strategy. Even for Constantine, despite the emperor's growing interest in Christianity, emperorship was an essentially pagan office. The emperor was the chief priest of the official pagan cults and was worshipped as divine. The emperor's role could not suddenly lose its traditional character. Official religion continued. Court poets and orators classified Constantine's victims in battle as divine sacrifices and his birth as a gift of the gods. One of them constructed a framework of paganism over which the emperor's Christianity could fit: "you have secret communion with the Divine Mind, which, delegating our care to lesser gods, deigns to reveal itself to you alone." Constantine continued to personify the Unconquered Sun in official portraits. Even later Christian emperors were honored and portrayed as gods. A sumptuous ivory plaque of the late fourth century in the British Museum shows winged spirits bearing an emperor up to his ancestors among the gods by way of the signs of the zodiac. The sacredness of the emperor's person, however, could now be redefined in Christian terms by calling him God's deputy on Earth and, in deserving cases, making him a saint after his death. In coins his sons issued, the hand of God guides Constantine into heaven on a chariot, like the prophet Elijah's in the Bible.

Imperial patronage profoundly affected Christianity. Constantine himself became, according to his own propaganda, "like an apostle"—settling disputes between quarreling theologians, influencing the election of bishops, summoning church councils. During the fourth century, Christianity gradually began to displace the old pagan cults as the official religion of the empire. Pulpits spread

Christian and pagan cultures were so similar and so mixed in the fourth-century Roman Empire that it is sometimes hard to tell them apart. Here an emperor, having ridden in life in triumph on an elephant, is hoisted skyward by the chariot of the sun, which pagans worshipped as a god and Christian artists used as an image for Christ. Winged spirits ascend with the emperor's soul, through the spheres of heaven, marked by the signs of the zodiac, top right, to the heavenly home of his ancestors. This is one of the last works of art that portrays a Roman emperor in a predominantly pagan setting.

imperial propaganda. The church supplied the state with a ready-made bureaucracy. Millions of subjects of the empire began to go to church—without necessarily embracing, or even understanding, Christian doctrines. More than ever, learned and aristocratic classes, who had previously despised Christianity, blended its teachings with the philosophy of classical antiquity. God became "the divine mind." Christian virtues blended with those of stoicism (see Chapter 6). Traditional Christian pacifism withered as Christians felt obliged to support the empire's wars.

Ezana

The adoption of Christianity at the court of Ethiopia at Axum in the 340s illustrates a similar dilemma for a war leader seeking to appropriate a religion of peace. The inscriptions of King Ezana were bloodthirsty documents, full of the numbers of his conquests and the tally of his captives. As his reign unfolded, they remained bloody but became increasingly high minded, full of the concept of the good of the people and service to the state. The king still waged wars but grew moralistic about justifying them. One adversary "attacked and annihilated one of our caravans, after which we took to the field." The king of neighboring Nubia (see Chapter 4) was guilty of boastfulness, raiding, violation of embassies, refusal to negotiate. "He did not listen to me," Ezana complains, "and uttered curses." The new tone reflects the influence of Christian clergy.

Before the 340s, Ezana described himself as "son of Mahreb"—a war god synonymous with the Greek god Ares in Greek versions of the inscriptions. Suddenly, he dropped the claim and waged war in the name of "Lord of Heaven and Earth" or "the Father, Son and Holy Spirit." His last monument proclaims, "I cannot speak fully of his favors, for my mouth and my spirit cannot fully express all the mercies he has done to me. . . . He has made me the guide of my kingdom through my faith in Christ." He toppled the great stone pillars of Axum or ceased to erect them and began to build churches. Fragments from his sanctuary are still visible in the Old Cathedral of St. Mary of Zion at Axum.

Trdat

To become Christian was to join the growing common culture—at the vertex of a triangle of Christian states, Ethiopia, Rome, Armenia. For Armenia, the evidence is too indistinct to yield a clear picture of what happened. The supposedly contemporary sources exist only in late, contradictory, and probably corrupt versions. A supposed letter King Trdat wrote in the late third century to an anti-Christian Roman emperor declares "loathing for Christians" and a promise to persecute them. His submission to baptism arose, according to the traditional story, in revulsion from the fate of 33 nuns whom he had put to death. The case of Gregory the Illuminator—Trdat's former friend, whom he imprisoned in a pit of snakes—accentuated his remorse. This looks like a theologically crafted tale of a change of heart induced by divine grace. The number of nuns was probably conventional, chosen to represent the Christian Trinity of Father, Son, and Holy Spirit and the supposed years of Jesus' life. The whole story seems loosely modeled on that of the Apostle Paul in the Bible—the persecutor turned converter. The date of Trdat's conversion cannot be fixed more exactly than between 301 and 314. The latter date seems likely, as by then Constantine had begun to favor Christianity, and Trdat favored alignment with Rome against Persia.

Diplomatic Conversions

In the Caucasus Mountains near Armenia, at about the same time, tradition credits an unnamed slave woman (whom later tradition called Nino) with converting the people we now know as the Georgians. Her prayers cured a queen's illness. When the king proposed to shower the slave with rewards, "She despises gold," said the queen. "She feeds on hunger as if it were food itself. The only way we can repay her is to worship divine Christ who cured me thanks to her prayers." The story sounds made up. The invocation of a miracle cure seems contrived to make the new religion attractive. The verifiable fact, however, is that the priests who launched the Georgian state church came, by general agreement among the sources, from Constantine's empire. Christianity was a political option for small states in imperial hinterlands, striving to preserve their independence and playing Persia against Rome. It made sense to associate with Rome, which was the more distant threat.

The Georgian kingdoms of Iberia and Lazica pried themselves free of Persian dominance, partly by opting for Roman support. By the early sixth century, a Roman ambassador to Lazica could hardly restrain his enthusiasm for a people who were "in no way barbarians, long association with the Romans having led them to adopt a civilized and law-abiding way of life." From 522, the kings of Lazica ceased to accept election by the emperors of Persia and chose to be invested by those of Rome. King Ztathius had the Roman emperor's portrait embroidered on his robes. His successor, King Gobazes, had the official rank of usher (an honored post) at the court of Constantinople.

It became normal for religious allegiances to change with political alliances. Poised between Christian and Muslim powers, the rulers of the Khazars (HAH-zahrs)—Turkic pastoralists between the Black Sea and the Caspian, who built up a state that endured for 400 years from the early seventh century—adopted, at different times, Christianity, Islam, and Judaism in their efforts to preserve their independence.

(a)

(b)

The monastery church at Jvari ("the Cross") in Georgia occupies a hilltop where St. Nino, a female evangelist traditionally credited with helping to spread Christianity in Georgia in the fourth century, is said to have paused to pray. A church on the site is documented from the seventh century, but the existing building resembles Western churches of the ninth and tenth centuries (a). Above the entrance, angels brandish a cross from which the "living water" of Christian baptism flows (b).

Buddhist Politics

Buddhist missionaries, like their Christian counterparts, displayed partiality for royal and imperial disciples. In the late first century, the Chinese emperor Ming was supposed to have introduced Buddhism as the result of a vision. This was untrue, but it is evidence of the importance the Buddhist clergy who invented the tale attached to imperial patronage. As we saw in the last chapter, Buddhism became the favorite spiritual resource of usurpers of the Chinese throne who wanted to legitimize their rule and of monarchs who needed a propaganda machine. In Dunhuang paintings, pious emperors preside at debates between rival schools of Buddhism. But however personally committed to Buddhism, or reliant on Buddhist support, no Buddhist emperor ever suspended the traditional rites and sacrifices that Chinese emperors were required to

Chronology: Early Conversions to Christianity

312	Emperor Constantine of Rome
ca. 301–314	King Trdat of Armenia
ca. 325	Georgia (King Mirian and Queen Nana)
340s	King Ezana of Ethiopia

"Indeed, the measure of Buddhism's success is that, until "Westernization" began in the late nineteenth century, it was the only movement of foreign origin ever really to catch on in China."

perform. Only Yang Jian in the sixth century (see Chapter 8)—a skeptic contemptuous of all religion—had the nerve to do that.

So Buddhism could never monopolize the Chinese imperial court. Not only the venerability of the traditional rites, but also the strength of Confucianism and Daoism ensured that. Buddhism also had to contend with Chinese belittlement of anything foreign. Indeed, the measure of Buddhism's success is that, until "Westernization" began in the late nineteenth century, it was the only movement of foreign origin ever really to catch on in China. Sporadic bursts of imperial favor enabled Buddhists to establish an enormous network of monasteries that became magnets of piety for millions of people. The scale of Buddhism's ascent was revealed during one of the spasms of persecution of Buddhism in which emperors occasionally indulged. In the 820s through the 840s, thousands of monasteries were dissolved, and 250,000 monks and nuns were forced back into lay life.

Korea

In the neighboring Korean kingdom of Koguryo, the beginnings of the rise of Buddhism were inseparable from the context of the late fourth century, when barbarian invasions of China enriched Koguryo with refugees. A series of fugitive Chinese monks made themselves indispensable at court and devised ways to reconcile Buddhism with royal responsibilities under the old, indigenous religion. King Kwanggaet'o dedicated one of Korea's first royally endowed temples with the inscription, "Believing in Buddhism, we seek prosperity." King Changsu, who ruled for most of the fifth century and died in 491, is depicted at the tomb of his predecessor at Pyongyang in what is today the capital of North Korea performing Buddhist as well as native rites. The rest of Korea resisted Buddhist intrusions at first, perhaps because of the importance of local religious rites as part of the ceremonial of kingship. The kings of Silla, for instance, derived prestige from their claim to have arisen from a dynasty of holy men. State formation in Korea was essentially a process of extending uniform religious rites to one community after another.

The launch of Buddhism as a royal religion in southern Korea is traditionally ascribed to the conversions of King Song in Paekche and King Pophung of Silla in the 520s or 530s. The bone ranks (nobility) opposed Pophung's choice, but the martyrdom of a young Buddhist official, Ich'adon, awed them. Both the king's wives became Buddhist nuns. Monks, like the chief minister Hyeyong in the mid–550s, became useful state servants. Won'gwang, who returned from China in 602 to head the bureaucracy, adapted dharma for political purposes. Serve your lord with loyalty and "face battle without retreating" became precepts of the faith. Having adapted to one political system in the sixth century, Korean Buddhism did so again, under new political conditions, in the tenth century, when the reform of the Korean administration along Chinese lines filled the bureaucracy with men trained in the study of Confucianism. The scholar-administrator Ch'oe Sungno expressed the ensuing compromise well in 982: "Carrying out the teachings of Buddha is the basis for the cultivation of the self. Carrying out the teachings of Confucius is the source for regulating the state."

Japan

Japan was the scene of the most remarkable working compromise between a new, universal religion and kingly commitment to traditional paganism. The first image of the Buddha in Japan was said to have arrived as a diplomatic gift from Korea in 538. The pious efforts of the Soga clan—immigrants from China—supposedly spread the new religion around the end of the sixth century. Underlying the tale is a political saga. The Soga aimed to replace the ruling imperial dynasty, which claimed descent from the Sun-goddess. The Soga saw Buddhism as the path to power. The traditional "way of the gods"—**Shinto** in Japanese—was the reigning dynasty's special responsibility. The same word in Japanese meant "shrine" and "palace." The word for *government* also meant "religion."

A traditional anecdote captures the true lines of the debate that raged in the mid-sixth century. "All neighboring states to the west already honor Buddha," Soga no Iname pointed out. "Is it right that Japan alone should turn her back on this religion?" But native ministers replied, "The rulers of this country have always conducted seasonal rites in honor of the many heavenly and earthly spirits of land and grain."

The search was on for a synthesis that would harness Buddhism for the state without disturbing the traditional Shinto ideology and magic of the monarchy. Prince Shotoku (574–622), the first great royal patron of Buddhism in Japan, realized the value of the Buddhist clergy as potential servants of the state. He wrote learned commentaries on Buddhist doctrine and founded monasteries. Shotoku saw that the emperor could take on the roles and advantages of a Buddhist patron while adhering to the old Shinto rites. His injunctions include, "The emperor is heaven and his ministers are Earth. . . . So edicts handed down by the emperor must be scrupulously obeyed. If they are not obeyed, ministers will bring ruin on themselves." Endorsed from the court, Buddhism flourished. The Japanese census of 624 counted 816 monks. By 690, 3,363 monks received gifts of cloth from the throne.

A reaction set in. The traditional elite feared Buddhism as a foreign intrusion and a menace to the imperial rites. Early eighth-century law codes banned wandering monks from "speaking falsely about misfortunes or blessings based on mysterious natural phenomena," "deluding the people," and begging without permit. Various measures attempted to prevent monasteries from abusing their tax-exempt status.

The advances of Buddhism, however, were irresistible. A Buddhist scripture warned kings that "if they do not walk in the law, the holy men go away and violent calamities arise." In the 730s, the monk Gembo returned from China with 5,000 volumes of Buddhist scriptures and endeared himself by curing an empress's depression. In 747, 6,563

Prince Shotoku. As regent for the first reigning Japanese empress in the early seventh century, Prince Shotoku, shown here with two of his sons in a Korean painting of nearly two centuries later, used his influence to promote contacts with China, remodel the Japanese government on Chinese lines, and spread Buddhism in Japan.

Chronology: The Introduction of Buddhism in Korea and Japan

Late fourth century	Chinese refugees introduce Buddhism in Koguryo
ca. 520–530	Kings of Paekche and Silla convert to Buddhism
538	First image of Buddha arrives in Japan
574–622	Prince Shotoku, first great royal patron of Buddhism
Seventh century	Rapid expansion of Buddhism in Japan under royal patronage

"No one in Japan, it is often said, was purely Buddhist. The traditional Shinto shrines played a part in the devotions even of monks, as they still do."

monks were ordained at a palace ceremony. As we shall see in the next chapter, emperors found socially useful ways to channel the dynamism of Buddhist devotion. Buddhist rituals originally intended in India to treat snakebites, poison, and disease were used in Japan to protect the state. The outcome was a characteristically Japanese compromise. No one in Japan, it is often said, was purely Buddhist. The traditional Shinto shrines played a part in the devotions even of monks, as they still do. Even Empress Shotoku in the 760s, whose Buddhist devotion was unsurpassed, never tried to tamper with the traditional rites.

Tibet

According to a legend crafted in Tibet about 500 years after the supposed event, a Chinese or Nepalese wife of King Songtsen Gampo brought Buddhism there in the sixth century. The true story was of long, slow monastic colonization. Though Songtsen Gampo probably patronized Buddhist monks and scholars, who frequented his court in the households of the Nepalese and Chinese princesses of his harem, he continued to represent himself as divine.

Even King Trisong Detsen in the second half of the eighth century, whom Buddhists hailed as a model of piety and whom their opponents denounced as a traitor to the traditional royal religion, depicted himself as both the divine defender of the old faith and the enlightened enthusiast of the new. In 792, he presided over a great debate between Indian and Chinese champions on the question of whose traditions better represented the Buddha's doctrine. The issue was decided in favor of the Indian traditional moral disciplines of **Theravada Buddhism**, as it is usually called, by which the soul might advance to Buddhahood by tiny incremental stages of learning and goodness, lifetime after lifetime in the course of reincarnation, rather than the **Mahayana Buddhism**, advocated by Chinese spokesmen, who claimed that the soul could achieve Buddhahood in one lifetime. Mahayana Buddhism, which also took root in Japan, is known as the "greater vehicle" because its proponents believe that it can carry more people to salvation than Theravada Buddhism, the "lesser vehicle," can.

But this debate was premature. Tibet was hardly yet a Buddhist country, nor could one tradition of Buddhism be imposed in the contexts in which Buddhism spread: missionary work and monastery founding; the ebb and flow of armies, who transmitted ideas as the tide shifts pebbles; and the spread of culture, including religion, along the routes of merchant caravans.

By the time of Tibet's treaty with China in 821, Buddhism had made real progress. The treaty invoked Buddhist as well as pagan gods, and after traditional sacrifices and blood-smearing rites, the Buddhists among the treaty's negotiators withdrew for a celebration of their own. King Ralpachen was so devout that he let monks sit on his prodigiously long hair. But a reaction set in at his death in 836, and Buddhism survived in Tibet only precariously into the next century, awaiting renewal by a new wave of monastic colonization. Its main rival was not the old religion but **Bon**. Of the origins of this faith, we know nothing reliable, but it was similar and heavily indebted to Buddhism. The sayings of the great Bon-po sage, Gyerspungs, closely resembled those of Buddhist masters: Existence is like a dream. "Validity is vacuity." Truth must "transcend sounds and terms and words." The main difference lay in the sages' attitude to India. Buddhists acknowledged that their teaching came from there, whereas Bon-pos traced it to a legendary land in the west, and regarded their mythical founder, Shen-rab, as the original Buddha.

Samye monastery. The first Buddhist monastery in Tibet was reputedly founded at Samye in the valley of Lhasa. It illustrates the importance of royal patronage in bringing Buddhism to Tibet. According to legend, King Trisong Detsen in the 770s invited an Indian sage into the kingdom, who consecrated the site of the monastery after a battle with the demons who infested it.

India

Ironically, the effort to combine Buddhism with traditional kingship failed most conspicuously in India itself, the Buddha's homeland. In the sixth century, kingdoms multiplied in India, and kings issued many grants of revenue and property to holy men to found religious establishments, in an effort to gain their support. Kings made relatively few grants, however, to Buddhists. The circumstances of the period—the conflicts with the Huns (see Chapter 8) and the crumbling of political unity—seem to have driven popular piety back to its roots in the worship of local gods, as if the troubles of the time were proof that Buddhism had failed.

Rites and practices associated with the traditions we now call **Hinduism** were taking hold. Indeed, some holy men set out to systematize them as an alternative to Buddhism. The development of the caste system—in which an unchangeable ritual rank, defined at birth, determines everyone's place in society—indicates how Hinduism was spreading. The caste system was not yet fully defined, but according to the description of India between 630 and 645 written by Xuanzang (shoo-en-tzang), the greatest Chinese Buddhist manuscript collector, butchers, fishermen, actors, executioners, and scavengers were ritually unclean and had to live outside city limits. Almost everyone acknowledged the superiority of the highest caste, the priestly Brahmans. The spread of blood sacrifice also shows that Buddhism was in retreat. The Guptas (see Chapter 8) sacrificed horses, in defiance of Buddhist teaching, but protected cows, which Hinduism regards as especially sacred. The first **sati**—the burning to death of a widow on her husband's funeral pyre—was recorded in 510. The Palas dynasty of Bengal in the eighth to the eleventh centuries was the last Buddhist reigning family in India, and their Buddhism, embodied in images of animal-shaped deities sprouting with heads and limbs, seems hardly recognizable as the doctrine of Buddha the founder. Most Indian kings preferred to stake their power on devotion to particular traditional gods rather than on Buddhism.

The Margins of Christendom

In Christendom, the *Constantinian model*, according to which conversion begins with the ruler, prevailed for most of what we think of as the Middle Ages. Almost every conversion of a nation or a people, as related in medieval sources, began with the conversion of a king. There were, of course, some exceptions or possible exceptions. Clovis, the Frankish chief who took over most of Gaul (modern France) in the 480s, gave up his claim to descent from a sea god when he converted to Christianity for the advantage of allegiance to a God who could deliver victory and equip him with administrators who could read and write. But conversion among the Frankish people preceded or accompanied Clovis's. In the traditional story, the Franks responded directly to the appeal of Bishop Remigius, not to any initiative by the king. In Iceland, where supposedly "democratic" decision making is generally supposed to have prevailed, the collective adoption of Christianity was resolved in the assembly of the people in 1000, but the lay speaker who presided over the assembly, Thorgeirr Thorkelsson, withdrew to meditate or commune with the gods for a day and a night before lending his decisive influence to the debate. Of course, Christianity was also spread in undocumented or barely documented ways: movements of population, journeys of merchants and envoys. But missionary strategy remained focused on leaders as means of mobilizing peoples.

In northern and Eastern Europe, a great sequence of royal conversions in the late tenth and early eleventh centuries more or less established the frontier of Christendom, beginning with Harold Bluetooth in the 960s in Denmark and Mieszko of Poland in 966. In Norway, an exchange of stories and attributes in the earliest chronicles between St. Olaf and his predecessor, Olaf Tryggvason has confused the outline of events, but it is clear that a year or two after Tryggvason's confirmation as a Christian in England in 995, a popular assembly in Norway endorsed the new religion. In Sweden Olof Skötkunung of the Svear began minting coins with Christian symbols on them before 1000. His reception as king established an uninterrupted sequence of Christian rulers. The coronation of Stephen of Hungary in 1001 settled the Christian destiny of that country.

Vladimir and the Rus

No case was more significant for the future than that of Vladimir, ruler of Kiev in what is today Ukraine, in 987–988, for his adherence ensured that Christianity would be privileged among the eastern Slavs—including the Russians, who became Europe's most numerous Slav community. Like the culture of his country, formed by the interaction of native Slavs with Scandinavian migrants who spread along the valley of the river Volga, Vladimir was the descendant of Scandinavians as well as Slavs, pagans on both sides (see Chapter 10). Like many great saints, he sinned with gusto. His harem was said to contain over 800 girls. Russians trace proverbs in praise of drunkenness to his invention. He left a reputation, in the words of a German chronicler, as "a cruel man and a fornicator on a huge scale."

Among his people, paganism was entrenched by the psychological power of terror. The horror of a human sacrifice among the Rus profoundly impressed the caliph's ambassador, Ibn Fadlan, who witnessed it in 969. The slave girl chosen to die with her master sang songs of farewell over her last cups of liquor before

The Jelling Stone. The Norse King Harold Bluetooth adopted Christianity in 965 and had commemorative stones carved with Christian symbols in memory of his parents, to atone for their paganism. The detail here shows the Crucifixion. "This Harold," claims the inscription on the stones, "conquered all Denmark and Norway and turned the Danes to Christianity."

ritually copulating with her executioners. An old woman called the Angel of Death then wound a cord around her neck and handed the slack to men standing on either side. Warriors beat their shields to drown the victim's screams. While the cord was tightened, the Angel of Death plunged a dagger repeatedly in and out of the girl's breast. The funeral pyre, built on a ship, was then lighted, and the fire fed until it burned to ashes. "After this, on the spot where the ship had lain, when they dragged it from the river, they built something that looked like a round mound. In the middle of it, they set up a big post of birch wood, on which they wrote the name of the dead man and of the king of the Rus. Then they went away."

Chronology: The Spread of Christianity	
ca. 500	Clovis, king of the Franks, converts to Christianity
960	Harold Bluetooth of Denmark converts
966	Conversion of King Mieszko of Poland
ca. 988	Vladmir of Kiev adopts Orthodox Christianity
ca. 997	Norway and Sweden convert to Christianity
1000	Iceland converts to Christianity
1001	Coronation of Stephen of Hungary as a Christian monarch

To replace this religion, and break the power of its priests, Vladimir needed something equally powerful. The traditional story of his emissaries' quest for a perfect religion led first to the Muslim Bulgars, who "bow down and sit, look hither and thither like men possessed, but there is no joy in them, only sorrow and a dreadful stench. Their religion is not good. Then we went to the Germans, and we saw them celebrating many services in their churches, but we saw no beauty there. Then we went to the Greeks, and they led us to the place where they worship their God [the church of Hagia Sophia that Justinian had built in Constantinople]; and we knew not whether we were in heaven or on Earth; for on Earth there is no such vision or beauty and we do not know how to describe it. We only know that there God dwells among men."

In fact, Vladimir's decision in favor of Orthodox Christianity owed more to politics than aesthetics. Conversion was the price he paid for the hand of a Byzantine princess whom he demanded with threats. (The Russians had tried to attack Constantinople several times in the ninth and tenth centuries.) Imperial Byzantine princesses were not normally permitted to marry foreign suitors, for, according to the tenth-century emperor, Constantine VII, "just as each animal mates with its own species, so it is right that each nation should also marry and cohabit not with those of other race and tongue but of the same tribe and speech." Put more bluntly, his point was that marriages between imperial princesses and foreign rulers diminished the sacred, divinely sanctioned dignity of the Byzantine monarchy and opened the way for foreign rulers to claim the Byzantine throne. Vladimir solemnly evicted the occupants of his sacred grove of idols. The golden-haired, silver-moustached thunder god, Perun, was buffeted, insulted, and dragged through the dust before being flung in a muddy river. Vladimir imposed Christianity by violence, while making it more acceptable and perhaps more intelligible by ordering that Christian liturgy be conducted in the Slavonic language the Rus spoke, rather than in Greek.

Islam and the Turks

The magnetism Christianity exerted on the frontiers of Christendom was paralleled in the Islamic world. Around the middle of the tenth century, the Karakhanids (kah-rah-HAHN-ihds) became the first Turkic people to subscribe to Islam—apparently as a result of the favorable impression they derived from raiding Islamic territory. This was an event pregnant with consequences for the future, because the Turks would bring to the Islamic world a vital infusion of manpower and expertise in war—"the army of God, whom I have installed in the East," according to a legendary saying of the Prophet. Islam's attraction for them is easier to express than explain. The memories they conserved of the time of their paganism reveal warlike values. Boys were not named until they had "lopped off heads in battle." A hero was judged by the number of times he could plait his moustache behind his head. Even women were war trained and "made the enemy vomit blood." Yet some of their leaders continued to see attractions or advantages in Islam. In 962, Altigin (AHL-tee-geen), a Turk who had adopted Islam while serving as a slave in Persia, founded at Ghazni in Afghanistan a Muslim state that was to exert great influence in the future. In about 985, a Turkic chief, Seljuk (SEHL-jook), who dreamed of "ejaculating fire in all directions" and conquering the world, ruled a small state, cobbled together by conquest, in Central Asia. His decision to become a Muslim was of enormous significance, as his descendants supplied some of the Islamic world's most effective frontiersmen.

TRICKLE DOWN: CHRISTIANIZATION AND ISLAMIZATION

When they converted rulers and conquered elites, religions trickled down to the rest of society. For Christians, for example, Constantine's patronage was an extraordinary windfall. At the time, despite the gradual—and, in some eastern provinces, formidable—accumulation of converts among the socially respectable and intellectual, Christianity had remained essentially one of many eastern cults popular in the Roman Empire. Christianity still bore the marks of its origins as a Jewish heresy, founded by a rabbi whose birth and death were, in the world's eyes, equally disreputable, and whom many saw as just another failed messiah or prophet. Its scriptures were, by the sophisticated standards of the Greek schools of rhetoric and philosophy, so badly written as to embarrass all educated Christians.

Now, after the conversion of Constantine, according to the fourth-century Christian historian Eusebius, who had chronicled the persecutions of previous reigns, "It felt as if we were imagining a picture of the kingdom of Christ and that what was happening was no reality but a dream." There were subsidies for the Church, exemptions from fiscal and military obligations for the clergy, jobs in the state service for Christians, and the assurance, from the emperor's own hand, that the worship of Christians benefited the empire.

The rise of the Church from persecution to predominance was completed in 395, when the emperor Theodosius proclaimed Christianity the official religion of the Roman Empire and reduced pagan traditions to the underprivileged status formerly imposed on Christians. From the late fourth century onward, nobility and sanctity converged. So many young aristocrats became monks that monasteries came to resemble "noblemen's clubs." Christianity guaranteed the best opportunities for promotion in the army and bureaucracy and for personal enrichment. Those who accepted it subscribed to a cultural package associated with success. Ethiopian sources are too meager for certainty, but in Armenia, too, the continuing progress of Christianity depended, at least until the Arab conquest in the eighth century, on royal and aristocratic initiatives.

To some extent, the same considerations applied within the Islamic world. Because the Muslim conquests were vast, and the conquerors relatively few in number, Muslim rulers could not exclude non-Muslims from positions of authority. The caliph Umar I expelled non-Muslims from Arabia in 635, but without the services of Christians and Jews in the rest of the Middle East, or of Zoroastrians in

"Christianity guaranteed the best opportunities for promotion in the army and bureaucracy and for personal enrichment. Those who accepted it subscribed to a cultural package associated with success."

Making Connections | FACTORS AIDING THE SPREAD OF UNIVERSAL RELIGIONS

RELIGION	WAR	TRADE	MISSIONARIES	ELITES
Buddhism	Early rulers Asoka, Kaniska, Anuruddha invoke "dharma" (teachings of Buddha) in violent conquests	Silk Roads fundamental to spreading Buddhism via traveling monks and monasteries housing merchants, pilgrims	Missionaries/pilgrims important—Xuanzang (China); conversion of kings a primary means of accelerating social acceptance	Emperor Ming (China); King Song (Korea); Prince Shotoko (Japan); Trisong Detsen (Tibet)
Christianity	Charlemagne, other rulers (Alfred the Great of England, Olaf of Norway) justify war, conquest by forcible conversion	Few long-distance Christian traders along Eurasian trade routes; Nestorians a thin and patchy presence along Silk Roads	Converting kings and elite groups a fundamental strategy	Constantine (Roman Empire); Ezana (Ethiopia); Trdat (Armenia); Vladimir (Kiev, Russia)
Islam	Jihad justifies both interior struggle and warfare against polytheists, idolaters, apostates; continual warfare against non-Islamic neighboring states	Effectively spread via land and sea routes across Africa. Dispersal of Muslim–merchant communities throughout south and southeast Asia	Traveling merchants; conversion encouraged by specific social/political policies favoring Muslims (beneficial tax system, legal codes)	Especially important in Turkic areas (Central Asia): tenth-century leaders Altigin, Seljuk

Persia, the administrations of the eighth- and ninth-century caliphates would have been understaffed. Still, by favoring Muslims, discriminating against non-Muslims, and insisting on the exclusive use of Arabic as the language of administration, rulers created a climate of prejudice in favor of Islam among elites. The caliph Abd al-Malik (ahbd al-MA-lihk) effectively proclaimed Islam's superiority to Christianity by building the Dome of the Rock and the al-Aqsa (ahl-AHK-sah) mosque in Jerusalem in the late seventh century to dwarf the Church of the Holy Sepulchre built on the site where Jesus had supposedly been buried. The new Islamic buildings symbolized the sacredness to Islam of what had been only a Christian and Jewish holy city—indeed, *the* holy city, the reputed center of the world. Even mild persecution could exert considerable pressure. The caliph Umar II (r. 717–720) tried to exclude Christians and Jews from public offices. He also forbade them to build places of worship or lift their voices in prayer. They had to wear distinctive clothing and were forbidden saddles for their horses. If a Muslim killed a Christian, his penalty was only a fine. Christians could not give valid testimony against Muslims in legal cases. Later caliphs sporadically renewed persecution. In 807, Caliph Harun al-Rashid (hah-ROON ahr-rah-SHEED) ordered all churches on the frontiers of his empire demolished and reenforced the clothing laws against Christians. In the 850s, the caliph al-Mutawakkil (ahl-moo-tah-WAH-keel) ordered that Christian and Jewish graves should be level with the ground. Converts to Islam, on the other hand, could rapidly ascend through the ranks of society. The leader of the coup that dethroned the Umayyads (oo-MEYE-yadz), the first caliphal dynasty, in

The Dome of the Rock in Jerusalem marks the spot where, according to Muslim tradition, the Prophet Muhammad ascended to paradise. The Caliph Abd al-Malik had it built in the late seventh century, marking as sacred to Islam a city that Christians and Jews already revered. The splendor and scale of the building out-dazzled and dwarfed the nearby Church of the Holy Sepulchre and the remains of the last Jewish temple.

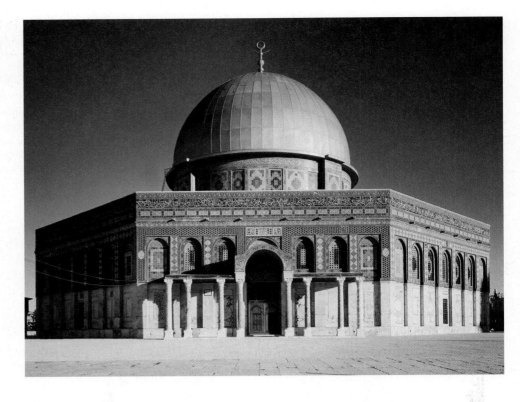

"Partly because Islam tolerated some other religions, the conquered societies were slow to become Islamized. Indeed, substantial Christian minorities have survived in Egypt, Iraq, Syria, and, especially, Lebanon to this day."

750, was a freed slave, and not even an Arab by birth, but a Persian. The second caliph of the next dynasty, the Abbasids, was the son of a Berber slave woman from North Africa.

For most Christian and Jewish subjects of Islamic states, the tax system—which exempted Muslims from most charges—was the focus of discrimination. Umar II declared that he would be happy to see Islam spread and revenues diminish, even if it meant he had to till the soil with his own hands. Indeed, many people proclaimed themselves Muslims simply to take advantage of reduced tax rates, until Al-Hajjaj, the brutal governor of Iraq in the 690s and early 700s, reimposed the old tax levels on supposedly phoney converts.

Partly because Islam tolerated some other religions, the conquered societies were slow to become Islamized. Indeed, substantial Christian minorities have survived in Egypt, Iraq, Syria, and, especially, Lebanon to this day. Some historians have tried to measure the rate of acceptance of Islam by calculating the number of people who gave their children Muslim-sounding names. This method suggested to Richard W. Bulliet, its greatest exponent, that only 2.5 percent of the population of Iran were converted to Islam in the seventh century. Not until the early ninth century was the majority of the population Muslim. The remainder was Islamized during the ninth and tenth centuries. In most places, the significance of name giving is broadly cultural, rather than specifically religious. But the names people were given or adopted do help to demonstrate roughly the rate at which Islam became the dominant influence on the culture of Iran. Though—strictly speaking—it tells us nothing about the personal religion or depth of conviction of the individuals who bestowed or received Islamic names, the evidence of personal names is consistent with the view that, once a new religion commands the allegiance of the elite, the rest of society can adopt the same religion without having their conversion significantly change their lives.

RELIGIOUS LIVES: THE WORLD OF MONKS AND NUNS

In Buddhism and Christianity, monasticism grew as these religions spread and, in turn, became a major cause of their continuing success.

Christian Monasticism

As a result of the triumph of Christianity as an elite religion, the Church became the great upholder of Roman standards of learning, art, and government. This is not surprising among aristocratic bishops, whose family traditions were of power. In the sixth century, Pope Gregory the Great organized the defense of Rome against the Lombards (see Chapter 8), launched missions of spiritual reconquest to parts of Western Europe, such as England, that had become paganized, and reimposed on the western empire a kind of unity by the sheer range of his correspondence. In Visigothic Spain, Isidore of Seville (ca. 560–636) passed the learning of classical Greece and Rome on to future generations in the form of an encyclopedia. Martin of Braga dedicated to a Germanic king a book about virtue, based on a lost Roman work.

It was harder to domesticate the church's own barbarians—the antisocial ascetics and hermits, whose response to the problems of the world was to withdraw from them or rail at them from their caves. The monastic movement made their lives "regular," concentrating them in houses of work, study, and prayer to benefit society as a whole. There is no scholarly consensus on the origins of monasticism. Christians perhaps got it from Buddhists, or maybe it arose independently in various cultures as hermits and holy men banded together for mutual support. The earliest recorded Christian monastic communities emerged in Egypt in the second century, among ascetics seeking to imitate Jesus' period of self-exile in the desert. Of the many rules of life for monks written in the following centuries, the most influential rule in the western church was that of Benedict of Nursia.

The only certain date in Benedict's life is 542, when the Ostrogothic king Totila visited him at his monastery of Monte Cassino in southern Italy. Benedict started as a typical, obsessive ascetic, in a cave, where food was lowered to him while he disciplined the lusts of the flesh in a convenient thornbush. In one of the earliest surviving illustrations of his life, the cave mouth is jagged and bloody. When he established his own community, he rededicated the pagan shrine of the Roman god Jupiter on the spot to St. Martin, the patron of poverty, who gave half his cloak to a beggar. The nearby pagan shrine of Apollo became the chapel of John the Baptist, the biblical voice crying in the wilderness. These rededications disclose Benedict's program: the practice of charity in refuge from the world.

Benedict's book of rules for monks borrowed freely from others. Most of it was filtered out of a rambling earlier rule. But its superiority and universality were recognized almost at once, and there has hardly been a monastic movement or revival in the West since then that has not been based on or deeply influenced by it. Its animating principles are the quest for salvation in common and the subordination of all individual willfulness. Benedict banned extremes of mortification in favor of steady spiritual progress, manual labor, study, and prayer in private and in common. Pope Gregory the Great showed how well he had interpreted Benedict's spirit when he dictated the last line of his biography of Benedict: "I must stop talking

St. Catherine's Monastery, Sinai. For almost 1,800 years, Christian monks have sought the desert, imitating Jesus and John the Baptist, who, the Bible says, both withdrew into the wilderness to think and pray. St. Catherine's monastery in Sinai in Egypt is in an oasis in a desert gorge, nearly 5,000 feet deep. Its remoteness protected it for centuries and helped to keep its collection of early Christian writings intact.

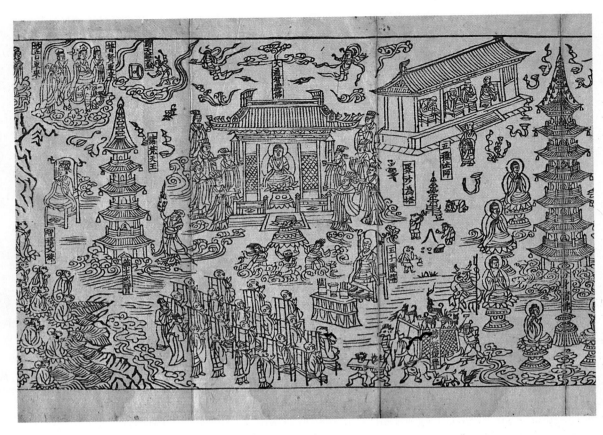

The Lotus Sutra. Composed between the first century B.C.E. and the second century C.E., the Lotus Sutra is the most important text of Mahayana Buddhism. The detail from this printed version, from around 1000 C.E., shows the Western Paradise of the Amitabha Buddha and his court of Bodhisattvas.

now for a while so that by silence I may repair my strength and be able to narrate the miracles of others." Benedict had sought a way to imitate paradise here on Earth. He had found a means to make civilization survive, for monastic study also embraced the learning of ancient Greece and Rome. Monasteries became centers for colonizing wasteland and wilderness. Monks sought "desert" frontiers to build new monasteries, and lay people followed them.

Buddhist Monks

Monasticism was even more important in Buddhism than in Christianity, since, in principle, most of the Buddhist clergy were subject to monastic discipline. In practice, however, Buddhist monasteries performed particular functions, especially in transmitting learning, that made their contributions similar to those of monasteries in Christendom. The 50,000 ancient manuscripts preserved in the library cave of Dunhuang—a precious time capsule, sealed for 800 years in the tenth century—are a measure of the importance of scholarship in Buddhist monasteries. The business of retrieving, translating, editing, and purifying the best written evidence of the Buddha's teachings turned the monks responsible for it into giants and heroes of learning. The first Chinese to be ordained as a Buddhist priest, for instance, in about 250, was Zhu Shixing (joo she-shing). He was nearly 80 years old when he made a pilgrimage to India to procure a manuscript of the Buddha. Exhausted by the journey, he handed it to his disciples to carry to China before he died. Kumarajiva, translator into Chinese of the most famous of Buddhist scriptures, the **Lotus Sutra**, in the early fifth century, was said to be able to memorize 30,000 words a day. As in Christendom, Buddhist monastic libraries diversified into secular learning, imaginative literature, and administrative and historical records of life way beyond the monastery walls. They were centers of lay life, too, hosting reading clubs for believers, including groups of women, who would pay fines—such as a jug of wine or bowl of cereal—for failure to attend meetings. And monasteries functioned as objects of pilgrimage, inns for travelers, and granaries to store food against hard times.

Chronology: Early Monasticism	
ca. 250	Zhu Shixing is the first Chinese to be ordained Buddhist priest
Second century	Earliest Christian monastic communities (Egypt)
Sixth century	Life of Saint Benedict
Seventh century	Abbess Hilda rules important religious establishments
Late eighth century	Rabia al-Adawiyya, Islamic Sufi mystic

Sufism

Strictly speaking, nothing like monasticism should exist in Islam. The Quran warned against the asceticism of Christian monks, which Muhammad evidently regarded as blasphemous. But Christian influence was not easy to filter out of early Islam. In the early eighth century, Hasan al-Basri quoted Jesus to support his view that asceticism is God's "training ground that his servants might learn to run to him." He advocated fasting and meditation to induce a mystical sense of identity with God. When, toward the end of the same century, the female mystic, Rabia al-Adawiyya, experienced a vision of Muhammad, the prophet asked her if she loved him. "My love of God has so possessed me," she replied, "that no space is left for loving or hating any but him." Groups of devotees who increasingly organized themselves into orders and sometimes founded houses of common life, or, at least,

Making Connections | THE RELIGIOUS LIFE

RELIGION	EXAMPLES OF RELIGIOUS COMMUNITIES	MONASTERY FUNCTIONS/ACTIVITIES
Christianity	Egyptian monasteries, second century; Benedictine monasteries, Italy and Europe, sixth century onward	Scholarly (preservation, translation of ancient manuscripts); cultural (laypeople followed monks in reclaiming desert regions); religious (Benedict's widely followed program focused on steady spiritual progress, manual labor, study, and prayer)
Buddhism	Silk Road monasteries (ca. 200–800)	Scholarly (transmission of learning; translation and preservation of texts); secular and religious education, centers of lay life (reading groups, pilgrimage sites, inns for travelers, and granaries for food storage)
Islam	Sufi monasteries, Middle East (ninth century and after)	Mystical orders focusing on intense spiritual practices (dancing, prayer, study) organized into brotherhoods, sisterhoods.

schools in which they trained in mystical techniques cultivated the tradition these thinkers established. Though fellow Muslims often suspected these **Sufis** of being heretical, Sufism supplied Islam with some of its supplest thinkers and most dedicated and successful missionaries.

Religious Women

In Christianity, Buddhism, and the Islamic world, women acquired new roles, inside the home as guardians of religious tradition for their children, and outside the home as members of religious orders, seeking sanctity in common with other women. Nuns played the same role as monks in prayer and scholarship. In some places, both sexes shared the same houses of religion, often under female leadership. At Whitby in seventh-century England, the formidable Abbess Hilda ruled one of the largest religious establishments of the day, with one of the highest reputations for learning. Nunneries played an important part in Buddhist life in China and Japan, often serving as nurseries and places of education for women. The empresses Shotoku of Japan (see Chapter 10) and Wu of China (see Chapter 8) were nuns before their ascent to power. In the Buddhist world, indeed, the nun's vocation was often a stage before returning to secular life, often in households where husbands had several wives and concubines. In Islam, which also allowed men to have up to four wives, there was relatively little spare woman power. So female monasticism never developed, and female Sufis—though often individually influential—were rare. Only exceptionally strong-minded women like Rabia al-Adawiyya could pursue their vocations in a life of renunciation of marriage.

Buddhist nun. In this painting of 910 from the Buddhist shrines at Dunhuang, the learned nun Yanhui and her brother, an imperial Chinese chamberlain, offer lotus flowers and incense to Avalokitesvara, the Buddhist personification of compassion, "in the hope," says the inscription, "that the empire may be peaceful and that the wheel of the law may continually turn therein."
© The Trustees of the British Museum

In Perspective
The Triumphs of the Potential World Religions

The story of this chapter has been of cultural change rather than religious conversion. Some cases of societies that Christianity, Islam, and Buddhism recruited happened in conditions similar to those pinpointed for individual conversions by psychological research. Violence, mass migration, enforced refugeeism, pestilence, famine, natural disaster, "culture shock," and demographic collapse constitute, on a large scale, influences comparable to the disturbing, dislocating events that often precede individual conversion. Yet, when we monitor the public progress of Christianity, Islam, and Buddhism, we glimpse, at best, shadows of individual religious experience. Instead, we see shrines multiplying; congregations growing; influence deepening on laws, rites, customs, and the arts.

By around 1000, all three religions had demonstrated their adaptability to different cultures and climates (see Map 9.2). Buddhism had big followings in China, Japan, Tibet, and Southeast Asia and had spread into Central Asia along the Silk Roads. Christianity had a near monopoly in Western Europe and was spreading east and north into Scandinavia and the Slav lands, while retaining the allegiance of communities scattered through Asia. Islam, dominant in Southwest Asia and

The Kaaba. Promoters of new religions often had to reconsecrate pagan sites—it was easier to do that than to persuade worshippers to abandon them. Muhammad, for instance, made pilgrimage to the black rock housed in a building known as the Kaaba in Mecca compulsory for Muslims. As the picture shows, tens of thousands of pilgrims circle the site each year at the beginning of a series of annual rituals called the hajj. But the rock had already been a place of pagan pilgrimage in Arabia, and a shrine of many gods, for generations, perhaps centuries, before Muhammad's time.

North Africa, spread by conquest, conversion, and migration among Turkic peoples and around the trade routes of the Indian Ocean and the Sahara. Among them, the three religions seemed to have carved up the world known to Ibn Wahab, whom we encountered at the start of this chapter discussing religion with the Chinese emperor. The bases from which all three religions would expand further, especially in the sixteenth and seventeenth centuries (see Chapter 18), to encompass even more of the world, had been laid.

Their competitive advantages with the religions they displaced were already evident. From an archaeological perspective, the decline of the old religions is as noticeable as the progress of the new. Pagan groves and temples became the sites of churches and Islamic and Buddhist shrines. Local deities reemerged as saints. Excavations at the shrine of the Irish saint, Gobnet, for instance, have yielded 130 anvils dedicated to the smith god, Goibhnin. In Scotland, the pagan goddess Brigid, associated with childbirth, became St. Bride. In the Islamic world, the sacred sites of paganism blended into the new religious landscape. The holiest site of Islam, the black stone of the **Kaaba** in Mecca, where Muslims have to perform pilgrimage at least once in their lifetimes if possible, was a pagan shrine in the time of Muhammad, housing 360 deities. Muslims still perform the same rites—kissing the sacred stone, running the course of the sacred stream that flows nearby—as their pagan predecessors did. Buddhists had no difficulty incorporating local gods into the vast

Scale varies with perspective

4,444 km
(2,762 miles)

3,867 km
(6,228 miles)

ICELAND

SCOTLAND   NORWAY
                        SWEDEN

IRELAND   Whitby   DENMARK   RUS

ATLANTIC   ENGLAND   Baltic Sea
OCEAN   Saxons   POLAND
                Rhine GERMANY   Slavs
                                            Kiev
            FRANKISH
            KINGDOM   UKRAINE
                        Alps Po   HUNGARY
    Braga   Khazars
                    ITALY   Dneiper   Volga
                        Nursia   Danube
    Seville   Rome   Caucasus
                    Monte Cassino   Black Sea   GEORGIA
                              Balkans   Constantinople   ARMENIA
                        GREECE
            Sicily   to Central Asia

North Africa   Mediterranean Sea   SYRIA   Baghdad
                                            Jerusalem   IRAQ
                        Alexandria   Muslim ruled
                              EGYPT   by 750 C.E.
                                                    Arabian
                                      Red Sea   Peninsula
                                      Nile
                                    ETHIOPIA   Mecca

MAP 9.2

The Christian World, ca.1000 C.E.

- Catholic Christianity
- Orthodox Christianity
- Christian churches believing Jesus to be wholly divine (Monophysite)
- Nestorian Christianity
- area with significant Christian minorities today

→ missions
✝ important church or monastery
Saxons people

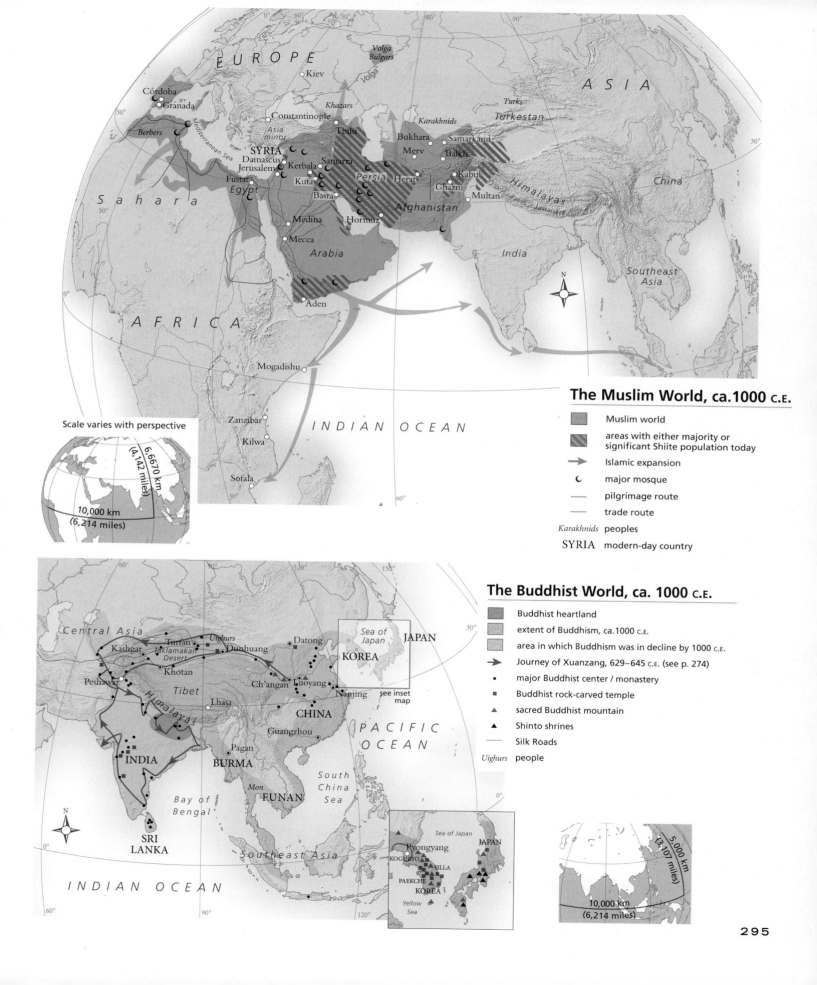

The Muslim World, ca.1000 C.E.

- Muslim world
- areas with either majority or significant Shiite population today
- → Islamic expansion
- ☾ major mosque
- ── pilgrimage route
- ── trade route
- *Karakhnids* peoples
- SYRIA modern-day country

Scale varies with perspective

6,6670 km (4,142 miles)
10,000 km (6,214 miles)

Map labels (upper map):

EUROPE
ASIA
Córdoba
Granada
Berbers
Kiev
Volga Bulgars
Volga
Khazars
Turks
Turkestan
Constantinople
Tbilsi
Bukhara
Samarkand
Karakhnids
SYRIA
Damascus
Jerusalem
Fustat
Egypt
Asia minor
Kerbala
Kufa
Samarra
Basra
Merv
Balkh
Persia
Herat
Kabul
Ghazni
Multan
Himalayas
China
Mediterranean Sea
Sahara
Medina
Mecca
Arabia
Hormuz
Afghanistan
India
Southeast Asia
AFRICA
Aden
Mogadishu
Zanzibar
Kilwa
Sofala
INDIAN OCEAN

The Buddhist World, ca. 1000 C.E.

- Buddhist heartland
- extent of Buddhism, ca.1000 C.E.
- area in which Buddhism was in decline by 1000 C.E.
- → Journey of Xuanzang, 629–645 C.E. (see p. 274)
- • major Buddhist center / monastery
- ■ Buddhist rock-carved temple
- ▲ sacred Buddhist mountain
- ▲ Shinto shrines
- ── Silk Roads
- *Uighurs* people

Map labels (lower map):

Central Asia
Kashgar
Turfan
Uighurs
Taklamakan Desert
Dunhuang
Datong
Sea of Japan
JAPAN
KOREA
see inset map
Khotan
Peshawar
Tibet
Ch'angan
Luoyang
Nanjing
Himalayas
Lhasa
CHINA
PACIFIC OCEAN
Guangzhou
INDIA
Pagan
BURMA
Mon
FUNAN
South China Sea
Bay of Bengal
SRI LANKA
Southeast Asia
INDIAN OCEAN

Inset (Korea/Japan):

Sea of Japan
Pyongyang
KOGURYO
SILLA
PAEKCHE
KOREA
JAPAN
Yellow Sea

5,000 km (3,107 miles)
10,000 km (6,214 miles)

Chronology

Second century	Earliest Christian monastic communities (Egypt)
ca. 250	Zhu Shixing becomes first Chinese to be ordained as Buddhist priest
ca. 314	King Trdat of Armenia converts to Christianity
ca. 340	King Ezana of Ethiopia converts to Christianity
366	Founding of Dunhuang monastery, western China
395	Proclamation of Christianity as official religion of Roman Empire
ca. 520	Conversion of kings of Paekche and Silla to Buddhism
538	First image of Buddha arrives in Japan
Sixth century	Life of Benedict of Nursia
Seventh and eighth centuries	Rapid expansion of Islam; spread of Buddhism in Tibet
Ninth century	Seaborne Muslim pilgrims begin to arrive in Mecca
ca. 988	Vladimir of Kiev converts to Orthodox Christianity

(All dates are C.E.)

"Even as they changed the societies in which they triumphed, the new religions changed in their turn, compromising with vested interests, modifying their messages to suit mighty patrons, serving the needs of warriors and kings, even becoming organs of the state, instruments of government, and means of training bureaucrats and communicating with subjects."

Buddhist pantheon, or sanctifying local shrines with relics of Buddhas.

This flexibility and adaptability made Christianity, Islam, and Buddhism suitable for projection around the world. These religions could combine local with universal appeal. This does not explain, of course, why other religions failed in this respect, or never made the attempt. The blend, which we now call Hinduism, of local Indian religions with the universally applicable philosophy of the Vedas (see Chapter 3) spread throughout India and parts of Southeast Asia, but no farther. Similarly, Daoism never reached beyond China. Nor, until migrants carried it to small colonies abroad, did Zoroastrianism penetrate beyond Southwest Asia, where it struggled to compete with Islam. Traditional paganism, Manichaeanism, and the many cults that came and went, leaving little trace in the record, withered in the face of Christian, Muslim, or Buddhist competition. Some religions, such as Bon in Tibet, Shinto in Japan, and, as far as we know, the religions of sub-Saharan Africa, had no universal aspirations and were designed only for their traditional followers. To judge from later evidence, there was a good deal of exchange between the local and regional religions of Mesoamerica. Though expressed in different languages and called by different names, the divine attributes personified in the arts of the peoples of what we now think of as Mexico and Central America were highly similar, or, at least, showed considerable overlaps, from the twelfth century to the sixteenth. We cannot say how much farther they might have spread had Christianity, arriving in the 1500s, not transformed the religious profile of the region. In the Americas, in sub-Saharan Africa, and in regions of which we know even less, such as Australia and the Pacific, the same reasons that inhibited the spread of other forms of culture also tended to limit the communicability of religions. There were no great, long-range avenues of communication, such as the Silk Roads and the monsoonal ocean. The kind of competition that Islam, Christianity, and Buddhism generated never took effect.

Even as they changed the societies in which they triumphed, the new religions changed in their turn, compromising with vested interests, modifying their messages to suit mighty patrons, serving the needs of warriors and kings, even becoming organs of the state, instruments of government, and means of training bureaucrats and communicating with subjects. A further consequence of expansion was that different traditions within each of the religions lost patience or touch with each other. Christians in different parts of the world adopted different theologies. In Ethiopia, for instance, the church believed that Jesus was wholly divine, with no distinctly human person. The Nestorian Christian communities of the Silk Roads preached the opposite doctrine: that the human Jesus was wholly human, leaving his divine nature in heaven. Theological differences gradually drove Christians in Europe apart. After 792, most congregations in Western Europe followed the pope in modifying the creed, the basic statement of Christian belief, to make the Holy Spirit "proceed" from "the Father and the Son" rather than "the Father" alone. Most churches in eastern, Byzantine Europe denounced—and still denounce—the new wording as heresy. Different Islamic states subscribed variously to Shiism and Sunnism (see Chapter 8) and to different interpretations of Islamic law. In Buddhism divisions between followers of the Theravada and Mahayana traditions were sometimes just as bitter, as rival sects multiplied.

Although all these religions had started by appealing to people of modest or marginal social position, they "took off" by converting rulers and elites. In any case of mass adhesion to a new religion, relatively few individuals experience personal conversion. Most become adherents by attraction, in imitation of converted leaders; or by compulsion, when rulers or conquerors impose the new religion by force; or by default, as the old religion withers; or by birth, as subsequent generations join a community more or less educated in the new religious self-description. More important for changing the religious profile of a whole society than promoting the new religion is banning or underprivileging the old one.

Ultimately, elites supported new religions—spiritual merits apart—because they saw advantages in doing so. The support of the church, for instance, was expensive for rulers and aristocrats. But it was worth it because it meant that God and his angels and saints became one's allies and friends. We can measure the value a typical royal convert got from the deal in the weight of gold and jewels in the votive crown that the seventh-century Spanish Visigothic king Reccesvinth hung in the sanctuary of his royal church. In return for such rich gifts, matched by comparable generosity in land, he got the prayers of the priests and monks, the services of a clerical bureaucracy, and the miraculous power of the relics of an army of martyrs. There was also a hidden advantage that no ruler could have banked on and that the next chapter must disclose. In the last three centuries of the first millennium, Islam, Buddhism, and, to a lesser extent, Christianity played vital and spectacular roles in new forms of environmental management.

Crown of Reccesvinth. Even by the high standards of the jewel work of Germanic invaders of the Roman Empire, Visigothic goldsmiths were outstanding. Crowns like this one from Spain were made not to be worn but to hang over the altars of the churches as offerings from pious kings. The fringe of gold filigree, pearls, and crystals spells the name of the donor, King Reccesvinth (d. 672), although the initial R is lost.

Making Connections | COMPARING THE WORLD RELIGIONS

	CHRISTIANITY	ISLAM	BUDDHISM
Core beliefs	Jesus of Nazareth is the Son of God and the Savior of humankind	There is no God but Allah and Muhammad is His Prophet	The Four Noble Truths: • Suffering is always present in life • Desire is the cause of suffering • Freedom from suffering can be achieved through nirvana (perfect peace and bliss) • The Eightfold Path leads to nirvana
Sacred texts	Bible (Old and New Testaments)	Quran	The *Tripitaka*, various Sutras
Core practices/ rites	Baptism, holy Eucharist	The "five pillars" of Islam: • bearing witness • praying five times a day • giving alms • abstinence and fasting during holy month of Ramadan • pilgrimage to Mecca during one's lifetime	The Eightfold Path: • right view • right intention • right speech • right action • right livelihood • right effort • right mindfulness • right concentration
Major traditions	Catholicism, Protestantism, Eastern Orthodox	Sunni, Shia	Mahayana, Theravada

PROBLEMS AND PARALLELS

1. What were the four chief ways in which world religions were spread? Why were merchants more important in the spread of Islam and Buddhism than of Christianity?

2. What advantages did Buddhism, Christianity, and Islam enjoy over older religions?

3. How did rulers and elites use religion to consolidate and justify their power and control over societies? Why was the conversion of Vladimir of the Rus to Orthodox Christianity so important? What was the relationship between Buddhism and Confucianism in China?

4. Why is Japan a unique example of a world religion coexisting with a traditional native religion? Was such a working compromise possible in other areas of the world? Why or why not?

5. How did differing forms of Christianity arise on the margins of Christendom?

6. How did Christianity and Islam trickle down to the masses after the elites adopted these religions in Eurasia and Africa? How did average citizens benefit from adopting (or not adopting) these religions?

7. Why did monasticism play such a large role in the early history of Buddhism and Christianity? Why has Benedict of Nursia's book of rules for monks been so influential? Why was monasticism less important in the Islamic world? What new roles did women acquire in the world religions?

8. How did the triumph of Buddhism, Christianity, and Islam change the societies and cultures where they triumphed? How were they in turn changed and modified?

READ ON ▶ ▶ ▶

To understand the problems of what conversion means, A. D. Nock, *Conversion: The Old and the New in Religion from Alexander the Great to Augustine of Hippo* (1933) is an indispensable classic, and K. F. Morrison, *Understanding Conversion* (1992) is an up-to-date introduction.

On Buddhism H. Bechert and R. Gombrich, eds., *The World of Buddhism: Buddhist Monks and Nuns in Society and Culture* (1984) is a superb survey, much wider in scope than the title implies. Works that deal with the reception of Buddhism in particular cultures are E. Zürcher, *The Buddhist Conquest of China* (1959), which is a work of outstanding scholarship; K. Lal Hazra, *Royal Patronage of Buddhism in Ancient India* (1984); M. T. Kapstein, *The Tibetan Assimilation of Buddhism* (2000); and the collections of essays edited by L. R. Lancaster and C. S. Yu, *Introduction of Buddhism to Korea* (1989); *Assimilation of Buddhism in Korea* (1991); and (with K. Suh) *Buddhism in Koryo* (1996). *The Cambridge History of Japan* (1988) deals expertly with all aspects of Japanese history in the period, including the reception of Buddhism. The travels of Xuangzang and other Chinese monks in search of Buddhist learning are covered in J. Mirsky, *The Great Chinese Travelers* (1964).

On Manichaeanism, P. Mirecki and J. BeDuhn, *Emerging from Darkness: Studies in the Recovery of Manichaean Sources* (1997) is a fascinating insight into the development of current scholarship. C. Mackerras, *The Uighur Empire* (1972) is a masterly survey.

On the spread of Islam it is helpful to consult G. S. P. Freeman-Grenville, *Historical Atlas of Islam* (2002). For the Indian Ocean, K. Chaudhuri, *Asia before Europe* (1990) is again to be recommended, with a word of caution about the demanding nature of this work.

For Africa, T. Insoll, *The Archaeology of Islam in Sub-Saharan Africa* (2003) is of great importance. M. Hiskett, *The Course of Islam in Africa* (1994) is a useful introduction. On East Africa, J. Trimingham, *Islam in East Africa* (1964), and M. Horton and J. Middleton, *The Swahili* (2000) (which is a good general history of the coastlands) can be recommended. For West Africa, M. Hiskett, *The Development of Islam in West Africa* (1984) and J. S. Trimingham, *A History of Islam in West Africa* (1962) are standard. For the Turks, an interesting source from the pre-Muslim period is G. Lewis, ed., *The Book of Dede Korkut* (1974). The important work I cite on Per-

sia is R. W. Bulliet, *Conversion to Islam in the Medieval Period: An Essay in Quantitative History* (1979).

On Christianity, W. H. C. Frend, *The Rise of Christianity* (1984); R. MacMullen, *Christianizing the Roman Empire* (1984); and R. Fletcher, *The Barbarian Conversion: From Paganism to Christianity* (1997) are fundamental and between them take the story down to the late Middle Ages. Exemplary case studies can be found in H. R. Mayr-Harting, *The Coming of Christianity to Anglo-Saxon England* (1972), J. Muldoon, ed., *Varieties of Religious Conversion in the Middle Ages* (1997), and B. Sawyer et al., eds., *The Christianization of Scandinavia* (1987), and N. Berend, ed., *Christianization and the Rise of Christian Monarchy* (2007).

For works on Constantine, see Chapter 8.

For the rise of Christianity in Ethiopia, S. Munro-Hay, *Aksum* (1991) is vigorous and makes much use of the stela texts; D. W. Phillipson, *Ancient Ethiopia* (2002) is a superb survey based on archaeological evidence; G. W. B. Huntingford, *The Historical Geography of Ethiopia* (1989) is a basic and classic work.

For the Caucasus, N. Garsoian, *Church and Culture in Early Medieval Armenia* (1999), and *Armenia Between Byzantium and the Sasanians* (1985) are collections of significant essays. C. Toumanoff, *Studies in Christian Caucasian History* (1963), and D. Braund, *Georgia in Antiquity* (1994) are also useful and important.

On Vladimir, F. Butler, *Enlightener of the Rus* (2000) is an interesting work, tracing the subject's historical reputation. The work of S. Franklin is fundamental.

On the origins of monasticism, G. Gould, *The Desert Fathers on Monastic Community* (1993), and W. Harmless, *Desert Christians* (2004) are highly instructive; and M. Dunn, *The Emergence of Monasticism* (2000) is a good introduction. There are many editions of *The Rule of St. Benedict*.

On Sufism, F. Meier, *Essays on Islamic Piety and Mysticism* (1999) contains many interesting pieces, while A. D. Knysh, *Islamic Mysticism* (2000) surveys the whole history of the subject efficiently. For Buddhist monasticism, the already-cited work edited by Bechert and Gombrich is excellent.

The long quotation on page 285 is from S. H. Gross and O. P. Sherbowitz, eds., *The Russian Primary Chronicle: Laurentian Text* (1953), p. 111.

CHAPTER 10

Remaking the World: Innovation and Renewal on Environmental Frontiers in the Late First Millennium

▲ **The monastery of Debra Damo.** In Ethiopia, as in Europe, monks were agents of colonization on remote and inhospitable frontiers. In northern Tigre, the founders of the monastery of Debra Damo—as early as the sixth century, according to tradition—took the search for seclusion in desert wastes to extreme: They located their house on top of a high outcrop, accessible to visitors only by means of ropes and pulleys, like the Orthodox monasteries of Mount Athos in Greece and many others in eastern Christendom

Chroniclers 500 years later recalled Queen Gudit with horror, but they could not agree about who she was or where she came from. For some she was an Ethiopian rebel, who seized control in the late tenth century by violence and enforced it by terror. For others she was a pagan or Muslim or Jewish invader, laying the country waste, destroying churches, toppling monuments, and exterminating the line of ancient rulers, who claimed descent from the biblical monarchs Solomon and Sheba. In some versions of the story, she was the descendant of an excluded branch of the Ethiopian imperial family, who was seeking revenge. In others she was the wife of the Jewish king of a realm in southern Arabia. One thing most later Ethiopian writers agreed on was that her example showed how dangerous women in power can be. Or perhaps, some said, Gudit was not really a woman, but a demon in disguise.

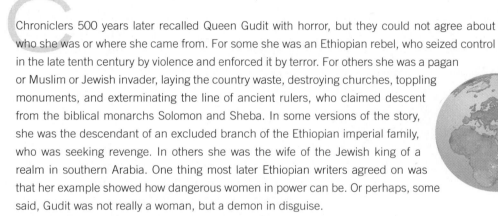

ETHIOPIA

Gudit, however, was no myth. A geographer writing in Iraq during the time of her ascent knew of a woman, whom he did not name, who "has ruled Ethiopia for some years now. She it was who killed the emperor of Ethiopia and she still rules her own country and controls the inland regions that formerly belonged to the emperor." So it looks as if, in the Arab world, Gudit was seen as a conqueror from an adjacent land—and probably not a Muslim, as an Iraqi source would surely have mentioned such a fact. Meanwhile, Christians in Alexandria, where the Egyptian Church was headquartered, received a desperate appeal from their co-religionists in Ethiopia reporting that an unnamed woman was subjecting the land to devastation and the dynasty to persecution. "God has become angry with us," the letter complained. "We have become wanderers. . . . The heavens no longer send rain and the earth no longer gives its fruits." The Alexandrians interpreted this scourge as divine punishment for the Ethiopians' failure to accept Egyptian nominees to the leading bishopric in the Ethiopian church, but the terms of the letter suggest that more than a spiritual crisis—more even than a devastating invasion or rebellion—was undermining Ethiopia. The vanishing rain and diminishing harvests were part of a long-term environmental problem.

The problems had been accumulating since the eighth century. At that time, Ethiopia was not yet in the state of collapse that had overcome the Roman and Persian empires, but it was in trouble. Ethiopia had its own "barbarian" hinterlands. The infiltration of nomadic peoples from the north seems to have driven Ethiopian families to resettle southward. No coinage was being issued. Monumental building had stopped. Squatters began to take over abandoned mansions in Axum, the Ethiopian capital. At the port of Adulis on the Red Sea, eighth-century ash lies

FOCUS questions

How did geography influence the transmission of culture in sub-Saharan Africa and the Americas?

What where the environmental consequences of the Islamic conquests?

How did Japan, China, and the states of Southeast Asia seek to stimulate economic growth?

How did Pacific islanders succeed in colonizing the Pacific?

Where did Christendom expand in the eighth and ninth centuries?

Where—if anywhere—did civilizations experience "dark ages" in this period?

How widespread during this period was ecological experiment?

thickly over ruined buildings, evidence that fire had wrecked the city. By the ninth century, central political control was hard or impossible to maintain.

Environmental influences played a big part in Ethiopia's eclipse. The surviving literary evidence, written by monks, blames the bad times on pagan revivals. According to the same sources, Christian resurgence brought recovery in the twelfth century. The archaeological record tells a different story. Increasing hardship drove the royal court from Axum. Trees vanished from hills overexploited for wood and charcoal. Intensive farming exhausted the soil. Heavy rains aggravated erosion, stripping slopes down to the stony subsoil. Mudslides buried buildings. Below the old volcanic hills, once-rich earth turned to dust. Axum never recovered its ancient greatness but remained a place of coronation for kings seeking to legitimize their rule. To renew the state and resume expansion, Ethiopians had to find new resources, new frontiers, new techniques.

From around 700 to 1000, states all over the world responded to similar problems. Slowly, uncertainly, unspectacularly, the discovery and exploitation of new resources, and the colonization of previously underexploited lands, equipped widely dispersed societies, in parts of Eurasia, Africa, the Americas, and the Pacific, with the means to sustain bigger populations, longer-range trade, and more ambitious environmental exploitation. The effect was to stimulate recovery and renewal in some of the regions the events discussed in Chapter 8 had disrupted, and to encourage rare or unprecedented initiatives elsewhere. Previously underrepresented parts of the world seem to leap into the historical record, because intense new activity leaves marks in the environment and, in some cases, memorials of art, thought, and high politics.

New ways to manage the environment multiplied during these centuries. They constitute something like a global story—or at least, a story that spans most of the world. Outcomes, however, continued to vary, and in some regions, such as the Islamic world, China, and Japan, the innovations of the period proved more durable than in others. What we might call the **axial zone** of the world expanded. The densely populated central belt of Eurasia, stretching from China to Europe and North Africa—the region that had seen so many experiments in civilization for so long—got bigger, as it incorporated new frontiers. In the Americas, sub-Saharan Africa, and the Pacific, similar but smaller zones began to take shape but remained fragile (see Map 10.1).

ISOLATION AND INITIATIVE: SUB-SAHARAN AFRICA AND THE AMERICAS
African Geography

In sub-Saharan Africa, it is tempting to treat Ethiopia as the exception that proves the rule: the one region where developments that historians usually treat as crucial—states and empires, radical modifications of the environment, maintenance of a literate tradition—have been comparable with those in the most favored parts of Eurasia. Geography is often said to imprison sub-Saharan peoples. While

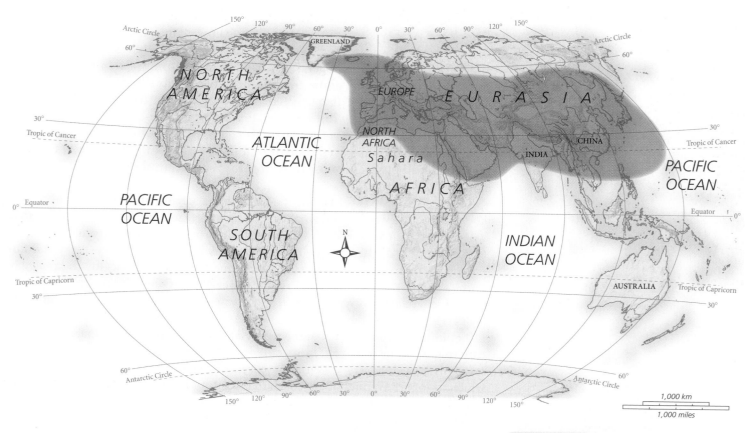

MAP 10.1

The Axial Zone, ca. 1000

☐ Axial zone

great axes of communication cross-fertilize much of the Old World, the Sahara and the Indian Ocean separate most of Africa from those highways of cultural exchange. Geography also separates African peoples from each other. Except on the Mediterranean and along the coast north of the Mozambique Channel in East Africa, shores exposed to the wind—*lee shores,* as sailors call them—make communication difficult by sea. The continent's high ground has relatively abrupt breaks, so that rivers fall sharply and are hard to navigate. In any case, Africa has only five or six major river basins, widely separated. Half of Africa's river drainage never reaches the coast. Dense forest impedes communications across the heart of the continent, where malarial mosquitoes are deadly to outsiders who have not developed resistance to the disease. Some of the flows of culture that we can detect, such as the spread of farming and of Bantu languages (see Chapter 5), took centuries longer than comparable transmissions in Eurasia.

The Emergence of Ghana and Gao Still, it is surprising that there has never been much exchange along the obvious axis of transcontinental communication in Africa: the Sahel, the belt of grassland that links East Africa, where Ethiopian civilization took shape, to another precocious region in the Niger valley in West Africa. Here, urban life, commerce, and industry show up in the archaeological record from the third century B.C.E. onward. By the first century C.E., at Jenne-Jeno, where floods fed the soil, farmers and ironworkers grew millet and rice. The population was reputedly so dense that royal proclamations could be "called out from the top of the city's walls and transmitted by criers from one village to the next."

The region was a natural crossroads where traders from the north could deal in slaves from the south, desert salt, local copper, and gold from the mines of Senegambia and the middle Volta River. Toward 1000, two states impressed Arab visitors: Ghana and Gao (gow). Ghana inspired particularly vivid reports. It was located in the territory of the Soninke (son-in-KAY) people, west of the middle Niger River. Its capital at Kumbi Saleh had houses of stone and acacia wood, and a royal compound. It was said that a sacred snake with a sensitive snout that sniffed out royal quality from among the contenders chose the king. Enriched by taxes on trade, the monarchs of Ghana and Gao attracted the reverence paid to sacred beings. At royal audiences, subjects prostrated themselves and covered their heads with dust. When the king of Gao ate, all business in the town was suspended, until shouts announced he had finished.

Sacred kingship spread along the Sahel. The Zaghawa of the Chad region in the late ninth century had "no towns," according to an Arab traveler's report, but "they worshipped their king as if he were Allah." There was a difference from the setup in Gao. To appear divine, the Zaghawan king took his meals in secret. Perhaps influenced by Ghana and Gao, evidence of divine kingship also begins to appear in Yoruba (YOH-roo-bah) territory on the lower Niger River from the tenth century, in the form of clay portraits of men and women with elaborate headgear and hairstyles. Had contacts developed across the Sahel between West African realms and Ethiopia, rather in the way that the steppeland linked Europe to China, African history might, in the long run, more closely have resembled that of Eurasia. But the West African kingdoms remained focused on relations north across the Sahara, while Ethiopia's avenues of approach to the rest of the world led in every direction but westward: north to the Nile, east to the Indian Ocean, south along the Rift valley (see Map 10.2).

American Geography

It is tempting to use similar arguments about the geography of the Americas to explain why the New World developed differently from the Old. The shape of the American hemisphere slowed diffusion of new culture and new crops, which had to travel across climate zones through the narrow, central continental funnel. Most of the great rivers flow east and west from the mountain spines that run up and down the Americas, and only the Mississippi traverses much distance from north to south.

Still, the effects of isolation could be overcome. The peoples of the Andes knew little or nothing, as far as we are aware, about those of Mesoamerica, until Spanish conquerors put them in touch with each other in the 1500s. But that isolation did not prevent civilizations from developing in the Andean region, in parallel with those of Mexico and Central America, taking advantage of the different ecosystems that a world of slopes and valleys, microclimates, and diverse plants and animals provided. The highlands of North America, on the other hand, housed nothing comparable. This may have been, in part, because the Andes and the Sierra Madre in Central America and Mexico are better placed than the mountains of the north: close to rain forests, seas, and swamps for maximum biological diversity. But the Rocky Mountains presented, in one respect, a more favorable environment. They provided a habitat for the bighorn sheep, a large animal that could have been domesticated but that for unknown reasons was not, perhaps because it likes to inhabit relatively high altitudes in regions where humans have, for most of history, preferred to live at lower altitudes and exploit the abundant game, such as bison and deer.

Figure of a sacred king. The Oni, or king, of Ile-Ife, excavated at Ita Yemoo, Nigeria in 1957, eleventh or twelfth century C.E. The king is shown draped in beads, a symbol of royalty. The fleshy naturalism is typical of the finest of Ife works, and the proportions emphasize the king's sacred head.

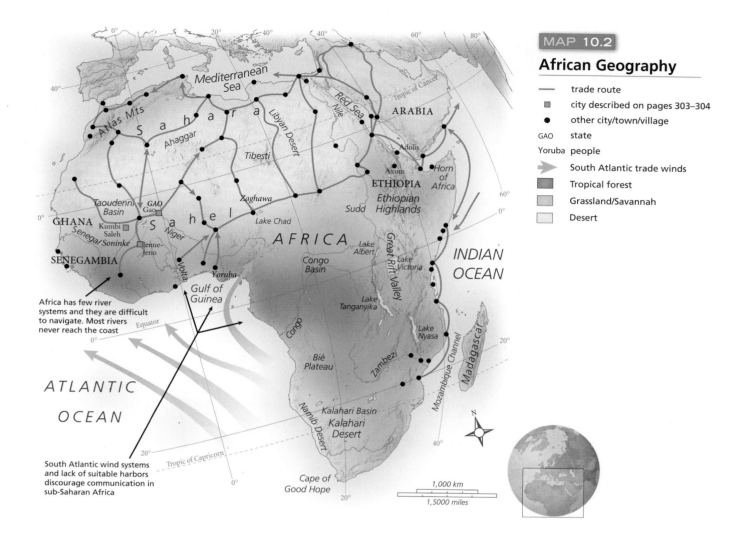

MAP 10.2

African Geography

— trade route
■ city described on pages 303–304
● other city/town/village
GAO state
Yoruba people
➤ South Atlantic trade winds
■ Tropical forest
■ Grassland/Savannah
□ Desert

Africa has few river systems and they are difficult to navigate. Most rivers never reach the coast

South Atlantic wind systems and lack of suitable harbors discourage communication in sub-Saharan Africa

1,000 km
1,5000 miles

Moche and Nazca Similarly, although North and South America both have arid deserts, the effort to civilize them encountered earlier success in the south (see Map 10.3). One of the strangest deserts in the world is in northern Peru. Except when El Niño drenches the land, almost no rain falls there. The region is cool, although only five degrees south of the equator, and dank with ocean fog. Little grows naturally, but modest rivers streak the flats, creating an opportunity to irrigate. The sea is at hand, with rich fishing grounds. Sea birds' excreta provide rich fertilizer to turn desert dust into cultivable soil. From the third century to the eighth, the civilization known as Moche (MOH-cheh) made this desert rich with turkeys and guinea pigs, corn, squash, peppers, potatoes, and peanuts, which the people admired so much that they modeled them in gold and silver.

Under platforms built as stages for royal rituals, their rulers' graves lie: divine impersonators in golden masks, with earspools decorated with objects of the hunt, scepters and bells with scenes of human sacrifice, necklets with models of shrunken heads in gold or copper with golden eyes, and portraits of a divine sacrificer wielding his bone knife. At San José de Moro, a woman was buried with limbs encased in plates of precious metals. In 2006, archaelogists in southern Peru found another female Moche mummy who had been buried not only with gold jewelry but also with weapons. Farther south, in the same period, in the even more inhospitable desert of northern Chile, the people known as the Nazca (NAS-cah)

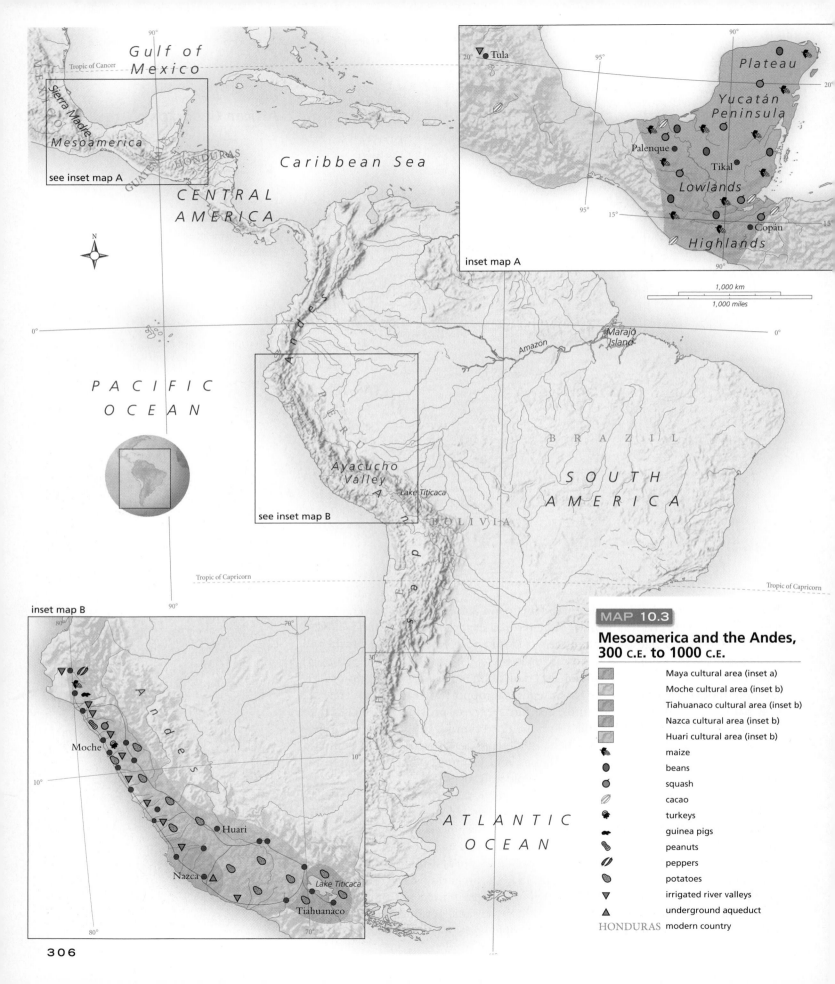

inset map A

Tula ▽●

Plateau

Yucatán
Peninsula

Palenque ●

Tikal

Lowlands

Copán ●

Highlands

20°

20°

95°

95°

15°

15°

90°

90°

1,000 km

1,000 miles

Gulf of
Mexico

Tropic of Cancer

MEXICO

Sierra Madre

Mesoamerica

see inset map A

GUATEMALA

HONDURAS

Caribbean Sea

CENTRAL
AMERICA

N

PACIFIC
OCEAN

Amazon

Marajó
Island

0°

0°

Andes

PERU

Ayacucho
Valley

Lake Titicaca

BOLIVIA

BRAZIL

SOUTH
AMERICA

see inset map B

Tropic of Capricorn

Tropic of Capricorn

90°

70°

30°

10°

Andes

ATLANTIC
OCEAN

inset map B

80°

70°

Moche

Andes

Huari

Nazca

Lake Titicaca

Tiahuanaco

80°

70°

10°

10°

MAP 10.3

**Mesoamerica and the Andes,
300 c.e. to 1000 c.e.**

Maya cultural area (inset a)

Moche cultural area (inset b)

Tiahuanaco cultural area (inset b)

Nazca cultural area (inset b)

Huari cultural area (inset b)

maize

beans

squash

cacao

turkeys

guinea pigs

peanuts

peppers

potatoes

▽ irrigated river valleys

△ underground aqueduct

HONDURAS modern country

built underground aqueducts to protect irrigation water from the sun. Above ground, they created some of the most ambitious works of art in the world: stunning representations of nature—a hurtling hummingbird, a cormorant spread for flight, sinuous fish—and bold abstract lines, triangles, and spirals, scratched in ochre deposits that film the rock. The dry air has preserved them to this day. Some of the images are 1,000 feet wide, too vast to be visible except from a height the artists could not reach, capable of permanently arousing the imagination.

Despite these achievements, the desert remained a fragile environment for such ambitious ways of life as those of the Moche and Nazca. They survived repeated droughts, which archaeologists have inferred from cores sampled from nearby mountain glaciers. El Niño events periodically drove away the fish and washed away the irrigation works. These were occurrences frequent enough for the locals to learn to live with. After the mid-eighth century, however, no mounds were built, no great artworks were made, and the irrigated land dwindled. No one knows why, though most scholars speculate that the people may have overexploited their environment, or an unusually protracted drought may have defeated them.

Andean Developments
The center of gravity of large-scale innovation shifted inland and upslope to the high Andes, though with little long-term gain in security. The city of Huari, 9,000 feet up in the Ayacucho valley in Peru, lasted, as a metropolis, only from the seventh century to the ninth. It had garrison buildings, dormitories for the elite, and communal kitchens, with a population of at least 20,000 clustered around it. It also seems to have had satellite towns dotted about the area.

At over 12,000 feet above sea level, potatoes fed the city of Tiahuanaco (tee-ah-wahn-AH-koh) in Bolivia because its altitude was hostile to growing grains. The city had already reached its greatest extent before Huari was founded, spreading over 40 acres. Mound agriculture could feed up to 40,000 people there. The tillers built stone platforms topped with clay and silt. They drew water from Lake Titicaca through channels to irrigate their mounds and protect them from violent changes of air temperature. Beds in this form stretched more than 9 miles from the lakeside and could produce 30,000 tons of potatoes a year. By about 1000, building had ceased, and the site was becoming abandoned—again, for unknown reasons, but perhaps because of overexploitation of the soil, or a shift in the regional balance of power. Tiahuanaco, as it gradually subsided into ruins, became a source of inspiration for all subsequent efforts to cultivate and build in the Andes. In short, the problem of initiating and sustaining civilization in the Americas remained acute throughout the period.

The Maya
No case has excited more curiosity than that of the Maya. They inhabited (and their descendants still inhabit) three contrasting environments: the abrupt, volcanic highlands of Guatemala, where microclimates create diverse eco-niches at different altitudes; the dry, gently hilly, limestone plateau of Yucatán (yoo-kah-THAN), the peninsula on Mexico's Caribbean coast, where agriculture depends on irrigation from pools and wells; and tropical lowlands in Central America with dense forests of heavy seasonal rain. There is bound to be some cultural diversity across such varied environments, and the chronology of Maya civilization

Nazca lines. The Nazca made the vast images for which they are famous by scraping the surface of the desert in Peru to reveal the bare rock underneath. But why did they do it? Vivid, intricate designs, such as this monkey, were too big to be fully visible except from the air. The people who made them can only have experienced them by walking the pathways the patterns made. The straight lines that accompany the images may have served as maps, perhaps indicating underground irrigation channels, but the pictorial devices themselves remain a mystery.

varied considerably among these regions. The lowlands experienced a Classic Age of monumental-scale building and art from about the third to about the tenth centuries, whereas the plateau "peaked" later in these respects. But Maya civilization has some surprisingly uniform features.

The Maya demonstrated, in spectacular ways, common threads of Native American civilizations seen from the Olmecs onward (see Chapter 4). Maya rulers had three areas of responsibility: war; communication with the gods and the dead; and building and embellishing monumental ceremonial centers. Royal portraits, often engraved on slabs of stone and displayed in the grand plazas where their subjects assembled, show rulers in roles similar to those of professional shamans, wearing divine disguises, or engaged in rituals of bloodletting designed to induce visions. Amazingly, we can still confront the images of many kings. At Palenque (pa-LEHN-keh), in the rain forest of southern Mexico, the seventh-century King Pacal (pa-KAL) is depicted on his tomb—dead, but refertilizing the world. A ceiba tree, sacred to the Maya, springs from his loins. In Copán (koh-PAN) in Honduras, the kings of the Macaw dynasty from the fifth century to the ninth, are shown communing together, as if at a celestial conference. At Tikal, when the sun is in the west and gilds the huge temple where he was buried, you can still pick out the vast outline of the fading image of King Jasaw Chan Kaui'il (ha-SA-oo chan kah-wee-EEL), molded onto the temple facade.

Politically, the Maya world, like that of classical Greece (see Chapter 5), was divided among city-states that sometimes engaged in territorial expansion, sometimes in close alliance, and sometimes in attempts at regional overlordship. But, in the period under consideration, they did not form large empires. They were perhaps too equally matched for imperialism to succeed. They were competitive in trade and in war, which, for most of them, seems to have been almost constant. Wars were fought by terror. Boasts of captives sacrificed are common in the texts. Mayan art often depicts scenes of sacrifice—including torturing to death and dismemberment while the victim was still alive.

Everything the Maya thought important—everything on Earth that they thought worth recording—happened in and around the ceremonial centers. The countryside was there to support and sustain those centers. In these cities were monumental buildings, intended to house elites and display rites to appease the

"Everything the Maya thought important—everything on Earth that they thought worth recording—happened in and around the ceremonial centers. The countryside was there to support and sustain those centers."

Mayan kings. The legitimacy that royal ancestry conferred was an important part of Maya kingship—especially, perhaps, when things were going badly. Yax Pasaj, who became king of Copán in 763, when he was still a small boy, ruled in a time of economic decline and political unrest. This may be why he had himself depicted in the company of all Copán's previous rulers, seated as if in conference around a small stone platform designed, perhaps, for the king to sit on. The kingdom dissolved shortly after Yax Pasaj's death.

gods and promote civic solidarity. Elite dwellings were imposing and built of stone, but the facades of some of them are adorned with carvings of humble dwellings, such as the Maya peasantry still inhabit today, built of reeds and thatch with a single stone lintel. The temples, which often doubled as tombs, always evoked the mounds on which, in the lowlands, farming was practiced: structures resembling pyramids or Mesopotamian ziggurats, with vast, terracelike flights of steps, surmounted by platforms on which rituals were enacted. Typically, especially in the highlands and lowlands, they were topped by false facades jutting into the sky, decorated with molded reliefs, displaying the symbols of the city, the portraits of the kings, the records of war, and the rewards of wealth. Even today, though faded and decayed, many of these roof combs still rise gleaming over forest treetops. In their time, for travelers, traders, or would-be aggressors, they carried an unmistakable message of propaganda: an invitation to commerce, a deterrent against attack.

These monumental centers were surrounded by markets and thousands—sometimes many thousands—of peasants' flimsy dwellings, in a landscape adapted for intensive agriculture. Small fields called *milpas*, were carved into highland terraces or dredged, in the lowlands, between canals that were used for irrigation or fish farming. The fields were sown with the three Native American staples: maize, beans, and squash, supplemented with other foods according to region or locality. Or they were devoted to cash crops, like cacao, which was in high demand as the source of the luxury beverage that accompanied rituals and feasts.

The Maya possessed a singular feature—it is tempting to say, a secret ingredient—because their writing system, the most expressive and complete known in the Native American world before the arrival of Europeans, did not spread to other culture areas. Much more common in lowland regions than in the plateau and highlands, these writings were carved in stone and therefore able to withstand destruction and decay. Despite the efforts of Christian missionaries in colonial times, who labored to erase memories of paganism at the cost of destroying valuable old texts, a vast body of Mayan inscriptions survives from the cities of the classic age from about the third to about the tenth centuries. Since the 1950s, heroic scholarship has gradually deciphered it.

Virtually all Maya writing falls into two categories: (1) records of astronomical observations and priestly timekeeping, which was a vital area of interest in Maya efforts to communicate with the gods and appease nature; and (2) dynastic records—the genealogies of kings, the records of their conquests, sacrifices, and acts of communion with their ancestors. On commemorative stone slabs and altars, on the facades of buildings, and in Copán, on a monumental stairway, the records of ruling dynasties are transmitted in such detail, with such a wealth of meticulous chronological and genealogical information, that we are better informed about the political history of some Maya states than about many European ones of the same era. A prominent theme of the royal records is always the observation, celebration, and commemoration of the movements of stars and planets. Especially in the lowlands, astronomical computations were a Maya obsession. In that region, the Maya dated almost every recorded event, from the third century to the tenth, in at least three different ways: according to the cycle of the planet Venus, as well as of the sun, and according to the number of days since an arbitrary starting point more than 3,000 years in the past.

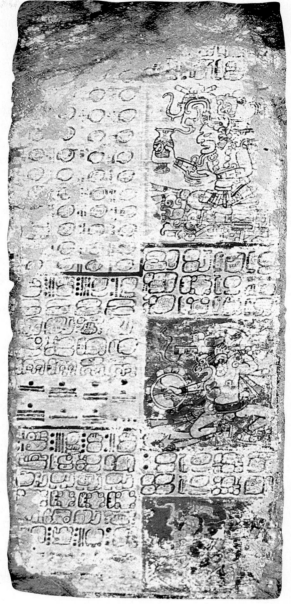

The Maya almanac known as the Dresden Codex contains a wealth of data on agriculture, divination, and religion. But its most remarkable contents, perhaps, are the detailed astronomical observations and predictions, especially the table recording the cycle of Venus, one page of which is shown here. The red bars and dots at bottom left are numbers, adding up to 584—the average number of days between the dates on which Venus rises with the sun. Such dates were favorable for war and sometimes foretold drought and death. The gods depicted represent from top to bottom, the Morning Star, Venus as bringer of war, and Venus demanding sacrifice.

Chronology: Civilizations of the Americas, ca. 200–1100	
ca. 200–900	Flourishing of Moche and Nazca civilizations
ca. 200–1100	Maya Classic Age (lowlands)
1000	Andean city of Tiahuanaco abandoned
ca. 1106–1200	Tula abandoned

Of course, all the surviving written evidence is propaganda, produced under the patronage of states. The claims and counterclaims of conquests and captures are evidence not of what the kings actually did but what they thought important. The central drama of kingship—the ritual the inscriptions most often commemorate—was the spilling of royal blood. A king would use a bone needle or spike to draw blood from his penis or scatter it from his hand. A queen might perform the ceremony by dragging a knotted thong, studded with sharp bones or spines, through a perforation in her tongue. Blotted onto bark, the blood would burn with hallucinatory drugs in an open fire. Enraptured by the fumes and by loss of blood, the monarch would succumb to a vision, characteristically depicted as a serpent rising from the smoke. The serpent was the mouthpiece of the ancestors. Their message usually justified war.

Maya civilization largely abandoned the lowlands in the ninth and tenth centuries. New building in ceremonial centers ended. Inscriptions ceased. The royal cult disappeared. Evidence vanished of rich elites and professions specialized in learning and the arts. Squatters occupied the ruins of decaying ceremonial centers. Traditional scholarship has dramatized and mystified these events as the collapse of classic Maya civilization—an echo of the decline and fall of the Eurasian civilizations of the axial age. It seems more helpful to see what happened as the displacement of the centers of the Maya world from the lowlands to the plateau. Still, it is mysterious. None of the explanations scholars suggest fit the chronology or the evidence. War is unlikely to have put an end to the lowland tradition. The Maya practiced wars so constantly that warfare must have served a useful purpose in their society. Spells of severe and prolonged drought certainly overlapped with the period of decline, but do not seem to have matched it. Political revolutions—rebellions of the masses or struggles within the elite—might have overthrown the regimes. But even if there were direct evidence of such upheavals, we would still need to explain why they occurred at roughly the same time in so many states.

That elite activities ended only in one eco-zone suggests that an environmental explanation should help us understand what happened. The lowlands were always a vulnerable environment, hostile to intensive agriculture and monumental building. In some ways, it is more surprising that such practices should have happened at all, and attained such impressive achievements, than that they should ultimately have failed. To sustain hundreds of cities and what were evidently densely packed populations, the Maya probably had to exploit their environment close to the limit of its possibilities.

Tula For a while, the influence and, to some degree, the power of the central Mexican empire of Teotihuacán stretched into the Maya world. For instance, on a carving at Tikal, Teotihuacano bodyguards flank a fifth-century king. Yet, as we saw in Chapter 8, Teotihuacán itself withered in the eighth and ninth centuries. This vast metropolis—once the center of a population that could probably be numbered in six figures—was never reoccupied, but became something like what we today would call a heritage site: revered and remembered by peoples who imitated its art and recalled its grandeur and its passing in their poetry. A new metropolis arose, well to the northwest, at Tula, the "garden of the gods," where groves of stone pillars and ceremonial enclosures, irrigated by blood sacrifices, justified the garden name. The environment at Tula was similar to the almost

Royal Bloodletting

The reign of Itzamnaaj B'alam ("Shield Jaguar") II of Yaxchilán (681–742), in what is today Mexico, produced some of the finest stone reliefs in which Maya rulers commemorated their performance of important rituals. The most common ritual was royal bloodletting, which was intended to provoke visions. During these bloodlettings, kings communicated with ancestors or gods.

The date of the ritual, shown here, was October 26, 709.

The carvings announce that the king and queen are shedding their blood.

The king wears a sacrificed captive's skull on his headdress and an emblem of the sun on his breast.

The queen draws a spiked thong through her tongue to spill her blood. A king would draw blood from his penis. Bark paper in the bowl below the monarchs absorbed the blood, which was then burned. The monarchs would inhale the smoke to induce a trance.

What does this stone relief tell us about Mayan kingship?

rainless limestone hills the Maya favored when the center of their civilization removed from the lowlands to Yucatán—except that at Tula, rivers could supply irrigation. The region already had a history of unstable settlement, and, by comparison with most earlier Maya cities or with Teotihuacán, Tula did not last long. Its site was abandoned in the twelfth century, but the ruins continued to inspire experiments in urbanization.

The Maize Frontiers

We can sum up all these New World histories of the late first millennium as efforts to open up new frontiers of exploitation for intensive agriculture, state formation, and city-building—activities formerly confined to narrowly limited areas, and vulnerable to periodic extinction. Hunter–gatherers, too, could engage with their environment in more productive ways. On the northwest coast of North America, houses got bigger as fishhooks got more plentiful and became more specialized. Along the northern edge of America, whale hunters were working their way along the Arctic coast, spreading new hunting and fishing techniques as they went, reaching Greenland by about 1000.

In other parts of the Americas, new crops and new technologies were extending farmers' frontiers, sometimes with transforming effects. Between the Missouri and Ohio River valleys, for instance, a large trading network flourished among peoples of similar material culture from about 200 to about 400. They buried their dead extravagantly, with copper earrings and breastplates, clay figures and smoking pipes, and ornaments carved from flat sheets of silicate in the shape of leaves and claws. They built tombs into mounds of astonishingly elaborate design: One in Ohio is in the shape of a long, coiling serpent—detectable as such only from a practically unattainable height, like the artworks of the Nazca in Chile. Their way of life, or, at least, of death ended sometime after 500. Leadership of society changed as maize cultivation spread through the region, and population grew.

This was the period of the great extension of maize cultivation into regions of North America formerly inhabited almost exclusively by hunter–gatherers, displacing former power groups, coaxing chiefdoms into existence and existing chiefdoms toward statehood. Farmers brought maize and beans into the central plains and, in some places from the Dakotas to the Red River in Canada, built burial mounds and earthworks similar to those found earlier along the Ohio and Missouri rivers. In some respects, this process looks like another case of a culture not extinguished, but changed and displaced from its former heartland. Maize farming reached the Great Basin of the North American plains, at sites where pottery and rock art were also made for the first time in this period. Beginning after 700, in the North American Southwest, where maize had been long established (see Chapter 5), large dwellings of adobe or stone displaced the semiunderground houses in which people formerly sheltered. Villages got larger, building toward the urban network that emerged around 1000 and that is a subject for the next chapter. Meanwhile, in the Southeast, the arrival of maize and, by around 1000, beans fed the ancestors of the large-scale builders of the early part of the next millennium.

Bird claw. Cut from a sheet of silicate, this sublime representation of the claw of a hawk or eagle was buried in a chief's grave in what is now Ross County, Ohio, in about 400 C.E. Hands and birds of prey were the symbols most often placed in the graves of the region's chieftains in this period.

Making Connections | EXPANDING STATES OF THE AMERICAS, 200–900

REGION/CULTURE	ENVIRONMENT	POLITICAL ORGANIZATION	ACHIEVEMENTS
South America			
Moche and Nazca	Desert; adjacent to Pacific Ocean; cool weather; little precipitation; abundant fish; small rivers	Communities governed by elites	Highly developed ceramics, gold/silver work; pottery; elaborate irrigation systems, some underground
Andean highlands (Huari)	Mountainous; glacier-fed streams and lakes; cultivable soil	Empire governing highlands and coast after decline of Moche; administrative centers; satellite towns	Intensive mound agriculture (potatoes); religious centers; road networks
Mesoamerica			
Maya	Contrasting environments: volcanic highlands of Guatemala; limestone plateau of Yucatán; tropical lowlands	City-states with rulers responsible for war, communication with gods; numerous ceremonial sites	Large-scale cities with monumental architecture; writing system and literature; long-distance trade networks; intensive agriculture, industry fueling population growth
Tula	Highlands with access to rivers, trade routes	City-states with ceremonial enclosures; use of blood sacrifice	Successor to Teotihuacán, largest city-state in Mesoamerica; monumental architecture; intensive irrigation
North America	Wide range of environments from mountains, to forests, deserts, open plains	Primarily chiefdoms, with larger-scale communities in Mississippi, Missouri, Ohio River valleys	As maize agriculture spreads, agricultural populations increase, displacing hunter–gatherer groups; large-scale mounds, tombs mark large population centers

On Marajó Island, in the mouth of the Amazon River in Brazil, although there is no evidence of new crops or techniques, people were practicing traditional agriculture with enhanced efficiency in an expanded area. Clusters of villages got denser after the mid-first millennium, with mounds raised for ceremonies as well as for agriculture. Here, the bones of the elite, boiled of their flesh, were buried in pots with clay representations of female genitals and gifts of beads, axes, and other valuables dependent on rank. The richly decorated burial urns provide glimpses of the creatures of their myths: turtles, scorpions, snakes, lizards, alligators, and almond-eyed humans.

THE ISLAMIC WORLD AND THE ENVIRONMENT

The garden of Islam. Enclosed from the world, enraptured by music, scented by flowering trees, cooled by drinks, and enlightened by conversation, the inmates of the garden of Islam inhabit an earthy paradise, in an illustration to a courtly romance about amorous intrigue.

Cultures widely scattered around the New World showed how basic tool kits or new crops could have profound effects. This feature was paralleled in the Old World—especially, on a huge scale, in the Islamic world. Although Islamic conquests slowed in the eighth century, an even more significant kind of expansion followed them: ecological expansion, as cultivators developed new crops and introduced them to new environments (see Map 10.4). For the desert pastoralists who bore Islam abroad, every frontier was a revelation. When, for example, the followers of Muhammad captured Basra on the Persian Gulf in what is today Iraq in 637, an eyewitness reported how they found two food baskets that the retreating Persians had abandoned. They ate the basket of dates but assumed the other contained poison, until a horse ate its contents without ill effects. "And their commander said, Pronounce the name of Allah over it and eat. And they ate of it and they found it a most tasty food." It was the Arabs' first taste of rice. When they took the Persian city of Ctesiphon (suh-TEHS-ih-fahn), they mistook medicinal camphor for salt.

They soon learned about the world that conquest had spread at their feet. The outreach of Islam was a process of discovery and renaissance in which a great array of new foods was gathered, adapted, and relocated in new environments. The Islamic world extended over the Mediterranean and touched Sahel, savanna, and tropical forests in sub-Saharan Africa, as well as monsoon lands in Yemen and northwest India, and regions of severe continental climate in Central Asia. The result was an unparalleled opportunity to exchange useful plants and animals among diverse environments.

Most of the new plants transmitted to the Middle East were exotics, reared in tropical or semitropical climates far from the areas in which they became adapted. Rulers encouraged new introductions, employing agronomists to manage their gardens, enhance their collections of medicinal plants, supply their tables, and improve their estates. Under the caliph al-Mahdi, for example, between 775 and 785, Yahya ibn Khalid led a mission to India to study medicinal drugs. Abd al-Rahman, ruler of Muslim Spain in the mid-eighth century, sent plant collectors to Syria. By the tenth century, Cordova, his capital, had, in effect, a special garden to grow exotic plants with fields for cuttings and seeds from abroad.

Plants from the tropics made a new summer growing season possible in the Middle East. Sugarcane, for instance, originated in South or Southeast Asia. From India, "a reed that produced honey without bees" had reached Persia. The Arabs extended its cultivation to the Mediterranean. Eggplant, too, was unknown in the Mediterranean or Middle East before this period. Other introductions from India included safflower, an herb pressed for cooking oil, with seeds used in cosmetics, and the Indian mung bean. The tenth-century geographer, Ibn Hawqal, tells of a

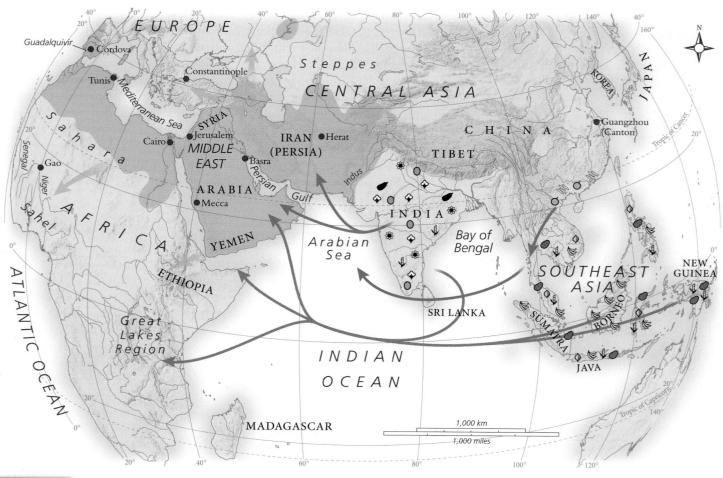

MAP 10.4

Transmission of New Crops to the Islamic World, ca. 1000

Islamic world, ca. 1000		eggplant	sugarcane
spread of crops from India		safflower	bananas
spread of crops from South and Southeast Asia		mung bean	taro
spread of crops from China (by way of Southeast Asia/Indian Ocean)		cotton	orange
Transmission of crops beyond Islamic frontier		lemon/lime	rice

landowner in northern Iraq who doubled his revenues by planting cotton and rice. The most important development to improve mass nutrition was of hard durum wheat in the Middle East. Some crops were transmitted onward, beyond the frontiers of the Muslim world. West Africa got cotton, taro, bananas, plantains, sour oranges, and limes in this period, probably across the Sahara. Christian Europe, by contrast, was slow to receive the benefits of Muslim agronomy. Spinach and hard wheat were not cultivated there until the thirteenth century, and rice not until the fifteenth.

Along with the new crops, technology and extended settlement further increased productivity. The new crops required watering during summer, stimulating irrigation by underground tunnels and wells, which led, in turn, to the adoption for agriculture of more previously marginal land. Forest clearance was practiced

Food and Plants with Arabic or Persian Word Origins

Aubergine (eggplant)*

Camphor

Caraway (seeds)

Coffee (by way of Turkish)

Cotton

Henna

Lemon

Orange

Saffron

Sherbet

Spinach

Sugar

Syrup

*Italic words are of Persian origin.

more widely and intensively than before. Fertilizer increased crop yields. Fertile land left uncultivated seems to have been rare in the Muslim world. Islamic law favored farmers. Landowners could use and dispose of their land as they liked. The enforcement of a free market in land meant that farms tended to fall into the hands of owners who used them most productively. Tenants acquired farms, as conquest broke up big holdings that had stagnated under the previous regimes. Tax rates in regions under the rule of the caliphs in Baghdad were low after reforms in the late eighth century—commonly a tenth of output, with summer crops often being exempted. Villages thrived. There were 12,000 villages along the Guadalquivir River in Muslim Spain by the tenth century. In seventh-century Sawad in Syria, 48,000 square miles were subject to land tax—virtually the entire cultivable area.

FRONTIER GROWTH IN JAPAN

The vast extent of the Islamic world made this rich environmental history possible. But on a smaller scale, a similar program, including the development of new foodstuffs, the exploitation of underexploited frontiers, and the adaptation of new areas for cultivation, was possible even in relatively small and isolated Japan. Here, a sense of struggle against nature animated the most persistent and consistent effort any state of the time made to boost food resources. Bureaucrats carefully totted up the hostility of the natural world. Between 806 and 1073, official records list 653 earthquakes, 134 fires, 89 cases of damage to crops, 91 epidemics, 356 supernatural warnings (including volcanic eruptions), and 367 appearances by ghosts. They recorded only 185 favorable events in the same period. In the *Nihongi* of the early eighth century, one of the earliest native Japanese chronicles, the rise of the

Watermill. Increased agricultural output caused demand for more and bigger mills to grind grain. Most have not survived, but a fine example of medieval watermill technology, pictured here, is on the Orontes River at Hama, Syria. Water wheels on this scale also hoisted water from riverbeds to aqueducts and irrigation channels.

imperial dynasty is linked with the overthrow of Susa-no-o, a god who "brought many people to an untimely end" by "making green mountains wither" and wrecking rice fields. Japanese rulers took seriously their responsibility to regulate their subjects' relations with the natural world. Unlike their counterparts in most other cultures, they did not limit themselves to acts and sacrifices intended to appease the forces of nature. From the early eighth century, they had ambitious environmental policies.

Some growth in the yield of agriculture would have happened even without state guidance. Rice yields improved thanks to new, labor-intensive techniques in which whole communities cooperated: growing seedlings in nurseries and transplanting them to the fields. Heavy plows arrived from Korea in the fifth century. It is doubtful, however, whether they made much impact until the ninth or tenth century because Japan had little iron for making plows. Most cultivation was on wetlands. Dry farming, which made the heavy plow familiar, spread slowly. Evidence of the increased stabling of animals implies systematic exploitation of them as resources for power, and suggests that farmers were using more and more land to grow crops. Meanwhile, barley gradually replaced millet as the country's second most important crop after rice, with some benefits for nutrition. Although we lack reliable figures, population was obviously growing. Census returns show—by global standards—exceptionally large households of an average of 10 persons each. Family customs helped. Young mothers commonly spent the first 5 to 15 years of married life in their parents' home, where their husbands visited them. This spread the burden of child care.

The government drive to boost food production was under way by 711, when a decree authorized aristocrats to apply to provincial governors for permission to cultivate virgin land at their own expense. The aim, according to a proclamation of 722, was to add 2.5 million acres to the area devoted to rice production. In 723, farmers became eligible to inherit newly cultivated fields for three generations if they irrigated those fields from new ditches or ponds. In 743, farmers acquired absolute ownership of such lands.

As well as a state-sponsored, aristocratic enterprise, the conquest of new environments was a preserve of freelance holy men. In 735, the dismay caused by a devastating smallpox epidemic boosted the appeal and numbers of these zealots. Most of them were Buddhists. The most effective holy man was the monk Gyoki. Traditionalists accused him of embezzling alms, impiously burning the bodies of the dead, and aggressively pursuing converts. But everyone approved of the way he organized his followers to perform public works—building bridges and roads, digging ponds and embankments. The state soon contracted Gyoki's workers to undertake official projects. In 741, 750 of his disciples joined the Buddhist priesthood after building a bridge over the Kizu River.

Frontier expansion at the expense of the "barbarians" of Japan's northeast Honshu Island also increased the amount of available land. The native Emishi (eh-MEE-shee) were denounced as "hairy people," who dwelt among "evil deities in the mountains and perverse devils on the plains." They were described in terms that seem almost universal among imperial peoples who want to conquer, dispossess, or exterminate others. They were "fierce and wild," dangerous, lacking a recognizable political or legal system. Without chiefs, they "all rob each other. . . . In winter they lodge in holes, in summer they dwell in nests." By 796, the state had settled 9,000 colonists in fortified households on Honshu to cultivate conquered lands.

By the early ninth century, the state was growing more confident about its ability to manage the environment and keep disaster at bay. After performing a successful

"Japanese rulers took seriously their responsibility to regulate their subjects' relations with the natural world. Unlike their counterparts in most other cultures, they did not limit themselves to acts and sacrifices intended to appease the forces of nature. From the early eighth century, they had ambitious environmental policies."

Map of Japan. Though it is now hard to separate facts about him from legends, the eighth-century Japanese Buddhist monk, Gyoki, is credited, like many medieval European saints, with important public works and contributions to what would now be called the infrastructure of the state: improving roads, building bridges, organizing labor for irrigation, and establishing inns for travelers and pilgrims, as he roamed the land, making converts. Whether he actually made maps is uncertain, but the earliest maps of Japan, which date from his era, go under his name, A typical example—reproduced on porcelain in 1839—shows the islands of Honshu, Shikoku, and Kyushu, divided into provinces. The Japanese state had barely penetrated the northern island of Hokkaido at the time. Korea, the Ryukyu Islands, and mythical lands are visible around the rim of the dish.

rainmaking rite, the hermit Kukai began his song of self-praise with a conventional reflection. Nature, he said, responded to human decadence. "And thus," he continued, "even though it is time for rain to fall, the four horizons are blazing with heat: the sun burns up everything, and rice and millet ears are all dry. The entire natural world dries up and hardens, and animals of fur and scale alike perish. With nothing to see but aridity in the land, court and peasants alike pour tears ceaselessly." In such circumstances, the emperor intervenes. He fasts and orders appropriate rites in all temples. "As the venerable monks chant the sacred scriptures . . . waterfalls gush forth from high peaks and soak wild animals, while rain fills the fields enough to drown water buffaloes. . . . Peasants! Do not lament any more. . . . See the storehouses, where grain piles up like islands, like mountains."

CHINA AND SOUTHEAST ASIA

In Japan, as in the Islamic world, the human assault on the natural frontier had effective states of growing power to back it. But in the same period, similar developments occurred even in politically unstable and apparently unfavorable conditions in China and India. After the collapse of the Gupta Empire (see Chapter 9), kingdoms in south India and the Deccan boosted their revenues, reach, and power by granting wasteland to priests, monks, and warriors to promote agriculture. In land grants recorded in conquered forest areas in the sixth century, monks and holy men are the biggest beneficiaries. This should not be seen merely—or perhaps at all—as evidence of kings' religious priorities but of monasteries' ability to transform the environment. An inscription on copper, dated 753, shows what happened when a priest received a royal land grant. "We the inhabitants went to the boundaries which the headman of the district pointed out, circumambulated the village from left to right, and planted milk-bushes and placed stones around it. . . . The donee shall enjoy the wet land and the dry land included within these four boundaries, wherever the iguana runs and the tortoise crawls, and shall be permitted to dig river channels and inundation channels." The king would receive taxes on the use of these facilities. The inscription also includes a list of payments that the priest did not have to pay, revealing the full range of collective activities that community contributions supported. The settlers made and operated oil presses and looms. They dug wells. They paid taxes to support the king, the district administration, and the priestly caste out of the yield of crops, including water lilies, "the share of the potter," the price of ghee (butter) and cloth. They supplied huntsmen, messengers, dancing girls, servants, fodder, cotton, molasses, "the best cow and the best bull," and "the fourth part of the trunks of old trees," including areca palms and coconut trees, to the royal court. When fines were due from the village "to the accountant and the minister," the priest-landlord did not have to contribute to them. Irrigation and double cropping appear in many Indian inscriptions of the following two centuries. Marginal land was coming under the plow. In a land grant of 994, in an arid region, for instance, the landlord was only entitled to a third of the water from a single well.

In China, although the emperors of the early seventh century were unable to sustain a lasting dynasty, they did contribute to the enduring infrastructure of the economy, building a canal system that crisscrossed the country. This alone stimulated the internal grain trade and therefore the productivity of the regions that grew rice and millet. The canals also improved irrigation. In 624, in Shaanxi province, imperial waterworks irrigated more than 80,000 acres. Meanwhile, large-scale land reclamation proceeded by drainage, as population growth and improving food supply stimulated each other. The policy of the Tang dynasty (see Chapter 8) was usually to break up large landholdings and distribute them among taxpayers. A major land reform of 737 divided great estates among their workers. This may have discouraged large landowners from investing in reclamation, but it encouraged cultivation because peasants farmed their holdings more intensively than large landowners did. It was part of an ideology of imperial benevolence that also established price-regulating granaries where food stocks accumulated at government expense when prices were low for redistribution at a discount when prices were high. The resulting stocks helped cushion disaster in the plague-ravaged, famine-fraught 730s through 740s. Improved rice strains, adapted from varieties of rice that Tang armies brought back from campaigns in Vietnam, helped.

Imperial policy also stimulated the southward shift of settlement, and therefore of the centers of production, into regions, far from the threat of steppeland invasion, where rice grew, with beneficial effects on nutrition and therefore on levels of population. In 730, vagrant families were ordered to be resettled in agricultural colonies under military discipline. Such proclamations often failed to produce results, but some colonies did take shape under this program, cultivating rice on the Huai River in 734. Although governments were prone to periodic bouts of hostility against Buddhism and Daoism, which Confucians tended to despise as superstitious, monasteries were generally encouraged because they were effective colonizers that could kick start development in underexploited areas. By the mid-eighth century, a third of China's people lived in the Huai and Yangtze River valleys, and, by the eleventh century, over half did. As colonization proceeded, Chinese villages replaced aboriginal populations, which were exterminated, assimilated, or driven into marginal areas. Population figures—statistics untrustworthy anywhere at the time except in China—suggest Tang environmental policies paid off. China had about 50 million people after An Lushan's rebellion in the 750s (see Chapter 8). Its population had grown to 60 million by the year 1000.

The Grand Canal. China's ancient canals are still useful to commerce. Here, long lines of barges sail the Grand Canal, an artificial waterway that was first built in the seventh century C.E.

Chronology: Population of China, 730–1000

730	Vagrant families ordered to resettle in agricultural colonies
734	Rice cultivation on the Huai River
750	China's population is 50 million
Mid-eighth century	One-third of China's population lives in the Huai and Yangtze valleys
1000	China's population is 60 million
Eleventh century	Half of China's population lives in the Huai and Yangtze valleys

The extension of the frontier of settlement and of rice cultivation in southern China was part of a bigger phenomenon, extending over the moist, hot, dense forests of mainland Southeast Asia (see Map 10.5). In the sixth century, Chinese geographers ceased to refer to Funan (see Chapter 8) and located a state they called Chen-la in the interior of what is now Cambodia. This was the first sign of an important change under way in the region. Alongside the maritime states, founded on trade that lined the routes from China to India, agrarian kingdoms were growing up, based on rice production. For centuries small chiefdoms and aspiring states had dotted the lower Mekong River valley, but in the eighth century, the people of the region, the Khmer (k-MER), began to coalesce into a single kingdom, centered at the new city of Angkor (AHNG-kor), on the north shore on the Tonle Sap—a natural reservoir of monsoonal rains. This region had no mines, no great commercial fleets, and no great industries. The wealth of the Khmer derived from a peculiar feature of the way the Mekong works. Swollen by the monsoon, the river becomes, in effect, too heavily charged to empty into the sea through its own delta. The water begins to flow backward, flooding the plain of the Tonle Sap. The soil there is so rich that, provided the waters are channeled into reservoirs, it yields three rice crops a year. Angkor was also well placed for contact with other major rice lands in the Maenam and Chao Phraya basins. In 802, it became a capital with explicitly imperial pretensions, when King Jayavarman II proclaimed himself monarch of the universe, and priests in his employ performed a ceremony nullifying all former oaths of loyalty.

Similar experiments occurred across Southeast Asia. The growth of the Viet and Cham kingdoms—the other big states that took shape in Indochina in the period—owed something to the traditional wealth of the region in ivory, rhinoceros horn, and aromatic woods, and much to the bureaucracy that arrived with Buddhism. But it was based mainly on taxes from lumber, as forests fell, and food products, as new fields replaced the forests. By 1000, a comparable transformation was taking shape in the northwest corner of the region. Here, in the Irawaddy valley on the borders between India and Bangladesh, dry rice cultivation began to transform a near-desert where little rain fell. Meanwhile, offshore, the axis of maritime state building shifted outward, toward the Indonesian islands.

Here, in the seventh century, the realm of Srivijaya (sree-vee-JEYE-ah), on the Sumatran coast, impressed the first Chinese sources to notice it. When the pilgrim I-ching (yee-jing) stopped there in 671, the capital had a community of Buddhist monks, said to number 1,000. The court employed Hindu and Buddhist scholars. But a tradition of pagan magic fascinated Muslim observers. Magic was meant to control the sea. The maharajah, as the sources called the king of Srivijaya, was said to have enchanted crocodiles to guard the mouth of his river. He supposedly bought the goodwill of the sea with annual gifts of gold bricks.

Srivijaya's economy relied on harbor tolls and the profits of piracy. A river-linked domain behind it supplied it with soldiers and rice, because even trading states needed their own food supplies. Srivijaya had big commercial resources in the form of spices and aromatic woods, but the inhabitants still worked to expand rice production. According to a legend of the foundation of Palembang, the fathers

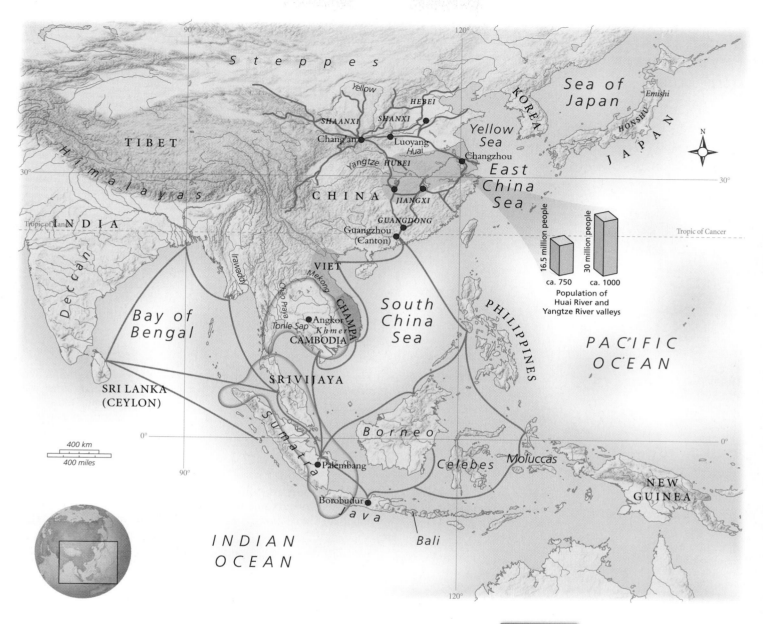

MAP 10.5

China and Southeast Asia, ca. 1000

- Huai River and Yangtze River valley
- Champa
- Viet
- Cambodia
- Srivijaya
- — maritime trade route
- — canal
- *Khmer* people

of the city chose its site by weighing the waters of Sumatra's various rivers for silt and finding that those of the Musi would be best for irrigating rice lands. Palembang's earliest inscription, dated 685, expresses a king's concern that "all the clearances and gardens his people made should be full, that the cattle of all species raised by them and their bondsmen should prosper."

The capital, where even the parrots spoke four languages, attracted merchants. The maritime strength of Srivijaya was concentrated in the ragged east coast of Sumatra, with its fringe of islands and mangrove swamps, its deep bays and shelters for shipping, its natural coral-reef defenses, its abundant fish and turtles. Its greatness and survival—for it was "invariably described as great," according to a Chinese administrator of its trade in the early eleventh century—depended on Chinese commerce, especially for the sandalwood and frankincense in which it established a dominant trading position.

Making Connections | EXPANDING STATES IN EAST AND SOUTHEAST ASIA, 600–1000

REGION/CULTURE	ENVIRONMENT	POLITICAL ORGANIZATION	ACHIEVEMENTS
Japan	Temperate climate; mountainous; volcanoes; relatively small areas of fertile soil	Centralized dynasty with provincial governors; high degree of social coordination	Productive rice, barley agriculture with community cooperation; creation of public infrastructure; frontier expansion to northeast island of Honshu
China and Southeast Asia Yangtze River valley	Moist, semitropical and crisscrossed with rivers	Large canal building; irrigation and drainage projects	Imperial-controlled land distribution; improved rice strains; state-controlled granaries; population increases; growth of Buddhist, Daoist monasteries
Indochina Angkor/Viet/Cham kingdoms	Coastal areas: Mekong River delta in south; Red River in north with adjacent forests; inland: mountainous areas	Small chiefdoms coalesce into single states	Combines highly productive rice agriculture and maritime trade (South China Sea); population increases; large-scale Buddhist temple complexes
Sumatra Srivijaya kingdom **Java** Sailendra dynasty	Tropical coastal regions; frequent earthquakes and volcanoes; thick forests	Chiefdoms and kingdoms with Muslim and Chinese merchants, advisers	Plentiful trade in agricultural goods, fish, wood, incense, spices; development of large-scale Buddhist and Hindu temple complexes

In eighth-century Java, the Sailendra dynasty rivaled Srivijaya. They built a huge Buddhist temple, Borobodur, which seemed to proclaim their patrons' privileged access to heaven. Built of half a million blocks of stone, it arose between about 790 and 830. Buddhism was a relative newcomer. The site of Borobodur had been intended for a Hindu temple when the ruling ideology abruptly changed. Terraces lead the pilgrim upward. The climb is like a mystic's spiritual ascent toward heaven. At the top, the pinnacle of experience awaits: a representation of the central world-mountain of Buddhist belief. Carvings that depict tales from Buddhist scriptures are a stone book, reminders of the stages that prepare the soul for nirvana.

The maritime economy of Sailendra has left no archives, but it comes to life in the carvings. One of the most famous depicts a legendary voyage to a prom-

(a) **The temple of Borobodur** on the Indonesian island of Java began to receive pilgrims in the early ninth century. Visitors, emerging from the dense tropical forest that surrounded the site, would ascend through four galleries, where stories of virtuous Buddhists were carved in relief (and, in their day, plastered and brilliantly painted), eventually reaching the realm of Enlightenment—the circular platform, guarded by statues of Bodhisattvas.

(b) **The galleries of Borobodur** relate legends of individuals who achieved Enlightenment by practicing virtue. The story of Hiru, the royal counselor who narrowly eluded death and endured exile for urging virtue on a wicked ruler is shown in the lower of these reliefs. The realistic depiction of his windblown ship is a vivid reminder of the maritime culture of Java under the Sailendra kings.

ised land that Hiru, the faithful minister of the mythical monk-king Rudrayana, made. Hiru earned the goodwill of heaven by intervening with the king's wicked son and successor, who proposed, among other evil acts, to bury his father's spiritual counselor alive. Miraculously advised to flee in advance of a sandstorm that would smother the court, Hiru fled by sea in a windborne ship to a happy shore. He found granaries, peacocks, varied trees, and hospitable inhabitants. The artist who carved the story had seen such scenes. He knew what a ship looked like and how it worked. The kind of art he produced—evidence, too, of a kind of spirituality—could only come from a world that regarded travel and trade as noble, virtuous activities.

According to later inscriptions—in which we must make allowance for mythical distortions or propagandistic exaggerations—a rival kingdom to the Sailendras arose in regions of Java where forest had been newly converted to rice cultivation on the plains of the Solo and Brantas rivers. Inscriptions credit the expulsion of the Sailendras from these regions in the mid-ninth century to Pikatan, a king who doubled as a holy man, forest clearer, and temple builder.

THE PACIFIC

Growing trade stimulated these developments in maritime Southeast Asia. But an even more impressive drive to colonize new lands and exploit new resources occurred deep in the Pacific, where, as far as we know, the commerce of the monsoonal seas barely reached (see Map 10.6).

To judge from the currently available archaeological evidence, the Caroline Islands in Micronesia were probably first colonized about 2,000 years ago, not from the relatively nearby Asian mainland but from the southeast, in the Solomon Islands and New Hebrides (the modern-day country of Vanuatu), by people who made distinctive round pots, intricately patterned by pressing tooth-shaped stamps into the clay, and whose houses were raised on stilts. The

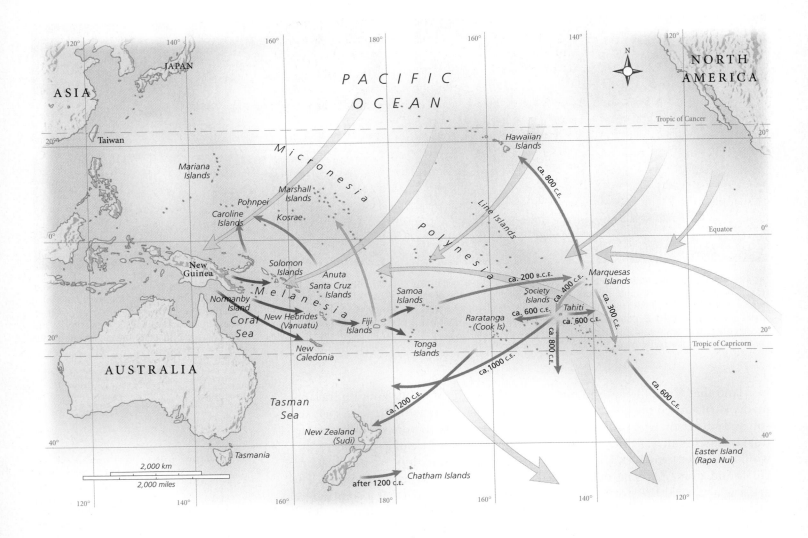

The Colonization of the Pacific to 1000 C.E.

➤ migrations before 1500 B.C.E.

➤ migrations 1500–1000 B.C.E.

➤ migrations 1000–1 B.C.E.

➤ migrations 1–500 C.E.

➤ migrations after 500 C.E.

➤ Trade Winds

way this culture changed—relatively suddenly and at vastly different rates on different islands—awaits explanation. The most precocious island was Pohnpei, at the Carolines' eastern end. It is small—probably incapable of supporting more than 30,000 people—but it was a center of ambitious activity toward the year 1000. Large-scale labor was mobilized to carve out artificial islets with increasingly monumental ceremonial centers—for tombs and rites including turtle sacrifices and the nurture of sacred eels. On nearby Kosrae Island, a similar history began soon after. Within a couple of centuries, cities were arising around paved streets within high walls of massive construction—observed with "total bewilderment" by the French expedition that came on the city of Lelu by accident in 1824.

Beyond the Carolines, in the South Pacific, lay one of the world's most daunting frontiers: an ocean too big to traverse with the technology of the time, where the winds blew almost without stop from the southeast and where vast distances separated islands that could support human life. Polynesians conquered this environment mainly after 500. Polynesians are easily defined as speakers of closely related languages. It is harder to find a common cultural profile for them in other respects. Using archaeological and linguistic evidence, however, we can piece together how they lived during the early centuries of their dispersal through the

Pacific. They grew taro and yams, supplemented with coconut, breadfruit, and bananas. They kept chickens and pigs. They named 150 kinds of fish, and exploited them for tools—files made of sea-urchin spines, fish hooks from oyster shells. They consumed kava, a fermented drink made from a plant whose roots have narcotic properties, to induce trances and celebrate rites. Although archaeology cannot retrieve their notions of the sacred, we can infer it from language and later evidence. **Mana**—a supernatural force—regulated the world. The mana of a net makes it catch fish; the mana of an herb makes it heal.

The Polynesian culture was a frontier culture in origin. It grew up in the central Pacific, probably in the islands of Tonga and Samoa, beginning about 2,000 to 3,000 years ago. The chronology of Polynesian expansion is relentlessly debated and deeply uncertain. Like the Caroline Islanders and the inhabitants of most of the islands of the South Pacific, the Polynesians shared a genetic background with some peoples in Taiwan and Southeast Asia, but—to judge from such DNA evidence as has come to light—belonged to a distinct wave of migration from their neighbors in the Carolines and Melanesia. The Polynesians were, from their first emergence in the archaeological record, constant voyagers, venturing ever farther into the paths of the southeast trade winds, which restricted the range of navigation but which at least promised explorers a good chance of getting home. Around 600, however, there was clearly a period of "takeoff," in which archaeological finds multiplied across the ocean and thousands of islands, as far as Easter Island (see Chapter 14). In further phases of expansion, Polynesians colonized northward as far as Hawaii, by about 800, and ultimately settled New Zealand and the Chatham Islands.

"Beyond the Carolines, in the South Pacific, lay one of the world's most daunting frontiers: an ocean too big to traverse with the technology of the time, where the winds blew almost without stop from the southeast and where vast distances separated islands that could support human life."

Polynesian canoe. Hokule'a is a modern Hawaiian reconstruction of a traditional Polynesian catamaran, in which members of the Polynesian Navigation Society demonstrated the navigability of the island systems of the Pacific in the 1970s, using navigation without instruments, under the guidance of Mau, a pilot fron the Caroline Islands. *© Monte Costa*

To colonize so many islands, many of which seemed dauntingly far apart, was such a surprising achievement that scholars who investigated it long assumed that it must have happened by accident—as a result of seafarers or regional traders drifting off course or being blown to new lands by freak winds. But long-range navigation is part of the logic of life on small islands—a characteristic way to maximize resources, extend economic opportunities, and diversify the ecosystem. The Polynesians, in common with the Caroline Islanders and other sailors of the northern and western Pacific, had impressive maritime technology: double-hulled canoes big enough to carry 200 people, or smaller vessels with outriggers for longer journeys, rigged with claw-shaped sails that kept the mast and rigging light. Their direction-finding techniques were the best in the world. Chants helped navigators remember the complex guidance of the stars in a hemisphere where no single polestar is available to guide voyagers, as it is north of the equator. Navigation was like "breadfruit-picking," star by star. They mapped the ocean's swells—mentally or perhaps with maps made of reeds, of which later examples survive. Eighteenth-

Making Connections | ENVIRONMENTAL/GEOGRAPHIC OBSTACLES TO DEVELOPMENT OF STATES

REGION	ENVIRONMENTAL/ OBSTACLES	ADAPTIVE STRATEGIES
Sub-Saharan Africa	Isolation—desert in north and lee winds offshore impede communication; widely separated river basins; lack of navigable rivers near coasts; dense forests, malarial jungles	Exploitation of agricultural, mining resources near Sahel grassland; West Africa; trans-Sahara trade routes focusing on copper, salt, gold
North and South America	Bounded by vast oceans—Atlantic and Pacific oceans; most rivers flow east–west preventing north–south contacts; mountainous terrain	Taking advantage of South/Mesoamerican highlands' proximity to rain forests, seas, swamps for resource exploitation; intensive development of fishing/hunting techniques in North America; introduction of new crops and technologies aided by trade networks from Mesoamerica to Mississippi River Basin
Japan	Isolated geography; few navigable rivers; poor soil; earthquake prone	Labor-intensive wetland agricultural techniques; highly regulated society; systematic exploitation of animals as sources of power
Pacific	Vast and isolated region; few food crops, little cultivable soil on many islands;	Skillful development of navigational, boat-building techniques; unsurpassed knowledge of ocean and night sky; introduction of basic "tool kit" (fish-hooks, taro, coconut, breadfruit, kava, banana plants, chickens, pigs) to uninhabited islands

century European observers noted that Caroline and Polynesian navigators could literally feel their way around the ocean, identifying their position by the way that waves felt on their own bodies.

By about 1000, the Polynesians may have gotten close to the limits of navigation accessible to them with the technology at their disposal. Oral traditions recall and presumably embellish their history. The most heroic tale is perhaps that of Hui-te-Rangiora, whose journey from Raratonga in the Cook Islands in the remote Pacific in the mid-eighth century took him through bare white rocks that towered over a monstrous sea, to a place of uninterrupted ice. Myths ascribe the discovery of New Zealand to the godlike Maui, who baited giant stingray with his own blood. A less shadowy figure is the indisputably human Kupe, who claimed that a vision of the supreme god Io guided him to New Zealand from Raratonga. Maybe, however, he just followed the migration of the long-tailed cuckoo birds. His sailing directions were: "Let the course be to the right hand of the setting sun, moon, or Venus in the second month of the year."

Chronology: Polynesian Expansion	
3,000–2,000 years ago	Origins of Polynesian civilization
600	"Takeoff" of Polynesian expansion
ca. 800	Settlement of Hawaii
ca. 1000	Colonization of New Zealand

THE FRONTIERS OF CHRISTENDOM

At the opposite end of Eurasia, in the eighth century, Christendom began to outgrow the frontiers of the Roman Empire (see Map 10.7). Here conquest was the main agent of change. Christendom developed no new crops or technologies. The heavy plow had long been in use. Rye and barley—the grains suitable for the frost-rimmed, dense soils of northern Europe—were ancient crops. Colonization, however, accompanied conquest and transformed environments, as conquerors encouraged settlers in underexploited territories, and armies drove gangways through forests, while monks tamed wilderness and attracted farmers in frontier regions.

Beyond Rome's farthest northern and western frontiers, monastic exiles took memories of antiquity into Scotland and Ireland, like the monk Columba, longing to compose his hymns "on a rocky outcrop, overlooking the coiling surface of the sea." A similar—more dangerous—enterprise flickered in Germany, where Boniface traveled from England in 719 to share the gospel with his fellow Saxons. Boniface was martyred around 754, but the task of converting the Saxons was taken up 30 years later, from inside the most dynamic spot on the frontier of Christendom: the kingdom of the Franks.

Two events transformed the Frankish ruler, Charlemagne, into the self-styled renovator of Rome. His journey to Italy in 774 opened his eyes to the ruined splendors of ancient Rome and enabled him to gather books and scholars. From the 790s, he could afford unprecedented ambitions when he captured the treasure of invading steppelanders, the Avars. Taking advantage of the fact that Irene, an empress of dubious legitimacy, ruled in Constantinople, he proclaimed himself successor of the ancient Roman emperors. Charlemagne—while remaining first and foremost a Frankish king—fancied himself in his new role. He affected what he thought was imperial Roman taste. He appeared on coins in a laurel crown. His seals were stamped with slogans of imperial revival. His court writers, who must have known what he wanted to hear, compared him to Constantine and Justinian (see Chapter 8). The manuscript painters, scribes, and ivory carvers of his palace copied ancient models.

"Beyond Rome's farthest northern and western frontiers, monastic exiles took memories of antiquity into Scotland and Ireland, like the monk Columba, longing to compose his hymns 'on a rocky outcrop, overlooking the coiling surface of the sea.'"

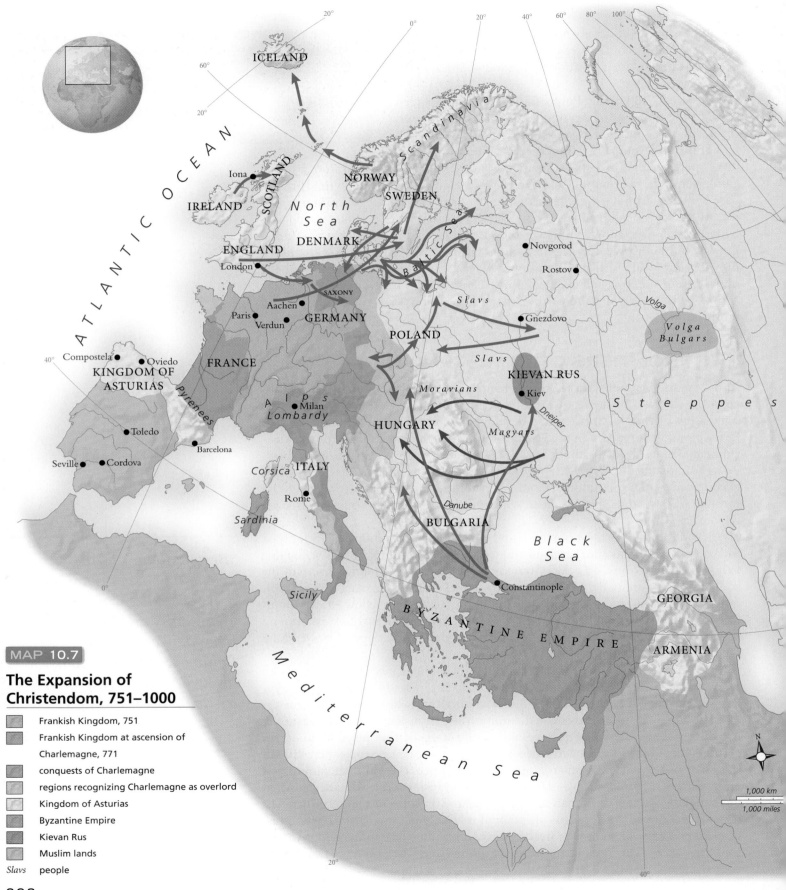

MAP 10.7

The Expansion of Christendom, 751–1000

Frankish Kingdom, 751

Frankish Kingdom at ascension of Charlemagne, 771

conquests of Charlemagne

regions recognizing Charlemagne as overlord

Kingdom of Asturias

Byzantine Empire

Kievan Rus

Muslim lands

Slavs people

Charlemagne's chapel. The Palace Chapel at Aachen Germany, consecrated in 805, shows how thoroughly his journeys in Italy in the 770s affected Charlemagne (r. 768-814). No building in Northern Europe had matched this scale and grandeur since Roman times. Charlemagne took the title of Roman Emperor in 800, and wanted a chapel similar to the churches founded by earlier Roman emperors that he had seen in Ravenna.

Even before Charlemagne came to the throne, the Frankish realm had incorporated lands beyond the margins of the old empire, especially along the North Sea and in central Germany. Charlemagne's conquest of Saxony, which took 18 years to complete, was the first annexation of a large new province in Europe by a self-consciously "Roman" Empire since the Emperor Trajan had conquered Dacia in the early second century. More significant yet was the enduring nature of this conquest. Saxony, wrested—said Charlemagne's servant and first biographer—from devil worshippers, became a parade ground of Christendom, converted from an insecure frontier into an imperial heartland.

On Christendom's other exposed flanks, similar expansion made slow progress. In the early ninth century, Mojmir I established a Slav state patterned

Irish cross. Outside the Roman Empire, Christianity was slow to take root in Europe—except in Scotland and Ireland. Isolation made Irish Christian art highly distinctive. This eighth-century bronze crucifix was probably made to adorn the cover of a gospel book. The artist was apparently concerned to represent scripture authentically—hence the soldiers who pierce Jesus' side and hoist a sponge to his lips. The angels who perch on the arms of the cross display fragments of what may be intended to represent Christ's shroud, or the cloth used to wipe his face.

on Charlemagne's monarchy, beyond the Danube in Bohemia, in a region where the Avar Empire used to rule. In 864, the Bulgar Tsar Boris decided to accept Christianity and impose it on his people. The Bulgars rapidly became like the Franks, rival claimants to the mantle of Rome, under a ruler who called himself "emperor of all the Greeks and Bulgars." Yet if the Bulgar Empire was a threat to Constantinople, it was a bulwark for Christendom against pagan steppelanders from farther east.

Despite an isolated position and scant resources, Asturias in northern Spain in the ninth century successfully defended Christendom's frontier against the Muslims at the opposite end of the Mediterranean. Part of the sacred armory of its kings lies in Oviedo Cathedral—vessels of gold, ivory, and lapis lazuli, housing even more precious scraps of wood and bone from the saints that could have a magical effect on the battlefield. On a hill above the town, Ramiro I could look out on his kingdom from his summer palace, or receive ambassadors in a hall decorated with carvings molded after Persian silverwork that must have been inherited from the Roman past. By the end of the century, the kingdom ruled from here had begun to expand beyond the mountains that screened it to the south.

Exploitation of the shrine attributed to the Apostle James the Great at Compostela gave Asturias advantages over other Christian states in Spain—in pilgrim wealth, monastic colonization, and the chances of recruiting knightly manpower. But a frontier position generally was good for state-building. In the 890s, Wilfrid the Hairy, Count of Barcelona, claiming the hairy man's birthright that God promised in the biblical story of Esau, conquered almost all the counties around his own, south of the Pyrenees. Laborious settlement of underpopulated areas is the subject of all the documents that survive from his time. A church synod at Barcelona recalled Wilfrid's generosity a few years later: "Moved with pity for that land, the Lord made arise the most noble prince Wilfrid and his brothers, who, filling men of diverse provenance and lineage with pious love, managed to return the famous church with its dependencies to its former state." Here, and in later charters, are hints of Wilfrid's success in attracting population to the lands of his border state. Wilfrid's story was typical of the edges of Christendom. In lands reclaimed from pagan conquest on the northern frontier, in England, Alfred the Great (r. 871–899) was securing a similar reputation as a state builder by lavish generosity to monks, the custodians of the historical record. By 924, Alfred's heirs had completed their reconquest of northern and eastern England. The extension or restoration of the frontier of Christendom was pushing Europe outward.

At the same time, a secular political tradition was being spread even farther afield. Christianity, as we saw in the last chapter, was barely beginning to penetrate Scandinavia, which—in terms of the colonists it generated and the new lands it explored—was the most dynamic part of Europe. A letter from the northern Russian city of Novgorod is said to have reached a Viking prince in 862. "Our land," it read, "is great and rich. But there is no order in it. Come and rule us." In response, he founded the state that eventually became Russia.

Vladimir of Kiev, whose conversion to Orthodox Christianity we discussed in Chapter 9, was a descendant of the Scandinavian founding fathers of Russian principalities. The story may have gotten oversimplified in the record, but it shows how territorial statehood was exported, far beyond the limits of the old Roman Empire, to relatively immature political worlds in northern and Eastern Europe. Meanwhile, Scandinavian expansion was also going on northward, spreading the frontiers of farming and statehood within its own peninsula, and turning seaward, colonizing Iceland.

Chronology: Christian Conquest and Expansion	
Ninth century	Growth of kingdom of Asturias
ca. 802	Charlemagne completes conquest of Saxony
ca. 860	Beginning of Scandinavian colonization of Iceland
864	Bulgar Tsar Boris accepts Christianity
884	Kiev becomes capital of Russian state
890s	Expansion of Barcelona under Wilfrid the Hairy
924	Completion of conquest of formerly pagan lands in England

In Perspective
The Limits of Divergence

On the face of it, the histories of sub-Saharan Africa and the Americas seem to diverge from that of Eurasia and North Africa from the eighth century to the year 1000. In Christendom, the Islamic world, China, Southeast Asia, and the western and central Pacific, states came and went, but economies and civilizations were robust—extending frontiers, colonizing new areas, founding new states and empires, or reviving old ones. These regions seem to have bucked the patterns detected by traditional historiography: to have endured beyond periods of decline and fall and dark ages. At first glance, the contrast with sub-Saharan Africa looks glaring. Ethiopia's dark age really was dark, in the sense that we know virtually nothing about it. Ghana's frustration, and the absence of any evidence of comparable state-building initiatives elsewhere, confirm the traditional picture of sub-Saharan Africa in this period as a region—like far northern Asia or Australia—about which historians of the period can find almost nothing to say. The myth of Maya collapse has long dominated the way we conventionally think of the Americas in this period. This was a hemisphere in which it was more usual for civilizations to perish than to grow outward or renew themselves. This is an exaggeration—perhaps even a caricature. But there is something in it. Teotihuacán, the Moche, the Nazca, the lowland Maya, Huari, Tiahuanaco—these casualties of the era were replaced, if at all, by unstable successors.

Nevertheless, a theme that, if not quite global, genuinely embraces the Old and New Worlds underlies the apparent differences between them. Broadly stated, this was a period of unusual ecological experiment: the exploration or conquest of new environments. In some cases, new frontiers were breached by expansion into neighboring regions and already-familiar environments, like those of the Islamic world or Southeast Asia or most of Christendom. In others, like the Caroline Islands or the Scandinavian expansion, apparently unprecedented adventures were launched from origins that present knowledge cannot adequately explain. In others again, as in China and Japan, internal colonization adapted and transformed previously underexploited wastelands. In others, such as the Andes, central Mexico, and the Maya world, the centers of activity were displaced to new environments—the limestone hills of Tula or Yucatán, the almost incredibly high altitude of Tiahuanaco. In others, which remain necessarily underrepresented in history books because of the absence of evidence, the business of locating resources,

"Broadly stated, this was a period of unusual ecological experiment: the exploration or conquest of new environments."

Chronology

ca. 200–400	Flourishing of mound-building culture in eastern North America
ca. 600	"Takeoff" of Polynesian expansion
ca. 750	China's population reaches 50 million
754	Martyrdom of Boniface
Third through tenth centuries	Maya Classic Age
Seventh through tenth centuries	Ecological expansion of Islam
Eighth century	Government drive to boost food production in Japan
Eighth through ninth centuries	Decline of Ethiopia
790–830	Construction of Borobodur temple, Java
ca. 800	Settlement of Hawaii
ca. 802	Charlemagne completes conquest of Saxony
ca. 860	Scandinavians begin colonization of Iceland
884	Kiev becomes capital of Russian state
ca. 1000	Andean city of Tiahuanaco abandoned; China's population reaches 60 million
1100s	Tula abandoned

(All dates are C.E.)

developing foodstuffs, and improving production techniques continued without leaving much trace in the record. In the 800s and 900s, for instance, all we have is linguistic evidence for two enormously important developments in the ecology of East Africa. An explosion of new terms shows that banana cultivation and cattle breeding spread inland from the Indian Ocean coast to the Great Lakes of Central Africa. Against this background, the history of the next three centuries, which is the subject of the next part of the book, becomes intelligible. Vibrancy and innovativeness, which became characteristic of most of these regions—and of others where the evidence only begins to mount up from this point onward—grew out of preceding, painstaking efforts to find new, more productive ways to exploit the environment.

The story of the last few centuries of the first millennium C.E. suggests an important point about how history happens. In the past, the search for patterns that help to explain it, and that make it easier to write textbooks about it, has driven historians to grotesque oversimplifications: seeing history as a continuous story of "progress" or decline; or representing it as a kind of swing between revolutions and counterrevolutions, or between decadence and dynamism, or between dark ages and rebirths. The reality, it seems, as we get to learn more about the past, is much more subtle and intriguing. At one level, the slow growth of compatible changes—what historians' jargon sometimes calls "structures"—gradually gave the world a new look. Simultaneously, and often with contradictory effect, random or short-term changes stimulate, impede, interrupt, or temporarily reverse those trends, and—sometimes—permanently deflect or end them. So both continuity and discontinuity tend to be visible in the story, pretty much all the time. A picture that omits either is almost certain to be distorted.

In these respects, history is rather like climate, in which many cycles of varying duration all seem to be going on all the time, and where random or almost-random changes frequently intervene. With increasing intensity in recent years, historians have struggled to match changes in the human record to knowledge of how these cycles and changes have interacted since the end of the Ice Age. As we are about to see, some of the most remarkable insights to have emerged from this quest illuminate worldwide changes that began—or that we can first begin to detect—around 1,000 years ago.

PROBLEMS AND PARALLELS

1. What were new ways of managing the environment during the late first millennium? How did societies exploit new resources and colonize new lands?

2. How did geography impede the diffusion of culture and crops in sub-Saharan Africa and the Americas?

3. What factors contributed to the flourishing of South American and Mesoamerican cultures and states?

4. What were the effects of environmental expansion under Islam? How did Muslim rulers like Abd al-Rahman and the Caliph al-Mahdi encourage the adoption of new plants and crops?

5. What roles did monumental architecture and religious ritual play in many of the cultures discussed in this chapter? Why were monks and holy men important to the conquest of new environments and the expansion of states in Europe and Asia? How did Charlemagne expand the frontiers of Christendom?

6. Why was ecological experiment and the conquest of new environments in Christendom, China, Southeast Asia, and the Pacific so important in the late first millennium?

7. What do the histories of such varied regions as the Islamic world, China, Japan, and Mesoamerica tell us about the relationship between the exploitation of the environment and the growth and decline of human societies? Are such long-ago transformations relevant or meaningful today?

READ ON ▶ ▶ ▶

The written sources on West Africa are collected in J. F. P. Hopkins and N. Levtzion, eds., *Corpus of Early Arabic Sources for West African History* (2000). J. Diamond, *Guns, Germs, and Steel* (2003) sets out the case for the isolating effects of American geography.

On the Moche, G. Bawden, *The Moche* (1996) is standard. For the Nazca, A. F. Aveni, *Nazca: Eighth Wonder of the World* (2000) is useful. B. Fagan, *Floods, Famines, and Emperors* (1999) is a lively romp through the history of the effects of El Niño. For Tiahuanaco, A. Kolata, *Tiwanaku and Its Hinterland* (1996), 2 vols., is exhaustive. R. Keatinge, ed., *Peruvian Prehistory* (1988) collects important essays on the Andean background. On the Maya, M. Coe, *The Maya* (2005), and N. Hammond, *Ancient Maya Civilization* (1982) are the most useful overviews. The exhibition catalog by L. Schele and M. Miller, *The Blood of Kings* (1992), is important for understanding royal rituals. D. Webster, *The Fall of the Ancient Maya* (2002) is a brilliant and provocative study of the crisis of the ninth and tenth centuries. On Copán in particular, W. Fash, *Scribes, Warriors, and Kings* (1993) is a vivid and engaging study. On Tula, R. A. Diehl, *Tula* (1983) is authoritatie. On Marajó and related topics, the exhibition catalog by C. McEwan et al., *Unknown Amazon* (2001), contains a wealth of exciting data.

For maize, see W. C. Gallinat, "Domestication and Diffusion of Maize" in R. I. Ford, ed., *Prehistoric Food Production in North America* (1985).

A. M. Watson, *Agricultural Innovation in the Early Islamic World* (1983) is the standard work on Islam's agrarian revolution in this period. K. W. Butzer, *Archaeology as Human Ecology* (1982) is classic, and D. W. Phillipson, *African Archaeology* (1994) is a survey by the leading living expert on Ethiopia.

The Cambridge History of Japan (1993) is unsurpassed on Japanese environmental history in this period.

R. Thapar, *Early India* (2004); and B. Chattopadhyaya, *Aspects of Rural Society and Settlements in Early Medieval India* (1990), and *The Making of Early Medieval India* (1994) are the best works to consult on environmental aspects of Indian history at the time.

M. Elvin, *The Retreat of the Elephants* (2004) is a sparkling historical study of the Chinese environment, focusing on the history of deforestation, about which there is much, too, in N. K. Menzies, "Forestry," in J. Needham, ed., *Science and Civilisation in China*, vi (2000). *The Cambridge History of China*, 3 (1979) is fundamental for Chinese history generally in this period.

On Angkor, the classic by G. Coedes, *Angkor, an Introduction* (1986) remains fundamental, supplemented now by the ingenious work of E. Mannika, *Angkor Wat: Time, Space, Kingship* (1996). M. D. Coe, *Angkor and the Khmer Civilization* (2005) is of special interest from a comparative point of view, as the author is a Mayanist. On Southeast Asia generally, D. G. E. Hall, *A History of South-East Asia* (1981) and the same author's contribution to *The Cambridge History of South-East Asia*, 1 (2000) are important.

On the Pacific, important contributions are collected in P. V. Kirch and T. L. Hunt, eds., *Historical Ecology in the Pacific Islands* (1997). P. V. Kirch, *On the Road of the Winds* (2001) is immeasurably helpful. P. Bellwood, *The Polynesians* (1987) is a useful introduction. The classic by B. Malinowski, *Argonauts of the Western Pacific* (1984) can still be read for pleasure and profit.

On Christendom, useful essays are collected in the forthcoming series, edited by F. Fernández-Armesto and J. Muldoon, *The Expansion of Christendom: The Middle Ages*, especially in my volume, "The Internal Frontier." C. Wickham, *The Mountains and the City* (1988), and R. Bartlett, *The Making of Europe* (1994) are fundamental.

The World in 1000 C.E.

There were few signs by the turn of the millennium that the era of divergence was reaching its end. But it was. This was partly because the huge states we call empires acted as arenas for transmitting culture. Some empires had functioned in this way for a long time. As we saw in Chapters 7 and 9, the Roman Empire transmitted Greek learning and the Christian religion from the eastern Mediterranean to as far away as the Atlantic edge of Europe. In Mesoamerica, as we discussed in Chapter 8, Teotihuacán had influenced fashion and politics in the Maya world. Over many centuries, China had forged a common identity in a vast domain, and the influence of its arts, learning, and political thinking had spilled over into Korea, Japan, and other parts of Asia. China had also been the conduit by which Buddhism spread from India to Korea and Japan (Chapter 9). The most spectacular cases were relatively recent. In Chapters 9 and 10, we saw how Muslim empire builders spread Islam across a great swathe of the Old World from Spain to the borders of India and deep into Africa. With Islam came scholars and texts that put the learning of India and of the former Roman world back in touch with one another. Muslim rulers and the gardeners and agriculturalists they patronized exchanged unfamiliar crops back and forth across Eurasia and North Africa. In about the year 1000, when Norse from Europe and Thule from the Pacific met in Greenland, it became possible, in theory, to circle the world by intercommunicating routes.

▶ QUESTIONS

1. Compare this map with the Big Picture map on pages 226–227. How are the two maps similar? How are they different? If the world in 100 C.E. was a world of empires, how is the world in 1000 C.E. a world of civilizations?

2. How does an environmental perspective make it possible to see common themes between the Old and the New Worlds in the period from 100 C.E. to 1000 C.E.?

To view an interactive version of this map, as well as a video of the author describing key themes related to this Part, go to www.myhistorylab.com

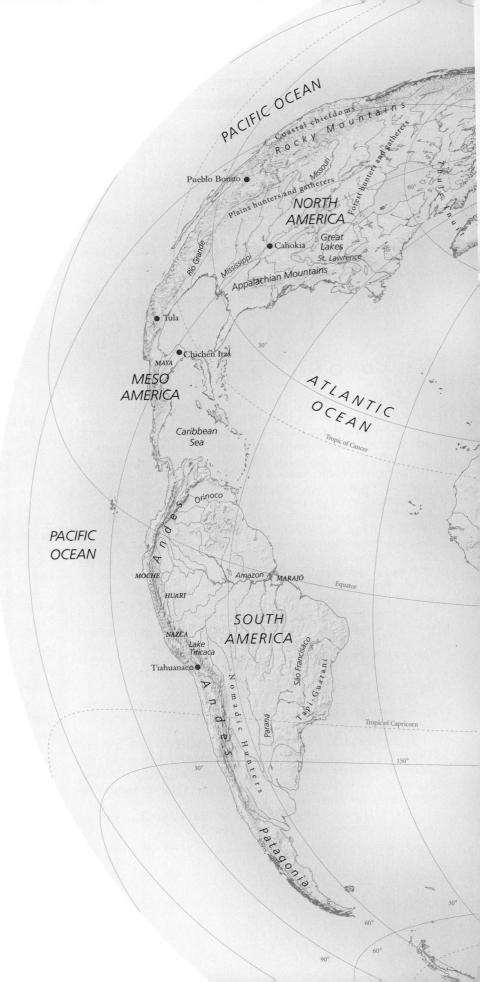

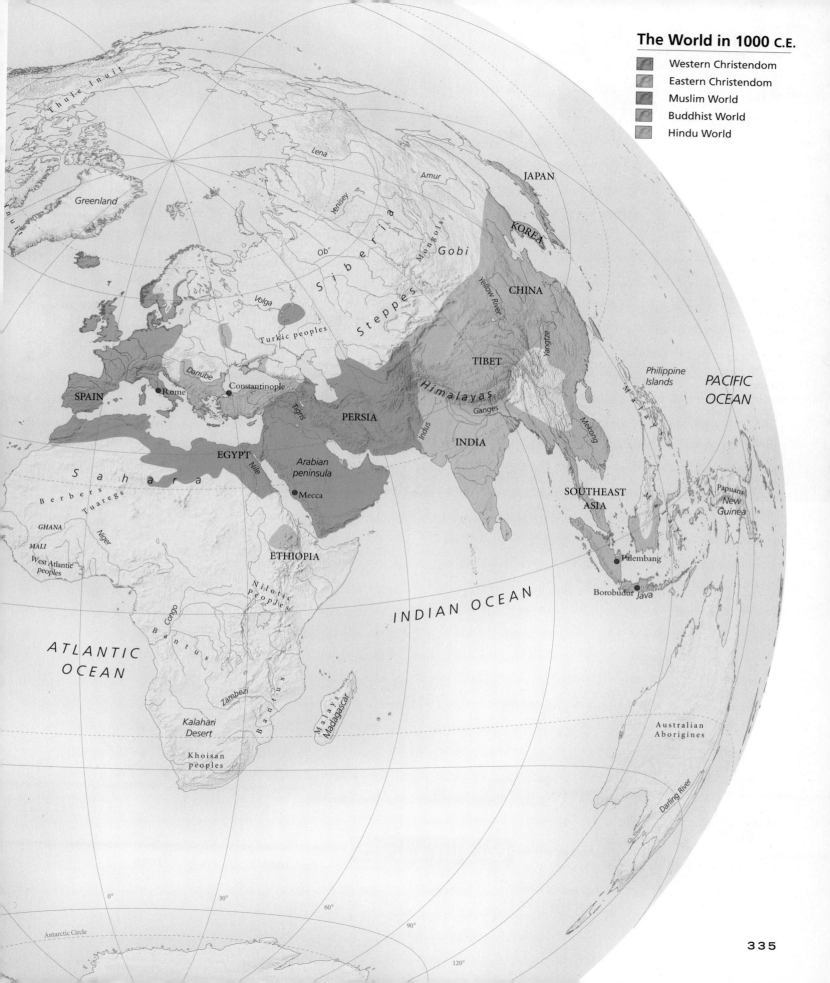

The World in 1000 C.E.

- Western Christendom
- Eastern Christendom
- Muslim World
- Buddhist World
- Hindu World

Thule Inuit

Greenland

Inuit

Lena

Amur

JAPAN

Yenisei

Siberia

Ob'

Mongols

Gobi

KOREA

Steppes

CHINA

Yellow River

Volga

Turkic peoples

TIBET

Yangtze

Danube

Himalayas

SPAIN

Rome

Constantinople

Tigris

PERSIA

Ganges

Indus

Mekong

Philippine Islands

PACIFIC OCEAN

EGYPT

Nile

Arabian peninsula

INDIA

Sahara

Berbers

Tuaregs

Mecca

SOUTHEAST ASIA

Papuans New Guinea

GHANA

Niger

MALI

West Atlantic Peoples

ETHIOPIA

Nilotic Peoples

Malays

Palembang

Congo

INDIAN OCEAN

Borobudur Java

ATLANTIC OCEAN

Bantus

Zambezi

Madagascar

Malays

Australian Aborigines

Kalahari Desert

Bantus

Khoisan peoples

Darling River

0°

30°

60°

90°

120°

Antarctic Circle

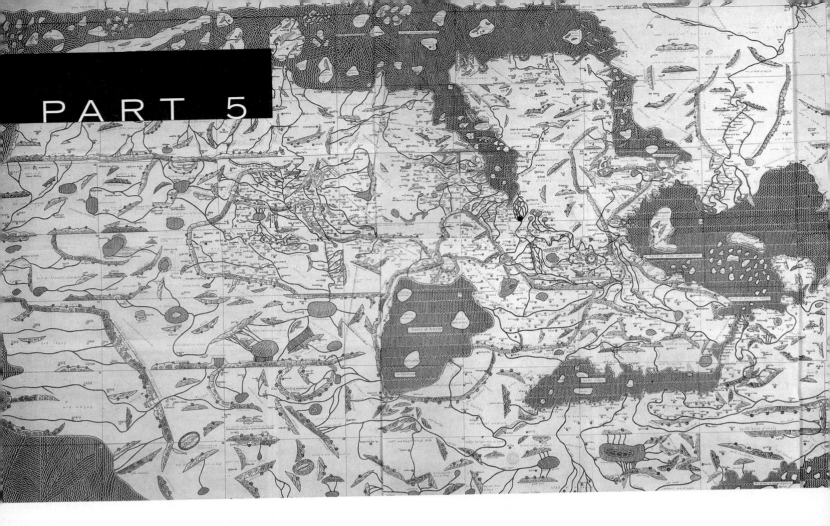

PART 5

Contacts and Conflicts, 1000 C.E. to 1200 C.E.

◀ **The World Map of Al-Idrisi,** a Muslim geographer who worked in Christian-ruled Sicily in the mid-twelfth century. He tried to follow the advice of the ancient Greek geographer, Ptolemy, and constructed his map on a grid. South is at the top. The shape of Arabia is clearly recognizable to a modern eye (upper center).

1000–1200
Transfer of crops from South and Southeast Asia to Islamic world

1040s–1090
Increased steppelander migrations into Middle East

ca. 1070–1122
Chola maritime expansion

900–1200
Growing population, especially in Europe and China

1000–1200
Spread of Islam to West Africa

ca. 1125
Angkor Wat

ca. 1200
Cahokia, height of Mississippian mound building

CHAPTER 11

Contending with Isolation: ca. 1000–1200

▲ **A ferocious sea.** The pilgrimages of Buddhist monks inspired Japanese stories about the ferocity of the sea. One of the most popular tales in the late twelfth and early thirteenth centuries was about Gisho, a monk who renounced the love of a beautiful woman and set sail for Korea. But in the incident depicted here, she followed him and flung herself into the sea, where, transformed into a dragon, she protected him from storms.

JAPAN

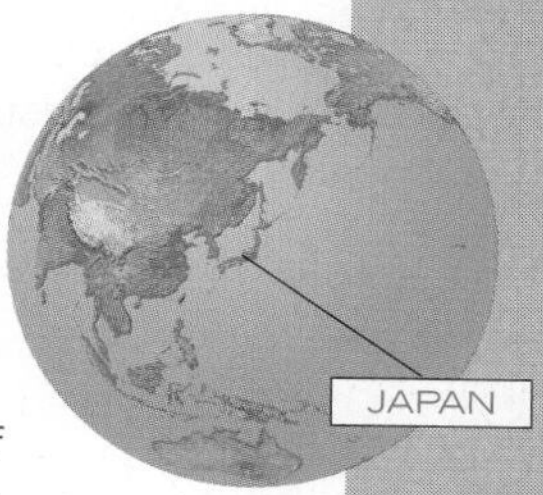

The farewells lasted "all day and into the night." Aboard ship, the travelers prayed for a peaceful crossing. When the clouds cleared, before dawn, "oars pierced the moon's reflection." Winds lashed. Typhoons threatened. Pirates lurked. The voyagers appealed to the gods by flinging tokens, charms, and cupfuls of rice wine into the sea. When perils threatened, they even sacrificed jewels and precious mirrors. It was a routine journey along the coast of Japan in 936. The governor of Kochi—at that time, one of the remotest provinces of the Japanese Empire on southern Shikoku Island in southwest Japan—was on his way home to the capital in what is now the city of Kyoto.

A journal that the governor's wife supposedly wrote carefully recorded the events of the journey. Scholars have doubted whether a woman really wrote the work, which is full of ironies and has flashes of male humor—as when, for instance, the wind gets up the writer's skirts. But soon after the date of the diary, literature in Japan became a suitable occupation for rich, intelligent women who did not have to worry about money but were barred from Japanese public life. So the "Tosa lady," as the diarist is called, could really have been a woman. In some ways, the work is obviously a literary creation and a moral tale. The ship navigates between perils. The sea is the arena of the "gods and Buddhas." Only prayer and sacrifice can save the travelers. When clouds recede, pirates emerge. When fear turns the voyagers' hair white, "Tell us, Lord of the Islands," prays the lady to the local god, "which is whiter—the surf on the rocks or the snow on our heads?"

Despite these dramatizations and fictional conventions, the sailing conditions the diarist described were true to life. The coast was so strewn with dangers that sailors dared not sail at night, except to elude pirates. Persistent and unpredictable head winds kept the voyagers cowering in harbor, yearning for home, passing the time writing poetry. The journey from Tosa to the ship's terminal in the port of Osaka can hardly have covered more than 400 miles; yet it took nearly three months. Hostile seas penned in the Japanese, despite their skill in nautical technology. This fact helps to explain why, for most of their history, the Japanese have been confined in their own islands and remained in a relatively small country, despite considering themselves to be an empire.

The experiences of the Tosa Lady, moreover, highlight a startling truth about her times. In other parts of the world, long-range navigations were leaping oceans. For in the amount of time the Tosa Lady took to get to Osaka, an Indian Ocean

[handwritten margin note: isolated due to poor sea conditions]

How did geography influence the spread of culture and state-building in North America and Mesoamerica?

Why was the Indian Ocean so important for the spread of culture?

Why were the land routes across Eurasia less significant than the sea routes across the Indian Ocean?

Which areas of India were most prosperous in the tenth and eleventh centuries, and what was the basis of their prosperity?

How did their relative cultural isolation affect Japan and Western Europe during these centuries?

Pilgrim ship. The monsoon helped to make the Arabian Sea a Muslim lake. The Indian pilgrim ship depicted in this Iraqi manuscript of the *Maqamaat* of al Hariri of 1238 is equipped with square sails to make the most of the winds on the outward and homebound crossings of the sea.

trader, with the benefit of the reversible wind system, could get all the way from the Persian Gulf to Sumatra (in modern Indonesia): a distance of more than 5,000 miles. The lady's Persian contemporary, Buzurg ibn Shahriyar, told stories of Persian and Arab mariners in *The Book of the Wonders of India*. One Persian captain made the journey to China and back to Persia seven times. The Japanese could only imagine such journeys. Not long after the Tosa diarist wrote, a fanciful Japanese sea story told of a ship—a "hollow tree"—blown by accident nonstop all the way from Japan to Persia.

As well as by commerce, pilgrim traffic to Mecca stimulated Indian Ocean navigation, as Muslim merchant communities spread across Asia and Muslim holy men took the increasing opportunities to travel and make converts. Meanwhile, beyond the range of the monsoon, migrants from what is now Indonesia crossed the ocean across the path of the southeast trade winds and colonized Madagascar, off the east coast of Africa. Their descendants are still there, speaking the same language the navigators brought—though what inspired such an extraordinary voyage remains unknown. Meanwhile, Polynesian navigators, as we have seen, were penetrating deep into the Pacific Ocean with the aid of some of the world's most regular long-range winds (see Chapter 10). Even more remarkably, around the year 1000, Thule Inuit, as archaeologists call them, from the Pacific and Norse from Scandinavia crossed the Arctic and Atlantic oceans from opposite directions and met in Greenland.

These extraordinarily long-range migrations were part of a double dynamic, as people stretched the resources available to them in one of two ways: exploring for new resources and exploiting existing opportunities in new ways. Region by region, culture by culture, in this chapter and the next, we can see people in widely separated parts of the world using similar strategies: felling forests, extending areas of cultivation and pasture, expanding into new terrain, enhancing muscle power with new technologies.

In the eleventh and twelfth centuries, these forms of expansion were widespread themes of world history; but, as we shall see, they followed divergent courses in different regions. As was so often the case, relative isolation was usually the key to the difference between long-lasting innovation and faltering, short-lived change. Cultures that exchanged information and artifacts were relatively robust. Peoples isolated from fruitful contacts found it much harder. In the Americas, therefore, as so often before, experiments in new ways of life were arrested by checks, frustrated by failures, interrupted by discontinuities. Meanwhile, however, some parts of the Old World, where long-range contacts were easier and more frequent, experienced enduring transformations.

The new opportunities of the period arose partly from the environmental changes of the preceding centuries, described in the last chapter. To see how people responded, we can devote this chapter to a world tour of some of the regions most affected—starting in the Americas, before turning to the world around the shores of the Indian Ocean, including the parts of East Africa that face that ocean, and ending with the extremities of Eurasia in Japan and Western Europe. In these parts of the world, we see societies contending with isolation with varying degrees of success. It would be neat if the history of the world only reflected common themes throughout the planet; but there have always been times and places conspicuous for being different, or for allowing or encouraging people to respond to common problems in peculiar ways. Isolation makes for divergence, and the places we look at in this chapter are bound to seem different from each other.

In other regions of Africa and Eurasia—China, Central Asia, West Africa, the Byzantine Empire, and the Islamic world—the single most important source of new pressures for change arose from a common experience: the stirrings of nomadic peoples. These are the subject of the next chapter.

AMERICAN DEVELOPMENTS: FROM THE ARCTIC TO MESOAMERICA

The history of the Americas in the eleventh and twelfth centuries is scattered with stories of new frontiers, developed by new migrations or new initiatives. But the effects of isolation and, sometimes, the challenges of hostile environments checked or restricted the achievements. We can start in the north and work, patchily, southward.

Greenland and the North

About 1,000 years ago, a relatively warm spell disturbed the lives of the ice hunters all along North America's Arctic edge. Taking advantage of improved conditions for hunting and navigating, migrants worked their way across the southern edge of the Arctic Ocean, following, from west to east, the line of what we now call the Northwest Passage along the northern coast of the New World in what is today the Canadian Arctic. The Thule Inuit traveled in vessels made of walrus hides, stretched across wooden ribs and sewn with sealskin thongs. They drew their bone needles only halfway through the hides to create waterproof seams. Their vessels were shallow, so that they could hug the shore, and light, so that the voyagers could lift them from between ice floes. When ashore, their crews could camp under the upturned hulls.

The Thule people hunted at sea for whales and polar bears. They mounted their harpoons on floats made from seal bladders, which they blew up like balloons. Game could then be towed home through the sea. Alternatively, they attacked their prey on rafts of ice, which they attached to the harpooned creatures until it was time to haul them in. On land, they hunted with dogs of a breed new to North America. Their spear-armed boatmen trapped reindeer in rivers. For warfare against human enemies, they reintroduced the bow and arrow (see Chapter 1). By about 1000 they had reached Greenland and the western extremities of North America (see Map 11.1). The navigation of the Arctic was an astonishing feat, unrepeated until the twentieth century.

Inuit seacraft. European technology was unable to make a ship that could sail around the Arctic coast of North America between the Atlantic and the Pacific until 1904. But the Thule Inuit accomplished the task with hide-covered craft by about 1000 C.E. Their boats were shallow enough to hug the shore, light enough to hoist onto the ice, and buoyant enough to avoid being crushed by ice floes.

MAP 11.1

Thule Inuit and Norse Migrations to ca. 1200

→	Thule Inuit migrations to ca. 1000
●	Thule Inuit settlements
▨	extent of Inuit, ca. 1200
⇢	assumed route of Norse settlement, late 9th century
⇒	assumed route of Eric the Red, late 10th century
➤	conjectural route of Leif Eriksson, late 10th century
➤	westerlies
⇢	ocean current
CANADA	modern country
●	Norse settlement/town

At the same time, almost equally heroic migrations were under way in the opposite direction, toward the same destinations, across the North Atlantic. A series of exploitable currents helped navigators from Scandinavia cross the ocean, via Iceland, below the Arctic Circle. It seems extraordinarily daring to risk such a long journey across the open sea, but the Scandinavians knew that the prevailing winds blew from the west in the latitudes they inhabited. So they could always hope to get home if the Atlantic venture proved fruitless. Even so, it was remarkable to navigate so far without chart or compass. The voyagers probably steered, like the Polynesians (see Chapter 10), by now-unrecoverable techniques, judging their latitude by observing the polestar with the naked eye on cloudless nights. By day, the only technical aid they had, as far as we know, was the so-called sun compass—a stump of wood with a protruding stick. The shadow it cast would tell the navigator whether his latitude had changed.

Whereas the Thule Inuit were blazing a trail of abundance, drawn by the fat-rich foods of the Arctic, the Norse—or Northmen—as the Atlantic voyagers are called, were usually escapees or exiles from poverty or restricted social opportunity. Erik the Red, traditionally celebrated as the first colonizer of Greenland, arrived there in 982, having been expelled from Iceland for murderous feuding. Most of the colonists he induced to follow him must have been extreme types—extremely desperate or extremely

Chronology: The Norse and Thule Inuit

900–1100	Warm spell in Arctic
ca. 982	Erik the Red reaches Greenland
c.a. 986	Founding of Brattahlid
ca. 1000	Thule Inuit reach Greenland
1189–1200	Construction of cathedral at Gardar

optimistic. "As to your enquiry what people go to seek in Greenland and why they fare thither through such great perils," said a medieval Norwegian book, the answer is "in man's threefold nature. One motive is fame, another curiosity, and the third is lust for gain."

In the early years of their settlement, the environment, harsh as it was, had a lot to offer the newcomers: plenty of fish and game, including luxury items valuable as potential exports to Europe, such as hunting falcons and walrus ivory. Greenland was not, however, a land the Norse cared to settle without changing the environment profoundly. They introduced grain and European grasses for grazing. They developed a breed of sheep whose wool was prized. The big wooden ships the Norse used, held together with iron nails, in a land with little timber or iron, must have seemed wildly extravagant to the Inuit in their skin canoes. The Norse town of Brattahlid in western Greenland—the remotest outpost of medieval Christendom—was heroically elaborate, with 17 monasteries and churches of stone with bells of bronze. The cathedral at Gardar was built between 1189 and 1200, of red sandstone and molded soapstone, with a bell tower, glass windows, and three fireplaces. The largest farms supported an aristocratic way of life, with big halls in which to feast dependents. But it remained an extremely precarious and isolated colony. Adam of Bremen, a canon of the cathedral of that north German city and a learned geographer of the late eleventh century, confided what little he knew: "Greenland is situated far out in the ocean opposite the mountains of Sweden. . . . The people there are greenish from the saltwater, whence, too, that region gets its name."

Brattahlid. The ruins of an eleventh-century Norse church at Brattahlid in Greenland show how ambitious—and, therefore, perhaps, ultimately how unsuccessful—the Norse colonists there were. Huge stone buildings, imported materials, dense settlements, ecologically revolutionary methods of agriculture, adherence to the culture of distant Europe in an environment where that culture could hardly be sustained—all these features of Norse life in Greenland made their colonies fragile.

The North American Southwest and the Mississippi Region

Beyond the colony in Greenland, the shore station that Greenlanders or Icelanders set up in Newfoundland off the east coast of Canada in about 1000 did not last. There were simply not enough wealthy or settled communities in the area with whom the Norse could establish contact, trade, and cultural exchange. A glance at the map of North America at the time shows similar cases, deep inland, of peoples struggling with isolation. The new way of life traveled along two routes: from the heartlands of maize in what is now Mexico into the arid lands of the North American Southwest; and from the Gulf of Mexico into the wetlands of the Mississippi valley and parts of what is now the United States' Deep South. The results included the rise of cultures with unmistakable similarities to predecessors in Mesoamerica (see Chapter 4), with urban life, irrigation, elaborate ceramics and shellcraft, gold work and copper work, ball games in some cases, and unmistakable signs of statehood (see Map 11.2).

In parts, for instance, of what are now the states of Colorado, New Mexico, and Arizona, evidence of some sort of political network spread over 57,000 square miles: from high in the drainage area of the San Juan River in the north to beyond the Little Colorado River in the south, and from the Colorado River to the Rio Grande. An extraordinary system of roadways, up to 12 yards wide,

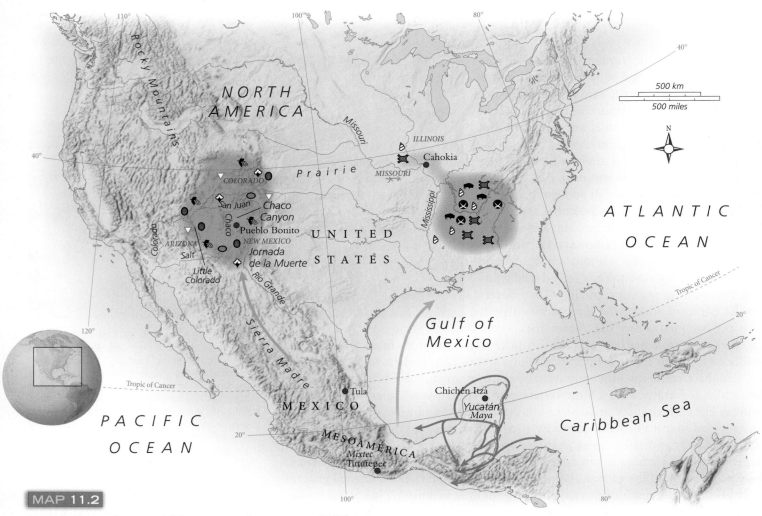

MAP 11.2

North America and Mesoamerica to ca. 1200

▨	canyon cultures
●	major city or ceremonial center
▨	Mississippian cultures
➔	roads leading north from Mesoamerica
➔	sea route from Mesoamerica to Mississippi River valley
→	Mayan trade route
Mixtec	peoples
ARIZONA	modern state

Economic Basis of Canyon People

🌾	maize
●	beans
◉	cotton
▽	irrigation
⬭	turquoise

Mississippian Trade Goods

𓆟	seashells
✕	deerskins
✕	bison pelts
❂	horn

radiated from a cluster of sites around the great canyon near the source of the Chaco River. Only two needs can account for such an elaborate network. Either some unknown ritual was being enacted, demanding and reinforcing close ties between the places linked; or the roads were there to move armies.

The environment is surprising: parched and—one would think—unsuitable for settled life. Apart from turquoise, which became the basis of a limited export trade, natural wealth was scarce. But the region was densely settled, at least in patches. The canyon people built ambitious cities or ceremonial centers around irregular plazas, surrounded by large, round rooms and a honeycomb of small rectangular spaces. Massive outer walls enclosed them. The main buildings were of stone, faced with fine masonry. Roofs were made of great timbers from pine forests in the hills—a dazzling show of wealth and power in a treeless desert. To construct the ceremonial center at Chaco Canyon, 200,000 trees were felled. We do not know what the political system was. But we know it was tough. Mass executions have left frightening piles of victims' bones, crushed, split, and picked as if at a cannibal feast.

The economic basis of this civilization was fragile. Sometimes the Chaco River would flood, though not regularly enough to create rich, silty soils. Rainfall levels are likely to have been higher than now, though irrigation was essential to help crops grow in the virtually rainless summer. If water could be delivered to the fields, cotton, maize, and beans would grow predictably, without danger from the sort of fluctuating temperatures that threatened at higher altitudes. Long irrigation canals did the job.

From the twelfth century onward, the climate got drier, which put the irrigation system under a constant strain. Faced with this kind of ecological crisis, communities usually try to adapt, at first, before giving up or moving on. The rulers of the canyon people responded by expanding into new zones, building more ambitiously, organizing labor more ferociously. But decline, punctuated by crisis, shows through a series of periodic contractions of the culture area and reorganizations of the settlements. Meanwhile, the harsh peacekeeping methods seem to have stopped working. Around the mid-twelfth century, settlements withdrew to high ground, where defense was easier, but where it was much harder to make an ample living from the fields. Revivals of a similar way of life happened frequently, but the problems of isolation defeated or limited all of them until the nineteenth century.

The canyon cultures were at least as remote from Mesoamerican civilizations as the Norse of Greenland were from Europe. Roads north from Mesoamerica led across dangerous territory. Nomadic peoples patrolled the northern edges of the Mesoamerican culture area, practicing raids and conquests, like those launched in Eurasia from the steppes into China or Europe, albeit on a smaller scale. The high road north from what is now Mexico to the nearest patch of easily cultivable soil led through a 61-mile pass known in modern times as the *Jornada del Muerto*: the "dead man's march," through rock-strewn defiles and dunes where the glare was so fierce that a traveler's eyes "boiled and bulged" and seemed to burst from their sockets, and men "breathed fire and spat pitch."

It was hard to travel that road—harder still to transmit Mesoamerican crops and traditions beyond the world of Chaco Canyon. The prairie, though a flat expanse, was an ecological barrier, where few patches could sustain sedentary life. It is more likely that Mesoamerica's tool kit, food, and ways of life and thought traveled across the Gulf of Mexico, by seaborne trade, to reach the North American Southeast. In parts of this region, the environment was promising. In

Canyon Culture. The adobe-built settlement of Pueblo Bonito in New Mexico enclosed large underground ceremonial spaces and storehouses for the maize painstakingly grown by irrigation in this parched region. The builders seem to have stuck to a single, coherent plan over the many generations it took to build the complex. In the twelfth century, before drought or some unknown disaster overwhelmed the place, Pueblo Bonito was a genuine imperial center, with outlying dependent pueblos built in imitation of it and a network of roads radiating from it.

the Mississippi valley and other riverside floodplains, natural ridges accumulated over centuries, wherever the floods dumped soil. These ridges were the nurseries of the farmers' crops and the inspiration for mounds dredged from the swamps to provide gardens. A hinterland of pools and lakes provided ideal centers for fish farming to supplement the field plants, among which maize was increasingly dominant.

In this region, between the ninth and thirteenth centuries, people laid out ceremonial centers in patterns similar to those of Mesoamerica. Platforms, topped with chambered structures, were loosely grouped around large plazas. The platform mounds grew. In generation after generation, people enlarged and enhanced them, as if to commemorate their own passage through the world. Each generation piled its structures on top of those of its predecessors.

Cahokia, east of St. Louis, is the most spectacular site. Cahokia stands almost at the northwestern limit of the reach of the culture to which it belongs. Its frontier position may have allowed it to act as a commercial gateway between zones of interrelated environments and therefore of interrelated products: shells from the Gulf, deerskins from the eastern woodlands, bison pelts and horn from the prairies. It is hard to calculate its overall size, because modern developments cover much of the area, but it probably covered 5.5 square miles. Cahokia's central platform is over 100-feet high—"a stupendous pile of earth" in the opinion of one of the first explorers to record its appearance in 1810. At about 13 acres, the base of the great mound is as big as that of the biggest Egyptian pyramid.

The city first arose in the tenth century. The remains of monumental building works date from the eleventh and twelfth centuries. At its height, in about 1200, Cahokia probably had around 10,000 inhabitants in its built-up area. It was the most intensely and elaborately constructed of a great arc of mound clusters from the site of present-day St. Louis in the west to the easternmost edges of the Mississippi floodplain. Farther away, smaller, similar sites extend from the riverbanks to the uplands of Illinois and Missouri. Cahokia's size gives it the look of a focal point for this scattering of settlements. Its air of importance tempts some scholars to think of it as something like the capital of something like a state, or, at least, a cultural center from which influence radiated. The chronology of Cahokia's development is uncertain in the present state of our

Cahokia. In the eleventh and twelfth centuries, Cahokia, near modern St. Louis, Missouri, was the most ambitious city north of the Rio Grande. As this reconstruction, with huge temple mounds surrounding a central plaza, suggests, Mesoamerican influence must have been at work here. Maize—a hardy northern variety developed from strains originating in Mexico—fed over 10,000 inhabitants and sustained an imperial society. The ambition of Cahokia's rulers demanded huge efforts to work the porous clay soil, exploit nearby forests, fight wars of domination, and control floods and mudslides.

knowledge, but a spate of sudden growth and intensive building around the mid-eleventh century seems to have coincided with the abandonment or decline of smaller sites in the same region. This coincidence makes it tempting see the rise of Cahokia as an example of successful imperialism.

Graves at Cahokia have given up honored dead. Their treasures included tools and adornments of copper, bones, and tortoiseshell covered in copper. One grave had gold and copper masks. Thousands of seashells, from the Gulf of Mexico, must have possessed the highest imaginable status and value in this deeply inland place. As time went on, increasing numbers of finely made stone arrowheads were buried in elite graves. This is a precious clue to how Cahokian culture changed, but it is hard to interpret. Were the arrows trophies of success—or imputed success—in war or hunting, or simple counters of wealth? In any case, the arrows were aristocratic possessions in a society graded for status and equipped for conflict. When Cahokia lost political power in the thirteenth century, the place retained a sacred aura: its manufactures—pots, shell work, soapstone carvings, and small axe heads that presumably had a place in forgotten rites—circulated over hundreds of miles and for hundreds of years after the mound dwellers died out or dispersed.

Chronology: North America and Mesoamerica, 10th to 13th Centuries	
Tenth century	Flourishing of canyon culture in American Southwest; founding of Cahokia in Mississippi River valley; founding of Chichén Itzá in Mesoamerica
Eleventh century	Mixtec first appear in historical record
1063–1125	Life of Eight-Deer Tiger-Claw
ca. 1100	Climate in American Southwest gets progressively drier
Eleventh–twelfth centuries	Maya intensively exploit Yucatán peninsula
ca. 1150	Canyon settlements withdraw to higher ground
ca. 1200	Cahokia population reaches 10,000
ca. 1300	Decline of upper Mississippi valley culture sites

When objects of great value are concentrated without evidence of a dwelling, grave, or warehouse, it is tempting to talk of a temple. An impressive cache of this type, found at what is now an automobile showroom, at a site somewhat to the southeast of Cahokia, contains carvings that give us glimpses into a mythic history or symbolic system that attached a high value to two themes: fertility and farming, and especially to maize and squash. One female figure tames a snake whose multiple tails are in the form of squash plants. Another female, kneeling on a mat, holds a stalk of maize. Images and fragments from other sites repeat some of these themes: female guardians of corn and serpents, some of whom also hold dishes as if offering a sacrifice.

The people who built Cahokia inaugurated a way of life that was economically successful and artistically productive for not much more than a couple of hundred years—not a bad tally for its place and time, but much shorter than the span major cities in Eurasia achieved. After a spell of stagnation or decline, their inhabitants deserted the upper Mississippi valley culture sites over a period of about four generations around the thirteenth and fourteenth centuries.

Yet culture of the kind that climaxed at Cahokia did not disappear. Rather, it was displaced and some of its more ambitious features—the huge mounds, the vast reach of trade—were abandoned. Mound building continued on a smaller scale, at sites scattered over the lower Mississippi valley and across the North American Southeast. Here, traditions of burying chiefs, with rich grave goods and sometimes with large-scale sacrifices, were also maintained.

"Yet culture of the kind that climaxed at Cahokia did not disappear. Rather, it was displaced and some of its more ambitious features—the huge mounds, the vast reach of trade—were abandoned."

Mesoamerica

In a similar way in Mesoamerica, the collapse of the cities of the classic Maya in the ninth and tenth centuries in Central America and southern Mexico (see Chapter 10) did not put an end to Maya experiments in civilization. Although the Maya cities of the lowlands never revived, and their peculiar culture, with its heavy investment in inscriptions on stone, never reappeared in quite the same form elsewhere, Maya city life and state-building continued in a new environment on the limestone peninsula of Yucatán in eastern Mexico. Here the environment contrasted with the old lowland heartlands of the Maya. The climate was dry, and irrigation relied on pools and wells. But it was possible to reconstruct the old Maya way of life with remarkable fidelity. In Yucatán, lowland tradition met links with central Mexico, which was accessible through a mixture of seaborne and overland routes (see Map 11.2).

The greatest Yucatán city, Chichén Itzá, began to arise in the tenth century, at about the time the lowland Maya culture withered. Its groves of columns resemble those of Tula (see Chapter 10), which it probably influenced. Some reliefs have undecipherable inscriptions and images that recall central Mexican art. Marked cultural continuities with the former Maya world are evident in the way the buildings are arrayed in the cities of Yucatán, in layouts that reflect an abiding interest in the observation of the movements of the stars and planets, and in the huge temple facades decorated with the snouts of curl-nosed gods or the jaws of feathered serpents. The ball court of Chichén Itzá is the biggest in the Mesoamerican world, and its sides are smothered with scenes of human sacrifice. If traditions recorded later are reliable, a dynasty with imperial ambitions, the Cocom, ruled in this city, and their wars with dynasties in rival centers dominated the history of the region for centuries.

Yucatán was a new frontier for the Maya: a region of unprecedentedly intense exploitation in the eleventh and twelfth centuries. It was not the only such area in Mesoamerica. The Pacific-facing regions of Mexico, beyond the Sierra Madre, leap into the historical record in the same period. This is the region where the people known as Mixtec (MEESH-tehk) lived, in relatively small communities that one could hardly call cities but that were densely settled and famed for their specialized professions of elite craftsmen, especially in gold work and books made of bark. One of the greatest of all Mesoamerican heroes came from here: Eight-Deer Tiger-

Chichén Itzá. With the end of monumental building, inscription-making, and royal rites among the lowland Maya in the tenth century, Maya civilization did not "die out." Its centers were displaced northward to the limestone peninsula of Yucatán, where Chichén Itzá arose to be the greatest city of the region. Some ways of life continued—lavish building, city-states almost constantly at war with one another, reliance on maize as a staple food, divination, human sacrifice, and elite rituals including chocolate-drinking and ball games. But the cities all have original architectural features. Chichén Itzá, for example, has a ball court of unprecedented size, and the unique, round-chambered building known as El Caracol, shown here in the foreground.

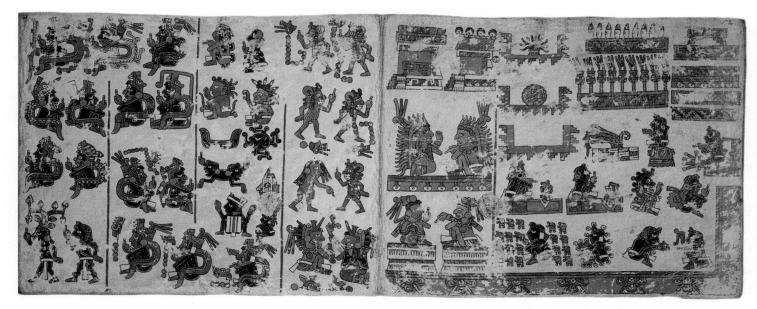

Mixtec creation myth. This Mixtec manuscript about the origins of the Earth predates the fifteenth century. Known as the Vienna Codex and painted on deer hide, it depicts Lord and Lady One-Deer, the legendary ancestors of all the Mixtec rulers, offering sacrifices of incense and tobacco to the gods.

Claw. From surviving royal genealogies, we can date his life with some confidence to the years 1063 to 1125. He came from Tututepec in the lowlands of Mexico and spent most of his career among Mixtec communities of the coastal region. His conquests have encouraged scholars to believe in an "empire of Tututepec," but we can best understand them as part of a violent power game to acquire deference, tribute, and victims for sacrifice.

Eight-Deer's wars did not necessarily lead to extensions of territorial power or of direct rule, but they did spawn a great reputation. He figures prominently in all surviving Mixtec histories. His activities show what was expected of a Mesoamerican king. He married frequently and had many children. He visited shrines, mediating between gods and men, offering sacrifices, consulting ancestors. He sent and received ambassadors, played the ball game against rival kings, negotiated peace, and—above all—made war. He died as he had lived. This model of Mesoamerican kingship was defeated, sacrificed, and dismembered by his enemies—entombed with his royal symbols in an episode vividly recorded in the genealogy of the kings of two small Mixtec towns, who wanted to be remembered as his descendants.

AROUND THE INDIAN OCEAN: ETHIOPIA, THE KHMER, AND INDIA

In the Americas, poor communications kept peoples apart and made it hard for them to exchange wealth and ideas. The Indian Ocean, by contrast, was, as we have seen, the world's great arena of exchange, crossed by trade routes and rimmed with rich societies. In the eleventh and twelfth centuries, the effects increased. In East Africa and Southeast Asia, the evidence of increasing wealth—and therefore the power of rulers able to harness that wealth—became more plentiful than ever, and new or renewed states and trading communities grew in size and influence. Meanwhile, in India, though political troubles convulsed many states, and their cultural influence shrank, trade across the ocean remained buoyant, prosperity survived, and some new or newly powerful kings emerged. We can continue our tour of the world by looking at each of these areas in turn.

"In the Americas, poor communications kept peoples apart and made it hard for them to exchange wealth and ideas. The Indian Ocean, by contrast, was, as we have seen, the world's great arena of exchange, crossed by trade routes and rimmed with rich societies."

East Africa: The Ethiopian Empire

The effects of isolation and of hostile environments, which inhibited so much long-term change in America, had also characterized the history of eastern Africa until this time (see Chapters 5 and 7). Gradually, as we have seen, links across the Indian Ocean lessened East Africa's isolation. By the twelfth century, important changes were occurring there.

Arabic-speaking geographers recorded the names of places along the east African coast as far south as the Limpopo River in Mozambique and knew of Muslim communities as far away as the island of Zanzibar. Arab traders already frequented Mogadishu (moh-gah-DEE-shoo) in modern Somalia. By 1200, Muslims from the Persian Gulf—the Shirazi dynasty—ruled it. Muslim geographers mentioned Mogadishu's transoceanic trade, bound for India and China, via the Maldive and Laccadive Islands in the Indian Ocean. Indeed, some places in Africa occur in Chinese books on geography as early as the tenth century, and East Africa, which formed part of the Indian Ocean world, bound to the trade of the ocean by the winds that linked it to Asia is well marked on thirteenth-century Chinese maps (see Map 11.3).

The increased trade of coastal kingdoms and cities could affect state-building far inland. This is important, not because state-building is necessarily good or progressive in itself, but because it is a measurable indicator of thoroughgoing, long-term change. In twelfth-century Ethiopia, a new dynasty recovered political unity and began a modest recovery. In this land, which had now been predominantly Christian for over 700 years (see Chapter 9), a time of internal crusade began, recorded in the lives of trailblazing frontier saints. On tireless pilgrimages, for instance, Takla Haymanyot made converts, dethroned idols, and chopped down forests, seizing "devils' trees" to build churches. An ideology of holy war seems to have taken hold. As early as the seventh century, some texts began to identify the ancient Ethiopian capital of Axum (see Chapter 9) as the "nursling of Zion" and her kings as "the children of Solomon," the biblical king of Israel. By the end of the twelfth century, kings regarded themselves as the heirs of Solomon and custodians of the Hebrew Ark of the Covenant, which had disappeared from the temple in Jerusalem centuries earlier. From Ziqwala, near Addis Ababa (ah-dees AH-bah-bah), the modern capital of Ethiopia, a monk called Gebre-Menfas-Qeddus challenged the surrounding Muslims and pagans to convert to Christianity.

On the Ethiopian frontier, the monastery churches of Lalibela began to emerge from the rocks: literally so, for they are hewn out of the ground. King Lalibela after whom their location is named, and who is credited with building most of them, is known only from semilegendary sources. His archives were lost in later wars or, as some scholars think, the next dynasty deliberately erased them. But the traditional tales are revealing. Emphasis, for instance, on the king's personal beauty "without defect from head to foot" reflects esteem for the artistic perfection of the buildings of his time. According to legend, a vision of heaven, which he then sought to realize on Earth, inspired Lalibela. After showing him what churches are like in heaven, God said to Lalibela, "It is not for the passing glory of this world that I will make you king, but that you may construct churches, like those you have seen, . . . out of the bowels of the earth." Stories of angels who worked on the buildings reflect the superiority of the craftsmanship. The monks who wrote Lalibela's life story emphasized that he used wage labor to supplement angelic work. Hatred of slavery was common in the writings of Ethiopian monks.

The Zagwe (ZAHG-way), as the kings of Lalibela's dynasty were called, were themselves frontiersmen. The metropolitan elites of the central highland region around Axum despised them for speaking a provincial language and regarded

> "Indeed, some places in Africa occur in Chinese books on geography as early as the tenth century, and East Africa, which formed part of the Indian Ocean world, bound to the trade of the ocean by the winds that linked it to Asia is well marked on thirteenth-century Chinese maps."

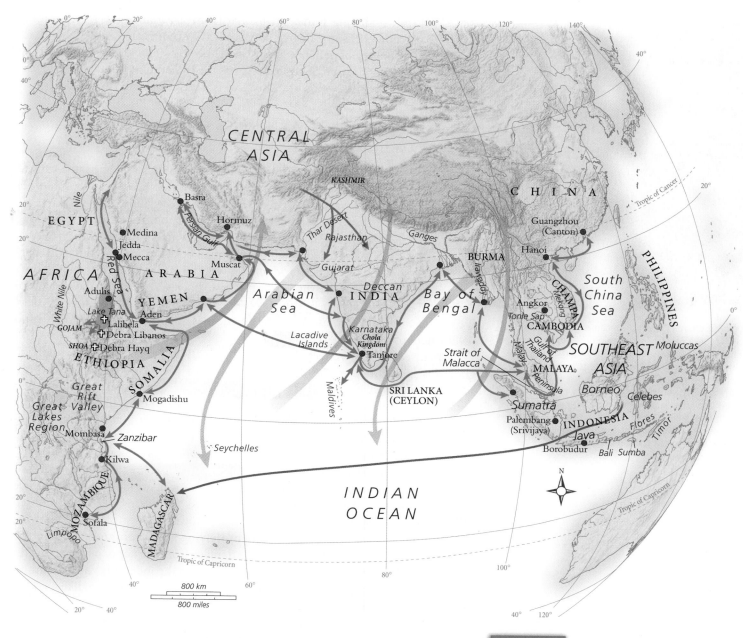

MAP 11.3

The Indian Ocean: From Ethiopia to Cambodia, ca. 1000–1200

- ▨ Zagwe dynasty, Ethiopia
- → Ethiopian expansion under the Solomids
- ✚ monastery
- → maritime trade route
- → colonization route to Madagascar
- → warm monsoon (April to September)
- → cold monsoon (October to March)
- → Muslim raids into northern India, 11th century

them as intruders. Nor perhaps did the Zagwe carry total conviction when they claimed to be heirs of Solomon. Everyone knew that they were upstarts who were not related to the old kings of Axum. Propaganda increasingly identified Ethiopia with the realm of the biblical Queen of Sheba, Solomon's concubine. Ethiopia was even proclaimed as "the new Israel." These claims to ancient roots favored rivals for the throne, who emerged in the second half of the thirteenth century, representing themselves as the rightful heirs of the Axumite monarchs, or calling themselves Solomids (meaning that they claimed to be descended from the biblical King Solomon). In 1270, they seized power. The state was organized for war, its court turned into an army, and its capital into an armed camp. The monasteries of Debra Hayq and Debra Libanos, the little world of religious communities on the islands of Lake Tana, became schools of missionaries whose task was to consolidate Ethiopian power in the conquered pagan lands of Shoa and Gojam.

Rock-cut church. Perhaps because of its relative isolation in a mountainous region, Ethiopian civilization has always shown great originality. The political and cultural revival of Ethiopia in the late twelfth and early thirteenth centuries is associated with King Lalibela, who began to build a new sacred capital in a frontier region, where masons dug churches out of the rock. Lalibela seems to have conceived this work as a place of pilgrimage, a "New Jerusalem," and an embodiment of what he claimed was a vision of heaven.

Ethiopia remained primarily an agrarian state, not a trading center. In some degree, it was always a mountain kingdom, with an ideology of defiance against neighboring states and peoples. But the multiplication of contacts across the Indian Ocean enabled Ethiopia to struggle against the effects of isolation with increasing success.

Southeast Asia: The Khmer Kingdom

At the opposite end of that ocean in Southeast Asia, the same context helps to explain the rise to fabulous wealth and power of another inland, agrarian kingdom: that of the Khmer in Cambodia. As we have seen (see Chapter 10), the Khmer homeland on the Mekong River, around the Tonle Sap, is ideal for rice growing. The fertility of the soil, enriched by silt from annual floods, nourishes three rice harvests a year. That productivity was the foundation of the kingdom's greatness. The rhythms of its rise, however, matched the growth of Indian Ocean trade, which opened outlets for the Khmer farmers' surplus. The ascent of the kingdom is documented in the growth and embellishment of its great city of Angkor.

The plan of the city reflects influences from India across the Bay of Bengal. Angkor was laid out to evoke the divine design of the world common to both Hindu and Buddhist beliefs: the central mountain or *Meru,* the mountains that ring it, the outer wall of rock, the seas flowing beyond in circlelike patterns. The royal palace built in the eleventh century centered on a tower that bore the characteristic inscription: "He thought the center of the universe was marked by Meru, and he thought it fitting to have a Meru in the center of his capital."

The architecture of the twelfth-century King Suryavarman II proclaims a new era. He had himself carved in the walls of his greatest foundation, the biggest temple in the world, Angkor Wat. Previously, monumental sculptures had only honored dead monarchs or royal ancestors. Suryavarman appears repeatedly in one of the temple galleries, surrounded by environment-defying goods: umbrellas against the sun, fans against the humidity. A dead snake dangles from his hand, perhaps in allusion to an anecdote about his accession. He seized the throne in his youth from his aged predecessor by leaping on the royal elephant and killing the king, like a god in a legend, who, "landing on the peak of a mountain, kills a serpent." Carvings he commissioned reenact the creation of the world, as if his reign were the world's renewal. They show the cosmic tug of war between good and evil gods. Scenes of the churning of the magic potion of life from the ocean suggest that the fortunate age of the world is about to begin. According to Hindu myth, peace and unity will prevail in the new age, and the various ranks of society will willingly perform their roles.

Hindu tradition predicted that this new age would last 1,728,000 years. Suryavarman's was over by 1150. But his ambitious building programs continued, especially under King Jayavarman VII later in the century. Jayavarman surrounded Angkor with shrines and palaces, way stations, and—it was said—more than 100 hospitals. A proclamation of his public health policy reads:

> He felt the afflictions of his subjects more than his own. . . . Full of deep sympathy for the good of the world, the king expresses this wish: all the souls who are plunged in the ocean of existence, may I be able to rescue them by virtue of this good work. May all the kings of Cambodia, devoted to the right, carry on my foundation, and attain for themselves and their descendants, their wives, their officials, their friends, . . . deliverance in which there will never be any sickness.

Angkor Wat. By the time of King Suryavarman II (r. 1113–1150), the great central temple of Angkor Wat, rising like the sacred mountain Hindus and Buddhists imagined at the center of the world, already dominated the skyline of Angkor. Thanks to silt deposited by the Mekong River, intensive rice cultivation generated huge food surpluses, making possible the investment of work and wealth required to build the stupendous city.

The allocation of resources for the hospitals hints at both the scale and the basis of Khmer wealth. Over 80,000 tributaries provided rice, healing spices, 48,000 varieties of fever medicines, salve for hemorrhoids, and vast amounts of sugars, camphor, and other antiseptics, purgatives, and drugs. From no other realm of the time—not even China—do we have figures of this sort or on this scale.

Even amid all this medication, the favorite remedy for illness was prayer. In 1186, Jayavarman dedicated a temple to house an image of his mother as "the Perfection of Wisdom." Again the statistics recorded in surviving documents are dazzling for their precision—which reveals the participation of meticulous bureaucrats—and the sheer volume of wealth they display. The temple received tribute from over 3,000 villages. Its endowments included vessels made of a mixture of gold and silver weighing more than 1,100 pounds and a similar set in silver. The records itemize thousands of precious stones, together with imported and locally produced luxury textiles. Daily provisions for a permanent establishment of 500 residents included rice, butter, milk, molasses, oil, seeds, and honey. Worshippers at the temple required annual supplies of wax, sandalwood, camphor, and sets of clothing for the temple's 260 cult images of Buddhas. This is all ample evidence of the penetration of Cambodia by Indian Ocean trade.

The same source adds evidence on a revolution of Jayavarman's reign: the triumph of Buddhism over Hinduism as the court religion. "Doing these good deeds," the inscription concludes,

> the king with extreme devotion to his mother, made this prayer: that because of the virtue of the good deeds I have accomplished, my mother, once delivered from the ocean of transmigration, may enjoy the state of Buddhahood.

Meanwhile, in the inner chamber of the gilded tower that the king added to the city, a Buddha replaced the Hindu images of previous reigns. The triumph of Buddhism in a state deeply rooted in Hinduism is remarkable. It owed something to the piety of the queen, who sought consolation in Buddhist devotions when her husband was away on campaign. But it was also part of a broader trend. Though Buddhism dwindled in India, it showed its potential for making converts elsewhere, slowly spreading in East, Southeast, and Central Asia.

"Though Buddhism dwindled in India, it showed its potential for making converts elsewhere, slowly spreading in East, Southeast, and Central Asia."

India: Economy and Culture

The strength of the cultural links across the Bay of Bengal, linking India and Southeast Asia, is a reminder of another problem. India had long been a fertile source of influences exerted across Eurasia: Buddhism and Hinduism; the science, logic, and technology of the Indian sages (see Chapter 6). The Indian subcontinent's central position athwart Indian Ocean trade routes guaranteed it against isolation and gave it privileged access to far-flung markets (see Map 11.3). India's long, open coasts could soak up ideas and influences from across the oceans, like the pores of a sponge.

Yet there are signs that from the eleventh century India's role in originating and recycling cultural influences began to diminish. Whereas earlier generations of Muslim scholars had looked to India as a source of useful learning, Al Biruni, who came from Persia in the 1020s, found Indian science and scholarship disappointing. He was widely regarded as the most learned man of his time, so he should have been in a position to know. Hindu science, he found, "presumed on the ignorance of the people." He found the Indian sages of his day complacent and uninterested in learning from abroad. His picture was exaggerated, and perhaps distorted by a hidden agenda: the desire to advocate the superiority of Islam over native Indian religion.

There was, however, some truth on al Biruni's side. At least in the north—the part of India he knew—political dissolution accompanied a decline in the quality and output of works of art and learning. The large states that had filled most of the subcontinent since the early ninth century collapsed under the strain of trying to compete with each other and the impact of invaders and rebellions. Much of central and northern India was not divided among territorial states but among competing royal dynasties who found it hard to sustain the loyalties of their followers. The rich Hindu temples of northern India became the prey of Muslim raiders from Afghanistan.

Nevertheless, though states provide the peace commerce requires—and, if the rulers are wise, the infrastructures that help trade thrive—economies can sometimes function well despite political troubles. In some parts of India, the economy was booming. Records of tribute paid to the temples in Rajasthan (RAH-jahs-tahn) in northwest India reveal the range of produce sold in local markets and the lively pace of trade in sugar, dyes, textiles, salt, areca nuts, coconuts, butter, salt, sesame oil. Charcoal makers, distillers, and shopkeepers had to pay taxes in cash. A local ruler in Shikar in Rajasthan in 973 levied tribute in pearls, horses, "fine garments," weapons, camphor, betel nuts, sandalwood, "and endless quantities of gold and with spirited rutting elephants, huge like mountains, together with their mates." From the eleventh century, we can reconstruct merchant lineages from inscriptions that are astonishing, because they reveal how merchants saw themselves. The Pragvata family, for instance, whose activities extended across Rajasthan and into Gujarat (goojah-RAHT), considered themselves warriors in a trade war against Muslim competitors and advanced loans to rulers to fight real wars. Not only the warrior caste, says one inscription, can fight in "the shop of the battlefield." This is amazingly ambitious, arrogant language for merchants, who, in most societies of the time, would not have dared to liken themselves to the warrior elite. Clearly, however turbulent the politics of the time may have been, the economy was doing well.

The most spectacular effect was the revival of Indian cities after what seems to have been a long period of relative stagnation. This effect was particularly strong in the south, where political troubles were fewer and invasions infrequent. In Karnataka (kahr-NAH-tah-kah) in southwest India, eleventh-century inscriptions mention 78 towns—three times the number recorded for the eighth century. A grant to a temple in northern Karnataka in 1204 reveals how a city was laid out, with streets leading

> "The Indian subcontinent's central position athwart Indian Ocean trade routes guaranteed it against isolation and gave it privileged access to far-flung markets."

between white-plastered temples, many bazaars, water tanks, flower gardens, and food plots, with arterial roads at the city's edges. The grant lays the economy of the region and the wealth of the cities before us. It enumerates 24 city precincts, both residential and commercial. Merchants and manufacturers met in the town assembly, which decided how to tax produce passing through the town, including foodstuffs, common drugs and medicines, raw cotton, cloth, perfumes, and horses. Local manufacturers mentioned in the same text included clothiers, perfumers, and jewelers.

India: The Chola Kingdom

Far from the political disorder of the north, states in southern India could enjoy the increase of strength that the wealth of the Indian Ocean made possible. The Chola kingdom was the most remarkable. Like that of the Khmer or of Ethiopia, its heartland lay away from the coasts, in rice fields and pastures. The Chola kings almost invariably attached more importance to landward security and expansion than to the sea. A raid that touched the Ganges River did more for the prestige of the monarchy than the remotest seaborne adventure. The Chola labored to extend their landward frontiers and develop their landward resources by ruthless exploitation. Indeed, they felled forests on a gigantic scale. The founding myth of the dynasty concerns King Chola, who was out hunting antelope when, lured deep into the forest by a demon, he came to a place where there were no Brahmans to receive alms. So he cleared the forest and planted temples. His successors followed this pattern.

The power, wealth, and ambitions of the Chola kings fused with those of the merchant communities on the coast. In the kingdom's grand ports, gold was exchanged for pearls, coral, betel nuts, cardamom, loudly dyed cottons, ebony, amber, incense, ivory, and rhinoceros horn. Elephants were luxuriously warehoused and were stamped with the royal tiger emblem before being shipped out for export.

The merchants' vocation blended with the pirates'. Chola merchants had private armies and a reputation "like the lion's" for "springing to the kill." The imperial itch seemed strongest in kings whose relations with merchants were closest. King Kulottunga I (r. 1070–1122), who relaxed tolls paid to the crown, imagined himself—there is a pillar inscription to prove it—the hero of songs "sung on the further shore of the ocean by the young women of Persia." Most Chola seaborne "imperialism" was probably just raiding, though there were Chola footholds and garrisons on Sri Lanka and the Maldives and perhaps in Malaya. Its impact, however, crippled Srivijaya in Indonesia (see Chapter 10) and enriched the temples of southern India.

Hindu temples were the allies and support of the Chola kings in managing the state and the biggest beneficiaries of victories in war. While the seaward drive lasted, the registers of gifts inscribed on temple walls show its effects: a shift from livestock and produce of the soil to dazzling bestowals of exotic goods and cash, especially from about 1000 to about 1070. The treasures of the city temple of Tanjore included a crown with enough gold to buy enough oil to keep 40 lamps alight in perpetuity, and many hundreds of precious gemstones and jewels, with plenty of umbrellas and fly whisks for the comfort of the worshippers at ceremonies.

Chola temple. The great era of Chola temple building in stone began in the reign of Queen Sembiyan Mahadevi in the late tenth century. Her grandson Rajendra dwarfed her achievements with this towering example—over 200 feet high—at Tanjavur. All the villages of the kingdom had to subscribe to its upkeep.

Chronology: The Chola Kingdom

1012–1042	Reign of Rajendra; new capital to commemorate Ganges campaign
1070–1122	Reign of Kulottunga I, proponent of seaborne imperialism
Thirteenth century	Decline of Chola

When King Rajendra (r. 1012–1042) built a new capital to commemorate his campaign on the sacred river Ganges, he gave the temples an extravagant new look. Concave, sinuous forms were meant to match the supple figures of queens and goddesses, who shimmied and sashayed in the bronzes earlier kings commissioned. Into the artificial lake, 16 miles long and 3 miles wide, Rajendra poured water drawn from the Ganges. The site of the building, according to a twelfth-century poet, could overwhelm with joy "all fourteen worlds encircled by the billowing ocean. . . . The very landscape around was made invisible."

The temples are the best evidence of the grandeur of the Chola Empire and the reach of its power and trade. But they also suggest why, ultimately, the Chola withdrew from overseas ventures. The temples invested heavily in land and in the revenues of farmers whom they supplied with capital to make agricultural improvements. In consequence, they may have contributed to a shift of priorities toward agriculture and land-based wealth, and therefore, in the long term, to weakening Chola maritime imperialism—an enfeeblement that became marked in the thirteenth century. So, although India remained as rich as ever, some forms of Indian enterprise turned inward.

EURASIA'S EXTREMITIES: JAPAN AND WESTERN EUROPE

The Indian Ocean enclosed the main routes of communication around maritime Asia and between Asia and Africa. Of secondary importance were the land roads across Central Asia and the Sahara, which are subjects for the next chapter. For travelers on both the ocean roads and the land roads, Japan and Western Europe—the regions at the easternmost and westernmost extremities of Eurasia—were hard to get to and from. They were distant from the centers of the system. Europe could not communicate directly with Asia by sea. Africa was in the way. Little of the land-based trade reached the extreme west. Trade was far more intense between the relatively rich markets concentrated in the region between Byzantium in the west, India in the south, and China in the east. As we saw at the start of the chapter, the typhoon-torn seas that plagued the Tosa Lady surrounded Japan.

Societies, therefore, threatened with isolation occupied the extremities of Eurasia. But they were placed close enough to the major communications routes to tap into the great exchanges of culture of the time. During the eleventh and twelfth centuries, both areas emerged from relative isolation. For Western Europe, as we shall see in the next chapter, the revitalization even led to ambitious attempts to make conquests from the Islamic world.

Japan

While in much of the world people struggled to overcome isolation, in Japan rulers had formerly tried to make a virtue of it. Japanese rulers were fearful of losing migrants to richer regions and apprehensive of Chinese power. They had suspended diplomacy and trade with China in 838 and with Korea nearly a century later (see Map 11.4). Permission to trade abroad was hard to obtain. Even Buddhist monks had to get permission to leave the country on pilgrimage. Of course, illicit trade—or "piracy" as officials called it—went on. But self-sufficiency remained the object of government policy.

The best-known Japanese literature of the tenth and eleventh centuries focuses on a narrow, closed court society in a narrow, closed country. The fiction of Murasaki Shikibu in *The Tale of Genji*, one of the earliest realistic novels ever written, unfolds in palace chambers and corridors dark enough to make her stories of mistaken identity among lovers believable. She depicts a world in which the supreme values seem to be snobbery and sensitivity. Struggles for precedence dominate court life. The emperor grants his favorite cat the privileges "of a lady of middle rank." A nurse can tell from the sound of a visitor's cough to what level of the nobility he belongs. Murasaki's male heroes are excited to love by exquisite penmanship, a girl by the "careless dexterity of a folded note." "Sometimes, people of high rank sink to the most abject positions," muses her main character, Prince Genji, "while others of common birth rise to be high officers, wear important faces, redecorate the insides of their houses, and think themselves as good as anyone." The court is everything. Even an appointment as governor of a province is a disgrace. Court literature scarcely mentions the peasants, beaten down by famine and plague, whose rice production sustained the court aristocracy through a system of grants of "public-allowance rice" or *kugeto*.

Murasaki was an acute observer, and her work portrayed the vices of a faction-ridden system. Genji was an underemployed prince demoted from the imperial family, like scores of surplus sons, for reasons of economy. The author was a spokeswoman for courtiers excluded from power by the man she hated, whose amorous advances she claimed to have turned down: the all-powerful courtier, Fujiwara no Michizane, who manipulated the political system by marrying his womenfolk into the imperial family and providing an effective bureaucracy from his own household. He was the brother-in-law of two emperors, uncle and father-in-law to another, uncle to one more, and grandfather to another two. After three emperors died in factional struggles, he was left as regent of the empire in 1008. He exploited his opportunities so well that, according to one embittered critic, "not a speck of earth was left for the public domain." Emperors were so preoccupied with ritual duties that the only way they could bid for power was by abdicating and attempting to control their heirs.

Provincial rule was left to administrators, supported by retinues of hired tough guys. Despised at court for their "badly powdered faces," these local leaders wielded real power and handled real wealth. Many of them, like Murasaki's Genji, were the descendants of imperial princes who had been sent to the provinces for want of employment at court, or who had opted for provincial careers to pursue autonomy, wealth, and authority of their own. Increasingly they became warriors whose authority depended on force. As the court began to lose control of the provinces, these provincial warmongers allied in rival bands. In the early twelfth century, Taira no Tadamori was a warrior-descendant of one of the most powerful clans and the son of a provincial governor. His feats against pirates, bandits, and a rebel army of disgruntled Buddhist monks won him a reception at court, but the court aristocracy despised his provincial origins and ridiculed his efforts at poetry.

In the 1070s, however, courtiers, temples, and merchants succeeded in opening Japan to foreign trade in their own economic interests. Trade with Korea resumed for a while as a result of the initiative of Korea's energetic King Munjon (r. 1046–1083). Direct relations between Japan and China followed. The results

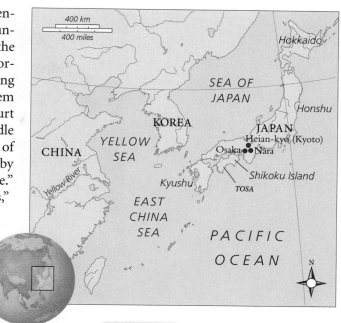

MAP 11.4

Japan, Korea, and Northern China

Genji. The earliest illustrated manuscripts of *The Tale of Genji* date from the 1120s, more than 100 years after the novel was written. But they demonstrate its enduring popularity and faithfully capture its atmosphere: the leisured opulence of the imperial palace at Heian, the learning and luxury of the court ladies, and the difficulty of leading a private life—let alone conducting the complex love affairs that the story depicts—behind frail partitions that were literally paper-thin.

were dramatic: Newly rich families became players for power. The greatest profiteers were the Taira clan, who relentlessly, during the twelfth century, built up their power by acquiring provincial governorships and penetrating and, by early in the second half of the twelfth century, dominating the imperial court. In a series of civil wars, culminating in 1185, their rivals and relatives, the Minamoto clan, had replaced them as imperial "protectors" or **shoguns**. From then on the emperors never recovered real power. The renowned monk Mongaku was an adviser to successive shoguns. Invited to pray for a new shogun in 1200, he showed just what he thought of the request: "In the dwellings of those who offend, prayer is of no avail."

As the diary of the Tosa Lady shows, it was hard to get around Japan's home islands—even that relatively small part of the islands the Japanese state occupied. Overseas contacts were genuinely difficult, the surrounding seas genuinely daunting. Yet even at its most restrictive, Japan's isolation had never shut out Chinese cultural influence. Some of Murasaki's characters showed impatience with "Chinesified" styles, appealing to the "spirit of Japan." And popular literature did depict China as strange and exotic. But educated Japanese were well aware of their dependence on China for almost all their models of learning, art, and government. Chinese was the language of the upper administration as well as of all serious literature. The elite used handbooks of quotations from Chinese classics to clinch arguments. Confucian ceremonies and Chinese poetry contests (on such subjects as "the thin, solitary voice of the first cicada" and "the freshness of mountains and streams after the sky has cleared") were among the main occupations at court. Murasaki Shikibu, by her own account, repelled Fujiwara's unwanted attentions by capping his Chinese verses.

Chronology: Japan: Official Isolation

838	Trade and diplomacy with China suspended
ca. 1000	*The Tale of Genji* written
1070s	Opening of Japan to limited foreign trade; restoration of direct relations with China
1160	Taira clan ascendant
1185	Minamoto replaces Taira as shoguns

Western Europe: Economics and Politics

Nowhere else in the world were there long-range trade routes to match those of the Indian Ocean. But—though the subject is poorly documented in this period—the land routes across Eurasia, from Europe to China, and across the Sahara, between the Mediterranean and the Sahel, were probably carrying increasing amounts of traffic through the eleventh and twelfth centuries. Western Europe lay at or just beyond the western and northern extremities of these land routes.

Its relative isolation always threatened the region with backwardness. The Atlantic clouded Europe's outlook to the west. The Sahara cut it off from access to much of Africa. Europe's frontier on the east to the great civilizations of Asia was vital but hard to keep open across plains that hostile steppelanders patrolled or forests, flanked by vast marshlands, obstructed. There was no direct access to the Indian Ocean. Western European merchants rarely went there—and, when they did, they had to undertake epic overland journeys via the Nile valley or across Arabia or what are now Turkey and Iraq. Unlike in Japan, no one in Western Europe wanted to stay outside the great circuits of Eurasian exchange. But isolation was hard to overcome.

A Muslim geographer, al-Istakhri, contemplating the world from Persia in 950, hardly noticed Western Europe at all. In his map, the West was squeezed almost out of the picture, dangling feebly off the edge of the known world. Meanwhile, Latin Christians who looked out at the world in their own imaginations probably saw something like the version mapped at about the same time by the monks who drew the illustrations in the *Commentary on the Apocalypse* of Beatus of Liébana in northern Spain: Asia takes up most of the space, Africa most of the rest. Europe consists mainly of three peninsulas—Spain, Italy, and Greece, jutting into the Mediterranean—with a thin strip of hinterland above them. In 1095, urging fellow Christians to new efforts against the Muslims, Pope Urban II expressed the feeling of being under seige:

> The world is not evenly divided. Of its three parts, our enemies hold Asia . . . Africa, too, the second part of the world, has been held by our enemies for two hundred years and more. . . . Thirdly there is Europe. . . . Of this region we Christians inhabit only a small part, for who will give the name of Christians to those barbarians who live in the remote islands and seek their living on the icy ocean as if they were whales?

"Unlike in Japan, no one in Western Europe wanted to stay outside the great circuits of Eurasian exchange. But isolation was hard to overcome."

A Muslim view of the world. The world, mapped by the Muslim geographer al-Istakhri in the tenth century. The map is now in the library of Leiden University in the Netherlands. Persia, the map-maker's homeland, is in the center. Europe is the tiny triangle at the lower right. The Caspian and Aral seas are represented as two large round blobs in the middle of Asia in the lower portion. West Africa is the landmass at the top.

Otto III. The workshop of the Abbey of Reichenau in Germany was one of the finest art studios in tenth- and early eleventh-century Europe, producing the Gospel book of Emperor Otto III on gilded pages. The enthroned emperor grasps the orb of the world, stamped with the cross of Christ. He towers over clergy and aristocracy alike, while the regions of Europe, led by Rome, shuffle humbly toward him with their tribute.

Urban wanted Christendom to combine to redress what he saw as an imbalance of power. But it crumbled into competing states with no strong focus of common allegiance. It became what political scientists call a state system, with lots of interlocking territorial states, rather than an imperial system that a single state dominated or covered, as it had been in the time of the Roman Empire. From 962, the German ruler Otto I called himself—more in hope than in reality—"Roman emperor" and made a big investment to recover a sense of unity. As he understood it, his empire was "holy"—serving the whole of Christendom—and the emperor's duty was to guard and extend its frontier. When his grandson, Otto III, looked back at the reflection of himself that stared, enthroned in power, from an illustration in his gospel book, he could see lavish images of Germany, Gaul, and the Slav lands humbly bearing their tribute toward him, led by a personification of Rome. These pretensions were hollow. The empire of the Ottos was essentially a German state, covering not much more than modern Germany. Map 11.5 shows where other major states of the system took shape in the eleventh century.

The rise of the state system did not necessarily make Christendom weaker or less able to expand. On the contrary, competition between states can stimulate innovation and promote expansion. Great unitary empires, like China, are vulnerable to bad central decision making, whereas, in the complexity of a system of many states, one state may fail without incapacitating the rest.

Although Latin Christendom failed to reunite, it continued to respond to the growing sense of being under attack by outsiders. As we have just seen in the case of Ethiopia, expansion does not only happen outward. There are often inward cracks and gaps to fill, slack to take up. From the eleventh to the early fourteenth centuries, a process of internal expansion, accompanied by new economic activity, was under way in Western Europe. Latin Christendom emerged as a genuinely expanding world, as it stretched between increasingly remote horizons (see Map 11.5).

Settlement encroached on marginal soils and headed uphill. In mountain settings, Western civilization spread up slopes formerly unoccupied or abandoned to the domain of hostile highlanders, whom their lowland neighbors despised as barbarians. The new accessibility of highlands to settlement from below is intelligible

MAP 11.5

Europe, ca. 1200

○   major centers of population

▨   Muslim frontier in Spain, ca. 1200

▨   predominantly pagan lands

—   Hanseatic trade route

Economic Activities

🌿   region of commercially produced cereals

🍇   region of commercially produced wine

📖   major textile area

▯   silver mine

🐝   wax

🌲   timber

⊛   salt

🐟   fish

🦡   furs

🐑   wool

against a long background of climate change: a "warm spell" that lasted from the late tenth to the mid-thirteenth centuries.

Meanwhile, other environments were transformed and ecologies disturbed. Forests fell. Bogs were drained. Farmers moved in. Church and state grasped communities formerly isolated by forest, marsh, or mountain, whose conversion to Christianity, before this period, was sometimes sketchy and whose habitats were often blanks on the map. This was more than an economic enterprise: it was a sacred undertaking—reclaiming for God part of the terrain of paganism. The forest was stained with pagan sensuality and alive with sprites, demons, and "wild men of the woods." The pious felled trees sacred to pagans.

Cistercian monastery, Catalonia. Cistercians sought to colonize wastelands, like those where John the Baptist, Jesus, and the first Christian monks withdrew from the world. But the world caught up. Peasants settled near the monasteries; rulers called upon monks to serve them; and princes chose to be buried among Cistercians, as in the monastery at Poblet, shown here, which became the pantheon of the rulers of Catalonia in northern Spain.

The most famous example is the best. Unable to sleep "on a certain night" in 1122, Abbot Suger of Saint-Denis, a monastery near Paris, rose to search the forest for 12 trees mighty enough to frame the new sanctuary he was planning for his abbey church, built—he hoped—to be full of light and "to elevate dull minds to the truth." The foresters smiled at him and wondered if the abbot was "quite ignorant of the fact that nothing of the kind could be found in the entire region"; but he found what he needed "with the courage of faith." It was a representative incident in a vast project to tame little-exploited and underexploited environments.

The Cistercians, one of the most dynamic new monastic orders of the period, directed their efforts into "deserts" where habitation was sparse and nature hostile. They disputed Suger's views on church architecture—advocating simplicity and austerity in worship—but favored building and tree felling on at least a comparable scale. They razed woodlands and "made rough places plain"—fulfilling one of the conditions the Bible specifies for the end of the world. They drove flocks and ox teams into wildernesses where today, all too often, the vast abbeys lie ruined in their turn. Sometimes, in their craving to escape the greedy secular society that put their souls at risk, Cistercians actually drove existing settlers away from their lands, extending the frontiers of colonization even farther as peasants imitated Cistercian practices on even more marginal lands.

Engineering came to the aid of environmental adaptation. Drainage helped extend the land on which people could dwell. In Holland, rapid population growth seems closely linked with the success of a project Count Floris V (r. 1256–1296) launched to reclaim waterlogged land. New embankments and canals made rivers easier to navigate. Searching out new routes and building roads and bridges were urgent tasks for the common good, for which monarchs accepted some responsibility and for which—for example—Domingo de la Calzada, who built causeways and bridges for pilgrims to the shrine of St. James at Compostela in northern Spain, was made a saint.

Behind the expanding frontiers, modest technical revolutions were boosting production. Among inventions originating in Europe at this time were windmills, ground lenses, and clocks. Others, brought there thanks to improved communications across Eurasia, were paper mills, the compass, firearms, and—a little later in the fourteenth century—the blast furnace. Large, heavy plows with curved blades bit deeply into the land, which enabled farmers to exploit the dense, wet soil of northern Europe. More effective harnesses enabled horses to pull the plows and take over a lot of hard work in the fields. More efficient windmills and water mills, more exact metallurgy and new products, especially in arms and glassware, extended the range of business and the flow of wealth. The advances in agriculture that began in the Islamic world toward the end of the previous millennium (see Chapter 10) spread hesitantly, across Western Europe, improving farming with new strains of wheat and—where it would grow—of rice. More varieties of beans improved nutrition and added nitrates to the soil.

Historians debate who was responsible for extending tillage and coaxing new wealth from the soil. Was it primarily the work of "free peasants"? Or did landowners force peasant dependants into greater productivity? There were many different patterns of landholding, which varied regionally and locally, and the drive to improve efficiency probably happened no matter what form landholding took. In any case, the colonization of new lands created opportunities of enrichment at all social levels. More food meant more people. The population of Europe may well have doubled, from about 35 million around the year 1000, while these changes took place.

As production and population increased, so did opportunities for trade. New trade routes knitted Atlantic and Mediterranean seaboards in a single economy. This was an important development, because Western Europe has two natural economic zones—formed, respectively, along the Mediterranean and Atlantic coasts. The Strait of Gibraltar separates them, with widely different sailing conditions along the two seaboards. Inland a chain of breakwaters splits the continent, determining the flow of rivers and, therefore, the directions of exchange. For much of Europe's history, communication between these two zones was not easy. Limited access through routes across France and the Alpine passes kept restricted forms of commerce alive, even when commercial navigation from sea to sea was abandoned.

New kinds of economic activity became possible in growing towns. Lübeck, founded in 1143, was the pioneer city of what became the **Hanseatic League**— a network of allied ports along the North Sea and Baltic coasts that collaborated to promote trade. Soon after, Mediterranean craft, mainly from the Italian city of Genoa, the island of Majorca, and Spain, resumed large-scale ventures along Atlantic coasts, such as had not been recorded since the Western Roman Empire collapsed in the fifth century (see Chapter 8).

Exchange across vast distances made geographical specialization and genuine industrialization possible. The industries served by the trade of Genoa depended on geographical specialization. Textiles depended on concentrating wools and dyestuffs from widely separated places of origin. Food processing relied on matching fresh foodstuffs with salt, oil or wine. Shipbuilding demanded a similar marriage of raw materials—wood, iron, sailcloth, and pitch.

The results included urbanization: the revival of old cities and the building of new ones. The best way, indeed, to measure the economic progress of the period in much of Europe is by the growth of towns—ways of organizing life, which, at the time, were prized as uniquely virtuous. "The order of mankind," according to Gerald of Wales in the 1180s, "progresses from the woods to the fields and

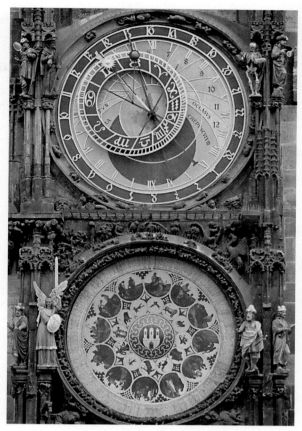

Town hall clock. The early fifteenth-century town hall clock of Prague—now capital of the Czech Republic—illuminates the growing concern among the citizens of late medieval European cities to know what time it was. Prague's clock divides the day into arbitrary hours of equal length, while also marking the passage of the hours of daylight, which varied from one day to another. Christian ideology also has its place on the clock. Every hour, the Archangel Michael appears to do battle with a Muslim Turk, and the Twelve Apostles move across the clock face.

Chronology: Technology and Growth in Europe	
Late tenth century	Beginning of warm spell in climate
1000	Population of Europe approximately 35 million
1143	Founding of Lübeck; beginning of Hanseatic League
ca. 1200	Introduction of new technologies: heavy plows, better harnesses, windmills, water mills, ground lenses, clocks
1300	Population of Europe approximately 79 million

REGION/PEOPLE OR KINGDOM	OPPORTUNITIES	EXPLOITATION STRATEGIES
Arctic/Inuit	Change in climate: warming weather allows for navigation across Canadian Arctic; introduction of new breed of pack dogs for transportation; introduction of bow and arrow	New techniques for constructing walrus-hide boats; new uses for sealskin, other animal hides for transport, hunting, food
Greenland/Norse	Warming climate; wealth of fish and game in almost uninhabited region; availability of export items such as hunting falcons, walrus ivory	Improved navigational techniques; new understanding of prevailing winds, ocean currents to improve chances of successful voyages; introduction of European grains and grasses for grazing animals; development of new breed of sheep
North American Southwest and Mississippi region/Native Americans	Southwest: introduction of maize from Mexico; defensible canyons with water supply; growing population	Southwest: irrigation canals to expand agriculture; many ceremonial centers; expansion into new zones; intensive organization of labor; development of multistoried residential structures
	Mississippi: introduction of Mesoamerican "tool kit," food, way of life, thought; expanded trade routes bring deerskin, shells, bison hides, metals, and minerals	Mississippi: expansion of trade routes; new forms of agriculture with maize, beans, squash, and fish farming; larger populations lead to more intensive crafts development/industry.
Mesoamerica/Yucatán: Maya	Abundant forests, wildlife, coastal resources	New forms of irrigation, wells; new communities lead to expanded sea and land trade routes
East Africa/Ethiopia	Wider access to trade goods	Increased Indian Ocean trade with Arabs, Chinese, Indians helps equip Ethiopian dynasties to expand into new terrain
Southeast Asia/Khmer kingdom (Cambodia)	Growth of Indian Ocean trade opens outlets for Khmer rice surplus; wealth from trade and taxes funds Angkor Wat	Expansion of kingdom coincides with monumental temple complexes at Angkor, complete with expanded amenities for subjects—hospitals, shrines, etc.
India/Chola kingdom	Expansion of frontiers through inland raids brings additional natural resources (forests, agricultural land)	Landward strategy of clearing forests, planting crops and building large temples; coastal merchant communities merge with pirate expeditions sponsored by Chola kings to raid foreign ports
Japan	Provincial warriors break away from imperial court, open Japan to foreign trade; new wealth	Taira and other newly rich families, begin to dominate imperial court, develop shogunate system of government to rule more efficiently
Western Europe	Expanding settlements into marginal agricultural areas; new engineering techniques to manage rivers, build infrastructure	Intensive land management—felling forests, draining bogs combines with Christianizing efforts to "civilize" barbarian areas; increased commerce leads to economic specialization, growth of towns and communes

from the fields to the towns and the gatherings of citizens." In Italy, the **commune**—as the citizen body was collectively called—became an institution of government in most cities only in the late eleventh or early twelfth century. In what seems to have been a conscious reaching back to a Roman model, many Italian cities acquired "consuls" in this period. By the mid-twelfth century, instead of deferring to some great protector—bishop, nobleman, or abbot— Italian cities became their own "lords" and even extended jurisdiction into the countryside. In effect, some cities were independent republics, forming alliances in defiance of, or in spite of, their supposed lords. Others tried unsuccessfully for the same status.

Self-ruling city-states were most common in Italy, where, perhaps, memories of Rome remained most alive. But similar phenomena occurred over much of Europe, as urban awareness and the number and size of towns grew. On the edges of Christendom, planned towns were laid out with the measuring rod and peopled by wagon trains. In Spain, the granting by monarchs of founding documents to tiny new communities marked the progress of settlement on the frontier with the Islamic world. These usually gave the inhabitants some share in judicial or administrative power. All towns of the time were small by modern standards. As few as 2,000 citizens could make a town if it had walls and a charter. "Feelings," it was said, "make the town." If the people felt urban, in other words, they *were* urban. Thirty thousand inhabitants was a metropolis.

For the sake of comparison, it is worth glancing at the farther edge of Christendom, beyond the reach of the Latin Church, in western Russia. Here the cities of Novgorod and Pskov contended against a hostile climate beyond the grain lands on which they relied for food. Famine besieged them more often than human enemies did. Yet control of the trade routes to the River Volga made Novgorod cash rich. It never had more than a few thousand inhabitants, yet its monuments record its progress: its *kremlin* (or palace-fortress) walls and five-domed cathedral in the 1040s; in the early twelfth century, a series of buildings that the ruler paid for; and in 1207, the merchants' church of St. Paraskeva in the marketplace.

From 1136, communal government prevailed in Novgorod. The revolt of that year marks the creation of a city-state on an ancient model—a republican commune like those of Italy. The prince was deposed for reasons the rebels' surviving proclamations specify. "Why did he not care for the common people? Why did he want to wage war? Why did he not fight bravely? And why did he prefer games and entertainments rather than state affairs? Why did he have so many gerfalcons and dogs?" Thereafter, the citizens' principle was, "If the prince is no good, throw him into the mud!"

> "Self-ruling city-states were most common in Italy, where, perhaps, memories of Rome remained most alive. But similar phenomena occurred over much of Europe, as urban awareness and the number and size of towns grew."

Western Europe: Religion and Culture

Transformations in art, thought, and worship matched the dynamism of the economy and of political change in Europe. New forms of religious dissent, for instance, were among departures of enormous importance for the future of Western Christendom. If popular dissent existed in Western Europe before the eleventh century, no one noticed it. After the year 1000, however, it emerged as a threat. A French peasant named Leutard had a vision in which bees—a traditional symbol of supposedly sexless reproduction—entered his body through his penis. The vision drove him to renounce his wife, shatter the images of Jesus and the saints in the local church, and preach universal celibacy. Among fellow peasants, he attracted a following that survived his death, albeit not for long. In 1015, the first

Hell's mouth. The Archangel Michael locks the gate of hell, pictured as a monster's jaws. Note that some of the tortured souls in this thirteenth-century miniature painting are monarchs and monks, with crowns and tonsures. Whatever their wealth or social position, all Christians were equally subject to God's judgment.

burnings of heretics in the West for over 600 years were kindled. From then on, popular heretical movements were a continuous and, on the whole, a growing feature of Western European history.

Two long, slow changes seem to underlie this phenomenon. First, by the late eleventh century, a movement of Christian renewal and evangelizing fervor (known to historians as the Gregorian Reform after Pope Gregory VII [r. 1073–1085], its greatest sponsor) was demanding new and exacting standards both of clerical behavior and of lay awareness of the faith, and challenging kings and noblemen for control over appointments in the church. More than a power struggle, it was a drive to purge the church of profanity.

The evangelical fervor of the clergy was also lowering its sights to include the peasantry, to whom clerics had, up to then, paid little attention. This was the result, in part, of a long buildup of dissatisfaction with the shallowness with which Christianity had penetrated popular minds. Among its effects was a new or increased emphasis in saints' lives on how saints could—in today's jargon—"relate" to ordinary people by doing menial jobs. A French count, for instance, who joined a monastery in about 990, was set first to keep the hens, then the sheep, then the pigs, and was astonished at his own delight in each successive task.

Second, the rise of popular dissent bears some signs of a revolution born of prosperity. Laypeople were themselves stepping up the demands they made of their clergy. The really popular heresies of the eleventh and twelfth centuries were those ministered to by men of ferocious sanctity, like the preachers who called themselves "the perfect," and whose fanatical renunciation of worldly pleasures made them seem holier than the church. At the same time, the new security of life, the opportunities to gather harvests without being attacked, the leisure that increased yields from the soil gave to people, all bought time for a luxury unavailable in hard times: time to think about the Christian mysteries and to develop a desire to get involved in them. At a relatively high level of education, the church could satisfy these stirrings by providing pilgrimages, private prayers, devotional reading matter, and, ultimately, orders of chivalry for the warrior class. Spiritual-minded peasants, like Leutard's enthusiasts, could not be accommodated so easily.

In the struggle to save their souls, European laymen in the Middle Ages were at a disadvantage. The religious life opened heaven's gates; the warrior's life, stained with bloodshed, distracted by the world, closed them. The religious model suggested the idea that obedience to rules—like those of monks and nuns—could sanctify the lay life. The first such rules or "codes of chivalry" in the twelfth century emphasized religious vows of chastity, poverty, and obedience, but lay virtues gathered prominence, redirected against deadly sins: generosity against greed, self-control against anger, loyalty against lies and lust. **Chivalry** became the prevailing disposition among the

A CLOSER LOOK

Vézelay

Clouds, stormy and serene, signify the powers to pardon and condemn that Jesus gave the apostles.

This is no mere "Jesus" but a divine Christ. Rays of light fly from his fingertips to empower the apostles. His garment swirls and whirls—he is clothed in the cosmos. Yet he remains human, with a face oppressed by compassion.

Though damaged by anti-Christian vandals in the 1790s during the French Revolution, the doorway of the monastery church of Vézelay, carved in the early thirteenth century, remains one of the masterpieces of Western art. It is a startling attempt to depict the world in all its diversity of peoples and cultures, activities, woes, and hopes.

In the outer curve of the arch, signs of the zodiac are interspersed with depictions of workers performing the labors of the corresponding seasons. Between Aries and Taurus, for instance, a shepherd feeds kids with new buds. Between Taurus and Gemini, a naked dancer wreathes flowers.

The peoples of the Earth come to Christ—the pagan Greeks, Romans, Persians, and Scythians, and even the "monsters" of legend: dog-headed, pig-snouted, elephant-eared, stunted. Some philosophers denied that such deformed creatures could be fully human, but Christ's love includes them all.

Carved with stunning realism, the inner curve of the arch depicts ordinary people experiencing miracles of healing and conversion.

What does this portal reveal about its makers' view of the world?

aristocracy of the age. It did not make warfare any more gentle or moral; nor did it make all aristocrats good. But it did widen the range of the virtues to which aristocrats aspired.

The art of the West in the eleventh and twelfth centuries reveals a sort of cult of the commoner. Images of peasants and artisans appeared alongside those of saints and angels around church door-ways, engaged in the productive economic activities that paid for this art. Here were arrayed the members of a peace-ful and orderly society, with everyone in their place and doing well out of it. The new mood affected the way artists showed heaven. Most people nowadays unfairly associate the art of the era with a cold and distant style of other-worldly portraits: with images of the Virgin staring, passionless, and kingly, judg-mental Christs. Yet the humanization of heaven was the essence of the artists' inspiration: the evocation of piercing emotions. Early in the eleventh century, the painter of the gospel book of Abbess Hilda of Meschede painted a scene of Jesus asleep in a storm on the Sea of Galilee, in which the ship leaps into life and the anxiety of the apostles burdens their brows. The Jesus carved for Archbishop Gero of Cologne in Germany dates from before the end of the tenth century, but no modern master ever chiseled the face of the suffering Jesus with more exqui-site agony: drawn lips, taut cheeks, nerveless lids, and a trickle of blood at the brow.

In art, literature, and scholarship, a strong sense of continuity with ancient civ-ilization shines through. Sculptors and builders copied classical works wherever they could find them. The ideas of Abbot Suger on the beauty of light were derived from what he thought was a Greek text from the early first century. The twelfth-century English historian, Geoffrey of Monmouth, claimed to trace the "British" monarchy back to characters from the ancient Greek poet Homer. Poets in Eng-land and Germany tried to write like ancient Romans. Lectures in Paris introduced students to the logic of Aristotle. Abelard (1079–1142), the most renowned Parisian teacher of the era, gave audiences the impression that there was nothing logic could not do. In his book, *Sic et Non* (*Yes and No*) of 1122, he exposed the contradictions in many treasured assumptions of the theology and philosophy of his day. The twelfth-century Archbishop of Canterbury, Anselm, too, wrote about God using reason as his only guide—suppressing references to Scripture or the tra-dition of the church. Indeed, Anselm sought to prove the existence of God—or at least of a real being with the perfection Christianity ascribed to God—by unaided reason. Roughly, his proof says that the most perfect being we can think of must exist, since, if he did not, we should be able to think of another, more perfect being who did.

By the twelfth century, students of nature were beginning to "stand on the shoulders of giants" of antiquity and see farther than they had. In 1092, Walcher of Malvern fixed the difference in time between Italy and England by tim-ing an eclipse. Adelard of Bath noted that light travels faster than sound. He agreed with his younger contemporary, William of Conches, that God likes to work through nature and that miraculous explanations should never be invoked when scientific ones will do. Practical observations piled up: the heights of tides, the habits of volcanoes. Carvers of capitals on pillars in churches imitated natural forms. From this time onward, sculptors chiseled plants and flowers into monastery cloisters.

Romanesque art has a reputation for stylization and formality. But in this early example that Arch-bishop Gero of Cologne in Germany commissioned before the end of the tenth century, the artist was evidently already interested in anatomical realism and in depicting intense emotion. Instead of a remote, divine, judgmental Christ, we see the sor-row and resignation of Jesus, a suffering human being.

In Perspective
The Patchwork of Effects

The great leap of Latin Christendom—the renaissance or rebirth in art and thought that began after the year 1000—was possible because people in Western Europe found ways to cope and contend with their relative isolation. Scholars in the late tenth and eleventh centuries went to Muslim centers of learning in Spain to acquire groundings in science and mathematics and to learn Arabic. Gerbert of Aurillac—the Emperor Otto III's tutor—sweated to learn mathematics in the Spanish Muslim city of Toledo. Adelard of Bath studied Arabic to get access to Arabic translations of classical Greek books, lost in the West. In the late eleventh and twelfth centuries, as we shall see in the next chapter, pilgrimages, wars, and trade took Western Europeans in unprecedented numbers to the eastern Mediterranean, and to contact with the Islamic world and Eastern Christendom at Constantinople. At the same time, the westward trickle of communications from South and East Asia probably increased along the Silk Roads.

For Japan, too, isolation might have been frustrating. But there was just enough contact with Korea and China to stoke Japanese art and learning with Chinese influences. The delicately folded poems written by Genji and his friends and real-life counterparts were all in Chinese—part of an ancient renaissance, as influential as anything Europeans wrote or sculpted in imitation of antique models.

In the preindustrial world, the size of states and the scope of economies were functions of time as well as distance. Messages, armies, revenues, and cargoes took a long time to travel across broken country or, by sea, through variable winds. Around the Indian Ocean, increased traffic brought areas in East Africa and Southeast Asia out of isolation and kept India rich, despite its political troubles. Despite the heroic efforts of the Norse in the Atlantic, the Thule Inuit in the Arctic, and the Polynesians in the Pacific, the wealth-creating effects of sustained transoceanic or interoceanic commerce could not yet be reproduced outside the region of the monsoons around the Indian Ocean.

Even so, India was much less influential in world history—far less productive of ideas and movements that affected the rest of the world—after 1000 than it had been before. This is only one of many ways in which India seems to have reached a "peak" of achievement. According to the best available studies, India's population was over 200 million in 1000 and fell for the rest of what we think of as the Middle Ages. The Chola kingdom was the last Indian empire to exert major influence in Southeast Asia, where Hinduism began to decline—ultimately, to survive only in patches outside India itself.

In the Americas and parts of sub-Saharan Africa, the arresting effects of isolation could not be overcome. Cultural contacts between Mesoamerica and parts of North America

> "In the preindustrial world, the size of states and the scope of economies were functions of time as well as distance. Messages, armies, revenues, and cargoes took a long time to travel across broken country or, by sea, through variable winds."

Chronology

Tenth century	Flourishing of canyon culture in American Southwest; Chichén Itzá founded
Late tenth century	Norse reach Greenland
ca. 1000	*The Tale of Genji* (Japan); Thule Inuit reach Greenland
1000–1300	Rapid population growth in Europe and development of new technologies; Maya intensively exploit Yucatán peninsula
1000–1100	Flourishing of Chola kingdom (India)
1070s	Opening of Japan to limited foreign trade; restoration of direct relations between China and Japan
Early twelfth century	Building of Angkor Wat (Cambodia) begins
1150	Canyon settlements in American Southwest withdraw to higher ground
1200	Population of Cahokia reaches 10,000
1270	Solomids seize power in Ethiopia
1300	Decline of upper Mississippi valley culture

helped, for a while, to produce spectacular experiments in building states and modifying environments. But the networks were still too fragile and temporary for the effects to endure.

In the next century, the thirteenth, changes in the pattern of communications across Eurasia would heighten the differences between the Old and the New Worlds. To understand these events and their effects, we have to turn first to the other great theme of the history of the eleventh and twelfth centuries: the growing contacts and conflicts between sedentary and nomadic peoples in Eurasia and parts of Africa, and their effects on the interactions of surrounding regions.

PROBLEMS AND PARALLELS

1. How did societies around the world contend with their relative isolation between 1100 and 1200? What does the diary of the Tosa Lady tell us about the difficulties Japanese navigators faced compared with those around the Indian Ocean? What effect did those difficulties have on Japan?

2. How were the Thule Inuit able to expand around the Arctic? Why was the Norse attempt to colonize Greenland so fragile?

3. What roles did Cahokia play in central North America? What evidence is there that it was influenced by the civilizations of Mesoamerica? Why was the Mixtec King Eight-Deer Tiger-Claw considered a model of Mesoamerican kingship?

4. How did Buddhism and Hinduism spread through Southeast Asia? Why did the Khmer kingdom adopt Buddhism in place of Hinduism?

5. How did the lands on the extremities of Eurasia (Japan and Europe) overcome their isolation and emerge with powerful political, cultural, and economic systems?

6. How did urbanization affect religious, economic, and political life in Europe between 1000 and 1200? Why did religious dissent increase in Western Europe after the year 1000?

7. How did increased trade across the Indian Ocean affect East Africa during the eleventh century? Why did the Chola kingdom ultimately withdraw from overseas imperialism?

8. How do the histories of the American Southwest, Ethiopia, and Western Europe during this period illustrate the benefits and drawbacks of cultural and economic isolation?

READ ON ▶ ▶ ▶

A convenient version of the Tosa diary is printed in D. Keene, ed., *Anthology of Japanese Travel Literature* (1960). *The Book of the Wonders of India* is available in an edition by G. S. P. Freeman-Grenville (1984). G. R. Tibbetts, *Arab Navigation in the Indian Ocean before the Coming of the Portuguese* (2002) gives the background.

On Greenland, K. Seaver, *The Frozen Echo* (1997), is a brilliant work, with contentious conclusions.

On the North American Southwest, S. Lekson et al., *Great Pueblo Architecture of Chaco Canyon* (1986) is outstanding; pages in B.G. Trigger and D. Washburn, eds., *The Cambridge History of the Native Peoples of North America*, v. 1, Part I, bring it up to date. The Mississippi sites are covered in T. R. Pauketat and T. E. Emerson, *Cahokia: Domination and Ideology in the Mississippian World* (2000); T. E. Emerson and R. B. Lewis, eds., *Cahokia and the Hinterland* (2000); and T. R. Pauketat, *The Ascent of Chiefs* (1994). On the Mixtec, R. Spores, *The Mixtec Kings* (1967) cannot be bettered.

For Ethiopia under the Zagwe, some sources appear in R. B. Pankhurst, *The Royal Chronicles of Ethiopia* (1967). On Ethiopia and Angkor the works recommended for Chapter 9 are good for the period covered here.

Al Biruni's *India*, ed. C. Sawyer, is the classic text. M. A. Saleem Khan, *Al Biruni's Discovery of India* (2001) attempts an interpretation. The works of Chattopadhyaya and Thapar mentioned above remain fundamental for this period in India. For the Cholas, V. - Dehejia, *Art of the Imperial Cholas* (1990) is a breathtaking work; B. K. Pandeya, *Temple Economy under the Colas* (1984) is important.

V. K. Jain, *Trade and Traders in Western India* (1990) and B. Stein, Peasant, *State and Society in Medieval South India* (1994) are useful on their subjects.

There are many editions of *The Tale of Genji*. For Japan in this period, *The Cambridge History of Japan*, 2 (2002) is comprehensive.

On Western Europe, R. Southern, *The Making of the Middle Ages* (1961) is a classic work, unsurpassed. R. Bartlett, *The Making* of Europe (1994) is fundamental. Classic essays on some of the topics covered here are collected in F. Fernández-Armesto, ed., *The Internal Frontier of Christendom (forthcoming)*. A useful little collection of Cistercian sources is in P. Matarasso, ed., *The Cistercian World* (1993). Abbot Suger is best approached through E. Panofsky, ed., *Abbot Suger on the Abbey Church of St Denis and Its Art Treasures* (1979). On technology, J. Gimpel, *The Medieval Machine* (1977) is superb and standard. On peasants, G. Astill and J. Langdon, eds., *Medieval Farming and Technology* (1997) provides an excellent introduction.

On heresy, M. Lambert, *Medieval Heresy* (2002) is spirited and comprehensive. A. Murray, *Reason and Society in the Middle Ages* (1978) is an ingenious work, full of insights. C. H. Haskins, *The Renaissance of the Twelfth Century* (2005) is a classic, once pioneering, now enduring. P. Lasko, *Ars Sacra* (1995) is a good introduction to the art of the period.

CHAPTER 12

The Nomadic Frontiers: The Islamic World, Byzantium, and China, ca. 1000–1200

▲ **Scenes of steppeland life in the Middle Ages.** Two warriors do their washing. A shaman writhes by the campfire. Weapons are stacked. Horses graze. Starving dogs hope for scraps. A chief mends his saddle.

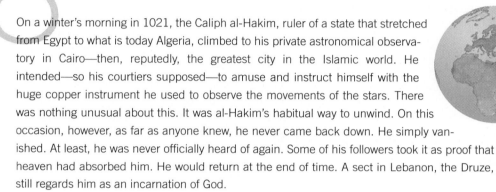

CAIRO

On a winter's morning in 1021, the Caliph al-Hakim, ruler of a state that stretched from Egypt to what is today Algeria, climbed to his private astronomical observatory in Cairo—then, reputedly, the greatest city in the Islamic world. He intended—so his courtiers supposed—to amuse and instruct himself with the huge copper instrument he used to observe the movements of the stars. There was nothing unusual about this. It was al-Hakim's habitual way to unwind. On this occasion, however, as far as anyone knew, he never came back down. He simply vanished. At least, he was never officially heard of again. Some of his followers took it as proof that heaven had absorbed him. He would return at the end of time. A sect in Lebanon, the Druze, still regards him as an incarnation of God.

To most observers, however, he was just mad. His "deeds were without reason," said a typical critic, "and his dreams without interpretation." Some of his actions were certainly erratic. At different times, he outlawed dogs, churches, evening traffic, canal trade, and women's shoes. He expected the end of the world—which perhaps explains his habits of personal austerity and reckless alms giving. His main defect, in his critics' eyes, was that he was a Shiite (see Chapter 9). The two chief doctrines of Shia clearly mattered to al-Hakim. He thought that supreme power in Islam passed by heredity—through Fatima, Muhammad's daughter, and her husband, Ali, to his own so-called Fatimid dynasty. And he saw himself as the fulfillment of Shiite belief in the divine appointment of an infallible **imam,** or holy ruler, to supplement Muhammad's own teaching.

For a while, it looked as if Fatimid success in war was a sign of God's favor and a prelude to the triumph of the divine imam. The conflict between rival caliphs, the Shiite in Cairo and the Sunni in Baghdad, divided the Islamic world into roughly equal portions. To make matters worse, from the 920s, a third dynasty, with its court in Cordova in Spain, also claimed to be the caliphs. At intervals in the tenth and eleventh centuries, Shiite rebels or invaders seized Baghdad and humiliated or manipulated the Sunni caliphs. From 1090, the Shiite sect known as the Assassins occupied Alamut—a mountain fortress in Persia—from where they launched raids and unleashed allegedly drug-crazed fanatics to execute political murders. The word *assassin* comes from "hashish."

FOCUS questions

How did the Islamic world deal with its steppeland neighbors?

How did Islam become implanted in West Africa?

How did Byzantine civilization combine religious and secular values?

Why did Byzantium survive for so long?

How did the Crusades affect the Islamic world and Byzantium?

How did Song China deal with the northern barbarians?

Why do nomads and settled peoples tend to be enemies?

Important threads of cultural unity still linked the rival political and religious traditions in the Islamic world: veneration of the Prophet Muhammad, adherence to the Quran, use of Arabic as the language of religion and learning, and the unifying force of the pilgrimage to Mecca that every Muslim was required to make once in a lifetime if possible. Mutual obligations among Muslims were still strong, even between Shiites and Sunnis. In 1070, for instance, when famine threatened Cairo, the Fatimid caliph sent his womenfolk to Sunni Baghdad to escape starvation. Islam was still the most widely dispersed civilization the world had ever seen. Muslims ruled a continuous band of territory from northern Spain, across North Africa and into Asia, to the Indus, the Jaxartes River (now called Syr Darya) in Central Asia, and the Arabian Sea (see Map 12.1).

Nonetheless, political disunity was strange and disturbing for Muslims. Fragmentation weakened the states it created and wasted their strength in wars against each other. The strain told. In the early eleventh century, the Spanish caliphate crumbled. In most of Iran and Kurdistan, the seizure of power by minor dynasties made the rule of the caliph in Baghdad no more than symbolic. The Fatimid caliphate had reached the limits of its expansion, and its North African provinces began to slip from its grasp after the Fatimids moved their court from Tunisia to Cairo in 973. On the western frontiers of the Islamic world in Spain, southern Italy, and Anatolia, aggressive Christian states were active. Both a challenge to and the salvation of Islam came from unlikely directions: the Sahara and the steppes of Central Asia.

THE ISLAMIC WORLD AND ITS NEIGHBORS

The Islamic world was caught up in a sweeping Eurasian confrontation. Settled societies in Europe, Africa, and Asia faced warlike, nomadic, pastoral societies that had emerged in Central Asia and North Africa. Sometimes the relationship was hostile. It was always tense. In this chapter, we look in turn at the societies most affected—the Islamic world, with its western neighbors in Spain and West Africa, and then the Byzantine and Chinese empires.

The Coming of the Steppelanders

The steppelands—home of unruly and warlike pastoral peoples—seemed more full of threat than promise to the Muslim world. The Turkic peoples of the Asian steppe, in particular, had a fearsome reputation for courage and stubbornness in battle. The *Dede Korkut*—the epic that celebrated their virtues—vividly captured the Turks' love of virility and violence (see Chapter 9). Turks had filtered into Islamic lands for centuries, usually as slaves and soldiers, as individuals or in small bands. Now Turkic peoples overspilled the steppeland in waves of migrants and invaders. As so often with

Pilgrim caravan. "I cling to journeying, I cross deserts, I loathe pride." The freedom and frequency of travel across the Muslim world are among the main themes of one of the most popular Arabic works of the thirteenth century, the *Maqamat* (or *Scales of Harmony*) of al-Hariri, which inspired some of the finest illustrated manuscripts of the time.

movements of peoples in the steppelands, we do not know what set them off. But once the shifts of population began, they ignited a kind of chain reaction, with some migrant groups pushing others ahead of them.

The city of Bukhara in modern Uzbekistan, once "the focus of splendor" and "the horizon of the literary stars of the world," according to an account based on the childhood recollections of a palace official's son, became for a while the headquarters of the Seljuk Turks (see Chapter 9), who overran Iran between the 1030s and the 1050s. One of Seljuk's brood seized Baghdad in 1055 and turned the caliph into a client—"a parrot in a cage." Farther east, in Afghanistan, the warlord Mahmud of Ghazni was the self-appointed guard of Islam, whose 17 raids into India gathered so many captives that prices in the slave markets of Afghanistan tumbled. He was the descendant of a Turkish adventurer. Seljuk's sons and grandsons first took service with, then turned on him. Their cavalry overwhelmed Mahmud's elephants. Muslims called them "the army of God"—not in approval but in fear. God had unleashed these ferocious pagans to punish Muslims' sins.

Turkish hostility might have shattered the Islamic world—just as the Arabs had destroyed the Persian Empire and the western barbarians had broken Rome. The Turks certainly altered the political framework of Islam. After a stunning series of conquests, however, they stopped, converted by the culture they had conquered. The first Turks to embrace Islam were a people of Central Asia known as the Karkhanids, whose conversion, according to traditional dating, occurred in 960. Their fervor set a precedent that almost all other Turkic peoples followed in placing themselves at the service of Islam.

Seljuk and his sons were among the next wave of converts. The effect was to change their whole way of life. The ruins of the capital they built at Konya in Anatolia show how thoroughly they abandoned pastoralism and absorbed the urban habits of the peoples they conquered. By the end of the twelfth century, 108 towers enclosed the city. Vast market gardens stretched far into the surrounding plain, feeding a population of perhaps 30,000. Charters of charitable foundations mention a marketplace and shops of all kinds. Inns with high-arched aisles were built to accommodate traveling merchants and their camels. But the Seljuks never entirely forgot the steppe. Their coins showed hero-horsemen with stars and haloes round their heads. Their sultans lay in tombs, shaped to recall the tents in which their ancestors dwelled.

The Seljuk experience was typical of that of pastoralists in and around the Muslim world at the time. No one knows how it happened, but the Islamic world absorbed most of the Turkic invaders and transformed them into its strength and shield. The newly converted Turks brought badly needed strength. They turned on the enemies—or alleged enemies—of orthodox, Sunni Islam. They conquered Anatolia and Armenia from Christians, Syria and Palestine from Shiites. In India and, later, on the frontiers of Europe, they began to drive back the bounds of the dominant cultures—Hindu and Christian, respectively—and advance those of Islam (see Map 12.1).

Success in attracting, converting, and domesticating pastoral peoples—and recycling their violence in Muslim

> *"The Turks certainly altered the political framework of Islam. After a stunning series of conquests, however, they stopped, converted by the culture they had conquered."*

Caravanserai. In 1229, a Seljuk sultan built this imposing structure in Anatolia near Aksaney on the road to Konya as a place where caravans could halt. On either side of the gateway, which had to be big enough to admit laden camels, the slender columns are topped by capitals that still seem to be in the tradition of ancient Rome. There were over 200 such structures known as *caravanserai*, around the Seljuk realms, facilitating the movement of armies and officials as well as of merchants.

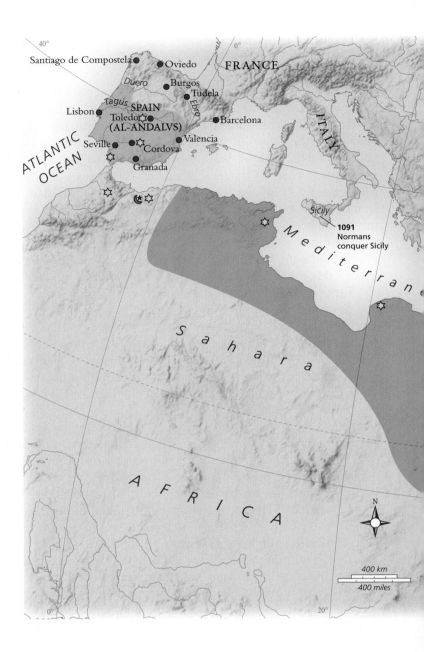

MAP 12.1

The Middle East and the Mediterranean, ca. 900–1100

	extent of caliphate, ca. 900
	area controlled by Ghaznavids, ca. 1000
➤	raids by Mahmud of Ghazni
BUWAYHIDS	Muslim dynasty with dates
➤	Seljuk conquests, ca.1040–1090
○	Seljuk capital (from 1077)
☻	Assassin stronghold
UZBEKISTAN	modern country
	Byzantine Empire, ca. 1050
----	Byzantine frontier with Seljuk Rum after 1077
⚔	battle
Karkhanids	people
✡	Jewish communities
☾	Sufi shrines, ca. 1250
✚	Christian communities
	caliphate of Cordova
	Fatimid dynasty

service—is one of the decisive and distinctive features of the history of the Islamic world. Its importance is apparent when one compares the Islamic record with those of other settled agricultural societies in Christendom, China, India, and Africa. Christendom usually dealt with steppelander threats by trying to fight them off or buy them off. The Magyars and Bulgars, who settled in Hungary and Bulgaria, respectively, were the only cases in which Europe successfully absorbed steppeland invaders. China seduced steppeland conquerors to Chinese ways of life, but was unable or unwilling to turn them permanently into a favorable fighting force. In India invading pastoralists frequently became ruling elites, sometimes adopting parts of Indian culture, but usually remaining alien intruders on the Indian scene. In none of these regions did native cultures manage to harness nomad energies for wars of aggression of their own. Yet the nomads brought new energy to the Islamic world and revitalized Muslim states' capacity for war.

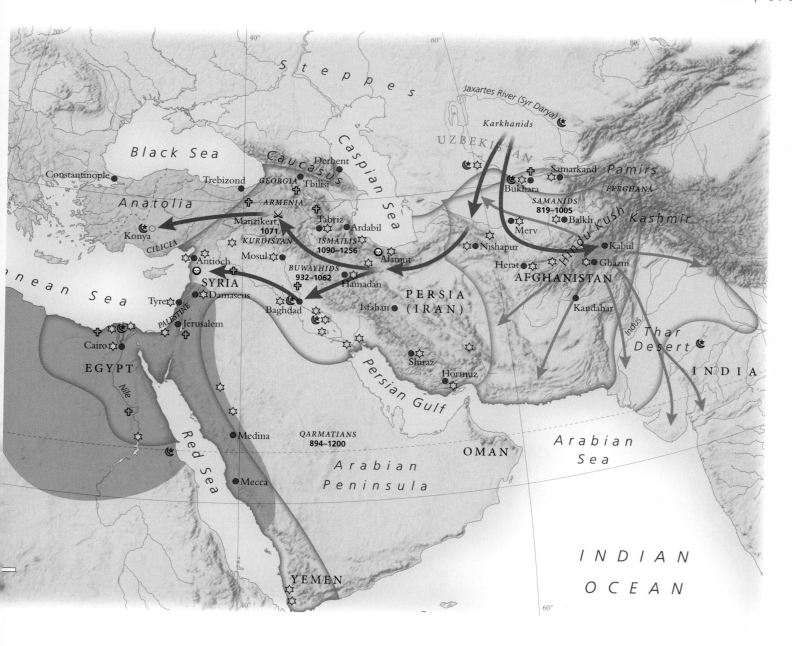

The Crusades

It is worth comparing the Islamic world's response to the steppeland invaders with the fate of the other intruders: the crusaders, who attacked from Christian Europe. Writers of world history usually give the Crusades a lot of attention, seeking signs of the vitality of the West—the capacity of Western Europeans to reach overseas and make war way beyond their frontiers. For the Islamic world, however, the Crusades were a minor nuisance. There were few crusaders. The states they founded were small and mostly short lived. Crusaders could not be converted to Islam, but—thanks to the availability of Turkish manpower and leadership—their threat to the Islamic world was neutralized or contained.

The Crusading movement started as an outgrowth from pilgrimage. Increasingly in the tenth and eleventh centuries, Christians made pilgrimages as an act of penance for their sins. Pilgrimages—in theory, peaceful journeys, on which the pilgrims relied on the mercy and charity of people whose lands they crossed—became armed expeditions. Simultaneously, Christians began to adopt what had formerly been a Muslim notion: holy war. The land where Jesus had walked, and where so many saints' bones lay buried, sanctified those who fought and died for it. Knights need no longer envy monks their easy route to salvation. Warriors could fulfill their vocation for violence and still be saved. "The blood of Muslims," declared a French poet in the early twelfth century, "washes out sins." Even if it were not holy, war for the recovery of Jerusalem would be just, according to Christian theorists: Palestine had once been Christian land, and Muslims had "usurped" it—so it was right to try to win it back.

These trends in thought and devotion came together in the 1090s. Preachers whipped up collective hysteria that sent thousands of poor, ill-armed pilgrims to their deaths in an effort to get to Jerusalem. Pope Urban II (r. 1088–1099) orchestrated a relatively well-planned military expedition. It is often claimed that the crusaders were younger sons, with inadequate inheritances, and adventurers "on the make," escaping from restricted social and economic opportunities. This claim seems false as many crusaders were rich men with a lot to lose. The church is also often thought to have encouraged the Crusades, so that it could increase its own wealth. That was one of the effects, as crusaders left property to monasteries and churches to look after in their absence, and, once they got to the East, made grants of conquered land and treasure to religious institutions there.

Association with the Holy Land and with pilgrimage made the Crusades special. But for contemporaries, especially for Muslims, they were part of a bigger phenomenon—the tide of conquest that flowed from north to south and west to east across and around the Mediterranean. From the 1060s, adventurers from Normandy in northern France conquered the central Mediterranean island of Sicily. In the 1080s, King Alfonso VI of Castile drove the frontier of his Spanish kingdom south from the valley of the River Duero to that of the Tagus. In the next decade, the Spanish mercenary chief known to tradition as El Cid carved out a short-lived realm of his own around Valencia, on Spain's Mediterranean coast. In none of these conflicts did religion motivate the conquerors. El Cid spent most of his mercenary career fighting for Muslim rulers. The outcome of the campaigns owed much to an inescapable fact of Mediterranean geography: because of the winds and currents, it is hard to defend most places in and around the sea from determined assaults from the west or north. But it so happened that the rulers on the losing sides in all these conflicts were Muslims, and religious rhetoric featured in the belligerents' propaganda. When the Crusades followed, Muslim chroniclers assumed a generalized strategy was afoot to dispossess them. They immediately dubbed it a "holy war."

The early crusaders blundered to surprising success, capturing Jerusalem in 1099 and lining the shores of the Levant with states their own leaders ruled (see Map 12.2). Muslim divisions made these successes possible. Muslim indifference and infighting prolonged them. The crusader kingdoms got support from Italian merchant-communities, which welcomed access to trade, and, occasionally, they received reinforcements from Europe. The newcomers from Europe, however, were often religious zealots who tended to disrupt the delicate tolerance between Christians and Muslims on which the crusader states relied for stability.

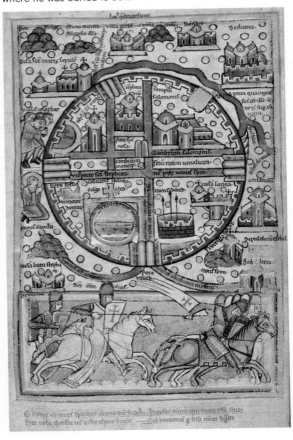

A medieval tourist-guide. This late twelfth-century guide was made to help English pilgrims find the major tourist attractions and useful spots in and around Jerusalem. The money exchange is in the center, and the food market is to its right. The Temple of Solomon occupies the upper right quarter of the city (surrounded by circular walls), and the Golden Gate "where Jesus entered sitting on a donkey" leads to it. The cross marks Golgotha where Jesus was crucified. The Holy Sepulcher where he was buried is below it.

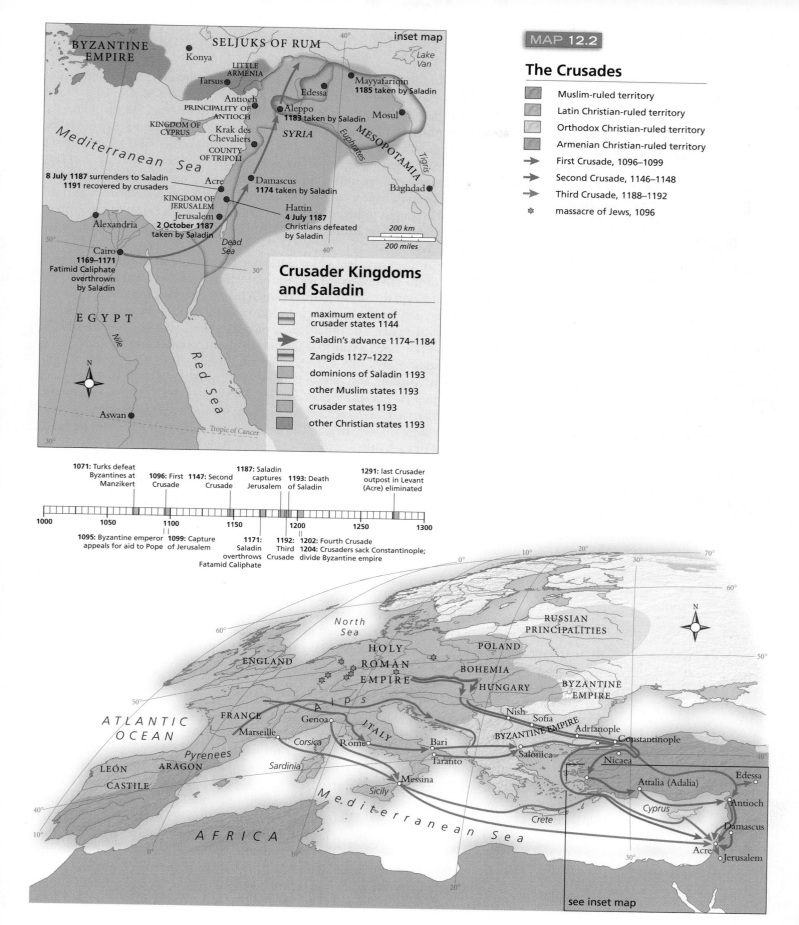

inset map

BYZANTINE EMPIRE

SELJUKS OF RUM

Konya

Lake Van

LITTLE ARMENIA

Tarsus

Mayyafariqin
1185 taken by Saladin

Edessa

Antioch
PRINCIPALITY OF ANTIOCH

Aleppo
1183 taken by Saladin

Mosul

KINGDOM OF CYPRUS

Krak des Chevaliers

SYRIA

MESOPOTAMIA

Mediterranean Sea

COUNTY OF TRIPOLI

Euphrates

Tigris

**8 July 1187 surrenders to Saladin
1191 recovered by crusaders**

Acre

Damascus
1174 taken by Saladin

KINGDOM OF JERUSALEM

Jerusalem
2 October 1187 taken by Saladin

Hattin
4 July 1187
Christians defeated by Saladin

Baghdad

Alexandria

Dead Sea

200 km
200 miles

Cairo
1169–1171
Fatimid Caliphate overthrown by Saladin

EGYPT

Nile

Red Sea

N

Aswan

Tropic of Cancer

MAP 12.2

The Crusades

Muslim-ruled territory
Latin Christian-ruled territory
Orthodox Christian-ruled territory
Armenian Christian-ruled territory
First Crusade, 1096–1099
Second Crusade, 1146–1148
Third Crusade, 1188–1192
massacre of Jews, 1096

Crusader Kingdoms and Saladin

maximum extent of crusader states 1144
Saladin's advance 1174–1184
Zangids 1127–1222
dominions of Saladin 1193
other Muslim states 1193
crusader states 1193
other Christian states 1193

1071: Turks defeat Byzantines at Manzikert
1096: First Crusade
1147: Second Crusade
1187: Saladin captures Jerusalem
1193: Death of Saladin
1291: last Crusader outpost in Levant (Acre) eliminated

1000 — 1050 — 1100 — 1150 — 1200 — 1250 — 1300

1095: Byzantine emperor appeals for aid to Pope
1099: Capture of Jerusalem
1171: Saladin overthrows Fatamid Caliphate
1192: Third Crusade
1202: Fourth Crusade
1204: Crusaders sack Constantinople; divide Byzantine empire

North Sea

RUSSIAN PRINCIPALITIES

ENGLAND

HOLY ROMAN EMPIRE

POLAND

BOHEMIA

HUNGARY

BYZANTINE EMPIRE

N

FRANCE

Alps

ITALY

Nish

Sofia

Adrianople

Constantinople

ATLANTIC OCEAN

Genoa

Marseille

Corsica

Rome

Bari

BYZANTINE EMPIRE

Salonica

Nicaea

Pyrenees

LEÓN

ARAGON

Sardinia

Taranto

CASTILE

Messina

Sicily

Attalia (Adalia)

Edessa

Crete

Cyprus

Antioch

Mediterranean Sea

Damascus

AFRICA

Acre

Jerusalem

see inset map

379

Christian and Muslim harmony. Songs in praise of the Virgin Mary, written by King Alfonso X of Castile (r. 1252–1284), could be played and enjoyed by both Christian and Muslim musicians. Both traditions upheld—and still uphold—the virginity of Jesus' mother. Food, dress, language, and even some religious practices spanned the frontier between Christian- and Muslim-ruled areas.

A Moor and a Christian playing the lute, miniature in a book of music from the 'Cantigas' of Alfonso X 'the Wise' (1221–1284). 13th Century (manuscript). Monasterio de El Escorial, El Escorial, Spain/Index/Bridgeman Art Library.

In the mid-twelfth century, Zangi—a Turkish chief who dubbed himself "pillar of the faith"—lost patience with the chaos of what we call the Middle East. Or, at least, he saw the opportunities it presented to build an empire. He proclaimed a *jihad* against infidels and Shiites. Zangi and his heirs began to reconquer the lands lost to the crusaders. Saladin, the Kurdish professional soldier who seized Zangi's empire in 1170, largely completed the job. He recaptured Jerusalem in 1187, reduced the crusader states to tiny enclaves on the coast, and beat off attempts by new crusaders from Europe to recover Jerusalem. Yet that was not Saladin's greatest achievement. He sought to be remembered above all as the "reviver of the empire of the Commander of the Faithful," a restorer of Islamic unity, a torch of Sunni Islamic orthodoxy.

The defeat of the crusaders was a sideshow. More important, in the long run, for the future of the Islamic world was the extinction of the Fatimid caliphate and the conquest of Egypt for Sunni Islam. Though heresy continued to disrupt Islamic uniformity, no such large or menacing Shiite state outside Iran ever again challenged Islamic solidarity. The other legacy of the Zangids and Saladin was Islamic militancy. Jihad remained a way to legitimize upstart dynasties and regimes.

The Crusades, meanwhile, left an equally sad legacy. For most of the Middle Ages, Christian, Muslim, and Jewish communities in the Middle East, Egypt, and Spain lived alongside one another in relative peace (see Map 12.1). Christians and Muslims intermarried, exchanged culture, and, in some frontier zones, even worshipped at the same shrines. In war, Christian and Muslim states rarely behaved as if they thought of each other as natural enemies. They often made alliances against third parties, regardless of religious affiliation. The Crusades, however, fed on religious propaganda and encouraged the two traditions to demonize each other. Crusading fervor also contributed to growing hostility in Europe between Christians and Jews, since Jews were often the victims of rioting aroused by laments over the loss of the Holy Land. In most places, Jews were the only non-Christian communities the mob found to hand (see Map 12.2).

The common opinion that the Crusades demonstrated the growing power of Latin Christendom seems—at best—exaggerated. There *was* dynamism in the Western Europe of the eleventh and twelfth centuries, but most of it was expended on inward development and on expanding the frontiers. If anything, the Crusades contributed indirectly. Their failure helped alert people in Europe to the backwardness and vulnerability of their part of the world compared to the cultures of the Near East.

The Invaders from the Sahara

It was not only in Asia that Islam successfully mobilized pastoralists for jihad. On their westernmost frontier, in Spain and Portugal, Muslims badly needed new strength. Since the eighth century, Muslim rulers had held territory as far north as the Duero and Ebro River valleys. But **al-Andalus**, as Muslims called the region, was a sprawling state, with a structure hard to hold together and frontiers hard to defend. The original Muslim settlers—mostly Berbers from North Africa—were scattered in towns or strung out around the southern and eastern river valleys and coasts, uneasily holding down large subject Christian populations. Internal communications relied on roads that the Romans had built centuries earlier to link widely scattered communities. The vast region between the rivers Tagus and Duero was a frontier in depth, strewn with fortifications, protecting the Islamic world's long flank against raids from the small Christian states that huddled in the mountains of the northwest. Wealth made al-Andalus viable: wealth gathered from the

Making Connections | THE CRUSADES

HISTORICAL BACKGROUND	CAUSE FOR ACTION	EUROPEAN CONSEQUENCES	CONSEQUENCES IN EASTERN MEDITERRANEAN
Tradition of pilgrimage—Christians go to Jerusalem	By 1050, increased danger, disorder, and occasional persecution in Middle East	Transformation of pilgrimage into armed expeditions; adoption of Islamic idea of holy war	Transformation of Holy Land into region of continual battle
Jerusalem formerly a Christian, Muslim, and Jewish city	Muslim kingdoms control the region	Religious leaders whip up mass movement—disorganized expeditions lead to disastrous results; Pope Urban II organizes a military expedition (First Crusade)	Quick capture of Jerusalem; creation of small "crusader kingdoms"
Catholic Church most important institution in Western Europe	Church needs land, wealth to fund its clerics, infrastructure, and religious activity; new spirituality favors pilgrimages as a form of penance	Bishops and papacy help coordinate, orchestrate Crusades; crusaders left property to monasteries and churches while abroad	Conquered land and treasure often granted to church institutions
European aristocracy needs means of salvation	Development of chivalric ethos; founding of knightly orders	Aristocratic violence exported on Crusades	Crusades become ruling elite over large Muslim population
Defeat of Muslims by crusaders	Weak, disorganized Muslim kingdoms in eastern Mediterranean	Initial success of crusaders; occupation of Jerusalem and Holy Land	Proclamation of *jihad* by Zangi, Turkic chief; reconquest of Jerusalem by Saladin; overthrow of crusader kingdoms

huge agricultural surplus of rich soils in the south and east; wealth spent on the fabulous luxuries—ivory work, jewels, palaces, lavish gardens—for which Spanish art of the time is renowned.

In the late tenth century, a strong-arm general, Almanzor, kept the potentially mutinous armies and regional aristocracies of the Spanish "caliphate," as its rulers called it, busy with wars against the Christians. Almanzor died in 1002. In 1009 Berber mutineers sacked his headquarters, "wilder now than the maws of lions, bellowing the end of the world." The caliphate dissolved into numerous competing kingdoms. The Islamic world's defense in the west was divided among more and weaker hands. The Christian frontier stole and lurched southward, as the northern Christian kingdoms took advantage of the disunity in the Islamic south. By the 1080s, the Tagus valley was in Christian hands. In alarm, some of the Spanish Muslim kingdoms called on warrior ascetics from North Africa, the Almoravids, for help.

In Arabic the Almoravids' name is a pun, suggesting both hermits and soldiers. They emerged as an alliance of pastoral bands from the Sahara, who, through firebrand preaching, were aroused into self-dedication to holy war.

A CLOSER LOOK

A Cordovan Ivory Jar

Richly carved ivory jars for holding rare and costly essences, such as camphor, ambergris, and musk, show how luxurious life was in the palace of Madinat al-Zahra in Cordova in Muslim Spain in the late tenth century. This example was made for a brother of the reigning caliph.

The domed shape suggests the architecture of palaces and mosques. The missing knob would have had the form of a rich fruit, such as a pomegranate.

The scenes depict hunters picking dates, court attendants, boys stealing eagles' eggs, and lions devouring bulls. The exact meaning of the images—if there ever was any—is lost, but all hint at royal power and well-being.

The inscription reads: "Blessings from God, goodwill, happiness, and prosperity to al-Mughira, son of the Commander of the Faithful, may God's mercy be upon him," with the date, 967.

Ivory pyxis of Al–Mughira. Scene of harvesting dates. 968 C.E. From Cordoba, Spain. Inv. 4068. Photo: H. Lewandowski/Musee du Louvre/RMN Reunion des Musees Nationaux, France. Art Resource, New York.

How does this ivory jar reflect the civilization and sophistication of Muslim Spain?

From the mid-tenth century, reports began to cross North Africa of large alliances of nomads, belonging to the veiled Sanhaja (sahn-HA-jah) peoples whose territory covered most of the western Sahara. By the 1040s, the Sanhaja, apparently united in the cause of jihad, broke out of the desert to conquer Morocco. They were not the first such invaders. Nomads whom the Fatimids had expelled from southern Egypt had already wrought havoc in the region. The Almoravids, however, were apparently more numerous and more effective.

Chronology: The Almoravids and Almohads	
1040s	Sanhaja conquer Morocco
1076	Kumbi Saleh falls to Almoravid armies
1080s	Muslim kingdoms in al-Andalus call on Almoravids for help
1140s	Almoravid Empire falls to the Almohads

When they received the summons to Spain to help its Muslim rulers fend off the Christian states, the Almoravids already had a reputation for military efficiency, having created a state that spanned the Sahara. In the tradition of many Saharan tribes, they had—at least at an early stage of their history—a surprisingly egalitarian attitude to women. A woman, Zaynab al-Nafzawiya (ZAY-nab ahn-nahf-zah-WEE-yah), dominated, for a time, Almoravid politics and nominated generals. "Some said the spirits spoke to her," said orally transmitted traditions, "others that she was a witch."

In Spain, the Almoravids drove back the Christians and preserved most of the peninsula for Islam. The Almoravids spent much of their fury, however, on the rulers of the petty Muslim kingdoms, whom they swept away, first denouncing their luxury, then seizing it for themselves. The corruption to which the Almoravids submitted in their turn became a provocation and an enticement to other religiously inspired desert pastoralists. In the 1140s the Almoravids' empire was conquered by a new ascetic alliance, the Almohads—the name means "people of the oneness of God"—who again invaded Spain from North Africa and, for a while, succeeded in propping up the Islamic frontier (see Map 12.3).

These movements of desert zealots also turned south Islam's frontier with paganism in Africa. The most celebrated of Almoravid generals, Abu Bakr al-Lamtumi (AH-boo BA-kuhr ahl-lam-TOO-mee), was said to have abandoned the embraces of Zaynab herself to take up the war against the black pagans. Almoravid efforts focused on Ghana, the kingdom of the Soninke (sohn-ihn-KAY) of the upper Niger River (see Chapter 10). Ghana was enviably gold-rich, for it controlled access to the routes of trans-Saharan trade, where gold was exchanged for salt. It was also offensive to the Almoravids as the home of "sorcerers," where, according to collected reports, the people buried their dead with gifts, "made offerings of alcoholic beverages," and kept a sacred snake in a cave. Muslims—presumably traders—had their own large quarter in or near the Ghanian capital Kumbi Saleh, but were kept apart from the royal quarter of the town. The Soninke fought off Almoravid armies with some success until 1076. In that year, Kumbi fell, and its defenders were massacred. The northerners' political hold south of the Sahara did not last, but Islam was firmly implanted in West Africa.

The main reasons for Muslims to go to the "the lands of the blacks" were commercial, although they also went south to make war, to find patronage if they were scholars or artists, and to make converts to Islam. Travelers' accounts recorded in Sicily and Spain in the eleventh and twelfth centuries give us snapshots of the history of the state known as Ghana in the West African interior, in the grassland region known as the Sahel, on the trade routes where salt from the Sahara was exchanged for gold (see Map 12.3).

The most extensive account is full of sensational and salacious tales, praising the slave women, excellent at cooking "sugared nuts and honeyed donuts" and with

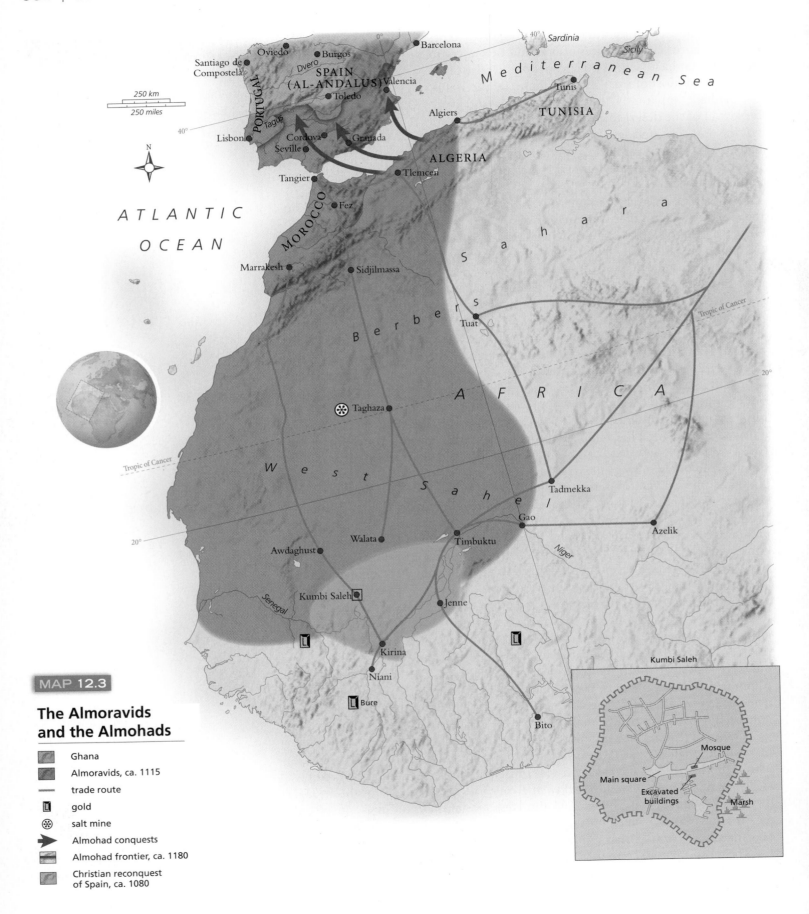

Oviedo
Burgos
Barcelona
Sardinia
Sicily
Santiago de Compostela
Dvero
SPAIN (AL-ANDALUS)
Valencia
Mediterranean Sea
Tunis
Lisbon
PORTUGAL
Tagus
Toledo
40°
Cordova
Granada
Algiers
TUNISIA
Seville
ALGERIA
Tangier
Tlemcen
MOROCCO
Fez

ATLANTIC OCEAN

N

250 km
250 miles

40°
0°

Marrakesh
Sidjilmassa
Berbers
Sahara
Tuat
Tropic of Cancer

20°

Taghaza
A F R I C A
20°

Tropic of Cancer

West Sahel
Tadmekka
Azelik
Gao
Walata
Timbuktu
20°
Awdaghust
Niger
Kumbi Saleh
Jenne
Senegal

Kirina
Niani
Bure
Bito

Kumbi Saleh

Mosque
Main square
Excavated buildings
Marsh

MAP 12.3

The Almoravids and the Almohads

- Ghana
- Almoravids, ca. 1115
- trade route
- gold
- salt mine
- Almohad conquests
- Almohad frontier, ca. 1180
- Christian reconquest of Spain, ca. 1080

"good figures, firm breasts, slim waists, fat buttocks, wide shoulders and sexual organs so narrow that one of them may be enjoyed as though she were a virgin indefinitely." But a vivid picture emerges of a kingdom with three or four prosperous, populous towns, productive in copperwork, cured hides, dyed robes, and Atlantic ambergris as well as gold. The authors also make clear how Islam spread in the region, partly by settlement of North African merchants in the towns and partly by the efforts of individual holy men or pious merchants who established relationships of confidence with kings. Interpreters and officials were already typically Muslims, and every town had several mosques, but even rulers sympathetic to Islam maintained their traditional court rituals, and what Muslims called "idols" and "sorcerers."

By the mid-twelfth century, Islam was clearly ascendant. Arab writers regarded Ghana as a model Islamic state, whose king revered the true caliph in Baghdad and dispensed justice with exemplary openness. They admired his well-built palace, with its objects of art and windows of glass; the huge natural ingot of gold that was the symbol of his authority; the gold ring by which he tethered his horse; his silk clothes; his elephants and giraffes. "In former times," reported a Muslim scholar based in Spain, "the people of the country professed paganism. . . . Today they are Muslims and have scholars, lawyers, and Quran readers and have become pre-eminent in these fields. Some of their chief leaders . . . have traveled to Mecca and made the Pilgrimage and visited the Prophet's tomb."

Archaeology confirms this picture. Excavations at Kumbi reveal a town of nearly 1.5 square miles, founded in the tenth century, housing perhaps 15,000 to 20,000 people, with a regular plan and evidence of large, multistoried buildings, including what excavators have designated as "mansions" of up to nine rooms, and a mosque measuring 100 feet by 140 feet. Artifacts include glass weights for weighing gold, many finely wrought metal tools, and evidence of a local form of money (see Map 12.3).

"Arab writers regard Ghana as a model Islamic state, whose king revered the true caliph in Baghdad and dispensed justice with exemplary openness."

A Quranic School in West Africa. Among the Dogon of Mali, Islamic penetration was superficial in the Middle Ages, but something of the atmosphere of the Quranic teachers who took Islam south of the Sahara in those days is detectable today in village schools kept by marabouts, who teach boys to master the Quran by heart, typically from the age of about four. Their pupils beg alms for the teacher's sustenance.

This magnificence did not last. After a long period of stagnation or decline, pagan invaders overran the Soninke state and destroyed Kumbi. But Islam had spread so widely by then among the warriors and traders of the Sahel that it retained its foothold south of the Sahara for the rest of the Middle Ages.

The Progress of Sufism

For all the achievements of the strong men who emerged from steppes and deserts to champion Islam, it is doubtful whether war alone could heal the divisions among Muslims and equip the Islamic world to expand. For that, inventive intellectuals were necessary—shapers of a religion that could appeal to a diversity of cultures and engage human sympathies and sensibilities without provoking conflict. Sufism (see Chapter 9) had enormous popular appeal. But most of the Muslim elite rejected it. In the early tenth century, for instance, ordinary people revered the great spokesman of Sufism, al-Hallaj, as a saint, but the Islamic authorities put him to death, because he claimed to have achieved self-extinction and mystical union with God. Gilani, his successor, who became one of the most popular preachers in mid-eleventh-century Baghdad, had a popular reputation as the "perfect man." He offered a simple morality of dependence on God—based on the rule, "Expect nothing from human beings"—as an alternative to the rigid legalism of Islamic scholars.

The divergence between legal-minded and mystic-minded Muslim theologians seemed unbridgeable until Abu Hamid Muhammad al-Ghazali entered the debate. He was blessed, or cursed, with an intellect he described as an "unquenchable thirst for investigation . . . an instinct and a temperament implanted in me by God through no choice of my own." At the height of a career as a conventional theologian in Baghdad, he experienced a sudden awareness of his ignorance of God. He became a Sufi, retired to his native Nishapur in Persia, and, before his death in 1111, wrote a dazzling series of works reconciling Sufism and Sunni orthodoxy. He was a master of reason and science but demonstrated, to the satisfaction of most of his readers, that human minds could not grasp some truths without direct illumination from God. Study could tell you about God, but only a mystical experience can show you who God is. Al-Ghazali likened the effect of mysticism to the difference between knowing what health is and being healthy. He valued the faith of the poor and uneducated as highly as the learning of the officials of the mosques. Al-Ghazali's rehabilitation of Sufism was vital for the future of Islam. Because Sufis were indifferent to externals, Sufi mystics could tolerate cultural differences among Muslims and between Muslims and non-Muslims in a way the legal-minded Islamic intellectuals could not. Though most people found Sufis' mystical practices as difficult to understand as any of the doctrines of the conventionally learned, Sufis' emphasis on experience, faith, and emotions was universally accessible. Their habits of holiness satisfied ordinary people's craving for saints. They were Islam's most effective missionaries in subsequent centuries (see Map 12.1).

"Though most people found Sufis' mystical practices as difficult to understand as any of the doctrines of the conventionally learned, Sufis' emphasis on experience, faith, and emotions was universally accessible."

THE BYZANTINE EMPIRE AND ITS NEIGHBORS

If the pastoralists contributed to the salvation of the Islamic world, their attacks were disastrous for the many non-Muslim states that proved less skillful at absorbing them or deflecting their power. A dramatic case in point is that of the state—

centered on Constantinople—whose rulers called it "The Roman Empire." In Western Europe, the Roman Empire was little more than a pious memory and its revival an impractical dream. But in Eastern Europe, the empire still existed—at least, in some people's perceptions. Today, historians usually balk at using the word *Roman* and prefer to call it the Byzantine Empire—from Byzantium, Constantinople's ancient Greek name. The rulers, after all, had no authority at Rome and spoke Greek rather than Latin. But the Byzantines claimed the exclusive right to regard themselves as heirs of ancient Rome. When ambassadors arrived in Constantinople in 968 from the "august emperor" Otto I in Germany (see Chapter 10), Byzantine officials laughed at "the audacity of it! To style a poor barbarian creature 'Emperor of the Romans.'" And the Byzantine emperors did maintain a principle of government that went back to the Emperor Constantine himself—they ruled both state and church. The kind of clergy the popes strove to give to the Latin Church in the eleventh century—"purified" of lay power, privileged by its own system of appointments, laws, and courts—was unacceptable in Byzantium, where emperors appointed all bishops, and the church accepted state control.

Byzantium and the Barbarians

The Roman-ness of Byzantium dwindled by degrees. Under Justinian (r. 527–565), the government at Constantinople was actively engaged in trying to reconstruct the Roman world, and Latin was still the official language (see Chapter 8). In the early seventh century, Byzantium still ruled substantial parts of the Western Roman Empire, with enclaves as far away as Spain. But events of the seventh and eighth centuries shifted its frontiers and changed its character. The Arab expansion after the death of Muhammad (see Chapter 9) stripped away the empire's territory south of the Mediterranean—Syria, Egypt, and North Africa. Meanwhile, from the sixth century to the eighth, speakers of Slav languages slowly colonized much of the Balkans, including Greece. Arabs, Bulgars, and Russians threatened Constantinople itself.

In defense of the empire, missionaries and diplomats were as important as armies. The church virtually monopolized literacy in the areas of the Balkans and Russia where Byzantine missions were active. Missionaries invented the alphabets in which Slav languages were written. They also helped to spread statehood, legitimating strong rulers, sanctifying weak ones. Many Balkan states slipped and slid between allegiance to the Latin- and Greek-speaking churches, but for a while, thanks to missionary efforts launched from Constantinople, Moravians, Croats, and Hungarians hovered in Byzantium's orbit before finally opting for the Latin Church. The greatest success for this religious diplomacy was the conversion of the rulers of much of what is now Russia (see Chapter 9). The policy was most effective when lavish gifts and the hands of Byzantine princesses, who married Bulgar khans and Russian princes, backed it. Instead of an empire like Rome's, a Byzantine "commonwealth" of Christian states was being built up—a diplomatic ring of outer defenses.

Byzantine diplomacy was exceptionally good at economizing on force by intimidating visiting barbarians with elaborate ceremonials. The Emperor Constantine VII (r. 913–959) laid down rules for courtly displays that were designed to embody imperial power and, in effect, to wield it. There was even an official whose job was to bribe paupers to line the streets for imperial processions—or, perhaps, reward those who would turn out anyway. The effect designers aimed for was unashamedly theatrical. When an ambassador arrived at Constantinople

The crown of King Geza I of Hungary. (r. 1074–1077) received from Byzantium was not a disinterested gift, but an attempt to imply that the king was a subject of the empire and dependent on Byzantium for the legitimacy of his rule. Hungary, however, remained firmly attached to the Church of Rome and to Latin culture.

in 924, the artificial roar of mechanical lions that guarded the imperial throne surprised him.

The deftness of Byzantine diplomacy, its rulers' ability to impress or intimidate surrounding "barbarians," is part of the repertoire of strategies with which all successful states managed the surge of migrations of the period. The wealth of the empire underpinned those strategies and paid for vital military backup. The Byzantine economy relied on the productivity of the peasantry of Anatolia and the trade that passed through Byzantine territory, for the empire enjoyed a privileged position, close to where great arteries of trade converged: the Silk Roads, the Volga, the Mediterranean.

Yet the system was rickety. Wealth depended on security, which was hard to guarantee. And the effectiveness of Byzantine diplomacy had its limits. While a zone of Byzantine influence took shape in the Balkans, Russia, and the Caucasus, most steppeland peoples, and the Muslims who predominated to the east and south, were indifferent to Byzantine religion and unintimidated by Byzantine methods. Caught between the Bulgars and the Turks, Byzantium seemed to lie at the eye of the steppelander storm. Byzantines tended to see their predicament as a test of faith—an episode of sacred history. In 980, the miracle at Chonae first appeared in a collection of Byzantine writings: the story of how the Archangel Michael diverted a river that evil pagans had turned to threaten his church. It is tempting to read this story as an allegory for the hoped-for, prayed-for escape of the "Roman Empire" from destruction at barbarian hands.

> *"The Byzantine economy relied on the productivity of the peasantry of Anatolia and the trade that passed through Byzantine territory, for the empire enjoyed a privileged position, close to where great arteries of trade converged: the Silk Roads, the Volga, the Mediterranean."*

Basil II

The longed-for savior appeared from an unlikely quarter. The Emperor Basil II barely survived adolescence. Successive usurpers surprisingly allowed him to live on after his father's death until he succeeded to the throne peacefully on coming of age in 976. His image appears on a page from his surviving prayer book—heavily armed, attended by angels, while barbarians cringe at his feet. This is how he liked to see himself and wished to be remembered.

Basil ruled intuitively, as if coping with a constant state of emergency, enforcing his own will, administering rough justice, respecting no laws or conventions. In 996, he dealt with a landowner he saw exploiting peasants: "we had his luxurious villa razed to the ground and returned his property to the peasants, leaving him with what he had to begin with and reducing him to the peasants' level." This was an instance of a long conflict between great landowners and the throne. Emperors needed prosperous, independent peasants to provide bedrock taxes and manpower for the armies. Landowners wanted to control the peasants themselves. Aristocratic revolts and resistance to taxation were commonplace.

Basil dealt with the most troublesome of Byzantium's satellite peoples, the Bulgars, by blinding—so it was said—14,000 of their captured warriors and cowing them into submission. His nickname was Bulgaroctonus—the Bulgar-Slayer. He incorporated Bulgaria into the empire in 1018. On the southern front, he made peace with the Arabs, whom the Byzantines had fought, strenuously but successfully, for half a century under previous emperors. In consequence, he gave the empire virtually ideal borders, with frontiers on the Danube and the Euphrates rivers, beyond which direct rule by Byzantium seemed neither practicable nor desirable. In Bulgaria he followed up his terror stroke by a policy of conciliation, cooperating with the native elite, appointing a Bulgar as the local archbishop. In

Greece he relied on repression, forcing the empire's religion and language on the immigrant Slavs. In the Caucasus he attacked Georgia. In Armenia, his successors lost patience with diplomacy and reconquered the region (see Map 12.4).

Force was expensive by comparison with the waiting game, bribes, and tricks characteristic of traditional Byzantine policy. Basil paid for a professional army by heavily taxing the aristocracy. When he died in 1025, his treasury was full, bigger than any emperor's since the sixth century. The empire he left to his heirs exerted influence and drew deference from far away. Prayers cited Basil's name in cities as distant as Kiev and Vladimir in the lands of the Rus and Ani in Armenia. Hungary's kings deferred to the pope on religious matters, but they still felt the pull of Constantinople. As late as the 1070s, a Hungarian king accepted a crown from Constantinople. The so-called crown of St. Stephen depicts the king reverencing the rulers of the Byzantine Empire.

The Era of Difficulties

Basil's legacy was unsustainable. His methods of government were personal and arbitrary. The aristocracy could afford his taxes only while his power protected their lands from invaders. Their restiveness and rebelliousness grew even worse after his death. As Turkish migrations and invasions began to roll over Byzantine Anatolia, the revenues failed. The succession to the throne, moreover, was problematic. Basil had no children, and his brother, who succeeded him, had only daughters. These were unusual circumstances: an opportunity for strong women to come to the fore. In the background, deeper, ill-understood social changes were under way. The family—formerly, in theory, a second-best lifestyle to monastic chastity—rose in Byzantine esteem in the tenth century. Women began to be admired for fertility as well as virginity.

In the eyes of influential classes—clergy, landowners, courtiers—eleventh-century experiments did not seem to justify the empowerment of female rulers. Princesses spent their lives confined to the palace, and though they got the same formal education as men, they were denied the opportunity to accumulate useful experience of the world. Basil's niece, Zoe, regarded the throne as a family possession and responsibility. Her "family album" is laid in mosaic in her private enclosure in the gallery of Hagia Sophia, Constantinople's cathedral. Her third husband's portrait smothers that of her second, who murdered his predecessor at Zoe's behest. Zoe outraged Constantinople's snobbish elite by adopting a workman's son as her heir—an upstart "pygmy playing Hercules," said the snobs. Zoe's sister Theodora ruled alone in 1055–1056, "shamefully" and "unnaturally"—according to her opponents—refusing to marry. These judgments lack objectivity, but show the outrage the sisters provoked among the elite.

Meanwhile, relations between the Latin- and Greek-speaking churches broke down. Differences had been growing over rites, doctrines, language, and discipline between the sees of Constantinople and Rome for centuries. Underlying the theological bitterness were deep cultural differences. Language was in part to blame. The Greek-speaking Byzantine Empire could not share the common culture of the Latin-speaking elites of Western and Central Europe, while few in the Latin West could speak or read Greek with fluency. Subtle theological distinctions, inexpressible in Latin, came easily in Greek.

Basil II. This is how the Byzantine emperor Basil II (r. 976–1025) liked to see himself. Unlike the German emperor Otto III (see Chapter 11), Basil needs no human helpers. He leans on his own sword while defeated barbarians crawl at his feet and angels crown him and invest him with a scepter. Isolated above the earth, he is perfumed with incense and adorned with a halo. Images of the saints guard him on either hand. Basil may have stressed these divine sanctions for his rule because his family had peasant origins. But the proof that God was on his side was the many victories he won against the empire's foes.

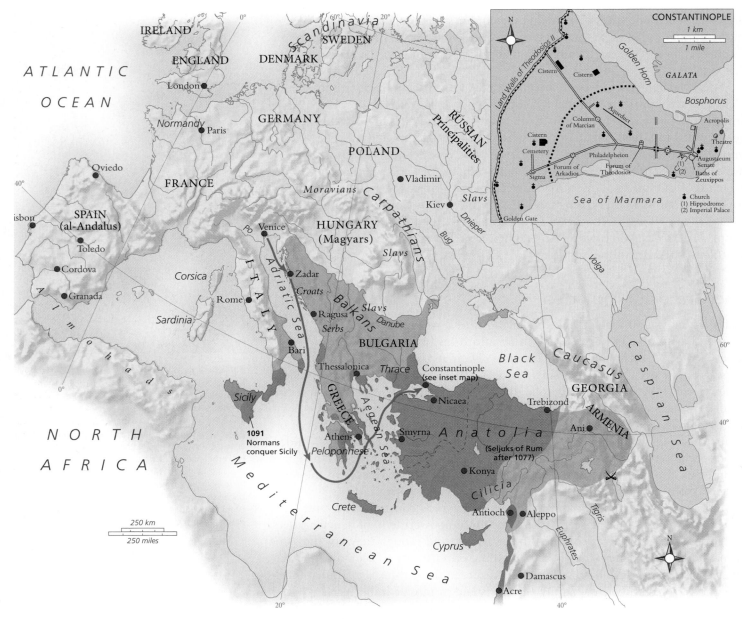

MAP 12.4

Byzantium and Its Neighbors, ca. 1050

- Byzantine empire, ca. 1050
- Byzantine empire, ca. 780
- ⚔ battle of Manzikert, 1071
- --- frontier with Seljuks of Rum after 1077
- ▮ maximum extent of crusader kingdoms, 1144
- *Croats* people
- → Fourth crusade route 1202–1204

Dogmas that were supposed to be universal turned out differently in the two tongues. For most people, religion is more a matter of conduct than of creed. In this respect, differences between the Roman and Byzantine traditions built up over centuries of relative mutual isolation. The process began as early as the mid-sixth century, when the Eastern churches resisted or rejected the supremacy of the pope. The effects were gradual but great. From the 790s, Greek and Latin congregations recited slightly different versions of the creed, the basic statement of Christian belief. By about 1000, the pope was the supreme authority regarding doctrinal questions and liturgy and the source of patronage in the church throughout Western Europe from the Atlantic to the River Bug and the Carpathian Mountains. The Western church still enclosed tremendous local diversity, but it was recognizably a single communion. Eastern Orthodox Christians felt no particular allegiance to the pope. In the West, moreover, the popes generally maintained, with difficulty, their own political independence. In the east, the patriarchs of Constantinople, as that city's bishops were titled, were the emperor's subjects and generally deferred to imperial power.

A moment when it might have been possible to restore Christian unity occurred in the mid-eleventh century. Constantinople and Rome faced common enemies. Norman invaders, the descendants of the Vikings, threatened the pope's political independence and the Byzantine emperor's remaining possessions in southern Italy and Sicily. On June 17, 1053, a Norman army cut the pope's German guard to pieces and, imploring the pope's forgiveness on bended knees, carried him off as a hostage.

Eventually, the papacy would win the Normans and turn them into its sword bearers. At first, however, the pope turned to the Byzantines for help. A Byzantine cross of the period is engraved with his message: Constantine the Great, founder of Byzantium, bows before images of the patron saints of Rome, Peter, and Paul held by a pope. Meanwhile, in 1054 in Constantinople, the patriarch, who was the head of the Byzantine church, saw an opportunity to exploit the pope's weakness. He closed the churches of the city's Latin-speaking congregations. The pope, teaching himself Greek, in the grip of a mortal sickness, sent an uncompromising mission to Constantinople. His representative, Cardinal Humbert, after weeks of bitter insults, served notice of excommunication on the "false patriarch, now for his abominable crimes notorious." The patriarch responded by excommunicating the pope. At the time, most people assumed this was just a political maneuver, soon to be rescinded or forgotten. In fact, relations between the Eastern and Western churches never fully recovered. A cultural fault line was opening across Europe.

The shenanigans of the imperial family and the quarrelsome habits of the church have given Byzantium a bad name as a society doomed by its own decadence. But it was not doomed. There are no irreversible trends in history. Nor, even when beset by difficulties, was the Byzantine Empire particularly decadent. On the contrary, the most unsuccessful emperor of the era was a model of energy and courage. Becoming emperor in 1068, Romanus IV Diogenes had to cope with aristocratic unrest while fighting on two fronts. In the west, the Normans threatened Byzantium's last possessions in Italy. In the east, Turks were penetrating Armenia and Anatolia, stealing the empire's vital food-producing zone. Romanus's military record made him look insuperable, but his generalship proved unequal to the task. In 1071, at the battle of Manzikert (MAHN-zih-kehrt), the Turks forced the emperor to kiss the ground before the feet of their leader, Alp Arslan (ahlp ahrs-LAHN)—a great-grandson of Seljuk's. Romanus could only raise a fifth of his ransom. He was released but deposed by a coup in Constantinople. Feuding at Constantinople between aristocratic factions paralyzed the government and allowed the Turks to overrun much of Anatolia.

Empress Zoe. The gallery of the great church of Hagia Sophia in Constantinople functioned as a private enclosure for members of the imperial family and was decorated with portraits of rulers and their spouses in pious attitudes. The mosaic dedicated to the Empress Zoe (980–1050) betrays the questionable complexities of her sex life. The face of Constantine IX Monomachus, her third husband, shown offering gold to Christ, was remodeled to replace the likeness of her second spouse, Michael IV, whom she had first employed to murder his predecessor, then banished to a monastery in 1041 when she tired of him. The squashed lettering above Constantine's halo to the left is clear evidence of a botched job.

Byzantium and the Crusaders

In 1097, crusaders arrived at Byzantium, ostensibly to help. But by then, the Byzantines had already begun to recover the lost ground on their own. The Byzantine princess Anna Comnena considered the newcomers more of a hindrance. Superbly educated in the classics, she was the official biographer of her father, the emperor. To her, the crusaders seemed "a race under the spell of Dionysos and Eros"—a classical way of saying they were lustful drunkards. A minority among them "undertook this journey only to worship at the Holy Sepulchre" (the tomb of Jesus at Jerusalem). Most crusaders, however, were enemies whose object was "to dethrone the emperor and capture the capital." The newcomers arrived already embittered by the religious squabbles that had divided the churches of Rome and Constantinople.

Tense cooperation between Byzantium and the crusaders, which characterized the First Crusade, broke down completely in the twelfth century. The crusaders failed to return to the empire most of the Byzantine territory they recaptured from the Muslims. Instead, they kept it for themselves. The crusaders blamed "Greek treachery" for their failures against the Muslims. The Byzantines were convinced of their own moral and cultural superiority over impious, greedy Westerners. The crusaders might have saved Byzantium, as the Turks saved the Islamic world. Instead, they undermined the empire.

Byzantium's difficulties multiplied. Agriculture was stagnant, despite the boom in other parts of Eurasia. The empire's hinterland beyond Constantinople was too insecure to prosper. In the twelfth century, in a serious reversal of earlier emperors' policy of nurturing the peasants at the landowners' expense, emperors tried to revive their rural revenues by granting control of peasant lands to great lords and encouraging monastic colonization of new lands. To some extent, this was another case of the attempt to exploit new resources, familiar in other societies of the time. The Emperor Isaac II Angelus (r. 1185–1195), for instance, gave a port to a monastery that settled a site at Vera in Thrace, formerly "devoid of men and dwellings, a haunt of snakes and scorpions, just rough ground, overgrown with spreading trees." Measures like these—which so dramatically increased the farmland of Western Christendom, Ethiopia, or, as we shall see, of China at the time—were of limited usefulness in a state whose territory was much diminished. Byzantium never recovered most of inland Anatolia from the Turks.

Increasingly, the empire was obliged to look to trade and industry for its wealth. There were, as a Byzantine poet observed, "big merchants" who "for large profits disdain terrors and defy seas." Self-made upstarts coveted money "as a polecat gazes at fat." The huge city of Constantinople, crowded and riotous as it was, benefited from its uniquely favorable position for trade, where Mediterranean and trans-Asian routes met. The Jewish merchant, Benjamin of Tudela, who visited in about 1170, celebrated "a busy city" with inhabitants so rich they "they look like princes" where "merchants come from every country by sea and land." With revenues of 200,000 gold pieces a year from rents, market dues, and the tolls on passing trade, "Wealth like that of Constantinople," Benjamin wrote, "is not to be found in the whole world. Here also are men learned in all the books of the Greeks, and they eat and drink, every man under his vine and his fig tree." For William of Tyre, a Latin bishop who visited at about the same time, the city seemed equally splendid on the surface. But William was a moralist, not a merchant. He was more aware of underlying squalor and inequalities of wealth. "The wealthy overshadow the streets," he wrote—alluding to the teetering mansions of the rich—"and leave dark, dirty spaces to the poor and to travelers." William's prejudices are obvious, but, precisely because he was so keen to criticize the city, we can trust his witness to its wealth.

A special relationship developed between Byzantium and Venice, a maritime republic near the northernmost point of the Adriatic Sea, where trade routes across the Alps converged with the main axis of north Italian commerce, the River Po. Venice's position on marshy, salty islands allowed little scope to accumulate wealth except by piracy, which Venetians practiced, mainly at the expense of Muslim shipping. In the ninth and tenth centuries, however, they began to build up enough

"The crusaders might have saved Byzantium, as the Turks saved the Islamic world. Instead, they undermined the empire."

St. Mark's Basilica, Venice, is and always has been a Roman Catholic church of the Latin rite, but it looks more like a Byzantine cathedral—smothered in dazzling mosaics, a form of decoration typical of Eastern Christianity, but rare in the West. The prototype of St. Mark's was found in Constantinople. Venetian merchants supposedly stole the relics of St. Mark—whose life is narrated in the mosaic—from Egypt in the ninth century. Venice looked east for both inspiration and trade.

capital to become major traders, channeling toward Europe a share of the valuable trade in silks and spices that was concentrated at Byzantium. Culturally, as well as economically, Venice was close to Byzantium. Though Venetians belonged to the Latin Church and spoke a language derived from Latin, Byzantine models saturated their taste in art and buildings. It could not be otherwise. They knew Byzantium well, and so they had to admire it—and, in some measure, to covet what they saw there.

To would-be attackers, Byzantium's wealth was a magnet and its weakness a motive. Toward the end of the 1190s, in Western Europe, popular enthusiasm revived for a new effort to launch a Crusade to recapture Jerusalem. The Venetians agreed to ship the crusading army out at what was to prove an unaffordable price. While the army gathered, an embassy arrived from the pretender to the Byzantine throne, Alexius IV, proposing a detour. If the crusaders put Alexius on the throne, he would reward them with treasure and help them against the Turks. Gradually, faced with their inability to pay the Venetians' bill, most of the crusaders agreed to a diversion. The Fourth Crusade, launched in 1202 as a "pilgrimage" under arms to recapture Jerusalem, ended in 1204 by shedding Christian blood, capturing and sacking Constantinople and dividing most of what was left of the Byzantine Empire in Europe among the victors. The big gainer was Venice, which seized—in the words of the treaty that divided the empire—"one quarter and one half of one quarter" of Byzantine territory, achieving virtual monopoly rights in Byzantine trade and

Chronology: Byzantium	
527–565	Reign of Justinian
Sixth to eighth centuries	Colonization of Balkans by Slavs
Seventh and eighth centuries	Arabs seize Syria, Egypt, and North Africa
Ninth century	Missions to convert Balkans and Central Europe to Byzantine Christianity
1018	Bulgaria incorporated into Byzantine Empire
1054	Schism between Orthodox and Latin Churches
1071	Battle of Manzikert; Seljuk Turks defeat Byzantines and overrun Anatolia
1095	First Crusade
1204	Sack of Constantinople

suddenly becoming an imperial power in the eastern Mediterranean (see Map 12.4). Meanwhile, in the remnants of the Byzantine Empire in western and coastal Anatolia, rival dynasties disputed claims to the imperial title.

Byzantine Art and Learning

Throughout the period this chapter covers, even amid the most severe difficulties of the twelfth century, Byzantium remained a beacon of learning and art. It is easy to get starry-eyed about the excellence of Byzantine culture. In 1078, Kekaumenos, a self-educated Byzantine ex-general who took learning seriously, complained that babblers "picked passages to gossip about." The most constant and careful Byzantine work in copying and analyzing the texts of classical authors and of the fathers of the Church was probably over by the tenth century. Mystics, represented by Saint Symeon the New Theologian (as he is called), who died in 1022, proposed an alternative route to learning, through divine illumination. "Orators and philosophers" could not access the wisdom of God. Painters developed a tradition that seemed consciously unclassical, abandoning realism in favor of stylized, formal figures, usually set against abstract or sketchy backgrounds, more indebted, perhaps, to the mosaic tradition, in which Byzantine artists excelled, than to classical painting or sculpture. Most painters worked only on religious commissions and accepted the artistic vocation as a sacred obligation, aiming at work that captured the spirit of its subject and that would be revered as holy in itself. Innovation happened slowly and subtly, for artists had to treat every subject strictly in accordance with tradition and church dogma.

Nonetheless, in most arts, and in learning, Byzantium preserved and developed the classical legacy, which, in the eleventh and twelfth centuries, revived in an intellectual movement comparable with the renaissance of the same period in the West (see Chapter 11). The historian and biographer Michael Psellus (1018–1078), for instance, wrote in an antique style based on classical Greek models, interpreted the meanings of ancient art, and lectured on Plato and Aristotle (see Chapter 6). Anna Comnena's historical work was saturated in knowledge of Homer (see Chapter 5), and she commissioned commentaries on previously neglected works of Aristotle. A renaissance of classical pagan themes in art followed in the twelfth century. A famous ivory carving of that time in classical style shows Europa, a princess whom the god Zeus, in bull's guise, abducted. She plays with satyrs and

The Veroli casket. Classical stories with an erotic edge decorated Byzantine trinket boxes in the twelfth century. The panels visible in this picture of a famous example, the Veroli casket, finely carved in ivory, show Helen of Troy, Bellerophon with his winged horse, and the chaste Hippolytus on the right resisting the sexual advances of his wicked stepmother. Such were the subjects that entertained a rich lady's mind while she donned her jewels.

centaurs, pouting prettily at her pursuers. In Byzantine scholarship of the late twelfth century, nothing commanded more prestige than classical research. Michael Choniates, archbishop of Athens from 1182 to 1204, was delighted to have the famous temple of the goddess Athena, the Parthenon, as a church to preach in and classical Greek poets to read for pleasure. Another Byzantine bishop wrote commentaries on ancient Greek poetry and searched through old manuscripts to improve the texts of classical plays.

Rather than the title of Roman Emperor, or the claims to diminished power that rivals disputed after the collapse of 1204, this tradition of art and learning is Byzantium's most significant legacy. As in the Islamic world, texts and art works inherited from ancient Greece and Rome survived in the Byzantine portion of the former Roman Empire, while, in the West, they were lost among the far more destructive invasions that transformed the Roman world in the fifth century. The recovery of classical traditions in the West would probably have been impossible without cross-fertilization with the Islamic world and Byzantium.

CHINA AND THE NORTHERN BARBARIANS

Beyond the limits of the Turkish steppe, other steppeland peoples were even harder to deal with. Not even the Seljuks seemed able to win battles against them. Fortunately, however, for the Islamic world, none of these remoter nomads yet seemed willing to extend their conquests beyond the steppeland in the west. Their critical relationships lay to the east, with China. We thus need a brief account of what had happened in China in the ninth and tenth centuries.

The End of the Tang Dynasty

Superficially, the history of China, in the 800s and 900s, looks like a series of disasters. An era of political disintegration began in the ninth century. Eunuchs controlled the succession to the imperial throne. The Xuantong (shoo-ehn-tuhng) emperor, who died in 859, never named an empress or an heir lest he be "made idle," that is, murdered. Steppelander incursions continued. In 840, in a typical incident, 10,000 Uighurs (see Chapter 9), driven from their Central Asian homeland by rival nomads, arrived on the bend of the Yellow River proposing to garrison the Chinese frontier. A new menace—or, at least, one of unprecedented scale—was the rise of banditry. In a land as densely populated as China, every dislocation, invasion, war, or natural disaster had profound environmental consequences, impoverishing many peasants and driving them to survive by any available means. In the late ninth century, bandit gangs grew into rebellious armies led by renegade members of the elite—students who had failed to pass the examinations for the civil service and Buddhist clergy forced out of monasteries the government had confiscated.

An imperial decree of 877 complained that the bandit forces "come and go just as they please." The emperor's professed wish to "equalize food and clothing so that all might be prosperous" was an admission of weakness. His threat to apply "force without remorse" against those who refused to lay down their arms was empty. In 879, the bandit leader, Huang Chao (hwang chow), unified most of the gangs and crossed the Yangtze River with, reputedly, 600,000 men. He took Chang'an, the seat of the court, with effects described in the verses of one of the most striking poems of the time, the *Lament of Lady Qin*: rape, pillage, and

"In a land as densely populated as China, every dislocation invasion, war, or natural disaster had profound environmental consequences, impoverishing many peasants and driving them to survive by any available means."

Cultural superiority. In the Confucian scale of values, superior wisdom outweighed superior strength. The cringing figures with their caps, furs, pelt banners, and armored horses are Uighurs, Turkic steppe nomads, whom General Guo Ziyi, unarmed and simply attired, graciously enlists in Chinese service. The scene supposedly depicts an eighth-century episode of the wars against Tibet. For the Song artist who painted it in the eleventh century, it represented emotions invested in the program, advocated by political theorists such as Ouyang Xiu, to use the barbarian world to benefit China (see p. 397).

bloodshed. Huang's successor, Zhu Wen (joo wehn), emerged as the most powerful man in China, effectively replacing the Tang dynasty in 907. His state fell in turn in 923 to Turkic nomads whom the Chinese had tried to use against the bandits. The Chinese Empire dissolved into "ten kingdoms."

China's situation recalls that of Western Europe, striving to maintain the ancient sense of unity and—for some rulers—even actively seeking to recover it, in times of political dissolution. The Chinese predicament also parallels those of the Islamic world and Byzantium, beset by nomadic migrants and invaders. Chinese responses, as we shall see, were also similar. They tried to fend off the "barbarians" by methods akin to those of the Byzantines: diplomacy, bribery, intimidation, displays of cultural superiority. As in the Islamic world, Chinese worked to convert invaders to their own culture, usually successfully. As in all the states we have looked at, the reexploitation of internal resources—especially by converting forest to farmland—made an important contribution.

For China, however, the outcome was different from those of other comparable regions. Throughout the period this chapter covers, the reconstruction of unity never seemed perfect or stable, but unity remained an actively pursued and—as we shall see—ultimately recoverable ideal. Divisions over religion, which deepened disunity in Christendom, or in the world of al-Hakim, had no parallel in China. China survived the invaders from the steppes but surrendered much territory to them. And, unlike the Islamic world, China never wholly succeeded in turning invading warriors into a force it could use for its own expansion.

The Rise of the Song and the Barbarian Conquests

The fight for unity after the collapse of the 920s began in 960, when a mutinous army proclaimed its general as emperor. The dynasty he founded, the Song (soong), lasted until 1279, but it always had to share China's traditional territory with steppeland invaders who created empires and dynasties of their own in parts of the north. These barbarian states adopted Chinese political ideas and bureaucratic methods and claimed the mandate of heaven—or, at least, a share in it—for themselves. But none of them were able to extend their conquests south of the Huai River, into the intricately patterned lands of rice paddies and dense population the Song retained.

First, from the early tenth to the early twelfth centuries, the Khitan state of Liao (lee-ow) loomed over China from heartlands in Mongolia and Manchuria. Under the warrior-empresses Chunjin (926–947) and Xiao (982–1009), the Liao state acquired a southern frontier across the Yellow River valley. The Khitans remained faithful to their pastoral traditions, but in the tenth century, they split their empire into two spheres, creating a Chinese-style, Chinese-speaking administration for their southern provinces. They began to build cities, following Chinese urban planning models, apparently to attract migrants. The Khitan Empire had its own civil service, selected on Confucian principles, issuing documents that scholars still do not fully understand. In a treaty of 1004, the Song conceded equality to Liao, which became known as the Northern Kingdom, alongside the Southern Kingdom of the Song. The Song paid Liao 100,000 ounces of silver and 200,000 bolts of cloth annually. This was tribute, which the Chinese disguised as "gifts" in a face-saving formula. The two dynasties affected kinship in an elaborate exchange of titles. The Liao empress mother, for instance, became the Song emperor's "junior aunt." In 1031, they jointly proclaimed "reunification of the universe," but this was a wild exaggeration. The two states lived together in uneasy equilibrium, punctuated by occasional hostilities.

Toward the end of the 1030s, a second steppeland state proclaimed itself an empire—the Tangut (tan-goot) realm of Xia (hsia). The axis of the state was a strip of grazing land, 900 miles long, squeezed between Tibet and the southern Gobi Desert. In 1044, a great Tangut victory forced another treaty out of the Song. Xia was accorded the status of a kingdom superior to all others except Song and Liao, and received annual tribute from the Song of about half the value that the Song paid to the Liao. Xia, too, had its own system of writing, its own bureaucracy, and an iron coinage much used along the Silk Roads. It also had a considerable scholarly establishment, largely devoted to acquiring and commenting on Buddhist scriptures.

The last state builders to intrude into the region were the Jurchen (juhr-chehn), who from 1115 began to build up conquests that eventually included the whole Liao Empire and covered northern China as far as the Huai River (see Map 12.5). Their homeland was in the forests of northern Manchuria. Their traditional economy relied on hunting rather than herding. They were "sheer barbarians," Chinese envoys reported, "worse than wolves or tigers." On this occasion, for once, we can be reasonably confident about the events that provoked their migration. It coincided with several years' exceptional cold and rain.

The Jurchen wars forced the Chinese to acknowledge Jurchen claims to the mandate of heaven. A treaty of 1127 imposed annual tribute on the Song of 300,000 ounces of silver, 1,000,000 strings of copper cash, and 300,000 bolts of silk. Jurchen campaigns penetrated far into the south of China. In 1161, however, the invaders despaired of creating a river navy strong enough to permanently dominate the Yangtze. The Song and Jurchen states learned to live with each other.

Meanwhile, the Jurchen adopted Chinese habits and traditions more fully than even the Khitans and Tanguts had. The Jurchen emperors were uncertain about this trend. On the one hand, they were quick to adopt Chinese bureaucracy and courtly customs themselves. On the other hand, they were afraid that the Jurchen would lose their warlike strength and will to dominate. The Jurchen, after all, were few in number—perhaps a few hundred thousand—compared with their more than 50 million Chinese subjects recorded in a census of 1207. Despite legislation forbidding Jurchen to adopt Chinese language or dress, distinctive Jurchen culture largely vanished.

Chinese thinkers found it hard to adjust to a world in which "barbarians" seemed at least their equals. On the whole, the Song coped by accepting the reality of the new distribution of power and opting for coexistence and peaceful persuasion, bribing and coaxing the foreigners into remaining quiet. One of the supplest intellects of the Song era was that of the early eleventh-century palace official, Ouyang Xiu (oh-yahng shoo). Earlier barbarian attacks, he thought, had been like "the sting of gadflies and mosquitoes." Now they were more serious and could not merely be brushed aside. He advised,

> Put away . . . armor and bows, use humble words and . . . generous gifts. . . . Send a princess to obtain friendship . . . transport goods to establish firm bonds. Although this will diminish the emperor's dignity, it could for a while end fighting. . . . Who would exhaust China's resources . . . to quarrel with serpents and swine? . . . Now is

Barbarian crown. Although the scalloped form is typical of the headgear of Central Asian nomads, this Khitan cap of the eleventh century—which is so magnificent that it must have been worn by someone of very high status—shows the influence of Buddhist religion and Chinese art. From a stylized mountain, a lotus grows upward, symbolizing the ascent of the soul to enlightenment, toward a sun-like flaming jewel—a common Buddhist symbol for wisdom. Dragons, symbolizing benevolence, reach for the same goal.
Khitan headgear with repousse decoration of two dragons chasing a flaming jewel. Chinese, early 11th century Photograph © 2007 Museum of Fine Arts, Boston.

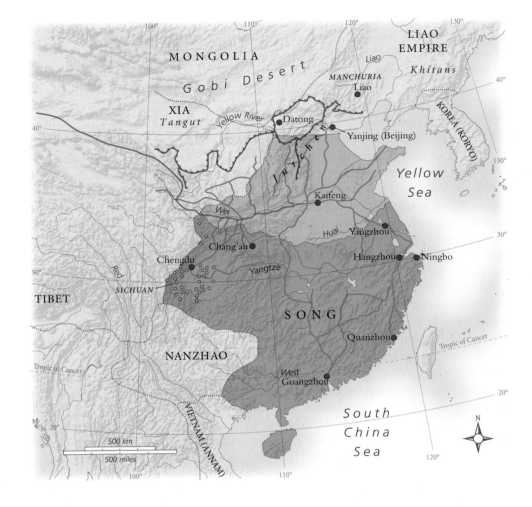

MAP 12.5

Song Empire, ca. 1150

- Song empire, ca.1050
- Song empire, 1127–1234
- Silk Road
- Great Wall
- ○ salt mine
- imperial highways
- *Khitans* people

"*Barbarian invaders always did get seduced by Chinese ways and adopt Chinese culture. But military defeats usually preceded these cultural victories, and the adoption of Chinese ways by barbarians usually followed bloody wars and costly destruction.*"

the moment for binding friendship. . . . If indeed Heaven causes the rogues to accept our humaneness and they . . . extinguish the beacons on our frontiers, which will be a great fortune to our ancestral altars.

According to Ouyang Xiu, civilization would always win encounters with savagery. Barbarians might be invincible in battle, but in the long run, they could be shamed into submission. There was a lot to be said for this point of view. China always survived. Barbarian invaders always did get seduced by Chinese ways and adopt Chinese culture. But military defeats usually preceded these cultural victories, and the adoption of Chinese ways by barbarians usually followed bloody wars and costly destruction.

In their way, Ouyang Xiu's arguments simply rewrote the old script—Chinese superiority would ultimately prevail. This kind of thinking made defeat by the Jurchen even harder to bear. The traumas the victims of the wars suffered come to life in pages by the poet Li Qingzhao (lee ching-jhao): a memoir of her life with her husband, whom she had married for love when he was a student and she was a teenager. The couple played intellectual games at teatime, rivaling each other in being able to identify literary quotations. Their books were their most cherished possessions. When the Jurchen invaded in 1127, the fleeing couple "first gave up the bulky printed volumes, the albums of paintings, and the bulkiest ornaments." They still had so many books that it took 15 carts to bear them and a string of boats to ferry them across the Yangtse. Another Jurchen raid scattered more of the collection "in clouds of black smoke." When Li Qingzhao finally got beyond danger, after the couple's parting and her husband's death, only a few baskets of books were left—and most of those were later stolen.

Economy and Society under the Song

Under pressure from the barbarian north, Song rule shrank toward the south (see Map 12.6). The Yangtze became the axis of the Song Empire. This potentially traumatic adjustment—the amputation of the ancient Yellow River heartlands, the "cradle" of Chinese civilization—was bearable because population, too, had shifted southward. About 60 percent of Chinese lived in the Yangtze valley by the last years of the tenth century. The trend continued under the impact of barbarian conquests in the north (see Map 12.6).

Away from the steppeland frontier, Chinese expansion went on. Loss of traditional territory, combined with the growth of population, stimulated colonization in new directions. The census of 1083 reported 17, 211, 713 families. By 1124, the number had grown to 20,882,258. Censuses tended to underestimate numbers, because tax evaders eluded the count. The Jurchen wars brought the growth of population to an end, but by then, Song China must have had well over 100,000,000 inhabitants—perhaps about half as many again as the whole of Europe. The state had the most basic resource: labor. It needed food and space.

The founder of the Song dynasty, Zhao Guangyin (jaow gwang-yeen), known as the Taizu (teye-tzoo) emperor, realized that China's new opportunities lay in a further shift in the center of gravity of the empire to the southwest: the vast, underpopulated region of Sichuan (seh-chwan). Colonization needed peaceful conditions. So the native tribes had to be suppressed. In a heavily forested, mountainous region, where tribal chiefs had a demonic reputation, this was not an easy task. By repute, the wildest inhabitants were the Black Bone Yi, led by a chief the Chinese called the "Demon Master." In 1001, the Song divided the region into two administrative units called "routes." A campaign in 1014 began the pacification. In 1036, the Demon Master became a salaried state official. The "forbidden hills" of Sichuan were stripped of forests and planted with tea and with mulberries for silk production. The salt mines became resources of the Chinese Empire. A land that

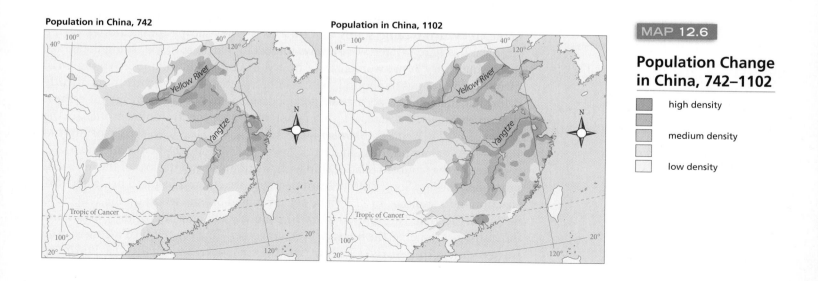

Population in China, 742

Population in China, 1102

MAP 12.6

Population Change in China, 742–1102

high density

medium density

low density

Rice cultivation. In the second half of the thirteenth century, Zhen Ji illustrated poems on rice cultivation in a long series of paintings, all copied—like the poems—from twelfth-century originals. His art demonstrates the continuity of Chinese agriculture. Even after revolutionary new strains of rice were introduced in China, older varieties of the crop were still cultivated in traditional ways.

poets formerly praised as a romantic wilderness of "streams and grottoes" became China's "heavenly storehouse."

Alongside the colonization of new land, new methods of exploitation enriched China, in a process of internal expansion strikingly reminiscent of what was going on at the same time in many other regions, notably in Europe and Ethiopia (Chapter 11). Environmental change fed the growing population. Wetlands were drained. New varieties of rice arrived from Vietnam, adapted to local conditions by trial and error. Planting and harvesting two crops a year effectively doubled the capacity for food production in the Yangtze valley. From the 1040s, the state promoted agriculture by making loans to peasants for seed grain, at favorable rates. Deforestation continued, stimulated by a tax on unharvested timber. By the end of the eleventh century, the forests around the city of Kaifeng (keye-fung) had disappeared, sacrificed to huge iron-smelting works, employing 3,000 men. In 1132, a new palace at Kaifeng was built with timber from the Qingfeng (chihng-fung) Mountains, reputedly inaccessible for centuries, like the enchanted forests of fairy tales.

Meanwhile, the money economy boomed. Song mints were always busy, always pumping out new coins—a million strings of coins a year in the early years of the century, six million in 1080—and always devaluing the currency by putting less precious metal—gold and silver—into coins. Paper money became a state monopoly from 1043. Towns grew spectacularly. Until the Jurchen captured it, Kaifeng was not just a seat of government but a thriving place of manufacture and trade. A famous twelfth-century painting by Zhang Zeduan (jwang tzeh-dwan) depicts the bustling life of the city—perhaps somewhat idealistically. On a roll more than 22-yards wide, all the life of Kaifeng at festival time unfolds—craftsmen, merchants, peddlers, entertainers, shoppers, and gawking crowds. Groaning grain ships bring the extra food. A river thick with traffic intersects the criss-cross framework of the neat streets with buildings roofed with thatch. Zhang also shows restaurant diners enjoying their meals. Kaifeng had 72 large restaurants, each of up to five pavilions, three-storeys high, and connected by delicate bridges. In 1147, the poet Master Meng (mung) recalled in his *Dream of the Eastern Capital's Splendor* how in Kaifeng the entertainers' din "could be heard for miles . . . Wildman Zhao would eat and drink while hung upside down . . . Li Waining (lee weye-ning) would pop up puppets with explosives."

Women, however, rarely appear in Meng's verses or on Zhang's scroll. They never enjoyed the same status in China as among the pastoral cultures of the steppeland, where women were always important partners in managing the herds. Increasingly, in China, women were traded as commodities, and as young girls, their feet were tightly bound with cloth, so that they became permanently deformed, in a practice perhaps originally designed to hobble them against escape. It soon, however, became a fashion that men supposedly found erotic. In the *Romance of the Western Chamber*—the sublime Chinese love classic of around 1200—feet "dainty but firm, like lotus flower buds" excite the hero's interest.

Despite the troubled relationship with the nomads and the loss of the northern provinces, the late Song Empire brimmed with wealth and inspired pride and satisfaction in its subjects. In 1170, a newly appointed official set off up the Yangtze to his job in Sichuan. He admired everything he saw: the newness of the bridges, the flourishing commerce, the boats crowded together "like the teeth of a comb." The war readiness of 700 river galleys, with their "speed like flight," excited him.

He celebrated ample signs of prosperity. The province to which he was traveling possessed enviable wealth. Two districts in Sichuan had between them 22 centers of population producing annual tax revenue of between 10,000 and 50,000 strings of cash—more than any other district of the Song Empire outside the lower Yangtze. The frontier had been drawn into the empire.

Kaifeng. In this most famous of Song dynasty scroll-paintings, Zhang Zeduan captures the vitality of life on the Yellow River at the city of Kaifeng in the early twelfth century and the wonderful commercial opportunities that the approach of the Spring Festival brought. Hundreds of wares arrive by cart, mule, or camel train or on poles slung across peddlers' backs.
The Art Archive/Picture Desk, Inc./Kobal Collection.

Song Art and Learning

The era left an enduring legacy of intellectual and artistic achievement. To the eleventh-century elite, philosophy was not an occupation of luxury or leisure, but the basis and business of government. On one side of the debate, Ouyang Xiu aimed to restore "the perfection of ancient times"—an ideal age "when rites and music reached everywhere." His writings capture the agenda and atmosphere of a sort of renaissance, a revival of ancient ethics and letters. He belonged to a type familiar in almost every great courtly society: urbane, world-weary, and with highly sophisticated sensibilities. His poems in praise of singing girls and strong drink made him vulnerable to attack by moralists. During a struggle among rival groups at court in 1067, he was disgraced in a sex scandal. Ouyang Xiu retired to what he called his "old tippler's pavilion" in the country.

Wang Anshi (wahng ahn-sheh), who led the party on the other side of the debate, thought life was like a dream and valued "dreamlike merits" equally with practical results. He carried the notion of socially responsible government to extremes and consulted "peasants and serving girls" rather than relying on Confucian principles and ancient precedents. The policies he pursued, when he was in charge of the government in the 1070s, included progressive taxation, the substitution of taxes for forced labor, cheap loans for farmers, and state-owned pawnshops. Wang mistrusted Confucian confidence in China's ability to tame the steppelanders—he introduced universal conscription. To combat banditry, and prevent the desertion of young peasants to bandit

Chinese Night Revels. A female musician entertains members of the scholar-gentry in The Night Revels of Han Xizai, painted in the tenth century by Gu Hongzhong. Chinese paintings rarely show men and women together in this kind of interior setting. The elaborately laid and decorated table, the porcelain ware, and the luxury and sexual appeal of female entertainment provide an intimate glimpse of courtly life during the Song dynasty.

Misty mountains. Chinese landscape painters under the Song dynasty celebrated the mountains and caves of newly colonized lands in southwest China. Mi Fei was one of the outstanding exponents of this type of painting, developing what came to be known as the "misty mountain style." No Western artist even began to show a similar appreciation of nature before the thirteenth century, and no Westerner painted landscapes without people in them until the sixteenth century. "Mountains are rivers," says the line from Confucius that captions Mi Fei's painting, "that put forth clouds."
Pavilion of Rising Clouds, Mi Fu. Freer Gallery of Art, Smithsonian Institution, Washington, D.C.: Gift of Charles Lang Freer, F. 1908. 171

gangs, he organized village society in groups of ten families, so that each family was held responsible for the good behavior of the others.

Both parties supported reform of the examination system that produced the imperial officials with two objectives in mind: to encode in it an ethic of service to society, and to recruit the state's servants from as wide a range of social backgrounds as possible. The old examination tested only skill in composition, especially in verse, and in memorizing texts. The new test asked questions about ethical standards and about how the state could serve the people better. It was a conservative revolution.

While Wang's agenda shaped policy, Ouyang Xiu's dominated the intellectual mainstream. The dominant trend in philosophy for the rest of the Song era was the effort to reinterpret the Confucian classics for the readers' own times. The work of Zhu Xi (joo shi) (1130–1200) summarized and synthesized all previous thinking on this subject. In his own mind, he was an orthodox Confucian, but in some ways, he was what we would now call a secular humanist. He upheld the doctrine of the natural goodness of human beings. He doubted whether "there is a man in heaven judging sin" and dismissed prayer in favor of self-examination and study of the classics. Morality, he thought, was a matter of individual responsibility, not heavenly regulation. But he did accept the tradition on which the Chinese state was based: "heaven" decreed the fortunes of society according to the merits of its rulers. Zhu's synthesis was so influential that it defined what subsequent ages called Confucianism.

The intellectual and economic environment of the Song Empire was highly favorable to the arts. There was money and enthusiasm for abundant patronage of artists. In the early twelfth century, the Huidzung (hway-dzuhng) emperor, who was an accomplished painter himself, founded a school of painting and expanded the palace gallery to exhibit paintings and ceramics. The painting of the era has always attracted special admiration, not just because it was prolific and technically excellent, but also because it specialized in scenes from the natural world. Admiration for the beauty of nature, untouched by human hands, is, perhaps, a measure of the maturity of a civilization. It is doubtful, however, whether Song artists painted nature, as modern romantics do today, for its own sake. To them, the natural world was a book of lessons about humankind and from which they could make comparisons about human nature. Every subject for a painting demanded long meditation in which the artist strove to understand the essence of what he was going to paint. Su Dongpo (soo dohng-pwoh) (1036–1101) painted virtually nothing but bamboo, because its fragility suggested human weakness. Li Longmian (lee lung-mee-en) (1049–1106) favored gnarled trees, defying weather, as symbols of the resilience of the sages. Mi Fei (mee fay) (1051–1107) perfected the representation of mist—which is the breath of nature, with power to shape the image, like the spiritual dimension of human beings. With other painters of the same era, they produced some of the world's most influential, most imitated images.

In Perspective
Cains and Abels

The North African Muslim Ibn Khaldun (1332–1406), one of the world's best historians, saw history as a story of struggle between nomads and settled people. To some extent, he based his view on the experience of the eleventh and twelfth centuries, when, as far as he could make out, pastoralist invaders wrecked the peace

Making Connections | NOMADIC THREATS TO SEDENTARY PEOPLES

CHARACTERISTICS OF EURASIAN NOMADS		CONSEQUENCES
Nomadic way of life requires extensive land	→	Constant threat of attack on sedentary peoples
Nomads ill equipped for certain economic activities and the manufacture of favored commodities	→	Dependence on theft and tribute from, or trade with, sedentary peoples
Nomads are expert horsemen	→	Until development of firearms and better fortifications, sedentary peoples at a disadvantage in war
Nomads cherish ideologies of superiority	→	Clash between nomads and settled peoples
Nomads can easily exploit farmers' lands	→	Until development of steel plows and mechanized harvesters, farmers could not exploit grasslands

and prosperity of his native region and Spain: first, Arab herders whom the Fatimids released or expelled from southern Egypt; then the Almoravids and Almohads from the Sahara. Modern historians have challenged his interpretation. The mutual disdain between tillers and herders was neither as deep nor as destructive as Ibn Khaldun thought. But the tension he perceived was real. The biblical story of Cain and Abel traces the origins of human conflict to the mutual hatred and murderous rivalry of a tiller of the soil and a keeper of flocks.

Nomads threatened their farming neighbors in various ways. The nomadic way of life demanded immeasurably more land per head of population than the intensive agriculture that fed dense farming populations. Nomads were ill equipped for some economic activities, including mining and silk manufacture, and the production of favored commodities, such as tea, fruit, and grain. For these things, therefore, they depended on theft, tribute, or trade from farming communities. The nomads were better equipped for war. Horsemanship made their way of life a preparation for battle. Sedentary peoples had not yet developed firearms or fortifications good enough to tilt the balance in their own favor. The nomads tended to cherish ideologies of superiority—variously of jihad or of divine election for empire—that clashed with the equal and opposite convictions of the settled peoples. Nomads could exploit farmers' lands, but agricultural communities did not yet have the technology—steel plows, mechanical harvesters—needed to turn the unyielding soils of the grasslands into productive farmland.

Yet the hostility of nomads and farmers arose less, perhaps, from conflicts of interest than from mutual misunderstanding: a clash of cultures, incompatible ways of seeing the world and coping with it. There is no moral difference between settled and nomadic lifeways. Each type of community, however, tended to see the other as morally inferior. This was probably because for followers of each way of life, those of the other came to represent all that was alien. Their mutual descriptions were full of incomprehension and even disgust.

Real differences underpinned this mutual revulsion. Pastoralist diets were, for farmers, literally stomach churning. Pastoralists relied on dairy foods, which most farmers' digestive systems rejected, because after early childhood they did not naturally produce lactase—the substance that makes milk digestible. It was also normal for herders to open their animal's veins for fresh blood to drink. This practice enabled nomad armies to take nourishment without halting on the march. Nomad

"Yet the hostility of nomads and farmers arose less, perhaps, from conflicts of interest than from mutual misunderstanding: a clash of cultures, incompatible ways of seeing the world and coping with it."

Chronology

907	End of Tang dynasty
960	Beginning of Song dynasty; conversion of Karkhanid Turks to Islam
1040s	Sanhaja conquer Morocco
1054	Schism between Latin and Orthodox Christianity
1071	Battle of Manzikert; end of Byzantine dominance in Anatolia
1076	Kumbi Saleh falls to Almoravid armies
1080s	Muslim kingdoms in al-Andalus call on Almoravids for help
1095	Pope Urban II calls for crusade to capture Jerusalem
1099	Jerusalem falls to crusaders
1111	Death of al-Ghazali, Sufi mystic and theologian
1140s	Almoravid Empire falls to the Almohads
1187	Crusader kingdom of Jerusalem falls to Saladin
1204	Crusaders sack Constantinople

diets tended to be short on plant foods. So to balance their intake, nomads would usually eat the raw organ meats of dead animals. This sort of food contains relatively high levels of vitamin C, which, in other cultures, people get from fruit and vegetables. Indeed, meat processed without cooking was important in the treeless environments of the steppe and the desert, where the only cooking fuel was dried animal dung. One of the great resources of the Eurasian steppe was the fat-tailed sheep, specially bred to drag its tail—as broad as a beaver's—behind it. Its fat is wonderfully soft. Even if nomads have no time to heat this fat, or no available kindling with which to cook it, they can eat it raw and digest it quickly. These were all elements of a rational food strategy for the nomadic life, but they inspired denunciations of the "barbaric" customs of eaters of raw meat and drinkers of blood. The nomads responded with equal contempt. For them, the settled life was soft and corrupted by luxury. Farming involved grubbing and groveling in mud. Cities and rice paddies were cramped and unhealthy.

After successful conquests, the nomads could usually be absorbed and induced to adopt or tolerate settled ways of life; but the conquerors kept coming. The relative success of the Islamic world in absorbing and converting the invaders of the tenth and eleventh centuries was a decisive feature of the history of the period. Byzantium, by contrast, failed to tame the intruders, while Western Christendom could recruit no more pastoralists after the Magyars. China developed no strategy to cope with the nomads, except to retreat and wait for them to adopt Chinese ways. Unprecedented changes in the steppeland, however, were about to upset the balance between nomads and settled peoples and unleash the most formidable steppeland conquerors of all, the Mongols. The outcome would transform the history of Eurasia.

PROBLEMS AND PARALLELS

1. Was the Islamic world's disunity an inevitable outcome of its vast geographic expansion by 1000? What parallels, if any, are there to earlier empires?

2. Why was the Islamic world more successful than Christian Europe or China in absorbing nomads? What strengths did the Turks bring to the Islamic world?

3. The Crusades started as an outgrowth of the tradition of pilgrimage. How was a religious process transformed into a series of violent military campaigns? What were the ultimate effects of the Crusades?

4. Why were the Almoravids and Almohads unable to prevent the decline of Islamic power in Spain Islamic power there? Why was the conversion of Ghana to Islam so significant?

5. Why did most Muslim elites and clerics reject the Sufis? Why were the teachings of Sufis like al-Ghazali important for the spread of Islam?

6. Why did the Byzantines claim to be the Roman Empire? Why was it strategically important for the rulers of Constantinople to build a Byzantine "commonwealth"? Why was Basil II so successful, and why were his successors unable to sustain his legacy? Why was there a rupture between Latin and Orthodox Christianity?

7. How did China under the Song deal with nomadic invaders? Why was Song China able to prosper despite the loss of the Yellow River valley?

8. Why did Ibn Khaldun see history as a story of struggle between nomads and settled people? Why have relations between pastoralists and sedentary peoples often been so hostile?

READ ON ▶ ▶ ▶

B. Lewis, *The Middle East* (1997) is a broad introductory narrative. M. S. Hodgson, *The Venture of Islam* (1977) is as always fundamental for anything in Islamic history. L. Yaacov, *State and Society in Fatimid Egypt* (1991) is an important collection of studies on the background to the caliphate of al-Hakim. T. Talbot-Rice, *The Seljuks in Asia Minor* (1960) is important for understanding the assimilation of the Turks. The *Dede Korkut* (1974) is available in an excellent edition by G. Lewis.

T. Asbridge, *The First Crusade* (2005) is a vigorous, up-to-date account. C. Tyerman, *God's War* (2006) is an efficient general introduction, as is J. Riley-Smith, *The Crusades* (2005). J. Riley-Smith, *Atlas of the Crusades* (1990) is a useful standby. K. M. Setton, ed., *A History of the Crusades* (1969) is exhaustive. J. Pryor, *Geography, Technology and War: Studies in the Maritime History of the Mediterranean, 649–1571*, makes what happened at sea intelligible.

H. Kennedy, *Muslim Spain and Portugal*, (1997) and R. Fletcher, *Moorish Spain* (1993) are helpful as introductions. D. Wasserstein, *The Rise and Fall of the Party Kings* (1985) deals with the dissolution of the caliphate of Cordova and its successor states. For the Spanish background, R. Fletcher, *The Quest for El Cid* (1991) is scintillating and highly readable. E. W. R. Bovill, *The Golden Trade of the Moors* (1992) and *Saharan Myth and Legend* are classic works that unfold the background to the Almoravids. N. Levtzion, *Ancient Ghana and Mali* (1980) is an authoritative and concise study. On Ghana, N. Levtzion, *Corpus of Early Arabic Sources for West African History* (1981) and T. Insoll, *The Archeology of Islam in sub-Saharan Africa* (2003) provide the main sources. J. S. Trimingham, *The Sufi Orders in Islam* (1998) is the great classic treatment of its subject.

On Byzantium, as well as works recommended in earlier chapters, C. Mango, *Byzantium and Its Image* (1984) is particularly good on cultural aspects, and D. Obolensky, *The Phoenix: The Byzantine Commonwealth*, (2000), which is particularly good on diplomacy, are helpful. B. Hill, *Imperial Women in Byzantium* (1999) is an indispensable modern study. A. J. Toynbee, *Constantine Porphyrogenitus and His World* (1973) is a timeless classic by one of the great historians of the twentieth century. Among the texts referred to in this chapter, *The Embassy to Constantinople and Other Writings of Liutprand of Cremona*, ed. J. J. Norwich, is instructive, and there are many editions of the *Alexiad* of Anna Comnena and *The Itinerary of Benjamin of Tudela*. On relations with the Latin church, S. Runciman, *The Eastern Schism*, (1955) though now half a century old, is concise and readable. J. J. Norwich, *A History of Venice* (1982) is a richly detailed narrative. D. E. Queller, *The Fourth Crusade* (1999) nicely blends narrative and analysis. There are many editions of the most engaging source: G. de Villehardouin, *The Conquest of Constantinople* (2006). N. Wilson, *Scribes and Scholars* (1991) is a lively account of Byzantine learning.

On Liao, J. S. Tao, *Two Sons of Heaven* (1988) is valuable; for the Jurchen, Y. S. Tao, *The Jurchen in Twelfth-Century China* (1977) is particularly good on sinicization. R. von Glahn, *The Country of Streams and Grottoes* (1988) is scholarly and well-written, bringing the internal frontier of China to life. R. Egan, ed., *The Literary Works of Ou-yang Hsiu* (1984) is an invaluable source. J. T. C. Liu, *Reform in Sung China*, which originally appeared in the 1950s, has not been replaced as far as I know.

THE BIG PICTURE

The World in 1200 C.E.

Hostility became routine between societies that relied mainly on tilling the soil and those that had to move frequently from one place to another with the herds they lived off. Grazing needs a lot of space, relatively speaking, to turn the plant life livestock eat into humanly edible food. So practitioners of the two types of culture became competitors for land. Their differences of culture were so marked that, as we have seen so often throughout this book, farmers and nomad herders found it easy to hate each other and hard to establish mutual understanding.

Christendom, Islam, and China had contrasting experiences of relationships with nomads. The Magyars and Bulgars settled inside Christendom, setting up states similar to those of their neighbors, but most of the herder-peoples who raided or invaded Europe remained excluded and hostile. Nomad invaders of China typically adopted Chinese ways and became vulnerable in their turn to further waves of invasion from the steppes. In Islam, however, the Turks' vocation for war outlasted conversion to Muslim religion and more settled ways of life. They became the sword-bearers of Islam, renewing manpower for defence and expansion to an extent unparalleled in Europe or China.

Despite turbulence in the steppes, contacts between China and Europe, though feeble and indirect, were never altogether interrupted. Though separated by turbulent seas, Japan was never quite out of touch with the other civilizations of east Asia. So the extremities of Eurasia were able to cope with—and, increasingly, emerge from—their relative isolation. Societies that fringed the Indian Ocean enriched and influenced each other. The relative stagnation of parts of Africa and the Americas showed, meanwhile, how isolation can inhibit change, whereas interactions between cultures exert mutual magnetism and make changes happen faster.

▶ QUESTIONS

1. How did different societies cope and contend with their relative isolation in the period from 1000 to 1200 C.E.?

2. Which settled societies were most threatened by nomadic peoples from 1000 to 1200 C.E.? Which sedentary societies were able to absorb pastoralists? In which societies did nomadic peoples remain excluded and hostile?

To view an interactive version of this map, as well as a video of the author describing key themes related to this Part, go to www.myhistorylab.com

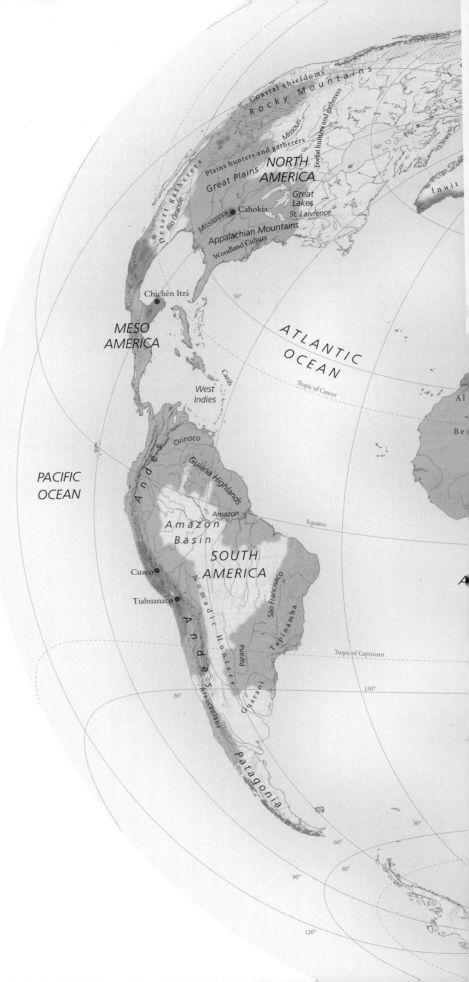

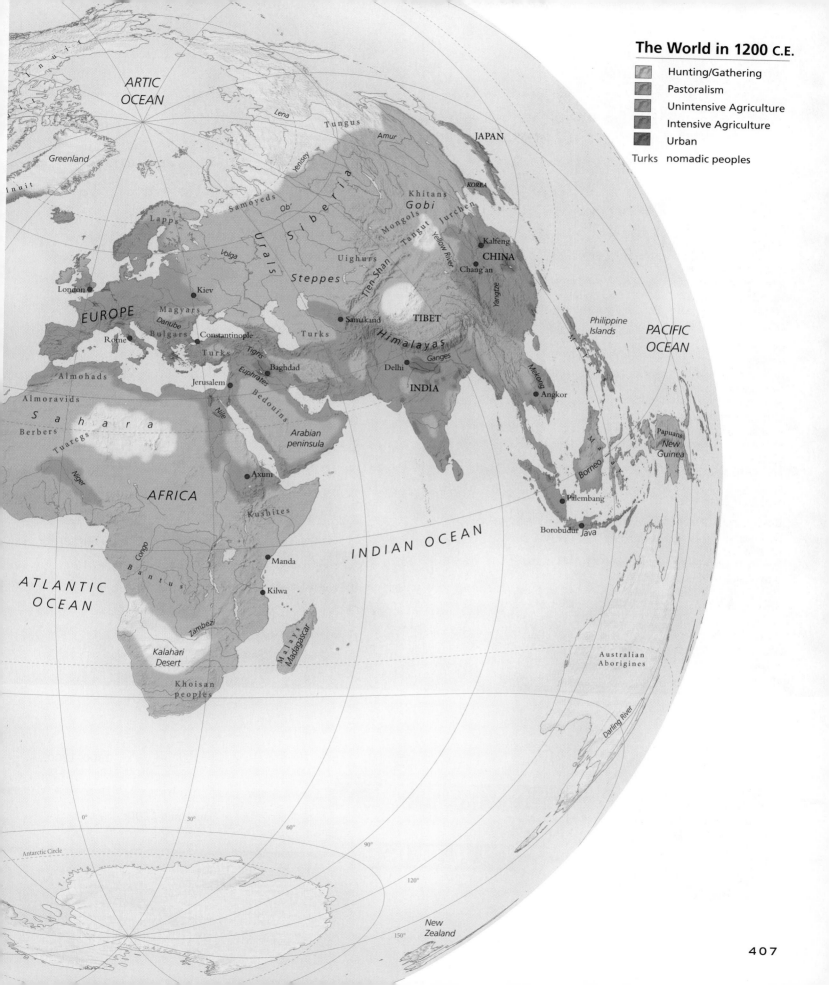

The World in 1200 C.E.

Hunting/Gathering
Pastoralism
Unintensive Agriculture
Intensive Agriculture
Urban

Turks   nomadic peoples

ARTIC
OCEAN

Greenland

Inuit

Lena

Tungus

Amur

JAPAN

Samoyeds

Ob'

Yenisey

Siberia

Khitans

Gobi

Mongols

Tangut

Jurchen

KOREA

Lapps

Urals

Uighurs

Yellow River

Kalfeng

Volga

Steppes

Tien-Shan

CHINA

London

Kiev

Samakand

Chang'an

Yangtze

EUROPE

Magyars

TIBET

Philippine
Islands

PACIFIC
OCEAN

Danube

Bulgars

Turks

Himalayas

Rome

Constantinople

Turks

Tigris

Ganges

Mekong

Almohads

Jerusalem

Euphrates

Baghdad

Delhi

Angkor

Almoravids

Bedouins

INDIA

Sahara

Nile

Papuans
New
Guinea

Berbers

Tuaregs

Arabian
peninsula

Borneo

Niger

Axum

AFRICA

Kushites

Palembang

Congo

Bantus

Borobudur   Java

INDIAN OCEAN

ATLANTIC
OCEAN

Manda

Kilwa

Zambezi

Madagascar

Malays

Australian
Aborigines

Kalahari
Desert

Khoisan
peoples

0°

30°

60°

90°

Darling River

120°

Antarctic Circle

New
Zealand

150°

PART 6

ENVIRONMENT

1300–1800
Little Ice Age

since mid-1200s
Lenses and clocks in Europe

CULTURE

1206–1360s
Mongol hegemony

The Crucible: The Eurasian Crises of the Thirteenth and Fourteenth Centuries

◀ **This Korean world map,** from about 1402, known as the Kangnido, is the earliest known map of the world from East Asia. It is also the oldest surviving Korean map. Based on Chinese maps from the fourteenth century, the Kangnido clearly shows Africa (with an enormous lake in the middle of the continent) and Arabia on the lower left. The Indian subcontinent, however, has been merged into a gigantic land-mass that represents China. The Korean peninsula, on the upper right, is shown as much bigger than it actually is, while Japan, on the lower right, is placed much farther south than where it is actually located.

1330s–mid-1400s (and sporadically to 1700s)
Plague in Eurasia

since mid-1400s
Growth of Atlantic navigation

from 1350s
Rise of the Ottomans

1368–1644
Ming dynasty (China)

from 1440s
Rise of Muscovy

from mid-1400s
Rise of Incas, Aztecs
Beginnings of oceanic imperialism

FRONT

BACK

FRONT

BACK

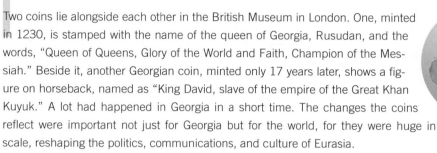

GEORGIA

T wo coins lie alongside each other in the British Museum in London. One, minted in 1230, is stamped with the name of the queen of Georgia, Rusudan, and the words, "Queen of Queens, Glory of the World and Faith, Champion of the Messiah." Beside it, another Georgian coin, minted only 17 years later, shows a figure on horseback, named as "King David, slave of the empire of the Great Khan Kuyuk." A lot had happened in Georgia in a short time. The changes the coins reflect were important not just for Georgia but for the world, for they were huge in scale, reshaping the politics, communications, and culture of Eurasia.

Georgia, protected by the high Caucasus Mountains, had been remarkably successful in resisting the nomad armies of the eleventh and twelfth centuries. Though the Seljuk Turks (see Chapter 12) had briefly terrorized the kingdom and exacted tribute, the Georgians fought back. They refused to pay tribute, recovered their lost territories, and extended their frontiers over parts of neighboring Armenia. In the early thirteenth century, Georgia was a formidable state, capable of imposing rulers as far afield as the Byzantine city of Trebizond on the Black Sea coast of Anatolia and the Muslim city of Ahar in Azerbaijan on the Caspian. In the 1220s, James of Vitry, a Catholic bishop and historian of his own times, admired Georgian pilgrims he saw in Jerusalem, who "march into the holy city with banners displayed, without paying tribute to anyone, for the Muslims dare in no way molest them."

As James of Vitry noted, Georgia was "surrounded by infidels on all sides". That did not seem to matter. The Georgians even promised the pope that they would assist in a new crusade. Suddenly, however, in 1224, letters from Georgia arrived in Rome, withdrawing the promise. "A savage people of hellish aspect have invaded my realm," wrote Rusudan, "as voracious as wolves in their hunger for spoils, and as brave as lions." In the next decade, her letters got increasingly desperate. The Mongols were coming. The world would never be the same again.

◀ **The Mongols arrive in Georgia.** Two coins from the kingdom of Georgia, minted less than two decades apart, show that the Mongols had conquered that Caucasian state. The front of the top coin, minted by Queen Rusudan of Georgia in 1230, features a bust of a bearded Jesus Christ, draped in a mantle and backed by a cross-shaped halo. The Greek abbreviations for the words "Jesus" and "Christ" flank his right and left shoulders respectively. A Georgian inscription runs along the border. The back of the coin shows inscriptions in both Georgian and Arabic. In contrast, on the bottom coin, minted by King David in 1247, a figure on horse back has replaced the image of Jesus Christ (front), while the inscription on the back of the coin is exclusively in Arabic and identifies the king as "the slave of the Great Khan."

FOCUS questions

Why were the Mongols able to conquer such a vast empire?

What were the effects of the Mongol conquests?

Why did the Mongols fail to conquer Egypt, India, and Japan?

How did Kubilai Khan's reign blend Mongol and Chinese traditions?

What technologies did the West develop in the thirteenth century, and what were the consequences?

Why did nothing comparable to the Mongol Empire develop in Africa or the Americas?

The effects of the events of the rest of the thirteenth century refashioned Eurasia, destroying old states, creating new ones, disrupting existing communications and reforging stronger, wider-ranging links. Eurasian civilizations benefited from enhanced contacts the Mongols fostered. Mongol methods were at first pitilessly bloody. They used terror and massacres to overawe their enemies. They razed cities, destroyed crops, slaughtered elites, and depleted peoples. Yet it looked as if a safer, richer, more interconnected, more dynamic, more expanding, and more enlightened world might emerge—as if something precious were to form in an alchemist's crucible, out of conflicting ingredients, flung at random and stirred with violence. Then a century of environmental disasters arrested these changes in most of Eurasia. Catastrophes reversed the growth of populations and prosperity. But previously marginal regions began to be drawn more closely into a widening pattern of contacts and cultural exchange. Some peoples, in Africa and Southeast Asia, for example, looked outward because they escaped disaster. Others, especially in Europe, did so because their reverses were so enormous that there was nothing else they could do.

THE MONGOLS: RESHAPING EURASIA

The earliest records of Mongol peoples occur in Chinese annals of the seventh century. At that time, the Mongols emerged onto the steppes of the Central Asian land now called Mongolia, from the forests to the north, where they seem to have been hunters and small-scale pig breeders. On the steppes they adopted a pastoral way of life. They became horse-borne nomads and sheepherders. Chinese and Khitan writers used versions of the names "Mongols" and "Tatars" for many different communities, with various religions and competing leaderships. One thing they had in common was that they spoke languages of common origins that were different from those of the Turks. In the early twelfth century, the bands or alliances they formed got bigger, and their raids against neighboring sedentary peoples became more menacing. In part, this was the effect of the growing preponderance of some Mongol groups over others. In part, it was the result of slow economic change.

Genghis Khan

Contact with richer neighbors gave Mongol chiefs opportunities for enrichment as mercenaries or raiders. Economic inequalities greater than the Mongols had ever known arose in a society in which blood relationships and seniority in age had formerly settled every person's position. Prowess in war enabled leaders to build up followers in parallel with—and sometimes in defiance of—the old social order. They called this process "crane catching"—comparing it to caging valuable birds. The most successful leaders enticed or forced rival groups into submission. The process spread to involve peoples who were not strictly Mongols, though the same name continued to be used—we use it still—for a confederation of many peoples, including many who spoke Turkic languages. In 1206, Temujin (TEH-moo-jeen), the most dynamic leader, proclaimed himself ruler (**khan**) "of all those who live in felt tents"—staking a claim to a steppe-wide empire. He was acclaimed by a title of obscure meaning, perhaps signifying "Ocean-King" and therefore, by implication, king of everything the ocean encloses. The title is traditionally rendered in the Roman alphabet as "Genghis Khan" (GEHN-gihs hahn).

We know maddeningly little about Temujin. Today, his memory is twisted between myths. When Mongolia was a communist state between 1921 and 1990, he was an almost unmentionable figure, inconsistent with the "peace-loving" image the communists tried to project. Now he is Mongolia's national hero. In his own day, he toyed with similarly contradictory images: a warlord who intimidated enemies into submission by massacre; an avenger of insults to his dynasty and tribe; an embodiment of Mongol convictions of superiority over sedentary peoples; a scourge of heaven, divinely appointed to chastise a wicked world; a lawgiver and architect of enduring empire.

In surviving documents, Genghis Khan addressed different audiences with conflicting messages. To Muslims, he was an instrument of God, sent to punish them for their sins. To Chinese, he was a candidate for the mandate of heaven. To Mongols, he was a giver of victory and of the treasure it brought. When he addressed monks and hermits, he stressed his own asceticism. "Heaven is weary of the inordinate luxury of China," he declared. "I have the same rags and the same food as cowherds and grooms, and I treat the soldiers as my brothers."

The violence endemic in the steppes now turned outward to challenge neighboring civilizations. Historians have been tempted to speculate about the reasons for the Mongols' expansion. One explanation is environmental. Temperatures in the steppe seem to have fallen during the relevant period. People farther west on the Russian plains complained that a cold spell in the early thirteenth century caused crops to fail. So declining pastures might have driven the Mongols to expand from the steppes. Population in the region seems to have been relatively high, and the pastoral way of life demands large amounts of grazing land to feed relatively few people. It is not a particularly energy-efficient way to provide food because it relies on animals eating plants and people eating animals, whereas farming produces humanly edible crops and cuts out animals as a wasteful intermediate stage of production. So perhaps the Mongol outthrust was a consequence of having more mouths to feed. Yet the Mongols were doing what steppelanders had always sought to do: dominate and exploit sedentary peoples. The difference was that they did it with greater ambition and greater efficiency than any of their predecessors.

Genghis Khan enforced or induced unity over almost the entire steppeland. The confederation of tribes he put together really did represent a combined effort of the steppe dwellers against the sedentary peoples who surrounded them. A single ideology came to animate, or perhaps reflect, that effort: the God-given terror-enforced right of the Mongols to conquer the world. The way events were recorded at the Mongol court in the next generation, it seemed as if from the moment of Genghis Khan's election as supreme ruler, "eternal heaven" had decreed that his conquests would encompass the world. The ruler is depicted as a constant devotee of **Tengri** (tehng-REE)—the sky, conceived as a supreme deity. The early Mongol-

Genghis Khan. Rashid al-Din (1247–1318) was a former Jewish rabbi, converted to Islam, who became the chief minister of the Mongol rulers of what is now Iran. His Compendium of Chronicles was propaganda that depicted Mongol rulers in Persian style. This is the image of Genghis Khan his successors liked to project—a lone, simple tent-dweller who was the arbitrator and lawgiver to petitioners from many nations.

"Exceptionally adaptable warmongers." This fourteenth-century Muslim painting shows the Mongols capturing Baghdad in 1258, with the help of siege craft and specialist engineers as well as their traditional cavalry. The last caliph appears behind a screen in his palace in the left background. In the center background, he emerges on a white horse to meet the Mongol leader, Hülegü. The painting seems to show the Mongols respecting the sacredness of the city and its ruler. Indeed, they showed their respect by putting the caliph to death without spilling his blood—a sign of reverence for the condemned in their culture.

inspired sources constantly insist on an analogy between the overarching unity of the sky and God's evident desire for the Earth to echo that unity through submission to one ruler.

It is more likely, however, that the sky cult was invented during the Mongol conquests to explain Genghis Khan's uniformly successful fortunes in war. The khan's imperial vision probably grew on him only gradually, as he felt his way from raiding, tribute gathering, and exacting ransom to constructing an empire, with permanent institutions of rule. Tradition alleges a turning point. When one of his generals proposed to exterminate ten million Chinese subjects and convert their fields into pasture for Mongol herds, Genghis Khan realized that he could profit more by sparing the peasants and taxing them to the tune of 500,000 ounces of silver, 400,000 sacks of grain, and 80,000 bolts of silk a year. The process, however, that turned the khan from destroyer to builder was tentative. He may have been only dimly aware of it.

Genghis Khan's initially limited ambitions are clear from the oath the Mongol chiefs swore to him at his election as khan, recorded in the earliest surviving Mongol record of the events. "If you will be our khan, we will go as your vanguard against the multitude of your enemies. All the beautiful girls and married women that we capture and all the fine horses we will bring to you." The khan acquired an unequaled reputation for lust and bloodlust. "My greatest joy," he was remembered for saying, "is to shed my enemies' blood, wring tears from their womenfolk and take their daughters for bedding." Meanwhile, he made the streets of Beijing—according to an admittedly imaginative eyewitness—"greasy with the fat of the slain." His tally of victims in Persia amounted, believably, to millions. When his army captured the city of Herat (heh-RAHT) in Afghanistan, it killed the entire population. Even after Genghis Khan had introduced more constructive policies, terror remained an instrument of empire. Mongol sieges routinely culminated in massacre. When the Mongols captured Baghdad in 1258, the last **caliph** and his sons were trampled to death—a ritual form of death reserved for rulers, which was designed to demoralize the enemy.

Wherever the Mongol armies went, their reputation preceded them. Armenian sources warned Westerners of the approach of "precursors of Antichrist . . . of hideous aspect and without pity in their bowels, . . . who rush with joy to carnage as if to a wedding feast or orgy." Rumors piled up in Germany, France, Burgundy, Hungary, and even in Spain and England, where Mongols had never been heard of before. The invaders looked like monkeys, it was said, barked like dogs, ate raw flesh, drank their horses' urine, knew no laws, and showed no mercy. Matthew Paris, the thirteenth-century English monk who, in his day, probably knew as much about the rest of the world as any of his countrymen, summed up the Mongols' image: "They are inhuman and beastly, rather monsters than men, thirsting for and drinking blood, tearing and devouring the flesh of

Chronology: The Rise of the Mongols

Seventh century	Earliest records of the Mongol people
Early twelfth century	Larger Mongol bands attack sedentary peoples
1206	Temujin proclaims himself khan

dogs and men. . . . And so they come, with the swiftness of lightning to the confines of Christendom, ravaging and slaughtering, striking everyone with terror and with incomparable horror."

The Mongol conquests reached farther and lasted longer than those of any previous nomad empire (see Map 13.1). After Genghis Khan's death, the energy that the conquests generated took Mongol armies to the banks of the Elbe River in eastern Germany and the Adriatic Sea. Invasions of Syria, India, and Japan failed, and the Mongols withdrew from Europe without attempting to set up a permanent presence west of Russia. They completed the conquest of China, however, in 1279. At its fullest extent, therefore, the empire covered the region from the Volga River to the Pacific, encompassing the whole of Russia, Persia, China, the Silk Roads, and the steppes. This made it by a big margin the largest empire, in terms of territorial extent, the world had seen.

Efforts to explain this unique success appeal to Genghis Khan's military genius, the cunning with which the Mongols practiced feigned retreats only to encircle and destroy their advancing enemies, the effectiveness of their curved bows, the demoralizing psychological impact of their ruthless practices. Of course, they had the usual steppelander advantages of superior horsemanship and unrivaled mobility. It is likely that they succeeded, in part, through sheer numbers. Though we call it a Mongol army, Genghis Khan's was the widest alliance of steppelander peoples ever. And it is probable—though the sources are not good enough for certainty—that, relatively speaking, the steppeland was more populous in his day than ever before.

Above all, the Mongols were exceptionally adaptable warmongers. They triumphed not only in cavalry country, but also in environments where previous steppelander armies had failed, pressing into service huge forces of foot soldiers, mobilizing complex logistical support, organizing siege trains and fleets, appropriating the full potential of sedentary economies to finance further wars. The mountains of Georgia could not stop them. The Mongols captured the Georgian capital, Tbilisi (t-BEE-lee-see), in 1234, turning Georgia into a puppet kingdom. Nor, in the long run, could the rice paddies and rivers of southern China where the Mongols destroyed the Song dynasty in the 1270s. Toward the end of the century, when another supreme khan wanted to conquer Java and Japan, they were even willing to take to the sea. But both attempts failed.

"Though we call it a Mongol army, Genghis Khan's was the widest alliance of steppelander peoples ever."

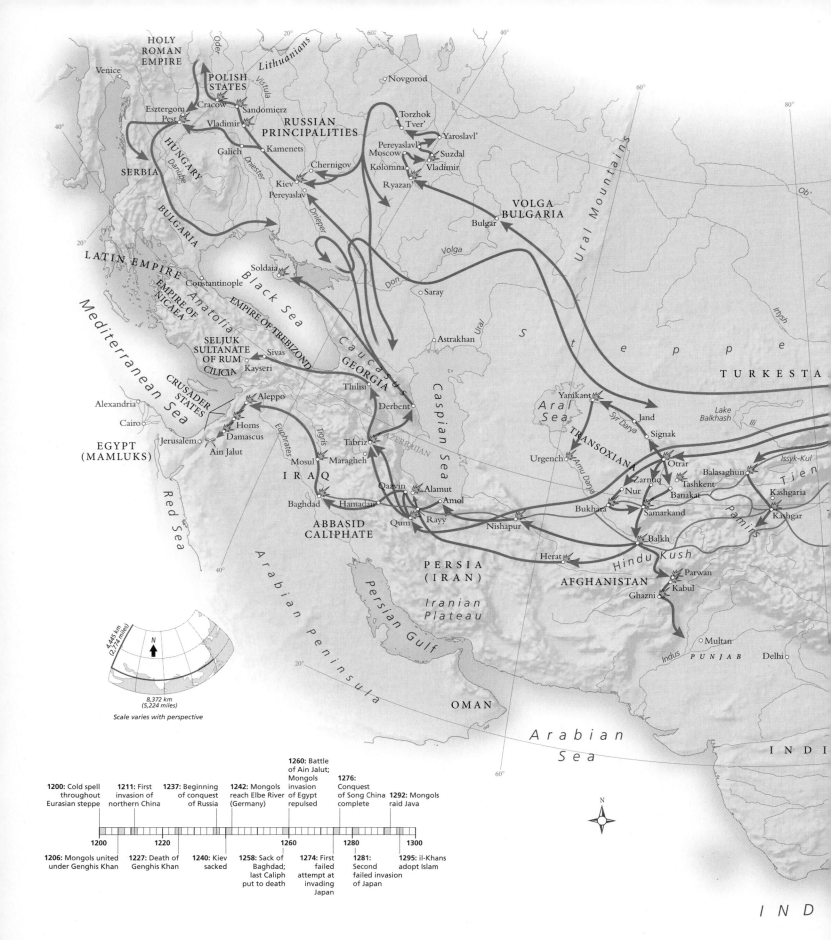

HOLY ROMAN EMPIRE

Venice

POLISH STATES

Esztergom
Pest
Cracow
Sandomierz
Vladimir

Oder
Vistula
Lithuanians

Novgorod

RUSSIAN PRINCIPALITIES

Torzhok
Tver'
Yaroslavl'
Pereyaslavl'
Moscow
Suzdal
Vladimir
Kolomna
Ryazan'

HUNGARY

SERBIA

Galich
Kamenets
Chernigov
Kiev
Pereyaslav

Danube
Dniester
Dnieper

BULGARIA

VOLGA BULGARIA

Bulgar

Ural Mountains

Volga

Don

Saray

Astrakhan

Ural

LATIN EMPIRE

Soldaia

Constantinople

Black Sea

EMPIRE OF NICAEA

Anatolia

EMPIRE OF TREBIZOND

SELJUK SULTANATE OF RUM

Sivas
Kayseri

CILICIA

CRUSADER STATES

Aleppo

Alexandria

Homs
Damascus
Jerusalem
Ain Jalut

Cairo

EGYPT (MAMLUKS)

Mediterranean Sea

Red Sea

Euphrates
Tigris

Mosul
IRAQ
Baghdad
Hamadan

ABBASID CALIPHATE

Caucasus

GEORGIA

Thilisi

Derbent

Caspian Sea

AZERBAIJAN

Tabriz
Maragheh

Qazvin
Alamut
Amol
Qum
Rayy

Nishapur

PERSIA (IRAN)

Iranian Plateau

Persian Gulf

Aral Sea

TRANSOXIANA

Urgench

Amu Darya

Syr Darya

Yanikant
Jand
Signak

Lake Balkhash

Ili

TURKESTA

S   t   e   p   p   e

Otrar
Zarnuq
Nur
Tashkent
Banakat
Bukhara
Samarkand
Balkh

Balasaghun

Issyk-Kul

Tien

Kashgaria

Kashgar

Pamirs

Herat

Hindu Kush

AFGHANISTAN

Parwan
Kabul
Ghazni

Multan

PUNJAB

Delhi

Indus

Arabian Peninsula

OMAN

Arabian Sea

I N D I

I N D

N

4,445 km
(2,774 miles)

8,372 km
(5,224 miles)

Scale varies with perspective

N

1200: Cold spell throughout Eurasian steppe

1211: First invasion of northern China

1237: Beginning of conquest of Russia

1242: Mongols reach Elbe River (Germany)

1260: Battle of Ain Jalut; Mongols invasion of Egypt repulsed

1276: Conquest of Song China complete

1292: Mongols raid Java

1200   1220   1260   1280   1300

1206: Mongols united under Genghis Khan

1227: Death of Genghis Khan

1240: Kiev sacked

1258: Sack of Baghdad; last Caliph put to death

1274: First failed attempt at invading Japan

1281: Second failed invasion of Japan

1295: il-Khans adopt Islam

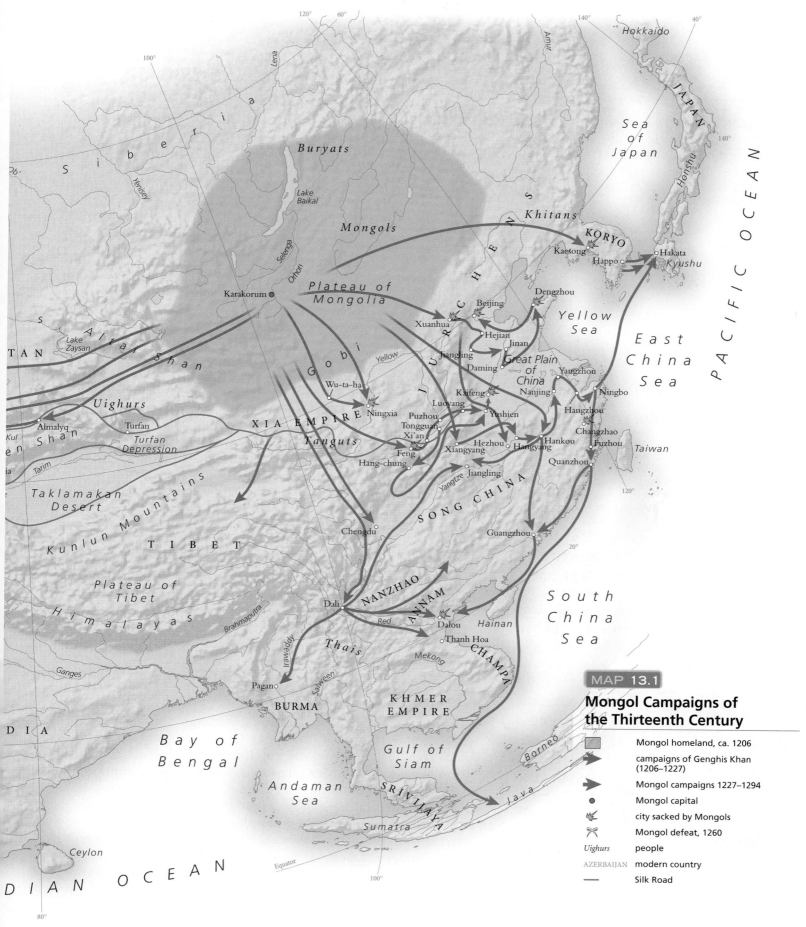

Mongol Campaigns of
the Thirteenth Century

MAP 13.1

Mongol Campaigns of the Thirteenth Century

- Mongol homeland, ca. 1206
- campaigns of Genghis Khan (1206–1227)
- Mongol campaigns 1227–1294
- Mongol capital
- city sacked by Mongols
- Mongol defeat, 1260
- *Uighurs* people
- AZERBAIJAN modern country
- Silk Road

Siberia

Buryats

Lake Baikal

Mongols

Khitans

Sea of Japan

Hokkaido

JAPAN

Honshu

KORYO

Kaesong

Happo

Hakata
Kyushu

PACIFIC OCEAN

Karakorum

Plateau of Mongolia

Selenga

Orhon

Yenisey

Lena

Amur

Altai Shan

Lake Zaysan

Almalyq

Uighurs

Turfan

Turfan Depression

Shan

Kul

Tarim

Gobi

Yellow

Wu-ta-ha

XIA EMPIRE

Tanguts

Ningxia

Puzhou

Tongguan

Xi'an

Feng

Hang-chung

Chengdu

Beijing

Xuanhua

Hejian

Jinan

Great Plain of China

Daming

Jiangling

Kaifeng

Luoyang

Yushien

Xiangyang

Hezhou

Hangyang

Dengzhou

Yellow Sea

Yangzhou

Nanjing

Ningbo

Hangzhou

Changzhao

Hankou

Fuzhou

East China Sea

Taiwan

Quanzhou

Taklamakan Desert

Kunlun Mountains

TIBET

Plateau of Tibet

Himalayas

Brahmaputra

Ganges

SONG CHINA

Yangtze

Jiangling

Guangzhou

Dali

NANZHAO

ANNAM

Red

Dalou

Thanh Hoa

Hainan

CHAMPA

South China Sea

Pagano

BURMA

Irrawaddy

Salween

Thais

Mekong

KHMER EMPIRE

Gulf of Siam

Bay of Bengal

Andaman Sea

SRIVIJAYA

Sumatra

Borneo

Java

Ceylon

INDIAN OCEAN

DIA

417

Making Connections | REASONS FOR MONGOL MILITARY SUCCESS

TACTICS/STRATEGIES	TECHNOLOGIES	PRACTICES
Psychological warfare; feigned retreats; unrivaled mobility	Superior horsemanship; curved bows; siegecraft	Ability to adapt to different environments and to overcome complex logistical obstacles; alliance formation with other steppeland peoples; recruitment of workers and administrators without favoritism

William of Rubruck. "He shall pass into the country of strange peoples. He shall try good and evil in all things." In the only surviving illumination that illustrates his report, Friar William of Rubruck looks alarmed at the instructions from King Louis IX of France to go on a mission to the Mongols. William's journey of 1253–1255 took him as far as the Mongol capital of Karakorum and generated an account full of vivid and faithful detail. The text illustrates how Western Europeans were becoming more aware of the wider Eurasian world.

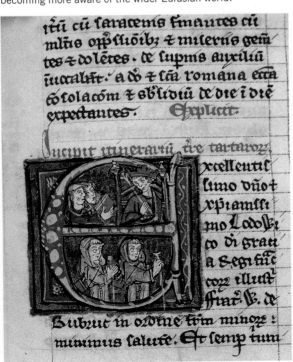

As well as for extent, the Mongol Empire was remarkable, by steppelander standards, for longevity. As his career progressed, Genghis Khan became a visionary lawgiver, a patron of letters, an architect of enduring empire. His first steps toward acquiring a bureaucracy and a judicial system more or less coincided with his election as khan. He then turned to lawmaking. Gradually, a code took shape, regulating hunting, army discipline, behavior at feasts, and social relationships, with death the penalty for murder, serious theft, conspiracy, adultery, sodomy, and witchcraft. Initially, the khan relied on Uighurs (see Chapter 9) for his administrators and ordered the adoption of the Uighur script for the Mongols' language. But he recruited as and where he conquered, without favoritism for any community or creed. His closest ministers included Muslims, Christians, and Buddhists.

In 1219, a Chinese Daoist sage, Changchun (chahng-chwuhn), answered the khan's call for wise experts. At the age of 71, he undertook an arduous three-year journey from China to meet the khan at the foot of the Hindu Kush Mountains in Afghanistan. There were sacrifices of principle Changchun would not make. He would not travel with recruits for the imperial harem, or venture "into a land where vegetables were unavailable"—by which he meant the steppe. Yet he crossed the Gobi Desert, climbed "mountains of huge cold," and braved wildernesses where his escort smeared their horses with blood to ward off demons. Admittedly, Changchun's meeting with the khan was disappointing. The question the conqueror was most eager to put was not about the art of government, but about a potion to confer longevity on himself.

The Mongol Steppe

Still, many lettered and experienced officials from the Jurchen, Khitan, and Tangut (THAN-goot) states (see Chapter 12) took service at the khan's court. The result was an exceptional, though short-lived, era in steppeland history: the **Mongol peace.** A European, who witnessed it in the 1240s, described it in an evident effort to reproach his fellow Christians with the moral superiority of their enemies: "The Mongols are the most obedient people in the world with regard to their leaders, more so even than our own clergy to their superiors. . . . There are no wranglings among them, no disputes or murders." This was obviously exaggerated, but Mongol rule did make the steppeland safe for outsiders. This was new. A previously inaccessible road through the steppes opened across

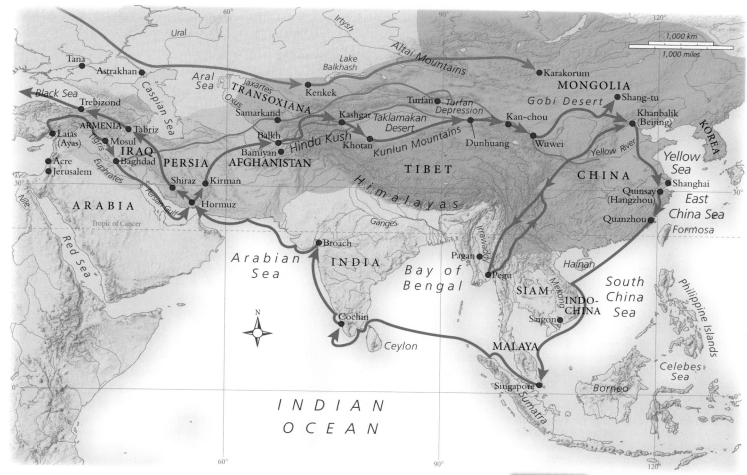

MAP 13.2

European Travelers of the Mongol Roads, 1245–1295

➤ John of Piano Carpini 1245–1247 and William of Rubruck 1253–1254

➤ Marco Polo 1271–1275

➤ Marco Polo 1275–1295

▢ Khanate of the Golden Horde

▢ Il-Khanate

▢ Chagatai Khanate

▢ Empire of the Great Khan

— Silk Road

Eurasia north of the Silk Road. Once they had learned the benefits of peace along the steppeland road, the Mongols became its highway police. Teams of Mongol horses, for instance, took the pope's ambassador, John of Piano Carpini, 3,000 miles in 106 days in 1246. Missionaries, spies, and craftsmen in search of work at the Mongol court also made the journey in an attempt to forge friendship between the Mongols and the Christian West, or, at least, to gather intelligence (see Map 13.2).

William of Rubruck—a Franciscan envoy recorded vivid details of his mission to Mongke Khan (MOHNG-keh hahn), Genghis Khan's grandson in 1253. As well as describing the road, William also described the Mongol way of life more accurately and completely than any Western visitor until the late nineteenth century.

After taking leave of the king of France, who hoped for an alliance with the Mongols against the Muslims, William crossed the Black Sea in May and set out across the steppe by wagon, bound for Karakorum (kah-rah-KOH-ruhm), the new city in Mongolia where the khan held court. "After three days," he recorded, "we found the Mongols and I really felt as if I were entering another world." By November, he was in the middle of Transoxiana, "famished, thirsty, frozen, and exhausted." In December, he was high in the dreaded Altai Shan (AHL-tay shahn), the mountain barrier that guarded the road to Karakorum. Here he "chanted the creed, among dreadful crags, to put the demons to flight." At last, on Palm Sunday, 1254, he entered the Mongol capital.

Friar William always insisted that he was a simple missionary, but he was treated as an ambassador and behaved like a master spy. And, indeed, he had more than one objective. The Mongols might be amenable to Christianity or at least to an alliance against common enemies in the Muslim world. On the other hand, they were potential enemies, who had already invaded the fringes of Europe and might do so again. Intelligence about them was precious. William realized that the seasonal migrations of Mongol life had a scientific basis and were calculated for military efficiency. "Every commander," he noted, "according to whether he has a greater or smaller number of men under him, is familiar with the limits of his pasture lands and where he ought to graze in summer and winter, spring and autumn."

Little useful intelligence escaped William. But he also showed interest in the culture he tried unsuccessfully to convert to Christianity. His description of a Mongol tent dwelling still holds good. The layout, social space, and way of life William saw have not changed much since his day. A frame of interlaced branches stretched between supports made of branches, converging at the top. The covering was of white felt, "and they decorate the felt with various fine designs." Up to 22 oxen hauled houses on wagons 20 feet broad.

Each wife of the master of the household had her own tent, where the master had a bench facing the entrance. In an inversion of Chinese rules of precedence, the women sat on the east side, the men to the right of the master, who sat at the north end. Ancestral spirits resided in felt bags arrayed around the walls. One each hung over the heads of master and mistress, with a guardian image between them. Others hung on the women's and men's sides of the tent, adorned with the udders of a cow and a mare, symbols of the sources of life for people who relied on dairy products for their diet. The household would gather to drink in the tent of the chosen wife of the night. "I should have drawn everything for you," William assured his readers, "had I known how to draw."

Shamans' trances released the spirits from the bags that held them. Frenzied drumming, dancing, and drinking induced the shamans' ecstasies. The power of speaking with the ancestors' voices gave **shamans** enormous authority in Mongol decision making, including the opportunity to interfere in making and unmaking khans. This was a point William missed. The Mongols leaders' interest in foreign religions, and their investment in the cult of heaven, were, in part at least, strategies to offset the power of the native priests.

Outside the tent, William vividly captured the nature of the terrain—so smooth that one woman could pilot 30 wagons, linked by trailing ropes. He described a way of life that reflected steppeland ecology. The Mongols had mixed flocks of various kinds of sheep and cattle. Mixed pastoralism is essential in an environment in which no other source of food is available. Different species have different cycles of lactation and fertility. Variety therefore ensures a reliable food supply.

The horse was the dominant partner of life on the steppe. Mare's milk was the Mongols' summer food. The intestines and dried flesh of horses provided cured meat and sausages for winter. By drawing blood from the living

Yurt. The shape and decoration of a Mongol tent dwelling—known as a *yurt* or *ger*—has not changed since William of Rubruck described those he saw in the thirteenth century. In the background of this photograph are the Pamir Mountains, which travelers westward on the Silk Roads had to cross when they emerged from the Taklamakan Desert.

creatures, Mongols on campaign could refresh themselves without significantly slowing the herds. This was the basis of their reputation for blood-sucking savagery among their sedentary neighbors. They made, said William, "very fine shoes from the hind part of a horse's hide." Fermented mare's milk was the favorite intoxicating drink. The Mongols revered drunkenness and hallowed it by rites: offerings sprinkled over the bags of ancestral spirits, or poured out toward the quarters of the globe. Challenges to drinking bouts were a part of nightly entertainment. To the accompaniment of singing and clapping, the victim would be seized by the ears, with a vigorous tug "to make him open his gullet."

William related in detail his conversations with the habitually drunken Möngke Khan. Despite the khan's bluster and self-righteousness, the conversations revealed some of the qualities that made the Mongols of his era great: tolerance, adaptability, respect for tradition. "We Mongols believe," Möngke said, if we can trust William's understanding of his words, "that there is but one God, in Whom we live and in Whom we die, and towards him we have an upright heart." Spreading his hand, he added, "But just as God has given different fingers to the hand, so He has given different religions to people." Later in the thirteenth century, Kubilai Khan, another of Genghis Khan's grandsons, expressed himself to the Venetian traveler, Marco Polo, in similar terms. So this was genuinely a Mongol saying.

THE MONGOL WORLD BEYOND THE STEPPES: THE SILK ROADS, CHINA, PERSIA, AND RUSSIA

The steppeland route was ideal for horseborne travelers. Trading caravans, however, still favored the traditional **Silk Roads,** which crossed Eurasia to the south of the steppe through the Taklamakan (tahk-lah-mah-KAHN) Desert. These routes had developed over centuries, precisely because high mountains protected them from steppeland raiders. But they had never been totally secure before the Mongol peace. The new security boosted the amount of traffic the roads carried. Mongol partiality for merchants also helped. Mongols encouraged Chinese trade, uninhibited by any of the traditional Confucian prejudices against commerce as an ignoble occupation. In 1299, after the Mongol Empire had been divided among several rulers, a Persian merchant was made the ambassador of the Supreme Khan to the court of the subordinate Mongol **Il-khan** (EEL-hahn) in Persia—an elevation unthinkable under a native Chinese dynasty, which would have reserved such a post for an official educated in the Confucian classics. The khans gave low-cost loans to Chinese trading companies. Chinese goods—and with them, patterns and styles—flowed to Persian markets as never before. Chinese arts, under Mongol patronage, became more open to foreign influences.

Geography still made the Silk Roads hard to travel. Marco Polo was a young Venetian who accompanied his father and uncle on a trading mission to Mongol-ruled China in the early 1270s. "They were hard put to it to complete the journey in three and a half years," Marco Polo reported at the start of his own account, first "because of

The Silk Roads. Cresques Abraham was the finest mapmaker of his day. He painted this image of a caravan on the Silk Roads in the late 1370s or early 1380s in an atlas probably commissioned for the king of France. By that date, the Mongols no longer controlled the whole of the route, though the lances of an armed escort, presumably of Mongols, are visible behind the merchants. The caption says the caravan is bound for China, but it is heading in the opposite direction.

A CLOSER LOOK

A Mongol Passport

Although they were in use in China before the Mongols arrived, documents called *paizi*, such as the one depicted here, were used as passports to regulate communication and administration in the vast Mongol Empire. Their use, the way they were designed, and the language in which they were written help us understand the massive movements of people and the rapid exchange of ideas and technology that occurred across Eurasia during the thirteenth and fourteenth centuries when Mongol rule was at its height. William of Rubruck and Marco Polo would have carried one of these passports on their return journeys to Europe from Mongol courts in Asia.

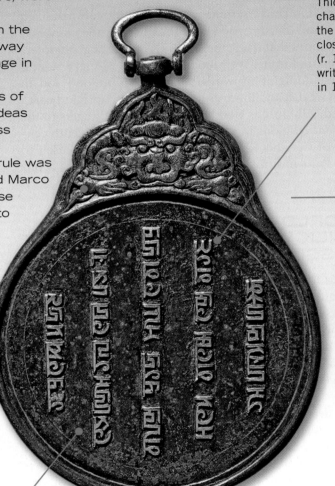

This passport is made of iron. Thick silver bands on it form characters in the script that the Tibetan monk Phagspa, a close adviser to Kubilai Khan (r. 1260–1294), devised for writing the Mongol language in 1269.

Most *paizi* were circular or rectangular and were either fastened on clothing or suspended from a person's neck, so that customs officers could easily see them.

Above the inscription is a handle with a silver lion mask inlaid on it that shows the influence of Tibetan and Indian art.

The inscription reads:
"By the strength of Eternal Heaven, an edict of the Khan. He who has no respect [for the edict] shall be guilty."

What does this passport reveal about the Mongol peace?

the snow and rain and flooded rivers and violent storms in the countries through which they had to pass, and because they could not ride so well in winter as in summer." The Taklamakan Desert was the great obstacle. The normal rule for caravans was the bigger the safer. But the modest water sources of the desert could not sustain many more than 50 men at a time with their beasts. The key to exploiting the desert routes was the distribution of water, which drains inland from the surrounding mountains and finds its way below the desert floor by underground channels. It was normal to go for 30 days without finding water, though there might be an occasional salt-marsh oasis or an unreliable river of shifting course, among featureless dunes. The worst danger was getting lost—"lured from the path by demon-spirits." "Yes," said Marco,

Demons. In Chinese and Mongol art, images of demons personify the torments of the desert—thirst, glare, sandstorms, extremes of heat and cold, the perils of being lost or attacked. William of Rubruck sang to drive away demons. Other travelers rang bells or deterred the demons with blood. In this fourteenth-century painting produced under Mongol patronage, the demon's dance evokes the swirling, stinging desert winds.

and even by daylight men hear these spirit-voices and often you fancy you are listening to the strains of many instruments, especially drums, and the clash of arms. For this reason bands of travelers make a point of keeping very close together. Before they go to sleep they set up a sign pointing in the direction in which they have to travel. And round the necks of their beasts they fasten little bells, so that by listening to the sound they may prevent them straying off the path.

As a fourteenth-century painter at Persia's Mongol court imagined them, the demons were black, athletic, and ruthless, waving the dismembered limbs of horses as they danced. As Friar William had seen, the Mongols recommended warding them off by smearing a horse's neck with blood.

A fourteenth-century guide included handy tips for Italian merchants who headed for East Asia to extend the reach of the commerce of their cities. At the port of Tana, on the Black Sea, you should furnish yourself with a good guide, regardless of expense. "And if the merchant likes to take a woman with him from Tana, he can do so." On departure from Tana, 25 days' supply of flour and salt fish were needed—"other things you will find in sufficiency and especially meat." The road was "safe by day and night," protected by Mongol police. But it was important to take a close relative for company. Otherwise, should a merchant die, his property would be forfeit. The text specified rates of exchange at each stop and recommended suitable conveyances for each stage of the journey: oxcart or horse-drawn wagon to the city of Astrakhan where the Don River runs into the Caspian Sea, depending on how fast the traveler wanted to go and how much he wanted to pay. Thereafter camel train or pack mule was best, until you arrived at the river system of China. Silver was the currency of the road, but the Chinese authorities would exchange it for paper money, which—Westerners were assured—they could use throughout China.

After the deserts, the next obstacles were the mountains on their rims. The Tian Shan, which screens the Taklamakan Desert, is one of the most formidable mountain ranges in the world: 1,800 miles long, up to 300 miles wide, and rising to 24,000 feet. The extraordinary environment these mountains enclose is odder still because of the deep depressions that punctuate them. That of Turfan (toor-FAHN) drops to more than 500 feet below sea level. Farther north, the Altai Shan Mountains guard

Chronology: Travelers during the Mongol Peace	
1245–1247	John of Piano Carpini
1253–1254	William of Rubruck
1271–1275; 1275–1295	Marco Polo
1275–1288	Rabban Bar Sauma

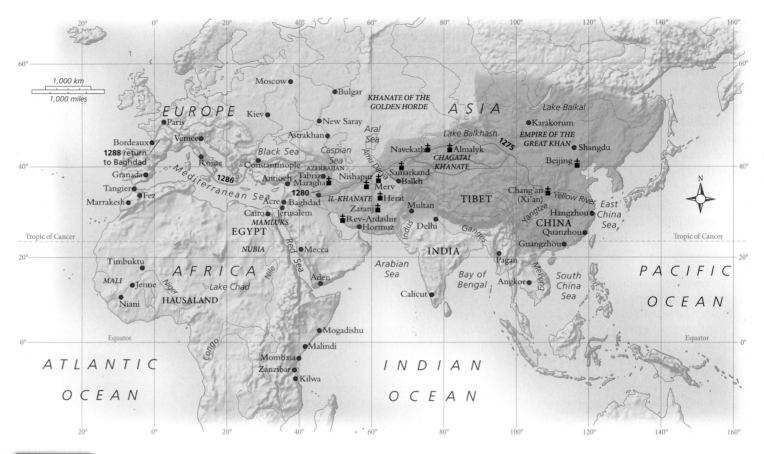

MAP 13.3

The Travels of Rabban Bar Sauma, 1275–1288

—— Silk Road

—— travels of Rabban Bar Sauma, 1275–1288

✝ Nestorian see

the Mongolian heartlands. "Before the days of the Mongols," wrote the bishop of the missionary diocese the Franciscans had established in China, "nobody believed that the Earth was habitable beyond these mountains, . . . but by God's leave and wonderful exertion the Mongols crossed them, and . . . so did I."

Europeans frequently made the journey to China. That reflects the balance of wealth and power at the time. China was rich and productive, Europe a needy backwater. We know of only one subject of the Chinese emperor who found it worthwhile to make the journey in the opposite direction. Rabban Bar Sauma was a Nestorian—a follower, that is, of a Christian tradition that had long flourished in Central Asia but the West had regarded as heretical since the fifth century (see Chapter 9).

When making a pilgrimage to Jerusalem, Bar Sauma planned a route between Nestorian monasteries, heading initially for Maragha (ma-rah-GEH) in what is now Azerbaijan, where the most respected bishop of the Nestorian church had his see. Maragha was a suitable way station: the intellectual capital of the western Mongol world, with a library reputedly of 400,000 books and a new astronomical observatory. There, Bar Sauma took service, first with the bishop, and later with the Mongol ruler of Persia, the Il-khan. He never completed his pilgrimage. In 1286, however, Bar Sauma did resume his travels. He was appointed the Mongols' ambassador to the kingdoms of the Christian West, to negotiate an alliance against Muslim Egypt (see Map 13.3).

When he got to Rome, Bar Sauma was accorded a signal honor: reception by the cardinals who had assembled to elect a pope. In Paris, he recognized the university there as an intellectual powerhouse reminiscent of Maragha, with schools of mathematics, astronomy, medicine, and philosophy. Persian was the only language in which Bar Sauma could communicate with Western interpreters. From the errors he makes in describing Western manners and politics, a lot evidently got lost in translation. He mistook diplomatic evasions for assent and vague expressions of Christian fellowship for doctrinal agreement. He returned to Persia with many assurances of friendship and exhortations to the Il-khan to convert to Christianity. The fact that he completed the journey at all shows how the Mongols made it possible to cross Eurasia.

China

The Mongols never ran their dominions as a centralized state. Nor did they apply consistent methods to govern territories as vast and diverse as theirs. Three main areas of conquest beyond the steppeland—in China, Persia, and Russia—were added after Genghis Khan's death. All were exploited in different ways, specific to the Mongols' needs and the peculiarities of each region.

The conquest of Song China was long and difficult for two reasons. It was a more powerful state than any the Mongols faced elsewhere, and it was highly defensible: compact, so that its armies could maneuver on interior lines of communication, and scored by terrain inhospitable to Mongol horsemen. But, fueled by resources from the Mongols' other conquests, and pursued with unfailing tenacity, the conquest unfolded relentlessly bit by bit. Letters from the Chinese court seeped desperation as the Mongols closed in for the kill. In 1274, the Chinese empress mother, Xie Qiao (shay chow), reflected on where the blame lay.

> The empire's descent into peril is due, I regret, to the instability of our moral virtue. . . . The sound of woeful lament reverberated through the countryside, yet we failed to investigate. The pall of hunger and cold enveloped the armed forces, yet we failed to console.

The real reasons for China's collapse lay in the superiority of the Mongols' war machine. Unlike previous steppelander invaders, the Mongols spared no resources to pursue all-out victory and hired the troops and equipment needed to subdue a country of cities, rice paddies, and rivers. Clearly, the size of the Mongols' existing empire helped. Persian engineers built the siege engines that helped overcome southern Chinese cities. The last battle was at Changzhao (chahng-jeeow) in 1275. The Chinese poet Yi Tinggao (yee teen-gow) was there, "smelling the acrid dust of the field," spying "the green irridescence of the dead." The human misery could be measured in the grief-stricken literature that survives: the suicide notes, the cries of longing for loved ones who disappeared in the chaos, massacred or enslaved. Years later, Ni Bozhuang (nee-bwo-chwang), bailiff of a Daoist monastery, recalled the loss of his wife: "I still do not know if you were taken because of your beauty, or if, surrounded by horses, you can still buy cosmetics." In 1276, with his advisers fleeing and his mother packed for

Kubilai Khan. Liu Guandao was Kubilai Khan's favorite painter. So we can be fairly sure that this is how the khan would like to be remembered: not just in the traditional inert Chinese pose (which Liu also painted), but also active, dressed and horsed like a Mongol ruler, engaged in the hunt. A woman, presumably his influential consort, Chabi, is at his side. The blank silk background evokes the featurelessness of the steppe, while also highlighting the human figures.

flight, the young Song emperor wrote his abdication letter to the Mongol khan. "The **Mandate of Heaven** having shifted, your Servant chooses to change with it, . . . yet my heart is full of emotions and these cannot countenance the prospect of the abrupt annihilation of the . . . altars of my ancestors. Whether they be misguidedly abandoned or specially preserved intact rests solely with the revitalized moral virtue you bring to the throne."

For the Mongols, the conquest of China was a logical continuation of the policies of Genghis Khan and a stage in fulfilling the destiny of world conquest heaven supposedly envisaged. But it was also the personal project and passion of Kubilai Khan (1214–1294), Genghis's grandson, who became so immersed in China that he never asserted his supremacy against those Mongol leaders in the extreme west of the Mongol world who resisted his claims. Some of his Chinese subjects resented Kubilai's foreign ways: the libations of fermented mare's milk with which he honored his gods, his barbarous banquets of meat, the officials he chose with great freedom from outside the Confucian elite and even from outside China. Marco Polo reported that all the Chinese "hated the government of the Great Khan, because he set over them steppelanders, most of whom were Muslims, and . . . it made them feel no more than slaves." In this respect, the khan indeed broke with Chinese tradition, which was to confine administrative positions to a meritocracy, whose members were selected by examination in the Confucian classics. Kubilai showed his reverence for Confucius by building a shrine in his honor, but he needed to recruit, as Genghis Khan had, from the full range of talent the Mongol Empire supplied.

Kubilai, indeed, remained a Mongol khan. In some respects, he flouted Chinese conventions. He showed traditional steppelander respect for the abilities of women, giving them court posts and, in one case, a provincial governorship. His wife, Chabi, was one of his closest political advisers. He introduced a separate tier of administration for Mongols, who became a privileged minority in China, ruled by their own laws, and resented for it by most Chinese. In defiance of Confucian teachings, Kubilai felt obliged to fulfill the vision of world conquest he inherited from Genghis Khan. But beyond China, he registered only fleeting success. In Java, the Mongols replaced one native prince with another, without making permanent gains. In Vietnam, the Mongols were only able to levy tribute at a rate too low to meet the cost of their campaigns there. So-called *kamikaze* winds—divine typhoons that wrecked the Mongol fleets—drove Kubilai's armies back from Japan.

While upholding Mongol traditions, Kubilai also sought, emphatically, to be a Chinese emperor who performed the due rites, dressed in the Chinese manner, learned the language, patronized the arts, protected the traditions, and promoted the interests of his Chinese subjects. Marco Polo, who seems to have served him as a sort of professional storyteller, called him "the most powerful master of men, lands, and treasures there has been in the world from the time of Adam until today."

Persia

In Persia, meanwhile, the Mongol rulers were like chameleons, gradually taking on the hues of the culture they conquered. But, as in China, they were anxious to maintain a distinct identity and to preserve their own traditions. The court tended to stay in the north, where there was grazing for the kinds of herds their

> *"For the Mongols, the conquest of China was a logical continuation of the policies of Genghis Khan and a stage in fulfilling the destiny of world conquest heaven supposedly envisaged."*

followers brought with them from the steppe. The Il-khans—"subordinate rulers," so called in deference to Kubilai Khan's nominal superiority—retained nomadic habits, migrating every summer and winter to new camps with palatial tents. At the end of the thirteenth century, Gazan Khan's tent took three years to make, and 200 men took 20 days to erect it. In southern Iran and Iraq, the Il-khans tended to entrust power to local dynasties, securing their loyalty by marriages with the ruling family or court nobility. In effect, this gave them hostages for the good conduct of provincial rulers.

Eventually in 1295, the Il-khans adopted Islam, after flirtations with Nestorianism and Buddhism. This marked an important departure from the tradition of religious pluralism Genghis Khan had begun and Kubilai upheld. From the moment the Il-khan Ghazan (r. 1295–1304) declared his conversion to Islam, the state began to take on a militantly religious character, excluding the Christians, Zoroastrians, Buddhists, and Jews formerly admitted to the khan's service. Moreover, the form of Islam the Il-khans finally adopted was Shiism, the prevailing tradition in Iran. Shiites (see Chapter 9) embraced doctrines most Muslims rejected: that Muhammad's authority descended by heredity from his nephew Ali; that a divinely selected leader or imam would perfect the Prophet's message; and that in the meantime the clergy had the right to interpret Islam. The Il-khan's option for Shiism ensured that eventually Persia would remain an exceptional region in the Muslim world as the only officially Shiite state.

Indeed, the religious art of the Il-khanate is strikingly unlike that of any other Muslim country. The painters freely painted human figures, especially those of Muhammad and his nephew, and even copied Christian nativity scenes to produce versions of the Prophet's birth. The Il-khans' Persia, however, was not isolated from neighboring states. On the contrary, as was usual in the Mongol world, the presence of rulers descended from Genghis Khan promoted trans-Eurasian contacts and exchanges of goods, personnel, and ideas. Persia supplied China, for instance, with engineers, astronomers, and mathematicians, while Persia received Chinese porcelain and paper money, which, however, did not take root in Persia before the twentieth century. Chinese designs influenced Persian weavers, and Chinese dragons appeared on the tiles with which Persian buildings of the time were decorated. Mongol rule ended in Persia in 1343 when the last Il-khan died without an heir.

Russia

Meanwhile, the Mongols who remained in their Central Asian heartlands continued to lead their traditional, unreconstructed way of life. So did those who formed the elite in the remaining areas the heirs of Genghis Khan inherited: in Turkestan and Kashgaria in Central Asia, and the steppes of the lower Volga River. From the last of these areas, where the Mongols were known as the Golden Horde, they exercised a form of overlordship over Russia, where they practiced a kind of imperialism different from those in China and Persia. The Mongols left the Christian Russian principalities and city-states to run their own affairs. But their rulers had to receive charters from the khan's court at Saray (sah-REYE) on the lower Volga, where they had to make regular appearances, loaded with tribute and subject to ritual humiliations. The population had to pay taxes

Il-Khan art. When Mongols converted to Islam, they did not necessarily accept all the beliefs and conventions of orthodox religion. In this four-teenth-century painting from what is now Iran, the white rooster symbolizes the Muslim call to prayer—but the rooster was also a traditional Zoroastrian symbol of dawn. The prophet Muhammad, moreover, is realistically depicted at bottom right—something most Muslim painters would regard as impious today. The other figures are of angels.

Novgorod. The cathedral of St. Sophia in Novgorod in Russia would have presented essentially the same outline in the thirteenth century that it does today. At the time, it was one of relatively few buildings in that mercantile city-state built of stone rather than wood. The tallest gilded dome shows the position of the sanctuary at the heart of the church.

directly to Mongol-appointed tax gatherers—though as time went on, the Mongols assigned the tax gathering to native Russian princes and civic authorities.

The Russians tolerated this situation—albeit unhappily, and with many revolts—partly because the Mongols intimidated them by terror. When the Mongols took the great city of Kiev in 1240, it was said, they left only 200 houses standing and strewed the fields "with countless heads and bones of the dead." Partly, however, the Russians were responding to a milder Mongol policy. In most of Russia, the invaders came to exploit rather than to destroy. According to one chronicler, the Mongols spared Russia's peasants to ensure that farming would continue. Ryazan, a Russian principality on the Volga, southeast of Moscow, seems to have borne the brunt of the Mongol invasion. Yet there, if the local chronicle can be believed, "the pious Grand Prince Ingvary Ingvarevitch sat on his father's throne and renewed the land and built churches and monasteries and consoled newcomers and gathered together the people. And there was joy among the Christians whom God had saved from the godless and impious khan." Many cities escaped lightly by capitulating at once. Novgorod, that hugely rich city (see Chapter 11), which the Mongols might have coveted, they bypassed altogether.

Moreover, the Russian princes were even more fearful of enemies to the west, where the Swedes, Poles, and Lithuanians had constructed strong, unitary monarchies, capable of sweeping the princes away if they ever succeed in expanding into Russian territory. Equally menacing were groups of mainly German adventurers, organized into crusading "orders" of warriors, such as the Teutonic Knights and the Brothers of the Sword, who took monastic-style vows but dedicated themselves to waging holy war against pagans and heretics. In practice, these orders were self-enriching companies of professional fighters, who built up territorial domains along the Baltic coast by conquest. In campaigns between 1242 and 1245, Russian coalitions fought off invaders on the western front, but they could not sustain war on two fronts. The experience made them submissive to the Mongols.

THE LIMITS OF CONQUEST: MAMLUK EGYPT AND MUSLIM INDIA

Mamluk Egypt

In the 1200s, Egypt was in chaos because of rebellions by pastoralists from the southern desert and revolt by the Mamluks, the slaves who formed the elite fighting force. It seems counterintuitive to arm slaves. But for most of the thirteenth century, the policy worked well for the heirs of Saladin who had ruled Egypt since 1192. The rulers handpicked their slave army. The slaves came overwhelmingly from Turkic peoples that Mongol rebels displaced or captured and sold. These slaves had nowhere else to go and no future except in the Egyptian sultan's service. They were acquired young. They trained in barracks, which became their substitutes for families and the source of their pride and strong sense of comradeship. They seemed, from the ruler's point of view, ideally reliable: a dependent class. Increasingly, however, the Mamluks came to know their own strength. In the 1250s, they rebelled. Their own later propaganda cites the sultan's failure to reward them fairly for their services in repelling a crusader attack on Egypt, and their outrage at the promotion of a black slave to one of the highest offices in the court. The Mamluks "threw themselves upon him like the onrush of an unleashed torrent." In 1254, the Mamluks replaced the last heir of Saladin with rulers from their own ranks.

The rebels, however, while contending with internal enemies, perceived the Mongols as a greater threat and turned to face them. In September 1260, they turned back the Mongol armies at one of the decisive battles of the world at Ain Jalut in Syria. It was the first serious reversal the Mongols had experienced since Genghis Khan united them. And it gave the Mamluk commander, Baybars (BEYE-bahrs), the chance to take over Egypt and Syria. He boasted that he could play polo in Cairo and Damascus within the space of a single week. The Mamluks mopped up the last small crusader states on the coast of Syria and Palestine between 1268 and 1291. In combination with the effects of the internal politics of the Mongol world, which inhibited armies from getting too far from the centers of power, the Mamluk victory kept the Mongols out of Africa.

Mamluk victory also marked a further stage in the Islamization of Africa. The Mamluks levied tribute on the Christian kingdoms of Nubia (see Chapter 9). Then, in the next century, they imposed Islam there. Cairo, as we shall see in the next chapter, became a normal stopping place on the pilgrimage route to Mecca for Muslim kings and dignitaries from West Africa. Islam percolated through the region of Lake Chad and into Hausaland in what is today Nigeria.

"It seems counterintuitive to arm slaves. But for most of the thirteenth century, the policy worked well for the heirs of Saladin who had ruled Egypt since 1192."

Muslim India: The Delhi Sultanate

After the disruptions caused by the violent Turkic migrations of the twelfth century, it took a long time for a state in the mold of Mahmud's (mah-MOOD) to reemerge in Ghazna (GAHZ-nah) (see Chapter 12). By the 1190s, however, a Muslim Turkic dynasty and people, the Ghurids

Chronology: Rise of the Mamluks	
1254	Mamluks depose sultan of Egypt
1260	Mamluk army victorious at the battle of Ain Jalut in Syria
1268–1291	Mamluks overthrow last of the crusader states

(see Map 13.4)

MAP 13.4

The Delhi Sultanate

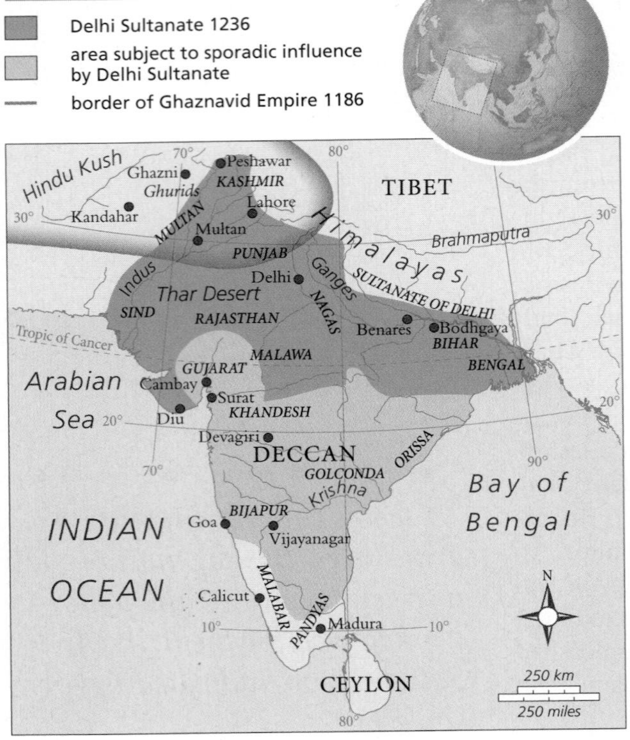

- Delhi Sultanate 1236
- area subject to sporadic influence by Delhi Sultanate
- border of Ghaznavid Empire 1186

(GOO-rids), had resumed the habit of raiding into Hindu India. As their victories accumulated, they began to levy fixed tribute in the Punjab and even established permanent garrisons in the Ganges valley. One of their most far-flung outposts—and therefore one of the strongest—was at the city of Delhi in northern India. The adventurer Iltutmish (eel-TOOT-mihsh) took command there in 1211. He was a former slave who had risen to general and received his freedom from his Ghurid masters. He avoided war with Hindus—which was, in essence, his job—in favor of building up his own resources. In 1216, exhibiting to his subordinates the letters that had granted him his freedom, he effectively declared himself independent. Over the next 12 years, he played the power game with skill, exploiting the rivalries of Muslim commanders to construct a state from the Indus River to the Bay of Bengal. Meanwhile, the effects of the Mongol conquests on Central Asia protected this new realm, which became known as the Sultanate of Delhi, against outside attack (see Map 13.4). The Mongols effectively eliminated any possible invader and drove many refugees to take service with Iltutmish. As one of the early chroniclers of the sultanate said, "Rulers and governors, . . . and many administrators and notables came to Iltutmish's court from fear of the slaughter and terror of the accursed Mongol, Genghis Khan."

There was no consistent form of administration. In most of the more remote territories, the Delhi sultan was an overlord, mediating between small, autonomous states, many of which Hindus ruled. Bengal was exceptional—a forest frontier, in which governors tried to promote Muslim settlement by making land grants to pioneering holy men and religious communities. But a core of lands was the sultan's personal property, exploited to benefit his treasury and run by administrators he appointed. Lands the sultan granted to warriors in exchange for military service ringed this core. For most of the rest of the century, the sultanate had a volatile history, punctuated by succession wars that were resolved at great oath-taking ceremonies, when the aristocracy of the realm—encompassing a great diversity of effectively freelance warriors and local rulers whom it was difficult or impossible for the sultan to dismiss—would make emotional but often short-lived declarations of loyalty.

Iltutmish's personal choice of successor set the tone on his deathbed in 1236. As an ex-slave, Iltutmish was no respecter of conventional ideas of hierarchy. Denouncing his sons for incompetence, he chose his daughter, Radiyya (rah-DEE-ah), as his successor. In the steppes, women often handled important jobs. In the Islamic world, a woman ruler was a form of impiety and a subversion of what was thought to be the natural order of the world. When, in 1250, a little before the Mamluks took over in Egypt, a woman had seized the throne there and applied to Baghdad for legitimation by the caliph, he is supposed to have replied that he could supply capable men, if no more existed in Egypt. Radiyya had to contend both with a brother who briefly ousted her—she had him put to death—and, what was harder, with male mistrust. Some of her coins emphasize claims to unique feminine virtues as "pillar of women." Others have modest inscriptions, in which all the glorious epithets are reserved for her father and the caliph in Baghdad. Her best strategy was to behave like a man. She dressed in male clothing, refused to cover her face, and, according to a slightly late source, "mounted horse like men, armed with bow and quiver." To conventional minds, these were provocations. She was ousted on grounds that—true or false—reflect male prejudices about female behavior. Accused of taking a black slave as a lover, she was deposed in 1240 in favor of a brother. Her real offense was self-assertion. Those modest coin inscriptions suggest that power brokers in the army and the court were willing to accept her, but only as a figurehead representative of her father, not as an active leader of men.

The sultanate had to cope not only with the turbulence of its own elite, but with its Hindu subjects and neighbors. Dominion by any state over the entire Indian subcontinent remained, at best, a dream. Frontier expansion was slow. Deforestation was an act of state, because, as a Muslim writer of the fourteenth century complained, "the infidels live in these forests, which for them are as good as city walls, and inside them they have their cattle and grain supplies of water collected from the rains, so that they cannot be overcome except by strong armies of men who go into these forests and cut down those reeds." In Bengal, the eastward shift of the Ganges River made Islamization easier. Charismatic **Sufis**, with tax-free grants of forest land for mosques and shrines, led the way.

For most of the thirteenth century, the Mongol menace overshadowed the sultanate. The internal politics of the dynasty of Genghis Khan caused dissensions and hesitancies that protected Delhi. Mongol dynastic disputes cut short periodic invasions. Moreover, a buffer state that dissident Mongols created in Delhi's western territories diminished the sultanate but also absorbed most of the khans' attacks. In the 1290s, however, the buffer collapsed. By what writers in Delhi considered a miracle, the subsequent Mongol attacks failed, faltered, or were driven off.

The Qutb Minar. The founder of the Ghurid dynasty began the Qutb Minar, near Delhi, as a monument to his own prowess in battle, toward the end of the twelfth century. Successors continued the project until, by the late fourteenth century, it was the tallest tower in India—much bigger than any minaret designed to hoist the call to prayer. The ridged form and decorative use of sandstone are typical of the stylistic traditions the Ghurids brought to India from Afghanistan.

EUROPE

With the scare the Mongol invasions caused and the loss of the last crusader states in Syria to the Mamluks, Latin Christendom looked vulnerable. Attempts were made to revitalize the crusading movement—especially by Louis IX, the king of France (r. 1226–1270) who became a model monarch for the Western world. But they all failed. A further reversal was the loss of Constantinople by its Latin rulers to a Byzantine revival. The Mongols destroyed or dominated most of the successor states that claimed Byzantium's legacy, but at the city of Nicaea in western Anatolia, rulers who continued to call themselves "Roman emperors" maintained the court rituals and art of Byzantine greatness. In 1261, they recaptured the old capital from the crusaders "after many failures," as the ruler at the time, Michael VIII, admitted, "because God wished us to know that the possession of the city was a grace dependent on his bounty."

Nevertheless, Latin Christendom grew on other fronts, extending the frontier deep into formerly pagan worlds along the Baltic in Livonia, Estonia, Prussia, and Finland. Between the 1220s and the 1260s, Christian kingdoms seized most of the Mediterranean seaboard of Spain and the Balearic Islands from the

MAP 13.5

Latin Christendom, 1200–1300

predominantly pagan lands

university/cathedral schools with date of foundation

important churches with stained glass

reconquest of Spain in thirteenth century

campaigns of Teutonic Knights and Sword Brothers

Maritime Trade Routes

Venetian

Genoese

Catalan

hands of Muslim rulers. Here the existing economy and population were not much disturbed. Conquests Castile and Portugal made over the same period in the Iberian southwest became a sort of Wild West of sparse settlements, tough frontiersmen, and vast cattle and sheep ranches. Meanwhile, traders of the western Mediterranean increased their commerce with northern Europe along the coasts the Spaniards conquered, through the Strait of Gibraltar (see Map 13.5). Toward the end of the century, as they became accustomed to Atlantic sailing conditions, some of them began to think of exploring the ocean for new routes and resources. In 1291, an expedition set off from the Italian city of Genoa to try to find "the regions of India by way of the ocean." The voyagers were never heard of again, but their voyage marked the beginning of a long, faltering effort by maritime communities of Western Europe to exploit the ocean at their feet.

The transforming influences, however, came from the east. The Mongol peace policing the routes that linked the extremities of Eurasia—ended Europe's relative isolation and stimulated trade and travel between Europe and China. The thirteenth century was the most intense period ever in trans-Eurasian communications, and European traditions were rechanneled as a result or, at least, guided more securely in directions they might have taken anyway. Paper, for instance, a Chinese invention that had already reached the West through Arab intermediaries, was a former luxury that came into general use in late-thirteenth-century Europe as a major contribution to what we would now call **information technology**, making written communication cheap, easy, and prolific. European maritime technology—a prerequisite of the prosperity borne by long-range trade and of the reach of most long-range imperialism—was especially primitive by non-European standards up to this time. The compass was first recorded in Europe in about 1190 in a text that explained the marvels of a pin well rubbed "with an ugly brown stone that draws iron to itself." As far as we know, the West had as yet no maritime charts. The earliest reference to such a device dates only from 1270. Gunpowder and the blast furnace were among the magical-seeming technologies that first reached Europe from China in the thirteenth and fourteenth centuries.

Meanwhile, with consequences for the future that can hardly be overestimated, Western science grew more **empirical**, more reliant on the reality of sense perceptions, more committed to the observation of nature. The renewal of this classical tradition in the West coincided with renewed contact with China, where empiricism had never been lost. At the University of Paris, which the Nestorian Rabban Bar Sauma so admired, scholars cultivated a genuinely scientific way of understanding the world. The end products were the marvelously comprehensive schemes of faith the encyclopedists of thirteenth-century Paris elaborated, especially in the work of the greatest intellect of the age, Thomas Aquinas (1225–1274), who arrayed in precise categories everything known by experience or report. In northwest Spain, an unknown, probably French artist of the thirteenth century depicted a similar vision of the whole cosmos in the stained glass windows of León Cathedral. The cosmos was measurable, portrayed between the dividers of Christ the geometer, like a ball of fluff trapped between tweezers (see page 434).

In the third quarter of the thirteenth century, Parisian teachers, of whom the most insistent was Siger of Brabant, pointed out that the doctrines of the church on the creation and the nature of the soul conflicted with classical philosophy and empirical evidence. "Every disputable question," they argued, "must be determined by rational arguments." Some thinkers took refuge in an evasive idea of "double truth," according to which things true in faith could be false in science and vice versa. The church condemned this doctrine in 1277 (along with a miscellany of magic and superstition).

Meanwhile, another professor in the thirteenth century at the University of Paris, Roger Bacon, stated that excessive deference to authority—including ancestral wisdom, custom, and consensus—was a cause of ignorance. He insisted that scientific observations could help to validate holy writ and that medical

Astrolabe. The Syrian instrument maker, al-Sarraj engraved his signature on this fine astrolabe in 1230–1231. The purpose of the astrolabe is to assist in astronomy—one of the many sciences in which the Islamic world excelled at the time. By suspending the instrument at eye level and swiveling a narrow central bar until it aligned with any observed star, the user could read the star's elevation above the horizon, as well as such additional information as the latitude, the date, and even the time of day from the engraved discs.
© National Maritime Museum Picture Library, London, England. Neg. #E5555–3

The measurable cosmos. This thirteenth-century illustrator of the creation of the world shows God as a well-equipped designer, measuring creation with an architect's or mathematician's dividers. The Earth is not the center of the cosmos, but a tiny blob in the corner, surrounded by chaos and dwarfed by God.

experiments could increase knowledge and save life. He also claimed—citing the lenses with which Archimedes reputedly set fire to a Roman fleet during the siege of the Greek city of Syracuse in Sicily in 212 B.C.E.—that science could cow and convert infidels. It was part of a modest scientific revolution in Western Christendom. The most relentless experimenter of the age was the German emperor and king of Sicily, Frederick II (r. 1212–1250). He was said to have had two men disemboweled to show the varying effects of sleep and exercise on the digestion, and to have brought up children in silence "in order to settle the question" of what language human beings "naturally" speak. "But he labored in vain, for all the children died."

Bacon was a Franciscan friar, a follower of Francis of Assisi (1181–1226), and his enthusiasm for science seems to have owed something to Francis's rehabilitation of nature: because the world made God manifest, it was worth observing. Francis was a witness and maker of the new European imagination. He was a rich man's son inspired by Jesus' advice to a rich youth ("Go, sell what thou hast and give to the poor. Then take up thy cross and follow me.") to seek a life of total dependence on God. In anyone less committed and charismatic, his behavior might have been considered insane or heretical. He launched his mission by stripping naked in the public square of his native city of Assisi in northern Italy, as a sign that he was throwing himself, unprotected, on God's mercy. He relied for sustenance on what people gave him. He attracted a following and modeled his followers' way of life on the way he thought Christ and the apostles lived, refusing to accept property, sharing everything the brethren received by way of alms.

The Franciscans became the spearhead of the church's mission to the poor and inspired other orders of friars—clergy who combined religious vows of poverty, chastity, and obedience with work in the world. In an age of urbanization, this was a particularly important mission, because friars could establish bonds of sympathy with the rootless masses who gathered in towns and faced the problem of adjusting to life away from the familiar companionship of rural parishes. Friars were also a valuable counterforce to heretics who denounced the church for worldliness. Friars, if they stayed true to their vocations, could match these enemies in holiness of life and in strict self-denial.

In his attitude toward nature, Francis was representative of his time and of the convergence of Western and Chinese attitudes to nature. In China, nature was the object of reverence and the subject of art. The same values now appeared in the West. Partly to rebut heretics repelled by the disorder of creation, Francis insisted on the goodness of God's creation, which was all "bright and beautiful." Even its conflicts and cruelties were there to elicit human love. He tried to enfold the whole of nature in love. He preached to ravens and called creatures, landscapes, sun, and moon his brothers and sisters, eventually welcoming "Sister Death." He communicated his sensibilities to his followers. As a result, Franciscans were prominent in scientific thinking in the West. Love of nature made them observe it more closely and keenly and scrutinize it for good uses.

Franciscans also became patrons of increasingly naturalistic art. The art they commissioned for their churches drew the onlooker into sacred spaces, as if in eye-

Francis of Assisi. Franciscan art patronage rewarded painters like Giotto, who were interested in creating vivid versions of sacred scenes in which the actors seemed real rather than abstract. Francis preached to the birds because humans failed to heed his message—but the image suggests, too, how the Franciscans promoted awareness of the natural world. Piety and science coincided in the observation of nature.

witness of the lives of Jesus and the saints. The devotion of the rosary, introduced early in the thirteenth century, encouraged the faithful to imagine sacred mysteries, while praying, with the vividness of scenes of everyday life, as if witnessed in person. Franciscan art stirred the emotions of the devout by unprecedented realism—looking at the world with eyes as unblinking as those of the new scientific thinkers. Considered from one point of view, the realism Western painting increasingly favored was a tribute to the enhanced prestige of the senses. To paint what one's eyes could see was to confer dignity on a subject not previously thought worthy of art. So art linked the science and piety of the age.

It is hard to resist the impression that the revolutionary experiences of the West at the time—the technical progress, the innovations in art, the readjustment of notions of reality through the eyes of a new kind of science—were owed in part to influences transmitted along the routes the Mongols maintained. None of this experimentation and imagination put Western science abreast of that of China, where observation and experiment had been continuous in scientific tradition since the first millennium B.C.E. (see Chapter 6). In two technologies, however—key technologies, as they later proved to be, for their influence on world history—Western Europe came to house the world's leading centers of development and production.

The first technology was glass making. In the thirteenth century, demand for fine glassware leaped in the West because of the growing taste for using church windows made of stained glass, penetrated by light, to illuminate sacred stories and to exhibit glowingly the wonders of creation as the windows at Chartres Cathedral did. Simultaneously, glassmakers adapted their skills to meet domestic demand for glass mirrors and optical lenses. These objects were not manufactured on a significant scale anywhere else in the world, though for centuries scholars writing in Arabic had known how to make them and use them as aids to scientific observation. Now Western savants could make the same experiments themselves and even improve on them. In the thirteenth century, Robert Grosseteste, the first chancellor of the University of Oxford in England, explained the geometry of the way lenses operate. "It is obvious," he concluded, "that they can make very large objects appear very small, and contrariwise very small and remote objects as if they were large and easily discernible by sight."

Second, the West drew ahead in the technology of clockwork. Mechanical clocks had a long history in China and the Islamic world. But clockwork never caught on except in Europe. This is a hard fact to explain. Clockwork is too regular to match the movements of the heavens. It divides the day into arbitrary hours of equal length that do not match those of the sun. But this way of organizing life suited Western monasteries, where, apart from the prayers prescribed for the dawn and nightfall, the services of prayer were best arranged at regular intervals, independently of the sun. For city churches in an age of urban growth, regular

Making Connections | EUROPEAN TRANSFORMATIONS AND INNOVATIONS, THIRTEENTH AND EARLY FOURTEENTH CENTURIES

TRADE AND TRANSPORTATION	TECHNOLOGY AND SCIENCE	POLITICS	RELIGION
Increased communication across Eurasia leads to introduction of Chinese and Arabic technology, medicine, and inventions	Imported inventions such as paper, magnetic compasses, gunpowder, and blast furnace combine with focus on empiricism	Christian kingdoms seize Muslim lands in Spain, Mediterranean islands; revival of Crusades, extension of frontier north to the Baltics, Finland, and Scandinavia	Francis and his religious order place new emphasis on observing nature, serving the poor, and renouncing wealth; increased emphasis on sacred mysteries
Increased transportation and trade links within Europe aided by new infrastructure (roads, canals); growth of towns; economic and political stability leads to larger towns and cities; more productive industry	Better maritime technology expands range of sea voyages; demand for elaborate church windows spurs glassmaking and innovation in glass lenses; clocks provide regularized timekeeping for monasteries and cities; availability of paper multiplies books and empowers states with a medium for their messages	Bigger, richer states with more scope to communicate and enforce commands; more church-state competition and conflict	Mendicants prominent in scientific thinking in West; spearhead Church's mission to poor in growing towns

timekeeping was also convenient. Clockwork suited the rhythms of urban life. Civic authorities began to invest heavily in town clocks in the thirteenth and fourteenth centuries. This was the beginning of the still-familiar Western convention of an urban skyline dominated by the town hall clock tower.

The combination of lenses and clockwork mattered in the long run because eventually—not until the seventeenth century, when telescopes were combined with accurate chronometry—they gave Western astronomers an advantage over Muslim and Chinese competitors. This in turn gave Western scientists the respect of their counterparts and secured the patronage of rulers all over the world in societies interested in astronomy either for its own sake or—more often—because of astrology—the belief that events on Earth reflected the movements of the heavenly spheres.

"The importance of the Mongols' passage through world history does not stop at the frontiers of their empire. It resonated across Eurasia."

In Perspective
The Uniqueness of
the Mongols

In the thirteenth century, a state arose that embraced the whole of the steppe. Like many great revolutions, the episode started bloodily and became constructive. When the Mongol alliance first challenged its neighbors, it seemed to threaten civilization with destruction—slaughtering settled peoples, razing cities, despising art and learning. Yet the Mongols came to play a unique and constructive role in the history of Eurasia. First, fear of the most devastating conquerors the interior had yet bred linked the peoples beyond the steppe, from Christendom to Japan. Then a peace that those same conquerors imposed connected them. For 100 years after the initial horror of the Mongol conquests, the steppe became a highway of fast communication, linking the extremities of the landmass and helping transfer culture across two continents. Without the Mongol peace, it is hard to imagine any of the rest of world history working out as it did, for these were the roads that carried Chinese ideas and technology westward and opened up European minds to the vastness of the world. The importance of the Mongols' passage through world history does not stop at the frontiers of their empire. It resonated across Eurasia.

The Eurasian experience was unique. Why did nothing like it happen in Africa or the Americas? Cultural exchanges across the grasslands of prairie, pampa, and Sahel never spread far until the nineteenth century. None of those regions saw conquerors like the Mongols, able to unify the entire region and turn it into a causeway of civilizations, shuttling ideas and techniques across a continent.

In the Americas, geography was an inhibiting influence. The North American prairie is aligned on a north–south axis, across climatic zones, whereas the

Chronology

1181–1226	Life of Francis of Assisi
1190	First European recorded reference to a compass
1206	Temujin proclaims himself khan
1211–1236	Reign of Iltutmish, sultan of Delhi
1225–1274	Life of Thomas Aquinas
1234	Mongols conquer Georgia
1241–1242	Mongol armies reach Elbe River, Germany
1253–1254	Mission of William of Rubruck to Mongolian court
1258	Mongols capture Baghdad, last caliph put to death
1260	Mamluks defeat Mongols at battle of Ain Jalut
1261	Byzantine Empire regains Constantinople
1268–1291	Mamluks overthrow last crusader states on coast of Palestine
1270	Earliest European reference to maritime charts
1271–1275	Marco Polo's first journey to China
1274, 1281	Failed Mongol attempts to invade Japan
1279	Mongol conquest of China completed
1286	Rabban Bar Sauma appointed Mongol ambassador to Christian West

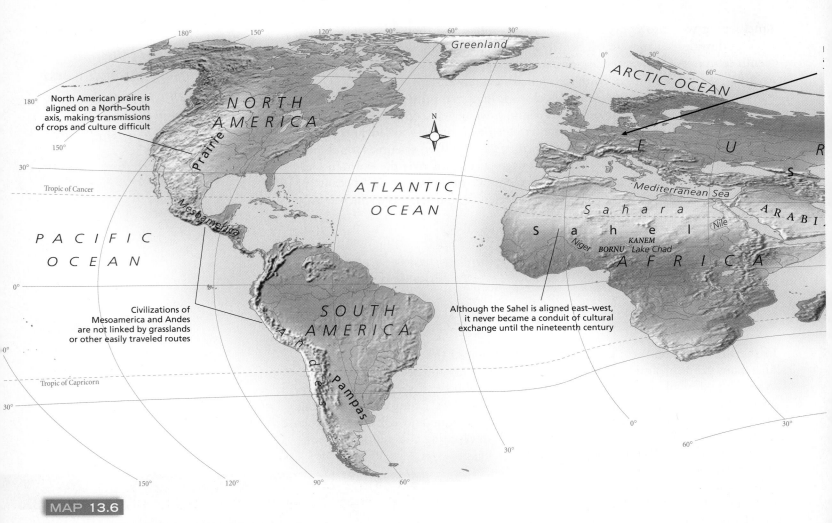

North American praire is aligned on a North–South axis, making transmissions of crops and culture difficult

Civilizations of Mesoamerica and Andes are not linked by grasslands or other easily traveled routes

Although the Sahel is aligned east–west, it never became a conduit of cultural exchange until the nineteenth century

MAP 13.6

Grassland Environments Compared

steppe stretches from east to west. Plants and animals can cross the steppe without encountering impenetrable environments. Seeds can survive the journey without perishing and without finding, at the end of the road, an environment too sunless or cold to thrive in. In North America, it took centuries longer to achieve comparable exchanges. As we have seen repeatedly—almost whenever the Americas have entered our story—transmissions of culture across latitudes are much harder to effect than those that occur within latitudes, which have relatively narrow boundaries, where climate and conditions are familiar.

Moreover, to function, an avenue of communications needs people at either end of it who want to be in touch. The Eurasian steppe was like a dumbbell, with densely populated zones and productive economies at either end of it (see Map 13.6). For people in Europe, Southwest Asia, and North Africa, access to the products of South, Southeast, and East Asia was highly desirable. For the suppliers of spices, drugs, fine textiles, and luxury products in the east, it was good to have customers who paid in silver. In the Americas, there was no chance to reproduce such relationships. The concentrations of wealth and population were in two regions—Mesoamerica and the Andes—that neither grasslands nor any other easily traveled routes linked. Though societies in other parts of the hemisphere drew lessons, models of life, technologies, and types of food from those areas, the results,

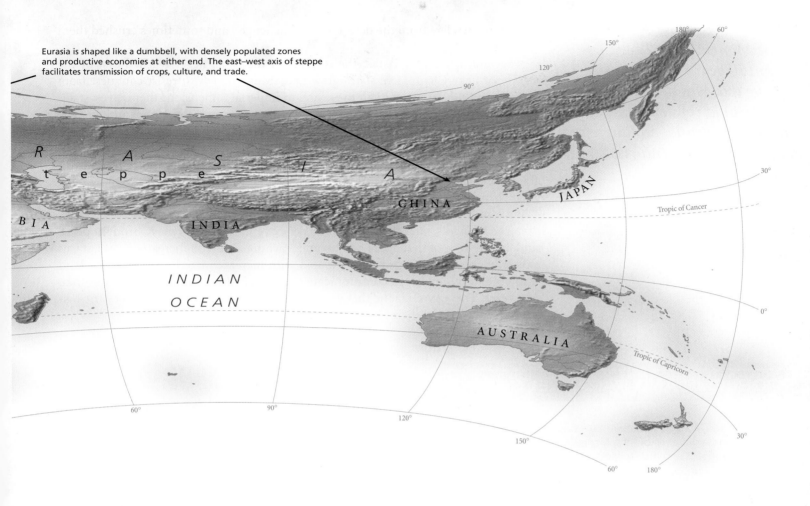

Eurasia is shaped like a dumbbell, with densely populated zones and productive economies at either end. The east–west axis of steppe facilitates transmission of crops, culture, and trade.

as we have seen (see Chapter 11) were hard to sustain because communications between these areas and outlying regions were difficult to keep up. Without the horse—extinct in the Americas for 10,000 years—the chances of an imperial people arising in the prairie or the pampa to do the sort of job the Mongols did in Europe were virtually zero. (Much later, as we shall see in Chapter 21, when European invaders reintroduced the horse in the Americas in the 1500s, experiments in grassland imperialism by peoples such as the Sioux followed.)

In Africa, the constraints were different. The **Sahel** might have played a role similar to that of the steppes in Eurasian history. There was a viable corridor of communication between the Nile and Niger valleys. In theory, an imperial people might have been able to open communications across the continent between the civilizations of East Africa, which were in touch with the world of the Indian Ocean, and those of West Africa, which the trade routes of the Sahara linked to the Mediterranean. But it never happened. For long-range empire building, the Sahel was, paradoxically, too rich compared with the Eurasian steppe. The environment of the Sahel was more diverse. Agrarian or partly agrarian states had more opportunity to develop, obstructing the formation of a Sahel-wide empire. Although pastoral peoples of the western Sahel often built up powerful empires, they always tended to run into either or both of two problems. First, as we have seen, and shall

> *"The Mongol peace lasted less than 150 years. The age of plague that was now about to begin would influence the history of Eurasia, and therefore of the world, for centuries."*

see again, invaders from the desert always challenged and sometimes crushed them (see Chapter 12).

Second, while they lasted, the empires of the Sahel never reached east of the region of Lake Chad. Here states grew up, strong enough to resist conquest from outside, but not strong enough to expand to imperial dimensions themselves: states like Kanem and Bornu—which were sometimes separate, sometimes united. The accounts of early Muslim visitors reviled the region for its "reed huts . . . not towns" and people clad only in loin cloths. But by the twelfth and thirteenth centuries, Kanem and Bornu commanded respect in Arab geography. Lakeshore floodplains for agriculture enriched them, together with the gold they obtained from selling their surplus millet. Around 1300, according to Arab sources, the region enclosed 12 "kingdoms."

The Mongols, after their initial bout of extreme destructiveness, brought peace and, in the wake of that peace, wealth and learning. But with increased travel, it was not only goods and ideas that circulated with increased freedom. The steppeland also became a highway to communicate disease. The Mongol peace lasted less than 150 years. The age of plague that was now about to begin would influence the history of Eurasia, and therefore of the world, for centuries.

PROBLEMS AND PARALLELS

1. How did the Mongols transform Eurasia in the thirteenth century? What techniques did the Mongols use to rule neighboring civilizations, and how successful were they?

2. How did the steppelanders' spiritual and religious life differ from that of their settled neighbors? Why did Genghis Khan believe that his empire should encompass the entire world?

3. How did the Mongol peace enable traders and travelers like Marco Polo and Rabban Bar Sauma to journey along the Silk Roads? How did Europe benefit from Chinese inventions in technology during the thirteenth century?

4. How did the civilizations of China and Persia affect the Mongols? How did Kubilai Khan combine Mongol and Chinese traditions of rulership? Why was the conversion of the Il-khans in Persia to Shiite Islam so important?

5. What were the consequences of the Mamluk victory over the Mongols at Ain Jalut? Why was the Delhi Sultanate able to survive in north India for so long?

6. How did Francis of Assisi and the Franciscan order remedy some of the social problems that medieval Europe faced? How did the Franciscans' interest in nature influence European culture?

7. What was the impact of empirical-based learning on European thinking at this time? Why were European advances in glassmaking and clockmaking so important?

8. How did geography hinder the development of continent-wide empires in Africa and the Americas? Why was it easier for ideas and trade to cross Eurasia than to cross the Americas or Africa?

READ ON ▶ ▶ ▶

D. Morgan, *The Mongols* (1986) is the best history of the Mongols: concise, readable, reliable. R. Grousset, *The Empire of the Steppes* (1970) is a translation of the unsurpassed classic history of steppeland peoples in antiquity and the Middle Ages. Samuel Adshead, *Central Asia in World History* (1993) is also helpful on this period.

P. Jackson, ed., *The Travels of Friar William of Rubruck* (1990) is an outstanding and informative edition of the most vivid of sources. Extracts from sources of the same kind are in I. de Rachewiltz, ed., *Papal Envoys to the Great Khan* (1971) and C. Dawson, ed., *Mission to Asia* (1980). A. Waley, ed., *The Secret History of the Mongols* (2002) collects some Mongol sources in lively translation. There is a scholarly edition by U. Onon (2001).

M. Rossabi, *Voyager from Xanadu: Rabban Sauma and the First Journey from China to the West* (1992), and *Kubilai Khan* (1989) are the best books on their respective subjects. On the voyage of Chang Chun, J. Mirsky, *Chinese Travellers in the Middle Ages* (2000) translates the main texts.

On the Silk Roads, the exhibition catalog edited by S. Whitfield, *The Silk Roads* (2004) is the best work. R. Latham, ed., *The Travels of Marco Polo* (1958) is a convenient and accessible abridgment in translation.

On China, R. Davis, *Wind against the Mountain: The Crisis of Politics and Culture in Thirteenth-century China* (1996) is an outstanding account written with close reference to the sources. The exhibition catalog edited by M. Rossabi, *The Legacy of Genghis Khan* (1996) is the best guide to the art of the Ilkhanate and other Mongol successor-states. M. Ipsiroglu, *Painting and Culture of the Mongols* (1966) is indispensable.

J.A. Boyle, ed., *The History of the World Conqueror* (1997) and *The Successors of Genghis Khan* (1971) translates some of the most important sources on the Ilkhanate.

On the Mamluks, R.Irwin, *The Middle East in the Middle Ages: The Early Mamluk Sultanate* (1986) is the best account of the their rise, and R. Amitai-Preiss, *Mongols and Mamluks* (2005) is a superb study of the wars against the Mongols, S.A. El-Banasi, ed., *Mamluk Art* (2001) covers a wide range of revealing objects.

P. Jackson, *The Delhi Sultanate* (2003) is a splendid introduction to the subject. The best edition of Ibn Battuta is by H.W. Gibb and C.F. Beckingham for the Hakluyt Society, *The Travels of Ibn Battuta* (1956).

On the transmission of Chinese technology westward, J. Needham, *Science and Civilisation in China* (1956) is fundamental–but it is a vast work still in progress. An abridged version in two volumes–*The Shorter Science and Civilisation in China* (1980)–is available. For Western science in the period, A. Crombie, *Robert Grosseteste and the Origins of Experimental Science* (1971) is controversial and stimulating. D.C. Lindberg, *The Beginnings of Western Science* (1992) gives an efficient and comprehensive account.

Of many studies of St Francis none is entirely satisfactory, but J.H.R. Moorman, *St Francis of Assisi* (1976) and A Mockler, *Francis of Assisi* (1976) can be recommended, the first for its scholarship and brevity, the second for its vivacity. K.B.Wolf, *The Poverty of Riches* (2003) is good on St Francis's theology.

On glassmaking see G. Martin and A. MacFarlane, *The Glass Bathyscape* (2003) and, on clockwork, D. Landes, *Revolution in Time: Clocks and the Making of the Modern World* (1983). On the general background of the thirteenth-century West, D. Abulafia, ed., *The New Cambridge Medieval History*, vol. 5, (1999) is as close as one can get to a comprehensive guide.

The Revenge of Nature: Plague, Cold, and the Limits of Disaster in the Fourteenth Century

▲ **City of the dead.** The fourteenth-century Arab traveler Ibn Battuta described Cairo's Southern Cemetery as "a place of peculiar sanctity" that "contains the graves of innumerable scholars and pious believers." The Mamluk domes and minarets visible here form part of the Sultaniyyah tomb complex that was built around 1360, a little over 10 years after the plague known as the Black Death had struck the city.

CAIRO

"The people of Cairo are fond of pleasure and amusement," wrote Ibn Battuta, when he first visited the Egyptian city in 1325. Wanderlust had made this Muslim pilgrim the world's most traveled man. Yet he had never seen, and would never see again, a city so big. Cairo had—so Ibn Battuta was told—12,000 water carriers, 30,000 donkey-rental businesses, and 36,000 river craft transporting food and goods. Among sources of pleasure he noted were "boys and maids with lustrous eyes" and the park and promenade along the Nile River, "containing many beautiful gardens." "Mother of cities, . . . mistress of broad provinces and fruitful lands, boundless in multitude of buildings, peerless in splendor. . . ." There seemed no end to Ibn Battuta's praise. The next time he visited Cairo, 23 years later in 1348, plague raged in the city, and corpses were piled in its streets. "I was told that during the plague the number of deaths there had risen to twenty-one thousand a day. I found that all the sheikhs I had known were dead. May God Most High have mercy upon them!"

Ibn Battuta was witnessing the most devastating natural catastrophe ever to have hit Eurasia: the so-called **Black Death.** This visitation of disease was not an isolated episode, but part of an enormous change, the consequences of which overtook the world. In the fourteenth century, Eurasia entered an age of plague (which would later spread worldwide), while the world entered an age of cold, as the climate got cooler. This combination of environmental disasters killed millions of people, disrupted states, and checked expansion. Themes of the story of global history, familiar from the last few chapters of this book, halted or were reversed as Eurasia's densely populated zone contracted. The growth of populations, trades, and states in Eurasia slowed or stopped. Cultural transmissions across the landmass diminished. Isolation from the main routes of trade and travel suddenly became, in some respects, an advantage.

Among the hardest-hit societies were the most ambitious—those with the longest and most active records in challenging their environments to suit themselves. Peoples that suffered most included those who had succeeded best in exploiting nature by turning land and energy sources to their own uses: those at and around the edges of Eurasia—in east, southwest, and south Asia; in Europe; and North Africa. Their contacts with each other, which had formerly enriched them with the benefits of cultural exchange, now communicated unprecedented deadly disease.

It was as if nature had struck back. Indeed, that was, more or less, how many Europeans and Muslims saw it. The weather, they thought, was a whiplash and the plague a scourge that God wielded to humble human arrogance and remind people of the unshakable power of death. One school of Muslim theologians accepted plague as God's punishment for sins, while others argued that plague, when Muslims suffered it, was "a martyrdom and a mercy from God," but "a punishment for an infidel." In China, too, conventional wisdom understood natural disasters as examples of what historian Mark Elvin calls "moral meteorology"—the corrections of heaven, unleashed to restore the balance of nature disturbed by human wickedness.

In history books, human agency tends to crowd out the rest of nature. Nonhuman life gets into the picture only as a source of analogies for human behavior, or as the means of human strategies—part of an Eden or an enemy to be used or abused. It is easy to forget that humans inhabit only a fraction of the biosphere, most of which is still outside our dominion. Currents in the ocean and the atmosphere change climate and shape our world despite us. Nor do we even control the whole of the ecosystem of which we form part. Our own bodies host microorganisms that feed on us whether we like it or not, sometimes benefiting us, sometimes doing us harm. Disease bearers can change their habits and patterns of attack with bewildering speed, leaving us unsure how to respond. Viruses, for example, are a part of the ecosystem that is largely beyond our control.

Climate and microbes belong to two rebellious realms of nature that resist human power. What happens when they combine—when sudden, unpredictable changes in both realms threaten humans simultaneously? To find out, we need only look back 700 years.

The fourteenth century was exceptional in human history because, in parts of the world, climate change and disease coincided to menace or undermine human activities. Procreation could make up the loss of life—eventually. The empires we shall see shaken and the states overthrown in this chapter and the next were restored or replaced. The regions and classes that profited from disaster—for there were some, as there are in every disaster—did not always retain their advantage for long. But the social shake-up that accompanied the changes had, for some of the people affected, irreversible effects. And it was impossible to undo the jarring psychological impact on societies that had accumulated self-confidence over a long period of expansion.

The best—or even, because of the evidence available, the only—way to approach the changes of the fourteenth century is to start in those parts of the northern hemisphere, especially in Eurasia and North Africa, where the effects of cold and plague combined. We can then turn to areas that escaped plagues, or escaped their worst consequences, in India, sub-Saharan Africa, Japan, and southeast Asia. Finally, we shall turn to far-away and out-of-touch societies in and around the Pacific to appreciate how isolation—which usually retards change—acted as a form of quarantine against disease. This should help us see some of the difference plagues made. As plagues affected some of the planet's previously most dynamic regions, other parts of the world leaped into the sight lines of global history, drawing our attention.

Readers should be aware that the distribution of material in the pages that follow reflects the distribution of sources and of scholarship. Most of what we know about the ecological disasters of the era comes from Eurasia, and, within that area, most relates to Europe. For some other areas, only scattered archaeological studies help us trace the course and character of the diseases of the time. Legal records of the kinds that help us establish the social consequences of ecological change in Europe are, at present, unavailable for most other places.

CLIMATE CHANGE

In the fourteenth century, temperatures fell. Broadly speaking, over the preceding four centuries or so, global temperatures had been relatively warm. The warm spell had been a period of expansion for most societies, with much erosion of natural environments as people converted previously underexploited land for farming or grazing (see Chapter 10). Peoples overcome by ecological disasters in the past had been victims of droughts or of their own over-exploitation of the land. Now a cool period—of fluctuating but relatively low temperatures—would last for about 500 years more. During the intense phases of the cool period, a fall in average temperatures of two or three degrees could reverse expansion, forcing people to abandon high ground, remote settlements, and northerly latitudes (such as, in the fourteenth century, parts of Greenland and of what are now Norway and Finland).

Though meteorologists scour tree rings and glaciers for evidence of weather cycles, hot and cold spells seem to alternate unpredictably. If a common cause—some cosmic rhythm—underlies all of them, we do not know what it is. Short-term fluctuations are sometimes traceable to particular causes. The middle of the second decade of the fourteenth century, for instance, was a cold period all over the Northern Hemisphere, probably because of a sudden, localized occurrence: the explosion of Indonesian volcanoes, pumping ash into the atmosphere and clouding the sun. But the fall in temperatures was not confined to a few exceptional years. It was part of a general, long-term trend.

The trend began in the Arctic in the thirteenth century. The ice cap crept southward. Glaciers disrupted shipping. From the fourteenth century, indicators of falling temperatures in the North Atlantic and parts of Eurasia are abundant, and it is fair to suppose that the Northern Hemisphere generally was registering the effects. Mean annual temperatures in China, which had stayed above 32 degrees Fahrenheit from the seventh century to the eleventh, remained below freezing from the thirteenth century—a period of abrupt fluctuations—until late in the eighteenth. Evidence of marginal glacier growth suggests that North America, too, felt the cold in the fourteenth century. Other indicators for the same century include the persistence of pack ice in summer in the seas around Greenland and the disappearance of water-demanding plants from the hinterland of Lake Chad in Central Africa from about 1300 onward. This is important, because glacier growth affects precipitation. When water ices over, less of it evaporates, and less therefore falls as rain. Weakening winds may also have contributed to changes in rainfall patterns and to the lack of moisture in deep interior regions with continental climates.

Worldwide effects—it is worth adding—of the continuing trend are detectable in glacier levels from the sixteenth century onward. A particularly marked period of glacier growth, even in low latitudes and in the Southern Hemisphere, occurred in

"The fourteenth century was exceptional in human history because, in parts of the world, climate change and disease coincided to menace or undermine human activities."

FIGURE 14.1 GLOBAL TEMPERATURE CHANGE, 1000–1900

Source: Hidore, John E. Global Environment Change: Its Nature and Impact, © 1996. Electronically reproduced by permission of Pearson Education, Inc., Upper Saddle River, New Jersey.

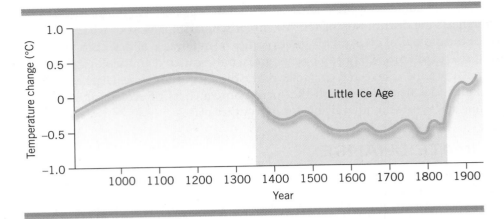

the seventeenth century. The cold therefore remained dominant, with some fluctuations, and intensified in the seventeenth century. Warming resumed gradually in the eighteenth and early nineteenth centuries, and, after a mid–nineteenth-century cold spell, has now been a constant and consistent feature of global climate probably for about the past 150 years (see Figure 14.1).

It is important to stress that the rhythms of climate change are full of fluctuating and conflicting shifts and contrasts of pace. Three levels are detectable. At one level, there is a long-term alternation between ice ages, which periodically smother great parts of the globe, and global warming, when some glacier-covered areas reemerge. We are between ice ages now. Historians, perhaps rather overdramatically, have adopted the **Little Ice Age** as a name for the protracted period of relative cold that began in the fourteenth century, but this term is misleading if it encourages readers to think of huge ice sheets spreading over the globe. All the fluctuations of the period this book covers have happened in a relatively warm era of the history of the planet.

Meanwhile, at another level, periods of a few hundred years of relative cold and warmth alternate within eras of global warming. But even within these periods, sudden changes in the winds and ocean currents can reverse the overall trend, producing spells, lasting from 10 to 50 years or so, of warmer or cooler temperatures.

Finally, there are sudden interruptions of normal conditions—occurring irregularly and, in the present state of our knowledge, unpredictably—when the normal distribution of atmospheric pressure is disturbed for unknown reasons. This produces the notorious **El Niño** effect in the tropics and the Southern Hemisphere (see Chapter 4). In Europe, reversals of normal patterns of atmospheric pressure in the North Atlantic produce longer spells, often of a decade or so, of extremely cold weather. And of course, above the deep and various rhythms of climate, the irregular lurches of the weather continue all the time.

Climate change is usually slow but can become perceptible suddenly. Contemporary descriptions show that people in Europe began to feel the cold, along with other unaccustomed weather, in the early fourteenth century. Of course, people felt the cold, and it affected their lives, because temperatures were lower than previously, not because it was cold in any absolute sense. Even after the intense global warming we have experienced recently, global temperatures have probably only recently returned to where they were when the Little Ice Age began. And European summers were probably, on average, hotter in the fourteenth century than in the twentieth.

The weather of the early fourteenth century, however, seemed hostile to people who had to endure it (see Map 14.1). In 1309–1310, the Thames River, which flows through London, froze and, wrote a chronicler, "bread wrapped in straw or other covering froze and could not be eaten unless it was warmed." Colder weather forced farmers to abandon formerly productive land above 1,300 feet in the southwest of England and 1,000 feet in the north. The cold was, an English poet wrote, "a new kind of affliction, . . . not known for a thousand years . . . . No horror left us e'er so like a ghost." Encroaching glaciers forced farmers into retreat in Norway.

During the prolonged cold of 1315–1316, before the icebergs grew sufficiently to disrupt rainfall, heavy rains were reported all over northern Europe, wrecking the crops, inflicting famine. Grain "could not ripen, nor had bread such power or essential virtue as it usually has," complained an English chronicler. A chronicler in Austria likened the rains to Noah's flood in the Bible. Fifteen or 16 people usually died each month in Bruges and Ypres in what is today Belgium. During 1316, the figure rose to 150 each month in Ypres and 190 in Bruges. From May to October, while these cities ran out of food, they lost over 5 percent and 10 percent of their population respectively. Calamitous flooding and coastal erosion became common around the North Sea, culminating in the "Great Drowning" of 1362, when the sea swallowed vast areas of Holland and 60 parishes in Denmark. On the North Sea coast of England, divers can still visit drowned villages, victims of the rips the floods of the era tore in the coastline.

Far from the sea, cooling in the Northern Hemisphere brought droughts and famines. In Central Asia, the accumulated abundance that fueled Mongol conquests in the previous century seems to have run out. The Mongol world began to contract. According to official chronicles, China experienced exceptionally severe winters for 36 of the fourteenth century's 100 years. In partial consequence, famines struck some part of China in every year of the reign of the Shun Ti emperor (r. 1333–1368).

Though the evidence is too slight for certainty, climate change at about the same time seems to have helped to destroy an impressive regional system of agriculture and urban life deep in the North American interior, between the Gila and San Juan Rivers and in the neighborhood of present-day Phoenix, Arizona. First the Hohokam (hoh–HOH–kahm) people—as archaeologists called them—re-located, from their scattered villages and small dwellings and sought for closer collaboration in relatively few, dense settlements with huge multistorey adobe houses. At Paquimé they huddled in a city with all the traditional amenities of earlier indigenous civilizations (see Chapter 11): ball courts, carved facades for temples and palaces, wells and irrigation works, workshops for copper workers and jewelsmiths. There was even a macaw hatchery to produce the ornamental feathers the elite coveted. It was a splendid effort, but it was clearly a response to stress. Every indicator shows severe population loss throughout the Southwest in the thirteenth and

"The Frozen Thames," 1677. The Thames River with old London Bridge in the middle distance and Southwark Cathedral on the right. People amuse themselves on the ice. Some shoot, and others skate. The river froze solid ten times in the seventeenth century.

Casa Grande. In the fourteenth century, Casa Grande—as this adobe structure is now called—stood five stories high. Massive outer walls and clusters of small dwellings surrounded it. It was part of the last phase of a long effort to raise monumental architecture and concentrate dense populations in what is now desert in Arizona, Colorado, and New Mexico.

Lack of rainfall
leads to population
loss throughout the
American Southwest

North American
glaciers increase

Polar ice cap begins
to creep southward in
the thirteenth century

PACIFIC
OCEAN

Phoenix *ARIZONA*
Casa Grande ● ● Paquimé

R o c k y   M o u n t a i n s

NORTH
AMERICA

M E X I C O

Mississippi

Hudson
Bay

Greenland

Falling temperatures
force abandonment of
settlements in northerly
latitudes and on high ground

Caribbean Sea

Iceland

Persistence of pack
ice in summer off
coast of Greenland

Thames River
freezes during
the winter of
1309–1310

North
Sea

NORWAY
SWEDEN
FINLAND

RUSSIA

DEN.
ENGLAND
London ● ● Bruges
Ypres

GERMANY
POLAND

S t e p p e

Cold, heavy rain and
flooding destroy crops
and erode coastlines
in northern Europe

Salzburg
● AUSTRIA

Danube

Black Sea

ATLANTIC
OCEAN

A n d e s

SOUTH
AMERICA

Amazon

A n d e s

FRANCE
ITALY

SPAIN

Mediterranean Sea

Anatolia

Euphra

M O R O C C O

North Africa

EGYPT

S a h a r a

Nile

1,000 km
1,000 miles
scale varies with perspective

Niger

Lake Chad

AFRICA

Water-demanding
plants disappear from
the Lake Chad region

N

30°
0°
120°
90°
60°

Tropic of Cancer
Equator

30°
150°
60°
180°

60°
30°
0°

PACIFIC OCEAN

JAPAN

KOREA

Yellow Sea

MONGOLIA

Yellow

CHINA

South China Sea

Mekong

SOUTHEAST ASIA

TIBET

Himalayas

Ganges

Bay of Bengal

Indus

INDIA

Caspian Sea

Steppes

PERSIA

Tigris

Euphrates

ARABIA

Arabian Sea

INDIAN OCEAN

Madagascar

AUSTRALIA

INDONESIA

Arctic Circle

Tropic of Cancer

Equator

Tropic of Capricorn

EURASIA

Severe winters and famines strike China throughout the fourteenth century

Cooling in Northern Hemisphere reduces food abundance, forcing Mongol world to contract

Between 1310 and 1315 Indonesian volcanoes pump ash into the atmosphere, clouding the sun.

MAP 14.1

Climate Change in the Fourteenth Century

⌂	ice pack
▢	polar ice pack
▲	major volcanic eruptions
➤	prevailing current, South Pacific (Humboldt Current)
➤	El Niño current
ARIZONA	modern state or country
●	city mentioned on pages 447–450

Making Connections | CLIMATE CHANGE IN EURASIA, AFRICA, AND THE AMERICAS

REGION/PERIOD	→	EVIDENCE AND ENVIRONMENTAL EFFECTS	→	EFFECTS ON HUMAN SOCIETY
Arctic / 1200s	→	Polar ice cap in Northern Hemisphere creeps southward	→	Glaciers disrupt shipping
North Atlantic, Arctic Ocean / 1300s	→	Falling temperatures, glaciation	→	Pack ice in summer around Greenland disrupts sea routes
Central Africa / 1300s	→	Disappearance of water-demanding plants near Lake Chad	→	Less rainfall reduces crop yields
Europe / 1300s	→	Thames River freezes; glaciers encroach in Norway; flooding and coastal erosion around North Sea	→	Formerly productive agricultural land abandoned in England; famine and mortality increase throughout northern Europe; flooding drowns many coastal villages in Holland, Denmark, England
Central Asia, China / 1300s	→	More severe winters	→	Abundance of food that fueled Mongol advances runs out; Mongol world contracts; famines strike China
American Southwest / 1300s	→	Less rainfall and water	→	Relocation of Hohokam villages in Arizona; severe population loss; major population centers abandoned

fourteenth centuries. By around 1400, even the new settlements were abandoned. Ruins remain. Casa Grande, in Pinal County, Arizona, leaves onlookers amazed at the ambition of the builders and clueless about what befell them. Some scholars have speculated that the conditions that crushed the Hohokam may also have driven migrants southward to colonize central Mexico and found the state that later became the kernel of the Aztec world (see Chapter 15). But the only evidence for this is in later, untrustworthy legends.

THE COMING OF THE AGE OF PLAGUE

In Eurasia the cold spell coincided with the beginning of an age of plague. Starting in the 1320s, unprecedented bouts of pestilence spread over much of Eurasia, culminating, in the late 1340s, in the disaster known to Europeans as the Black Death, which, in terms of the proportion of the population it wiped out, was probably the most lethal event ever experienced in human history up to that time. Recurrences—less widespread and less intense—of similar or identical diseases remained common and frequent in Eurasia until the eighteenth century. The age of plague was so unusual and significant that we want to know what the disease was, where it came from, what caused it, and how much damage it did. All these questions are hard to answer.

Most attempts to write the history of disease have foundered on a false assumption: that we can recognize past visitations of identifiable diseases, known to modern medical science, from symptoms historical sources describe. For two reasons, this is an unrealistic expectation.

First, people in the past looked at disease with perceptions different from ours. The symptoms they spotted would not necessarily be those an observer today would note, nor would they use the same sort of language we would to describe them. The signs we look for change as culture changes. From time to time, literary and scientific literature introduces new paradigms of disease and discards or displaces old ones.

Second, diseases themselves change. They change, perhaps, more than any other aspect of history because many of the microorganisms that cause disease are subject to rapid mutations. They evolve fast because they reproduce rapidly. They respond quickly to changing environments. The plagues of the age of plague need not all have been visitations of a single disease. They could have been "cocktails" of different diseases. They may have included some diseases that today's medical handbooks identify. But we must be open to the likelihood—it is stronger than a possibility—that some of the diseases that devastated Eurasia in the age of plague were peculiar to that period. They did not exist previously in the same forms and have ceased to exist since. New pathogens are deadly because they are unfamiliar. When they strike, no one has built up immunity to them.

So what can we say about the pathology of the Black Death? Of diseases now known to medical science, bubonic plague—not, perhaps, of the same variety we know today—most likely played a part in the age of plague. Bubonic plague is a rat-borne disease. Fleas that live on rats transmit it to humans. When they bite, fleas regurgitate the bacillus, ingested from rats' blood, into the bloodstream of human victims, or communicate infection by defecating into their bites. In cases of septicemic plague (a systemic, blood-poisoning disease), one of the first symptoms is generally death. Otherwise, swellings appear—small like Brazil nuts or big and ridged like grapefruit—over the neck and groin or behind the ears. Jitters, vomiting, dizziness, and pain might follow, often accompanied by an inability to tolerate light.

Fourteenth-century sources describe all these symptoms, together with sudden fainting, before victims, as one observer explained, "almost sleeping and with a great stench eased into death." The trouble is that during the first hundred years of the age of plague, of all the sources that describe the symptoms, fewer than one in six lists symptoms of this kind. Moreover, almost everyone at the time was convinced that plague spread by infection or contagion. Rats—the normal agent for the spread of bubonic plague—play no part in the accounts in the sources. The black rat, the culprit species in the transmission of bubonic plague, seems not to have existed at the time in plague-stricken Iceland, and was rare or absent in other afflicted places. Finally, it seems most unlikely that the frequent epidemics reported in China from the 1320s to the 1360s can have been of bubonic plague in the form now familiar to us, which, as we shall see, hit an unimmunized China in the late eighteenth century. The suddenness and virulence of the visitations that afflicted China suggest the arrival of a new and previously unexperienced pathogen. For the Chinese, with their long experience in farming and animal domestication, enjoyed highly developed natural immunities to the familiar diseases that breed in farming environments.

"The age of plague was so unusual and significant that we want to know what the disease was, where it came from, what caused it, and how much damage it did. All these questions are hard to answer."

Plague victims. The illustrator of an early fifteenth-century German chronicle imagined the plague of Egypt—sent by God, according to the Book of Exodus in the Bible, to make Pharaoh "let my people go"—with the same symptoms as the Black Death. In the background, Moses brings the plague down on Egypt by prayer. By implication, prayer and obedience to the will of God could also be remedies for plague.

Many accounts of the Black Death include a bewildering variety of symptoms that are not associated with bubonic plague: complications in the lungs, spitting blood, headaches, rapid breathing, discolored urine. The emphasis of some sources on lung disorders suggests a mixture of bubonic and pneumonic plague, which primarily attacks the lungs. To judge from other surviving descriptions, outbreaks of typhus, smallpox, various kinds of influenza, and hemorrhagic fevers coincided with some visitations of plague. In the Mediterranean, the plague usually struck in summer, while in northern Europe, autumn seems to have been the deadliest season. But, looked at as a whole, the plagues of the period had no seasonal pattern and no obvious connection with any particular weather systems or atmospheric conditions. This again points to the involvement of more than one pathogen.

Anthrax may have been a contributing factor. A form of anthrax certainly existed among cattle in Europe at the time. Whether or not anthrax was a factor, domestic animals were probably an essential part of the background—as carriers of disease, as a reservoir of infection, and even as sufferers. One of the curious features about the way some early plague victims described the disease is that they were sure that their domestic animals suffered from it, just as they did themselves. A chronicler in the city of Florence in Italy listed "dogs, cats, chickens, oxen, donkeys, and sheep" among the sufferers, with the same symptoms as human victims, including swellings in the groin and armpits. At the port of Salona on the Adriatic coast, the Black Death's first victims were "horses, oxen, sheep, and goats." The Egyptian chronicler, al-Maqrizi, who was among the most observant and thoughtful witnesses, believed that the disease started, like so many others, among animals before transferring to human hosts. It had spread from grazing flocks on the steppe in 1341, after which "the wind transmitted their stench around the world." Al-Maqrizi and other Muslim commentators thought wild animals caught it, too. If any of these sources are correct, the Black Death must have been—or included—a disease unknown today.

An unresolved question is, *How, if at all, were changes in climate and disease patterns linked?* The plague pathogens, as we have seen, were remarkably indifferent to weather, striking at different seasons and in climatically different regions of Eurasia, from the cold environment of Scandinavia and rain-drenched Western Europe to the hot, dry lands of the Middle East. The plagues were less penetrative, however, in hot, moist regions and do not seem to have gotten across the Sahara to tropical Africa, even though many potential disease carriers crossed that desert to trade. It is worth bearing in mind that the plague pathogens seem to have included new arrivals in the microbial world that remained active for as long as global cooling lasted.

The Course and Impact of Plague

The nature of the plague is hard to define, but the routes by which it traveled are easier to describe (see Map 14.2). The Italian chronicler Matteo Villani said the plague came "from China and upper India," by which he meant Central Asia, for which "India" at the time was a synonym, "then through their surrounding lands and then to coastal places across the ocean." Broadly speaking, Arabic sources specify the same, or a similar, path.

The age of plague indeed seems to have started in China. But that is not the same as saying that subsequent outbreaks elsewhere were the result of communication from China, or even that they were necessarily outbreaks of the same disease or diseases. Repeated occurrences—or, perhaps, a continuous visitation—of massively lethal maladies were recorded in southwest China, and over much of central China, north of the Yangtze River, in the early 1320s. In 1331, mortality rates in parts of northeast China that had endured five reported outbreaks of plague in the previous two decades reputedly reached 90 percent. Two years later, a plague claimed 400,000 lives in the Yangtze and Huai (hway) valleys. In 1353–1354, chroniclers reported that around two-thirds of the population perished from pestilence in eight distinct Chinese districts. Most of those areas experienced repeated bouts of disease of the same sort in the late 1350s or early 1360s.

Doubt persists, however, over whether the diseases rampant in China were the cause of—or even the same as—those found farther west. From the perspective of most commentators at the time in Europe and the Middle East, plague, like the Mongols, seemed to be an invader from the steppeland. Many observers at the time noted that the Mongols transmitted plague. A lawyer in northern Italy wrote one of the most detailed and doom-laden accounts of the arrival of plague in Europe. In 1346, by his account, "countless numbers of Tatars," as he called the Mongols, and Muslims "were struck down by a mysterious illness that brought sudden death." At the time, a Mongol army was laying siege to the Genoese trading colony of Kaffa on the nothern shore of Black Sea, where Italian merchants made contact with two great trade routes: those of the Silk Roads and the Volga valley. "But behold!" he continued, "the whole army was affected by a disease. . . which killed thousands every day. . . . But they ordered corpses to be placed in catapults and lobbed into the city in the hope that the intolerable stench would kill everyone inside."

The besiegers' stratagem worked. The disease proved highly contagious. "As it happened," the account went on, "among those who escaped from Kaffa by boat, there were a few sailors who had been infected with the poisonous disease. Some boats were bound for Genoa, others went to Venice and to other Christian areas. When the sailors reached these places and mixed with the people there, it was as if they had brought evil spirits with them."

Of course, there were multiple points of entry, as the same author acknowledged:

> Almost everyone who had been in the East, or in the regions to the south and north, fell victim to sudden death after contracting this pestilential disease. . . . The scale of the mortality and the form which it took persuaded those who lived, weeping and lamenting, . . . the Chinese, Indians, Medes, Kurds, Armenians, Cilicians, Georgians, Mesopotamians, Nubians, Ethiopians, Turks, Egyptians, Arabs, Saracens and Greeks (for almost all the East had been affected)—that the last judgement has come.

A pandemic on this scale was unprecedented. The pathogens responsible had found an eco-niche as wide as Eurasia.

Chroniclers' estimates of mortality are notoriously unreliable. Historians have been reluctant to believe claims that the plague wiped out half or more—sometimes much more—of the population where it struck, but verifiable evidence bears out some of the most shocking assessments of the damage. In Barcelona on the Mediterranean coast of Spain, 60 percent of jobs in the church fell vacant. Records of the archdiocese of York in northern England suggest the first visitation of the

"From the perspective of most commentators at the time in Europe and the Middle East, plague, like the Mongols, seemed to be an invader from the steppeland."

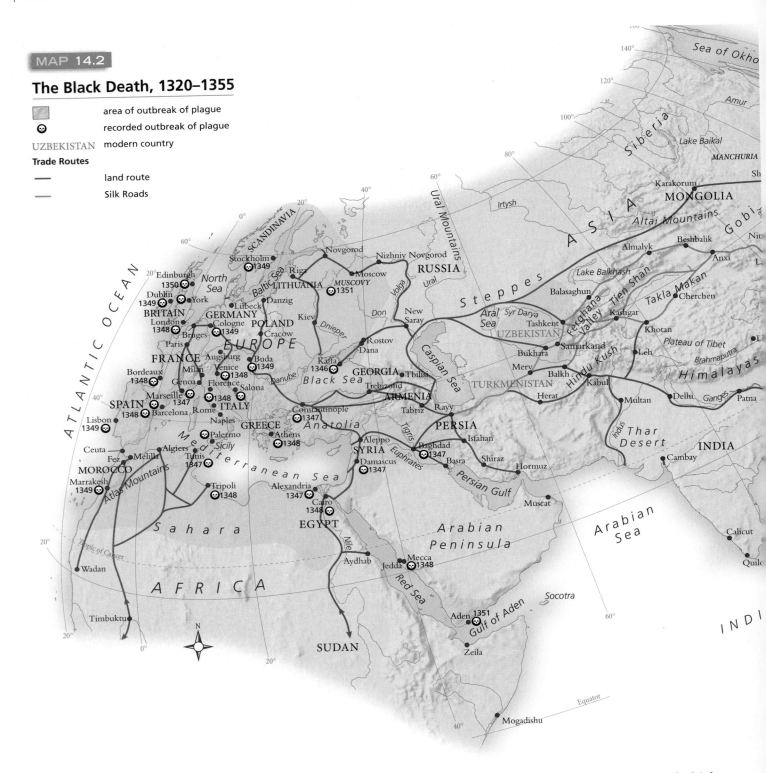

MAP 14.2

The Black Death, 1320–1355

▢ area of outbreak of plague

◉ recorded outbreak of plague

UZBEKISTAN modern country

Trade Routes

— land route

— Silk Roads

plague killed 40 percent of clergy there. Clergy were, perhaps, members of a high-risk profession, exceptionally exposed to infection by the need to minister to the sick. But the laity suffered just as much. In some manors in England, up to 70 percent of tenants died. Some villages in southern France lost 80 percent of their population. Towns ran out of cemetery space. The living had to pile the dead in pits with quicklime to speed decomposition and minimize rot. Half the villages of Sicily were abandoned, as were a third of those around Rome.

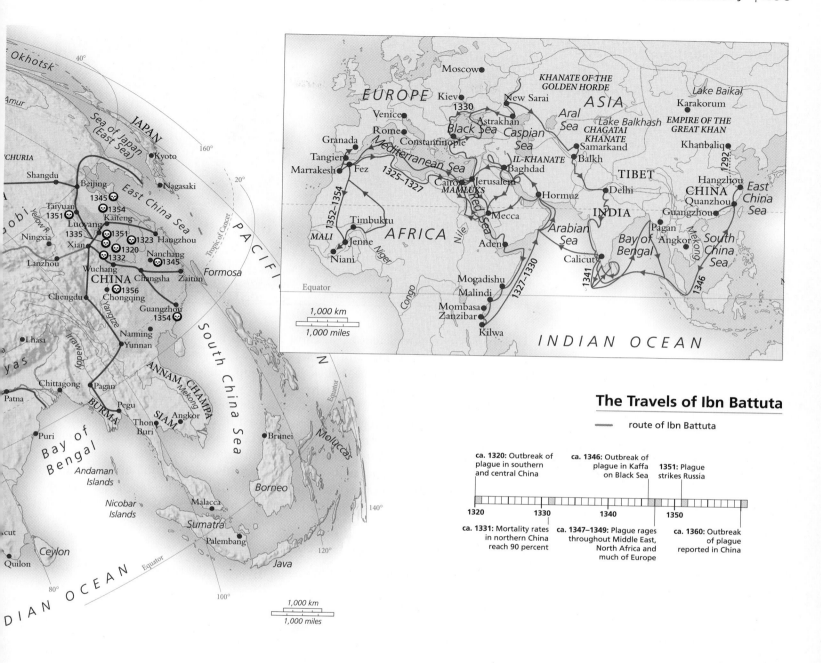

The Travels of Ibn Battuta

------- route of Ibn Battuta

ca. 1320: Outbreak of plague in southern and central China

ca. 1346: Outbreak of plague in Kaffa on Black Sea

1351: Plague strikes Russia

1320   1330   1340   1350

ca. 1331: Mortality rates in northern China reach 90 percent

ca. 1347–1349: Plague rages throughout Middle East, North Africa and much of Europe

ca. 1360: Outbreak of plague reported in China

When the plague reached the Middle East, the tireless traveler, Ibn Battuta, was there to observe it, on his way back to Cairo. Arriving in Syria in May 1348, he found that deaths in the city of Damascus reached 2,400 a day. In one town, three-quarters of the public officials had died. A sheikh delayed a banquet for Ibn Battuta until a day arrived when "I did not pray over a corpse." The plague spread along the coast of North Africa, causing—so people claimed—1,000 deaths a day at its height in Tunis, and reaching Morocco, where Ibn Battuta's own mother was among the victims.

In Central Asia, where plagues bred or where microorganisms traveled between the densely populated ends of Eurasia, we can also find indications of mortality. Arab sources reported that many steppeland dynasties and Mongol warriors succumbed to plague. Nestorian headstones at Chwolson in what is now

Flagellants. In 1349, the Black Death inspired thousands of penitents to organize processions and cults of self-flagellation across Europe in an attempt to deflect God's wrath. Like many others, the Flemish chronicler whose work is depicted here denounced the flagellants for claiming that their penance was a kind of baptism, that it could wipe out sin, and that it was a sacrifice akin to Christ's death on the cross. The king of France banned flagellation, and the pope outlawed it.

Turkmenistan refer to plague as the cause of deaths in 1338 and 1339. In 1345 and 1346, according to Russian chronicles, pestilence devastated cities in the Mongol-ruled parts of southern Russia. Uzbek villages emptied. In 1346–1347, an official in Crimea reputedly counted 85,000 corpses.

In China, too little work has been done on the demographic impact of plagues to make firm assertions. In general, there seems little doubt that the population of the empire fell in the relevant period. The census of 1393, with adjustments demographers made to compensate for the official habit of underestimating the numbers, suggests a total population of perhaps a little over 80 million—compared with about 120 million in the mid–fourteenth century. The loss of people was by no means uniform. Some regions even seem to have made slight gains.

Moral and Social Effects

"Although the Black Death killed people indiscriminately—the vicious and the virtuous alike—it was tempting, especially for Christians, to see it as a moral agent, even a divine instrument to call the world to repentance and make people good."

Natural disasters always inspire moralizing. Although the Black Death killed people indiscriminately—the vicious and the virtuous alike—it was tempting, especially for Christians, to see it as a moral agent, even a divine instrument to call the world to repentance and make people good. The plague was a leveler, attacking all sorts and conditions. For many who experienced it, the plague was a test of faith, first eliciting selfish reactions of terror and flight, profiteering and despair, then, as Matteo Villani observed, "people . . . began to help one another, so that many were cured, and people felt safe in helping others." Dice makers, claimed an abbot in northern France, turned to making rosary beads. In China, as we shall see, plague, combined with other natural disasters, helped to stir up religious movements that over spilled into political revolution (see Chapter 15). In the Islamic world, fear of plague stimulated a revival of features of popular religion the clergy normally condemned: summoning spirits, magical spells, and charms.

Medicine and Morals

As well as to prayer, penance, and superstition, plague was a stimulus to science as people searched for a cure. It was normal to speak of sin as if it were the cause of the plague. But most people did not take such talk literally. Moralistic explanations of

Treating the plague. In the mid–fifteenth century, a patron who was probably a plague survivor endowed a chapel in the high Alps at Lanslevillard. The chapel was dedicated to St. Sebastian, adopted by plague victims, perhaps because his arrow wounds resembled the pockmarks and pustules of so many diseases. The scene reproduced here shows the underarm buboes that are also a symptom of bubonic plague, the indiscriminate nature of the disease, its supposed origin as a punishment from God, and physicians' efforts to cure it by lancing pustules.

disease were hardly more convincing in the fourteenth century then they are today, and scientific inquiry soon replaced lamentations. The University of Paris medical faculty blamed "a year of many fogs and damps. . . . We must not overlook the fact that pestilence proceeds from divine will, . . . but this does not mean forsaking doctors." Astrologers produced fatalistic explanations. "Corrupt air" was widely blamed, perhaps caused by polluted wells, perhaps by earthquakes. In the Islamic world, too, religious interpretations of the origin of plague never inhibited scientific inquiry into its causes and possible cures. Muslim physicians also blamed corrupt air, caused in its turn by irregular weather, decaying matter, and astrological influences.

As for how to treat plague, practices were wildly different. In Cairo, healers smeared the swellings on the bodies of the afflicted with Armenian clay. In Muslim Spain, the physician Ibn Khatib advised abstention from grains, cheese, mushrooms, and garlic. Barley water and syrup of basil were widely prescribed as remedies or ways to prevent becoming ill. Gentile of Foligno in central Italy, who died of the plague in 1348, recommended dried snake's flesh, at least a year old. This was not as silly as it sounds. Snakes, whose venom can be beneficial in measured quantities, had a long and honorable therapeutic record with the medical profession. Another Italian, Gabriele de' Mussis, favored bloodlettings and plasters made of mallow leaves. Turks sliced off the heads of the boils on the bodies of the sick and supposedly extracted "green glands."

The overwhelming medical consensus among both Christians and Muslims saw infection and contagion as the main threats to the population. Where the authorities responded accordingly in time by imposing quarantine, lives were spared. Quarantine worked in places as busy as the great city of Milan in northern Italy.

Where it could not be averted, plague shattered morale. A poet in Cairo, al-Sallah al-Safadi, described the psychological effect of the disease. Those it spared were maddened. It "spread fear and misery in the hearts of women" and convinced even the mighty of their mortality. It entered houses "like bands of thieves," dispelling people's sense of security. "God has not just subdued Egypt,"

Burying the dead. "How come you feel no sadness when you bury a fellow-creature . . . that you remain unready for your own graves . . . that you pay no heed when warnings of death reach your ears?" The twelfth-century Muslim writer al Hariri asked this question in his *Maqamat*, a collection of moralistic stories. Al Hariri had no doubt that sickness, besides being a physical affliction, also served a moral purpose. God sent it to test human virtue and compassion. When the Black Death struck in the 1300s, many Muslims and Christians also saw the plague this way and tried to minister to the sick and dying. Yet the number of deaths could overwhelm the living, and many of the dead were dumped in mass graves.

al-Safadi concluded, "he has made her crawl on her knees." The Florentine poet, Petrarch, felt the guilt of survival among the corpses. He saw "just one comfort: that we shall follow those who went before." He raged at his fellow survivors: "Go, mortals, sweat, pant, toil, range the lands and seas to pile up riches you cannot keep. . . . The life we lead is a sleep; whatever we do are dreams. Only death breaks the sleep and wakes us from dreaming. I wish I could have woken before this."

The Jews

Plague had winners and losers. In Europe, Jews were among the losers. A skeptical German Franciscan reported the common opinion that Jews started the plague by poisoning wells "and many Jews confessed as much under torture: that they had bred spiders and toads in pots and pans, and had obtained poison from overseas. . . . Throughout Germany, and in all places, they were burnt. For fear of that punishment many accepted baptism and their lives were spared." The massacres that ensued, especially in Germany, were nearly always the result of outbreaks of mob violence, which the authorities tried to restrain. In July 1348, Pope Clement VI declared the Jews innocent of the charge of well poisoning and excommunicated anyone who harmed them. In January 1349, the city council of Cologne in the Rhineland warned authorities in other cities that anti-Jewish riots could ignite popular revolt. "Accordingly we intend to forbid any harrassment of the Jews in our city because of these flying rumors, but to defend them and keep them safe, as our predecessors did—and we are convinced that you ought to do the same." Not all authorities, however, were equally vigilant, equally effective, or equally committed to the defense of the Jews, and massacres continued.

Why did some people in Europe victimize Jews? Jewish communities had existed all over the Mediterranean since Roman times (see Map 14.3). Like other migrants from the east, such as Greeks, Syrians, and Arabs, Jews were an urban and often a commercial people. The itinerary of the twelfth-century Jewish merchant, Benjamin of Tudela, whose description of Constantinople we quoted in Chapter 12, describes their close-knit world, in which a structure of family firms and the fellow feeling of co-religionists gave Jews a commercial advantage and helped them to trade between the Christian and Muslim worlds. An isolated reference to Jews in Cologne occurs as early as 321 C.E. when the Rhineland was part of the Roman Empire, but Mediterranean communities were probably the springboard for Jewish colonization of northern European cities between the sixth and eleventh centuries.

Wherever they went, Jews were alternately privileged and persecuted: privileged, because rulers who needed productive settlers were prepared to reward them with legal immunities; persecuted, because host communities resented intruders who were given special advantages. Some scholars trace **anti-Semitism** to the influence of Christianity. Indeed, medieval anti-Semitism did exploit Christian prejudices. Gospel texts could be read—as they were, for example, at the time of the First Crusade (see Chapter 12)—to saddle Jews with collective responsibility for the death of Jesus. And Holy Week, when Christians prepare to commemorate Christ's death, was at best an expensive and at worst a fatal time for Jewish communities, who had to buy security from bloody reprisals.

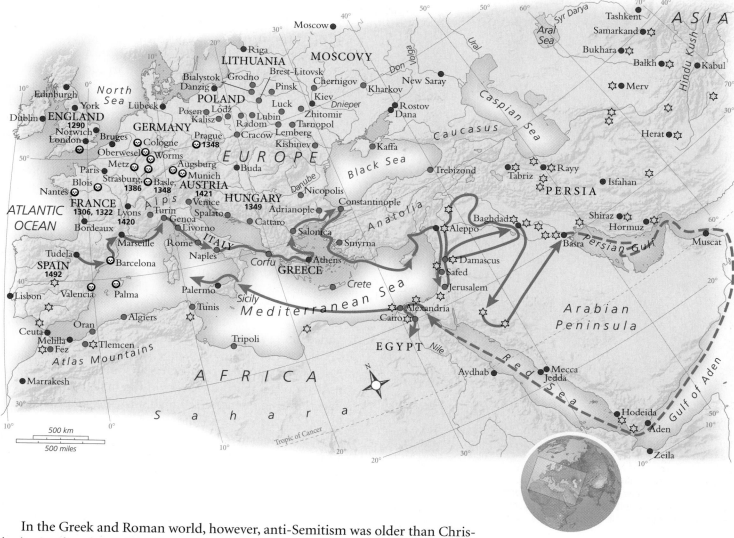

MAP 14.3

Jews in Medieval Europe and the Middle East, 1100–1400

● major centers of Jewish resettlement, 1200–1500

☺ massacres of Jews, ca. 1100–1400

1290 date of expulsion of Jews

➡ travels of Benjamin of Tuleda, ca. 1160–1173

▪▪➤ presumed route of Benjamin of Tuleda

☆ Jewish communities in Muslim world

In the Greek and Roman world, however, anti-Semitism was older than Christianity. Medieval anti-Semitism, moreover, was just one aspect of a wider phenomenon: society's antipathy for groups it could not assimilate—comparable, for instance, to the treatment of lepers, Muslims, and, later, Gypsies. Outbreaks of anti-Jewish hatred are intelligible, in part, as examples of the prejudice outsiders commonly attract. At the time of the Black Death, lepers were also accused of well poisoning. So were random strangers and individuals unpopular in their communities. We can find similar phenomena in almost every culture. The case of the Jews in Europe demands attention not because it is unique, but because it is surprising, given Western society's indebtedness to Jewish traditions, and to the individual genius of many Jews.

The increasing pace and intensity of persecution in the fourteenth century drove Jews to new centers. England had already expelled those Jews who did not convert to Christianity in 1290. The Jews were forced out of most of France in the early fourteenth century, and from many areas of western Germany in the early fifteenth century. (Spain and Portugal followed suit in the 1490s.) The effect was to shift Jewish settlement toward the central and eastern Mediterranean, Poland, and Lithuania (which first admitted Jews in 1321).

Christianity's Supremacy over Judaism. Church and Synagogue are clearly sisters, but the Church is crowned and upright, while the Synagogue is blindfold, with bare, inclined head. These examples are from Bamberg Cathedral in Germany but the pairing of Church and Synagogue appears, with remarkable consistency, all over Europe. Typically, the Synagogue has a broken staff, while the tablets of the law slip from her other hand. If the sculpture of the Church shown here were undamaged, she would almost certainly hold a cross and a chalice.

Distribution of Wealth

Though the evidence relates almost entirely to Europe, there were also people—whole groups of people—who benefited from the effects of plague. In Western Europe, propertied women were certainly among them. The aristocratic marriage market could be fatal to women who married young and faced repeated pregnancies, but it also left many young widows—the last wives of aging, dying husbands. So property law had to provide for widows by ensuring them an adequate share in their dead husbands' estates and reversion of the property the women had brought to their marriages as dowries. More widows burying more husbands could shift the balance of property ownership between the sexes.

Chroniclers, insisting on death as a leveler, often remarked that the plague carried off men and women alike. But, after the terrible devastations of 1348, contemporaries who noticed a difference in mortality rates between the sexes all saw men as the main victims. The plagues of the fourteenth century, taken as a whole, seem to have hit men harder than women, presumably because women led relatively more secluded, and therefore protected, lives than men. Rich widows, often accumulating property from successive marriages, wielded power in their own right. To some extent, the same considerations applied lower down the ranks of society. For instance, during the period of high mortality associated with cold and famine in the second decade of the fourteenth century, more than half the weddings among the peasants of the manor of Taunton in southwest England involved rich widows. After the Black Death, the lords of the manor introduced massive license fees for anyone who wanted to make such marriages, ostensibly to protect widows from predatory Romeos. In unprecedented numbers, widows became the administrators of estates. Women of leisure, education, and power played a bigger part in Western society after this. The increased prominence of women in political, literary, and religious life from the fifteenth century onward might not have been possible without the damage plague did to men.

In Western Europe peasants, if they survived the plague, also benefited from it. In the long run, owners could only keep great properties viable after plague had scythed the labor force by splitting the proceeds with their workers, or by breaking the estates up and letting peasants farm the parcels as tenants. Instead of taking orders from the lord's agent or bailiff, tenants paid rent and could manage their landholdings to their own best advantage. The trend toward "free" peasantries started long before the Black Death struck because in many cases it suited landowners, too. Peasants often made the land more productive. It made economic sense to allow them the initiative to improve their holdings. In England, where the royal courts encouraged peasant freedom to expand their own jurisdiction at aristocrats' expense, about half the peasants in the south of the country were already free when the plague arrived.

Lords wrote off their rights to labor services because, as a steward on an English estate admitted in 1351, "the lord's interest made it necessary." The contract peasant dependants of an English abbey renegotiated is revealing. "At the time of the mortality or pestilence which occurred in 1349, scarcely two peasants remained on the manor." They threatened to leave unless the abbey made a new contract. Most of their former services—including plowing, weeding, carting, and preparing soil for planting—were commuted for rent "as long as it pleases the lord—and would that it might please the lord for ever," added the scribe, "since the aforesaid services were not worth very much." It is remarkable, however, that the growth of leaseholding and the relaxation of lordly controls over peasant farmers happened on a large scale in the late fourteenth and fifteenth centuries in the parts of Western Europe plague affected. In areas the Black Death bypassed—such as Poland, much of Russia, and what is now the Czech Republic and Slovakia—the opposite happened. Peasants became tied to their lords' land and subject to the landholders' jurisdiction.

Were the effects on the European peasantry duplicated in other plague-ridden lands? Certainly, the rural population became more restive and mobile in Egypt and Syria, where, in 1370, one jurist railed against the laws that obliged justices to return peasant refugees to the places from where they had fled. Villages in Egypt often had their tax burdens reduced in acknowledgment of the loss of population. The cost of labor services rose as population fell, creating opportunities for economic mobility among peasants and urban workers, and stimulating a further decline in rural population levels as peasants migrated to towns. But these changes did not disturb landowners' grip on their holdings. Peasants and landowners seem to have suffered together the effects of declining rural productivity.

Peasant Millenarianism

Where peasants benefited, improved conditions took a long time to take effect. Combined with the effects of climate change, the immediate consequences of the plague disturbed, even subverted, the sense of security and stability associated with a traditional way of life. Moreover, most governments responded to the demographic disaster, loss of revenue, and loss of labor by raising taxes and trying to limit labor mobility. In previous centuries, ecological disasters and political oppression had often driven peasants into religious extremism or rebellion. Now, popular revolt took on a new agenda: revolutionary **millenarianism**—the doctrine that in an imminent, divinely contrived relaunch of history, God would empower the poor. This happened independently but in strikingly similar ways, in both Europe and China. A popular preacher who incited peasant rebels in England in 1381, expressed the doctrine of egalitarianism:

> How can the lords say or prove that they are more lords than we—save that they make us dig and till the ground so that they can squander what we produce? . . . They have beautiful residences and manors, while we have the trouble and the work, always in the fields and under the snow. But it is from us and our labor that everything comes with which they maintain their pomp. . . . Good folk, things cannot go well in England, nor ever shall until all things are in common and there is neither villein nor noble, but all of us are of one condition.

Prophecies helped nourish revolt. Some Franciscans (see Chapter 13), with their special vocation to serve the poor, excited expectations that the end of the world could not be far off, and that a new age was at hand when God would release riches from the bowels of the Earth and eliminate inequality. In China, a similar doctrine inspired peasant rebels in the 1350s. A new Buddha would inaugurate a golden age and give his followers power over their oppressors (see Chapter 15).

The Wife of Bath. "Thanks be to God, who is for aye alive, / Of husbands at Church door have I had five." "The Wife of Bath" was a fictional character of about 1400—shown here in a contemporary illustration to the English writer Geoffrey Chaucer's verses about her. But, like all good satire, she was representative of the society of her times: sexually shameless, irrepressibly bossy, and determined to exert "power, during all my life" over any husband "who shall be both my debtor and my slave."
"Facsimile of Ellesnere Chaucher, The Life of Bath" 1400–1410. VdA Museum, London. Picture Desk, Inc./Kobal Collection

According to both movements, a divinely appointed hero would put a bloody end to the struggle of good and evil.

The next chapter describes the politics of the ensuing revolt in China. According to popular traditions dating from soon after the time, the leader of the rebellion, the founder of the Ming dynasty, who claimed to be the prophesied hero, experienced the effects of ecological crisis himself. In one story, he rose to prominence by inventing a medicine that could cure a devastating new plague "which killed half the people and which no known medicine could combat." In another version, the plague and the great Yellow River flood of 1344 reduced him to beggary, and eventually he joined the rebellion that brought him to supreme power.

In addition to contributing to revolution and a change of dynasty in China, and to instability in Europe, the plagues helped transform the Mongol world. The region the Mongols dominated spanned the plague's trans-Eurasian corridors of transmission. Though the evidence comes from European observers, it is a safe assumption that Mongol manpower suffered and that population levels in some regions from which the Mongols levied recruits and collected taxes also fell. The loss of China in 1368 was, of course, the Mongols' most spectacular forfeiture of power. But the effects went further. Mongol control slackened in other dominions, and, on the Chinese front, it never recovered.

In general, plague-stricken societies showed more of what we now call social mobility. The ranks of aristocracies, which were always subject to rapid turnover as families died out, thinned and refilled faster than ever. This seems to have applied as much to China's scholar elite, whose hold on power lapsed and was not fully reasserted until well into the fifteenth century, as to Western European nobilities, whose composition changed. In Western Europe, the increase in the number of free peasants and tenants created a form of rural capitalism. Families formerly restricted to modest social ambitions could accumulate wealth and bid for higher status, buying education or business opportunities or more land.

THE LIMITS OF DISASTER: BEYOND THE PLAGUE ZONE

How far did the plagues of the fourteenth century reach? In terms of effects, the plague was a regional phenomenon, changing the history of China, Western Europe, the Middle East, and the steppeland empires. But much of Central and Eastern Europe escaped. So did areas that ought to have been vulnerable to a disease spread by contagion or infection, such as southeast Asia, and the parts of Africa that were in touch, by way of the Indian Ocean or the Saharan caravan routes, with affected regions. Its relative isolation protected Japan. Apart from a pestilence in the capital Kyoto in 1342, which chroniclers were inclined to attribute to the vengeful spirit of a former emperor, Japan suffered no visitations of any disease on a scale resembling that of the Black Death. The principalities and city-states of central and northern Russia suffered relatively little and late—not before 1350, which is surprising in view of Russia's openness to the steppeland and close contact with the Mongols. India was relatively little affected—references to pestilence are not much more frequent in fourteenth-century sources than for other periods, and recorded outbreaks were localized.

Beyond the reach of the plagues—or, at least, beyond the zone of their most severe effects—the fourteenth century was an era of opportunity in Eurasia. The Mongols were now troubled giants, from whom states in India, Japan, and

"Beyond the reach of the plagues—or, at least, beyond the zone of their most severe effects—the fourteenth century was an era of opportunity in Eurasia."

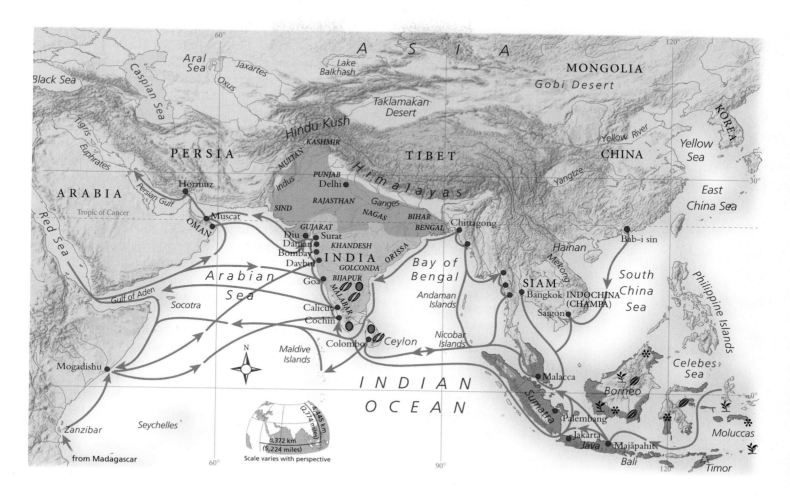

South and Southeast Asia, ca. 1350

- region where Majapahit claimed tribute
- Delhi sultanate at its greatest extent, ca. 1335
- area subject to sporadic influence by Delhi Sultanate
- — main trade route
- ● important trade centers

Traded Goods

- pepper
- cinnamon
- sandalwood
- nutmeg
- cloves
- mace

southeast Asia were at last safe. We can look at those regions first, before turning to sub-Saharan Africa and the Pacific where, as far as we know, the plagues never penetrated.

India

In India, the sultanate of Delhi profited from the Mongols' decline. Sultan Muhammad Ibn Tughluq (r. 1325–1351) was the driving force of a policy of conquest that almost covered the subcontinent with campaigns (see Map 14.4). Ibn Battuta, who knew the sultan well, called him "of all men the most addicted to the making of gifts and the shedding of blood. His gate is never without some poor man enriched or some living man executed." Emphasis on the sultan's generosity reflects Ibn Battuta's own priorities. He was always on the lookout for rich patrons. But the key facts about Ibn Tughluq's methods are clear. He ran his court and army by balancing lavish gifts with intimidating displays of wrath.

Ibn Tughluq's administration was a machine for recycling wealth. Ibn Battuta describes the regular arrival of revenue collectors from villages, casting gold coins into a golden basin: "These contributions amount in all to a vast sum which the sultan gives to anyone he pleases." Annually, "the daughters of the infidel kings and who have been taken as captives in war during that year" were distributed among the sultan's chief supporters, after performing a sort of audition—singing and dancing, presumably to establish which girls were the most valuable.

Daulatabad. The Delhi Sultan Ibn Tughluq (r. 1325–1351) transferred his court to the strongest fortress in India, which he called Daulatabad, or "City of Riches," near the frontier of his campaigns against Hindu kingdoms in the south. He planned to relocate the entire population of the city of Delhi to the surrounding slopes. The steep ascent made the place defensible. A narrow gangway was the only approach to the palace complex.

While praising Ibn Tughluq's sense of justice, Ibn Battuta indicts him for the use of terror, abuses of power, and judicial murder. "The Sultan was far too free in shedding blood. . . . Every day there are brought to the audience hall hundreds of people, chained, beaten and fettered, and those who are for execution are executed, those for torture tortured, and those for beating beaten." He put one of his brothers to death on a charge of rebellion, which Ibn Battuta clearly felt was trumped up—the first of many judicial murders. On one occasion, the sultan executed 350 alleged deserters at once. A sheikh who accused him of tyranny was fed with excrement and beheaded. Twice, Ibn Tughluq dealt with suspected conspiracies in Delhi by expelling the classes of Muslim notables whom he suspected of disaffection.

Ibn Tughluq's was a personal empire. His own dynamism and reputation, and a policy of religious toleration held it together—the only policy workable for a Muslim elite in a largely Hindu country. But Ibn Tughluq's state was not built to last. It relied on conquest to fuel the system. The Turkic elite, who provided the muscle for revenue collection at home and for war on the frontiers, demanded constant rewards. When they did not get them, they seceded from the state. This began to happen on a large scale toward the end of Ibn Tughluq's life. Conquest is, in any case, a gambler's game. Military fortunes change, and military systems, even of the most crushing superiority, can fail unpredictably. Disaster struck Ibn Tughluq, for instance, when a plague devastated his army. "The provinces withdrew their allegiance," Ibn Battuta reported, "and the outer regions broke away."

Moreover, the Delhi sultans were under constant pressure from the Muslim establishment to impose Islam by force, launch holy war, and ease the tax burden on Muslims at the expense of "infidels." The discontent evident among sheikhs and some Muslim notables during Ibn Tughluq's reign owed something, no doubt, to fear of the sultan's arbitrary measures. But frustration with his policies of toleration also inspired much of it. Ibn Tughluq's successor succumbed to these pressures. He forfeited Hindu allegiance. Beyond the frontier, Hindu states adopted a counter ideology of resistance to Islam—at least at the level of rhetoric, since religion rarely took priority over politics. In southern India, a Hindu state with imperial ambitions arose at Vijayanagar. The conquest juggernaut of the sultanate of Delhi stopped rolling, and provincial elites in outlying regions in Gujarat and Bengal dropped out of the empire. Again, as so often happened in Indian history, both the difficulties of and the capacity for an India-wide empire had been demonstrated. But again, the problems of maintaining such a large and diverse state were obvious. Future attempts would run into the same kinds of difficulties as those that caused the sultanate's control of the outer edges of the state to unravel and its expansion to come to a halt.

Southeast Asia

Rather as Delhi did in India, a native kingdom in Java, (the main island of what is today Indonesia), exploited the opportunity that emerged as the Mongol threat waned. The offshore world of Southeast Asia produced goods the Chinese market wanted. Some states in the region were in a position to threaten or control the passage of those goods by sea: pepper and cinnamon from southern India and Sri Lanka; sandalwood from Timor; timber and aromatic spices—nutmeg, cloves, and mace—from Borneo and the Moluccas. Control of the strait between Malaya, Java, and Sumatra was strategically vital for China-bound trade, and the shipping of Java made an important contribution to the commerce of the region. That is why Kubilai Khan focused on Java when he tried to extend his empire into Southeast Asia (see Chapter 15).

The establishment of a powerful state on Java, centered on the secure, inland city of Majapahit (Mah-jah-PAH-heet), was the achievement of Kertanagara, who died in 1292. Chroniclers credited him with magic powers or saintly virtues, according to their own prejudices. In fact, he seems to have balanced the rituals of Buddhist, Hindu, and indigenous religions to keep a diverse array of followers together. Kertanagara repulsed Kubilai Khan's Mongol invasion.

The king who launched Majapahit on its own imperial career in the mid–fourteenth century was Hayan Wuruk (died 1389). He had dazzling ambitions. We know this because his childhood playmate, who became one of his chief ministers, wrote a poem in his praise. The verses reveal what the king wanted people to think of him. The poem lovingly describes the royal palace at Majapahit, which had gates of iron and a "diamond-plastered" watchtower. Majapahit was like the sun and moon, while the villages of the rest of the kingdom are "of the aspect of stars." When Hayan Wuruk traveled the country, his court filled numberless carts. Through the streets of his capital, he paraded, clad in gold, borne on a throne carved with supporting lions, to the music of lutes and drums, conches and trumpets, and singers. Ambassadors from foreign courts brought him praises in Sanskrit verse.

Hayan Wuruk was both "Buddha in the body" and "Shiva incarnate"—worshipful to Buddhist and Hindu subjects alike. He was also a master of native rituals, skilled in the theater, dance, and song. "The king's song put them under a spell," the poet assures us, "like the cries of a peacock." Hayan Wuruk's realm, according to the poet, was more famous than any country in the world except India. In reality, the kingdom occupied little more than half the island of Java. The king, however, aimed to make it bigger. The poet listed tributaries in many islands in what is today Indonesia, and "protectorates" in northern Malaya, Thailand, and Indochina. Even China and India, he claimed, defer to Hayan Wuruk. "Already the other continents," he boasts, "are getting ready to show obedience to the illustrious prince" and a state "renowned for its purifying power in the world."

That was all the exaggeration of propaganda. But a disinterested chronicler, from Samudra-Pasai, a pepper-exporting port beyond the Strait of Malacca to the west, left a description of Majapahit that confirms much of the picture:

> The empire grew prosperous. People in vast numbers thronged the city. At this time every kind of food was in great abundance. There was a ceaseless coming and going of people from the territories overseas which had submitted to the king. . . . The land of Majapahit was supporting a large population. Everywhere one went there were gongs and drums being beaten, people dancing to the strains of all kinds of loud music, entertainments of all kinds like the living theater. . . . These were the commonest sights and went on day and night in the land of Majapahit.

"When Hayan Wuruk traveled the country, his court filled numberless carts. Through the streets of his capital, he paraded, clad in gold, borne on a throne carved with supporting lions, to the music of lutes and drums, conches and trumpets, and singers."

A CLOSER LOOK

A Javanese Queen

This fourteenth-century sculpture, carved before Islam had begun to dominate the culture of Java, depicts a Javanese queen as an incarnation of the Hindu goddess Parvati. Parvati is the wife of the supreme god Shiva, who is associated with destruction and transformation, and like him she has both benign and violent attributes.

The blooming lotus is one of the benign attributes of Parvati.

One of Parvati's sons, the elephant-headed god Ganesha, is depicted executing a dance step influenced by yoga.

Kartikkeya, another of Parvati's sons, is a god of war.

Posthumous Portrait of a Queen as Parvati. Eastern Javanese period, 14th century. Indonesia. Andesite, H. 6 ft. 8 in. (203.2 cm); W. 3 ft. 3 in. (99.1 cm). The Metropolitan Museum of Art, New York, NY, U.S.A. Image copyright ∞© The Metropolitan Museum of Art / Art Resource, NY.

Parvati is often shown riding a lion, but here she rests on Nandi, the divine bull, whom Shiva rode.

How does this sculpture reflect ideals of kingship in Java at this time?

Surviving temple reliefs show what the Java of Hayan Wuruk was like. Wooden houses, perched on pillars over stone terraces, formed neat villages. Peasants grew paddy rice, or coaxed water buffalo over dry fields to break up the soil. Women did the harvesting and cooking. Orchestras, beating gongs with sticks, accompanied masked dancers. Royal charters fill out the picture of economic activities. Industrial processes included salt making by evaporation, sugar refining, processing cured water-buffalo meat, oil pressing from seeds, making rice noodles, ironmaking, rattan weaving, and dyeing cloth. More sophisticated ceramics and textiles were imported from China. The same charters reveal the extension of royal power and impact into the hinterland. They establish direct relationships between the royal court and members of local elites. They favor the foundations of new temples and encourage the spread of communications, the building of bridges, the commissioning of ferries, and the erection of "rest houses, pious foundations, and hospitals" mentioned in the king's praise poem.

Majapahit was an expanding realm. As Mongol vigilance in the region relaxed, Majapahit's power increased. In the 1340s, a network of ports in the hands of Majapahit garrisons spread over the islands of Bali and Sumatra. Majapahit indeed seems to have annihilated commercial rivals in Sumatra and to have maintained fortified outposts on the coast of that island. In 1377, Hayan Wuruk launched an apparently successful expedition against Palembang, the major way station on the route from India to China. A struggle was on to profit from Southeast Asia's trade (see Map 14.4).

Japan

Japan, like Java, was a region that the plagues spared and the Mongols failed to conquer. Here, however, security from the Mongol menace had a contrasting effect. As the threat from the Mongols receded, so did pressure to stay united and serve the state. Potential rebels could now raise armies with increasing ease. Fourteenth-century Japan began to experience unprecedented instability. Familiar patterns in politics and social life were shaken like the contents of a kaleidoscope. Since the beginning of the rule of the shoguns, the hereditary chief ministers who controlled the government (see Chapter 11), Japan had enjoyed more than a century of stability. The warrior class had been pacified—maintained by grants of estates and their revenues. Now people at all social levels were accumulating wealth. Social status, which was supposedly protected by complicated standards of eligibility for different ranks, was up for grabs. Warriors began to diversify into new occupations, to sell or break up their estate rights, and, in increasing numbers, to resort to violence as a way of life.

At the top of this volatile society, rival branches of the imperial family contested the throne. The Emperor Godaigo (r. 1318–1339) fought to exclude family competitors and to take back the power the shoguns exercised in the emperor's name. He accused them of "drawing water from a stream and forgetting its source." Godaigo had his portrait painted showing himself with a sword—an accessory normally considered too active for an emperor, but one that signified his intentions to recover real power and keep hold of the symbols of imperial authority, which included a sacred sword.

Godaigo found, however, that he could not simply take up the reins of power himself. Traditional methods could no longer govern the country. Loyalty, though much talked of by writers at the time, became an unpredictable commodity, liable to change hands as circumstances changed. An oath the members of a warband took

"Fourteenth-century Japan began to experience unprecedented instability. Familiar patterns in politics and social life were shaken like the contents of a kaleidoscope."

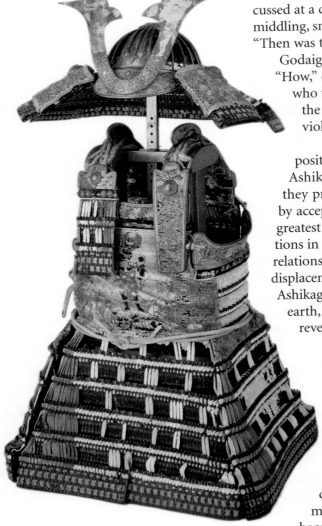

A Shogun's Armor. This armor is believed to have belonged to Ashikaga Takauji who was shogun from 1338 to 1358. The quality and costliness of the gilt copper breastplate and helmet mountings show that the armor belonged to a person of high status. Stenciled in lacquered doeskin, an image of Fudo Myo-o—the god who personified the samurai virtues of outward ferocity and inner calm—adorns the breastplate.
The Metropolitan Museum of Art, Gift of Bashford Dean, 1914 (14.100.121) Photograph © 1991 The Metropolitan Museum of Art.

in 1336 declared, "Let there be no differences of opinion. Everything shall be discussed at a council. If some disobey this, they shall suffer the punishment of all the middling, small, and great gods of the country of Japan in Heaven, Earth and Hell." "Then was then," proclaimed a saying of the time. "Now is now: rewards are lord!" Godaigo's army deserted in dissatisfaction over the rewards he could provide. "How," complained one of the officials who worked for his party, "can those who tend to have the outlook of a merchant be of use to the court?" Clearly, the new disorder was, for some, a kind of social revolution: the result of violations of the proper boundaries of class and rank.

In 1335, the most powerful of the warlords, Ashikaga Takauji, seized the position of supreme power as **shogun** in defiance of Godaigo's wishes. The Ashikaga dynasty emerged with the greatest share of authority because they promised the most rewards. They survived as shoguns almost until 1573 by accepting the realities of the changed world, withdrawing into a role as the greatest of a number of regional powers, and attempting only modest interventions in the spheres of other major warlords. The Ashikaga also restored the old relationship between shogun and emperor, in which pieties smothered the real displacement of power into the shogun's hands. "There is heaven," declared Ashikaga Takauji in his testament of 1357, "there is the sovereign, there is the earth, and there is the minister. . . . If the joint path of sovereign and subject is reversed, then there will be neither heaven nor earth, sovereign nor subject."

In 1336, the Ashikaga overwhelmed Godaigo's remaining supporters at the Battle of Minato River (see Map 14.5). Godaigo and his heirs, however, did not give up. Ashikaga victories confined them to a small enclave in the south of the country, but they resisted until the 1380s.

The chaos of the fourteenth century favored the rise of **Zen,** a tradition of Buddhism that valued personal extinction as a part of mystical experience. A twelfth-century Japanese text defined it: "a special transmission outside the scriptures, not founded on words or letters, which allows one to penetrate the nature of things by pointing directly to the mind." Zen made progress partly because of the influx of monks from China who were escaping from the Mongols, and partly because Zen ideas suited the warriors and warlords who now effectively ruled Japan. Discipline, self-denial, and willingness to die are martial virtues. The warriors recognized Zen monks as kindred spirits. Warrior families made Zen practitioners the custodians of their ancestral temples and tombs.

For the women of families of warrior and aristocratic rank, the changes of the period were oppressive. Women could attain responsible positions in the emperor's court. Hino Meishi, for instance, was in charge of the sacred imperial symbols in 1331, when the shogun tried to depose Godaigo. But changing marriage customs were unfavorable to women's personal independence. Until the fourteenth century, marriage in Japan was predominantly a private, essentially sexual relationship. Now it became increasingly formalized, as a union of two families. Wives moved into the homes of their husbands' families, instead of remaining in their own homes. Hino Meishi, for instance, started her experience of married life in 1333 in traditional manner, when her lover started visiting her openly. This publicly acknowledged the relationship as a permanent one. She worried, not because the arrangement was informal, but because her husband's family was of higher rank than her own. In the confused conditions of the civil war then raging, Meishi was forced to move house, but she ended up in her husband's home.

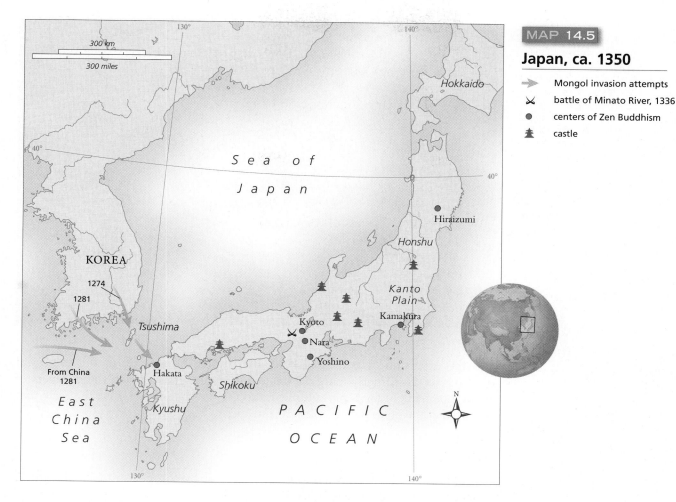

MAP 14.5

Japan, ca. 1350

→ Mongol invasion attempts

⚔ battle of Minato River, 1336

● centers of Zen Buddhism

🏯 castle

A sign of women's changed circumstances is that they stopped writing fiction and the kind of personal diaries familiar from earlier periods. Hino Meishi herself was the author of the last autobiographical memoir by a woman—which is why we know so much about her life. Self-expression was now considered inappropriate for the female sex. Wives came to be thought of as their husbands' property. In the same period, following changes in the practices of the imperial family, it became common for women aristocrats to receive a life interest in a share of family property, rather than inheriting property outright. Property rights were steered toward a single male heir. Among commoners, however, this practice failed to take hold, and women held growing amounts of property and engaged in more business in their own right.

The changes that were transforming the warrior class do not seem to have affected peasant prosperity. On the contrary, the peasants profited. Relaxation of central authority freed villagers from intrusive legislation. They could get on with improving crop yields as they saw fit. The new regime of rewards for military service meant that the landlords were always changing—dispossessed and replaced as the fortunes of war shifted. The rapid turnover of lords, who were usually absentees, also allowed the peasants to get on with their business. There were no epidemics in the fourteenth-century countryside in Japan, and serious crop failures were rare. Nor were population growth

Chronology: The Ashikaga Shogunate	
Fourteenth century	Changing marriage customs diminish women's independence
1318–1339	Emperor Godaigo seeks to regain imperial power
1335	Ashikaga Takauji defies Godaigo and seizes shogunate
1336	Godaigo's supporters defeated at Battle of Minato River

Zen garden. Zuiho-in is one of 24 temples within the temple complex of Daitokuji in Kyoto, one of the Japan's biggest Zen communities. Most temples have a garden of meditation designed to be observed from a single viewpoint to encourage solitude. The hallmarks of these gardens are the expanses of gravel raked to resemble waves, and rocks arranged like islands within it. Greenery is not a normal part of most Zen garden designs, perhaps because living plants are mutable—they change too easily with the passing seasons, whereas rocks are deceptively unchanging. But to ask what a Zen garden "means" is to invite an evasive answer.

and the extension of cultivated land interrupted. As a result of the successful exploitation of formerly marginal lands outside the great estates, the numbers of small independent farmers multiplied, though not on anything like the scale that occurred at the same time in Western Europe.

Mali

Just as Java and Japan seemed to grow in stature by comparison with the afflictions of China and the Mongols, so parts of West Africa projected an image of abundance toward the devastated Mediterranean world. A conspicuous piece of evidence for West African prosperity is the Catalan Atlas, made in the studio of the finest mapmaker in Europe, Cresques Abraham, on the Mediterranean island of Majorca, in the 1370s or 1380s. The map is smothered with gold paint, scattered with bright images in costly pigments, like the contents of a spilled jewel box. In the part of the map devoted to West Africa, a black king appears—bearded, crowned, enthroned, surrounded by depictions of rich cities of many turrets—holding a huge nugget of pure gold. "This is the richest king in all the land," says a caption.

His kingdom, Mali, occupied the Sahel region of grassland and mixed savanna between the Sahara Desert and the tropical forest. The desert sealed it from the effects of plague (see Map 14.6). According to tradition, a hero known as **Sundiata** founded the kingdom in the early thirteenth century. His story has obviously mythical features. He was a cripple, mocked and exiled, who returned home as a conqueror and avenger. The strength of his army, and those of his successors, was horsemen. Terracotta sculptures show us what they were like. Helmed and armed, with round shields and breastplates over slashed leather jackets, they kept their heads haughtily tilted and their horses on short rein, with elaborately braided bridles. Their great age of conquest came in the 1260s and 1270s when, according to the Muslim historian Ibn Khaldun, "their dominions expanded and they overcame the neighboring peoples . . . and all nations of the land of the blacks stood in awe of them."

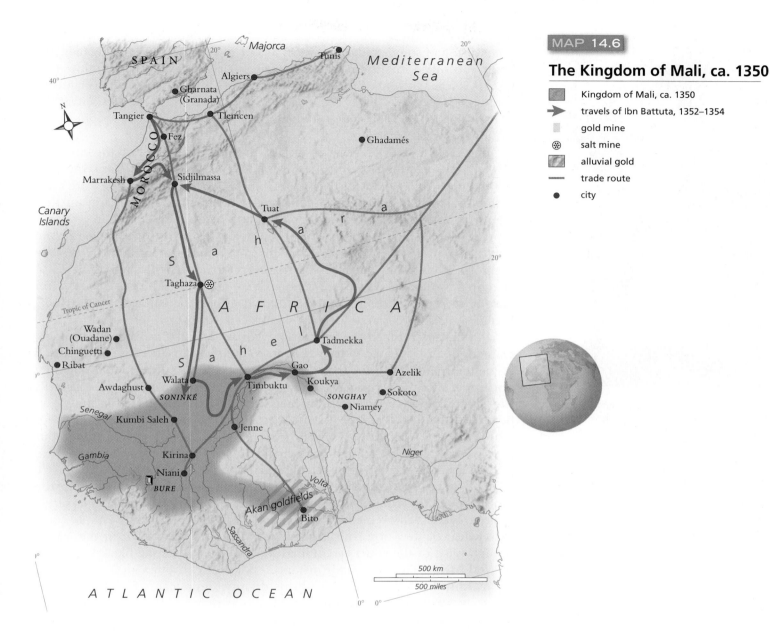

MAP 14.6

The Kingdom of Mali, ca. 1350

- Kingdom of Mali, ca. 1350
- → travels of Ibn Battuta, 1352–1354
- gold mine
- ⊛ salt mine
- alluvial gold
- — trade route
- ● city

The "mansas," as the kings of Mali were titled, made pilgrimages to the Muslim holy city of Mecca via Cairo at intervals from the late thirteenth century, spreading the fame of their land. Although all Muslims are supposed to make the *hajj*, as the pigrimage to Mecca is called, at least once in their life if possible, the mere fact that the mansas could leave their country for the year-long journey shows how stable the state must have been. In about 1324, Mansa Musa stayed in Egypt for about three months on his way to Mecca. He gave 50,000 gold coins to the Mamluk sultan and distributed ingots of raw gold to officials. He endowed so many mosques and shrines that he caused inflation. By various accounts, the value of gold in Egypt fell 10 to 25 percent as a result of his stay. On his homeward journey, he raised loans that, it was said, he repaid at the rate of 700 coins for every 300 of the same value.

The location of West Africa's gold mines was a closely guarded commercial secret, but it was probably in Bure (BOO–ray), around the upper reaches of the

Mansa. "All the peoples of the land of the Blacks stood in awe of them," wrote Ibn Khaldun of the mounted warriors of the Mansas of Mali. Many fired-clay representations of these soldiers survive from the thirteenth to the fifteenth centuries. Nearly all show the same erect posture, proudly uptilted head, and elaborate helmets and bridles.

Niger River and the headwaters of the Gambia and Senegal rivers. The Volta River valley also had some gold. The merchants of Mali handled the gold trade but never controlled its production. When they tried to take over the mines, the miners refused to work. But the gold had to pass through the mansa's lands to get to trading cities, such as Walata and Timbuktu (tihm-buhk-TOO) near the edge of the Sahara. The mansa took nuggets for tribute—hence the image on Cresques Abraham's map.

In 1352, Ibn Battuta—that relentless traveler—set off to find the kingdom of Mali. He journeyed south from his home in Morocco to Taghaza, the salt-mining town on the edge of the Sahara, where "houses and mosques are built with blocks of salt." There he joined one of the merchant camel caravans that regularly crossed the desert, trading salt for gold. Mali was so rich in gold and so short of salt that the price of salt reputedly tripled or quadrupled in the kingdom's markets. Ibn Battuta and his companions crossed the desert by night marches. They ate "desert truffles swarming with lice" in a land "haunted by demons. . . . There is no visible road or track in these parts," Ibn Battuta recorded, "nothing but sand blown hither and thither by the wind." Water sources were sparse—ten days' journey apart.

Ibn Battuta reached the frontier of Mali at Walata. "It was then," he complained, "that I repented of having come to their country because of their lack of manners and their contempt for white men." He found the food disgusting, not appreciating how lucky he was to be served expensive millet at the desert's edge. Outraged to find himself watched when he relieved himself in the Niger, he failed, at first, to realize that the spectator was there to guard him from crocodiles. He found the sexual freedom of the women alarming, but approved of the way children were chained until they learned the Quran. He praised the "abhorrence of injustice" he found among black people.

The mansa's court impressed him, as it impressed other visitors in the same period. This consensus is striking, because North African Muslims rarely praised black achievements. The mansa, according to Ibn Battuta, commanded more devotion from his subjects than any other ruler in the world, though most of the court ceremonial was traditional among black kingdoms in West Africa. The mansa, for instance, spoke only through an intermediary, for to raise his voice was beneath his dignity. Supplicants had to prostrate themselves and sprinkle dust on their heads as they addressed him. When his words were relayed to the people, guards strummed their bowstrings, and everyone else hummed appreciatively. Sneezing in the mansa's presence was punishable by death. Hundreds of servants attended him with gilded rods. Court poets and scholars came to serve the mansa from Muslim Spain and North Africa.

Meanwhile, the gold of West Africa inspired heroic European efforts to get to its source. Western Europe produced only small amounts of silver, and its economies were permanently short of precious metals with which to trade. There was a longstanding adverse trade balance with more productive Silk-Road economies. To keep it going, this trade always needed infusions of cash. So, as Mali's reputation grew, the search for African gold obsessed European adventurers. Cresques Abraham depicted the fate of one of them, the Spaniard Jaume Ferrer, lost to shipwreck off the West African coast in 1346 in an attempt to find a sea route to Mali. The endeavor was hopeless. Mali was landlocked, and the African coasts had little gold until well into the fifteenth century.

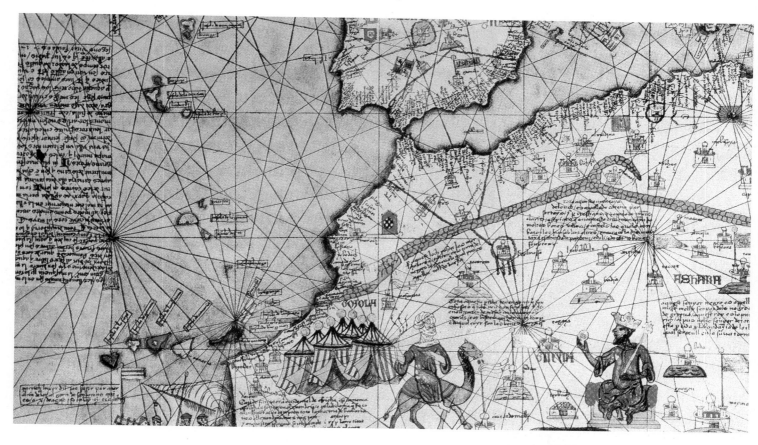

Mansa Musa. "Lord of the blacks of Guinea," reads the legend accompanying the portrait of Mansa Musa (r. ca. 1312–1327), the king of Mali in West Africa, on the fourteenth-century Catalan Atlas. "This lord is the richest and most noble lord of all this region owing to the abundance of gold which is gathered in this land." The Mansa's wealth was said to exceed that of all other kings. His European-style crown and ample beard are compliments bestowed by an artist who had not learned, as Europeans were to do in later centuries, to despise black African kingship.

THE PACIFIC: SOCIETIES OF ISOLATION

Beyond the world that escaped the worst of the Black Death lay regions contagion did not threaten. Isolation, which had arresting effects in so many cases already familiar to readers of this book, was a privilege in the fourteenth century. To understand this unaccustomed reversal of what can only be called the normal pattern of global history, we need to look at some relatively isolated societies. The vastness of the Pacific—which the technology of the time could not cross—ensured that exceptionally isolated cultures lay scattered around and about that ocean.

Easter Island

No part of the inhabited globe was more isolated than Easter Island, which lay, at the time, more than 2,000 miles away from any other human habitation. The island covers only 64 square miles of the Pacific Ocean, way off the usual routes of navigation and the usual course of the winds. It is hard to believe that the Polynesian navigators who first colonized the island, possibly over 1,500 years ago, would have stayed if they had been able to continue their journey or turn around and go home. Most of the soil is poor. Nowadays, there are no nearby fisheries, though native traditions recall a time when the island's elite feasted on porpoise and dolphin. The first settlers brought chickens and the starchy plant called taro. But not much that was edible was available to them when they arrived. Migrant birds were their renewable source of food. The oldest art on the island shows a birdman. Feasts of fowl and egg-stealing competitions greeted the annual arrival of flocks of sooty terns.

Moais. Monumental statue making on Easter Island was probably at its most intense in the fourteenth century. For a small population on a poorly provided and remote island, the investment of energy the practice required seems astounding. The images are similar to those of ancestor cults elsewhere in Polynesia, but they are exceptional in being carved from stone, rather than wood, huge, and numerous. Isolation apparently made Easter Island culture distinctive, but still recognizably like that of other Polynesian colonies.

MAP 14.7

Easter Island (Rapa Nui)

	main area of statues
◇	restored statue site
●	ceremonial center
●	settlement
◨	quarry for red topknots
◨	quarry for statues

Despite the natural poverty of the island and its isolation from other societies, in the fourteenth century it housed a people at the height of their ambition. Probably late in the first millennium, they had begun to erect monumental statues for reasons we can no longer determine. The statues, called *Moais*, resemble those other Polynesian peoples erected: tall, elongated, stylized faces hewn of stone. They were originally adorned with red topknots—sitting hatlike on their heads—and white coral eyes, looking out with a fixed stare. The Easter Island statues are unique compared with other Polynesian works of the same sort only because they are so big and there are so many of them—878 in all, including those abandoned, incomplete, in the quarries. Some 600 finished examples survive, most of them more than 20 feet tall (see Map 14.7).

It took real communal effort to make and erect the statues, each carved from a pillar of rock weighing between 30 and 40 tons. A single extended family—say, about 400 people—joining together to provide the labor and feed the workers, would have taken more than a year to complete the task. As time went on, the statues got bigger—a clear case of competition, driving up the costs of the culture, and, perhaps, condemning it to collapse, a century or two later. So an enterprising community could buck the effects of isolation, and even turn isolation to advantage—but, in an extreme case like that of Easter Island, the effort was evidently hard to sustain. Statue building slowed and, in the sixteenth or seventeenth century, stopped.

New Zealand

New Zealand was another, almost equally remote outpost of the Polynesian world, but with infinitely more resources than Easter Island, and therefore with better prospects of sustainable development. Although the date of the first settlement of New Zealand is disputed (see Chapter 11), fairly secure dates are possible for changes that were under way by the fourteenth century. Population increased. Hunting resources diminished in populated areas as the fur seal and moa began to get scarce, for the moa, a huge, flightless bird, with eggs as big as a hundred hen's eggs, was among the early settlers' main sources of food. Human overexploitation was almost certainly responsible for the moa's extinction. Its meat was processed in immense butcheries. At the biggest butchery, at the mouth of the Waitako River in South Island, up to 90,000 birds were dismembered with blades made of obsidian, a volcanic stone that can be honed to a razor-sharp edge. The same region had over 300 smaller sites, each handling at least 5,000 moa.

As the balance of the way of life shifted from hunting toward farming, mobile colonies settled down. The kind of wear the teeth of people buried in this period shows is different from that of their predecessors: fibrous foods and gritty mollusks ground their dental bites, which show fewer traces of the effects of a meat-rich diet. The results included stronger community identification with land and, therefore, more competition for cultivable resources. Part of the farming surplus was invested in war. From the fifteenth century, the number of places where weapons were made grew enormously. So did the number of fortified villages, especially in the North Island. War was only one of many forms of new or newly intensive activity that favored the power of chiefs. Farming required strong centers of power to organize collective activity and regulate the distribution of food. So did new fishing technologies with gigantic nets that needed many hands to operate them.

Ozette

Meanwhile, on the Pacific rim of the New World, people experimented with contrasting responses to isolation (see Map 14.8). Good evidence has survived for two different communities. One body of evidence comes from a community of hunters in the north of the hemisphere. Exact dates are hard to assign, but probably toward the end of the fifteenth century, a mudslide at Ozette, in Washington State, buried the homes of a community of whalers and seal fishers. The mud perfectly preserved the site. Archaeologists have revealed layers of sediment that show that ways of life had not changed here significantly for centuries before the disaster. The mud of Ozette gives us a unique glimpse into the lives of a hunting culture in what we think of in European terms as the late Middle Ages.

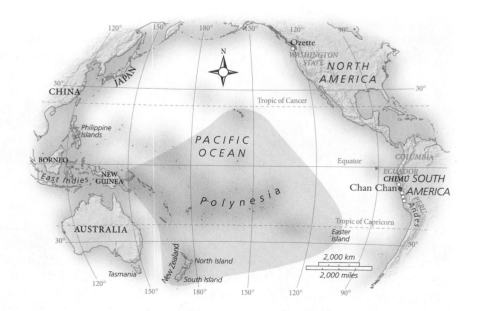

MAP 14.8

Societies of the Pacific, ca.1400

area of Polynesian settlement

PERU   modern country or state

The victims of the mudslide lived in big cedarwood buildings, each more than 50 feet long and 30 feet wide. Each building housed about 40 people, divided typically by partitions into half a dozen smaller family units with their own hearths. Hanging mats helped insulate the walls. The Ozette people ate almost no vegetable matter except wild berries. Though they hunted land animals and birds, the sea was their main hunting ground. Fur seals provided nearly 90 percent of their meat. For cooking, they filled watertight cedarwood boxes with hot water and boiled or steamed their food. They hunted and fished in dugouts. Whale images dominated their art, probably because the art had a ritual or magical function in bringing good fortune to the whale hunt. Carvers also made bowls in the shape of men, depicted realistically except for big cavities, where the belly should be, to hold food or offerings. Their way of life was, broadly speaking, similar to that of the Thule Inuit centuries earlier (see Chapter 11).

Chan Chan

On the Pacific's South American edge, we can trace new activity to roughly the same period. Of course, this was not a region as isolated as New Zealand, Easter Island, or even Ozette. As we have seen many times in this book, the coasts of what are now Peru, Ecuador, and Pacific-side Colombia were always in touch with the cultures of the high Andes and, through them, with the lowlands beyond. In South America, in and around the fourteenth century, the latest experiment in state-building, intensive agriculture, and city life was under way at Chan Chan. This city was in the coastal desert region of Peru where the Moche had formerly built complex irrigation works and prosperous cities in defiance of a hostile environment (see Chapter 10). The methods of the Chimú (chee-MOO) people of Chan Chan were different. They concentrated agriculture around the city, where 30,000 people lived. The population of Chan Chan's hinterland was thinly distributed and not much greater than that of the city itself.

Cotton production was a major economic activity. Fishing seems to have mattered little. For protein, the people of Chan Chan—or, perhaps, just the elite—

Huaca del Dragón. The date of the stacked platforms of Huaca del Dragón, near the site of Chan Chan in Peru, is much disputed, but the adobe reliefs—of which a recently restored section is depicted here—are probably of Chimú workmanship. Below a frieze of warriors, a divine feast is shown. A double-headed serpent, with a rainbow-like body surrounded by clouds, devours curl-nosed victims, framing similar scenes shown in profile. Food-storage areas were built into the structure, which seems to have been both temple and warehouse—a repository, perhaps, for food of the gods.

relied on llamas. Pasture was limited, so the llamas were farmed in corrals in and around the city. Fodder supplemented grazing.

The city of Chan Chan covered almost 7 square miles. Spaces in Chan Chan served as the tombs of kings, dwellings for elites, and warehouses to store and distribute food. The layout shows that the Chimú state was oppressive, with a security-obsessed elite. High walls, fortified gateways and dog-leg corridors, designed with sharp turns to delay attackers and favor defenders, protected the rulers' quarters from their own people.

The warehouses were the most important buildings. Access to them was through chambers where costly ceremonies unfolded: sacrifices of llamas and men, deposits of precious objects. The storerooms were vital—the most vital part of the state—because El Niño periodically and unpredictably washed away the irrigation works. Stockpiling enabled the Chimú to recover when disaster struck.

The rulers' tombs were so rich that colonial-era Spaniards spoke of "mining" them. The Chimú elite favored gold for their precious ornaments and ritual objects. But gold did not occur naturally in this part of Peru. Trade or tribute must have brought it to Chimú, which was evidently an expansionist state. Perhaps it had to be to boost its resources in a difficult and depleted environment. Sites of towns built in the style of Chan Chan stretch between the Sana and Supe Rivers.

In Perspective
The Aftershock

Ibn Khaldun left an often-quoted but unforgettable description of the effects of the Black Death on the Muslim world:

> Civilization shrank with the decrease of mankind. Cities and buildings were bared, roads and signposts were abandoned, villages and palaces were deserted. Tribes and dynasties were expunged. It was as if the voice of existence in the world had called out for oblivion, and the world had responded to the call.

But how serious and enduring were the consequences? For Latin Christendom in Western Europe, the picture looked bleak. After the achievements of the previous century, and the benefits of a long period of enhanced contacts with the Islamic world and China, the West seemed poised for a great age of expansion. Now many promising initiatives of the preceding period ended. North Atlantic navigation, which Norse seafarers had developed so heroically in previous centuries, dwindled. The last Icelandic voyage to mainland America was in 1347. The Norse Greenland colonies became increasingly isolated. When a bishop's representative sailed to the more northerly of them in the 1340s, he "found nobody, either Christians or heathens, only some wild cattle and sheep, and they slaughtered the wild cattle for food, as much as the ships would carry, and then sailed home therewith themselves." When the Greenland colony was finally extinguished in the fifteenth century, it was by mysterious raiders of savage ferocity known to the Norse as Skraelingar—presumably, the Thule Inuit with whom the Norse had long shared the island. Exploration of other parts of the Atlantic virtually stopped at the time of the Black Death. In the half century preceding the onset of the plague, explorers from maritime communities in Western Europe had made considerable progress. Mapping of the African Atlantic had begun, with the Canary and Madeira Islands, and navigators had begun to investigate the pattern of the

"After the achievements of the previous century, and the benefits of a long period of enhanced contacts with the Islamic world and China, the West seemed poised for a great age of expansion. Now many promising initiatives of the preceding period ended."

Making Connections | BEYOND THE PLAGUE ZONE

REGION	→	TENTATIVE REASON FOR ABSENCE OF PLAGUE	→	CONSEQUENCES
Japan	→	Protected by relative isolation	→	Protected from Mongols; new threats emerge from prosperous provincial warlords; the imperial family divides into rival factions; new dynasty of shoguns emerges; Zen Buddhism becomes influential
Northern Russia	→	Unknown—interaction with Mongols should have made Russians vulnerable	→	Grand Duchy of Moscow begins to throw off Mongol rule in late 1300s
India	→	Unknown—although Silk Roads and sea trade connected it to other parts of Eurasia and Africa	→	Sultanate of Delhi profits from Mongols' decline, initiating policy of conquest; Turkic elite responsible for war and revenue collecting eventually secedes; Hindu/Muslim relations are always problematic
Southeast Asia	→	Unknown—trade routes from China, Europe, Africa should have made the region vulnerable	→	Establishment of powerful state on Java (Majapahit), to control trade with China and India, creating stable and prosperous society
Pacific	→	Isolation	→	Existing societies expand; shift from hunting to agriculture in New Zealand; Chimú state (Chan Chan) flourishes in Peru
Sub-Saharan West Africa	→	Unclear— trans-Saharan trade routes should have carried plague	→	Mali becomes rich and powerful from control over gold trade; European need for gold creates obsession with reaching Mali

northeast trade winds. Jaume Ferrer's shipwreck was symbolic. Few similar voyages were recorded in the second half of the fourteenth century.

Human foes supplemented the plague, famine, and cold. In 1354, an earthquake demolished the walls of the Byzantine city of Gallipoli at the entrance to the Dardanelles, which divides Europe from Anatolia. Ottoman Turks were waiting to take over the ruins, inaugurating a history of European anxiety about the defensibility of Christendom's eastern Mediterranean frontier – anxiety that would last, with fluctuations, for over 200 years. In the northeast, pagan Lithuanians eroded the conquests of the Teutonic Knights along the Baltic (see Chapter 13). To some extent, the gradual diffusion of Catholic faith, under Polish influence, into Lithuania made good these losses—for Christendom, if not for the Germans. Meanwhile, in parts of Eastern Europe, state-building continued, under rulers whose longevity helped bring stability. The period of the Black Death was spanned by the reigns of Charles the Great in Bohemia (r. 1346–1378), Casimir the Great in Poland (r. 1333–1370) and Louis the Great of Hungary (r. 1342–1382). On the whole, even in Western Europe, the effects of plague favored the state, because afflicted populations turned to monarchs as potential saviors and were willing to trust them with enhanced powers. Even peasant rebels tended to focus their resentments on the rest of the elite and appealed for aid directly—albeit, usually, unsuccessfully—to monarchs.

In the Mongol dominions, the case was different. Mongol expansion ceased. Russian principalities began to pry themselves free of Mongol control. The Mongol state in Persia fragmented, and the last Il-khan died in 1343. From the ruins of Mongol domination, a new state arose in Anatolia, under a Turkish dynasty, known as the Ottomans, whose center of operations from 1326 was at the formerly Byzantine city of Bursa, in what is now western Turkey, from where they were able to profit from the dislocation the Black Death caused (see Map 14.9). They gradually came to dominate Byzantium, invaded the Balkans, and established a close trading relationship with the Italian city of Genoa. Toward the end of the fourteenth century, they began to construct a navy, to extend their power into the Mediterranean. In China, as we shall see in the next chapter, the strain of the ecological crisis of the mid–fourteenth century contributed to the dissolution of the Mongol state and its replacement by a new regime of native Chinese rulers, under the Ming dynasty.

At a deeper level than that of the rise and fall of states and political elites, the coming of the age of plagues, made worse by unpredictable changes in climate, affected the balance of population—and therefore of power—among Eurasian civilizations. Natural disasters do not usually affect population trends for long. Population can recover with surprising speed. Recovery was harder in the wake of the Black Death because, although plagues became less ferocious, and populations built up immunity, pestilence affected the same regions for centuries to come, at a rate too rapid to enumerate. In Egypt, for instance, visitations of plague struck more than once, on average, every four years in the two centuries following the Black Death. The population of Eurasia probably remained static during the late fourteenth century and for most of the fifteenth. In the long run, of the three culture areas that suffered most, it appears that the Islamic world may have been more affected than Christendom or China, both of which seem to have recovered faster and resisted better. This can only be a tentative conclusion, because the evidence is unreliable. It does seem,

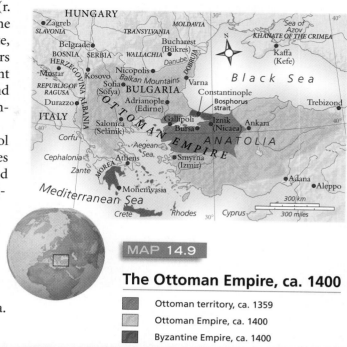

MAP 14.9

The Ottoman Empire, ca. 1400

- Ottoman territory, ca. 1359
- Ottoman Empire, ca. 1400
- Byzantine Empire, ca. 1400

Chronology

1290	England expels Jews
Thirteenth and fourteenth centuries	Climate change in Northern Hemisphere; population rises in New Zealand and agriculture replaces hunting as way of life; rise of Chimú state (Chan Chan) in Peru
1309–1310	Thames River freezes (London)
1315–1316	Heavy rains in northern Europe
1320s	Plague epidemics in southwest and central China
1324	Mansa Musa makes *hajj* to Mecca
1325–1351	Reign of Ibn Tughluq (Delhi Sultanate, India)
1330s	Mortality rates in northeast China reach 90 percent
1335	Ashikaga Tokauji seizes shogunate (Japan)
1343	Last Il-khan dies in Persia
1346	Plague reported in Crimea (Black Sea)
1347	Last Icelandic voyage to America
1347–1349	Plague rages in Western Europe, Middle East, and North Africa
1350s	Peasant rebellions spread in China
1351	Plague strikes southern Russia
1352	Ibn Battuta sets off for Mali
1354	Ottoman Turks cross Dardanelles to occupy Byzantine city of Gallipoli
1360	Plague in China
1389	Death of Hayan Wuruk (Majapahit in Java)
ca.1400	Settlements in American Southwest abandoned

FIGURE 14.2 THE POPULATION OF EUROPE, CHINA, AND THE ISLAMIC WORLD COMPARED

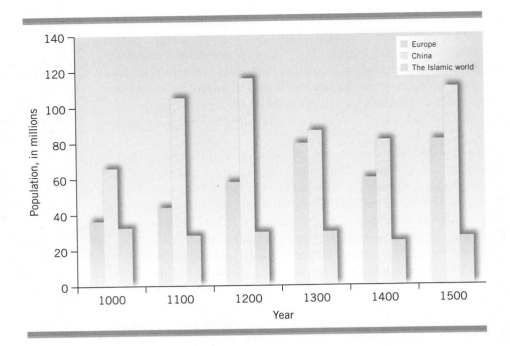

however, that the populations of Christendom and China recovered to preplague levels by the end of the fifteenth century, whereas in Egypt, Syria and, perhaps, other parts of the Islamic world, the recovery did not even begin until then. The increase of population thereafter was generally slower in the Islamic world than in Christendom and China until the twentieth century (see Figure 14.2). If correct, this conclusion may help to explain one of history's great shifts in wealth, power, and every kind of dynamism—away from the Islamic world. Whereas in what we call the Middle Ages, the Islamic world had contributed enormously— far more than Christendom—to cultural exchange in Eurasia, and had tended to win out in conflicts with Christendom, Muslim power dwindled over the succeeding centuries. The relative eclipse of the Islamic world and the relative ascent of Europe are major themes of the age of plague and, therefore, of the next two parts of this book.

PROBLEMS AND PARALLELS

1. How might Mongol rule have spread plague during the fourteenth century? How did rulers like Hayan Wuruk in Java and Ibn Tughluq in India profit from the decline of Mongol power? Why did the fading of the Mongol threat lead to political instability in Japan?

2. How did the climate change and age of plagues that began during the fourteenth century affect Western Europe, China, and the Islamic world? Why did peasants in China and Europe embrace millenarian ideas?

3. In what parts of the globe did plague and climate cause the most harm during the fourteenth century? Why was geographic isolation an advantage during the age of plague? Why was Mali under Mansa Musa so rich and powerful?

4. How was climate change related to plague? How did the onset of the Little Ice Age affect agriculture and settlement in Western Europe? How did climate change affect the people of the American Southwest?

5. Why is it difficult or impossible to understand the medical causes of the Black Death? What did West Europeans and Muslims believe caused the plague, and how did they try to treat it?

6. Who were the "winners" and "losers" in the plague years (other than the immediate survivors and victims)? Why did many Europeans blame the Jews for the Black Death? How did the status of upper-class women change in Western Europe and Japan during the fourteenth century?

READ ON ▶ ▶ ▶

H. Lamb, *Climate, History and the Modern World* (1995) is the classic work on its subject, complemented by B. Fagan's *The Little Ice Age* (2000). Classic works—now superseded on many points—on the global history of disease are H. Zinsser, *Rats, Lice, and History* (1996), and W. H. McNeill, *Plagues and Peoples* (1998). S. Cohn, *The Black Death* (2003) is indispensable for the plagues in Europe and for the epidemiology of the Black Death. N. Cantor, *In the Wake of the Plague* (2001) has some interesting material on social effects. R. Horrox, *The Black Death* (1994) is a valuable anthology of source material. M. W. Dols, *The Black Death in the Middle East* (1977)—though corrected in some respects by Cohn's work—is invaluable on its subject. As so often, the edition by H. Gibb and C. Beckingham of *The Travels of Ibn Battuta* (1994) is an indispensable guide.

On China, the *Cambridge History of China,* vols. 6–8, is fundamental, and the collection of essays edited by P. J. Smith and R. von Glahn, *The Song-Yuan-Ming Transition in Chinese History* (2003) crackles with revisionism. For Europe, M. Jones, ed., *The New Cambridge Medieval History* vi, (2000) is a comprehensive survey. On the problems of the status of women, G. Duby and M. Perrot, eds., *A History of Women* (2000) is the leading work; particularly useful work on the subjects touched in this chapter includes R. Smith, "Coping with Uncertainty: Women's Tenure of Customary Land in England," in J. Kermode, ed., *Enterprise and Individual in Fifteenth-Century England* (1997), and L. Mirrer, ed., *Upon My Husband's Death* (1992).

For Hohokam, the article by P. Crown, "The Hohokam of the American Southwest," *Journal of World History*, vol.iv (1990) is a good introduction. G. J. Gumerman, ed., *Themes in Southwest Prehistory* (1994) contains some important contributions.

On the Jews, N. Cohn, *Europe's Inner Demons* (2001) is a controversial but gripping attempt to trace the origins of anti-Semitism. P. Johnson, *History of the Jews* (1988)—though superseded in its coverage of the early period—remains the best general history. L. Kochan, *The Jew and his History* (1985) is a good introduction.

On peasant millenarianism, N. Cohn, *The Pursuit of the Millennium* (1970) remains unsurpassed. On Japan, J. Mass, ed., *Origins of Japan's Medieval World* (1997) amounts to a fine history of the fourteenth century. The Delhi sultanate is covered in R. Majumdar, *The History and Culture of the Indian People*, vol.4 (1951) and P. Jackson, *The Delhi Sultanate* (1999). On Java, T. Pigeaud, ed., *Java in the Fourteenth Century* (1960) is a marvelous edition of the poem I cite about Hayan Wuruk. D. G. Hall in N. Tarling, ed., *The Cambridge History of Southeast Asia*, vol.I (1992), provides further help. On Mali, N. Levtzion, *Ancient Ghana and Mali* (1986) is highly accessible, and D. T. Niane covers the subject expertly in *UNESCO History of Africa*, vol.iv (1998), but the classic work by E. W. R. Bovill, *The Golden Trade of the Moors* (1995), can still be read with pleasure. For the Pacific, J. van Tilburg, *Easter Island* (1995) is the only fully reliable work on that island. J. Belich, *Making Peoples* (2002) is insuperable on New Zealand. On Ozette, see R. Kirk and R. D. Dougherty, *Hunters of the Whale* (1998). On the Chimú, R. Keatinge, *Peruvian Prehistory* (1988) is standard.

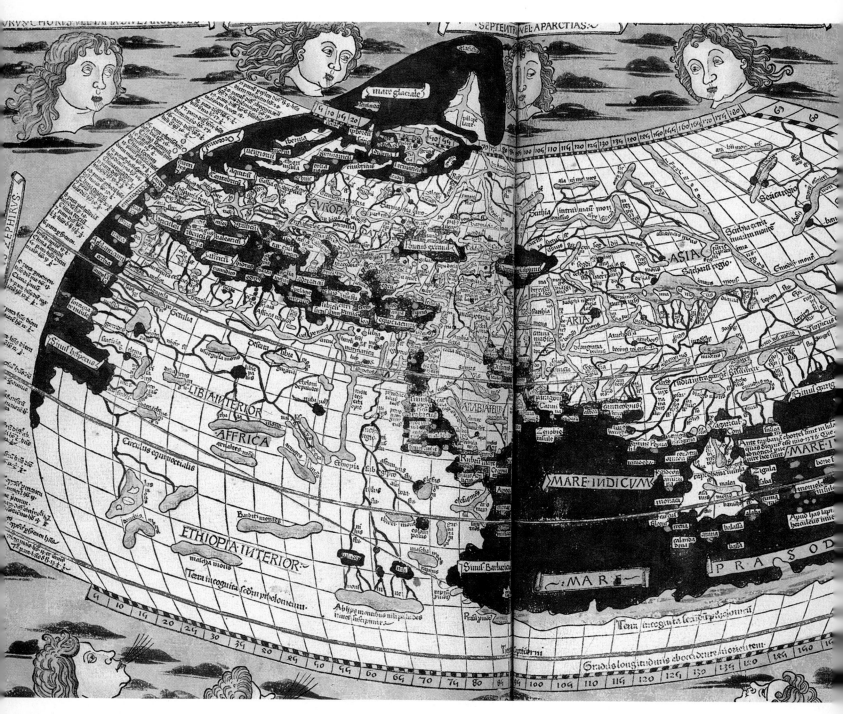

▲ **Claudius Ptolemy's Geography,** written in Alexandria, Egypt in the second century, was still the standard source for how educated Europeans saw the world in the fifteenth century. Printed editions, like this one of 1482, usually included attempts to map the world as Ptolemy described it. Common features include a grid of lines of latitude and longitude—the system Ptolemy devised for locating places in relation to one another; the exaggerated size and prominence of Sri Lanka; locating the source of the Nile in mountains beyond large lakes deep in Africa; and showing the Indian Ocean as landlocked, which undermined navigators' confidence that they could reach India and Asia by sea.

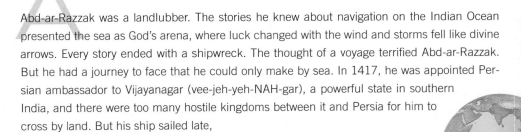

INDIAN OCEAN

Abd-ar-Razzak was a landlubber. The stories he knew about navigation on the Indian Ocean presented the sea as God's arena, where luck changed with the wind and storms fell like divine arrows. Every story ended with a shipwreck. The thought of a voyage terrified Abd-ar-Razzak. But he had a journey to face that he could only make by sea. In 1417, he was appointed Persian ambassador to Vijayanagar (vee-jeh-yeh-NAH-gar), a powerful state in southern India, and there were too many hostile kingdoms between it and Persia for him to cross by land. But his ship sailed late,

> so that the favorable time for departing by sea, that is to say the beginning or middle of the monsoon, was allowed to pass, and we came to the end of the monsoon, which is the season when tempests and attacks from pirates are to be dreaded. . . . As soon as I caught the smell of the vessel, and all the terrors of the sea presented themselves before me, I fell into so deep a faint that for three days breathing alone indicated that life remained within me. When I came a little to myself, the merchants, who were my intimate friends, cried with one voice that the time for navigation was past, and that everyone who put to sea at this season was alone responsible for his death.

Abd-ar-Razzak's predicament, however, had a positive side. The late monsoon is so fierce that ships speed before it. He made the journey in only 19 days, about two-thirds of the time one might normally expect.

Abd-ar-Razzak's voyage demonstrates the crucial importance of winds in world history. Most of the Earth's surface area is sea. Long-range communications have to traverse wide waters. Throughout the age of sail—that is, for almost the entire history of travel—winds and currents set the limits of what was possible: the routes, the rates, the mutually accessible cultures. More particularly, Abd-ar-Razzak's experience illustrates the paradox of Indian Ocean navigation in his day. The monsoon winds made travel speedy, but the Indian Ocean was stormy, unsafe, and hard to get into and out of. Access from the east was barely possible in summer, when typhoons tore into the shores. Fierce storms guarded the southern approaches. No one who knew the reputation of these waters cared to venture between about 10 and 30 degrees south and 60 or 90 degrees east during the hurricane season. Arab legends claimed the region was impassable. Many European maps of the fifteenth century depicted the Indian Ocean as landlocked—literally inaccessible by sea. Yet it was the biggest and richest zone of long-range commerce in the world.

FOCUS questions

Why were some African empires able to expand on such an impressive scale during this period?

What role did geographic diversity play in the Inca and Aztec Empires?

What strong new empires arose on the Eurasian borderlands?

Why did China turn away from overseas expansion in the fifteenth century?

Why did Europe begin to reach out across the oceans in the late 1400s?

By the end of the fifteenth century, European navigators had found a way to penetrate it. Meanwhile, the Atlantic was developing into a rival zone, with transoceanic routes ready to be exploited. Indeed, seafaring on the Atlantic would transform the world by bringing cultures that had been torn apart into contact, conflict, commerce, and cultural and ecological exchange. The divergent, isolated worlds of ancient and medieval times were coming together to form the interconnected world we inhabit today.

How did it happen? How did the world rebound from the plagues and climate changes of the fourteenth century? For one thing, populations gradually acquired immunity against plague, as susceptible people died and those who were naturally most resistant passed on their genes. As for worsening climates, survivors relocated or just got used to colder, wetter conditions. To some extent, technological advance made up for—indeed, was a response to—decreased population. As we have seen, across Eurasia, and in parts of Africa that were in contact with Eurasia, the long period of accelerated exchange in the Song and Mongol eras had equipped expanding economies with improved technology (see Chapter 13). In regions that escaped the catastrophes of the fourteenth century, long-term population growth continued to strengthen states and economies. So it is not surprising that the world of the late fourteenth and fifteenth centuries was a world in recovery and even a world of resumed expansion.

Toward the end of the period, from about 1460 on, in states in widely separated parts of the world, expansion speeded up like springs uncoiling. An age of expansion really did begin, but the phenomenon was of an expanding world, not, as some historians say, of European expansion. The world did not wait passively for European outreach to transform it, as if touched by a magic wand. Other societies were already working magic of their own, turning states into empires and cultures into civilizations. Beyond the reach of the recurring plagues that stopped demographic growth in much of Eurasia, some of the most dynamic and rapidly expanding societies of the fifteenth century were in the Americas and sub-Saharan Africa. Indeed, in terms of territorial expansion and military effectiveness against opponents, African and American empires outclassed any state in Western Europe until the sixteenth century.

As we shall see, some European communities played big and growing roles. And their expansion did have unique features—exceptional range, above all, which enabled people from Western Europe to cross unprecedented distances on previously unexplored routes. But to appreciate what was special about Europe, we have to see it in global context and acknowledge that expansion was a worldwide phenomenon. If we start in Africa and approach Europe only after looking at the Americas and following Abd-ar-Razzak's route in Asia, we can begin to make sense of the peculiar features of the history of Atlantic-side European peoples, as they launched empires that will take up more and more space in the rest of the book.

FRAGILE EMPIRES IN AFRICA

East Africa

Ethiopia emerged relatively early from its period of quiescence following the rise and stagnation of the Solomid dynasty in the thirteenth century (see Chapter 11). In the late fourteenth century, the highland realm again began to reach beyond its mountains to dominate surrounding regions. Monasteries became schools of missionaries whose task was to consolidate Ethiopian power in the conquered pagan lands of Shoa and Gojam. Rulers, meanwhile, concentrated on reopening their ancient outlet to the Red Sea and thereby the Indian Ocean. This they accomplished by conquering the hostile lowlanders and recapturing the port of Massaweh in 1403. By then, Ethiopian rule stretched into the Great Rift valley. Trade northward along the valley was in slaves, ivory, gold, and ingredients of perfumes. Ethiopia largely controlled it. The resulting wealth funded defense of the empire and fueled expansionist ambitions. European visitors multiplied, as Ethiopia's Massaweh road became a standard route to reach the Indian Ocean.

Although Ethiopia conquered no more territory after 1469, the lives of saints, which are a major source for Ethiopian history in this period, tell of internal expansion. Wasteland was converted to farmland and settled by monks. In 1481, the Ethiopian church resumed contact with Rome, where the pope provided a church to house visiting Ethiopian monks. When Portuguese diplomatic missions began to arrive in Ethiopia—the first in the 1490s, a second in 1520—"men and gold and provisions like the sands of the sea and the stars in the sky" impressed them. As we shall see in the next chapter, however, they overestimated the empire's stability. Ethiopia had probably already overreached its resources.

"The world did not wait passively for European outreach to transform it, as if touched by a magic wand. Other societies were already working magic of their own, turning states into empires and cultures into civilizations."

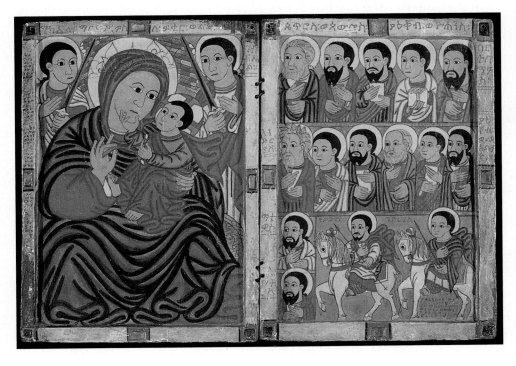

Virgin and Child. In the dynamic reign of Emperor Zara Yacob (1434–1468), Ethiopia conquered an outlet to the sea, extended and fortified its land frontier, pacified and Christianized pagan peoples, and made contact with Europe. But the enforcement of religious orthodoxy was perhaps closest to the emperor's heart. He commissioned many paintings of the Virgin and Child, often shown guarded, as here, by armed angels and worshipped by warrior saints.

Chronology: The Reemergence of Ethiopia	
Late fourteenth century	Ethiopia expands into surrounding regions
1403	Recapture of port of Massaweh
1469	End of period of conquest
1481	Ethiopian church resumes contact with Rome
1490s	First Portuguese diplomatic missions arrive in Ethiopia

Southward from Ethiopia, at the far end of the Rift valley, lay the gold-rich Zambezi valley and the productive plateau beyond, which stretched to the south as far as the Limpopo River, and was rich in salt, gold, and elephants. Like Ethiopia, these areas looked toward the Indian Ocean for long-range trade with the economies of maritime Asia.

Unlike Ethiopia, communities in the Zambezi valley had ready access to the ocean, but they faced a potentially more difficult problem. Their outlets to the sea lay below the reach of the monsoon system and, therefore, beyond the reach of the normal routes of trade. Still, adventurous merchants—most of them, probably, from southern Arabia—risked the voyage to bring manufactured goods from Asia in trade for gold and ivory. Some of the most vivid evidence comes from the mosque in Kilwa (Kil-WAH), in modern Tanzania, where fifteenth-century Chinese porcelain bowls line the inside of the dome.

Further evidence of the effects of trade lie inland between the Zambezi and the Limpopo Rivers, where fortified, stone-built administrative centers—called **zimbabwes**—had been common for centuries. Now, in the late fourteenth and fifteenth centuries, the zimbabwes entered their greatest age. The most famous, Great Zimbabwe, included a formidable citadel on a hill 350 feet high, but remains of other citadels are scattered over the land (see Map 15.1). Near stone buildings, the beef-fed elite were buried with gifts: gold, jewelery, jeweled ironwork, large copper ingots, and Chinese porcelain that Arab traders brought across the Indian Ocean to Kilwa and Sofala, another great coastal city.

In the second quarter of the fifteenth century, the center of power shifted northward to the Zambezi valley, with the expansion of a new regional power. Mwene Mutapa (MWEH-nee MOO-TAH-pah), as it was called, arose during the northward migration of bands of warriors from what are now parts of Mozambique and KwaZulu-Natal. When one of their leaders conquered the middle Zambezi valley—a land rich in cloth, salt, and elephants—he took the title Mwene Mutapa, or "lord of the tribute payers," a name that became extended to the state. From about the mid–fifteenth century, the pattern of trade routes altered as Mwene Mutapa's conquests spread eastward toward the coast. But Mwene Mutapa never reached the ocean. Native merchants, who traded at inland fairs, had no interest in a direct outlet to the sea. They did well enough using middlemen on the coast and had no incentive for or experience of ocean trade. Like Mali (see Chapter 14), Mwene Mutapa was a landlocked empire, sustained by trade in gold and salt. The colonists were drawn, not driven, northward, though a decline in the navigability of the Sabi River may have stimulated the move.

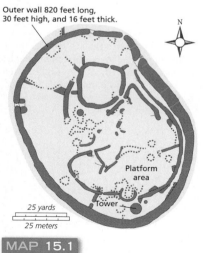

Outer wall 820 feet long, 30 feet high, and 16 feet thick.

Platform area

Tower

25 yards

25 meters

MAP 15.1

Great Zimbabwe

■ stone construction
⋯⋯ walls in ruin
— drain

West Africa

New states emerged in West Africa, too, but here the opportunities were the result, at least in part, of the decline of the old regional power, Mali (see Map 15.2). Like many empires of promise in out-of-the-way places, Mali became a victim of its relative isolation. From about 1360, a power struggle pitted the descendants of Mansa Musa against those of his brother, Mansa Sulayman. At

The turreted walls of Great Zimbabwe surround a 350-foot-high hill, crowned by a formidable citadel, which housed the elite, who ate beef and were buried with gifts of gold, copper, jewels, and Chinese porcelain. Though it was the biggest of the stone-built settlements of the period, Great Zimbabwe was typical, in style and substance, of other buildings in the region south of the Zambezi River during what we think of as the late Middle Ages.

about the end of the century, the Songhay, a people from lower down the Niger River, broke away and Mali lost Gao (gow). This was disastrous for Mali, because Gao was one of the great trading cities between the rain forest and the desert. Traders could now outflank Mali's trading monopoly. Mali was further weakened in the 1430s when invaders from the Sahara seized its northernmost towns.

Two decades later, in the 1450s, when Portuguese expeditions, pushing up the river Gambia, made the first recorded European contact with Mali, the Mansa's power was virtually confined to the original heartland. The result was a tragedy for the history of the world, for the absence of a strong African state undermined Europeans' view of black Africans as equals. The Portuguese expected to find a great, rich empire. Instead, they found Mali a ramshackle wreck. Their disappointment prejudiced them, and they wondered if black Africans had any capacity for political greatness. Thus, in maps, instead of the magnificent depictions of the Mansa of Mali typical of the fourteenth century—bearded and costumed in European fashion—the ruler of Mali became a figure of fun. Though some Europeans continued to treat black Africans as equals—and the Portuguese crown, in particular, maintained the affectation that black kings were fellow monarchs on a par with those of Europe—from now on, white people in Africa could nourish convictions of superiority. Although, as we shall see, other African realms or regions replaced Mali in European esteem and became famous for wealth or as places of opportunity for European adventurers, their elites never again commanded the same prestige in Europe.

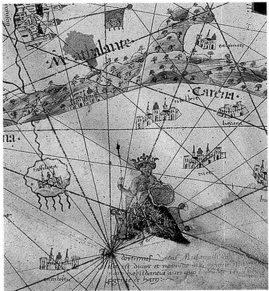

A European view of the King of Mali, ca. 1480. By the 1430s, familiarity with the West African kingdom of Mali had caused disillusionment among European visitors, who expected magnificence of the sort depicted in the previous century in the Catalan Atlas (see Chapter 14). But Mali had declined, and its ruler appeared in this map by Gabriel Vallseca of Majorca, and others of the time, as a comically dressed and even laughable figure.

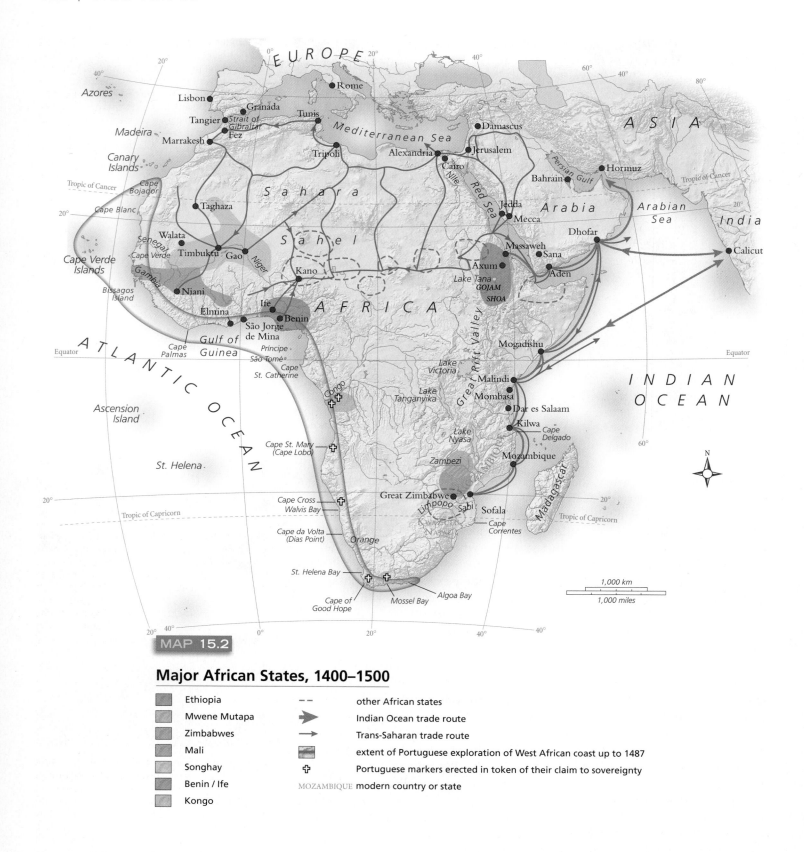

MAP 15.2

Major African States, 1400–1500

▨	Ethiopia	--		other African states
▨	Mwene Mutapa	➤		Indian Ocean trade route
▨	Zimbabwes	→		Trans-Saharan trade route
▨	Mali	▨		extent of Portuguese exploration of West African coast up to 1487
▨	Songhay	✚		Portuguese markers erected in token of their claim to sovereignty
▨	Benin / Ife	MOZAMBIQUE		modern country or state
▨	Kongo			

Songhay (SOHNG-eye) gradually succeeded Mali as the most powerful state in the region, but it never controlled as much of the Saharan trade as Mali had. At first, isolated areas were converted to Islam, but Muhammad Touray Askia, an upstart general who used Islam to justify seizing the throne, wrenched Songhay into the Islamic mainstream in the late fifteenth century. In 1497, he undertook a pilgrimage to Mecca on a scale of magnificence calculated to echo that of Mansa Musa in 1324–1325 (see Chapter 14). Askia's ascent to power represented the triumph of Islam over the pagan magic that some of his predecessors and opponents claimed to wield. His victory also ensured that Sahelian Africa—the band of dry grasslands south of the Sahara—would be predominantly Muslim. His alliance with the Muslim intelligentsia made Songhay a state "favored by God" in the eyes of religious Muslims—the class on which the state depended for administrators. He stimulated trade by imposing peace and so increasing Saharan merchants' sense of security. He promoted a modest sort of capitalism by concentrating resources in the hands of religious foundations, which had the personnel and range of contacts to maximize their holdings' potential. New canals, wells, dikes, and reservoirs scored the land. Cultivated terrain was extended, especially for rice, which had long been known in the region but never previously farmed on a large scale.

Songhay, like Mali before it, benefited from the trade routes of the Sahara, which linked the Mediterranean coast to the Niger valley. The Niger River is navigable for almost its entire length, providing access to rich goldfields and the best national communications system in Africa. At the same time, the Atlantic's adverse winds and currents limited opportunities for long-range communications by sea. The states and cultures of the tropical forest and coast in the African "bulge" were therefore limited to contending for strictly regional power and wealth. Nevertheless, they have left plenty of evidence of economic expansion and of the growing wealth and power of their kings in the fifteenth century. There are, for instance, the fortifications of the city-state of Benin and the splendid metal weapons, adornments and courtly furnishings of Benin and the Ife.

The whole African coast from Senegambia to the mouth of the Niger impressed Europeans at the time. In 1486, the Portuguese crown celebrated the baptism of a Senegambian chief in Lisbon with a lavish display. The trading post that Portugal opened at São Jorge da Mina, on the underside of the African bulge, in 1482, appeared on maps as a fantasy city. It suited the purposes of the Portuguese monarchs to exaggerate the grandeur, but their propaganda reflected the reality of a region of rich kingdoms, busy commerce, and patches of urban life.

Farther south, too, in the Congo Basin, the opportunities for states to reach out by sea were limited. The Kingdom of Kongo dominated the Congo River's navigable lower reaches, probably from the mid–fourteenth century. The ambitions of its rulers became evident when Portuguese

Chronology: The Portuguese in West Africa and the Congo	
1450s	First reported Portuguese contact with Mali
1480s	Portuguese make contact with kingdom of Kongo
1482	West African trading post of São Jorge da Mina established
1486	Senegambian chief baptized in Lisbon

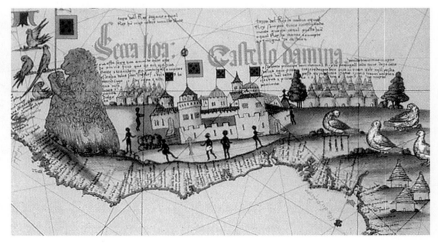

The fort of São Jorge da Mina, founded by the Portuguese in 1482 on the underside of West Africa's bulge, never really looked like this depiction on a richly decorated world map sold to an Italian ambassador in Lisbon in 1502. The turrets and spires are fanciful, but convey the image the mapmaker wanted to show: of exotic grandeur and financial success, since the fort attracted much of the region's trade in gold and slaves.

A CLOSER LOOK

A West African view of the Portuguese

The court art of Benin, in the Niger Delta of West Africa, preserves precious images of Portuguese visitors, as native artists saw them in the sixteenth century. The Obas, as the rulers of Benin were called, frequently asked for Portuguese military help, sometimes offering to adopt Christianity in exchange.

The Portuguese soldier, carved in ivory, is supporting the Oba's saltcellar. Salt was a precious commodity in Benin.

The soldier's short spear, feathered straw hat, and sweatband are local touches, but the rest of his clothes, his beard, his sword, and his pectoral cross were exotic emblems to the African artist who carved them.

African, Nigeria, Edo peoples, court of Benin, Salt-cellar: Portuguese Figure, 15th-16th century, Ivory; H. 7–1/8 in. (18.1 cm). The Metropolitan Museum of Art, Louis V. Bell and Rogers Funds, 1972. (1972.63ab) Photograph by Stan Reis. Photograph © 1984, The Metropolitan Museum of Art

How is this ivory carving evidence of West African expansion in the fifteenth century?

explorers established contact in the 1480s. Kongo enthusiastically adopted the religion and technology of the visitors. The kingdom became host to Portuguese missionaries, craftsmen, and mercenaries. The royal residence was rebuilt in Portuguese style. The kings issued documents in Portuguese, and members of the royal family went to Portugal for their education. One prince became an archbishop, and the kings continued to have Portuguese baptismal names for centuries thereafter. In emulating Portugal, the kings of Kongo were, of course, serving their own self-interest. Equipping their armies with European firepower, for example, gave the kings a military advantage over their neighbors. They gained territory and, more importantly, slaves, many of whom they sold to the Portuguese for export.

The Portuguese connection made Kongo the best-documented kingdom in West Africa in the sixteenth century. Missionary reports extolled the zeal of the "angelic" ruler Affonso I (r. 1506–1545) and commended him for "burning idolaters along with their idols," but the monarch's own letters to the king of Portugal reveal tensions with white slavers, who infringed the royal monopoly of European trade goods and seized slaves indiscriminately.

Although Ethiopia, Mwene Mutapa, Songhay, and Kongo were all formidable regional powers, and although many small states of the West African coast expanded commercially and territorially, little of this activity was on an unprecedented scale (see Map 15.2). Ethiopia's resumed rise was part of a sequence of expansion and decline that had been going on for centuries. Songhay was the latest in a series of empires in the Sahel. Trading states had long studded the underside of the West African bulge. Mwene Mutapa was the successor state of the builders of the zimbabwes. If there was something new out of the Africa at this time, it was part of a wider phenomenon. The empires grew at impressive rates and to impressive extents because they were in touch with other phenomena of commercial and political expansion: Songhay across the Sahara, Ethiopia and Mwene Mutapa across the Indian Ocean, the coastal trading cities and Kongo with the Portuguese. In the Americas, however, in the late fifteenth century, even states that had to contend with isolation could expand on a new scale.

"If there was something new out of the Africa at this time, it was part of a wider phenomenon. The empires grew at impressive rates and to impressive extents because they were in touch with other phenomena of commercial and political expansion . . ."

ECOLOGICAL IMPERIALISM IN THE AMERICAS

Since the inventive historian, Alfred Crosby, coined the term **ecological imperialism** in 1972, historians have used it to refer to the sweeping environmental changes European imperialists introduced in regions they colonized. The term also suits Native American empires, especially in mountainous regions of Mesoamerica and the Andes, where, as we have seen, the key to success in large-scale state-building lay in combining diverse regions and exploiting the complementary products of contrasting ecosystems.

The Inca Empire

In the late fifteenth century, the world's fastest-growing empire was the Inca Empire of Peru. Inca chronology is always uncertain because until the 1530s, the Incas made records in forms that are now indecipherable. Nonetheless, evidence suggests that they built their empire within a concentrated period—all during the reigns of three rulers in the late fifteenth and early sixteenth centuries.

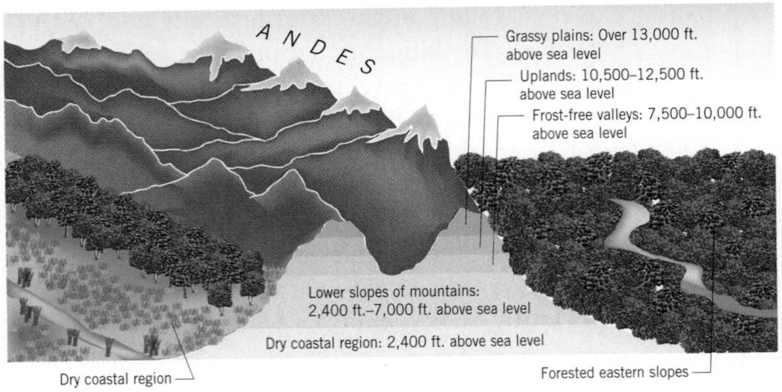

FIGURE 15.1 MICROCLIMATES OF THE ANDES. The Andean environment packs tremendous ecological diversity into a small space, with various climatic zones at different altitudes, contrasting microclimates in the valleys, and tropical forest and the ocean close at hand.

Grassy plains: Over 13,000 ft. above sea level

Uplands: 10,500–12,500 ft. above sea level

Frost-free valleys: 7,500–10,000 ft. above sea level

Lower slopes of mountains: 2,400 ft.–7,000 ft. above sea level

Dry coastal region: 2,400 ft. above sea level

Dry coastal region

Forested eastern slopes

ANDES

"The Inca realm encompassed coastal lowlands and the fringes of the Amazonian rain forest. The tribute system was based on the exchange of products between contrasting zones, as a form of insurance against disaster."

Probably early in the second half of the fifteenth century, the founders of the Inca state descended from the highlands to find fertile land. They occupied Cuzco in what is today Peru, which became their biggest city, and began subjugating their neighbors. Their story was typically Andean. They gathered many diverse environments into one state to facilitate exchanging and stockpiling a wide range of products. It was the story of Chavín de Huántar in 1000 B.C.E. (see Chapter 4). The Incas, however, took this well-established practice to new lengths. Theirs was one of the most environmentally diverse empires of the time. It was long and thin, with the Andes forming its spine and creating valleys and microclimates. Abrupt mountains multiplied microclimates, where sun, wind, and rain hit different slopes in different ways (see Figure 15.1). The Inca realm encompassed coastal lowlands and the fringes of the Amazonian rain forest. The tribute system was based on the exchange of products between contrasting zones, as a form of insurance against disaster. When the maize of the lowlands failed, for instance, potatoes from the highlands might still be abundant. The Inca uprooted populations and transferred them to new locations according to the needs of the system.

Economic security, however, came at a political price. To maintain the state, the Incas had to acquire new territories, leading to hectic and, in the long run, perhaps, unsustainable expansion. Moreover, their methods of subjugation were extreme. For example, they extinguished the coastal civilization of Chimú (see Chapter 14), razing its capital at Chan Chan almost to the ground and deporting its entire population. An Inca ruler was said to have drowned 20,000 enemy warriors when he conquered the Cañaris. The survivors became irreconcilable opponents. Many subject-peoples harbored grievances arising from memories of massacred warriors and forced migrations. Even the Incas' allies and elites were dissatisfied. The Checa, for instance, a people important to the Inca system of control, because their homeland straddled the route from Cuzco to the coast, never forgave the Inca for breaking his promise to perform ritual dances at their principal shrine in acknowledgment of their alliance. The Inca never seemed to have enough rewards to go around. The cults of dead leaders—who lay, mummified, in expensive shrines maintained by huge payrolls—existed to appease key Inca clans and factions, whose resources they boosted at the state's expense because tribute had to be diverted to meet the costs. Toward the end of the fifteenth century, the Inca Empire approached its greatest extent, from Quito (KEE-toh) in what is today Ecuador in the north, to the Valle Central in what is today Chile in the south. But at its core, the empire was shaky.

The Aztec Empire

In the same period, rapid expansion and environmental diversity characterized Mesoamerica. Here, an exceptionally dynamic state grew from the city of Tenochtitlán (tehnoch-teet-LAHN) in the valley of Mexico (and some neighboring, allied cities). Tenochtitlán stood in the middle of a lake, some 5,000 feet above sea level. It could not grow some of the staples of Mesoamerican life or any of the luxuries elites demanded for social or ritual purposes. The ground was swampy, and there was too little cultivable soil to grow enough maize and beans to feed the city. Tenochtitlán was too high and the climate too severe for cacao and cotton. Its people, whom we have traditionally called Aztecs, had only two options: poverty or warfare. They chose the latter.

Aztec expansion, like Inca expansion, was largely a late fifteenth- and early sixteenth-century phenomenon (see Map 15.3). At its peak, the Aztec Empire stretched from the Pánuco River in the north to what is now the Mexican-Guatemalan border on the Pacific coast, covering nearly 100,000 square miles and including hundreds of tributary communities.

The tribute collected demonstrated the power and reach and the ecological diversity of the regions from which the Aztecs extorted tribute. The Aztec bureaucracy meticulously listed and depicted it. From the "hot countries" in the south came ornamental feathers and jaguar pelts, jade, amber, gold, rubber for ritual ball games, and resin for incense. Overlapping regions supplied cacao, the essential ingredient of the addictive, high-status drink essential at Aztec ceremonies and parties. Ornamental shells arrived from the Gulf Coast and live eagles, deerskins, and tobacco from the mountain lands that fringed the valley of Mexico. For war and for the ball game, which was a form of mock warfare and an aristocratic exercise, Aztec nobles and priests dressed as gods, So on almost every folio of the tribute roll appear magnificent ritual garments and divine disguises. The tribute system brought necessities as well as luxuries: hundreds of thousands of bushels of maize and beans every year, with hundreds of thousands of cotton garments and quilted cotton suits of armor. Finally, there was the product that best expressed Aztec power and—perhaps in Aztec minds—supplied the blood that fueled the universe: human-sacrifice victims, captured in war or tendered in tribute. In 1487, for instance, at the dedication of a temple in Tenochtitlán, thousands of captives were said to have been slaughtered at once.

The Aztec system was complex, in the sense that tributary networks linked hundreds of communities. Some communities exchanged tribute, often collecting it from some tributaries to pass part of it on to others. Tenochtitlán was at the summit of the system, but it left most communities to govern themselves as long as they paid tribute. This was contrary to the highly interventionist politics of the Incas. According to records copied in the sixteenth century, Tenochtitlán only garrisoned or directly ruled 22 communities. The Aztecs did,

The Inca city of Machu Picchu in Peru is a miracle of urban engineering. It was built on a sharp 2,000-foot rise in the high Andes. Unrecorded in colonial times, it was discovered early in the twentieth century when the eccentric and adventurous American archaeologist, Hiram Bingham, was searching for another lost Inca city, Vilcamba. Unknown to Bingham, however, Vilcamba was in the tropical lowlands of Peru. The vast difference in climate between the two cities is stunning evidence of the environmental diversity of the Inca world.

MAP 15.3

The Aztec and Inca Empires, ca. 1500

- ▨ Maximum extent of Aztec Empire
- ▨ Maximum extent of Inca Empire
- ● Important center
- *MAYA* native state or people
- ECUADOR Modern country
- —— Aztec trade route
- —— Inca road

inset map 1

inset map 2

The Valley of Mexico

- ○ Aztec town or city
- —— aqueduct
- ═══ causeway
- —— dike
- ▨ marshland

Tenochtitlán

however, share some of the same problems that afflicted the Incas. They relied on fragile alliances, bore the resentment of tributary peoples, and expanded so rapidly that their reach always threatened to outrun the available manpower and technology.

The Aztecs and Incas saw themselves as continuing the traditions of earlier empires. They recalled ruined supremacies of the past: Tula and Teotihuacán in the Aztec case, Tiahuanaco for the Incas. The reach of their power seems, however, to have exceeded anything either region had witnessed before. So how did they do it? Long-range exchanges with other cultures helped to propel empires in Eurasia and Africa into expansion, but these advantages did not apply in the Americas. Indeed, the Andean and Mesoamerican worlds were so isolated that they do not even seem to have been in touch with each other. They did not benefit from new technology. Nor, as far as we know, were people in either region bouncing back from anything resembling the demographic catastrophe of parts of the Old World in the previous century. There was no momentum of recovery behind the enormous extensions of Aztec and Inca power. The most likely explanation is that demographic growth crossed a critical threshold in both areas. Probably, only imperial solutions could command the resources and compel the exchanges of goods needed to sustain the growing cities in which the Aztecs and Incas lived. In any case, both empires, as we shall see in the next chapter, were short lived. Essentially they were empires of types traditional in the region and overreached the realistic limits of their potential.

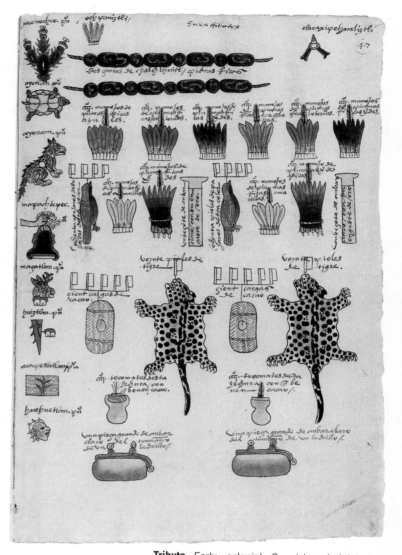

Tribute. Early colonial Spanish administrators were careful to copy tribute records from the archives of the preconquest Aztec state. The records show both the complexity if the tributary networks that linked the Aztec world and the amazing environmental diversity of the regions from which tribute flowed. This folio, from the Codex Mendoza, shows the tribute due to Tenochtitlán—the Aztec capital in central Mexico—from the "hot country" near what is now the Mexican-Guatemalan border. Among the items depicted are ornamental feathers, bird skins, jaguar pelts, and jade beads.

NEW EURASIAN EMPIRES

The expanding states of fifteenth-century Africa and the Americas were conspicuous in their day. However, they proved relatively fragile. Sixteenth-century European conquerors swallowed the Aztec and Inca states almost at a gulp. Ethiopia barely survived in the sixteenth century, eroded by Muslim invaders and waves of pagan, pastoralist immigrants. Songhay fell to invaders from Morocco in the late sixteenth century. Finally, though Mwene Mutapa survived into the seventeenth century, having fought off would-be conquerors from Europe, it then dissolved gradually and ingloriously into numerous petty states. It was the borderlands that straddle Europe and Asia that nurtured the really big, really enduring new or resumed empires of the age, those of the Turks and Russians.

The Russian Empire

The rise of a powerful Russian state was without precedent. Previously, the geography of the region produced volatile and therefore usually short-lived empires. Its

Chronology: Incas and Aztecs

ca. 1325	Aztecs found city of Tenochtitlán
ca. Mid-fifteenth century	Inca begin period of conquest and expansion
ca. Late-fifteenth century	Inca Empire approaches greatest extent
ca. Early sixteenth century	Aztec Empire reaches its peak

Making Connections | EXPANSION AND ITS LIMITS: AFRICA AND THE AMERICAS IN THE FIFTEENTH CENTURY

REGION/STATE OR EMPIRE	CAUSES FOR EXPANSION	EVIDENCE/EFFECTS OF EXPANSION	LIMITATIONS
East Africa / Ethiopia	Access to long-range trading routes to Indian Ocean via Red Sea ports	Recapture of coastal cities in 1400s, increased trade in slaves, ivory, gold, incense; creation of main access road to Indian Ocean	Limited agricultural land; need to control mountainous and lowland areas to access trade routes; major river systems to south and east with large populations; gradually encroaching Portuguese and Muslim influence by sixteenth century
East/Central Africa / Zambezi River Valley, Great Zimbabwe	Difficult access to Indian Ocean seaports; large populations with ivory, gold, metal resources	Manufactured goods from Asia (porcelain, silk, etc.) traded for gold, ivory; increasingly large administrative centers in stone, large amounts of coins, jewelry, gold, etc.	Landlocked; altered trade routes; decline in navigability of rivers
West Africa / Songhay Empire	Trade routes of the Sahara, linking Mediterranean and Niger valley; astute leadership (Muhammad Askia) and alliance with Muslim clerics, scholars	Canals, dikes, reservoirs; extension of cultivable land; rich trade with Niger valley goldfields	Limited long-range communication; adverse Atlantic winds/currents
Central Africa / Kongo	Domination of Congo River; alliance with Portuguese; abundant natural resources	Use of Western firearms, Christian religion and symbols to legitimate and maintain control; trading of slaves from conquered territories to Portuguese	Ultimate loss of control over slave trade to Portuguese leads to decline and fall
South America / Inca	Diversity of environments, resources; tribute system allows exchange of products between zones	Quick expansion and use of extreme methods of control; extensive road system; large shrines for dead leaders	Mass executions and other methods of subjugation alienate subject peoples and allies
Mesoamerica / Aztecs	Environmental diversity; hundreds of tributary communities; efficient recordkeeping; large array of natural resources	Intensive transformation of environment in/around capital (Tenochtitlán); abundance of commodities, both necessities (food, tools) and luxuries; widespread human sacrifice; monumental architecture	Loose administrative control; fragile alliances; alienation of tributary peoples; excessively rapid expansion

open, flat expanses of land and widely scattered populations contributed to an environment in which states could form with ease but only survive with difficulty. Most came and went quickly, vulnerable to external attack and internal rebellion.

In the fifteenth century, however, the rulers of Moscow established a state of imperial dimensions. Muscovy—as the early Russian Empire was called—has always been volatile at the edges, but it has been exceptionally enduring. One of the features that made Muscovy different was the shape of its heartland. It was based on control of the Volga River, a north–south axis of trade. Earlier empires, including the Mongols', were based on the east–west axis of the steppes, which served as highways for horse-borne armies.

The new empire's beginnings in the fourteenth century were almost imperceptible to those who experienced them or witnessed their effects. As we have seen, Russian princes could sometimes use Mongol dominance to their own advantage. Rulers of Moscow were the most adept in exploiting the Mongols to secure independence of and—increasingly—power over other Russians. Ivan I, known as Kalita or "Moneybags" (r. 1325–1340), got his nickname from his success as a tax collector for the Mongols. In 1378–1382, shortly after the collapse of Mongol rule in China, Muscovy attempted to drive the Mongols out of Russia. The challenge was premature, but Moscow's privileged relationship with the overlords survived. Mongol supremacy faded gradually.

The Russian world was expanding northward in the late fourteenth and early fifteenth centuries, as missionaries opened roads to convert people in the forests and tundra. An astonishing example of expansion by sea occurred in the 1430s. The evidence comes from a monastery on an island—bare, poor, and ice bound for much of the year—in the White Sea, on the edge of the Arctic. The monks painted their home not as it was but as they envisioned it, with a golden sanctuary and domes like candle flames. They showed the founders of their monastery rowing to the island, while whip-wielding angels expelled the original inhabitants. The paintings show merchants arriving, and monks rescuing shipwreck victims, with help from the ghosts of the monastery's saintly founders, who drive back the pack ice. Angels supply bread, cooking oil, and salt. All the ingredients of a typical story of European colonialism appear: the religious inspiration, the heroic voyage into a perilous environment, the ruthless treatment of the natives, the struggle to adapt and establish a viable economy, the quick arrival of commercial interests, and, finally, success through perseverance.

Muscovy's sudden take-off in the second half of the century, when conquests of neighboring peoples turned it into an imperial state, overshadowed early efforts at expansion. Indeed, when Constantinople fell to the Turks in 1453, Muscovites could see their city as, potentially, the "Third Rome," replacing Constantinople as Constantinople had replaced Rome, the former imperial capital (see Chapter 9). By the 1470s, Ivan the Great (r. 1462–1505) had absorbed most of Russia's other surviving principalities and was ready to throw off Mongol overlordship. He married a Byzantine princess, incorporated an imperial eagle into his coat of arms, forged a genealogy that traced his family back to the Roman Caesars, imported Italian technicians to fortify his palace complex, the Kremlin, and contemptuously dismissed an offer from the German emperor to invest him as king. "We have been sovereign in our land from our earliest forefathers," he replied, "and we hold our sovereignty from God."

"It was the borderlands that straddle Europe and Asia that nurtured the really big, really enduring new or resumed empires of the age, those of the Turks and Russians."

Russian expansion. The monastery these Russian Orthodox monks—Zosima and Savatti—founded in the White Sea off the Arctic coast of Siberia was really a modest and precarious little community, housed in wooden buildings in an icy desert. But the monks painted it as they would like it to be—big, grand, prosperous, and frequented by commerce.

During his reign, Ivan the Great more than trebled the territory he ruled—to over 240,000 square miles (see Map 15.4). His realm also took a new shape around most of the vast length of the Volga, stretching across the breadth of Eurasia, uniting the fur-rich north and the cash-rich fringes of Asia, and reaching for the Baltic and Caspian Seas. The city of Novgorod, which Muscovy absorbed in the 1470s, formed the northern pole of the state. Fur was the "black gold" of the north, inducing Russians to conquest and colonization, just as gold and spices lured other European peoples to Africa and the East.

War parties gathered pelts as tribute along a northern route that missionaries pioneered in the late fourteenth century, by way of the rivers Vym and Pechora. Repeatedly from 1465, Ivan sent expeditions to the rivers Perm and Ob to levy tribute. The expedition of 1499 numbered 4,000 men, equipped with sleds drawn by reindeer and dogs. They crossed the Ob in winter, returning with 1,000 captives from the forest-dwelling peoples who hunted for the furs. Ivan's ambassador to the rich Italian duchy of Milan boasted that his master received 1,000 gold ducats' worth of tribute annually in furs—five or six times an Italian nobleman's income. In the south, Russian dominance extended over Muslim-ruled Kazan (kah-ZAHN), near the Black Sea, Russia's great rival for control of Siberia's fur trade. While in the north missionaries, seeking to convert pagans, formed the vanguard for Russian conquests. Russian expansion therefore became a conscious crusade. Rulers justified it on religious grounds.

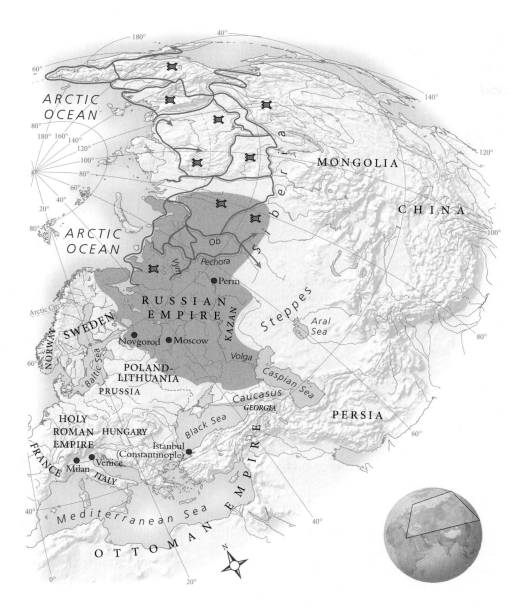

MAP 15.4

The Russian Empire, ca. 1505

- Russian Empire
- routes used by fur traders
- fur

Timurids and the Ottoman Empire

In the early fifteenth century, Turkish—and therefore Muslim—expansion resumed in southern Europe and Asia, still under the leadership of the Ottoman dynasty. The Mongol supremacy had been a traumatic challenge to the Islamic world, shattering the reputation of Muslim armies, breaking the monopoly of Sharia or Islamic law, exposing the limitations of the clergy, and inspiring the religious minded to withdraw from the world in a spirit of resignation. The Black Death had also battered the Islamic world. In some ways, indeed, it never fully recovered. Muslims' numerical preponderance over Christians never got back to earlier levels. But, for global history, the Islamic recovery is a much bigger story than the temporary setback.

To understand recovery, we turn to one of its most brilliant Muslim observers after the Black Death, the historian Ibn Khaldun (ihb-ihn hahl-DOON). In 1377,

"Everywhere in Ibn Khaldun's day, Islamic survival and success depended on Muslims' ability to tame the invaders challenging them from the deserts and the steppes, and turn their power to the service of Islam."

he sat down in a village in what is now Algeria "with ideas pouring into my head like cream into a churn." His efforts produced one of the most justly admired works of all time on history and political philosophy, the *Muqaddimah*. Its theme was the counterpoint of herder and tiller, which Ibn Khaldun saw as the motivating force of historical change. He had plenty of opportunity to observe the often violent interplay of nomads and sedentarists, their periodic collaboration, the incorporation of herder communities into Islamic states, and the way they launched new empires of their own. The consequences were clear. Everywhere in Ibn Khaldun's day, Islamic survival and success depended on Muslims' ability to tame the invaders challenging them from the deserts and the steppes, and turn their power to the service of Islam. Despite the disasters of the Black Death, new manpower stoked the Islamic world's potential for expansion. The pastoral peoples of Central Asia continued to provide converts. Islam's unique appeal to steppelanders was one of the great formative influences in the late medieval world. Most Turkic peoples and many Mongols were converted into warriors for Islam. Consequently, Central Asia stayed Muslim, and the Indian Ocean linked mainly Muslim shores. In other words, the Silk Roads and maritime routes of Eurasia had to pass through Muslim-ruled territory. Equally important, human fuel renewed the Islamic world's capacity to wage war and expand its frontiers.

The most conspicuous mobilizer of steppeland manpower in Muslim service in the late fourteenth and early fifteenth centuries, was the self-proclaimed "world conqueror," Timur (tee-MOOR) the Lame. Western writers, who traditionally call him Tamerlane, have tended to see him, romantically, as an embodiment of the superior virtues and simple lives of pastoral peoples. In reality, Timur was a nobly born townsman from Central Asia. Unlike most steppeland upstarts, he could justly claim to be descended from Genghis Khan (see Chapter 13). His court historian represented him as "the being nearest to perfection" and a pious devotee of holy war, but his role models were the pagans, Alexander the Great (see Chapter 5) and Genghis Khan.

When Turkic nobles rebelled against their Mongol masters in his homeland, Timur emerged as their leader. Deftly eliminating his rivals, he emerged as ruler of the region by 1370. By the time he died in 1406, he had conquered Iran, halted the growth of the Ottoman Empire, captured and caged its sultan, invaded Syria and India, and planned the conquest of China (see Map 15.5). Wherever he went, he heaped up the skulls of citizens unwise enough to resist his sieges. But this destruction was for efficiency, not for its own sake. It made most conquests submit cheaply. His success was by no means uniform, but it was impressive enough and consistent enough, to seem decreed by God. He addressed enemies in terms reminiscent of Mongol tradition: "Almighty God has subjugated the world to my domination, and the will of the Creator has entrusted the countries of the Earth to my power."

The day after his death, as his heirs turned on one another, his achievements seemed transitory. Even today, Timur's impact on the Islamic world is usually seen as negative. His success against the Ottomans gave Christendom a reprieve. By humbling the Mongols, he encouraged Christians in Russia. By weakening the Muslim sultans of Delhi, he liberated millions of Hindus. These reflections, however, overlook his psychological legacy. He was a champion of Islamic orthodoxy and exerted great influence as a patron of Muslim education. He is also important as an example of the process that converted pastoralists. Having been the scourge of the Islamic world, they became its sword.

Timurid horoscope. Despite their fearsome reputation, Timurid princes—the descendants of the Muslim Turkic conqueror whom Westerners called "Tamerlane"—were great patrons of both astronomers and astrologers. This horoscope was drawn up in Shiraz, Iran, in 1411 for one of Timur's grandsons, Iskandar Sultan. The date of his birth, 1384, is given in Persian, Uighur, and Chinese.

Timur was like a hurricane—his force soon spent. The Ottomans were more like a monsoon: Their armies returned and receded as each season came and went, but they constantly made new conquests. The fate of the Mongols—expelled from China, retreating from Russia—shows how hard it was for a great Eurasian empire to survive in the aftermath of the Black Death, which jarred economies and felled manpower. Yet, falteringly in the early fifteenth century but with renewed strength thereafter, the Ottoman Empire managed to do so.

The Ottomans' great advantage was location. The heartlands of the empire were at the crossroads of some of the world's great trade routes, where the Silk Roads, the Indian Ocean routes, the Volga, the Danube, and the Mediterranean almost converged (see Map 15.5). The history of the Byzantine Empire showed the importance of holding on to this location. Byzantium flourished while it occupied these lands, faltered when its control there slackened and ceased (see Chapter 12). From their own past, the Ottomans inherited the traditions of steppeland imperialism. They were content, at first, to levy tribute and allow their tributaries to govern themselves or to exist as puppet states to be manipulated according to Ottoman needs.

Gradually, the Ottomans adapted to the conditions of the environments they conquered, which were predominantly agrarian, urban, and maritime. As their conquests grew, their methods of governing became, necessarily, more bureaucratic and centralized. As their frontiers touched formidable foes, they modified their military traditions. Other empires of nomadic origins failed when required to adapt to new military technologies, but the Ottomans' readily became a gunpowder empire. Their forces could blow away cavalry or batter down city walls.

The Ottomans even took to the sea. In the 1390s, the sultans began to build permanent fleets of their own. It was a long process and hard to catch up with

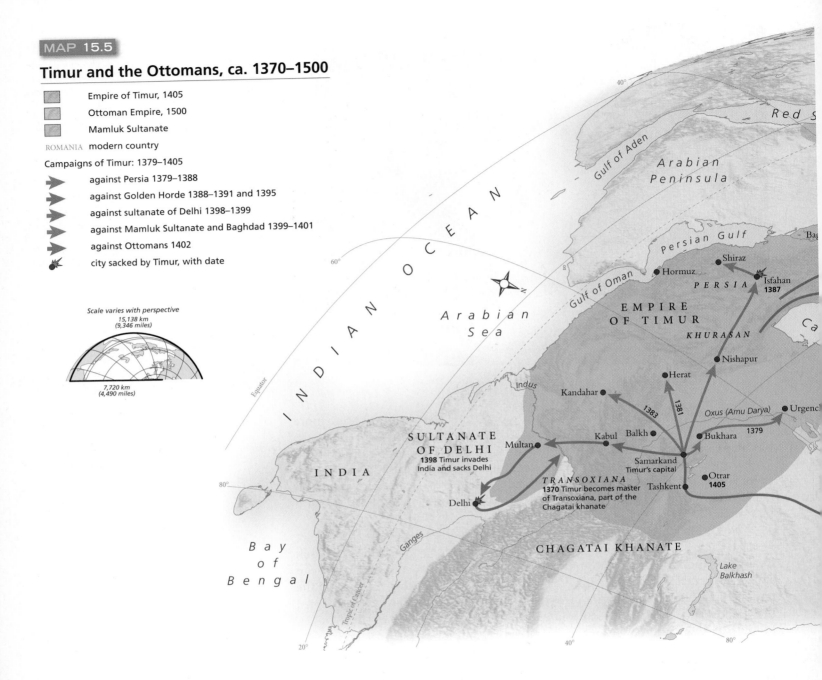

MAP 15.5

Timur and the Ottomans, ca. 1370–1500

- Empire of Timur, 1405
- Ottoman Empire, 1500
- Mamluk Sultanate
- ROMANIA modern country

Campaigns of Timur: 1379–1405

- against Persia 1379–1388
- against Golden Horde 1388–1391 and 1395
- against sultanate of Delhi 1398–1399
- against Mamluk Sultanate and Baghdad 1399–1401
- against Ottomans 1402
- city sacked by Timur, with date

Scale varies with perspective
15,138 km
(9,346 miles)

7,720 km
(4,490 miles)

Red S

Gulf of Aden

*Arabian
Peninsula*

Persian Gulf

Ba

Shiraz

Hormuz

P E R S I A Isfahan
1387

Gulf of Oman

EMPIRE
OF TIMUR

K H U R A S A N

INDIAN OCEAN

*Arabian
Sea*

Nishapur

Indus

Herat

Kandahar

Ca

60°

Oxus (Amu Darya) Urgenc

1383

1381

Kabul Balkh Bukhara 1379

SULTANATE
OF DELHI
1398 Timur invades
India and sacks Delhi

Multan

Samarkand
Timur's capital

Otrar
1405

TRANSOXIANA
1370 Timur becomes master
of Transoxiana, part of the
Chagatai khanate

Tashkent

INDIA

80°

Delhi

Equator

Ganges

CHAGATAI KHANATE

*Lake
Balkhash*

*Bay
of
Bengal*

Tropic of Cancer

20°

40°

80°

long-established naval powers. As late as 1466, a Venetian merchant in Constantinople claimed that to win a battle Turkish fleets needed to outnumber those of Venice by four or five to one. By the end of the century, however, the Ottomans had overturned the 400-year-old Christian maritime supremacy in the Mediterranean. Never since Rome defeated Carthage (see Chapter 7) had such an unlikely candidate become a naval power.

Like other imperialists of steppeland origin, the Ottomans mastered the art of keeping subjects of diverse religions loyal to them. At the same time, Ottoman leaders, as self-appointed warriors of Islam, took whatever steps were necessary to strengthen the Islamic state. They tolerated Jews, Christians, and Shiites, but had no qualms about levying punitive taxes on these minorities. On Christians, they imposed a levy of male child slaves, who were brought up as Muslims to form the **Janissaries**, an elite corps of the armed forces, and staff the ranks of the administration. The system provided servants for the state, and converts for Islam, while keeping Christian communities in submission. From the 1420s, consistently with the character of the empire as a Muslim state with people of many religions and customs, the sultan functioned as head of two linked systems of law and justice. The first consisted of secular laws and

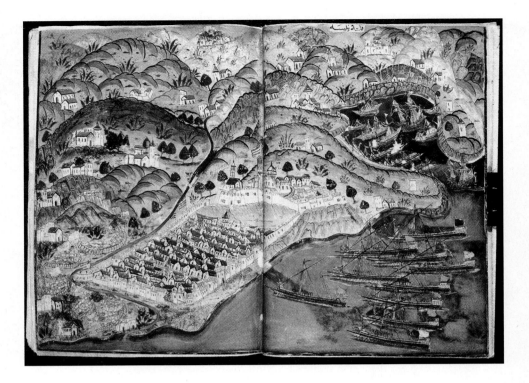

A Turkish fleet at anchor off Toulon, in southern France, in 1543, from a chronicle written to celebrate the wide-ranging campaigns of Sultan Suleiman the Magnificent (r. 1520–1566). The Ottomans were able to wage naval war in the western Mediterranean, thanks to the many harbors along the North African coast controlled by Muslim chiefs who were subjects of the sultans.

customs that the sultan's appointees administered. The second was enshrined in the Quran and the traditions of Islamic law, with a body of experts to run it, who met in the sultan's palace.

In 1451, Mehmet (MEH-meht) II became sultan at the age of 19, uninhibited by caution, committed to reform. This was a decisive step in the shift from indirect rule to centralized government. Mehmet's predecessors had prudently allowed self-rule to continue in the city of Constantinople and its few surviving dependencies—the last fragments of the Byzantine Empire that still proclaimed itself the heir of Rome. The Ottomans controlled what happened in Constantinople by threatening and bribing political factions there. But some factions in the city were determined to challenge the Turks and formed an alliance with Western Christendom. Mehmet laid siege to Constantinople. He built huge forts to command the sea approaches to the city and fired the heaviest artillery ever made at its walls. He transported ships overland in pieces to get round the great chain the defenders stretched across the entrance to the harbor. In the end, the sheer weight of numbers was decisive. The attackers climbed the walls over the bodies of dead comrades. The last Byzantine emperor, Constantine XI, fell fighting—only the eagles on his purple boots identified his corpse.

With the fall of Constantinople in 1453, Mehmet II could see his empire as a continuation of Rome. He looked westward for fashions to incorporate into his court culture and chose Italians to paint his portrait, sculpt his medals, and write some of his propaganda. The direction of Ottoman conquests tilted toward Europe as Mehmet attempted to recreate the Byzantine Empire. He extended his territory into most of what are now Greece, Romania, and Bosnia, seeking to control the shores of the Adriatic and Black seas.

THE LIMITATIONS OF CHINESE IMPERIALISM

Ottoman imperialism in the fifteenth century resumed its former course after setbacks caused by the Black Death and the rise of Timur. An observer at the time might have predicted that China, too, would resume expansion and even anticipate the Ottomans in bidding for a maritime empire. The best way to understand why such developments seemed likely—and why they were frustrated—is to look back at China's recovery from the mid-fourteenth-century plagues. Like so many decisive episodes of Chinese history, the story begins among the people on whose labor the empire depended: peasants.

The rhythms of peasant life sometimes seem slow and changeless, peasants' expectations low: deferring hope, shrugging off promises of improvement. Their response, in a surprisingly wide variety of cultural contexts, is to wait and pray for the millennium—a fabled future, when divine intervention will either perfect the world or end it. Often, however, in times of extreme disaster, peasant movements arise to try to trigger the millennium. One of the most explosive of all such movements began among Chinese canal workers in 1350.

Mid-fourteenth-century China was particularly wretched. Peasants were the victims of the slow-grinding effects of economic misery and the survivors of terrible environmental disasters. The plagues that began in the 1320s kept returning. Not until well into the 1350s did the plagues begin to lose their virulence or to encounter naturally immunized populations. In 1344, the Yellow River flooded. Persistent droughts followed. Decayed communications that prevented timely help made local famines worse. The population of the empire had fallen, by some calculations, to half what it had been at its height. In this setting, peasants were forced to repair the Grand Canal, which carried essential food supplies from southern and central China to Beijing.

The peasants' millenarianism—their hope of deliverance in a transfigured world—was based on a Buddhist myth. The lord Maitreya, the last of the earthly Buddhas, would come to prepare the world for extinction. Now, however, given the peasants' miserable lives, the myth acquired a political edge. Maitreya would put a triumphant end to the struggle of good against evildoers and give his followers power over their oppressors. A similar movement was current at the same time in Western Europe, where the Fraticelli, a group of Franciscan friars, identified with the needs and interests of the wretched of the Earth. The Franciscans predicted that a cosmic hero would come to wrest treasures from the soil and enrich the poor. Fulfilling the biblical prophecy uttered by the mother of Jesus that the prayers of the church repeated every day, he would put down the mighty from their seat and exalt the humble and meek.

In China, the mood was particularly dangerous. Along with their desire for deliverance, peasants harbored a folk memory of the Song dynasty (see Chapter 12) and a hankering for the good times supposed to have preceded the Mongol invasions of a century before. Peasant revolts are often revolutionary in the most literal sense of the word, wanting to turn the world back, "revolve" it full circle, to an imagined or misremembered golden age. Therefore, when the Mongol rulers executed a pretender to the throne who claimed to be the heir of the Song in 1351, a revolt broke out among his followers. They easily recruited thousands of peasants

Sultan Mehmet II (r. 1451–1481) extended the Ottoman Empire westward into Europe, taking great interest in the culture of lands that had once belonged to the Roman Empire—especially after he captured the old Roman capital of Constantinople in 1453. Gentile Bellini, who worked at Mehmet's court and was one of the best Venetian painters of the day, painted this portrait of the sultan in the realistic style that was popular in Italy at the time. Bellini framed the sultan's image with columns decorated in the European style.

to their cause. Some members of the elite even joined in, out of resentment at the ruling dynasty's partiality for foreign advisers.

The leader who emerged from the chaos of rebellion was Zhu Yuanzhang (joo yoo-ehn-jhang), the recruiting officer of a rebel band. By the end of the 1350s, the empire in the Yangtze region had dissolved into a chaos of small states run by similar upstarts. Between 1360 and 1363, in river warfare of reckless daring, Zhu conquered his rivals. At this stage, he was careful to represent himself as a mere servant of the rebel cause. By 1368, however, he was so powerful that he proclaimed the start of a new dynasty.

Zhu cleverly managed the coalition that had brought him to power. He juggled all the rebels' conflicting ideologies while reconciling former enemies. To please the Confucian establishment, he restored ancient court ceremonies and the examinations for public service. He kept the military command structure and even dressed in some of the same ways as the previous Mongol dynasty had. He renounced the cult of Maitreya, but only after making it clear that he had fulfilled it in his own person by adopting the name "Ming" for his dynasty. The word, which means bright, was traditionally used to describe the lord Maitreya.

Zhu had the self-educated man's typical contempt for the academic establishment. "Chewing on phrases and biting on words," he said, "they have never had any practical experience. When you examine what they do, it is nothing." But he recognized that the Confucian bureaucrats had expertise he could use. His empire—vast and literate, as it was—needed a civil service that would heed a traditional code of ethics. He also needed to keep the Confucian elite under his control. He therefore kept the traditional power centers of his court in balance: the military top brass, the eunuchs who ran the imperial household, the foreign and Muslim advisers and technicians, the Buddhist and Daoist clergies, and the merchant lobby. Together, they limited the power of the Confucian elite.

The result was a brief period when expansionist policies prevailed over Confucian caution. Zhu's son, the Yongle (yuhng-leh) emperor (r. 1402–1424) aggressively sought contact with the world beyond the empire. He meddled in the politics of Vietnam and enticed the Japanese to trade.

The most spectacular manifestation of the new outward-looking policy was the career of the Muslim eunuch-admiral, Zheng He (jehng heh). In 1405, he led the first of a series of naval expeditions. Their purpose has been the subject of long and unresolved scholarly debate, but in part, at least, it was to show China's flag all over the Indian Ocean (see Map 15.6). He replaced unacceptable rulers in Java, Sumatra, and Sri Lanka, founded a puppet state on the commercially important Strait of Malacca, and gathered tribute from Bengal in India. He displayed Chinese power as far away as Jiddah, on the Red Sea coast of Arabia and in major ports in East Africa as far south as the island of Zanzibar. "The countries beyond the horizon," he announced with some exaggeration, "and from the ends of the Earth, have become subjects." He restocked the imperial zoo with giraffes, ostriches, zebra, and rhinoceroses—all hailed as beasts bringing good luck—and brought Chinese geographical knowledge up to date.

Giraffe. "The ministers and all the people gathered to gaze at it and their joy knows no end," commented Zhen-tu, the Chinese court painter who recorded the arrival of one of several giraffes at China's imperial zoo in the early fifteenth century. Imperial propaganda identified giraffes with mythical beasts of good omen.

1977-42–1. Tu, Shen. "The Tribute Giraffe with Attendant". Philadelphia Museum of Art: Gift of John T. Dorrance, 1977.

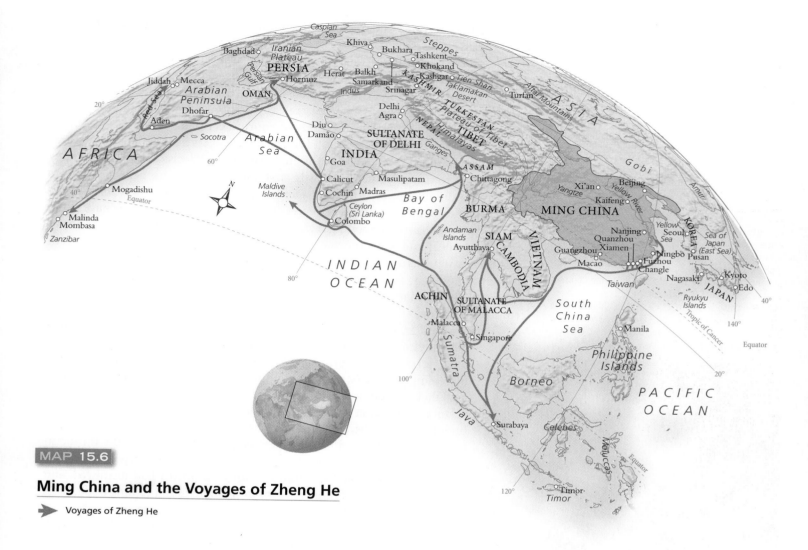

MAP 15.6

Ming China and the Voyages of Zheng He

➤ Voyages of Zheng He

Can Zheng He's voyages be called an imperial venture? Their official purpose was to pursue a fugitive pretender to the Chinese throne—but that would not have required such vast expeditions to such distant places. The Chinese called the vessels treasure ships and emphasized what they called tribute gathering (in the more distant spots Zheng He's ships visited, what happened was more like an exchange.) Commercial objectives may have been involved. Almost all the places Zheng He visited had long been important in Chinese trade. In part, the voyages were scientific missions: Ma Huan, Zheng He's interpreter, called his own book on the subject, *The Overall Survey of the Ocean's Shores,* and improved maps and data on the plants, animals, and peoples of the regions visited were among the expeditions' fruits. But flag showing is always, to some extent, about power or, at least, prestige. And the aggressive intervention Zheng He made in some places, together with the tone of his commemorative inscriptions, demonstrates that the extension or reinforcement of China's image and influence was part of the project.

Indeed, it is hard to see how else the huge investment the state made in his enterprise could have been justified. Zheng He's expeditions were on a crushing scale. His ships were much bigger than anything European navies could float at the time. His first fleet was said to comprise 66 junks of the largest ever built, 225 support vessels, and 27,870 men. The seventh voyage—probably the longest in reach—sailed 12,618 miles. The voyages lasted on average over two years each. Some silly claims have been made for Zheng He's voyages. Ships of his fleet did not sail beyond the limits of the Indian Ocean—much less discover America or Antarctica. His achievements, however, clearly demonstrated China's potential to become the center of a maritime empire of enormous reach.

But the Chinese naval effort could not last. Historians have debated why it was abandoned. In many ways, it was to the credit of Chinese decision makers that they pulled back from involvement in costly adventures far from home. Most powers that have undertaken such expeditions and attempted to impose their rule on distant countries have had cause to regret it. Confucian values, as we have seen, included giving priority to good government at home. "Barbarians" would submit to Chinese rule if and when they saw the benefits. Attempting to beat or coax them into submission was a waste of resources. By consolidating their landward empire, and refraining from seaborne imperialism, China's rulers ensured the longevity of their state. All the maritime empires founded in the world in the last 500 years have crumbled. China is still there.

Part, at least, of the context of the decision to abort Zheng He's missions is clear. The examination system and the gradual discontinuation of other forms of recruitment for public service had serious implications. Increasingly scholars, with their indifference to expansion, and gentlemen, with their contempt for trade, governed China. In the 1420s and 1430s, the balance of power at court shifted in the bureaucrats' favor, away from the Buddhists, eunuchs, Muslims, and merchants who had supported Zheng He. When the Hongxi (huhng-jher) emperor succeeded to the throne in 1425, one of his first acts was to cancel Zheng He's next voyage. He restored Confucian office holders, whom the Yongle emperor had dismissed, and curtailed the power of other factions. In 1429, the shipbuilding budget was cut almost to extinction. The scholar-elite hated overseas adventures, and the factions that favored them so much that they destroyed all Zheng He's records in an attempt to obliterate his memory. Moreover, China's land frontiers became insecure as Mongol power revived. China needed to turn away from the sea and toward the new threat.

By the late fifteenth century, the scholars' position seemed unshakable, and the supremacy of Confucian values could not be challenged. The Hongxi emperor aspired to Confucian perfection. He ordered the slaughter or expulsion of court magicians and exiled 1,000 Buddhist and Daoist monks. He resumed a Confucian priority: study of the penal code, which previous Ming emperors had neglected. He reintroduced the palace lectures, during which Confucian professors instructed the emperor. He endowed a library alongside the Confucian temple at the sage's birthplace in Qufu (choo-foo). He patronized artists whose work radiated Confucian serenity. Wu Wei (woo way), the emperor's favorite painter, had Daoist patrons, too, but his representations of ascetics meditating in sketchy landscapes demonstrate the triumph of thought over nature and, therefore, by implication, of Confucianism over Daoism.

By the end of the fifteenth century, there was little chance the Chinese would resume a strategy of expanding the empire and no chance

Wu Wei was one of the most original and influential artists of late-fifteenth-century China. But his values were those of his patrons, the conventional scholar-elite of the imperial court. This painting is typical. The scholar staring thoughtfully into the distance is drawn in delicate and flattering contrast to the heavy, blotchy ink used to depict the tree. *Wu Wei, "Scholar Seated Under a Tree," China. Ink & traces of colour on silk. 14.7 × 8.25. Chinese and Japanese Special Fund. Photograph © 2007 Courtesy Museum of Fine Arts, Boston*

that they would expand by sea. For the rest of the Ming period (1368–1644), China did not cease to be a great imperial power, but frontier stability became far more important to the ruling elite than frontier expansion. The transfer of the imperial capital from the southern citty of Nanjing to the northern city of Beijing under the Yongle emperor symbolized this concern. The state never resumed the active patronage of overseas expansion. The growth of trade and of Chinese colonization in Southeast Asia was left to the private initiative of merchants and migrants. China, the empire best equipped for maritime imperialism, opted out. Consequently, lesser powers, including those of Europe, were able to exploit opportunities in seas that Chinese power vacated.

Chronology: The Early Ming Dynasty	
1350s	Yangtze region dissolves into small warring states
1360–1363	Zhu Yuanzhang conquers his rivals
1368	Zhu Yuanzhang founds Ming dynasty
1405	Zheng He leads first naval expedition
1425	Hongxi emperor succeeds to throne; Zheng He's voyages cancelled; Confucian values ascendant

THE BEGINNINGS OF OCEANIC IMPERIALISM

Even under the Yongle emperor, China confined its seaward reach to the monsoonal seas of maritime Asia and the Indian Ocean—seas of terrible hazards and fabulous rewards. As we have seen, the Indian Ocean was relatively easy to cross but relatively hard to enter or exit. For most of history, therefore, it was the preserve of peoples whose homes bordered it or who traveled overland—like some European and Armenian traders—to become part of its world. Moreover, all the trade was internal. Merchants took no interest in venturing far beyond the monsoon system to reach other markets or supplies.

From Europe, however, access to the Indian Ocean was well worth seeking. Merchants craved a share of the richest trades and most prosperous markets in the world, especially the spices, drugs, and aromatics that were the specialities of producers in Sri Lanka, and parts of India and what is now Indonesia. These products, sold to rich buyers in China and Southwest Asia, and, to a lesser extent, in Europe, were the most profitable in the world, in terms of price per unit of weight. Many Europeans sought to find out where they came from and to take part in the trades. But the journey was too long, laborious, and hazardous to generate much profit. From the Mediterranean, merchants had either to travel up the Nile and proceed by camel caravan to a Red Sea port, or to negotiate a dangerous passage through the Ottoman Empire to the Persian Gulf. In either case, they obviously could not take ships with them. This was a potentially fatal limitation because Europeans had little to offer to people in the Indian Ocean basin except shipping services. For most of the fifteenth century, until the 1490s, Europeans were not sure if it was possible to approach the Indian Ocean by sea at all.

To understand why, until the late fifteenth century, Europeans were so backward in navigation compared with Indian Ocean peoples and unable to gain direct access to Asian markets and supplies, we must look at the wind map (see Map 15.7). For most of history, winds and currents have played a huge part in conditioning, and even determining, who and what went where in the world.

Europe's only effective access by sea to the rest of the world is along its western seaboard, into the Atlantic, which has a fixed-wind system. That is, instead of changing direction seasonally, as in monsoonal systems, the prevailing winds in the Atlantic are always the same. It took a long time to develop navigation with fixed-wind systems because, until navigators explored and decoded those winds' path-

"China, the empire best equipped for maritime imperialism, opted out. Consequently, lesser powers, including those of Europe, were able to exploit opportunities in seas that Chinese power vacated."

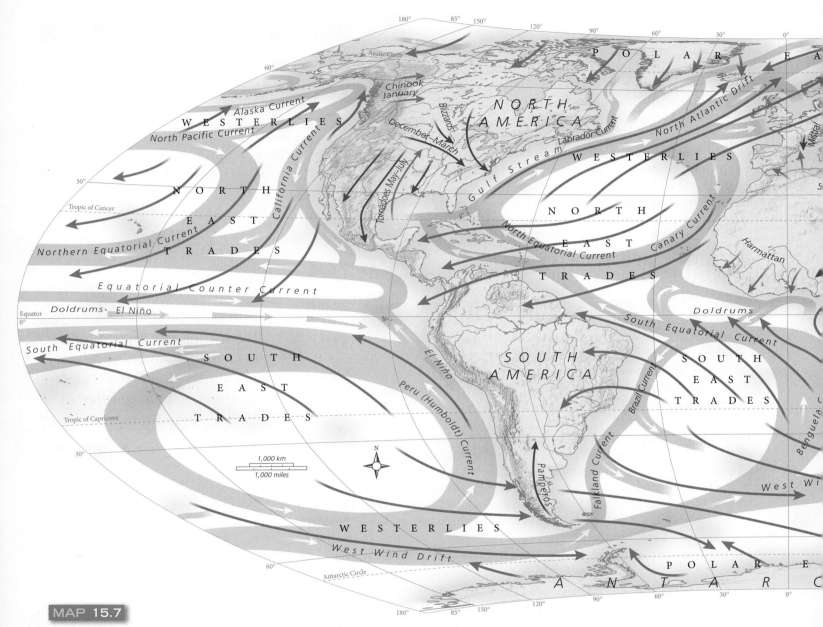

MAP 15.7

Winds and Ocean Currents Worldwide

Ocean Currents

| | warm |
| | cold |

Prevailing Winds

→ warm

→ cold

Local Winds

→ warm

→ cold

ways, adventurers could not get home. Navigators either sailed into the wind—which usually resulted in their being blown back without discovering any useful new lands or routes—or they sailed with the wind, never to be heard of again.

The Norse explorers of the North Atlantic in the tenth and eleventh centuries (see Chapter 11) overcame these limitations by sailing west with the currents that cross the Atlantic below the Arctic, and then picking up the westerlies, which took them home. But this route led only to relatively poor and underpopulated regions. For the Atlantic to become Europe's highway to the rest of the world, explorers had to develop ways to exploit the rest of the fixed-wind system. They had to discover the winds that led to commercially important destinations. There were, first, the northeast trade winds, which led to the resource-rich, densely populated regions of

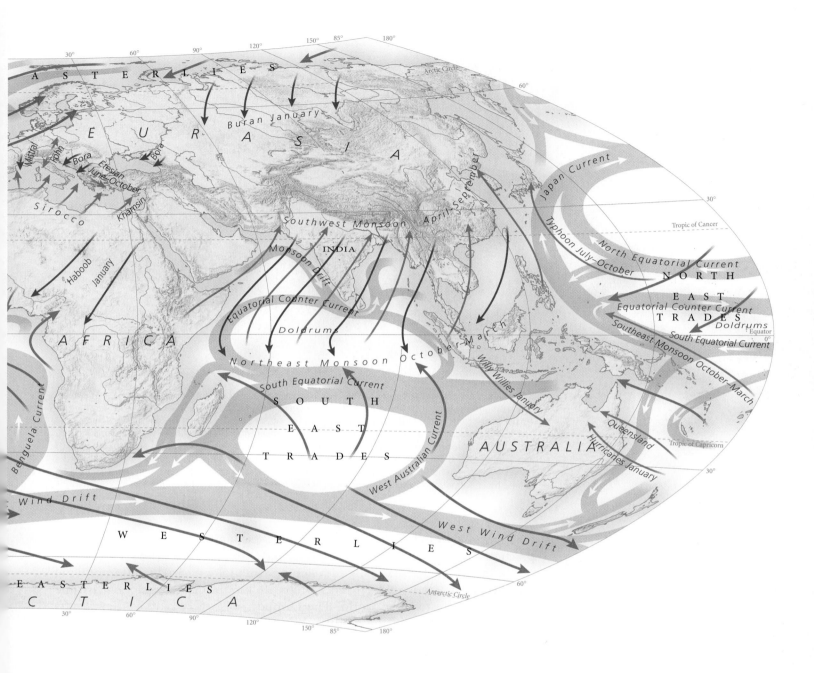

the New World, far south of the lands the Norse reached. There was also the South Atlantic wind system, which led, by way of the southeast trade winds and the westerlies of the far south, to the Indian Ocean.

The technology needed to exploit the Atlantic's wind systems only gradually became available during a period of long, slow development in the thirteenth, fourteenth, and fifteenth centuries. Like most technology, for most of history, it developed by trial and error. We know little about the process, because the work went undocumented. Humble craftsman labored to improve hull design and rigging—and therefore the maneuverability of ships—and to make water casks secure for the long voyages explorers had to undertake. Historians have traditionally emphasized the contribution of formal science in developing maritime charts and instruments

Spice box. This sixteenth-century leather box was used to house specimens of spices from Southeast Asia. Around the outer rim would have been different kinds of pepper, which accounted for as much as 70 per cent of the global trade in spices in the early modern period; cloves (the most valuable spice per unit of bulk, production of which was overwhelmingly concentrated in the islands of Ternate and Tidore); and ginger. The inner compartment would have contained nutmeg and mace (which are both products of the nutmeg tree, the former being the inner kernel of the seed, the latter its outer coating, grown in the Banda Islands in what is today Indonesia); and cinnamon (most of which came from what is now Sri Lanka, though production was widely diffused across the region as far as the Philippines).

for navigating by the stars. Now it seems that these innovations were irrelevant. No practical navigator of this period in Europe seems to have used them.

In addition to gradually developing technology, gradually improving knowledge of winds and currents prepared Europeans to explore maritime routes to the rest of the world. The European discovery of the Atlantic was launched from deep in the Mediterranean, chiefly by navigators from Genoa and the island of Majorca. They forced their way through the Strait of Gibraltar, where the strength of the adverse current seemed to stopper their sea, in the thirteenth century. From there, some turned north to the familiar European Atlantic. Others turned south into waters unsailed, as far as we know, for centuries, toward the Madeira and Canary Islands and the African Atlantic. Early efforts were long and laborious because explorers' vision was limited to the small patches of the ocean before them, with their apparently unremitting winds. Navigators were like code breakers deprived of information to work with. Moreover, the Black Death and the economic downturn of the mid–fourteenth century interrupted the effort, or at least slowed it down.

Only the long accumulation of information and experience could make a breakthrough possible. Navigators had no means to keep track of their longitude as they beat their way home against the wind. They made increasingly huge deep-sea detours to find westerlies that would take them home. Those detours led to the discovery of the Azores, a mid-ocean string of islands more than 700 miles west of Portugal. Marine charts made not later than the 1380s show all but two islands of the group. Much longer open-sea voyages now became common. From the 1430s, the Portuguese established way stations, sown with wheat or stocked with wild sheep, on the Azores, so that passing crews could find provisions.

Several attempts were made during the fifteenth century to explore Atlantic space, but most doomed themselves to failure by setting out in the belt of westerly winds. Presumably explorers chose this route because they wanted to be sure that they would be able to get home. We can still follow the tiny gains in the slowly unfolding record on rare maps and stray documents. In 1427, a Portuguese pilot called Diogo de Silves established for the first time the approximate relationship of the islands of the Azores to one another. Shortly after 1450, the westernmost islands of the Azores were reached. Over the next three decades, the Portuguese crown often commissioned voyages of exploration farther into the Atlantic, but none is known to have made any further progress. Perhaps they failed because they departed from the Azores, where the westerlies beat them back to base.

Not only was exploitation of the Atlantic slow, but at first it yielded few returns. One exception was Madeira, which paid enormous taxes to the Portuguese crown thanks to sugar planting in the mid–fifteenth century. The explorers' hope of establishing direct contact with the sources of West African gold proved false, though they were able to get gold at relatively low prices through trade with West African kingdoms. This trade also produced something that could be sold in European markets. From 1440, Portuguese desperadoes obtained increasing numbers of slaves through trading and raiding. But markets for slaves were limited because great slave-staffed plantations, of the sort later familiar in the southern United States, hardly existed in Europe, where most slaves were still domestic servants. The Canary Islands attracted investment because they produced natural dyestuffs and seemed exploitable for sugar. But their inhabitants fiercely resisted Europeans, and the conquest was long and costly.

In the 1480s, however, the situation changed, and Atlantic exploration began to pay off. In the North Atlantic, customs records of the English port of Bristol indicate that quantities of whaling products, salt fish, and walrus ivory from the ocean increased dramatically. In West Africa, the Portuguese post at São Jorge da Mina, near the mouth of the Benya River, was close to gold fields in the Volta River valley, and large amounts of gold now began to reach European hands. In 1484, sugar production at last began in the Canary Islands. In the same decade, Portuguese made contact with the kingdom of Kongo. Although voyages toward and around the southernmost tip of Africa encountered unremittingly adverse currents, they also showed that the far south of the Atlantic had westerly winds that might at last lead to the Indian Ocean. By the end of the 1480s, it was apparent that Atlantic investment could yield dividends.

Imperial marker. Portuguese explorers erected carved stone pillars to mark their route and to record their claim to have annexed territory for Portugal. Diogo Cão raised this example, the Padrão de Santo Agostinho, at Santa Maria, south of Benguela in Angola in 1482 (see Map 15.8).

The 1490s were a breakthrough-decade in Europe's efforts to reach out across the ocean to the rest of the world (see Map 15.8). In 1492–1493, Christopher Columbus, in voyages financed by Italian bankers and with backing from the Spanish monarchs, discovered fast, reliable routes across the Atlantic that linked the Mediterranean and the Caribbean. In 1496, John Cabot, another Italian adventurer, backed by merchants in Bristol and the English crown, discovered a direct route across the North Atlantic, using variable springtime winds to get across and the westerlies to get back. His route, however, was not reliable and, for over 100 years, was mainly used to reach the cod fisheries of Newfoundland.

Meanwhile, the Portuguese sought to determine whether the Indian Ocean was genuinely landlocked. In 1497–1498, a Portuguese trading venture, commissioned by the crown and probably financed by Italian bankers, attempted to use the westerlies of the South Atlantic to reach the Indian Ocean. Its leader, Vasco da Gama, turned east too early and had to struggle around the Cape of Good Hope at the tip of Africa. But he managed to get across the Indian Ocean anyway and reach the pepper-rich port of Calicut at the tip of India. The next voyage, in 1500, reached India without a serious hitch.

The breakthroughs of the 1490s opened direct, long-range routes of maritime trade across the world between Europe, Asia, and Africa. Success may seem sudden, but not if we view it against the background of slow developments in European chronology and knowledge and the accelerating benefits of Atlantic exploration in the previous decade. Was there more to it than that?

Making Connections | THE BEGINNINGS OF OCEANIC IMPERIALISM IN EUROPE

DESIRE	OBSTACLES	BREAKTHROUGHS, 1200–1500
European merchants crave access to Indian Ocean trade	Long, laborious journey across hostile territories Europeans have little to offer in exchange for the spices, drugs, and aromatics of the East Fixed-wind system of Atlantic makes oceanic voyages impractical Black Death and consequent economic downturn slow down efforts to explore Atlantic	Technology to exploit Atlantic wind system slowly develops Knowledge of winds and currents gradually improves Thirteenth century: Navigators from Genoa and Majorca force their way through the Strait of Gibraltar Portuguese discover the Azores in the late fourteenth century *1450–1480*: Portuguese commission Atlantic voyages of exploration *after 1480*: Exploration of Atlantic begins to pay returns *after 1490*: Europe begins to reach out across the ocean to the rest of the world.

Was there something special about European culture that would explain why Europeans rather than explorers from other cultures discovered the world-girdling routes, linking the Old World to the New and the Indian Ocean to the Atlantic? Some European historians have argued just that—that Europeans had something others lacked.

Such a suggestion, however, seems ill conceived. Compared to the peoples of maritime Asia, Europeans were special mainly in being slow to launch long-range voyages. The Atlantic, the ocean they bordered, really was special, however, because its wind system inhibited exploration for centuries but rewarded it spectacularly once it was launched. Moreover, the breakthrough explorations were not the work of "Europe" but of people from a few communities on the Atlantic seaboard and in the Mediterranean. What distinguishes them is not that they set off with the right kind of culture, but that they set off from the right place.

THE EUROPEAN OUTLOOK: PROBLEMS AND PROMISE

In some ways, indeed, Western Europe in the fifteenth century was beset with problems. Recovery from the disasters of the fourteenth century was slow. Though plagues were less severe, they remained frequent. And though used to the severe climate of their little ice age, Western Europeans did not reoccupy the high ground and distant colonies that they had abandoned in the fourteenth century. In most places, population increase was modest and probably did not reach levels attained before the Black Death. Food supplies were unreliable, and harvests frequently failed.

Human foes joined impersonal enemies—plague, war, and famine. In 1396, a crusade to drive the Turks from the Balkans failed. It marked the beginning of a long period of Turkish advance on the Balkan and eastern Mediterranean frontiers of Christendom. Meanwhile, in the northeast, Lithuanians, most of whom remained pagan until the late fourteenth or early fifteenth century, eroded the conquests of German knightly orders along the Baltic Sea (see Chapter 12). In the early fifteenth century, Thule Inuit raiders finally obliterated the Norse colony on Greenland (see Chapter 14).

Meanwhile, hard times created opportunities for those with the skill or luck to exploit them. High mortality opened gaps in elites, which bureaucrats could fill, thanks, in part, to a revolution in government. The use of paper made it cheap and easy to transmit rulers' commands to the farthest corners of their realms. To help legitimize the newcomers' power, Western moralists redefined nobility as the product of virtue or education rather than ancestry. "Virtue is the sole and unique nobility," declared a Venetian coat of arms. A doctrine of late fifteenth-century Italian social thought invoked Greek mythology to make its point: "Neither the wealth of Croesus [reputedly the richest man in the world] nor the antiquity of the blood of Priam [the king of Troy in Homer's epics] could rival reason as an ingredient of nobility."

New economic divisions appeared. The line of the Elbe and northern Danube Rivers and the lands between became a cultural fault line. To the west of this line, underpopulation boosted the value of labor. The effects were to liberate peasants and urban communities from landowners' control, split up landholdings, encourage tenancies, and convert cropland to pasture. In the east the opposite occurred. Landholders responded to the loss of manpower and revenue by clamping down on peasants' rights and forcing formerly free towns into submission. New definitions of nobility were rejected. East of the Bohemian forest, nobility was ancient blood or acquired "by martial discipline," and that was that.

Scored by heresies, trenched by conflicting social values, and riven by economic cracks, Western Europe nevertheless showed signs of self-confidence and optimism. Scholars and artists pursued, with renewed vigor, the project of recovering the legacy of classical antiquity—the cultural achievements of ancient Greece and Rome. The movement is commonly called "**the Renaissance**" on the grounds that the civilization of classical antiquity was reborn—but "the" is a much-abused word. Scholarship has now identified renaissances in almost every century for the previous 1,000 years. No radically new departure occurred in the fifteenth century from what had gone before—merely an accentuation of long-accumulating tendencies.

An event traditionally said to be representative of the Renaissance occurred in 1400, when the Cloth Importers' Guild of Florence launched a competition for a new set of bronze doors for the greatest monument in their care: the Baptistery that faced the city's cathedral. The Baptistery had been built in the eighth century as the place where infants and converts could receive the sacrament of baptism. Urban myth, however, claimed it was orginally a Roman temple of the god Mars. Two great geniuses were the finalists in the competition: Filippo Brunelleschi and Lorenzo Ghiberti both used classical models for their startlingly realistic and dramatic trial plaques depicting the Sacrifice of Isaac. Both works represent the moment in the biblical story when God stays Abraham's hand from sacrificing his son Isaac. Ghiberti won the commission, perhaps because he was technically more ingenious, using less bronze and therefore cutting the cost. In 1425, his second set of Baptistery doors genuinely marked a breakthrough in the power of the art of bronze reliefs: "gates of paradise," as Florentines called them, which acquired the realism of an extra dimension through the use of perspective. In 1440, Donato Donatello, the most devoted student of classical art in Florence, produced his free-standing bronze statue of David, which, under the form of a sacred subject,

"Scholarship has now identified renaissances in almost every century for the previous 1,000 years. No radically new departure occurred in the fifteenth century from what had gone before—merely an accentuation of long-accumulating tendencies."

(a)　　　　　(b)

Renaissance competition. In 1400, when the Cloth Workers' Guild of Florence sponsored a competition for new designs for the doors of the baptistry in the city's cathedral, Florence's leading designers competed for the job. The subject to be portrayed was the story from the Book of Genesis when God intervened to prevent Abraham from sacrificing his son Isaac. The model entered by Filippo Brunelleschi, the cathedral's architect, was more dramatic, with an angel literally staying Abraham's hand to save Isaac from being slain (a). But Lorenzo Ghiberti's winning design was more classical. The angel's foreshortening, the musculature of Isaac's body, which was copied from ancient Greek and Roman sculpture, and the technically dazzling way in which Abraham's elbow jabs from the plaque help explain Ghiberti's success (b).

again from the Bible, seemed to bring a vanished pagan world back to life: secular, sensual, homoerotic.

For there was no notion of "art for art's sake" in fifteenth- and sixteenth-century Italy. Artists were practical. The technology of bronze casting developed along with experience in casting cannon. Many masters of the Renaissance had sidelines in gunnery. Ironically, increased demand for bronze guns starved art of a vital raw material and even led to the melting down of antique bronzes, just when artists and collectors most valued them. Similarly, painters had to be good at every kind of design, including urban planning, architectural drawing, interior decoration, jewelwork, stagecraft, party-planning, and engineering. When Leonardo da Vinci—universally hailed as one of the greatest painters of the early sixteenth century—sought new patrons, he advertised himself as skilled in every kind of handiwork, including the making of weapons and the constructions of siege engines. When he worked for the dynasty that ruled Milan, one of his jobs was to paint their coat of arms on the ceilings of their apartments.

Admirers of classical learning adopted a predominantly secular curriculum: grammar, rhetoric, poetry, history, and moral philosophy, imbibed mainly from classical texts. The classics as well as—even, instead of—Christianity came to inform common ideas of morality, politics, and taste. Spreading, at first, from a few French and north Italian schools, **humanism** gradually became Europe's most prestigious form of learning. Political thinkers turned back to Greek and Roman history for instruction. Religious innovators modeled their ideas on evidence from early Christianity. Artists adopted realism and perspective from what they thought were Greek and Roman models.

Florence demonstrates humanism's power and limitations. In the fifteenth century, classical taste transformed its art and architecture. Comparisons with the Roman republic inspired its citizens to think of themselves as free and self-governing.

The Church of San Lorenzo. Filippo Brunelleschi, the trend-setting architect of Florence, got the commission to design the parish church of the ruling Medici family in 1418. He based his concept on laws of mathematical proportion that, he believed, ancient Greek and Roman architects had followed. He copied the ground plans of the most ancient churches he knew, and, to support the clergy's growing desire to make congregations participate actively in worship, he opened domes above the sacred spaces to fill them with light.

Yet power gradually fell into the hands of a single family, the Medici, who patronized art in the classical tradition but who actually spent more on jewels and on gaudy, gem-like artworks that could display their wealth. When they were temporarily overthrown in 1494, after their banking business collapsed, the state that replaced them was no Roman-style republic. Rather, it was the rule of a "godly" clique, inspired by a hell-fire preacher, who preferred piety to humanism. Botticelli (1444–1510), the great artist who had painted pagan erotica for a Medici villa, turned to biblical subjects.

Still, across Europe, the rise of humanism had lasting consequences for Christian culture. Humanists painstakingly scrutinized the language of the Bible and the historical traditions of the church, exposing incorrect translations and departures from the practices of early Christianity. New styles in church architecture reflected classical taste and, more deeply, arose from the desire to create a setting for the kind of devotion that humanism inspired. Open sanctuaries, brilliantly lit and approached through wide naves and aisles allowed worshippers to see and take part in events at the altar.

Humanism also helped arouse European interest in the wider world. Some important and provocative geographical writings of classical antiquity became widely known in the West. In the early fifteenth century, the work of the ancient Greek scholar Ptolemy, originally written in Alexandria in the second century, invited intense speculation about geography, mapping the world, and the limits of exploration. The first-century B.C.E. work of Strabo, a Greek geographer who sought to reconstruct Homer's mental map of the world, prompted questions

Chivalrous hero. When Albrecht Dürer painted an altarpiece for the family of wealthy merchants Stephan and Lucas Paumgartner in Nuremberg Germany, probably in 1498, both brothers wanted to appear as figures of chivalry. Stephan was shown as St. George, the knightly dragon-slayer, and Lucas, depicted here, took on the role of St. Eustace, displaying a banner with the image of Christ between a stag's antlers to recall the moment when Eustace, according to legend, was converted during a hunt.

about finding previously unknown continents in the ocean. Humanists' fascination with the history of language reinforced the search for "primitive" peoples who might cast light on the question of how language originated.

Magic was at least as much a part of the learned culture of the Renaissance as humanism. Florence, like everywhere else in the world at the time, as far as we know, was full of popular spells and superstitions. Three nights before the death of the Medici banker and art patron, Lorenzo the Magnificent in 1492, lightning struck the cathedral, sending stones from the famous dome crashing to the street. Florentines said Lorenzo had a demon trapped in his ring and had released it as he sensed his impending death. In 1478, when Jacopo Pazzi was hanged for his part in a conspiracy against Medici rule, heavy rains threatened the survival of the grain crop. Popular wisdom was that it was Jacopo's fault: His burial in consecrated ground had offended God; so he was dug up and dragged stinking through the streets, while the mob battered his remains before flinging them into the Arno River.

Belief in magic was not just a vulgar error. There was learned magic, too. The notion that human agency could control nature was a perfectly rational one. Promising approaches included techniques we now classify as scientific, such as observation, experiment, and the exercise of reason. Astrology, alchemy, conjuration, and sorcery had not yet proved to be false leads. For what is the difference between magic and science? Both are attempts to explain and therefore to control nature. Western science of the sixteenth and seventeenth centuries grew, in part, out of magic. The vocations of scientists overlapped with those of magicians—wielders of magical techniques for mastering nature.

In any case, chivalry was more characteristic than humanism in the values and education of most members of the elite. **Chivalry** could not, perhaps, make men good, as it was supposed to do. It could, however, win wars. In 1492, for instance, the monarchs of the Spanish kingdom of Castile extended the frontier of Christendom by conquering Granada, the last Muslim kingdom in Spain, in what the Venetian ambassador called "a beautiful war." "There was not a lord present who was not enamored of some lady," who "often handed warriors their weapons...with a request that they show their love by their deeds." Queen Isabella II of Castile (r. 1474–1504) died uttering prayers to the Archangel Michael as "prince of the chivalry of angels."

The typical chivalrous hero of the time took to the sea, conquered an island, married a princess, and became a ruler. Explorers—often men of humble social origins—tried to embody these fictions in real life. Adventurers in the service of the Portuguese Prince Henry (1394–1460), included former pirates and violent criminals. They indulged in chivalric rituals and gave themselves storybook names, like Lancelot and Tristram of the Island. They also colonized the Madeira Islands and parts of the Azores, and explored the coast of West Africa as far as Sierra Leone. The commercial sector that helped to back overseas adventures was looking for new opportunities—especially the Genoese, whose role in the eastern Mediterranean at this period was largely confined to high-bulk, low-profit shipping and trading. Marginal noblemen, shut out from advancement at home and imbued with chivalric ideas, were willing to take amazing risks. That, together with the availability of high-risk investment, helps to explain many early forays in Atlantic exploration.

Prince Henry himself—traditionally misrepresented as a navigator motivated by scientific curiosity—imagined himself a romantic hero, destined to perform great deeds and win a kingdom of his own. The truth is that he never went exploring, and his desperate efforts to make enough money to pay his retainers included slave raiding and a soap monopoly. His followers included the father-in-law of Christopher Columbus, a weaver by training who reinvented himself as a "captain of cavaliers and conquests," and who took to exploration to escape the restricted social opportunities of home.

Alongside chivalry, millenarian fantasies may have influenced overseas expansion. The first king of Portugal's ruling dynasty was actually called "Messiah of Portugal." Columbus claimed that the profits of his discoveries could be used to conquer Jerusalem and help complete God's plans for a new age. Franciscan friars who supported Columbus believed that an "Age of the Holy Spirit," which would precede the end of the world, was coming soon, and some of them came to see the New World as the place where such an age might begin.

Europe's outreach into the Atlantic was probably not the result of science or strength, so much as of delusion and desperation. This was a space race where it helped to come from behind. The prosperous cultures with access to the Indian Ocean felt no need to explore remote lands and seas for new resources. For cash-strapped Europe, however, the attempt to exploit the Atlantic for new products was like the efforts of underdeveloped countries today, anxiously drilling for offshore wealth from oil or natural gas. In some ways, it paid off.

> *"Europe's outreach into the Atlantic was probably not the result of science or strength, so much as of delusion and desperation. This was a space race where it helped to come from behind."*

In Perspective
Beyond Empires

The imperial habit was spreading, and new empires were forming in environments that had never experienced imperialism before. Russia, for example, extended empire to the Eurasian far north. Mwene Mutapa introduced it in sub-Saharan East Africa. The Aztecs and Incas practiced it in the Americas on an unprecedented scale. Nonetheless, most of Africa and the Americas, as well as the whole of Australia and most of the Pacific island world, as far as we know, had still not experienced anything like empire. While some empires revived, most of the world remained in the hands of communities with modest political ambitions. These were still organized as kinship networks, chiefdoms, or small states. More remarkably, perhaps, some regions with an imperial past, or under imperialist threat, shied away. Instead, they developed systems in which independent states coexisted with varying degrees of mutual hostility. The world of the late fourteenth and fifteenth centuries had four such areas.

In North Africa, Mamluk Egypt was an immensely rich and productive state but remained confined to the Nile valley, unable to expand beyond the deserts that fringed it. A second area lay westward, along Africa's Mediterranean coast. Here numerous small states, founded on the profits of trade or piracy, flourished where Mediterranean and Saharan trade routes met. At the western end of North Africa, Morocco emerged as a kingdom on the edge of the Islamic world, holding Christendom at bay.

South and southeast Asia was a third empire-free region. In India, the sultanate of Delhi never fully recovered from the setbacks of the mid–fourteenth century. Hindu states proliferated, some warlike, specifically, toward Islam. The most militaristic, perhaps, was Vijayanagar—the name means "City of Victories"—with its 60 miles of sevenfold walls (see Map 15.9). This was the state, for

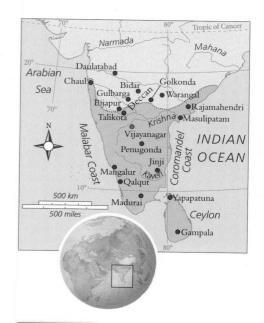

MAP 15.9

Vijayanagar

extent of Vijayanagar Empire, circa 1500

Absolute sovereignty. The artist of the Wilton Diptych is unknown, but it is regarded as one of the most exquisite paintings of the fourteenth century. It is a propaganda work, emphasizing the claims of King Richard II of England (r. 1377–1399), to sacred responsibilities. His heavenly patrons, St. John the Baptist, and two earlier, sainted English kings, present him to the Blessed Virgin Mary, whose angel-attendants wear Richard's badge—the emblem of the white stag—and carry the English flag. Most interpreters suppose that the message of the painting is that the Virgin is entrusting Richard with the realm of England, symbolized by the flag, but his hands seem open to receive the Christ Child himself—symbolism suitable to a traveling altarpiece, probably designed to be set up whenever the king wished to hear mass during a journey.

which Abd-ar-Razzak, the Persian ambassador mentioned at the start of the chapter, was bound in 1417. It impressed another Muslim visitor in 1443 as "such that the eye has seen nothing like it." Chinese expansion nibbled at the edges of southeast Asia, but China's renunciation of imperialism left the native states of the region free to try one another's strength. The Thai—founders of what is now called Thailand—certainly had expansionist ambitions. In the early fifteenth century, they created the region's largest state at the expense of their neighbors, the Burmese, Khmer, Mons, and Malays (see Map 15.8). Nonetheless, the region lacked a dominant empire and remained home to a state system in which a number of regional states contended with each other.

Finally, most of Europe continued to enclose a state system. East of the Vistula River, where geography favored the formation of large, unstable states by conquest, Russia, as we have seen, undertook a massive imperial enterprise. A brief union of the Polish and Lithuanian states in 1386 created what, on the map, at least, also looked like an empire of daunting dimensions, stretching from the Baltic to the Black Sea. Farther west, however, small states got stronger, and the dream of reuniting them and recreating the old Roman Empire faded—or began to look unrealistic.

Something like what we now call **nationalism** emerged. That is, group feeling developed where people's mutually intelligible speech and a common sense of identity defined by birth caused them to merge into a single community. In the fifteenth century, for instance, the kings of England began to use English, alongside

French and Latin, in official documents and correspondence. National communities adopted patron saints. At international gatherings, such as universities and church councils, people defined themselves according the nation to which they belonged and engaged in ferocious disputes over precedence. At a Council of the Church in 1415, the Castilian delegation settled such a dispute with the English by overturning the bench on which their rivals were sitting, so that the Castilians could occupy a higher place in the hall.

States increasingly asserted their absolute sovereignty, rejecting any obligation to defer to such traditionally supranational authorities as the church or the Holy Roman Emperor. When, for instance, the Emperor Sigismund visited England in 1415, a knight rode into the sea to challenge him to renounce all claim to authority in England before he was allowed to disembark. Kings of France called themselves "emperors in their own realm" and those of Castile in Spain asserted "my sovereign absolute power."

Some rulers developed ideological grounds for their claims to absolute sovereignty. French kings were supposedly endowed with divine powers to heal and able to perform "miracles in your own lifetime." Richard II of England (r. 1377–1399) had himself painted in a sumptuous image, attended by angels, opening his hands to receive the body of Christ from the hands of the Virgin Mary herself.

At the same time, the power of the state really did increase. One reason was improved communications. As paper replaced parchment, increasing the output of documents, royal bureaucracies reached more people in more parts of the realm. Changes in the concept of law also strengthened the state. Traditionally, the law was seen as a body of wisdom handed down from the past. Now it came to be seen as a code that kings and parliaments could endlessly change and recreate. The state's power also expanded over vast new areas of public life and common welfare: labor relations, wages, prices, forms of land tenure, markets, the food supply, livestock breeding, and even, in some cases, what personal adornments people could wear.

Finally, while the state was growing more powerful, the power of the church declined. Between 1378 and 1415, rulers in Latin Christendom could not agree whom to recognize as pope. The power vacuum eroded what little unity Christendom still had. Secular states became stronger as heresies arose. Under the influence of reformers who demanded—among other changes—lay control of appointments in the church and worship in everyday language instead of Latin, Bohemia for a time refused to recognize papal authority. Reformers known as conciliarists argued that the church should become a kind of republic, with power transferred from Rome to a council of bishops who would meet periodically in a kind of parliament.

Chronology

ca. 1325	Aztecs found city of Tenochtitlán
1368	Beginning of Ming dynasty
1370–1406	Reign of Timur
Late fourteenth century	Ethiopia expands into surrounding regions
1401	Lorenzo Ghiberti wins competition for the bronze doors of the Bapistery in Florence
1405	First voyage of Zheng He
1417	Voyage of Abd-ar-Razzak to Vijayanagar (India)
1430s	Portuguese establish way stations in Azores
1440s	Portuguese begin to obtain slaves from West Africa
ca. 1450	Inca begin period of expansion and conquest
1453	Ottomans capture Constantinople
1462–1505	Reign of Ivan the Great
ca. 1475	Center of power in southern Africa shifts from Zimbabwe to Mwene Mutapa
1480s	Portuguese make contact with kingdom of Kongo
1482	Portuguese establish trading post of São Jorge da Mina on West African coast
1484	Sugar production begins in Canary Islands
1490s	First Portuguese diplomatic missions arrive in Ethiopia
1492–1493	First voyage of Christopher Columbus; Spanish kingdom of Castile captures Granada, last Muslim kingdom in Spain
1496	John Cabot discovers direct route across North Atlantic
1497	Pilgrimage of Muhammed Touray Askia, ruler of Songhay, to Mecca; first voyage of Vasco da Gama
1500	Vasco da Gama reaches India; Aztec Empire at its peak

"The expanding empires of the age were reaching toward each other. Where they made contact, they became arenas of unprecedented scale for trade and for transmitting technology, ideas, sentiments, and ways of life."

How much difference did the state system make to Europe's prospects? Historians have engaged in a pointless debate over this question. On the one hand, the state system deprived Europeans of unified command, of the sort found, for instance, in the Chinese or Ottoman Empires. On the other hand, it stimulated competition among rulers, multiplying the possible sources of patronage available to innovators. For European maritime expansion, the state system was not decisive in launching most initiatives. The explorers and would-be empire builders relied on private enterprise, with little or no state backing. Columbus, for instance, got no direct financial support from the Spanish crown—the myth that Queen Isabella of Castile pawned her jewels for him is nonsense. Prince Henry's Atlantic enterprise was a private venture. Furthermore, as the example of Southeast Asia shows, a state system was not in itself sufficient to produce overseas imperialism; for that, the stimulus of coming from behind was necessary. Asian states were at the nodes of the world's richest trades. They had no need to explore new markets or conquer new centers of production, because everything came to them anyway. Europeans, on the other hand, had to expand if they were to gain access to anything worth exploiting.

For all its hesitations and limitations, fifteenth-century expansion was new and potentially world changing. The new routes pioneered in the 1490s linked the populous central belt of Eurasia to the Americas and Africa, and Europe to Asia by sea. We can see the beginnings of an interconnected globe—a **world system** able to encompass the planet. The expanding empires of the age were reaching toward each other. Where they made contact, they became arenas of unprecedented scale for trade and for transmitting technology, ideas, sentiments, and ways of life. The consequences would transform the world of the next three centuries: Worldwide encounters, commerce, conflict, contagion, and cultural and ecological exchange would follow.

PROBLEMS AND PARALLELS

1. Why was the last half of the fifteenth century an age of expansion? How did the beginnings of a world system emerge around 1500?

2. Why were African states fragile in this period? How did Muhammad Touray Askia use Islam to make Songhay the dominant power in West Africa?

3. What does the term *ecological imperialism* mean? How did the Inca exploit the many different ecosystems of their empire? What was role of tributary networks in the Aztec Empire?

4. How did the Russian and Turkish worlds expand in the fourteenth and fifteenth centuries? What was the impact of Timur's conquests on the Islamic world?

5. Why did the Chinese turn away from maritime expansionism after the voyages of Zheng He? Why was frontier stability more important than overseas expansion for China? Why did the Hongxi emperor reinstate Confucian values at the Chinese court?

6. Why were wind systems so important in world history? Why did the beginnings of European oceanic imperialism have as much to do with geography as with culture?

7. How did the rise of nationalism and the state system drive European expansion? Why were there no major empires in North Africa or in South Asia during this period?

READ ON ▶ ▶ ▶

The material on Abd-ar-Razzak comes from R. H. Major, ed., *India in the Fifteenth Century* (1964). D. Ringrose, *Expansion and Global Interaction, 1200–1700* (2001) gives the background.

On Ethiopia, S. C. Munro-Hay, *Ethiopia: the Unknown Land* (2002) and R. Pankhurst, *The Ethiopians: A History* (2001) are valuable general histories. W. G. Randles, *The Empire of Monomotapa* (1975) is excellent on Mwene Mutapa. On West Africa in this period, E. W. R. Bovill, *The Golden Trade of the Moors* (1995) is a readable classic. Songhay is not well served by books in English but a useful collection of sources is J. O. Hunwick, ed., *Timbuktu and the Songhay Empire: Al-Sa'di's Ta'rîkh al-Sudan down to 1613, and Other Contemporary Documents* (1999). Anne Hilton, *The Kingdom of Kongo* (1985) is outstanding.

Of histories of the Inca and Aztecs, J. V. Murra, *The Economic Organization of the Inca State* (1980), T.N. D'Altroy, *The Incas* (2003), and M. Smith, *The Aztecs* (2002) are particularly strong on ecological aspects.

My material on the White Sea comes from R. Cormack and D. Gaze, eds, *Art of Holy Russia* (1998). J. Martin, *Treasures of the Land of Darkness* (2004) is enthralling on the economic background to Russian expansion. I. Gray, *Ivan III and the Unification of Russia* (1972) is a businesslike introduction. Ibn Khaldun's great work is *The Muqaddimah: An Introduction to History*, tr. Franz Rosenthal (1969). B. F. Manz, *The Rise and Rule of Tamerlane* (1999) is the outstanding work on its subject.

For the Ottomans, see H. Inalcik, *The Ottoman Empire: the Classical Age* (2001). E.L. Dreyer, *Early Ming China* (1982) and *Zheng He: China and the Oceans in the Early Ming Dynasty* (2006) cover the Chinese topics of this chapter admirably. L. Levathes, *When China Ruled the Seas* (1997) is readable and reliable.

On Europe C. Allmand, ed, *The New Cambridge Medieval History, VII* (2005) is comprehensive, while M. Aston, *The Prospect of Europe* (1968) offers a short introduction. On Portuguese expansion, P.E. Russell, *Henry the Navigator* (2001) is admirable and F. Bethencourt and D. Curto, eds, *Portuguese Oceanic Expansion* (1998) provides a broad survey. P.O. Kristeller, *The Cambridge Companion to Renaissance Humanism* (1996) is an unsurpassed classic on its topic and M.H. Keen, *Chivalry* (1986) is on the way to attaining the same status.

The World in 1491

In the thirteenth century, as we pointed out in Chapter 13, the Mongol peace proved a greater stimulus to the migration of ideas and technologies across Eurasia than all previous empires had achieved. In part, the Mongols' outreach was a response to climate change, as cooling shriveled their grasslands. In the fourteenth century, observers began to notice unsteadily increasing cold. Glacial evidence shows that global cold lasted—with varying intensity—until the eighteenth century. In most of Eurasia and North Africa, climate change nourished the diseases contemporaries called plague. As long as the cold period lasted, so did frequent plagues.

The Mongol peace exceeded previous empires as a stimulus to the migration of ideas and technologies, while merchants, missionaries, and pilgrims pioneered ever more intensive communications that bound together Eurasia and parts of North, East, and West Africa. Gradually, with gathering pace in the fifteenth century and dramatic acceleration from the sixteenth century onward, convergence began to replace divergence as the dominant theme in the history of human cultures. After millennia of divergence, it seems amazing that the process should have been halted and reversed.

Explorers found routes across the Atlantic, which for the first time linked Europe and Africa to the Americas. They sailed around Africa to connect Europe by sea with the lands around the Indian Ocean, the world's richest zone of commerce. Cultural exchange stimulated Western arts and learning, though from the perspective of Islam, India, or China—Westerners remained relatively backward and poor. Over a longer period, empires and trade overleaped oceans, taking people, animals, plants, deadly microbes, and forms of culture with them. Parts of the globe that had grown unalike now began, slowly and selectively at first, to resemble each other once again as they had before the continents had drifted apart millions of years ago.

► QUESTIONS

1. Based on the globes shown here, which cultures were experiencing the most convergence in 1491? Which cultures were mostly divergent from other cultures?

2. In 1491, which ocean was the biggest and richest zone of long range commerce? Is there any evidence in the globes shown here that the Atlantic would emerge in the sixteenth century as a major zone of cultural and ecological exchange?

To view an interactive version of this map, as well as a video of the author describing key themes related to this Part, go to
www.myhistorylab.com

Chinese Exploration by c. 1491

- Known and mapped in detail
- Known by observation or report but not mapped in detail

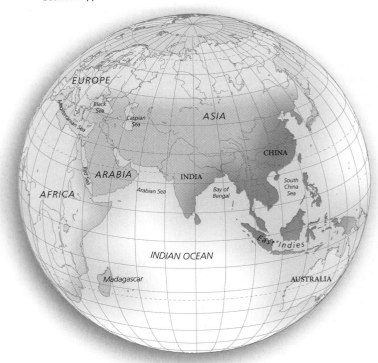

Japanese Knowledge of the World, c. 1491

- Known in detail
- Known by report

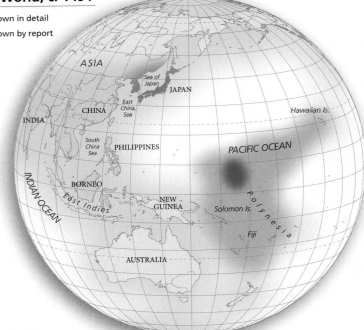

The World of Polynesian Navigators by c. 1491

- Known and mapped in detail
- Known but not mapped

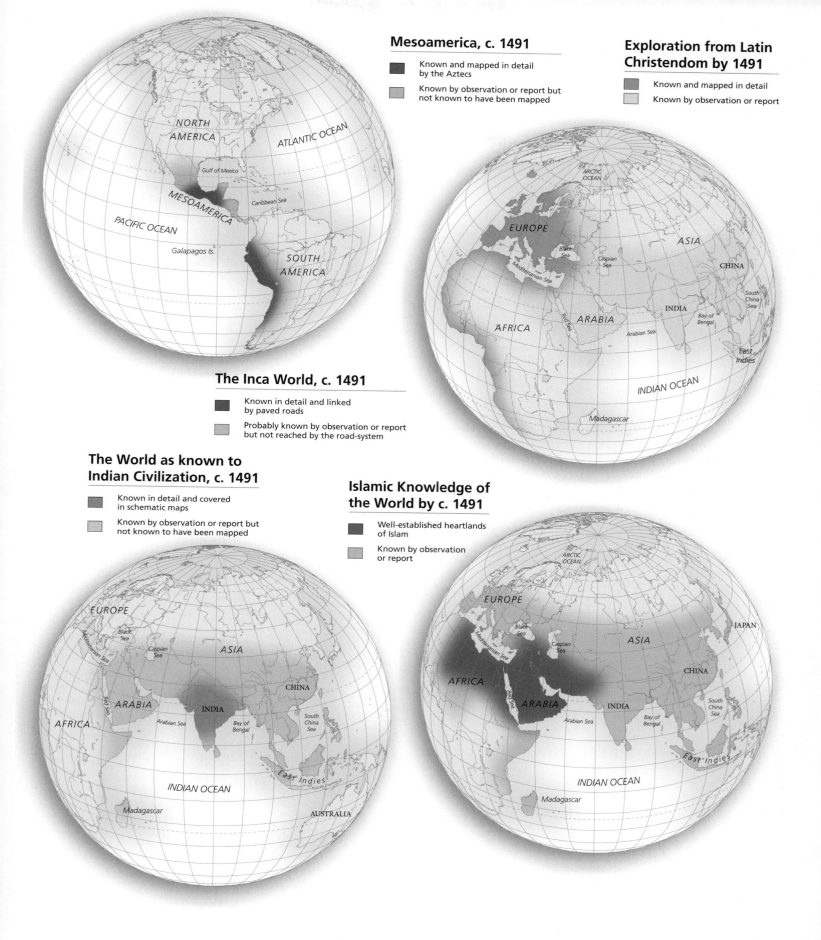

Mesoamerica, c. 1491

■ Known and mapped in detail
by the Aztecs

■ Known by observation or report but
not known to have been mapped

**Exploration from Latin
Christendom by 1491**

■ Known and mapped in detail

□ Known by observation or report

The Inca World, c. 1491

■ Known in detail and linked
by paved roads

■ Probably known by observation or report
but not reached by the road-system

**The World as known to
Indian Civilization, c. 1491**

■ Known in detail and covered
in schematic maps

■ Known by observation or report but
not known to have been mapped

**Islamic Knowledge of
the World by c. 1491**

■ Well-established heartlands
of Islam

■ Known by observation
or report

Abolitionism Belief that slavery and the slave trade are immoral and should be abolished.

Aborigine A member of the indigenous or earliest-known population of a region.

Aborigines Indigenous people of Australia.

Afrikaans An official language of South Africa, spoken mostly by the Boers. It is derived from seventeenth-century Dutch.

Age of Plague Term for the spread of lethal diseases from the fourteenth through the eighteenth centuries.

Ahriman The chief spirit of darkness and evil in Zoroastrianism, the enemy of Ahura Mazda.

Ahura Mazda The chief deity of Zoroastrianism, the creator of the world, the source of light, and the embodiment of good.

Al-Andalus Arabic name for the Iberian Peninsula (Spain and Portugal).

Alluvial plains Flat lands where mud from rivers or lakes renews the topsoil. If people can control the flooding that is common in such conditions, alluvial plains are excellent for settled agriculture.

Almoravids Muslim dynasty of Berber warriors that flourished from 1049 to 1145 and that established political dominance over northwest Africa and Spain.

Alternative energy Energy sources that usually produce less pollution than does the burning of fossil fuels, and are renewable in some cases.

Alternative medicine Medicines, treatments, and techniques not advocated by the mainstream medical establishment in the West.

Americanization The process by which other cultures, to a greater or lesser degree, adopt American fashions, culture, and ways of life.

Anarchists Believers in the theory that all forms of government are oppressive and undesirable and should be opposed and abolished.

Animal rights Movement that asserts that animals have fundamental rights that human beings have a moral obligation to respect.

Anti-Semitism Hostility or prejudice against Jews or Judaism.

Arthasastra Ancient Indian study of economics and politics that influenced the Emperor Asoka. The Arthasastra expresses an ideology of universal rule and emphasizes the supremacy of "the king's law" and the importance of uniform justice.

Artificial intelligence The creation of a machine or computer program that exhibits the characteristics of human intelligence.

Arts and Crafts Movement Nineteenth-century artists and intellectuals who argued that the products produced by individual craftsmen were more attractive than and morally superior to the mass, uniform goods produced by industry.

Assassins A secret order of Muslims in what is today Syria and Lebanon who terrorized and killed its opponents, both Christian and Muslim. The Assassins were active from the eleventh to the thirteenth centuries.

Atlantic Slave Trade Trade in African slaves who were bought, primarily in West Africa, by Europeans and white Americans and transported across the Atlantic, usually in horrific conditions, to satisfy the demand for labor in the plantations and mines of the Americas.

Atomic theory The theory that matter is not a continuous whole, but is composed of tiny, discrete particles.

Australopithecine (Trans.) "Southern ape-like creatures." Term used to describe prehuman species that existed before those classed under the genus *Homo*.

Axial Age A pivotal age in the history of world civilization, lasting for roughly 500 years up to the beginning of the Christian era, in which critical intellectual and cultural ideas arose in and were transmitted across the Mediterranean world, India, Iran, and East Asia.

Axial zone The densely populated central belt of world population, communication, and cultural exchange in Eurasia that stretches from Japan and China to Western Europe and North Africa.

Aztecs People of central Mexico whose civilization and empire were at their height at the time of the Spanish conquest in the early sixteenth century.

Balance of trade The relative value of goods traded between two or more nations or states. Each trading partner strives to have a favorable balance of trade, that is, to sell more to its trading partners than it buys from them.

Bantu African people sharing a common linguistic ancestry who originated in West Africa and whose early agriculture centered on the cultivation of yams and oil palms in swamplands.

Big bang theory Theory that the universe began with an explosion of almost infinitesimally compressed matter, the effects of which are still going on.

Black Death Term for a lethal disease or diseases that struck large parts of Eurasia and North Africa in the 1300s and killed millions of people.

Boers Dutch settlers and their descendents in southern Africa. The first Boers arrived in South Africa in the seventeenth century.

Bon Religion that was Buddhism's main rival in Tibet for several centuries in the late first millennium C.E.

Brahman A member of the highest, priestly caste of traditional Indian society.

British East India Company British trading company founded in 1600 that played a key role in the colonization of India. It ruled much of the subcontinent until 1857.

Bureaucratization The process by which government increasingly operates through a body of trained officials who follow a set of regular rules and procedures.

Business Imperialism Economic domination and exploitation of poorer and weaker countries by richer and stronger states.

Byzantine Empire Term for the Greek-speaking, eastern portion of the former Roman Empire, centered on Constantinople. It lasted until 1453, when it was conquered by the Ottoman Turks.

Cahokia Most spectacular existent site of Mississippi Valley Native American civilization, located near modern St. Louis.

Caliph The supreme Islamic political and religious authority, literally, the "successor" of the Prophet Muhammad.

Canyon cultures Indigenous peoples of the North American Southwest. The canyon cultures flourished beween about 850 and 1250 C.E.

Capitalism An economic system in which the means of production and distribution are privately or corporately owned.

Caste system A social system in which people's places in society, how they live and work, and with whom they can marry are determined by heredity. The Indian caste system has been intertwined with India's religious and economic systems.

Centralization The concentration of power in the hands of a central government.

Chaos theory Theory that some systems are so complex that their causes and effects are untraceable.

Chicago economics The economic theory associated with economists who taught at the University of Chicago that holds that low taxes and light government regulation will lead to economic prosperity.

Chimú Civilization centered on the Pacific coast of Peru that was conquered by the Inca in the fifteenth century.

Chinese Board of Astronomy Official department of the Chinese imperial court created in the early seventeenth century that was responsible for devising the ritual calendar.

Chinese diaspora The migration of Chinese immigrants around the world between the seventeenth and nineteenth centuries.

Chivalry The qualities idealized by the medieval European aristocracy and associated with knighthood, such as bravery, courtesy, honor, and gallantry.

Chola Expansive kingdom in southern India that had important connections with merchant communities on the coast. Chola reached its height around 1050 C.E.

Christendom Term referring to the European states in which Christianity was the dominant or only religion.

Cistercians Christian monastic order that built monasteries in places where habitation was sparse and nature hostile. Cistercians practiced a more ascetic and rigorous form of the Benedictine rule.

Citizen army The mass army the French created during the Revolution by imposing mandatory military service on the entire active adult male population. The army was created in response to the threat of invasion by an alliance of anti-Revolutionary countries in the early 1790s.

Civilizing mission The belief that imperialism and colonialism are justified because imperial powers have a duty to bring the benefits of "civilization" to, or impose them on, the "backward" people they ruled or conquered.

Clan A social group made up of a number of families that claim descent from a common ancestor and follow a hereditary chieftain.

Class struggle Conflict between competing social classes that, in Karl Marx's view, was responsible for all important historical change.

Climacteric A period of critical change in a society that is poised between different possible outcomes.

Code Napoleon Civil code promulgated by Napoleon in 1804 and spread by his armies across Europe. It still forms the basis for the legal code for many European, Latin American, and African countries.

Cold war Post–World War II rivalry between the United States and its allies and the Soviet Union and its allies. The cold war ended in 1990–1991 with the end of the Soviet Empire in Eastern Europe and the collapse of the Soviet Union itself.

Columbian Exchange Biological exchange of plants, animals, microbes, and human beings between the Americas and the rest of the world.

Commune Collective name for the citizen body of a medieval and Renaissance Italian town.

Communism A system of government in which the state plans and controls the economy, and private property and class distinctions are abolished.

Confraternities Lay Catholic charitable brotherhoods.

Confucianism Chinese doctrine founded by Confucius emphasizing learning and the fulfillment of obligations among family members, citizens, and the state.

Constitutionalism The doctrine that the state is founded on a set of fundamental laws that rulers and citizens make together and are bound to respect.

Consumerism A system of values that exalts the consumption and possession of consumer goods as both a social good and as an end in themselves.

Coolies Poor laborers from China and India who left their homelands to do hard manual and agricultural work in other parts of the world in the nineteenth and early twentieth centuries.

Copernican revolution Development of a heliocentric model of the solar system begun in 1543 by Nicholas Copernicus, a Polish churchman and astronomer.

Council of Trent A series of meetings from 1545 to 1563 to direct the response of the Roman Catholic Church to Protestantism. The council defined Catholic dogma and reformed church discipline.

Counter Reformation The Catholic effort to combat the spread of Protestantism in the sixteenth and seventeenth centuries.

Countercolonization The flow of immigrants out of former colonies to the "home countries" that used to rule them.

Country trades Commerce involving local or regional exchanges of goods from one Asian destination to another that, while often handled by European merchants, never touched Europe.

Covenant In the Bible, God's promise to the human race.

Creoles People of at least part-European descent born in the West Indies, French Louisiana, or Spanish America.

Crusades Any of the military expeditions undertaken by European Christians from the late eleventh to the thirteenth centuries to recover the Holy Land from the Muslims.

Cubism Artistic style developed by Pablo Picasso and Georges Braque in the early twentieth century, characterized by the reduction and fragmentation of natural forms into abstract, often geometric structures.

Cultural relativism The doctrine that cultures cannot be ranked in any order of merit. No culture is superior to another, and each culture must be judged on its own terms.

Cultural Revolution Campaign launched by Mao Zedong in 1965–1966 against the bureaucrats of the Chinese Communist Party. In lasted until 1976 and involved widespread disorder, violence, killings, and the persecution of intellectuals and the educated elite.

Culture Socially transmitted behavior, beliefs, institutions, and technologies that a given group of people, peoples, or animals share.

Cuneiform Mesopotamian writing system that was inscribed on clay tablets with wedge-shaped markers.

Czars (Trans.) "Caesar." Title of the emperors who ruled Russia until the revolution of 1917.

Dada An early twentieth-century European artistic and literary movement that flouted conventional and traditional aesthetic and cultural values by producing works marked by nonsense, travesty, and incongruity.

Dahomey West African slave-trading state that began to be prominent in the sixteenth century.

Daimyo Japanese feudal lord who ruled a province and was subject to the shoguns.

Daoism Chinese doctrine founded by Laozi that identified detachment from the world with the pursuit of immortality.

"Declaration of the Rights of Man and Citizen" Declaration of basic principles adopted by the French National Assembly in August 1789, at the start of the French Revolution.

Decolonization The process by which the nineteenth-century colonial empires in Asia, Africa, the Caribbean, and the Pacific were dismantled after World War II.

Deforestation The process by which trees are eliminated from an ecosystem.

Democracy Government by the people, exercised either directly or through elected representatives.

Devsirme Quota of male children supplied by Christian subjects as tribute to the Ottoman Sultan. Many of the boys were drafted into the janissaries.

Dharma In the teachings of Buddha, moral law or duty.

Diffusion The spread of a practice, belief, culture, or technology within a community or between communities.

Dirlik (Trans.) "Wealth." The term applied to provincial government in the Ottoman Empire.

Divine love God's ongoing love for and interest in human beings.

Dominicans Order of preaching friars established in 1216 by Saint Dominic.

Druze Lebanese sect that regards the caliph al-Hakim as a manifestation of God. Other Muslims regard the Druze as heretics.

Dualism Perception of the world as an arena of conflict between opposing principles of good and evil.

Dutch East India Company Dutch company founded in 1602 that enjoyed a government-granted monopoly on trade between Holland and Asia. The company eventually established a territorial empire in what is today Indonesia.

Dutch East Indies Dutch colonies in Asia centered on present-day Indonesia.

East India Trade Maritime trade between Western Europe and New England and Asia (predominantly India and China) between 1600 and 1800. Westerners paid cash for items from Asia, such as porcelain, tea, silk, cotton textiles, and spices.

Easterlies Winds coming from the east.

Ecological exchange The exchange of plants and animals between ecosystems.

Ecological imperialism Term historians use for the sweeping environmental changes European and other imperialists introduced in regions they colonized.

Ecology of civilization The interaction of people with their environment.

Economic liberalism Belief that government interference in and regulation of the economy should be kept to a minimum.

Edo Former name of Tokyo when it was the center of government for the Tokugawa shoguns.

El Niño A periodic reversal of the normal flow of Pacific currents that alters weather patterns and affects the number and location of fish in the ocean.

Elan vital The "vital force" hypothesized by the French philosopher Henri Bergson as a source of efficient causation and evolution in nature.

Empiricism The view that experience, especially of the senses, is the only source of knowledge.

Emporium trading Commerce that takes place in fixed market places or trading posts.

Enlightened despotism Reforms instituted by powerful monarchs in eighteenth-century Europe who were inspired by the principles of the Enlightenment.

Enlightenment Movement of eighteenth-century European thought championed by the *philosophes*, thinkers who held that change and reform were desirable and could be achieved by the application of reason and science. Most Enlightenment thinkers were hostile to conventional religion.

Enthusiasm "Religion" of English romantics who believed that emotion and passion were positive qualities.

Epistemology The branch of philosophy that studies the nature of knowledge.

Eugenics The theory that the human race can be improved mentally and physically by controlled selective breeding and that the state and society have a duty to encourage "superior" persons to have offspring and prevent "inferior" persons from reproducing.

Eunuchs Castrated male servants valued because they could not produce heirs or have sexual relations with women. In Byzantium, China, and the Islamic world, eunuchs could rise to high office in the state and the military.

European Union (EU) Loose economic and political federation that succeeded the European Economic Community (EEC) in 1993. It has expanded to include most of the states in Western and Eastern Europe.

Evolution Change in the genetic composition of a population over successive generations, as a result of natural selection acting on the genetic variation among individuals.

Examination system System for selecting Chinese officials and bureaucrats according to merit through a series of competitive, written examinations that, in theory, any Chinese young man could take. Success in the exams required years of intense study in classical Chinese literature. The examination system was not abolished until the early twentieth century.

Existentialism Philosophy that regards human existence as unexplainable, and stresses freedom of choice and accepting responsibility for the consequences of one's acts.

Expressionism Term describing a work of art in which forms are created primarily to evoke subjective emotions rather than to portray objective reality.

Factories Foreign trading posts in China and other parts of Asia. The chief representative of a factory was known as a "factor." Though the earliest trading posts were established by the Portuguese in the sixteenth century, the number of factories grew rapidly in the eighteenth and nineteenth centuries, with European and American merchants trading for silk, rhubarb, tea, and porcelain.

Fascism A system of government marked by centralization of authority under a dictator, stringent socioeconomic controls, and suppression of the opposition through terror and censorship.

Fatimids Muslim dynasty that ruled parts of North Africa and Egypt (909–1171).

Feminism The belief that women collectively constitute a class of society that has been historically oppressed and deserves to be set free.

Final Solution Nazi plan to murder all European Jews.

Fixed-wind systems Wind system in which the prevailing winds do not change direction for long periods of time.

Fossil fuels Fuels including peat, coal, natural gas, and oil.

Franciscans Religious order founded by Francis of Assisi in 1209 and dedicated to the virtues of humility, poverty, and charitable work among the poor.

Free trade The notion that maximum economic efficiency is achieved when barriers to trade, especially taxes on imports and exports, are eliminated.

French Revolution Political, intellectual, and social upheaval that began in France in 1789. It resulted in the overthrow of the monarchy and the establishment of a republic.

Fulani Traditional herdsmen of the Sahel in West Africa.

Fundamentalism The idea that a sacred text or texts contains fundamental truths that cannot be questioned, either by critical inquiry or by scientific evidence.

Futurism Artistic vision articulated by Emilio Filippo Marinetti in 1909. He believed that all traditional art and ideas should be repudiated, destroyed, and replaced by the new. Futurists glorified speed, technology, progress, and violence.

Gauchos Argentine cowboys.

General will Jean-Jacques Rousseau's concept of the collective will of the population. He believed that the purpose of government was to express the general will.

Genetic revolution Revolution in the understanding of human biology produced by advances in genetic research.

Genocide The systematic and planned extermination of an entire national, racial, political, or ethnic group.

Ghana A medieval West African kingdom in what are now eastern Senegal, southwest Mali, and southern Mauritania.

Global gardening The collecting in botanical gardens of plants from around the world for cultivation and study.

Globalization The process through which uniform or similar ways of life are spread across the planet.

Glyph A form of writing that uses symbolic figures that are usually engraved or incised, such as Egyptian hieroglyphics.

GM Crops that have been *genetically modified* to produce certain desired characteristics.

Golden Horde Term for Mongols who ruled much of Russia from the steppes of the lower Volga River from the thirteenth to the fifteenth centuries.

Grand Vizier The chief minister of state in the Ottoman Empire.

Greater East Asia Co-Prosperity Sphere Bloc of Asian nations under Japanese economic and political control during World War II.

Green revolution Improvements in twentieth-century agriculture that substantially increased food production by developing new strains of crops and agricultural techniques.

Greenhouse effect The increase in temperature caused by the trapping of carbon in the Earth's atmosphere.

Guardians Self-elected class of philosopher-rulers found in Plato's *Republic*.

Guomindang (GMD) Nationalist Chinese political party founded in 1912 by Sun Yat-Sen. The Guomindang took power in China in 1928 but was defeated by the Chinese Communists in 1949.

Habsburgs An Austro-German imperial family that reached the height of their power in the sixteenth century under Charles V of Spain when the Habsburgs ruled much of Europe and the Americas. The Habsburgs continued to rule a multinational empire based in Vienna until 1918.

Haj The pilgrimage to Mecca that all faithful Muslims are required to complete at least once in their lifetime if they able.

Han Dynasty that ruled China from ca. 206 B.C.E. to ca. 220 C.E. This was the period when the fundamental identity and culture of China were formed. Chinese people still refer to themselves as "Han."

Hanseatic League Founded in 1356, the Hanseatic League was a powerful network of allied ports along the North Sea and Baltic coasts that collaborated to promote trade.

Harem The quarters reserved for the female members of a Muslim household.

Herders Agriculturalists who emphasize the raising of animals, rather than plants, for food and products, such as wool and hides.

High-level equilibrium trap A situation in which an economy that is meeting high levels of demand with traditional technology finds that it has little scope to increase its output.

Hinduism Indian polytheistic religion that developed out of Brahmanism and in response to Buddhism. It remains the majority religion in India today.

Hispaniola Modern Haiti and the Dominican Republic.

Hohokam People Native American culture that flourished from about the third century B.C.E. to the mid–fifteenth century C.E. in south-central Arizona.

Holocaust Term for the murder of millions of Jews by the Nazi regime during World War II.

Holy Roman Empire A loose federation of states under an elected emperor that consisted primarily of Germany and northern Italy. It endured in various forms from 800 to 1806.

Homo erectus (Trans.) "Standing upright." Humanlike tool-using species that lived about 1.5 million years ago. At one time, Homo erectus was thought to be the first "human."

Homo ergaster (Trans.) "Workman." Humanlike species that lived 800,000 years ago and stacked the bones of its dead.

Homo habilis (Trans.) "Handy." Humanlike species that lived about 2.5 million years ago and made stone hand axes.

Homo sapiens (Trans.) "Wise." The species to which contemporary humans belong.

Human rights Notion of inherent rights that all human beings share. Based in part on the assumption that being human constitutes in itself a meaningful moral category that excludes nonhuman creatures.

Humanism Cultural and intellectual movement of the Renaissance centered on the study of the literature, art, and civilization of ancient Greece and Rome.

Hurons A Native American confederacy of eastern Canada. The Huron flourished immediately prior to contact with Europeans, but declined rapidly as a result of European diseases such as smallpox. They were allied with the French in wars against the British, the Dutch, and other Native Americans.

Husbandry The practice of cultivating crops and breeding and raising livestock; agriculture.

Ice-Age affluence Relative prosperity of Ice-Age society as the result of abundant game and wild, edible plants.

Icon A representation or picture of a Christian saint or sacred event. Icons have been traditionally venerated in the Eastern, or Orthodox Church.

Il-Khanate A branch of the Mongol Empire, centered in present-day Iran. Its rulers, the Il-Khans, converted to Islam and adopted Persian culture.

Imam A Muslim religious teacher. Also the title of Muslim political and religious rulers in Yemen and Oman.

Imperator A Latin term that originally meant an army commander under the Roman Republic and evolved into the term *emperor*.

Imperialism The policy of extending a nation's authority and influence by conquest or by establishing economic and political hegemony over other nations.

Incas Peoples of highland Peru who established an empire from northern Ecuador to central Chile before the Spanish conquest in the 1530s.

Indian National Congress Political organization created in 1885 that played a leading role in the Indian independence movement.

Indirect rule Rule by a colonial power through local elites.

Individualism Belief in the primary importance of the individual and in the virtues of self-reliance and personal independence.

Indo-European languages Language family that originated in Asia and from which most of Europe's present languages evolved.

Inductive method Method by which scientists turn individual observations and experiments into general laws.

Industrial Revolution The complex set of economic, demographic, and technological events that began in Western Europe and resulted in the advent of an industrial economy.

Industrialization The process by which an industrial economy is developed.

Information technology Technology, such as printing presses and computers, that facilitates the spread of information.

Inquisition A tribunal of the Roman Catholic Church that was charged with suppressing heresy and immorality.

Iroquois Native American confederacy based in northern New York State, originally composed of the Mohawk, Oneida, Onondaga, Cayuga, and Seneca peoples, known as the Five Nations. The confederation created a constitution sometime between the mid-1400s and the early 1600s.

Isolationism Belief that, unless directly challenged, a country should concentrate on domestic issues and avoid foreign conflicts or active participation in foreign affairs.

Jainism A way of life that arose in India designed to free the soul from evil by ascetic practices: chastity, detachment, truth, selflessness, and strict vegetarianism.

Janissaries Soldiers in an elite Ottoman infantry formation that was first organized in the fourteenth century. Originally drafted from among the sons of the sultan's Christian subjects, the janissaries had become a hereditary and militarily obsolete caste by the early nineteenth century.

Jesuits Order of regular clergy strongly committed to education, scholarship, and missionary work. Founded by Ignatius of Loyola in 1534.

Jihad Arabic word meaning "striving." Muhammad used the word to refer to the inner struggle all Muslims must wage against evil, and the real wars fought against the enemies of Islam.

Joint-stock company A business whose capital is held in transferable shares of stock by its joint owners. The Dutch East India Company, founded in 1602, was the first joint-stock company.

Kaaba The holiest place in Islam. Formerly a pagan shrine, the Kaaba is a massive cube-shaped structure in Mecca toward which Muslims turn to pray.

Keynesianism Economic policy advocated by J. M. Keynes, based on the premise that governments could adjust the distribution of wealth and regulate the functioning of the economy through taxation and public spending, without seriously weakening free enterprise or infringing freedom.

Khan A ruler of a Mongol, Tartar, or Turkish tribe.

Khedive Title held by the hereditary viceroys of Egypt in the nineteenth century. Although nominally subject to the Ottoman sultans, the khedives were, in effect, sovereign princes.

Khmer Agrarian kingdom of Cambodia, built on the wealth produced by enormous rice surpluses.

Kongo Kingdom located in west central Africa along the Congo River, founded in the fourteenth century. The Portuguese converted its rulers and elite to Catholicism in the fifteenth century.

Kulturkampf (Trans.) "The struggle for culture." Name given to the conflict between the Roman Catholic Church and the imperial German government under Chancellor Otto von Bismarck in the 1870s.

Laissez-faire An economic policy that emphasizes the minimization of government regulation and involvement in the economy.

Latin Church Dominant Christian church in Western Europe.

Latitude The angular distance north or south of the Earth's equator, measured in degrees along a meridian.

League of Nations International political organization created after World War I to resolve disputes between states peacefully and create a more just international order.

Legalism Chinese school of thought that emerged in the fourth century B.C.E. Legalists believed that morality was meaningless and that obedience to the state was the supreme good. The state thus had the right to enforce its laws under threat of the harshest penalties.

Levant The countries bordering on the eastern Mediterranean from Turkey to Egypt.

Liberation theology Religious movement in Latin America, primarily among Roman Catholics, concerned with justice for the poor and oppressed. Its adherents argue that sin is the result not just of individual moral failure but of the oppressive and exploitative way in which capitalist society is organized and functions.

Little Ice Age Protracted period of relative cold from the fourteenth to the early nineteenth centuries.

Logograms A system of writing in which stylized pictures represent a word or phrase.

Longitude An imaginary great circle on the surface of the Earth passing through the north and south poles at right angles to the equator.

Lotus Sutra The most famous of Buddhist scriptures.

Low Countries A region of northwest Europe comprising what is today Belgium, the Netherlands, and Luxembourg.

Magyars Steppeland people who invaded Eastern Europe in the tenth century and were eventually converted to Catholic Christianity. The Magyars are the majority ethnic group in present-day Hungary.

Mahayana One of the major schools of Buddhism. It emphasizes the Buddha's infinite compassion for all human beings, social concern, and universal salvation. It is the dominant branch of Buddhism in East Asia.

Mahdi A Muslim messiah, whose coming would inaugurate a cosmic struggle, preceding the end of the world.

Maize The grain that modern Americans call "corn." It was first cultivated in ancient Mesoamerica.

Mali Powerful West African state that flourished in the fourteenth century.

Malthusian Ideas inspired by Thomas Malthus's theory that population growth would always outpace growth in food supply.

Mamluks Egyptian Muslim slave army. The mamluks provided Egypt's rulers from 1390 to 1517.

Mana According to the Polynesians, a supernatural force that regulates everything in the world. For example, the mana of a net makes it catch a fish, and the mana of an herb gives it its healing powers.

Manchurian Incident Japanese invasion of Manchuria in 1931, justified by the alleged effort of the Chinese to blow up a Japanese train. In fact, Japanese agents deliberately triggered the explosion to provide a pretext for war.

Manchus A people native to Manchuria who ruled China during the Qing dynasty.

Mandarins High public officials in the Chinese Empire, usually chosen by merit after competitive written exams.

Mandate of Heaven The source of divine legitimacy for Chinese emperors. According to the mandate of heaven, emperors were chosen by the gods and retained their favor as long as the emperors acted in righteous ways. Emperors and dynasties that lost the mandate of heaven could be deposed or overthrown.

Manichaeanism A dualistic philosophy dividing the world between the two opposed principles of good and evil.

Manifest destiny Nineteenth-century belief that the United States was destined to expand across all of North America from the Atlantic to the Pacific, including Canada and Mexico.

Manila Galleons Spanish galleons that sailed each year between the Philippines and Mexico with a cargo of silk, porcelain, and other Asian luxury goods that were paid for with Mexican silver.

Maori Indigenous Polynesian people of New Zealand.

Marathas Petty Hindu princes who ruled in Maharashtra in southern India in the eighteenth century.

Maritime empires Empires based on trade and naval power that flourished in the sixteenth and seventeenth centuries.

Maroons Runaway slaves in the Americas who formed autonomous communities, and even states, between 1500 and 1800.

Marshall Plan Foreign-aid program for Western Europe after World War II, named after U.S. Secretary of State George C. Marshall.

Marxism The political and economic philosophy of Karl Marx and Friedrich Engels in which the concept of class struggle is the determining principle in social and historical change.

Material culture Concrete objects that people create.

Matrilineal A society that traces ancestry through the maternal line.

Maya Major civilization of Mesoamerica. The earliest evidence connected to Maya civilization dates from about 1000 B.C.E. Maya civilization reached its peak between 250 and 900 C.E. Maya cultural and political practices were a major influence on other Mesoamericans.

Meiji Restoration The overthrow of the Tokugawa *bakufu* in Japan in 1868 and the "restoration" of power to the imperial government under the Emperor Meiji.

Mercantilism An economic theory that emphasized close government control of the economy to maximize a country's exports and to earn as much bullion as possible.

Mesoamerica A region stretching from central Mexico to Central America. Mesoamerica was home to the Olmec, the Maya, the Aztecs, and other Native American peoples.

Messiah The anticipated savior of the Jews. Christians identified Jesus as the Messiah.

Mestizos The descendents of Europeans and Native Americans.

Microbial exchange The exchange of microbes between ecosystems.

Militarization The trend toward larger and more powerful armed forces and the organization of society and the economy to achieve that goal.

Military revolution Change in warfare in the sixteenth and seventeenth centuries that accompanied the rise of fire-power technology.

Millenarianism Belief that the end of the world is about to occur, as foretold in the biblical Book of Revelation.

Minas Gerais (Trans.) "General Mines." Region of Brazil rich in mineral resources that experienced a gold rush in the early eighteenth century.

Ming Dynasty Chinese dynasty (1368–1644) noted for its flourishing foreign trade and achievements in scholarship and the arts.

Mongols Nomadic people whose homeland was in Mongolia. In the twelfth and thirteenth centuries, they conquered most of Eurasia from China to Eastern Europe.

Monocultures The cultivation of a single dominant food crop, such as potatoes or rice. Societies that practiced monoculture were vulnerable to famine if bad weather or disease caused their single food crop to fail.

Monroe Doctrine The policy enunciated by President James Monroe in 1823 that the United States would oppose further European colonization in the Americas.

Monsoons A wind from the southwest or south that brings heavy rainfall each summer to southern Asia.

Mound agriculture Form of agriculture found in pre-Columbian North America.

Mughals Muslim dynasty founded by Babur that ruled India, at least nominally, from the mid–1500s until 1857.

Multiculturalism The belief that different cultures can coexist peacefully and equitably in a single country.

Napoleonic Wars Wars waged between France under Napoleon and its European enemies from 1799 to 1815. The fighting spilled over into the Middle East and sparked conflicts in North America and India and independence movements in the Spanish and Portuguese colonies in the Americas.

Nationalism Belief that a people who share the same language, historic experience, and sense of identity make up a nation and that every nation has the right to assert its identity, pursue its destiny, defend its rights, and be the primary focus of its people's loyalty.

Natural selection The process by which only the organisms best adapted to their environment pass on their genetic material to subsequent generations.

Nature versus nurture Debate over the relative importance of inherited characterizes and environmental factors in determining human development.

Nazis Members of the National Socialist German Workers' Party, founded in Germany in 1919 and brought to power in 1933 under Adolf Hitler.

Neanderthal (Trans.) "Neander Valley." Humanlike species, evidence for whose existence was found in the Neander River valley in northern Germany in the mid–nineteenth century. Neanderthals disappeared from the evolutionary record about 30,000 years ago.

Negritude The affirmation of the distinctive nature, quality, and validity of black culture.

Nestorianism The Christian theological doctrine that within Jesus are two distinct and separate persons, divine and human, rather than a single divine person. Orthodox Christians classed Nestorianism as a heresy, but it spread across Central Asia along the Silk Roads.

New Europes Lands in other hemispheres where the environment resembled that of Europe and where immigrants could successfully transplant a European way of life and European culture.

New Rich Rich people whose wealth was acquired in the recent past, often in industry or commerce.

New World Term Europeans applied to the Americas.

Nirvana The spiritual goal of Buddhism, when a person ends the cycle of birth and rebirth and achieves enlightenment and freedom from any attachment to material things.

Noble savage Idealized vision that some people in the West held about certain non-Europeans, especially some Native Americans and Polynesians. It was based on the notions that civilization was a corrupting force and that these peoples lived lives more in tune with nature.

Northwest Passage Water route from the Atlantic to the Pacific through the Arctic archipelago of northern Canada and along the northern coast of Alaska. For centuries, Europeans sought in vain for a more accessible route to the Pacific farther south in North America.

Obsidian Volcanic glass used to make tools, weapons, and mirrors.

Old regime Term for the social, economic, and political institutions that existed in France and the rest of Europe before the French Revolution.

Old World Term for the regions of the world—Europe, parts of Africa and Asia—that were known to Europeans before the discovery of the Americas.

Ongons Tibetan images in which spirits are thought to reside. Shamans claimed to communicate with the ongons.

OPEC The Organization of Petroleum Exporting Countries, an alliance of the world's major oil producers.

Oracle A person or group that claims to be able to have access to knowledge of the future by consulting a god. Ancient rulers often consulted oracles.

Oriental despotism Arbitrary and corrupt rule. Eighteenth-century Europeans saw it as characteristic of Asian or Islamic rulers.

Orthodox Church Dominant Christian church in the Byzantine Empire, the Balkans, and Russia.

Ottoman Empire Islamic empire based in present-day Turkey, with its capital at Istanbul. At its height in the sixteenth century, the Ottoman Empire stretched from Iraq across North Africa to the borders of Morocco and included almost all the Balkans and most of Hungary. The empire gradually declined, but endured until it was dismembered after World War I.

Pampas A vast plain of south-central South America that supports huge herds of cattle and other livestock.

Pan-African Congress A series of five meetings held between 1919 and 1945 that claimed to represent all black Africans and demanded an end to colonial rule.

Pangaea A hypothetical prehistoric supercontinent that included all the landmasses of the Earth.

Partition of India The division in 1947 along ethnic and religious lines of the British Indian Empire into two independent states: India, which was largely Hindu, and Pakistan, which was largely Muslim. The division involved widespread violence in which at least 500,000 people were killed.

Paternalism A social or economic relationship that resembles the dependency that exists between a father and his child.

Patrilineal A society that traces ancestry through the paternal line.

Philosopher's stone A substance that was believed to have the power to change base metals into gold.

Physiocrats Eighteenth-century French political economists who argued that agriculture was the foundation of any country's wealth and recommended agricultural improvements.

Plantation system System of commercial agriculture based on large landholdings, often worked by forced labor.

Polestar Bright star used for navigation.

Positivism Doctrine that asserts the undeniability of human sense perception and the power of reason to prove that what our senses perceive is true.

Pragmatism Philosophy advocated by William James that holds that the standard for evaluating the truth or validity of a theory or concept depends on how well it works and on the results that arise from holding it.

Proletariat The working class, which according to Karl Marx, would overthrow the bourgeoisie.

Protectorate A country or region that, although nominally independent and not a colony, is in fact controlled militarily, politically, and economically by a more powerful foreign state.

Protestantism The theological system of any of the churches of Western Christendom that separated from the Roman Catholic Church during the Reformation. The advent of Protestantism is usually associated with Martin Luther's break from the Catholic Church in the 1520s.

Psychoanalysis Technique developed by Sigmund Freud to treat patients suffering from emotional or psychological disorders by making them aware of their subconscious conflicts, motivations, and desires.

Public sphere Sites for the public discussion of political, social, economic, and cultural issues.

Qing dynasty Last imperial Chinese dynasty (1644–1912), founded when the Manchus, a steppeland people from Manchuria, conquered China. It was succeeded by a republic.

Quantum mechanics Mechanics based on the principle that matter and energy have the properties of both particles and waves.

Quran The sacred text of Islam dictated from God to the Prophet Muhammad by the Archangel Gabriel. Considered by Muslims to contain the final revelations of God to humanity.

Rape of Nanjing Atrocities committed by the Japanese during their occupation of the city of Nanjing, China, in 1937.

Rastafarianism A religious and political movement that began among black people in Jamaica in the 1930s. Its adherents believe that former Emperor Haile Selassie of Ethiopia (r. 1930–1974) was divine and the Messiah whose coming was foretold in the Bible.

Rationalism The doctrine that reason by itself can determine truth and solve the world's problems.

Realpolitik Political doctrine that says that the state is not subject to moral laws and has the right to do whatever safeguards it and advances its interests.

Reformation The Protestant break from the Roman Catholic Church in the sixteenth century.

Remittances Transfers of money by foreign workers to their home countries.

Renaissance Humanistic revival of classical art, architecture, literature, and learning that originated in Italy in the fourteenth century and spread throughout Europe.

Renewable energy Energy that is not derived from a finite resource such as oil or coal.

Rig Veda A collection of hymns and poems created by a sedentary people living in the area north of the Indus valley where northern India and Pakistan meet. The Rig Veda provides evidence for the theory that invaders destroyed Harappan civilization.

Romanticism Intellectual and artistic movement that arose in reaction to the Enlightenment's emphasis on reason. Romantics had a heightened interest in nature and religion, and emphasized emotion and imagination.

Rus A Slavic-Scandinavian people who created the first Russian state and converted to Orthodox Christianity.

Safavids Shiite dynasty that ruled Persia between 1501 and 1722.

Sahel A semiarid region of north Central Africa south of the Sahara Desert.

Saint Domingue A French colony on Hispaniola that flourished in the eighteenth century by cultivating sugar and coffee with slave labor. It became the modern republic of Haiti after a protracted struggle that began in the 1790s.

Samurai The hereditary Japanese feudal-military aristocracy.

Sati In Hinduism, the burning of a widow on her husband's funeral pyre.

Satyagraha (Trans.) "The force of truth." Nonviolent movement launched by Mohandas K. Gandhi, with the goal of achieving Indian independence.

Savanna A flat grassland of tropical or subtropical regions.

Scientific revolution The sweeping change in the investigation of nature and the view of the universe that took place in Europe in the sixteenth and seventeenth centuries.

Scientism The belief that science and the scientific method can explain everything in the universe and that no other form of inquiry is valid.

Scramble for Africa Late nineteenth-century competition among European powers to acquire colonies in Africa.

Sea Peoples Unknown seafaring people that contributed to the instability of the eastern Mediterranean in the twelfth century B.C.E., attacking Egypt, Palestine, Mesopotamia, Anatolia, and Syria.

Second Vatican Council Council of the Roman Catholic Church that convened at intervals in the 1960s and led to major changes in church liturgy and discipline.

Secularism Belief that religious considerations should be excluded from civil affairs or public education.

Self-determination Principle that a given people or nationality has the right to determine their own political status.

Self-strengthening Mid–nineteenth-century Chinese reform movement initiated in response to Western incursions.

Seljuks A Turkish dynasty ruling in Central and western Asia from the eleventh to the thirteenth centuries.

Serf Agricultural laborer attached to the land owned by a lord and required to perform labor in return for certain legal or customary rights. Unlike slaves, serfs could not usually be sold away from the land.

Shaman A person who acts as an intermediary between humans and spirits or gods. Such a person functions as the medium though which spirits talk to humans.

Sharia Islamic law The word *sharia* derives from the verb *shara'a*, which is connected to the concepts of "spiritual law" and "system of divine law."

Shiites Members of the most important minority tradition in the Islamic world. Shiites believe that the caliphate is the prerogative of Muhammad's nephew, Ali, and his heirs. Shiism has been the state religion in Iran since the sixteenth century.

Shinto A religion native to Japan, characterized by veneration of nature spirits and ancestors and by a lack of formal dogma.

Shogun A hereditary military ruler of Japan who exercised real power in the name of the emperor, who was usually powerless and relegated to purely ceremonial roles. The last shogun was removed from office in 1868.

Sikhism Indian religion founded by Nanak Guru in the early sixteenth century that blends elements of the Hindu and Muslim traditions.

Silk Roads Key overland trade routes that connected eastern and western Eurasia. The route first began to function in the aftermath of Alexander the Great's expansion into Central Asia at the end of the fourth century B.C.E.

Sioux A nomadic Native American people of central North America who, with the benefit of horses introduced to the Americas by the Spanish, formed a pastoralist empire in the late eighteenth and mid–nineteenth centuries.

Social Darwinism The misapplication of Darwin's biological theories to human societies, often to justify claims of racial superiority and rule by the strong over the weak.

Socialism Any of various theories or systems in which the means of producing and distributing goods is owned collectively or by a centralized government.

Socialist realism An artistic doctrine embraced by many communist and leftist regimes that the sole legitimate purpose of the arts was to glorify the ideals of the state by portraying workers, peasants, and the masses in a strictly representational, nonabstract style.

Sociobiology The study of the biological determinants of social behavior.

Solidarity Polish trade union founded in 1980 that played a key role in bringing down Poland's communist regime.

Solomids Dynasty that seized power in Ethiopia in 1270 C.E. and claimed descent from the Biblical King Solomon.

Song dynasty Dynasty (960–1279) under which China achieved one of its highest levels of culture and prosperity.

Songhay An ancient empire of West Africa in the present-day country of Mali. It reached the height of its power around 1500 C.E.

Soninke West African kingdom on the upper Niger River.

Soviet Russian term for a workers' collective.

State system Organization of early modern Europe into competing nation-states.

Steppe A vast semiarid, grass-covered plain, extending across northern Eurasia and central North America.

Stoicism Philosophy founded on the belief that nature is morally neutral and that the wise person, therefore, achieves happiness by accepting misfortune and practicing self-control.

Stranger effect The tendency some peoples have to esteem and defer to strangers.

Stream of consciousness A literary technique that presents the thoughts and feelings of a character in a novel or story as they arise in the character's mind.

Subsidiarity Doctrine that decisions should always be made at the level closest to the people whom the decisions most affect.

Suez Canal Canal linking the Mediterranean and the Red Sea. It was built by French engineers with European capital and opened in 1869.

Sufis Members of Islamic groups that cultivate mystical beliefs and practices. Sufis have often been instrumental in spreading Islam, but Muslim authorities have often distrusted them.

Sundiata Legendary hero said to have founded the kingdom of Mali in West Africa.

Sunnis Members of the dominant tradition in the Islamic world. Sunnis believe that any member of Muhammad's tribe could be designated caliph.

Surrealism Literary and artistic movement that attempts to express the workings of the subconscious.

Syllogisms A form of argument in which we can infer a necessary conclusion from two premises that prior demonstration or agreement has established to be true.

Syncretic Characterized by the reconciliation or fusion of differing systems of belief.

Taiping Rebellion Rebellion (1852–1864) against the Qing Empire that resulted in tens of millions of deaths and widespread destruction in southern China.

Tang dynasty Chinese dynasty (618–907) famous for its wealth and encouragement of the arts and literature.

Tengri "Ruler of the sky." The supreme deity of the Mongols and other steppeland peoples.

The Encyclopedia Twenty-eight volume compendium of Enlightenment thought published in French and edited by Denis Diderot. The first volume appeared in 1751.

The Mongol Peace Era in the thirteenth and fourteenth centuries when Mongol rule created order and stability in Central Asia and enabled goods and ideas to flow along the Silk Roads.

Theory of value The theory that the value of goods is not inherent, but rather determined by supply and demand.

Theravada A conservative branch of Buddhism that adheres to the nontheistic ideal of self-purification to nirvana. Theravada Buddhism emphasizes the monastic ideal and is dominant in present-day Sri Lanka and southeast Asia.

Third Rome Term Russians used for Moscow and Russian Orthodox Christianity. It expressed the belief that the Russian czars were the divinely chosen heirs of the Roman and Byzantine emperors.

Thule Inuit Indigenous Native American people who crossed the Arctic and arrived in Greenland around 1000 C.E.

Tillers Agriculturalists who emphasize the cultivation of plants for food and products, such as timber and cotton.

Tokugawa A family of shoguns that ruled Japan in the name of the emperors from 1603 to 1868.

Trading-post empires Term for the networks of imperial forts and trading posts that Europeans established in Asia in the seventeenth century.

Treasure Fleets Spanish fleets that sailed from the Caribbean each year to bring gold and silver from mines in the Americas back to Europe.

Tundra A treeless area between the ice cap and the tree line of Arctic regions.

Turks A member of any of the Turkic-speaking, nomadic peoples who originated in Central Asia. The Turks eventually converted to Islam and dominated the Middle East.

Uncertainty principle Niels Bohr and Werner Heisenberg's theory that because observers are part of every observation their findings can never be objective.

United Nations International political organization created after World War II to prevent armed conflict, settle international disputes peacefully, and provide cultural, economic, and technological aid. It was the successor to the League of Nations, which had proved to be ineffectual.

Universal love Love between all people, regardless of status, nationality, or family ties.

Upanishads The theoretical sections of the Veda (the literature of the sages of the Ganges civilization). The Upanishads were written down as early as 800 B.C.E.

Urbanization The process by which urban areas develop and expand.

Utilitarianism System of thought devised by Jeremy Bentham, based on the notion that the goal of the state was to create the greatest happiness for the greatest number of people.

Utopianism Belief in a system or ideology aimed at producing a perfect or ideal society.

Vaccination Inoculation with a vaccine to produce immunity to a particular disease.

Vernacular languages The languages that people actually spoke—as opposed to Latin—which was the language used by the Roman Catholic Church and was, for a long time, the language of scholarship, the law, and diplomacy in much of Europe.

Virtual reality A computer simulation of a real or imaginary system.

Wahhabbism Muslim sect founded by Abdul Wahhab (1703–1792), known for its strict observance of the Quran. It is the dominant form of Islam in Saudi Arabia.

Westerlies Winds coming from the west.

Westernization The process by which other cultures adopt Western styles or ways of life.

World system The system of interconnections among the world's population.

World War I Global war (1914–1918) sparked by the assassination of Archduke Francis Ferdinand of Austria by a Serb terrorist in June 1914.

World War II Global conflict that lasted from 1939 to 1945 and ended with the defeat and occupation of Fascist Italy, Nazi Germany, and Japan.

Zen A school of Mahayana Buddhism that asserts that a person can attain enlightenment through meditation, self-contemplation, and intuition.

Ziggurat A tall, tapering Mesopotamian temple. Ziggurats were the physical and cultural centers of Mesopotamian cities.

Zimbabwes Stone-built administrative centers for rulers and the elite in southern Africa. The zimbabwes flourished in the fifteenth century.

Zoroastrianism Iranian religious system founded by Zoroaster that posited a universal struggle between the forces of light (the good) and of darkness (evil).

CHAPTER 1

1. L. van der Post, *The Lost World of the Kalahari* (NY: Morrow, 1958), pp. 252–261.

CHAPTER 2

1. J. L. Harlan, *Crops and Man* (1992), p. 27.

2. Charles Darwin, *The Variation of Plants and Animals under Domestication*, 2 vols (1868), i, pp. 309–310.

CHAPTER 11

1. G. Coédès, Angor: *An Introduction* (1963), pp 104–105.

2. G. Coédès, Angor: *An Introduction* p. 96.

3. Patrologia Latina, cli, col. 0572; William of Malmesbury, *Chronicle of the Kings of England*, 68 IV, ch. 2 (ed. J. A. Giles [1857], p. 360).

CHAPTER 12

1. J. T. C. Liu, *Reform in Sung China: Wang An-Shih and His New Policies* (Cambridge, MA: Harvard University Press, 1957), p. 54.

CHAPTER 13

1. P. Jackson, ed., *The Travels of Friar Willam of Rubruck* (London, 1981), pp. 113–114.

2. R. Latham, ed., *The Travels of Marco Polo* (Harmondsworth, 1972), p. 85.

3. R. L. Davis, *Wind Against the Mountain: The Crisis of Politics and Culture in Thirteenth-Century China* (Cambridge, MA: Harvard University Asia Center, 1996), p. 62.

4. J. Fennell, *The Crisis of Medieval Russia* (Longman Publishing Group, 1983), p. 88.

CHAPTER 14

1. R. Horrox, *The Black Death* (Manchester University Press, 1994), p. 16.

2. N. Cantor, *In the Wake of the Plague* (New York: Perennial/Harper Collins, 2002), p. 199.

3. D. Hall in *Cambridge History of Southeast Asia*, ed. N. Tarling (Cambridge University Press, 1992), i. 218.

4. F. Rosenthal ed. *The Muqaddimah*, 3 vols. (New York: Pantheon Books, 1958), i, 64–65.